Juvenile Justice SOURCEBOOK

EDITED BY

Wesley T. Church II,
David W. Springer, and
Albert R. Roberts

Juvenile Justice
SOURCEBOOK

2nd Edition

OXFORD
UNIVERSITY PRESS

OXFORD
UNIVERSITY PRESS

Oxford University Press is a department of the University of Oxford.
It furthers the University's objective of excellence in research, scholarship,
and education by publishing worldwide.

Oxford   New York
Auckland   Cape Town   Dar es Salaam   Hong Kong   Karachi
Kuala Lumpur   Madrid   Melbourne   Mexico City   Nairobi
New Delhi   Shanghai   Taipei   Toronto

With offices in
Argentina   Austria   Brazil   Chile   Czech Republic   France   Greece
Guatemala   Hungary   Italy   Japan   Poland   Portugal   Singapore
South Korea   Switzerland   Thailand   Turkey   Ukraine   Vietnam

Oxford is a registered trademark of Oxford University Press
in the UK and certain other countries.

Published in the United States of America by
Oxford University Press
198 Madison Avenue, New York, NY 10016

Library of Congress Cataloging-in-Publication Data
Juvenile justice sourcebook : past, present and future / edited by Wesley T. Church,
David W. Springer, Albert R. Roberts.—2nd ed.
     pages cm.
Revised editon of: Juvenile justice sourcebook : past, present, and future /
[edited by] Albert R. Roberts.
Includes index.
ISBN 978–0–19–932461–3
1. Juvenile justice, Administration of—United States.   2. Juvenile courts—United States.
I. Church, Wesley T.
HV9104.J868 2014
364.360973—dc23
2013033914

To my family—Debra, Braeden, Paulina, Keaton, Maylie, and Lincoln

~WTC

To my son, Aidan

~DWS

Contents

Foreword   Kevin Corcoran   xi

Preface   xiii

Acknowledgments   xv

Contributors   xvii

SECTION   **I**   **Overview, Trends, and Critical Issues in Juvenile Justice**

I   An Overview of Juvenile Justice and Juvenile Delinquency:
Cases, Definitions, Trends, and Intervention Strategies   3
Albert R. Roberts, Katherine L. Montgomery, Wesley T. Church II, and David W. Springer

2   Juvenile Justice Policy: Current Trends and 21st-Century Issues   37
C. Aaron McNeece and Tiffany Ryan

3   The Second American Crime Drop: Trends in Juvenile and Youth Violence   61
Jeffrey A. Butts and Douglas N. Evans

4   Theories of Juvenile Crime and Delinquency   79
Cesar J. Rebellon

5   Risk and Protective Factors for Involvement in Juvenile Justice: Implications
for Prevention   101
Traci L. Wike and Caren L. Putzu

6   Brain Science and Juvenile Justice: Questions for Policy and Practice   123
Alexandra Cox

SECTION   **II**   **Juvenile Justice Processing**

7   Police Work with Juveniles   149
Jeremiah Jaggers, Sarah Young, and Wesley T. Church II

8 Juveniles' Competence and Procedural Rights in Juvenile Court   167
Barry C. Feld

9 Juvenile Detention   193
David W. Roush, Michelle Brazeal, and Wesley T. Church II

10 Juvenile Drug Courts, Juvenile Mental Health Courts, and Teen Courts   215
Matthew L. Hiller and Christine A. Saum

11 Waivers and Transfers of Juveniles to Adult Court: Treating Juveniles like Adult Criminals   241
Michele Deitch and Neelum Arya

SECTION **III**   **School- and Community-Based Programs**

12 Marginalized Students, School Exclusion, and the School-to-Prison Pipeline   267
Michael P. Krezmien, Peter E. Leone, and Michael G. Wilson

13 School-Based Delinquency Prevention   289
Katherine L. Montgomery

14 Community-Based Treatment Interventions   313
Robert Butters

15 Neighborhood Street Gangs: Patterns, Activities, and Community-Based Programs   337
Paul D. Steele

16 Re-entry and Aftercare   363
Laura S. Abrams

SECTION **IV**   **Evidence-Based Assessment and Treatment with Juvenile Delinquents**

17 Risk Assessment with Juvenile Offenders   387
Henrika McCoy, Joshua P. Mersky, John Leverso, and Elizabeth A. Bowen

18 Mental Health and Youth in the Juvenile Justice System: Current Status and Evidence-Informed Future Directions   413
Cynthia Weaver, Edward Byrnes, and Wesley T. Church II

19 Family-Based Interventions for Juvenile Offenders   439
Stephanie C. Kennedy and Stephen J. Tripodi

SECTION **V** **Special Issues and Populations**

20 Homelessness and Juvenile Justice   463
Sarah Young, Jeremiah Jaggers, and David E. Pollio

21 Disproportionate Minority Contact (DMC) in the U.S. Juvenile
Justice System   487
Susan A. McCarter

22 The Wayward Girl in the 21st Century: Female Pathways to Delinquency   507
Lisa Pasko, Scott K. Okamoto, and Meda Chesney-Lind

23 Juvenile Sex Offenders: History, Policies, and Assessment   531
Megan Schlegel

24 Serious, Chronic, and Violent Offenders   553
Bryanna Hahn Fox, Wesley G. Jennings, and Alex R. Piquero

25 Gender, Racially, and Culturally Grounded Practice   581
Keva M. Miller, Ben Anderson-Nathe, and Jana L. Meinhold

SECTION **VI** **Juvenile Justice Reform**

26 The Road Ahead: Progressive Possibilities and Challenges for Juvenile
Justice Reform   607
Laura Burney Nissen

Glossary   629

Index   647

Foreword for *Juvenile Justice Sourcebook*, 2nd edition

Alfred Lord Tennyson wrote, "Science moves, but slowly, creeping from point to point," and so, too, has juvenile justice and juvenile justice science moved slowly since Al Roberts' first edition of the *Juvenile Justice Sourcebook*. And yet while moving slowly much has changed in the last decade, all of which are reflected in Church, Springer, and Roberts' second edition. Since 2004 some of what was once "present" is now "past," and some aspects of the "future" that Al and his authors speculated about are now the "present" in the administration of justice for our youth. The new or current "future" is as it was with the first edition—elusive and unpredictable.

As observed by Professor Laura Moriarty pursuant to the first edition, "the *Juvenile Justice Sourcebook* [2nd] is remarkable for the breadth and depth that [Church, Springer and Roberts] and [their] esteemed author team bring to the topic. It truly is a 'sourcebook' that will be beneficial to both academicians and practitioners" (p. vii). This new edition continues to be "a 'must-read' for those interested in the topic of juvenile justice.

In this edition the editors divide the topics into six sections. Section I (Overview, Trends and Critical Issues) contains six chapters that range from a historical overview to the relatively new science of brain and behavior. Section II (Juvenile Justice Processing) contains five chapters on policy, juvenile courts, detention, mental health and substance abuse courts, and waivers and removal to being tried as an adult. Section III (School- and Community-Based Programs) contains five chapters on the school-to-prison pipeline, prevention programs including gang prevention, community interventions, reuniting offenders, and aftercare. Section IV considers the science of juvenile justice, with an emphasis on evidence-based assessment and treatment. The three chapters cover risk assessment, work with juveniles with mental health conditions, and family-based treatment. Section V (Special Issues and Populations) contains six chapters: homelessness and the ever-troubling disproportionality of youth of color in every phase of the justice system, female pathways to delinquency, sex offenders, violent offenders, and the promise of gender-specific and culturally grounded practices. The final section (Juvenile Justice Reform) comprises one chapter, which actually is about "the reform of reform of reform"; after all, we started reform efforts over a century ago with Judge Baker courts and the rehabilitative ideal. As this chapter reflects, the rehabilitative ideal has never died and continues to be the star that guides our continuous effort to make the administration of juvenile justice, in fact, justice for youngsters.

I wish to end this foreword with a personal note about the first edition and the seed of hope we plant for those who walk the mean streets in and out of the juvenile justice system. Al Roberts was a close and dear friend to me. For many years we would talk on the telephone every month for a couple of hours at a time, and often even longer. I knew him well, well enough to know the details of why he dedicated the first edition to his parents and why he noted the "turbulent adolescent years"; those years—and an understanding and compassionate judge—gave rise to the juvenile justice expert and reformer he became. Al's youth is testimony, indeed, to the rehabilitative ideal. And since I miss him so, I shall never forsake his confidence in me by disclosing his story. I will say, though, that his story as a youngster is reason we temper the cold steel of justice with the compassion of mercy. Justice without mercy is not justice at all, especially for our youth. And this edition of the *Juvenile Justice Sourcebook* illustrates how this is so.

Kevin Corcoran, Ph.D., J.D.
Professor of Social Work
Portland State University, School of Social Work

Preface

The first edition of the *Juvenile Justice Sourcebook* was the first comprehensive volume devoted to an in-depth discussion of the critical issues and basic controversies in the field of juvenile justice and the problems encountered by those who try to unravel the causes, processes, intervention programs, and outcomes for juvenile offenders. It truly was a sourcebook and was remarkable for the breadth of information that was compiled into one comprehensive source. It was touted as a "must read" for those interested in the topic of juvenile justice, and over the past 10 years has proven to be such.

The decision to write and edit the second edition was not taken lightly. However, based on our belief in the importance of the first edition, we saw a need for an up-to-date text for undergraduate and graduate students interested in juvenile justice trends, critical issues, policies, programs, and research. This volume should also prove useful to practitioners and administrators, both as a desktop reference and as a resource for updating their knowledge about the most effective interventions and practices with juvenile offenders.

The impetus for the second edition stems from our great respect for Al's work. He had great passion for improving the juvenile justice system and transforming the lives of juvenile delinquents. We share this passion, as does Al's widow, Beverly. We are grateful to Al for paving the way, for showing us over the years what it means to be a mentor, teacher, and friend. We are equally grateful to Beverly, for supporting and encouraging us to carry on his work and legacy through editing this second edition.

Al believed in pulling together the best team of chapter authors when editing a book, and we think that he would be thrilled with the lineup for this new edition. The chapter authors are leaders in their respective areas and have prepared chapters that are both grounded and cutting-edge. Building on Al's work, this new edition continues to trace the tremendous progress achieved toward resolving juvenile justice issues, dilemmas, and controversies presented in the first edition, while at the same time looking forward to the future of the juvenile justice field.

Acknowledgments

First and foremost, we thank our esteemed team of authors for writing their chapters. They are leaders in their field, and we are grateful for their willingness to share their time and expertise.

We are extremely appreciative of our diligent editorial and production team at Oxford University Press, including Dana Bliss, Nicholas Liu, and Brianna Marron. Katie Casstevens of The University of Texas at Austin was instrumental in the copyediting and camera-ready preparation of the book.

Finally, this second edition of Al Roberts' *Juvenile Justice Sourcebook* would not have been possible without the support and encouragement of Al's widow, Beverly Roberts.

Wesley T. Church II, Ph.D.   David W. Springer, Ph.D.
Tuscaloosa, Alabama   Austin, Texas

Contributors

Laura S. Abrams, Ph.D.
Associate Professor and Doctoral
Program Chair
UCLA Luskin School of Public
Affairs
Department of Social Welfare
Los Angeles, CA

Ben Anderson-Nathe, Ph.D.
Associate Professor
Portland State University
School of Social Work
Portland, OR

Neelum Arya, J.D., M.P.A.
Assistant Professor of Law
Barry University
Dwayne O. Andreas School of Law
Orlando, FL

Elizabeth A. Bowen
Doctoral Candidate
University of Illinois at Chicago
Jane Addams College of Social Work
Chicago, IL

Jeffrey A. Butts, Ph.D.
Director, Research and
Evaluation Center
The City University of New York
John Jay College of Criminal Justice
New York, NY

Robert Butters, Ph.D., L.C.S.W.
Assistant Professor
Director, Utah Criminal
Justice Center
University of Utah
College of Social Work
Salt Lake City, UT

Laura Burney Nissen, Ph.D.
Professor
Portland State University
School of Social Work
Portland, OR

Michelle Brazeal, M.S.W.
Doctoral Student
The University of Alabama
School of Social Work
Tuscaloosa, AL

Edward Byrnes, Ph.D.
Associate Professor
Undergraduate Program Director
Eastern Washington University
School of Social Work
Cheney, WA

Wesley T. Church II, Ph.D., L.C.S.W.
Associate Professor
Chair of the PhD Program
The University of Alabama
School of Social Work
Tuscaloosa, AL

Alexandra Cox, Ph.D.
Assistant Professor
SUNY-New Paltz
Sociology Department
New Paltz, NY

Meda Chesney-Lind, Ph.D.
Professor and Chair
Women's Studies
University of Hawaii at Mānoa
College of Social Sciences
Public Policy Center
Honolulu, HI

Michele Deitch, J.D., M.Sc.
Senior Lecturer
The University of Texas at Austin
Lyndon B. Johnson School of Public
Affairs
Austin, TX

Douglas N. Evans, Ph.D.
Assistant Professor
Mercy College
Visiting Scholar
John Jay College of Criminal Justice
Dobbs Ferry, NY

Barry C. Feld, J.D., Ph.D.
Centennial Professor of Law
University of Minnesota
Law School
Effie, MN

Bryanna Hahn Fox, Ph.D.
Assistant Professor
University of South Florida
Department of Criminology
Tampa, FL

Matthew L. Hiller, Ph.D.
Associate Professor
Temple University
Department of Criminal Justice
Philadelphia, PA

Jeremiah Jaggers, Ph.D.
Assistant Professor
East Tennessee State University
Department of Social Work
Johnson City, TN

Wesley G. Jennings, Ph.D.
Assistant Professor
University of South Florida
Department of Criminology
Tampa, FL

Stephanie C. Kennedy
Doctoral Student
Florida State University
College of Social Work
Tallahassee, FL

Michael P. Krezmien, Ph.D.
Assistant Professor
University of Massachusetts
Department of Student Development
Amherst, MA

John Leverso
Honors College Undergraduate
Research Experience Student
University of Illinois at Chicago
Jane Addams College of Social Work
Chicago, IL

Peter E. Leone, Ph.D.
Professor
University of Maryland
Department of Special Education
College Park, MD

Susan A. McCarter, Ph.D.
Assistant Professor
University of North
Carolina-Charlotte
College of Health and Human
Services
Charlotte, NC

Henrika McCoy, Ph.D.
Assistant Professor
University of Illinois at Chicago
Jane Addams College of Social Work
Chicago, IL

C. Aaron McNeece, M.A.,
M.S.W., Ph.D.
Dean and Walter W. Hudson
Professor (Emeritus)
Florida State University
College of Social Work
Tallahassee, FL

Jana L. Meinhold, Ph.D.
Assistant Professor
Portland State University
School of Social Work
Portland, OR

Joshua P. Mersky, Ph.D.
Associate Professor
University of Illinois at Chicago
Jane Addams College of Social Work
Chicago, IL

Keva M. Miller, L.C.S.W., Ph.D.
Assistant Professor
Portland State University
School of Social Work
Portland, OR

Katherine L. Montgomery, Ph.D.,
M.S.S.W.
Postdoctoral Fellow
Washington University
George Warren Brown School of
Social Work
St. Louis, MO

Scott K. Okamoto, Ph.D.
Associate Professor
Hawai'i Pacific University
School of Social Work
Honolulu, HI

Lisa Pasko, Ph.D.
Associate Professor
University of Denver
Department of Sociology and
Criminology
Denver, CO

Alex R. Piquero, Ph.D.
Ashbel Smith Professor in
Criminology
The University of Texas at Dallas
School of Economic, Political, and
Policy Sciences
Richardson, TX

David E. Pollio, Ph.D.
Hill Crest Foundation Endowed
Professor
The University of Alabama
School of Social Work
Tuscaloosa, AL

Caren L. Putzu
Doctoral Student
Virginia Commonwealth University
School of Social Work
Richmond, VA

Cesar J. Rebellon, Ph.D.
Associate Professor
University of New Hampshire
Department of Sociology
Durham, NH

Albert R. Roberts, Ph.D., D.A.B.F.E.,
D.A.A.E.T.S (deceased)
Professor of Criminal Justice and
Social Work
Rutgers–the State University of
New Jersey
Piscataway, NJ

David W. Roush, Ph.D.
Executive Director
Juvenile Justice Associates
Albion, MI

Tiffany Ryan, M.S.W.
Ph.D. Candidate
The University of Texas at Austin
School of Social Work
Austin, TX

Christine A. Saum, Ph.D.
Associate Professor
Rowan University
Department of Law and Justice
Studies
Glassboro, NJ

Megan Schlegel, Ph.D.
The University of Texas at Austin
School of Social Work
Austin, TX

Paul D. Steele, Ph.D.
Director, Center for Justice Studies
Professor of Criminology
Coordinator, Graduate Studies
Morehead State University
Department of Sociology, Social
Work and Criminology
Morehead, KY

David W. Springer, Ph.D., L.C.S.W.
Distinguished Teaching Professor
The University of Texas at Austin
School of Social Work
Austin, TX

Stephen J. Tripodi, Ph.D.
Associate Professor
Florida State University
College of Social Work
Tallahassee, FL

Traci L. Wike, Ph.D.
Assistant Professor
Virginia Commonwealth University
School of Social Work
Richmond, VA

Cynthia Weaver, Ph.D., M.S.W., MA
Adjunct Research Professor
University of Southern Mississippi
School of Social Work
Hattiesburg, MS

Michael G. Wilson
Assistant Professor
Columbia University
Teachers College
New York, NY

Sarah Young, M.S.W.
Doctoral Student
The University of Alabama
School of Social Work
Tuscaloosa, AL

Juvenile Justice SOURCEBOOK

I

Overview, Trends, and Critical Issues in Juvenile Justice

An Overview of Juvenile Justice and Juvenile Delinquency

Cases, Definitions, Trends, and Intervention Strategies

Albert R. Roberts, Katherine L. Montgomery,

Wesley T. Church II, and David W. Springer

several million juveniles commit delinquent acts each year. Violent and property crimes committed by juveniles are one of the major social and public health problems in American society. Newspapers and other media saturate us with graphic depictions of individual youths and gangs committing violence in the schools, in the streets, in parking lots, and in the home. In reality, although the National Center for Juvenile Justice and the Office of Juvenile Justice and Delinquency Prevention (OJJDP) reported almost 2 million juvenile arrests in 2009 (Puzzanchera, Adams, & Hockenberry, 2012), the approximate number of juvenile delinquent acts could be between 13 and 15 million annually. This could be attributed to the fact that many crimes committed by juveniles often go unreported or undetected, or no arrest is made. Nevertheless, almost all types of juvenile violent and property crimes have been declining since the mid-1990s. Many legislators, agency administrators, practitioners, and students are unaware of the latest model juvenile offender treatment and prevention programs and of the growing research evidence of their success in sharply reducing recidivism. Therefore, a major emphasis of this book is to present the latest information on prevalence trends and on policies and programs that are effective in reducing juvenile delinquency and juvenile status offenses.

This chapter provides an orientation to the critical issues, trends, policies, programs, and intervention strategies of the juvenile justice system. It discusses the functions and legal responsibilities of the various juvenile justice agencies and institutions. This overview chapter lays the foundation and groundwork for the study of juvenile delinquency and the juvenile justice process by providing case illustrations of the different types of delinquency and status offense cases, delineating the legal definitions of *juvenile status offenses* and *juvenile delinquency*, examining the nine steps in the juvenile justice case-flow process, and showing the scope of the problem in terms of official and unofficial delinquency statistics.

■ Case Illustrations

■ *A 15-year-old male runaway, Matt, is before the juvenile court judge for possession of a concealed, unloaded, .38-caliber handgun. The juvenile probation officer who conducted the pre-dispositional investigation recommends detention for the youth on the handgun charge. The public defender states that the 3 days that Matt has already spent in detention have had a profound effect on him and requests leniency. The judge rules that Matt and his parents must attend 12 sessions of family counseling provided through the probation department and that the stepfather, who works as a security guard, must keep his revolver in a lockbox, so that Matt is not able to take it again.*

■ *A 16-year-old female named Suzie fought with another girl when it was learned that Suzie had become pregnant by the other girl's boyfriend. During the argument, Suzie cut the other girl with a broken bottle. The juvenile court judge suspends commitment to the state girls' training school and places her in a group home for adolescent girls for 1 year.*

■ *Stephen, a 15-year-old male broke into the home of an elderly woman to search for cash and valuables. The woman returned home to find Stephen ransacking her house. In a fit of rage, he brutally assaulted and raped her. The judge rules that Stephen, although only 15 years old, is to be tried as an adult. Found guilty by a jury, he is sentenced to 6 to 10 years of incarceration.*

■ *Candace, a 14-year-old female, has repeatedly run away from the group home where she was placed because her mother could not handle her at home. Candace's mother has two jobs; the girl has never met her biological father. Candace recently stole a car and was suspended from school three times in the past year for possession of marijuana and twice for possession of designer drugs. Her case record reflects that she was sexually abused by her mother's boyfriend. The judge adjudicates Candace to the girls' training school until she reaches age 16.*

In general, youths can be charged with two types of wrongdoing: juvenile delinquency offenses, which are criminal acts (e.g., auto theft, forcible rape, breaking and entering) for which they would be held accountable if they were adults, and status offenses (e.g., truancy, incorrigibility, and running away from home), which are illegal only for juveniles. Violent juvenile crimes receive the most media attention and serve to intensify the fear and outrage of concerned citizens. This fear and outrage, in turn, frequently influences prosecutors, juvenile court judges, and correctional administrators to subject more juvenile offenders to harsher penalties. Far more prevalent than violent crimes are juveniles who commit status offenses or nonviolent property crimes, as in the following examples:

■ *A 13-year-old boy, Henry, was brought to the county juvenile detention center after his mother complained that he was on drugs and was uncontrollable. The social worker's investigation for the court revealed that the mother had been released from the state hospital 3 months earlier. She had a history of psychotic episodes. The judge ruled that Henry should live with the aunt and uncle with whom he lived while his mother was confined in the state hospital, and receive 90 days of substance abuse counseling.*

■ *A 16-year-old male, John, whose mother was an alcoholic had been reared in a home in which he was neglected and there was no discipline or limit setting. John had a history of 12 arrests for petty theft and shoplifting starting at the age of 11. Following the most recent arrest, he was sent to a rehabilitation-oriented juvenile training school that provided group therapy 6 days a week, a behavior modification program, and vocational training. John was learning to be an auto mechanic and proudly demonstrated his knowledge of automobile repair.*

Students and practitioners working in juvenile justice agencies, on either a volunteer or paid basis, sometimes encounter the discretionary, deficient, flawed, and often overcrowded system of juvenile justice. At other times, students and practitioners encounter caring and compassionate juvenile justice volunteers and other practitioners. Although the goal of justice-oriented agencies is to protect society and to humanely care for and rehabilitate our deviant children and youth, in actuality the juvenile justice system sometimes labels, stigmatizes, mistakenly punishes, and reinforces delinquent patterns of behavior. In a number of jurisdictions, the controlling, biased, and punitive orientation of some juvenile justice officials has led to a revolving-door system in which we find an overrepresentation of children and youth from Black, low-income, neglectful, and/or abusive homes. For example, in 2009 a disproportionate number of juvenile arrests involved minorities (Puzzanchera et al., 2012).

Although juvenile arrest rates have been declining overall, the proportion of delinquency cases that involved Black youth increased from 25% in 1985 to 34% in 2009 (Puzzanchera et al., 2012). After converting the total reported arrest numbers into arrest rates per 1,000 juveniles in each racial group, the number of delinquent arrests for Black youth (103.2) was more than double the rate for White (40.3) and American Indian juveniles (50.9). With regard to crimes against persons, the arrest rate for Black juveniles (30.2) was approximately three times the arrest rate for American Indian juveniles (11.6) and White juveniles (8.8), and 11 times the arrest rate for Asian American juveniles (2.8). In some states, juveniles who are members of minority races are more likely to be incarcerated than White juvenile offenders. For example, OJJDP conducted an analysis of studies that spanned over 12 years and found approximately two thirds of the studies to have a "negative race effect" (meaning that race explained why minorities remained in the system) during various stages of the juvenile justice process (Armour & Hammond, 2009). See Chapter 21 for a discussion of disproportionate minority contact with the juvenile justice system.

This chapter examines three primary areas related to learning about the juvenile justice system: definitions of juvenile delinquency and status offenses, the stages in the juvenile justice process, and the scope and extent of juvenile delinquency. The following 25 chapters focus on the full range of issues within the juvenile justice system, ranging from risk and protective factors, mental health, drug, and teen courts, waivers and transfers to the adult criminal system, the school-to-prison pipeline, reentry and aftercare, mental health issues, homelessness and the juvenile justice system, and female pathways to delinquency.

■ Defining Juvenile Justice

What is the juvenile justice system? It is the agencies and institutions whose primary responsibility is handling juvenile offenders. These agencies and their programs concern themselves with delinquent youths and with those children and youths labeled incorrigible, truant, or runaway. Juvenile justice focuses on the needs of the more than 2 million youths who are taken into custody, diverted into special programs, or processed through the juvenile court and adjudicated, and then placed on probation, referred to a community-based day treatment program, or placed in a group home or a secure facility.

The history of juvenile justice has involved the development of policies, programs, and agencies for dealing with youths involved in legal violations. As we examine the juvenile justice system, we focus on the interrelated, yet different, functions of several agencies and programs: the police, courts, detention facilities, schools, neighborhoods, family-based programs, and aftercare.

What has been done during the past 100 years to provide juvenile offenders with equal opportunities for justice? Which policies and program alternatives are currently prevalent within the juvenile justice system? What are the latest trends in processing and treating juvenile offenders? What does the future hold? This book explores the answers to these questions. The next section of this chapter focuses on the legal and behavioral definitions of juvenile delinquency and status offenses.

■ Defining Juvenile Delinquency

Juvenile delinquency is a broad term that includes many diverse forms of antisocial behavior by a minor. In general, most state criminal codes define juvenile delinquency as behavior that is in violation of the criminal code and committed by a youth who has not reached adult age. The specific acts by the juvenile that constitute delinquent behavior vary from state to state. A definition that is broad in scope and commonly used was developed by the U.S. Children's Bureau (1967):

> Juvenile delinquency cases are those referred to courts for acts defined in the statutes of the State as the violation of a state law or municipal ordinance by children or youth of juvenile court age, or for conduct so seriously antisocial as to interfere with the rights of others or to menace the welfare of the delinquent himself or of the community.

Other agencies define as delinquent those juveniles who have been arrested or contacted by the police, even though many of these individuals are merely reprimanded or sent home when their parents pick them up. Less than half of the juveniles handled by the police are referred to the juvenile court. These are the children and youths the Children's Bureau would classify as delinquents.

The legal definitions of what constitutes juvenile delinquency appear in state juvenile codes and statutes and vary somewhat from state to state. Generally, a criminal law definition of juvenile delinquency holds that any person, usually under 18 years of age, who commits an illegal act is considered a delinquent when he or she is officially processed through juvenile or family court. A juvenile does not become a delinquent until he or she is officially labeled as such by the specialized judicial agency (e.g., the juvenile court). For example, Ohio defines a *delinquent child* as a child:

a) Who violates any law of this State, the United States or any ordinance or regulation of a political subdivision of the state, which would be a crime if committed by an adult . . . .

b) Who violates any lawful order of the court. . . . (Chapter 2151.02. *Page's Ohio Revised Code Annotated*, 1994).

A Montana statute specifies that a delinquent youth is one who has either committed a crime or who has violated the terms of his or her probation, while the Mississippi statute defines a delinquent child broadly as a youth (10 years of age or older) "who is habitually disobedient, whose associations are injurious to the welfare of other children" (Binder, Geis, & Bruce, 1988, p. 6). Therefore, a youth who could be defined as a "delinquent" under the Mississippi statute in many situations would not be so considered under the Ohio or Montana codes.

It is important to carefully note the difference between a "delinquent" and a delinquent act. The specific act is the behavior that has violated the state criminal code, and the term *delinquent* is the official label frequently assigned to a youth who deviates from the accepted community norms. A juvenile who commits an illegal act is not immediately or automatically defined as a delinquent. Assaulting another youth or breaking a school window does not automatically make one a delinquent. Isolated single incidents usually are tolerated by the community or neighborhood. For the most part, society-at-large reserves judgment until after a number or series of legally defined delinquent acts are committed. Police officers and prosecutors handle juveniles differently depending on age and the nature, severity, and frequency of the juvenile's acts. See Chapter 7 for a detailed discussion of police work with juveniles. Prosecutorial and judicial discretion with juvenile offenders and their beliefs about punishment versus rehabilitation explain why two different youths are usually handled differently by the juvenile court, even if they commit the same offense. See Chapter 8 for a detailed discussion of juvenile court and procedural rights and competency.

There are two primary types of juvenile delinquency. As discussed above, the first are the criminal offenses: those acts considered illegal whether committed by an adult or a juvenile. Such illegal acts include aggravated assault, arson, homicide, rape, burglary, larceny, auto theft, and drug-related crimes. These types of serious offenses are the primary concern of juvenile corrections officials. According to the national and local statutes on juvenile criminality, burglary and larceny are the most frequently committed offenses. The brutal crimes of homicide and forcible rape represent only a small percentage of the total number of crimes committed by juveniles.

The second major type of juvenile delinquency is known as status offenses: misbehavior that would not be considered a crime if engaged in by an adult. Examples of status offenses are truancy, incorrigibility, curfew violations, and running away from home. Approximately half of the states include status offenses in their definition of juvenile delinquency offenses. Other states have passed separate legislation that distinguishes juveniles who have committed criminal acts from those who have committed status offenses. In those states, status offenders are viewed as individuals "in need of supervision" and are designated as CHINS, CINS, MINS, PINS, or JINS. The first letter of the acronym varies based on whether the initial word is *children, minors, persons,* or *juveniles,* but the rest of the phrase is always the same: "in need of supervision."

■ Juvenile Justice Processing and Case Flow

The juvenile justice process usually involves the formal agencies and procedures developed to handle those children and youths suspected or accused of violating their state's juvenile code. The juvenile justice agencies are police and sheriff's department's youth or juvenile aid divisions, juvenile and family courts, and community-based and institutional juvenile correctional facilities. There are nine stages in delinquency case processing through the juvenile justice system:

- ☐ Initial contact by law enforcement agencies
- ☐ Law enforcement informal handling, diversion, arrest, and/or referral to the juvenile court
- ☐ Court intake via the juvenile probation intake unit or the prosecutor's office
- ☐ Pre-adjudication juvenile detention
- ☐ Prosecutors filing a delinquency petition in juvenile court or waiving to adult criminal court
- ☐ Investigation or predisposition report prepared by a probation officer
- ☐ Juvenile court judge's adjudicatory decision and sanctions
- ☐ Participation and completion of mandated juvenile offender treatment program
- ☐ Juvenile aftercare plan

Because of discretion exercised by police and judicial officers, there is some variation from one city or county to the next in the processing of juvenile cases. Therefore, while there is a sequential series of critical decision points in case processing, there is also some variation in how, when, and which types of decisions are made. In general, alleged juvenile offenders have their first encounter with the juvenile justice system through police officers or sheriff's deputies.

■ Initial Contact and Handling by the Police

Law enforcement officers frequently divert juvenile delinquents and status offenders out of the juvenile justice system. However, in many instances an officer has sufficient evidence to arrest a juvenile and immediately bring the suspect to the police precinct or department. An *arrest* is defined as taking an individual into custody for purposes of interviewing or charging an individual with a delinquency offense. Upon arresting the youth, a decision is made based on whether there is sufficient evidence to either send the juvenile to probation intake and detention or to divert the case out of the system into alternative educational or recreational programs. In most cases, the police juvenile officer makes this decision, after discussions with the victim, the juvenile, and the parent or guardian, and after carefully determining the nature and extent of the youth's previous contacts with the police and juvenile courts. Federal regulations clearly discourage detaining juveniles in adult county or city jails and lockups. If a police officer believes that it is necessary to detain a youth in secure custody for a short period in order to allow a parent to pick up a youth or to arrange transport to the county juvenile detention facility, then federal regulations require that the youth be detained for a maximum of 6 hours and in a restricted area from where no adult detainees can be observed or heard.

■ Juvenile Court Intake and Pre-adjudication Juvenile Detention

The overwhelming majority of juvenile court referrals come from police sending the juvenile to the county or city probation intake unit. The remaining referrals usually come from parents, victims, and school personnel. In general, juvenile court intake units are staffed by the juvenile probation department or the prosecutor's office. At this decision point, the probation intake officer must decide whether to dismiss the case, handle the juvenile informally, or request formal adjudication by the juvenile court. Before making this decision, the intake officer is required to examine the type and seriousness of the alleged offense and to make a determination of whether there is clear and convincing evidence to prove the allegation. If there are no clear legal merits, such as eyewitnesses, then the case is dismissed. If there is sufficient evidence, then the intake probation officer makes a determination as to whether official juvenile court processing is appropriate.

Approximately half of all juvenile cases referred by intake officers are handled informally. The overwhelming majority of these cases are dismissed. In the other informally handled cases, the youth voluntarily signs a written agreement outlining specific conditions for an informal disposition for a specified time period. Typical conditions often include victim restitution, drug education and intensive counseling, school attendance, or a curfew. In many jurisdictions, a youth may be offered an informal disposition only after verbalizing remorse for the crime. Compliance with the agreement is frequently monitored by a probation officer and sometimes referred to as "informal probation." At the end of the specified period, and as long as the youth complies with the written agreement, the case is dismissed. If the youth fails to comply with the written agreement, then the probation officer may refer the case for formal prosecution. If that is the case, then the juvenile is mandated to an adjudicatory hearing.

■ Pre-adjudication Juvenile Detention

A youth may be held in a secure juvenile detention facility during the processing of his or her case if the intake officer believes detention is needed to protect the community or the child. When a youth is accused of having committed a serious crime, the police usually bring him or her to the juvenile detention facility. Most juvenile detention facilities have an intake unit where detention intake or juvenile probation officers review the facts of the case and the juvenile's background and home situation and then decide whether the juvenile should be detained, pending a hearing by a judge. In all states, a detention hearing should be held within a time period defined by statute, generally within 24 hours on a weekday or within 72 hours if the youth is referred on the weekend. At the detention hearing, a court-appointed referee or judge reviews the case and then determines if continued detention is necessary. Detention sometimes extends after the adjudicatory and dispositional hearings. Unfortunately, as a result of overcrowded state-operated juvenile facilities, short-term detention can continue beyond formal adjudication until a bed opens up at the state juvenile correctional or drug treatment facility.

■ Prosecutors File a Case in Either Juvenile or Criminal Court

In many states, prosecutors are mandated by the criminal code to file certain (generally serious violent) juvenile cases in the adult criminal court. These are violent cases in which the state legislature has decided the youth should be waived to criminal court and be handled as a criminal offender. In a growing number of states, the legislature has allowed the prosecutor the sole discretion of filing a defined list of serious cases in either juvenile court or adult criminal court. In these states, the prosecutor selects the court that will hear the case. If the case is handled by a juvenile court judge, then two types of formal petitions may be filed: delinquency or waiver to adult court. A delinquency petition formally describes the allegations and requests the juvenile court to *adjudicate* (or judge) the juvenile a delinquent, making the juvenile offender a ward of the court. This legal language is different from that applied in the criminal court system, where an offender is *convicted and sentenced*. With regard to delinquency petitions, an adjudicatory judicial hearing is scheduled. At the adjudicatory hearing (trial), the juvenile is represented by counsel, and witnesses are called to present the facts of the case. In most adjudicatory hearings, the judge (rather than a jury) determines whether the juvenile committed the offense(s).

■ Investigation or Pre-disposition Report Prepared by a Probation Officer

Between the time of processing the case through the juvenile court and the disposition hearing, the probation staff prepares a pre-disposition report. If the juvenile is adjudicated a delinquent by the judge, then a disposition plan is developed. A disposition can be defined as a decision to administer punitive sanctions as a result of a delinquency adjudication. The probation officer preparing this plan for the judge may order psychological testing and forensic evaluations, diagnostic tests, or a short period of confinement in a diagnostic and classification facility. At the disposition hearing, specific treatment and program recommendations are presented to the judge. The prosecutor and the youth's parent or the youth may also prepare and present dispositional recommendations. After reviewing all of the options, the juvenile court judge orders a disposition in the case.

There are three main types of juvenile dispositions: *nominal, conditional,* and *custodial* options. *Nominal* dispositions are frequently used with nonviolent first offenders and include reprimands or warnings that the juvenile will be incarcerated for a long time if he or she returns to the court for a new offense. *Conditional* dispositions often require juvenile offenders to comply with certain conditions of probation, such as participating in 2 months of addictions treatment, including 6 days per week of intensive group therapy, psychosocial assessment, and individual clinical treatment twice a week, completion of a vocational evaluation and placement program, or full restitution to victims and the juvenile court, which are monitored by the probation officer. *Custodial* dispositions limit juveniles' freedom of movement by placing them in non-secure custody foster homes, community-based temporary confinement, secure custody, or secure confinement, including home detention with electronic monitoring devices, group homes, forestry camps, structured wilderness programs, schools, and secure juvenile institutions (Fig. 1.1).

■ The Juvenile Court Judge's Decision and Sanctions

Juvenile court judges have the responsibility of ordering sanctions on adjudicated delinquents that can result in a turning point for juvenile

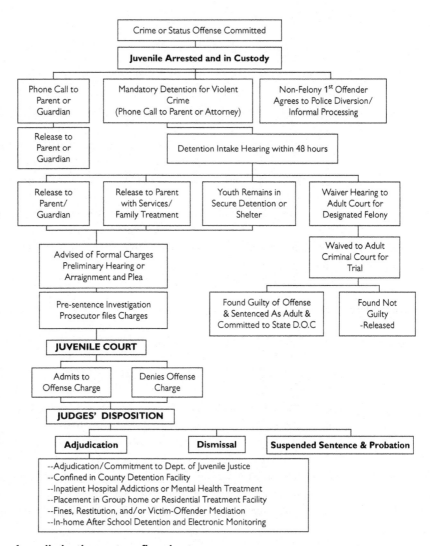

Figure 1.1   Juvenile justice system flowchart.

lawbreakers. Participation in short-term residential or community treatment programs can break the cycle of habitual delinquency and criminality. On the other hand, being sent to a state training school for 2 years or longer can further corrupt a young delinquent and eventually lead to a life of habitual crime and long periods of incarceration. Regular probation, intensive probation supervision, and probation-monitored restitution are the preferred sanctions of many juvenile court judges. However, about one third of these delinquents are committed to residential treatment programs. These commitments may be for a specific short term of 3 or 4 months or for an indeterminate time period. The juvenile residential facility may be publicly or privately operated and may have a secure lockup and institutional environment or an open setting with extensive educational and recreational facilities. In a large number of states, after the judge commits a youth to the state department of juvenile services or corrections, the department then determines in which facility the juvenile will be placed and the date the juvenile will be released. In other cases, the judge controls the placement and length of stay. In either situation, review hearings on a monthly basis are important in order to assess the progress of the juvenile.

A probation sanction may include individual drug counseling, daily participation in AA or NA meetings, weekend confinement in the local detention center, and community service or victim restitution. The term and conditions of probation are usually very specific. In some cases, however, the length of the probation order is open-ended and determined by the probation officer, based on the progress of the probationer. After the probation officer reports to the court that all conditions have been met, the judge terminates the case.

Juvenile Aftercare Plan

Upon release from a state training school, also known as a juvenile correctional institution, the juvenile may be ordered to a period of intensive aftercare or parole. During this period, the juvenile may be monitored or placed under the supervision of the juvenile court or corrections department. Aftercare programs should include a continuum of services and scheduled activities, such as afterschool recreational and creative arts programs, alternative dispute resolution programs, mentoring and tutoring programs, career development and vocational training programs, religious group meetings, family counseling, volunteer work with the homeless and disabled, and neighborhood crime prevention projects. The juvenile who does not adhere to the conditions of aftercare may be remanded to the same juvenile correctional facility or to another facility.

■ The Processing of Status Offense Cases Differs From That of Delinquency Cases

As discussed earlier in this chapter, a delinquency offense is an act committed by a minor for which an adult could be prosecuted in criminal court. However, status offenses are behaviors that are violations of the state juvenile code only for children and youths of minor status—for example, running away from home, chronic truancy, ungovernability, staying out all night without permission, and underage drinking. In a number of ways, the law enforcement and court processing of status offense cases parallels that of delinquency cases.

However, not all states consider all of these behaviors to be law violations. Most states view these behaviors as indications that the youth is in need of closer supervision and respond to the behavior by providing social and family services. This different perspective of status offenses often results in their being handled more like dependency than delinquency cases. Status offenders are just as likely to enter the juvenile justice system through a child welfare agency as through law enforcement.

The landmark Juvenile Justice and Delinquency Prevention Act of 1974 strongly discouraged holding status offenders in secure fixed juvenile correctional facilities, either for detention or placement. This important legislation and policy mandate is called *deinstitutionalization of status offenders*. An exception to this deinstitutionalization policy takes place when the juvenile status offender violates a valid court order, such as a probation order that requires the adjudicated status offender to reside in a group home for 30 days or one that requires attendance at school 5 days a week and an 8 p.m. curfew. The status offender who violates the court order or group home placement may then be confined in a secure detention or correctional facility.

■ Juvenile Court Referrals and Case Dispositions

The overwhelming number (83%) of juvenile delinquency cases processed by the juvenile courts during 2009 were referred by law enforcement agencies. The remaining referrals to juvenile courts came from social service agencies, schools, parents, probation officers, and victims (Puzzanchera, Adams, & Hockenberry, 2012). Juvenile delinquency cases that are referred to a county or city juvenile court are usually screened by a probation or juvenile intake department (either located within or attached to the court, or outside the court). The intake unit or department decides whether to dismiss the case because of a lack of sufficient legal cause or to resolve the matter through a formal petition or informally through referral to a social service or family counseling agency, substance abuse treatment program, or restitution. In 2009, 55% of all juvenile delinquency cases that were disposed of by the juvenile courts were handled formally while 45% were handled informally (Fig. 1.2). Among non-petitioned delinquency cases, 41% were dismissed at the intake or precourt level, frequently for a lack of legal justification. However, in the remaining 59% of cases, the troubled youths voluntarily accepted informal sanctions, such as referral to a social service or counseling agency, informal probation or restricted curfews, payment of fines, community service, or voluntary monetary restitution.

When the intake department makes a decision that a case needs to be formally processed within the juvenile court, a petition is filed and the case is then placed on the juvenile court's calendar (or docket) for an adjudicatory hearing and judicial disposition. The probation or juvenile detention intake officer may recommend that a case be removed from juvenile court and waived to adult criminal court. In these relatively few serious cases, a petition is often

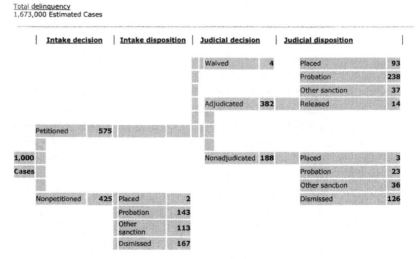

Total delinquency
1,673,000 Estimated Cases

| Intake decision | Intake disposition | Judicial decision | Judicial disposition |

Waived 4
Placed 93
Probation 238
Other sanction 37
Adjudicated 382 Released 14

Petitioned 575

1,000 Cases
Nonadjudicated 188
Placed 3
Probation 23
Other sanction 36
Dismissed 126

Nonpetitioned 425
Placed 2
Probation 143
Other sanction 113
Dismissed 167

Figure 1.2   Juvenile court processing for a typical 1,000 delinquency cases, 2010.

filed in the juvenile court to formally request a transfer or waiver hearing, at which time the juvenile court judge or referee is asked to waive or set aside jurisdiction over the juvenile case.

For example, during 2010, 58% (313,000 out of 536,000) of all the formally processed delinquency cases (adjudicated, nonadjudicated, or waived) in the United States resulted in the youth being adjudicated a juvenile delinquent. In approximately 41% of these alleged delinquency cases, the youths were not adjudicated, and the remaining 1% of formally processed cases were judicially waived to criminal court (see Fig. 1.2).

It is the juvenile court judge's responsibility at the disposition hearing to determine the most reasonable and appropriate sanction, as a result of carefully reviewing a predisposition psychosocial and delinquency history report prepared by the county or city probation department. The full range of adjudication options available to a typical juvenile court includes commitment to a juvenile institution or a residential drug treatment facility, placement in a group home or foster care, traditional or intensive probation supervision, court-monitored home-based electronic monitoring, referral to an outside community agency, prevocational program, psychosocial day treatment, or a community mental health program, a fine, community service in a local hospital, nursing home, or public works program, or restitution.

During 2009, clearly the most common sanction for adjudicated youth was formal probation, the result of 60% of formally adjudicated cases, compared with the 27% of adjudicated youths who were placed in a residential facility.

With regard to juvenile court dispositional hearings, judges usually do their best to determine appropriate and effective sanctions for delinquent youth in order to break the cycle of juvenile delinquency recidivism. In a growing number of delinquency dispositions, the juvenile court imposes a combination of sanctions, such as probation for 1 year with the first 3 months spent in a residential drug treatment facility or commitment to a group home for 6 months, with the stipulation that the adjudicated youth attend an alternative school 5 days a week and 2 hours of group therapy every night. Other sanctions include commitment to a juvenile correctional institution's maximum-security MICA unit (mentally ill and chemically dependent juvenile offenders), probation, and/or electronically monitored home detention.

The number and percentage of delinquency adjudications resulting in residential placements increased by approximately 27% from 1985 to 2009. This number, however, peaked in 1997 and decreased by 24% in 2009. Specifically, adjudicated delinquent youths were court-ordered to residential placement in 176,800 in 1997 compared to 133,800 delinquency cases in 2009. The overwhelming majority of residential placements were associated with drug offense cases, followed by offenses against persons, the public order cases. The number of adjudicated delinquency cases resulting in formal probation increased approximately 51% from 1985 to 2009. Similar to the residential placement increases, however, probation increases occurred between 1985 and 1997, and the number has decreased steadily since that time. In 2009, 60% (about 300,000) of all adjudicated delinquency cases led to formal juvenile probation. Furthermore, in 2009, other court-ordered sanctions, including community service, day treatment, and restitution, were imposed in 63,500 (13%) of the adjudicated delinquency cases.

According to the U.S. Department of Justice data, probation is the most common form of sanction given by the juvenile court. Between 1997 and 2009, the number of juvenile offenders formally placed on probation decreased across all four types of offenses. Specifically, the percentage of youth adjudicated to formal probation decreased the most for property offenses (40%), followed by drug offenses (17%), offenses against persons (12%), and public order offenses (5%).

With the decreases in the number of overall juvenile court cases from 1997 to 2009, decreases in the number of sanctions given out by the court should be expected. This trend has been reflected in other fields as well. Specifically, similar decreases have been reflected in youth substance use (Johnston, O'Malley, Bachman, & Schulenberg, 2013), school violence (Pitner, Astor, & Benbenishty, in press), and school dropout (U.S. Department of Education, 2012). Some have hypothesized that the emphasis on delivering evidence-based intervention to at-risk youth may be reducing and diverting youth from these problematic trajectories (Greenwood & Edwards, 2011).

Delinquency cases disposed, 1960–2010

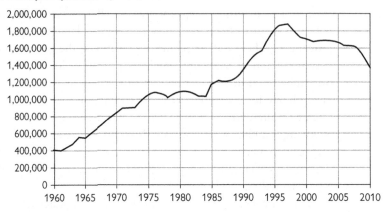

Figure 1.3   Juvenile court cases 1960–2010.

Source: *OJJDP Statistical Briefing Book*. Online. Available: http://www.ojjdp.gov/ojstatbb/court/qa06204.asp?qaDate=2010. Released on April 17, 2013.

■ Juvenile Court Jurisdiction and Upper Age Limits

According to Figure 1.3, during the last four decades of the 20th century, the number of juvenile court cases increased significantly from only 405,000 cases in 1961 to 1.75 million by the year 2000 (Puzzanchera et al., 2001; Snyder, 2002). More specifically, juvenile court cases rapidly increased from 405,000 in 1961 to 1.25 million in 1977, with a small decline to 1.1 million in 1984 and 1985, and then a gradual year-by-year increase to 1.83 million cases by 1996. By 1975, the number of juvenile court cases had more than doubled at 1,051,000 since the 1961 statistics. The all-time peak of 1,828,800 occurred in 1996. Since the peak in 1996, there has been a steady overall decline in juvenile court cases, as illustrated in Figure 1.3.

All 50 states and the District of Columbia have legal statutes that define an upper age limit for juvenile court jurisdictions. But states differ on the age at which a juvenile's wrongdoing is handled as a criminal (adult) offense rather than a juvenile offense. The oldest age at which an offender is still treated as a juvenile ranges from 15 to 18. In the overwhelming majority of states and the District of Columbia, an individual is under the jurisdiction of the juvenile court until the age of 18 (Table 1.1). However, youths in 10 states are treated as an adult at the age of 17 (Georgia, Illinois, Louisiana, Massachusetts, Michigan, Missouri, New Hampshire, South Carolina, Texas, and Wisconsin). In addition, youth living in New York and North Carolina who violate their state's criminal code at age 16 (or older) are within the jurisdiction of the criminal court (OJJDP, 2012).

In contrast to this practice of specifying maximum ages for juvenile court jurisdiction, only a few states designate a specific minimum age in their

Table 1.1   **Upper Age of Original Juvenile Court Jurisdiction, 2011**

State	Upper Age of Jurisdiction		
	Age 15	Age 16	Age 17
Alabama			X
Alaska			X
Arizona			X
Arkansas			X
California			X
Colorado			X
Connecticut		X	
Delaware			X
Florida			X
Georgia		X	
Hawaii			X
Idaho			X
Illinois		X	
Indiana			X
Iowa			X
Kansas			X
Kentucky			X
Louisiana		X	
Maine			X
Maryland			X
Massachusetts		X	
Michigan		X	
Minnesota			X
Mississippi			X
Missouri		X	
Montana			X
Nebraska			X
Nevada			X
New Hampshire		X	
New Jersey			X
New Mexico			X
New York	X		
North Carolina	X		
North Dakota			X
Ohio			X
Oklahoma			X
Oregon			X
Pennsylvania			X
Rhode Island			X

(continued)

19

Table 1.1   **(Continued)**

State	Upper Age of Jurisdiction		
	Age 15	Age 16	Age 17
South Carolina		X	
South Dakota			X
Tennessee			X
Texas		X	
Utah			X
Vermont			X
Virginia			X
Washington			X
West Virginia			X
Wisconsin		X	
Wyoming			X

Source: *OJJDP Statistical Briefing Book.* Online. Available: http://www.ojjdp.gov/ojstatbb/structure_process/qa04101.asp?qaDate=2011. Released on December 17, 2012.

juvenile code. Most state juvenile and criminal codes implicitly follow the English common-law position that a child under the age of 7 is incapable of criminal intent. Therefore, a child below the age of 7 who commits a crime is not held morally or criminally responsible for that act.

An increasing number of state legislatures have determined that juvenile offenders accused of brutal crimes should be processed by criminal courts rather than juvenile courts. Many states have authorized a waiver of jurisdiction that automatically gives the adult criminal courts jurisdiction over certain violent juveniles. For example, in 1978, New York State passed legislation creating a classification of juvenile offenses called "designated felonies." Under this state law, 14- and 15-year-olds charged with committing murder, kidnapping, arson, manslaughter, rape, or assault were tried in designated felony courts. If the accused offenders were found guilty of the charges, they could be imprisoned for up to 5 years (Prescott, 1981 p. 1). This is an increase over the typical sentence for a juvenile offender, which averages 12 months.

Until recently, 20 states permitted the death penalty as a sentencing option for 16- and 17-year-olds. In fact, there have been 22 executions of juvenile offenders since 1976, 13 of which occurred in Texas (Lane, 2005). In 2005, however, the U.S. Supreme Court ruled it unconstitutional to give the death penalty to anyone under the age of 18. The court's decision was supported by substantial evidence associated with the fact that an adolescent's brain is not fully developed and able to understand consequences. Chapter 24 provides further information on the criminal courts' handling of and intervention with repeat violent juvenile offenders.

■ Handling Juvenile Status Offenders

There has been considerable debate over the appropriate way to handle status offenders. The major issue is whether the juvenile court should retain authority over them. Those in favor of the court's continuing authority believe that a youth's habitual misbehavior will eventually lead to more serious delinquent acts; therefore, it is wise for the court to retain its jurisdiction over the status offender. An opposing view (often advanced by deviance theorists with a societal reaction or labeling-theory perspective) holds that status offenders who are defined as delinquents may actually become delinquents as the result of a self-fulfilling prophecy, leading to secondary deviance (Becker, 1963; Lemert, 1971; Schur, 1973).

Another belief held by a number of social workers is that the needs of status offenders can be better met within the community social service and child welfare service systems (Boisvert & Wells, 1980; Roberts, 1987; Springer, 2001). For example, Roberts's (1987) research documented the need for the full range of social services, including 24-hour telephone hotlines, short-term runaway shelters, family treatment programs, education and treatment services for abusive parents, and vocational training and placement services.

At issue is the type of treatment status offenders should receive. Should they be sentenced to a secure juvenile facility or referred to a community social service agency for counseling? For many years, it was common for juvenile status offenders to be sentenced to juvenile training schools, where they were confined in the same institution with youths convicted of serious crimes. The practice of sending status offenders to juvenile correctional institutions has become much less common in recent years because of the deinstitutionalization of status offenders. However, in certain circumstances a minor who has committed no crime can still be sent to a juvenile training school. For example, a youth with a history of chronic runaway behavior is placed in a group home by the court. If the juvenile then runs away from that facility, the court views that act as a delinquency offense, and the youth is usually sent to a secure juvenile institution.

Probation officers often believe that although most status offenders do not pose a danger to others, they do frequently exhibit destructive behavior patterns such as drug abuse, alcohol abuse, or suicidal ideation. They often come from dysfunctional, conflict-ridden families where physical, sexual, or emotional abuse is prevalent. Thus the social work perspective urges that a continuum of services be provided for status offenders and their families through a social service agency, a family service agency, or a juvenile court–based program. Available services should include family counseling, individual and group counseling, addiction treatment, alternative education programs, and vocational evaluation, education, and training.

For an in-depth analysis of the nature and types of social service and counseling programs to which status offenders are referred, see Chapters 13, 14,
and 15 on the emergence, proliferation, and characteristics of contemporary
juvenile diversion and community-based programs.

■ Official and Unofficial Statistics

Juvenile delinquency trends and estimates of the scope of the delinquency
problem come from both official statistics and unofficial self-report studies.
The four major sources of data on delinquency and victimization are:

1 **Official police statistics,** such as the FBI Uniform Crime Report, which
   is published annually by the FBI. These data are based on crimes cleared
   by arrest and are limited because they do not indicate the total number
   of juveniles adjudicated for the offense for which they were arrested and
   detained. To improve the accuracy of FBI crime statistics, the National
   Incident Based Reporting System (NIBRS) was implemented in 35 states
   and the District of Columbia to collect data on offenses reported to or
   observed by law enforcement officers. In addition, there are eight states
   that are testing the NIBRS, and only six states that are not currently
   participating (Alaska, Florida, Georgia, Hawaii, Nevada, and Wyoming).
   The NIBRS has individual incident records for the 33 crime categories
   and 46 other offenses (Bureau of Justice Statistics, 2011).

2 **Official statewide and national juvenile court statistics** and trend data
   are collected by the National Center for Juvenile Justice and the OJJDP
   on delinquency, child neglect, and dependency cases processed through
   juvenile and family courts nationwide.

3 **Self-report studies,** such as the National Youth Survey, involve asking
   youths whether they have engaged in one or more delinquent behaviors
   in the past year (e.g., damaging or destroying school property, making
   obscene phone calls, running away from home).

4 **Victimization studies,** like the National Crime Victimization Survey
   (NCVS), involve interviews each year with a large sample of individuals
   and household heads (approximately 40,000 households that represent
   about 75,000 people) in order to estimate the frequency of crimes,
   the characteristics of self-reported crime victims, and the likelihood of
   victimization.

Official Statistics

According to the latest U.S. Department of Justice report (Snyder, 2012), in the
year 2010, police agencies throughout the United States made almost 1.7 million arrests of youths under the age of 18. As documented by the FBI, children

and youths accounted for about 14% of all arrests and an estimated 18% of all arrests for violent crimes in 2010. While juvenile crime is a prevalent social and public health problem, the violent crime index offenses—murder, forcible rape, robbery, and aggravated assault—peaked in 1994 and have steadily declined over the past 16 years.

The most promising development is that the juvenile murder arrest rate has fallen to its lowest level since the mid-1960s. In 2010, there were 1,010 juvenile arrests for murder. The peak year for juveniles being murdered was 1993, with nearly 2,900 juvenile murder victims. The number of juvenile and adult murders combined also peaked in 1993 with 24,526 reported murders in the United States, in comparison with 11,200 murders reported to police agencies in the year 2010 (Snyder, 2012). Murder is a crime that is almost always reported. Therefore, the FBI statistics on murder are definitely the most accurate and valid in light of the limitations on the reporting of other offenses.

Since 1972, the U.S. Children's Bureau has issued periodic estimates on the number of juvenile delinquents in the United States. Their figures, based on reports from a sampling of juvenile courts across the country, show a significant increase in the number of crimes committed by juveniles. In 1930, they estimated that there were 200,000 delinquents; in 1950, the figure climbed to 435,000 (Robinson, 1960). In 1966, more than 1 million individuals under the age of 18 were arrested. Alfred Blumstein (1967) estimated that 27% of all male juveniles would probably be arrested before reaching age 18.

During the 1960s and 1970s, the federal Office of Youth Development reported a significant increase in juvenile court cases. This surge markedly exceeded the growth of the population of children in the 10- to 17-year-old age group. Between 1960 and 1970 the number of delinquency cases more than doubled, climbing from 510,000 to 1,052,000, while the child population increased by only 29%, from 25.4 million to 32.6 million (Youth Development and Delinquency Prevention Administration, 1973). In 1984, the total number of arrests for youths under age 18 had exceeded 2 million (2,062,448). The juvenile most likely to be arrested (regardless of the type of offense) was over 15 years of age, by a ratio of almost three to one (1,537,688 to 524,760). Table 1.2 lists the most frequent offense categories for older juveniles between the ages of 15 and 18.

We now turn our attention to the major index crimes. As shown in Table 1.3, the vast majority of juvenile arrests are for property offenses rather than violent crimes. Property crimes include burglary, larceny, theft, motor vehicle theft, and arson. Violent crimes include murder, forcible rape, robbery, and aggravated assault.

As documented in Table 1.3, juvenile crime increases dramatically with age. In comparing the crime rate for juveniles under 15 with those age 15 to 17, arrests for property crimes more than doubled while arrests for violent crimes nearly tripled. Although the number of arrests for property and violent

Table 1.2 **Most Frequent Offenses by Older Juveniles, 2012**

Offense Charged	Number of Juveniles Arrested
Larceny/theft	169,992
Burglary	40,351
Liquor law violations	62,380
Vandalism	44,578
Disorderly conduct	87,983
Curfew and loitering law violations	40,125
Drug abuse violations	100,498
Motor vehicle theft	8,991

Source: U.S. Department of Justice. (2013). *Crime in the United States: Uniform crime reports, 1984.* Washington, DC: U.S. Government Printing Office.

crime increase as juveniles become older, their percentages of total crime remain more or less stable. Property crime makes up about 23% of total crime over all age groups, while violent crime makes up a little over 4%. These data on juvenile arrests represent only the tip of the iceberg. They do not include status offenses, nor do they reflect the number of juvenile lawbreakers who were not apprehended or who committed offenses that were never reported to the police.

Table 1.4 provides a useful perspective on person offenses cases handled by the juvenile courts. Between 1985 and 2009, the number of cases handled increased by 30%. However, the biggest increase took place between 1989 and 1994. The period between 1994 and 1998 saw an increase of only 12%, minimal compared with the overall span. The cases handled after that time began to decrease, with a 12% decline between 2000 and 2009. This drop indicates a decrease in violent crimes committed by juveniles. It shows a promising trend with regard to juvenile violent crimes handled by the juvenile courts. It seems to show that in recent years, there has been a decrease among juveniles committing almost all violent crimes, while the rates of robbery revealed an increase.

Table 1.3 **Total Arrests of Juveniles for Property and Violent Crime, 2012**

Offense Charged	Number of Juveniles Arrested		
	Under 15	15–17	18 and over
Property crimes	64,321	158,337	1,008,628
Violent crimes	11,929	30,449	337,395
Total offenses charged	270,470	698,064	8,027,884

Source: U.S. Department of Justice. (2013). *Sourcebook of criminal justice statistics.* Washington, DC: U.S. Government Printing Office.

Table 1.4 **Persons Offenses Cases Handled by U.S. Juvenile Courts, 1989–2009**

| Cases Disposed | 2009 | Percentage Change | |
		1985–2009	2000–09
Total persons offenses[a]	365,700	99	−8
Violent crime index	80,300	24	−3
Criminal homicide	1,300	3	−10
Forcible rape	4,000	21	−5
Robbery	29,000	15	35
Aggravated assault	45,500	32	−18
Simple assault	243,900	143	−10

Note: Percent changes are calculated using rounded numbers.

[a]Total includes other persons offenses categories not listed.

Source: Puzzanchera, C., Adams, B., & Hockenberry, S. (2012). *Juvenile court statistics 2009*. Pittsburgh, PA: National Center for Juvenile Justice.

Table 1.5 clearly indicates that juvenile arrests for violent and property crimes peaked in 1996 and have steadily declined since then. In fact, the 2010 arrest rates reflect the lowest seen over the past several decades. During any given time period, the crime rate may shift. Sometimes this shift results in a decrease, a gradual increase, or a cyclical up-and-down pattern. The first half of the 1980s, mainly the period from 1980 to 1984, saw a gradual decline in the overall crime rate for juveniles. This decline was due to the decrease in both property and violent crimes. However, beginning in the mid-1980s through the mid-1990s, the number of crimes began to shift. Both violent and property crimes increased. The peak for juvenile property crimes was reached in 1991, and the peak for juvenile crimes of violence in 1994. Gradually, by the end of 2000, the overall juvenile crime rate once again shifted back to close to its level in 1980. Since 2000, the rates have trended downward to the lowest rates over the past 30 years. In large part, this was due to a major decrease in the number of both violent and property crimes, especially in the period between 1995 and 2009. This statistical trend bodes well for the future because not only did the violent crime rate fall below its 1980 annual rate, but so did the total number of property crimes and overall arrest rates.

According to Table 1.6, drug cases in the juvenile court have remained virtually steady. There was practically no change in gender from 1989 to 1998. The substantial change occurred on the race demographic variable. Between 1989 and 1998, there was a slow, steady increase in the number of juvenile cases committed by Whites. This increase from 58% to 68% had an obvious effect on the Black group variable, which decreased from 40% to 29% over the 10-year span. However, over the past 10 years, drug case arrests have slowly begun to shift, with an increased number of Blacks being arrested for substance-related incidents.

While the official statistics may be appropriate in examining the extent of the labeling process, law enforcement and juvenile court statistics do not

Table 1.5   **Juvenile (ages 10–17) Arrest Rates for 1980–2010 (per 100,000)**

Year	Violent Crime	Property Crime	All Crimes*
1980	334.09	2562.16	6396.6
1981	322.64	2442.85	6370.2
1982	314.48	2373.32	6607.7
1983	295.98	2244.41	6073.9
1984	297.46	2220.73	6110.1
1985	302.97	2370.74	6466.0
1986	316.70	2427.07	6728.5
1987	310.55	2451.39	6808.2
1988	326.48	2418.73	7263.8
1989	381.56	2433.80	7339.1
1990	428.48	2563.65	7244.6
1991	461.06	2611.51	7466.4
1992	482.14	2522.62	7294.5
1993	504.48	2431.01	7509.3
1994	526.64	2545.56	8157.2
1995	517.74	2445.62	8228.3
1996	460.27	2381.78	8476.1
1997	442.46	2265.12	8211.3
1998	369.64	1959.62	7421.4
1999	339.14	1750.75	6757.2
2000	298.7	1546.6	6493.6
2001	289.6	1450.6	6202.2
2002	272.2	1394.6	6232.4
2003	267.5	1334.4	6078.1
2004	263.9	1300.1	5998.2
2005	276.7	1207.0	5907.1
2006	290.3	1163.0	6072.8
2007	280.2	1208.5	5983.5
2008	280.3	1278.2	5833.6
2009	253.3	1231.6	5343.8
2010	224.5	1084.3	4857.1

Note: Rates are arrests of persons ages 10–17 per 100,000 persons in the resident population. The violent crime index includes the offenses of murder and nonnegligent manslaughter, forcible rape, robbery, and aggravated assault. The property crime index includes burglary, larceny-theft, motor vehicle theft, and arson.

*As of 2010, the FBI no longer considers runaways in the total crime number.

Source: Adapted from National Center for Juvenile Justice (2012). *Juvenile Arrest Rates by Offense, Sex, and Race (1980–2010).* Retrieved from http://www.ojjdp.gov/ojstatbb/dat.html

Table 1.6 **Drug Cases in Juvenile Court: 1989, 1994, 1998, and 2009**

	1989 (%)	1994 (%)	1998 (%)	2009 (%)
Male	86	86	84	82
Female	14	14	16	18
Race ethnicity				
White	58	61	68	64
Black	40	37	29	34
Other	2	2	3	2

Source: Puzzanchera, C., Adams, B., & Hockenberry, S. (2012). *Juvenile court statistics 2009*. Pittsburgh, PA: National Center for Juvenile Justice.

give the full picture of the extent and volume of delinquent behavior. In other words, official statistics provide only a limited index of the total volume of delinquency. Because not all delinquent behavior is detected (and, therefore, cannot be officially recorded), the acts that are officially recorded should be combined with unofficial national surveys in order to obtain a more representative sample of all delinquent acts.

■ Unofficial Methods of Measuring Delinquency

Researchers have been quite persistent in their attempts to identify juvenile delinquents and to measure juvenile delinquency. The primary sources of data have been self-reports, victimization surveys, and observational studies in gang hangouts and schools. The major limitation of these methods relates to the representativeness of the individuals reported as delinquent.

Self-Report Delinquency Studies

Self-report questionnaires were first introduced as a method of measuring delinquency by Short and Nye (1958). Several other prominent sociologists and criminologists used the self-report approach: Empey and Erickson (1966); Gold (1966, 1970); Hindelang, Hirschi, and Weis (1981); and Hirschi (1969). Some self-report studies focus on measuring the proportion of youths who have engaged in delinquent acts, asking such questions as "Have you ever stolen something?" or "Have you stolen something since you were 9 years old?" These types of studies gather data on the extent of participation in specific delinquent behaviors. Other self-report delinquency studies make inquiries about the frequency of individual involvement in delinquent behaviors over a specific period, such as within the past year or two. Studies having time bounds of four or more years have only limited usefulness because of memory decay and filtering of recall.

Most self-report surveys indicate that the number of youths who break the law is much greater than official statistics report. These surveys reveal that the most common juvenile offenses are truancy, alcohol abuse, shoplifting, use of false identification, fighting, marijuana use, and damaging the property of others (Farrington, 1973; Hindelang, 1973).

Some of the more striking findings of self-report studies relate to the extent of delinquency and status offenses. According to estimates of the President's Commission on Law Enforcement and Administration of Justice (1967), self-report studies indicate that the overwhelming majority of all juveniles commit delinquent and criminal acts for which they could have been adjudicated.

Erickson and Empey (1963) studied self-reported delinquency behavior among high-school boys aged 15 to 17 in Provo, Utah. Using a list of 22 criminal and delinquent offenses to question the youths about their illegal activities, the researchers found that 90% of minor offenses (such as traffic violations, curfew violations, minor thefts, liquor law violations, and destroying property) went undetected. They compared the self-reported delinquency of boys who were officially nondelinquent with a group of official delinquents—those who had been processed by the court only once, those on probation, and those who were incarcerated. The results were surprising: the nondelinquents admitted to an average of almost 158 delinquent or status offense acts per youth. However, official delinquents' self-reports greatly exceeded the reports of nondelinquents: youths with a one-time court appearance had an average of 185 delinquent acts, repeat offenders who had been on probation had an average of 855 delinquent acts, and incarcerated delinquents had an average of 1,272 delinquent acts. In sharp contrast, Williams and Gold (1972) found that "(e)ighty-eight percent of the teenagers in the sample confessed to committing at least one chargeable offense in the three years prior to their interview" (p. 213).

The "dark figure of crime"—the unreported delinquent acts—are difficult to determine. Self-report studies indicated that the dark or unknown figure may be more than nine times greater than the official estimate, given that about nine of every 10 juvenile law violations are either undetected or not officially acted upon. The overwhelming majority of juveniles have broken the law, even though their offenses are usually minor. Yet, there is a small group of chronic, violent offenders; these are the youths who habitually violate the law and, as a result, are more likely to be apprehended and formally adjudicated.

Empey (1982) offers an analogy comparing juvenile offenders to fish caught in a net in an ocean:

> The chances are small that most fish will be caught. And even when some are caught, they manage to escape or are released because they are too small. But because a few fish are much more active than others, and because they are bigger, they are caught more than once. Each time this occurs, moreover, the chances that they will escape or be thrown back decrease. At the very end, therefore, they form a very select group whose behavior clearly separates them from most of the fish still in the ocean. (p. 113)

The most important and enlightening developments in research on hidden delinquency came from the national youth surveys. Beginning in 1967, the National Institute of Mental Health implemented the first national survey of a representative sample of adolescents, focusing on their attitudes and behaviors, including delinquent behavior. In 1972, the national youth survey (NAYS) was repeated; in 1976, the National Institute of Juvenile Justice and Delinquency Prevention became the cosponsor of what developed into an annual survey of self-reported delinquent behavior, based on a national probability panel of youths from 11 to 17 years of age (Weis, 1983).

These longitudinal, national surveys were based on a carefully drawn sample ($N = 1,725$) of adolescents from throughout the United States who were asked to report on their delinquent behavior for five consecutive years.

The major survey findings indicated that the overwhelming majority of American youths (11–17 years old) in the sample admitted that they had committed one or more juvenile offenses. In agreement with other self-report studies, the NAYS has found that the majority of youths had committed minor offenses, especially as they grew older. Notably, less than 6% of the youths in the survey (Huizinga & Elliot, 1984) admitted having committed one of the more serious index offenses that are listed in the FBI Uniform Crime Reports. The trends in self-reported delinquency reveal that youths in the 1980s seemed to be no more delinquent than youths in the early 1970s.

The survey found that those youths living with both natural parents reported lower delinquency rates than juveniles who came from single-parent or reconstituted families. It also found that youths who stayed in school reported less involvement in delinquency than those who dropped out. In addition, school dropouts admitted they had participated in crimes such as felony assault and theft, hard drug use, disorderly conduct, and general delinquency to a much greater extent than the in-school youths. In contrast, higher percentages of in-school youth indicated they had participated in minor assaults, vandalism, and school delinquency (Thornberry, Moore, & Christenson, 1985). Finally, the 1978–1980 national youth surveys asked about attendance at religious services. Those youths who reported regular attendance at religious services also reported less involvement in virtually all types of delinquent behaviors.

■ Trends on Illegal Drug Use and Juvenile Crime

The National Household Survey on Drug Abuse collects self-report data from a representative sample of just over 90,000 youths 12 to 17 years of age in all 50 states and the District of Columbia on current use of illegal drugs (Substance Abuse and Mental Health Services Administration, 2013). Highlights of the report indicate that 26.8% of youths in the 12- to 17-year-old age group used drugs in 2009, compared with 25.7% in 2010. This was a statistically significant decrease. There was a significant reduction in lifetime inhalant use, 9.2% in 2009 to 8.2% in 2010. However, there was no change in lifetime use of marijuana between 2009 and 2010, with approximately 17% of 12- to 17-year-olds reporting use in both years.

The abuse of crack, cocaine, marijuana, and alcohol escalated in the 1980s and resulted in a large number of juveniles being arrested and adjudicated for the sale and distribution of narcotics, as well as liquor law violations. Then in the second half of the 1990s, adjudications of juveniles for drug-related offenses declined. Now in the early 21st century, we are witnessing abuse of methamphetamines, ice, crystal, speed, OxyContin, and Ecstasy. Heavy drug use can destroy the brain functioning and lives of adolescent and young adult addicts. Specifically, heavy use of cocaine or methamphetamines often leads to hallucinations, delusions, psychotic episodes, suicide attempts, and juvenile violence. Possession, sale, manufacture, and distribution of illegal substances are criminal offenses. In addition, adolescent drug users frequently commit burglaries, thefts, and robberies and prostitute themselves to support their drug cravings.

The most comprehensive compendium of official and unofficial criminal justice statistics is the *Sourcebook of Criminal Justice Statistics*, published each year by the Hindelang Criminal Justice Research Center at the State University of New York at Albany (Maguire & Pastore, 2001, 2002). This huge volume includes FBI Uniform Crime Reports, Bureau of Justice Statistics reports and bulletins, OJJDP reports, NCVS tables, and large-scale national surveys of high-school students on unreported crimes, such as the PRIDE school confidential questionnaire (Table 1.7).

Victimization Surveys

Victimization studies have been completed in a large number of cities throughout the United States. These studies have been conducted as joint efforts by the U.S. Bureau of Justice Statistics and the Bureau of the Census. The best-known victimization survey is the NCVS, a massive, annual, house-to-house survey of a random sample of 40,000 households and 75,000 individuals (Bureau of Justice Statistics, 2011). The NCVS provides annual estimates of the total number of crimes committed by both adult and juvenile offenders. The six types of crime measured are rape, robbery, assault, household burglary, personal and household larceny, and motor vehicle theft. Based on the 2011 survey data, it has been estimated that 22.9 million serious crimes occur each year in the United States. The NCVS estimate is approximately two times greater than that reported in the FBI Uniform Crime Reports (Truman & Planty, 2012). These data indicate that underreporting is far more pervasive than was generally recognized before the completion of the national victimization surveys (Roberts, 1998).

Table 1.7   **Students Reporting Problem Behaviors by Grade Level of Respondent, 2006–2007**

	Never (%)	Seldom (%)	Sometimes (%)	Often (%)	A lot (%)
Have you been in trouble with the police?	74.4	13.4	6.7	2.6	2.8
Grades 6 to 8	77.6	11.5	5.8	2.5	2.7
Grades 9 to 12	70.5	15.9	7.8	2.7	3.1
12th grade	70.5	17.0	7.7	2.2	2.8
Do you take part in gang activities?	87.8	4.7	3.2	1.4	2.9
Grades 6 to 8	87.8	4.9	3.2	1.4	2.5
Grades 9 to 12	87.6	4.3	3.3	1.4	3.4
12th grade	87.6	2.8	3.0	1.4	3.3
Have you thought about committing suicide?	75.8	11.3	7.0	2.5	3.4
Grades 6 to 8	79.0	9.8	6.0	2.1	3.1
Grades 9 to 12	71.9	13.2	8.3	2.9	3.8
12th grade	71.9	13.3	8.8	2.6	3.3
Have you driven a car after or while drinking alcohol?	91.0	3.8	2.3	1.0	1.9
Grades 6 to 8	96.2	1.5	0.9	0.4	1.0
Grades 9 to 12	84.6	6.8	4.0	1.7	3.0
12th grade	71.0	14.0	7.5	3.1	4.3

Note: These data are from a survey of 6th- through 12th-grade students conducted during the 2006–2007 school year by PRIDE Surveys. Participating schools are sent the PRIDE questionnaire with explicit instructions for administering the anonymous, self-report survey. Schools that administer the PRIDE questionnaire do so voluntarily or in compliance with a school district or state request. For the 2006–2007 academic year, survey results are based on students from 22 states; the following states participated: Alabama, Arkansas, Arizona, California, Georgia, Illinois, Kentucky, Minnesota, Mississippi, New Hampshire, New Jersey, New York, North Carolina, Ohio, Oklahoma, Pennsylvania, South Dakota, Tennessee, Texas, Virginia, West Virginia, and Wisconsin. To prevent any one state from having a disproportionate influence on the summary results, random samples of students were drawn from those states where disproportionately large numbers of students were surveyed. Therefore, no state represents more than approximately 10% of the sample. The results presented are based on a sample consisting of 98,086 students drawn from the 410,688 students who completed the PRIDE questionnaire.

[a]Percents may not add up to 100 because of rounding.

Source: PRIDE Surveys, 2006–2007 PRIDE Surveys National Summary, Grades 6 through 12 (Bowling Green, KY: PRIDE Surveys, 2008), p. 189, Tables 4.23 and 4.24; p. 190, Table 4.25; p. 192, Table 4.32. Table adapted by SOURCEBOOK staff. Reprinted by permission

This survey also provided estimates of the juvenile offense rates for a limited number of crimes: rape, robbery, assault, and personal larceny. Historically, Laub's (1983) analysis indicated that the rates of delinquency for the years 1973 to 1981 remained relatively stable. In addition, there has been very little change in the types of persons who are victimized by juveniles. For the most part, juvenile perpetrators victimized other youths, rather than adults; males were the victims twice as frequently as females.

Summary

Not every youth who violates the law is labeled a juvenile delinquent. Many either escape detection entirely or, when apprehended by the local police, receive a strict lecture or warning and then are taken home. Most authorities do not consider law-breaking youths to be juvenile delinquents unless they are officially processed through the juvenile court and adjudicated a delinquent.

Youths can be referred to the juvenile court for three types of offenses:

- ☐ Delinquency offenses: illegal acts that are considered crimes whether committed by an adult or a juvenile (e.g., aggravated assault, arson, burglary, drug-related offenses, theft, and rape)
- ☐ Status offenses: deviant acts or misbehavior that, if engaged in by an adult, would not be considered crimes (e.g., truancy, incorrigibility, and running away from home)
- ☐ Dependency cases: a documented pattern of child neglect, physical abuse, or sexual abuse and identification of a minor needing foster care or other residential placement outside the home

For status offenders, many states have separate legislation that views these juveniles as individuals "in need of supervision." An array of crisis intervention services, runaway shelters, youth service bureaus, addiction treatment programs, day treatment programs, and family counseling programs have been developed to serve these youths (Roberts, 1998; Springer, 2001).

This chapter laid the groundwork for an examination of the field of juvenile justice. This was done by presenting legalistic, sociological, and criminological information that focuses on the nature of the juvenile justice system and its subsystems, the definition of the terms *juvenile delinquency* and *status offenses*, and juvenile justice processing, including referrals by police and schools to juvenile court, intake decisions and dispositions, juvenile court judges' decisions and dispositions, and official and unofficial trends and statistics on the extent of juvenile delinquency in the United States.

As defined in this chapter, *delinquency* refers to a juvenile who has been apprehended for any activity that is a violation of a state juvenile code. The juvenile justice system is concerned with caring for, controlling, and rehabilitating these juvenile law violators. A number of the chapters in this book examine the policies, agencies, programs, treatment alternatives, and services that have been developed to control and rehabilitate juvenile offenders. Emphasis is placed on examining the juvenile offender treatment programs that have reduced recidivism based on consistent longitudinal research.

Discussion Questions

1 Define *juvenile delinquency.*

2 Compare and contrast the terms *juvenile delinquency offenses* and *status offenses.*

3 Divide the class into two groups for a debate. Ask one group to adopt and defend a conservative perspective and the other group to adopt and defend a progressive perspective on the following issues:

☐ Should state legislatures authorize a waiver of jurisdiction to process juvenile offenders in adult criminal court who have been accused of brutal crimes and are over the age of 14?

☐ Should the juvenile court retain jurisdiction over habitual status offenders, or should they be diverted to a continuum of community social services?

4 Using official juvenile court statistics, discuss the recent trends in juvenile delinquency.

5 According to the recent report by Puzzanchera, Adams, and Hockenberry (2012), identify and discuss what happened to the juvenile arrest rates between 1985 and 2009.

6 List and describe the functions of the juvenile and criminal justice agencies in your county or city that have primary responsibility for handling juvenile status offenders and juvenile delinquents.

References

Armour, J., & Hammond, S. (2009). *Minority youth in the juvenile justice system: Disproportionate minority contact.* Washington, DC: National Conference of State Legislatures.

Becker, H. S. (1963). *Outsiders: Studies in the sociology of deviance.* New York: Free Press.

Blumstein, A. (1967). Systems analysis and the criminal justice system. *Annals of the American Academy of Political and Social Science,* Vol. 374, 92–100.

Boisvert, M. J., & Wells, R. (1980). Toward a rational policy on status offenders. *Social Work, 25,* 230–234.

Bureau of Justice Statistics. (2011). *Background and status of incident-based reporting and NIBRS.* Retrieved from http://www.jrsa.org/ibrrc/background-status.shtml.

Empey, L. T. (1982). *American delinquency: Its meaning and construction.* Chicago: Dorsey.

Empey, L. T., & Erickson, M. L. (1966). Hidden delinquency and social status. *Social Forces, 44,* 546–554.

Erickson, M. L., & Empey, L. T. (1963). Court records, undetected delinquency, and decision making. *Journal of Criminal Law, Criminology, and Police Science, 54,* 456–469.

Farrington, D. P. (1973). Self-reports of deviant behavior: Predictive and stable? *Journal of Criminal Law and Criminology, 44,* 99–111.

Gold, M. (1966). Undetected delinquent behavior. *Journal of Research in Crime and Delinquency, 3,* 27–46.

Gold, M. (1970). *Delinquent behavior in an American city.* Belmont, CA: Brooks/Cole.

Greenwood, P. W., & Edwards, D. L. (2011). Evidence-based programs for at-risk youth and juvenile offenders: A review of proven prevention and intervention models. In D. W. Springer & A. R. Roberts (Eds.), *Juvenile justice and delinquency* (pp. 369–390). Sudbury, MA: Jones and Bartlett.

Hindelang, M. J. (1973). Causes of delinquency: A partial replication and extension. *Social Problems, 20*(4), 471–487.

Hindelang, M. J., Hirschi, T., & Weis, J. (1981). *Measuring delinquency*. Beverly Hills, CA: Sage.

Hirschi, T. (1969). *Causes of delinquency.* Berkeley: University of California Press.

Huizinga, D., & Elliot, D. S. (1984). *Self-reported measures of delinquency and crime: Methodological issues and comparative findings.* Boulder, CO: Behavioral Research Institute.

Johnston, L. D., O'Malley, P. M., Bachman, J. G., & Schulenberg, J. E. (2013). *Monitoring the future national results on drug use: 2012 overview, key findings on adolescent drug use.* Ann Arbor: Institute of Social Research, The University of Michigan.

Lane, C. (2005). *5–4 Supreme Court abolishes juvenile executions.* Retrieved from http://www.washingtonpost.com/wp-dyn/articles/A62584-2005Mar1.html

Laub, J. H. (1983). *Juvenile criminal behavior in the United States: An analysis of an offender and victim characteristics.* Albany, NY: The Michael J. Hindelang Criminal Justice Research Center, State University of New York at Albany.

Lemert, E. M. (1971). *Instead of court: Division in juvenile justice.* Chevy Chase, MD: National Institute of Mental Health, Center for the Studies of Crime and Delinquency.

Maguire, K., & Pastore, A. L. (Eds.). (2001). *Sourcebook of criminal justice statistics: 2000.* Albany, NY: The Hindelang Criminal Justice Research Center, State University of New York at Albany (Funded by the Bureau of Justice Statistics of the U.S. Department of Justice. Washington, DC: U.S. Government Printing Office).

Maguire, K., & Pastore, A. L. (Eds.). (2002). *Sourcebook of criminal justice statistics: 2001.* Albany, NY: The Hindelang Criminal Justice Research Center, State University of New York at Albany (Funded by the Bureau of Justice Statistics of the U.S. Department of Justice. Washington, DC: U.S. Government Printing Office).

National Center for Juvenile Justice (2012). *Juvenile arrest rates by offense, sex, and race (1980–2010).* Retrieved from http://www.ojjdp.gov/ojstatbb/dat.html

Office of Juvenile Justice and Delinquency Prevention. (2012). *Upper age of jurisdiction.* Retrieved from http://www.ojjdp.gov/ojstatbb/structure_process/qa04101.asp.

Pitner, R. O., Astor, R. A., & Benbenishty, R. (in press). Violence in schools. In P. Allen-Meares (Ed.), *Social work in schools* (7th ed.). Boston, MA: Allyn & Bacon.

Prescott, P. S. (1981). *The Child Savers.* New York: Alfred A. Knopf.

President's Commission on Law Enforcement and Administration of Justice. (1967). *Task force report: Juvenile delinquency and youth crime.* Washington, DC: U.S. Government Printing Office.

Puzzanchera, C., Adams, B., & Hockenberry, S. (2012). *Juvenile court statistics 2009.* Pittsburgh, PA: National Center for Juvenile Justice.

Puzzanchera, C., Stahl, A., Finnegin, T., Snyder, H., Poole, R., & Tierney, N. (2001). *Juvenile court statistics 1998.* Washington, DC: Office of Juvenile Justice and Delinquency Prevention, U.S. Government Printing Office.

Roberts, A. R. (1987). *Runaways and nonrunaways.* Chicago: Dorsey.

Roberts, A. R. (1998). *Juvenile justice: Policies, programs and services.* Chicago: Nelson-Hall.

Robinson, S. M. (1960). *Juvenile delinquency: Its nature and control.* New York: Holt, Rinehart & Winston.

Schur, E. (1973). *Radical nonintervention: Rethinking the delinquency problem.* Englewood Cliffs, NJ: Prentice-Hall.

Short, J. F. Jr., & Nye, F. I. (1958). Extent of unrecorded delinquency, tentative conclusions. *Journal of Criminal Law, 49,* 296–302.

Snyder, H. N. (2002). *Juvenile arrests 2000*. Washington, DC: Office of Juvenile Justice and Delinquency Prevention, Office of Justice Programs.

Snyder, H. N. (2012). *Patterns and trends: Arrests in the United States, 1990–2010*. Washington, DC: Office of Juvenile Justice and Delinquency Prevention, Office of Justice Programs.

Springer, D. W. (2001). Runaway adolescents: Today's Huckleberry Finn crisis. *Brief Treatment and Crisis Intervention, 1*(2), 131–152.

Substance Abuse and Mental Health Services Administration. (2002). *The National Household Survey on Drug Abuse: Preliminary findings 2002*. Rockville, MD: SAMSHA, Office of Applied Studies.

Substance Abuse and Mental Health Services Administration. (2012). *2010-2011 NSDUH state estimates of substance use and mental disorders*. Retrieved from http://www.samhsa.gov/data/NSDUH/2k11State/NSDUHsae2011/Index.aspx

Thornberry, T. P., Moore, M., & Christenson, R. L. (1985). The effect of dropping out of high school on subsequent criminal behavior. *Criminology, 23*, 3–18.

Truman, J. L., & Planty, M. (2012). *Criminal victimization, 2011*. Washington, DC: U. S. Department of Justice, Office of Justice Programs.

U.S. Children's Bureau. (1967). *Juvenile court statistics, 1966* (Statistical Series 90). Washington, DC: U.S. Government Printing Office.

U.S. Children's Bureau. (1973). *Juvenile court statistics, 1972*. Washington, DC: U.S. Government Printing Office.

U.S. Department of Education, National Center for Education Statistics. (2012). *The condition of education 2012* (NCES 2012-045).

U.S. Department of Justice. (1984). *Sourcebook of criminal justice statistics*. Washington, DC: U.S. Government Printing Office.

U.S. Department of Justice. (1985). *Crime in the United States, 1984: Uniform Crime Reports*. Washington, DC: U.S. Government Printing Office.

U.S. Department of Justice. (2001). *Sourcebook on criminal justice statistics 2000*. Washington, DC: U.S. Government Printing Office.

Weis, J. G. (1983). Crime statistics: Reporting systems and methods. In *Encyclopedia of crime and justice* (Vol. 1). New York: Free Press.

Williams, J. R., & Gold, M. (1972). From delinquent behavior to official delinquency. *Social Problems, 20*, 209–229.

Youth, Development and Delinquency Prevention Administration. (1973). *The challenge of youth service bureaus*. Washington, DC: U.S. Government Printing Office.

2

Juvenile Justice Policy

Current Trends and 21st-Century Issues

C. Aaron McNeece and Tiffany Ryan

During the past two decades a number of highly publicized juvenile crimes have occurred, such as the school shootings at Columbine High School in Littleton, Colorado (CNN 2003), leading to political support for harsher treatment for juvenile offenders. Yet statistics from state and federal agencies showed clearly that juvenile violent crime was decreasing (Snyder, 1999).

Between 1992 and 1997, 45 states modified state laws and juvenile procedures to make their juvenile justice systems more punitive (Snyder & Sickmund, 1999). However, the state of Missouri created a juvenile justice system so successful that it is known as the "Missouri Miracle" (Edelman, 2010). A few positive changes also have occurred in a handful of other states.

In the following discussion of trends in juvenile offenses and case dispositions, bear in mind that we are dealing only with estimates that are based on officially reported offenses. The official cases are those that proceed beyond police encounters with juveniles. When there are inadequate personnel and resources to deal with serious juvenile felony offenses, juvenile misdemeanors are ignored. In most cases, only the juvenile who has established a history of relatively serious delinquent behavior will be referred to the court for official handling.

■ Major Policy Shifts

Four major shifts in federal juvenile policy have occurred since the 1960s (Ohlin, 1983). Community organization models were used in the early 1960s by federal policymakers to foster local responsibility for juvenile misbehavior. The second shift in policy came from a number of presidential commissions studying the problems of crime and violence. In 1967 the first of these commissions recommended dramatic policy innovations such as the decriminalization of status offenses, the diversion of juvenile offenders from official court processing, and the deinstitutionalization of juvenile offenders.

The Juvenile Justice and Delinquency Prevention Act (JJDPA) of 1974 was the culmination of this policy shift (McNeece, 1980). The intent of this bill was to deinstitutionalize status offenders, provide additional funds to communities to improve delinquency prevention programs, establish new mechanisms for dealing with runaway youths, and remove juveniles from adult jails and lockup facilities (Bartol & Bartol, 1989).

A third major change in juvenile justice policy began in the mid-1970s with a federal shift toward a "law and order" philosophy. The JJDPA was amended in 1977, partly as a response to alleged increases in school violence and vandalism, in order to allow more flexibility in the deinstitutionalization process. Throughout the late 1970s, an "iron-fisted" punitive approach to non-status offenders emerged (Hellum, 1979), and a growing fear of crime pushed the juvenile justice system toward more repressive action (Ohlin, 1983).

The Reagan administration targeted serious or repetitive juvenile offenders for special attention in 1981, once more shifting the system in the direction of control. This new "get tough" approach was evident in the Comprehensive Crime Control Act of 1984 (Bartol & Bartol, 1989).

Another important shift took place on March 1, 2005, when the U.S. Supreme Court ruled it unconstitutional to execute juvenile defendants (*Roper v. Simmons*, 543 U.S. 2005). This shift signaled a possible weakening of the punitive approach to juvenile crime.

Between 1990 and 2000 most states adopted tougher laws regarding the prosecution of serious, violent, and chronic juvenile offenders. Such laws lowered the age at which a juvenile could be transferred to adult court, expanded the list of crimes for which a juvenile could be transferred, and made the process for transferring the juvenile easier (Mears, 2000; Office of Juvenile Justice and Delinquency Prevention [OJJDP], 1996; Snyder & Sickmund, 1999).

Beginning with the *Roper v. Simmons* decision, this "get tough" trend appears to be waning. Since 2005 there have been four other major policy shifts in several states. The first trend that has occurred in four states (Colorado, Maine, Virginia, and Pennsylvania) is the passage of laws prohibiting juveniles from being housed in adult prisons. The second policy shift (Connecticut, Illinois, and Mississippi) is the expansion of juvenile court jurisdiction to older youth. The third trend (Arizona, Colorado, Connecticut, Delaware, Illinois, Indiana, Nevada, Utah, Virginia, and Washington) is altering laws to make it more difficult to try juveniles as adults. Finally, the last trend (Colorado, Georgia, Texas, and Washington) is to change mandatory minimum sentencing laws to consider developmental differences between youth and adults (National Center for Juvenile Justice, 2010; Steinberg, 2008).

Additional policy shifts occurring throughout the United States include repealing life sentencing without parole for juveniles who have committed murder, reducing automatic transfer laws, increasing community-based treatment, increasing the age for those sent to adult court to 18, and allowing for youth to claim incompetence based on their developmental maturity (Children's Defense Fund, 2012; Steinberg, 2008).

■ Diversion and Deinstitutionalization Programs

The enthusiastic application of "diversion" programs actually has resulted in the creation of a new semi-legal, semi-welfare bureaucracy, which has broadened the effective social control mechanisms of the juvenile justice system without paying much attention to the legal rights of children (Blomberg, 1983; Empey & Stafford, 1991). The implementation of the JJDPA of 1974 resulted in a relatively small reduction in public institutional populations (McNeece, 1980). However, the number of status offenders in private institutions increased substantially between 1979 and 1989, roughly equivalent to the drop in the number of status offenders in public institutions (OJJDP, 1991). The bottom line is that there has been little or no change in the number of juvenile status offenders in custody, despite two decades of "reform." The 1980 amendments to the Juvenile Justice Act still permit juveniles who have run away from valid court placements to be charged with contempt of court, a delinquent act (U.S. Dept. of Justice, OJJDP, 1985), which may result in the offender being reclassified as a juvenile delinquent. Official statistics show that the number of juveniles held in public institutions did decrease between 1971 and 1977 (Bureau of Justice Statistics, 1981), but there was a corresponding increase in private correctional facilities, residential treatment programs, and psychiatric units of hospitals to serve juvenile offenders. Although confinement to traditional long-term public facilities did decline somewhat, the use of private facilities offset those declines (Lerman, 1980). Between 1974 and 1983, the total number of status offenders held in secure facilities increased from 79,017 to 80,097 (U.S. Dept. of Justice, OJJDP, 1985, p. 13). A subsequent report by OJJDP (U.S. Dept. of Justice, 1991), *Juveniles Taken into Custody*, indicated that the trend had continued, with declines in the number of status offenders in public facilities offset by increases in the number of such youths in private facilities (p. 6).

■ Jail Removal Programs

In the winter of 1973, Senator Birch Bayh, chair of the subcommittee, introduced the Juvenile Justice and Delinquency Prevention Act of 1974 which contained a strong provision on jailing juveniles. Juveniles "shall not be detained or confined in any institutions in which adult persons convicted of a crime or awaiting trial on criminal charges are incarcerated" (U.S. Congress, Senate, 1974). However, the bill that eventually passed was considerably weakened. A compromise allowed juveniles to be confined in jails so long as they were kept separate from adult prisoners.

In 1980 President Carter signed the reauthorization of the Juvenile Justice and Delinquency Prevention Act into law. Only those juveniles who are tried as adults for criminal felonies were allowed to be detained or incarcerated in adult jails. The degree of success varied considerably from state to state.

However, in 1990 the National Coalition of State Juvenile Justice Advisory Groups concluded that the jail removal program had been generally successful (OJJDP, 1991). Bureau of Justice Statistics (BJS) data indicated an average daily juvenile population of 2,527 in adult jails in 1992 (U.S. Dept. of Justice, BJS, 1993). However, "the proportion of juveniles who were housed in adult jails in accordance with [the 1980 amendment] is not available" (p. 10). As late as 2007, it was estimated that every day in America, an average of 7,500 youth were still incarcerated in adult jails (Campaign for Youth Justice, 2007). Perhaps the most important impact of this legislation is that states that are out of compliance with its juvenile jail removal mandates can be sued.

■ "New Age" Juvenile Justice: Mediation, Restorative Justice, Acupuncture, Boot Camps, Drug Treatment, and Privatization

Dozens of new approaches to the problems of juvenile delinquency have been introduced to the juvenile justice system within the past few years. The oldest of these "new" ideas is probably mediation, which has been around since the development of community dispute resolution centers in the 1950s (Ray, 1992). Mediation seems to have had a rebirth within the past decade, and recent evaluations indicate that outcomes are just as desirable as more costly alternatives (Umbreit, Coates, & Kalanj, 1994). Restorative justice is closely linked with mediation. It emphasizes three goals: (a) identifying the obligation created by the juvenile's offense and ensuring that he or she is held responsible for it (accountability), (b) returning the offender to the community competent to interact in a successful, pro-social manner (competence), and (c) ensuring that the community is not further injured by the juvenile's future delinquent behavior (public safety) (Ellis & Sowers, 2001).

Boot camps experienced a decade of political popularity as a promising new treatment option, with millions of dollars set aside for such programs in the Violent Crime Control Act of 1994. Their routine is characterized by harsh, summary discipline, a rigid dress code, and frequent inspections (Marlette, 1991). Despite the early enthusiasm for boot camps, research indicates that they are no more effective than the more traditional institutional approaches (Zhang, 2001).

Acupuncture is one of the more recent and more controversial treatment options for drug-involved juvenile offenders, but there is little evidence of its effectiveness with either juveniles or adults (Springer, McNeece, & Arnold, 2003).

An increasing trend in the justice system, for both juveniles and adults, is the privatization of services (Bowman, Hakim, & Seidenstat, 1992). Some fear that public accountability for justice system programs may suffer through privatization. Others fear the danger of sacrificing rehabilitation and treatment goals to the overriding concerns of cost efficiency within a completely privatized system (Coenen, 2010; McNeece, 1995). Research shows that states that have higher rates of privatization also have higher rates of recidivism, lending credence to the concern that private companies are more interested in profits than rehabilitation (Bayer & Pozen, 2004).

Another concern of privatization includes corruption. In 2008, two juvenile court judges in Pennsylvania were involved in a "kids for cash" scheme associated with the private juvenile detention centers in the state (Shelden, 2011). Private for-profit companies operated secure juvenile facilities in 23 states and the District of Columbia in 2003 (Building Blocks for Youth, 2003). Despite the controversies surrounding privatization (Ellis & Sowers, 2001), the trend continues. Citing cost concerns, Florida plans to completely privatize state-operated juvenile facilities by October 2013 (Huffpost Miami, Oct. 15, 2012).

■ Delinquency Prevention Programs

The 1992 amendments to the JJDPA of 1974 (P.L. 93-415) also expanded the funding for delinquency prevention programs. By 1996, more than 230 local governments were awarded grants for "community prevention" (OJJDP, 1996). The JJDPA of 2002 provides guidelines to the states in meeting federal requirements. In brief, states must (1) deinstitutionalize status offenders; (2) keep sight and sound separation between adult and juvenile detainees/inmates; (3) remove juveniles from adult facilities; and (4) reduce disproportionate minority contact (42 U.S.C. 5601). The JJDP Reauthorization Act of 2009 (S. 678, 2009) adds as a purpose of the original act the support of a continuum of programs (including delinquency prevention, intervention, mental health and substance abuse treatment, and aftercare programs) to address the needs of at-risk youth and youth who come into contact with the justice system. Equally important, it adds certain requirements relating to the protection of juveniles against placement in adult prison facilities and the treatment of juveniles equitably on the basis of gender, race, family income, and disability. It also defines "evidence based" as a program or practice that is demonstrated to be effective and that:

(1) is based on a clearly articulated and empirically supported theory,

(2) has measurable outcomes, and

(3) has been scientifically tested.

■ "Just Desserts" in Juvenile Justice

Certain policy reforms have spilled over into the juvenile justice system from the adult criminal justice system. More than a decade ago, the state of Washington adopted a determinate sentencing policy for juvenile offenders. Under the policy, juvenile offenders are sentenced to a specific term of incarceration related to the severity of the offense. The attempt is to "make the punishment fit the crime" (Sertill, 1980). This concept obviously is not congruent with the rehabilitative ideal prevalent in our juvenile justice system, but reformers believe it will be more equitable and just. Unfortunately, other states have followed suit (Ellis & Sowers, 2001; Mears, 2000; Merlo, 2000).

Such changes reflect a sense of frustration and powerlessness in dealing with juvenile offenders, as well as a shift in the public mood favoring punishment rather than rehabilitation. Evidence of this shift is reflected in the policy changes mentioned earlier, with 45 states making changes in their statutes to make it easier to place juveniles in the adult criminal justice system (Merlo, 2000). One organization (Building Blocks for Youth, 2003) estimates that 85% of the decisions to prosecute juveniles as adults are made by prosecutors, not judges. In addition, 82% of youths charged in adult court were minority youths. According to Amnesty International (1998), as many as 200,000 youths under age 18 were processed in adult criminal court annually. Of those, 180,000 were from 13 states that set the upper age of juvenile jurisdiction at 15 or 16 years, and the great majority of the others were from states that allow prosecutorial discretion in charging children as adults. At every stage of processing, minority youths were overrepresented and treated more harshly than other youths (Building Blocks for Youth, 2003; Krisberg, 1992; Snyder & Sickmund, 1999), especially those accused of drug-related offenses (see Table 2.8).

■ Due Process

Beginning in the 1960s, "the legal foundations of the juvenile justice system began to unravel completely" (Butts & Mears, 2001, p. 173). The less rigorous standards that were applied to juveniles were justified as being in the child's best interest. Children were also believed to have substantially different constitutional rights than adults. Beginning in the mid-1960s, however, a number of Supreme Court decisions strengthened some of the rights of children. *Kent* (1966) extended limited due process guarantees to juveniles. *In re Gault* (1967) provided juveniles with the right to notice of the charges, the right to counsel, the privilege against self-incrimination, and the right to confront and examine witnesses. *In re Winship* (1970) applied the "reasonable doubt" standard to juvenile cases.

Nevertheless, in *McKeiver v. Pennsylvania* (1970), the Supreme Court maintained some different standards for juveniles in rejecting the argument that children were entitled to a jury trial. Proof that the concept of *parens patriae* was still alive came in the *Schall v. Martin* (1984) decision, when the court said that "juveniles, unlike adults, are always in some form of custody." Thus, while children still do not have exactly the same constitutional guarantees as adults, the legal system has moved in that direction. Juveniles accused of criminal offenses may not be treated as arbitrarily or capriciously, as they were in the first half of the last century.

A unanimous decision in *Oklahoma Publishing Co. v. District Court in and for Oklahoma City* (1977) allowed the press to use the name and picture of a minor in a juvenile court proceeding in circumstances where members of the press were present during the court proceeding and no objection to their presence was made. The pretrial use of detention for juveniles presenting a serious risk of committing other offenses was upheld by the Supreme Court in *Schall v. Martin*, a New York case (1984).

In 1989 the Supreme Court held in *Stanford v. Kentucky* that the imposition of capital punishment on individuals for murders committed at the age of 16 or 17 years does not constitute cruel and unusual punishment in violation of the Eighth Amendment. In 1992 the Supreme Court held in *Reno v. Flores* that releasing alien juveniles who were detained pending deportation hearings only to parents, guardians, or other close relatives was not a violation of Fifth Amendment rights.

Beginning in the mid-1970s, several states adopted legislation that mandated minimal or determinate sentences for juveniles. At least 17 states have revised their purpose clause or mission statements for juvenile courts to emphasize public safety, punishment, and offender accountability (Torbet & Szymanski, 1998). This has virtually eliminated the differences between juvenile and adult sentencing in those states. The fact that "the purposes of the juvenile process have become more punitive, its procedures formalistic, adversarial and public, and the consequences of conviction much more harsh" was acknowledged in *In re Javier A.* (1984).

We have corrected a serious deficiency in the juvenile justice system by requiring closer attention to matters of procedural rights, but it will take much more than a mere declaration of those rights by appellate courts before much real change can be expected. For example, ensuring that accused juveniles are provided legal counsel will not per se make any significant difference in case outcomes. Several studies have shown that there is no substantial difference in adjudication or disposition decisions when attorneys are assigned to represent juveniles (Burruss & Kempf-Leonard, 2002). In fact, some studies show that juveniles who are represented by legal counsel are more likely to receive harsher depositions (McNeece, 1976; Stapleton & Teitlebaum, 1972).

The problem is the prevailing attitude concerning procedural rights that still exists in the juvenile justice system. Many attorneys who represent juvenile clients remain convinced that because the juvenile court is really an institution for providing treatment to their clients, they should not aggressively pursue the protection of the legal rights of such clients. Other attorneys (Feld, 2003) believe that *Gault* precipitated a revolution in the juvenile court system that has unintentionally sidetracked its original progressive and rehabilitative ideals and "transformed the juvenile court into a scaled-down, second-class criminal court for young offenders" (p. 16).

Several states have lowered the age at which youths may be tried as adult offenders for serious offenses, and other states have made it much easier to waive juveniles of any age to adult courts. Some have called for the abolition of the juvenile court altogether, arguing that the U.S. Supreme Court has made the juvenile and adult systems so similar that having separate systems no longer makes sense (Schichor, 1983). Other people have suggested that we abandon therapy or rehabilitation in favor of protecting the public.

On the positive side, due process has been enhanced through the court's decision mentioned above in *Roper v. Simmons* (543 U.S. 2005) that prohibited the execution of juvenile offenders. One could reasonably assume that the courts might respond to the current conservative backlash regarding juvenile offenders by taking somewhat more punitive actions in processing at least a portion of these clients. We will be looking for those trends in the data described in the following pages.

■ Funding for Juvenile Justice

Another useful way to analyze policy changes in juvenile justice is to examine the changes in funding patterns. If decision makers are serious about changes in policy, those changes will be reflected in budgets. A major change in funding programs in the area of juvenile justice occurred with the passage of the Law Enforcement Assistance Act (LEAA) in 1965 (P.L. 89-197) and the Omnibus Crime Control and Safe Streets Act of 1968 (P.L. 90-351). Together, these two laws provided money and the administrative apparatus for new grants to state and local agencies for law enforcement and related programs. In 1974, the Office of Juvenile Justice and Delinquency Prevention was created within LEAA to coordinate efforts to control delinquency (P.L. 93-415). For the fiscal years 1975 through 1977, 89,125 JJDPA formula grants to state and local agencies were approved (U.S. Dept. of Justice, OJJDP, 1979). In 1977, $47,625,000 was available through OJJDP for delinquency control and prevention programs.

Budget authority for OJJDP was scheduled to increase to $100 million in 1981 and $135 million in 1982 under the proposed Carter budget (Executive Office of the President, Office of Management and Budget [OMB], 1981b). The actual expenditure for juvenile justice formula grants in 1980 was $68 million (Executive Office of the President, OMB, 1981b).

Meanwhile, disenchantment of Congress with LEAA resulted in an order to dismantle the agency well before the end of the Carter administration. While the actual expenditure for all LEAA programs in 1980 was $444,781,000, the executive budget request for 1982 was only $159,691,000. The few remaining LEAA grants ended in 1982 (Executive Office of the President, OMB, 1981a), and funds that would have been allocated as grants through OJJDP were converted to block grants to the states (Executive Office of the President, OMB, 1981c). Few new federal funds have been directed specifically at delinquency prevention or delinquency programs. Many of the original advocates of the federal cost-sharing approach to crime and delinquency programs now believe that a serious mistake was made in funding criminal and juvenile programs. Some believe it might have made matters worse. Wilson (1975) believes that these billions of dollars did not add much to our knowledge about which approaches and programs were most effective, and that, rather than testing our theories about rehabilitation and prevention, we were merely "funding our fears."

For better or for worse, it appears that the federal largesse in juvenile corrections has ended. In the President's 2013 budget, the Office of Justice Programs is funded at $1.7 billion, down from $2.7 billion in 2011 and $2 billion in 2012 (Kelly, 2012). The juvenile justice programming funding by OJJDP was cut from $423.6 million in 2010 to $276 million in 2011, a 65% decrease. This loss in funding often cuts prevention programs for at-risk youth. President Obama's 2012 budget proposed juvenile justice funding levels at $280 million (Children's Defense, 2012). The budget would have increased spending on the juvenile justice and delinquency prevention programs at OJJDP, a division of the Office of Justice Programs.

States and localities will continue to bear the bulk of the financial burden for institutional programs and other post-adjudication dispositions, cities and counties will finance most law enforcement programs, and courts and probation staff will be supported by both state and local revenues. Because federal money was largely responsible for the development of delinquency prevention, there is a real possibility that states and communities may return to their previous pattern of funding only the more "traditional" juvenile programs—that is, institutions and probation.

■ Official Statistics

Since 1929, the primary source of information on activities of the nation's juvenile courts has been the series *Juvenile Court Statistics*. The first report described cases handled by 42 courts during 1927. This was (and still is) a voluntary reporting system, and few courts maintained and reported case-level data on juvenile clients. By 1937, case-level reporting was dropped for dependency cases, and a few years later the decision was made to switch the reporting system for both dependency and delinquency cases to aggregate counts only. In 1957 the Children's Bureau initiated a new data collection program that enabled the production of national estimates of juvenile court actions through a stratified probability sample of more than 500 courts. Although this early effort was aborted, the National Center for Juvenile Justice (NCJJ) was awarded a grant by OJJDP in 1975.

By this time many more courts were keeping automated records on juvenile cases to meet their own needs, so that estimating national trends became somewhat easier. Table 2.1 summarizes estimates of the delinquency cases disposed by juvenile courts in the United States for the years 2001 to 2009.

The official statistics indicate that more than 1.9 million juvenile arrests are made each year (FBI, 2011), and 78.9% of those arrested are referred to juvenile court. The others are not charged, or the charges against them are dropped. An unknown number of juveniles are referred to court without an arrest, by parents, schools, human service agencies, and others. Some of those may eventually result in formal processing. Of the total number of cases referred to juvenile court (approximately 1,504,100 in 2009), about one third subsequently involve a delinquency hearing.

Table 2.1	**National Estimates of Referrals to Juvenile Court (in Thousands)**								
	2001	2002	2003	2004	2005	2006	2007	2008	2009
	1,687	1,676	1,683	1,689	1,699	1,643	1,647	1,634	1,504

Table 2.2. **National Estimates of Juvenile Delinquency Cases: Offenses, 2001–2009**

	Person	Property	Drugs	Public Order	Total
2001	405,311	659,516	191,070	431,478	1,687,375
	(24%)	(39.1%)	(11.3%)	(25.6%)	
2002	403,719	654,780	183,844	434,115	1,676,458
	(24.1%)	(39%)	(11%)	(25.9%)	
2003	410,858	644,541	183,000	444,897	1,683,296
	(24.4%)	(38.3%)	(10.9%)	(26.4%)	
2004	418,568	631,443	184,985	454,393	1,689,389
	(24.8%)	(37.4%)	(10.9%)	(26.9%)	
2005	434,271	614,708	185,167	465,005	1,699,151
	(25.5%)	(36.2%)	(10.9%)	(27.4%)	
2006	415,350	588,059	181,671	458,350	1,643,430
	(25.3%)	(35.8%)	(11%)	(27.9%)	
2007	409,976	599,449	183,259	454,395	1,647,079
	(24.9%)	(36.4%)	(11.1%)	(27.6%)	
2008	400,611	613,177	178,097	442,697	1,634,582
	(24.5%)	(37.5%)	(10.9%)	(27.1%)	
2009	365,705	567,139	167,081	404,220	1,504,145
	(24.3%)	(37.7%)	(11.1%)	(26.9%)	
% change since 2001	−9.8%	−14.1%	−12.6%	−6.4%	−10.9%

Of those youths, half will be adjudicated as "delinquent" and placed on probation, made to pay fines or restitution, ordered to undergo counseling, or placed in an institution (NCJJ, 2010). The number of juvenile offenders processed by the courts has declined in recent years after several years of moderate growth (Table 2.1). Referrals have been decreasing slowly since 1997. The greatest increase in juvenile referrals was among those 17 years of age, with an increase of 36% between 1990 and 2000. However, referrals for 17-year-olds also peaked in 1997 and declined by 5% by 1999 and have continued to fluctuate roughly 10% between 1999 and 2009.

The distribution of offenses in four broad categories from 2001 through 2009 is provided in Table 2.2.

■ Recent Trends

The overall decrease of 10.9% between 2001 and 2009 masks some important changes in specific offense categories. All four offense categories steadily decreased, with property and drug crimes accounting for the largest percent of overall change. Juvenile property crimes, the largest category of juvenile crimes, dropped 12% from 1990–2000, but during the same period person offenses increased nearly 52%, public order offenses increased nearly 80%, and drug offenses increased by 179%. However, these trends have reversed since 1997, when juvenile offending was at its peak. Between 2001 and 2009, total juvenile offenses declined nearly 10.9%, led by a 14.1% drop in property crimes.

Drug crimes dropped by 12.6%, followed by person crimes dropping by 9.8%, and public order offenses decreased by 6.4% during that same period. While the proportion of drug crimes attributed to non-White juveniles rose 51% between 1990 and 2000, between 2001 and 2009 drug crimes decreased by 15%. Drug offenses among White youths between 1990 and 2000 rose 287% but have declined by 8.5% between 2001 and 2009. Between 1990 and 2000 person offenses rose 66% among White youths and only 32% among non-Whites, while between 2001 and 2009 they increased by only 2.6% for non-Whites and decreased by 20.9% for White youth.

The vast majority of all juvenile delinquency referrals are male (72.4% in 2009), and both male and female referrals have steadily decreased in all categories. These declines may be attributed to the overall waning of the "get tough" attitude in juvenile justice (National Center for Juvenile Justice, 2010; Steinberg, 2008). Between 1990 and 2000, person offenses increased almost 107% among female juveniles but only 38% among their male counterparts. Although the image of violent, gang-involved girls makes for dramatic news headlines and has even been blamed by some on women's increasing equality in the family and the workplace, recent research tells a different story.

Histories of physical and sexual abuse appear to be the rule rather than the exception among female offenders, and research suggests that much of their offending may be a result of abuse. In fact, some researchers have pointed out that female juveniles are often charged with domestic violence for incidents in which an adult caregiver is actually the aggressor (McNeece, Jackson, & Winokur, 2003). Although states and jurisdictions have increased their capacity to incarcerate female juveniles (Florida recently opened a maximum-risk juvenile prison for girls), insufficient attention is generally paid to the underlying problems that have resulted in higher rates of female delinquency.

Detention

Detention refers to the placement of a youth in a restrictive facility between referral to court intake and case disposition. Table 2.3 provides the national estimates for detention decisions between 2001 and 2009. While the *number* of juveniles detained decreased between 2001 and 2009 by 15.5%, the *percentage* of juvenile offenders detained has remained fairly steady. A decrease in the percentage of youths detained was observed for males and females as well as for both White and non-White youths. From 1989 to 1998, the increase in

Table 2.3   **National Estimates of Juvenile Delinquency Cases: Detention Decisions, 2001–2009**

	Detained	Not Detained	Total
2001	376,254	1,311,121	1,687,375
	(22.2%)	(77.8%)	
2002	384,999	1,291,460	1,676,459
	(22.9%)	(77.1%)	
2003	381,549	1,301,747	1,683,296
	(22.7%)	(77.3%)	
2004	375,737	1,313,651	1,689,388
	(22.2%)	(77.8%)	
2005	363,666	1,335,486	1,699,152
	(21.45)	(78.6%)	
2006	367,302	1,276,128	1,643,430
	(22.3%)	(77.7%)	
2007	359,970	1,287,108	1,647,078
	(21.9%)	(78.1%)	
2008	345,891	1,288,690	1,634,581
	(21.2%)	(78.8%)	
2009	317,958	1,186,186	1,504,144
	(21.1%)	(78.9%)	
% change since 2001	−15.5%	−9.6%	−10.9%

number of detained females (56%) was greater than for males (20%) because of the large increase in the number of female delinquency cases involving person offenses (157%). During the same time, the number of White juveniles detained grew more (33%) than for African American juveniles (15%), also because of the higher increase of person and drug offenses for White youths. It may be due in part to the much higher proportion of African American youths being processed in the adult system (OJJDP, 2009).

Manner of Handling

The manner of handling is a general classification of case processing within the court system. Petitioned (formally handled) cases are those that appear on the official court calendar in response to the filing of a petition or other legal instrument. Non-petitioned (informally handled) cases are those cases that are diverted or handled informally. The percentage of cases that were petitioned (Table 2.4) decreased from 57.2% to 54.7% between 2001 and 2009.

As overall delinquency cases decreased 10.1%, formally petitioned cases decreased 14.8%. The number of male youths formally petitioned decreased 15%, while the number of female youths petitioned decreased 14%. The

Table 2.4 **National Estimates of Juvenile Delinquency Cases: Manner of Handling, 2001–2009**

	Formal	Informal	Total
2001	965,945	721,430	1,687,375
	57.2%	42.8	100.0%
2002	960,705	715,754	1,676,459
	57.3%	42.7%	100.0%
2003	960,624	722,672	1,683,296
	57.1%	42.9%	100.0%
2004	935,739	753,649	1,689,388
	55.4%	44.6%	100.0%
2005	935,974	763,177	1,699,151
	55.1%	44.9%	100.0%
2006	927,808	715,622	1,643,430
	56.4%	43.6%	100.0%
2007	925,069	722,009	1,647,078
	56.2%	43.8%	100.0%
2008	909,912	724,669	1,634,581
	55.7%	44.3%	100.0%
2009	823,234	680,910	1,504,144
	54.7%	45.3%	100%
% change since 2001	−14.8%	−5.7%	−10.1%

number of White youths formally petitioned decreased 21.3%, while the number of non-White youths petitioned decreased only 2.3%. Earlier studies had indicated that juvenile courts did not handle alcohol and drug cases with a formal petition as often as they did other delinquency cases, but that drug cases (47%) were more likely than alcohol cases (38%) to be formally petitioned (National Institute of Justice, 1989). Unfortunately, current national data do not allow distinctions to be made between drug and alcohol offenses, only between drug and public order offenses (OJJDP, 2009).

Adjudication Decisions

A juvenile who is adjudicated is judicially determined (judged) to be a delinquent or status offender. Table 2.5 provides the national estimates of both adjudicated and non-adjudicated juvenile cases from 2001 to 2009. Adjudicated cases decreased faster (−17.4%) than the overall decrease in juvenile cases (−11%). The reduction in female adjudications (−17.6%) was nearly identical to the rate in male adjudications (−17.3%), but the reduction in adjudications of White youths (−23.8%) was much greater than the rate among non-White youths (−4.4%).

Table 2.5   **National Estimates of Juvenile Delinquency Cases: Adjudication Decisions, 2001–2009**

	Adjudicated	Not Adjudicated	Total
2001	591,268	1,096,106	1,687,374
	35%	65%	100.0%
2002	588,814	1,087,645	1,676,459
	35%	65%	100.0%
2003	585,545	1,097,751	1,683,296
	34.7%	65.3%	100.0%
2004	573,572	1,115,816	1,689,388
	34%	66%	100.0%
2005	565,347	1,133,805	1,699,241
	33.3%	66.7%	100.0%
2006	565,436	1,077,994	1,643,430
	34.4%	65.6%	100.0%
2007	556,925	1,090,154	1,647,079
	33.8%	66.2%	100.0%
2008	538,702	1,095,879	1,634,667
	33%	67%	100.0%
2009	488,788	1,015,356	1,504,144
	32.5%	67.5%	100.0%
% change since 1990	−17.4%	−7.4%	−11%

Dispositions

Dispositions are categorized here as the most severe action taken or treatment plan decided upon or initiated in a particular case. Case dispositions are coded into the following categories:

Waived—Cases that are waived or transferred to a criminal court
Placement—Cases in which youths are placed out of the home
Probation—Cases in which youths are placed on informal/voluntary or formal court-ordered probation or supervision
Dismissed—Cases that are dismissed (with no further disposition)
Other—A variety of dispositions, including fines, restitution, community service, and referrals outside the court

Table 2.6 provides national estimates of dispositions of juvenile delinquency cases. One category of dispositions merits attention: juvenile waivers to adult court, which rose for years and then peaked in 1994, dropping 51.4% by 2000. The decline was most dramatic among non-White youths, dropping 41.3%, compared with a 14.6% drop among White youths. White males experienced a 16% drop in waivers compared with a 43.4% drop among non-White

Table 2.6   **National Estimates of Juvenile Delinquency Cases: Dispositions, 2001–2009**

	Waived	Placed	Probation	Released	Other	Total
2001	8,086	160,607	614,797	539,484	364,401	1,687,375
	.0.4%	9.5%	36.4%	32%	21.6%	100.0%
2002	8,719	159,474	609,363	526,181	372,723	1,676,460
	0.5	9.5%	36.3%	31.4%	22.2%	100.0%
2003	8,525	157,777	608,428	522,182	386,383	1,683,295
	0.5%	9.4%	36.1%	31%	23%	100.0%
2004	8,260	150,905	599,989	543,639	386,595	1,689,388
	0.4%	8.9%	35.5%	32.2%	22.9%	100.0%
2005	8,433	154,711	584,391	557,789	393,827	1,699,151
	0.4	9.1%	34.4%	32.8%	23.2%	100.0%
2006	8,831	155,880	575,647	533,214	369,858	1,643,430
	0.5%	9.5%	35%	32.4%	22.5%	100.0%
2007	8,908	152,580	582,924	528,732	373,935	1,647,079
	0.5%	9.3%	35.4%	32.1%	22.7%	100.0%
2008	8,820	149,650	580,619	535,095	360,397	1,634,581
	0.5%	9.2%	35.5%	32.7%	22%	100.0%
2009	7,642	133,797	541,391	486,178	335,136	1,504,144
	0.5%	8.9%	36%	32.3%	22.3%	100.0%
% change since 2001	−5.5%	−16.7%	−12%	−9.9%	−8.1%	−10.9%

males. From 2001 to 2009, overall waivers remained steady. However, White youths saw a 14.8% decrease in waivers and non-White youths saw an 11.5% increase. Between 2001 and 2009 female waivers decreased 2.3%, compared with a 5.9% drop for males.

While waivers to adult court fell between 2001 and 2009, so too did out-of-home placements (−16.7%). Females experienced a decrease of 20.9% for out-of-home placements, compared with 15.9% for males. For White youths out-of-home placements decreased by 24.4%, compared with a relatively small decrease of 3.4% for non-White youths. In addition, the number of youths placed on probation decreased by 12% between 2001 and 2009.

■ Trends in Offenses and Case Processing

Since the 1990s, it appears that racial differences in formal handling decreased somewhat, as well as the proportion of cases resulting in detention and adjudication. The disparity between out-of-home placements and waivers to adult court has also decreased. Overall, waivers of minority youths were down 41%

Table 2.7   **National Estimates of Juvenile Delinquency Cases: Non-White Males Waived to Adult Court by Offense, 2001–2009**

Count	Person	Property	Drugs	Public Order	Total
2001	1,395	628	403	208	2,634
2002	1,345	660	422	171	2,598
2003	1,404	622	401	187	2,614
2004	1,468	634	347	189	2,638
2005	1,812	532	387	245	2,976
2006	1,969	642	425	250	3,286
2007	2,016	651	400	251	3,318
2008	2,185	799	360	334	3,678
2009	1,673	678	331	270	2,952
% change since 2001	19.8%	7.9%	8.2%	3%	12.1%

between 1990 and 2000. However, from 2001 to 2009 there was an increase in non-White males waived to the adult court system (Table 2.7).

Although disparities have eased in several areas, it appears that considerable racial disparity in juvenile justice persists. Earlier, we discussed the "get tough" legislation passed in 45 states between 1992 and 1997 (Snyder & Sickmund, 1999). The effect of that legislation was to increase prosecutorial discretion in trying juveniles as adults, to lower the statutory age for referral to the adult court, and to broaden the categories of offenses that go to adult court. Judges aren't issuing waivers as often today, but only 15% of those decisions to waive to adult court are made by judges; 85% are made by prosecutors or legislative bodies, and the great majority of waivers are minority youths (OJJDP, 2009). Neither are minority youths being treated more gently in the juvenile system. To further illustrate the risk of more severe handling experienced by non-White youths, we have compared dispositions for White and non-White 17-year-old male drug offenders in Table 2.8.

The non-White juveniles in this group are much more likely to be waived or placed, while White juveniles tend to have other consequences such as

Table 2.8   **National Estimates of Juvenile Delinquency Cases: 2009 Disposition by Race for 17-Year-Old Males Charged with Drug Offenses**

Count	Waived	Placed	Probation	Released	Other	Total
White	434	1,774	10,618	8,360	7,522	28,708
	0.1%	6%	36.9%	29%	26.2%	100.0%
Non-White	212	1,416	3,346	4,004	2,162	11,140
	1.9%	12.7%	30%	35.9%	19.4%	100.0%
Total	646	3,190	13,964	12,364	684	29,848

fines, restitution, community service, and referrals outside the court for services, with minimal or no further court involvement anticipated. The bottom line is that we seem to have decided that minority youth are not amenable to treatment in the juvenile system.

■ Females in Juvenile Justice

Approximately one third of juveniles who are arrested are female. Girls typically commit less serious offenses than their male counterparts, and the majority of female juvenile offending continues to consist of status offenses and relatively minor delinquency (OJJDP, 2009). However, between 1985 and 2009, the female proportion of those committing person offenses steadily increased from 20% to 30% (NCJJ, 2010).

Some research suggests that female juveniles are treated more harshly than their male counterparts (OJJDP, 1998). For example, a report published by the Florida Department of Juvenile Justice (2001) notes that girls committed to secure placement for their first commitment have less serious offense histories than boys given the same sanctions. An earlier study reported that girls are more likely to be placed in detention and are detained for less serious offenses than boys (OJJDP, 1998).

Research on delinquent girls reveals that they generally have backgrounds of victimization. Researchers have noted that girls who become involved in juvenile justice systems generally have been sexually or physically abused, and their offending is often related to the abuse. Chesney-Lind (1997) describes the "criminalization of girls' survival strategies," whereby abused girls run away from home and are arrested for running away or for engaging in crime to survive on the streets. Critics have noted that programs fail to address the gender-specific issues associated with female offenders (OJJDP, 1998).

The U.S. Congress acknowledged the apparent rise in female juvenile offending and the different issues underlying their delinquency. When the JJDP Act was reauthorized in 1992, it included funding to assist states in "developing and adopting policies to prohibit gender bias in placement and treatment" (Title 42, Chapter 72, Sub-chapter II, Part E, Sec. 5667c). A number of states have received research funding under this provision of the JJDP Act. However, gender inequities persist in the processing and rehabilitation of female offenders (American Bar Association and the National Bar Association, 2001).

■ Recommendations

We have responded to the rapid increase in female delinquency by treating female delinquents more or less as males. More research is needed on the causes of female delinquency and gender-specific ways of effectively treating female offenders. Until we know what is effective, we should try to maximize the degree of care we provide to juveniles and minimize the harm done to them. Let's put a moratorium on additional punitive legislation.

Some progress has been made on weakening racial bias in juvenile justice, but substantial racial equity remains. Although our courts, law enforcement agencies, and treatment programs may not be quite as prone to treat non-White youth as harshly as they did a half-century ago, there are still obvious advantages to being White in our juvenile justice system. We should take action immediately to address the differential processing of minority and non-minority juvenile offenders.

Three decades ago, I suggested in an article on juvenile justice policy that until we know how to provide effective treatment for juvenile offenders, we should concentrate on making the juvenile justice system as equitable, just, and humane as possible (McNeece, 1983). While we have not addressed the issue of humaneness in this chapter, it is obvious that we still have problems in achieving equity, and it is doubtful that justice is being done.

Conclusion

There does seem to be a gradual movement away from the punitive approach to juvenile justice that has dominated our system for the past several decades. However, media coverage and politics have usually interacted to the detriment of juveniles. Justice as a symbolic value is easily dispensed by political leaders: it is cost-free and very popular (Merlo & Benekos, 2000).

Although racial and gender inequities still abound, and there are yet far too many youths in adult jails and prisons, that picture does not seem to be quite so grim today. While the movement of a few states away from treating juveniles as adults is not exactly a move toward rehabilitation, it just might be grounds for hope.

Discussion Questions

1   What have been the major shifts in federal juvenile policy since the 1960s?

2   How would you describe the impact of juvenile diversion programs?

3   How successful has the deinstitutionalization movement been regarding juvenile offenders?

4   In what way(s) are minority youths treated differently in the justice system?

5   What impact has the provision of "due process" to juveniles had on the juvenile justice system?

6 Discuss federal financial support for juvenile justice programs.

7 What are the ways that children are processed into the adult criminal justice system?

8 What impact have the courts had on juvenile justice policy?

9 Discuss some positive trends in state juvenile justice policy.

10 How have things changed for females in the juvenile justice system?

References

American Bar Association and the National Bar Association (2001). *Justice by gender: The lack of appropriate prevention, diversion and treatment alternatives for girls in the justice system.* Retrieved from http://www.americanbar.org/content/dam/aba/publishing/criminal_justice_section_newsletter/crimjust_juvjus_justicebygenderweb.authcheckdam.pdf on November 27, 2012.

Amnesty International (1998, November). *Betraying the young.* Retrieved from http://web.amnesty.org on June 12, 2003.

Bartol, C., & Bartol, A. (1989). *Juvenile delinquency: A systems approach.* Englewood Cliffs, NJ: Prentice-Hall.

Bayer, P., & Pozen, D. (2004). *The effectiveness of juvenile correctional facilities: Public versus private management.* Yale University.

Blomberg, T. (1983). Diversion's disparate results and unresolved questions: An evaluation perspective. *Journal of Research in Crime and Delinquency, 20,* 24–38.

Bowman, G. W., Hakim, S., & Seidenstat, P. (1992). *Privatizing the United States justice system: Police, adjudication, and correction services from the private sector.* Jefferson, NC: McFarland.

Building Blocks for Youth (2003). *Transfer to adult court/trying kids as adults.* Retrieved February 4, 2003, from www.buildingblocksforyouth.org/issues/transfer/facts_transfer.html

Burruss, G., & Kempf-Leonard, K. (2002). Questionable advantage of defense counsel in juvenile court. *Justice Quarterly, 19,* 37–68.

Butts, J. A., & Mears, D. P. (2001). Reviving juvenile justice in a get-tough era. *Youth and Society, 33*(2), 169–198.

Campaign for Youth Justice (2007). *Key facts: Jailing juveniles. The dangers of incarcerating youth in adult jails in America.* Retrieved November 1, 2012, from http://www.campaignforyouthjustice.org/documents/CFYJFS_JailingJuveniles_000.pdf

CBS Miami (Oct. 20, 2012). *State report: S. Fla. teen in juvenile center 'neglected to death.'* Retrieved October 28, 2012, from http://miami.cbslocal.com/2012/10/20/state-report-s-fla-teen-in-juvenile-center-neglected-to-death/

Chesney-Lind, M. (1997). *The female offender: Girls, women, and crime.* Thousand Oaks, CA: Sage.

Children's Defense Fund (2012). *Supporting California's Senate Bill 9, the Fair Sentencing for Youth Act.* Retrieved on November 15, 2012, from http://www.childrensdefense.org/policy-priorities/juvenile-justice/.

CNN (Cable News Network). (2003). *Jefferson County Sheriff's Department.* Retrieved February 13, 2003, from http//www.cnn.com/SPECIALS/2000/columbine.cd/frameset.exclude.html

Coenen, R. (2010). Privatizing criminal justice. *The American Criminal Law Review*. Retrieved on November 15, 2012, from http://www.americancriminallawreview.com/Drupal/blogs/blog-entry/privatizing-juvenile-justice-11-03-2010.

Edelman, M. W. (2010). *Juvenile justice reform: Making the "Missouri Model" an American model*. Huffington Post, March 15, 2010. Retrieved October 28, 2012, from http://www.huffingtonpost.com/marian-wright-edelman/juvenile-justice-reform-m_b_498976.html

Ellis, R. A., & Sowers, K. M. (2001). *Juvenile justice practice: A cross-disciplinary approach to intervention*. Pacific Grove, CA: Brooks/Cole.

Empey, L. T., & Stafford, M. C. (1991). *American delinquency: Its meaning and construction* (3d ed.). Belmont, CA: Wadsworth.

Executive Office of the President, Office of Management and Budget (1981a). *Budget of the United States Government, Fiscal Year 1982*. Washington, DC: U.S. Government Printing Office.

Executive Office of the President, Office of Management and Budget (1981b). *Budget of the United States Government, Fiscal Year 1982, Appendix*. Washington, DC: U.S. Government Printing Office.

Executive Office of the President, Office of Management and Budget (1981c). *Budget of the United States Government, Fiscal Year 1982, Budget Revisions: Additional Details on Budget Savings*. Washington, DC: U.S. Government Printing Office.

Federal Bureau of Investigation (2000). *Crime in the United States—2000*. Washington, DC: U.S. Government Printing Office.

Federal Bureau of Investigation (2011). *Crime in the United States—2011*. Washington, DC: U.S. Government Printing Office.

Feld, B. C. (2003). *Juvenile justice administration*. St. Paul, MN: Thomson/West.

Florida Department of Juvenile Justice (2001). *2001 outcome evaluation*. Tallahassee, FL: Author.

Florida to completely privatize juvenile correctional facilities. (2012). Retrieved December 4, 2012, from http://www.huffingtonpost.com/2012/10/15/florida-privatize-juvenile-detention_n_1967464.html

Hellum, F. (1979). Juvenile justice: The second revolution. *Crime and Delinquency, 25*, 299–317.

Kelly, J. (2012). A look at youth-related spending in Obama's 2013 budget. *Youth Today*. Retrieved November 15, 2012, from http://www.youthtoday.org/view_article.cfm?article_id=5215.

Krisberg, B. (1992). *Juvenile justice: Improving the quality of care*. Washington, DC: National Council on Crime and Delinquency.

Lerman, P. (1980). Trends and issues in the deinstitutionalization of youths in trouble. *Crime and Delinquency, 26*, 281–298.

Marlette, M. (1991). Boot camp prisons thrive. *Corrections Compendium, 16*, 6–8, 10.

McNeece, C. A. (1976). *Juvenile courts in the community environment*. Unpublished doctoral dissertation, University of Michigan.

McNeece, C. A. (1980). "Justice" in the juvenile court: Some suggestions for reform. *Journal of Humanics*, May, 77–97.

McNeece, C. A. (1983). Juvenile justice policy. In A. Roberts (Ed.), *Social work in justice settings* (pp. 19–43). Springfield, IL: Charles C. Thomas.

McNeece, C. A. (1995). Adult corrections. In *Encyclopedia of social work*. Washington, DC: National Association of Social Workers.

McNeece, C. A., Jackson, S., & Winokur, K. (2003). *The impact of gender on domestic violence charges against juveniles*. Paper presented at the annual meeting of the Society for Social Work and Research, Washington, DC.

Merlo, A. V. (2000). Juvenile justice at the crossroads: Presidential address to the Academy of Criminal Justice Sciences. *Justice Quarterly, 17*(4), 639–661.

National Center for Juvenile Justice (2003). National juvenile court data archive. Retrieved from http//www.ojjdp.ncjns.org on September 23, 2003.

National Center for Juvenile Justice (2010). National juvenile court data archive. Retrieved from http//www.ojjdp.ncjns.org on November 15, 2012.

National Institute of Justice (1989). Juvenile courts vary greatly in how they handle drug and alcohol cases. In *OJJDP update on statistics*. Washington, DC: U.S. Government Printing Office.

Office of Juvenile Justice and Delinquency Prevention, U.S. Dept. of Justice (1991). *Juveniles taken into custody: Fiscal year 1990 report.* Washington, DC: U.S. Government Printing Office.

Office of Juvenile Justice and Delinquency Prevention, U.S. Dept. of Justice (1996). *1996 report to Congress, Title V, incentive grants for local delinquency prevention programs.* Washington, DC: U.S. Government Printing Office.

Office of Juvenile Justice and Delinquency Prevention, U.S. Dept. of Justice (1998). *Guiding principles for promising female programming: An inventory of best practices.* Washington, DC: U.S. Government Printing Office.

Office of Juvenile Justice and Delinquency Prevention, U.S. Dept. of Justice (2002, January). *Detention in delinquency cases, 1989–1999* (OJJDP Fact Sheet No. 01). Washington, DC: U.S. Government Printing Office.

Office of Juvenile Justice and Delinquency Prevention, U.S. Dept. of Justice (2003). *Easy access to juvenile court statistics.* Retrieved February 8, 2003, from http://ojjdp.ncjrs.org/ojstatbb/njcda/.

Office of Juvenile Justice and Delinquency Prevention, U.S. Dept. of Justice (2009). *Easy access to juvenile court statistics.* Retrieved November 15, 2012, from http://ojjdp.ncjrs.org/ojstatbb/njcda/.

Ohlin, L. (1983). Interview with Lloyd E. Ohlin, June 22, 1979. In J. Laub (Ed.), *Criminology in the making: An oral history.* Boston: Northeastern University Press.

Ray, L. (1992). Privatization of justice. In *Privatizing the United States justice system: Police, adjudication, and correction services from the private sector?* Jefferson, NC: McFarland.

Schichor, D. (1983). Historical and current trends in American juvenile justice. *Juvenile and Family Court Journal, 34,* 61–75.

Sertill, M. S. (1980). Washington's new juvenile code. *Corrections Magazine, 7,* 36–41.

Shelden, R. G. (2011). *Privatization of juvenile justice comes home to roost.* Center on Juvenile and Criminal Justice. Retrieved on November 15, 2012, from http://www.cjcj.org/post/juvenile/justice/privatization/juvenile/justice/comes/home/roost.

Snyder, H. N. (1999, December). Juvenile arrests 1998. *Juvenile Justice Bulletin,* 1–11.

Snyder, H. N., & Sickmund, M. (1999). *Juvenile offenders and victims: 1999 national report.* Washington, DC: Office of Juvenile Justice and Delinquency Prevention.

Springer, D. W., McNeece, C. A., & Arnold, E. M. (2003). *Substance abuse treatment for criminal and juvenile offenders: An evidence-based approach.* Washington, DC: American Psychological Association.

Stapleton, V., & Teitlebaum, L. (1972). *In defense of youth.* New York: Russell Sage.

Steinberg, L. (2008). Introducing the Issue. *Journal of Juvenile Justice, 18*(2), 3–14.

Torbet, P., & Szymanski, L. (1998). *State legislative responses to violent juvenile crime: 1996–1997 update.* Washington, DC: Office of Juvenile Justice and Delinquency Prevention.

Umbreit, M. S., Coates, R. B., & Kalanj, B. (1994). *Victim meets offender: The impact of restorative justice and mediation.* Monsey, NY: Willow Tree Press.

U.S. Congress, Senate (1974). Juvenile Justice and Delinquency Prevention Act. S.B. 821 (P.L. 93-415). Washington, DC: U.S. Government Printing Office.

U.S. Dept. of Commerce (1992). *1990 census of population, general population characteristics, United States.* Washington, DC: U.S. Government Printing Office.

U.S. Dept. of Commerce (2002). *2000 census of the population of the United States.* Washington, DC: U.S. Government Printing Office.

U.S. Dept. of Justice, Bureau of Justice Statistics (1981). *Sourcebook of criminal justice statistics.* Washington, DC: U.S. Government Printing Office.

U.S. Dept. of Justice, Bureau of Justice Statistics (1993). *Sourcebook of criminal justice statistics, 1992.* Washington, DC: U.S. Government Printing Office.

U.S. Dept. of Justice, Office of Juvenile Justice and Delinquency Prevention (1979). *Second analysis and evaluation, federal juvenile delinquency programs,* Vol. 1. Washington, DC: U.S. Government Printing Office.

U.S. Dept. of Justice, Office of Juvenile Justice and Delinquency Prevention (1980). *A national assessment of case disposition and classification in the juvenile justice system: Inconsistent labeling: Vol. 11. Results of a literature search.* Washington, DC: U.S. Government Printing Office.

U.S. Dept. of Justice, Office of Juvenile Justice and Delinquency Prevention (1985). *Reports of the National Juvenile Justice Assessment Centers: The impact of deinstitutionalization on recidivism and secure confinement of status offenders.* Washington, DC: U.S. Government Printing Office.

U.S. Dept. of Justice, Office of Juvenile Justice and Delinquency Prevention (1991). *Juveniles taken into custody: Fiscal year 1990 report.* Washington, DC: U.S. Government Printing Office.

Wilson, J. Q. (1975). *Thinking about crime.* New York: Basic Books.

Zhang, S. X. (2001). *Evaluation of the Los Angeles County juvenile drug treatment boot camp: Executive summary* (NCJ Report 187678). Washington, DC: U.S. Government Printing Office.

Cases

In re Gault, 387 U.S. 1 (1967).

In re Javier A., 159 Cal., App. 3d 913, 206 Cal Rptr. 386 (1984).

In re Winship, 397 U.S. 358 (1970).

Kent v. U.S., 383 U.S. 541, (1966).

McKeiver v. Pennsylvania, 403 U.S. 528 (1970)

Oklahoma Publishing Co. v. District Court in and for Oklahoma City, 430 U.S. 308 (1977).

Reno v. Flores, 507 U.S., 113 S. Ct., 123 L.Ed.2dl (1992).

Roper v. Simmons, 543 U.S. 551 (2005)

Schall v. Martin, 467 U.S. 253 (1984).

Stanford v. Kentucky, 492 U.S. 361 (1989).

3

The Second American Crime Drop

Trends in Juvenile and Youth Violence

Jeffrey A. Butts and Douglas N. Evans

■ Introduction

This chapter explores several questions. "Are today's violent crime rates different from the rates of 30 years ago?" "Do recent trends in serious and violent crime by juveniles (under age 18) differ from trends among older youth (i.e., young adults ages 18–24), and how much of the overall crime decline that began in the 1990s can be attributed to juveniles and older youth?" The discussion focuses primarily on serious and violent youth crime since 1981. This is about as far back as a careful analysis can go if the goal is to compare crime trends for offenders of various ages. It was not until the 1970s that arrest statistics for detailed age groups were even available at the national level. Furthermore, it was during the three decades after 1980 when crime rates suddenly spiked and then dropped again, capturing the attention of criminologists, policymakers, and citizens alike.

This chapter reviews these trends and shows that young people (juveniles and older youth) were disproportionately responsible for growing rates of serious crime in the 1980s and early 1990s, but they contributed an even larger share to falling rates since the mid-1990s. In fact, young people appear to be largely responsible for a second violent crime drop in the United States. The second crime drop appeared after a brief period of increasing violence between 2004 and 2006. Violent crime began to decline again after 2006 and continued to decline through 2011, with juveniles and older youth leading the change.

■ The First Crime Decline: 1991–2004

In the 1990s, and after a decade of rising violence, the volume and rate of serious crime began to fall significantly in many countries, including the United States. Cities and states across the country benefitted from plummeting rates of violence and other forms of serious crime. The total rate of violent crime fell nearly continuously for almost 15 years. A short violent crime rebound then occurred. Crimes like murder, robbery, and weapons offenses grew between 2004 and 2006. The resurgence ended before the severe economic recession hit the U.S. economy in 2007. After 2006, crime rates resumed their downward trajectory, resulting in a second American crime drop. By 2011, the second crime decline had resulted in levels of violent crime not seen since 1970 (Fig. 3.1).

Scholars proposed many theories to explain the first crime drop, but no single theory seemed to offer a complete understanding (Blumstein & Rosenfeld, 2008; Blumstein & Wallman, 2006; Greenberg, 2013; Zimring, 2007). The decline in serious crime between the early 1990s and 2004 may never be fully explained. Most researchers in the 1990s assumed that violent crime would rise into the early 21st century because crime rates had been growing before the 1990s (Barker, 2010). Popular explanations for the growth

Violent Crimes Reported per 100,000 Population

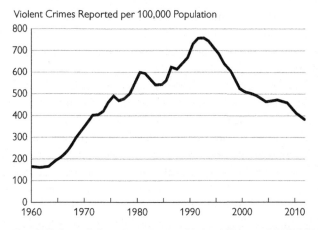

Figure 3.1   Total Violent Crime Rate in the United States: 1960–2011.

Source: Uniform Crime Reports, Federal Bureau of Investigation (FBI), U.S. Department of Justice. Data for 1960-2010 prepared by the National Archive of Criminal Justice Data. Available on the Internet: http://bjs.gov/ucrdata/Search/Crime/Crime.cfm.

in violent crime prior to 1990 included the expansion of the youth population from the post-World War II baby boom as well as perceived declines in the legitimacy of social institutions. After 1980, many blamed the emergence of the crack cocaine market for particularly sharp crime spikes. Some scholars noted that a variety of cultural factors were partly the cause for rising violence. Of course, most of these explanations suggested that serious crime would continue to grow (Baumer, 2011).

The sharp increase in violent crime ended suddenly in the early 1990s when adult crime rates began to fall. For several years, the declining rate of serious crime among older adults was overshadowed by ongoing increases in youth crime (Levitt, 1998). Then, to the surprise of criminologists and citizens in general, serious and violent crime rates also began to decline among juveniles and youth under age 25 (Levitt, 2004). Between 1991 and 2001, the homicide rate fell 43%, the total violent crime rate dropped 34%, and the rate of serious property crime decreased 29%. The crime drop had clearly begun.

Juveniles and older youth are always implicated in the rise and fall of violent crime rates. Young people commit serious crime at a rate that is disproportionate to their percentage of the population (Lawrence & Hesse, 2010). Indeed,

Definitions

This chapter uses the terms "youth" and "young" to describe individuals who are 10 to 24 years of age. Some but not all youth are legal juveniles. The term "juvenile" is used in popular discourse as a synonym for young, but the legal definition of the term is more specific. It does not include all young people or even all people under age 18. Legal definitions vary according to state laws that set the age threshold for criminal prosecution. Most states extend juvenile status through age 17, but some extend it only through age 15 (e.g., New York) or age 16 (e.g., Georgia, Louisiana, Massachusetts, Michigan, Missouri, South Carolina, Texas, and Wisconsin).

the fluctuations in homicide and robbery during the 1980s and 1990s were in large part due to changes in youth violence (Blumstein, 2002) and to the sharp decrease in youth homicide rates that began after 1994 (Blumstein & Wallman, 2006).

There are many possible explanations for the unexpected drop in youth crime after 1994. Youth growing up in the 1980s and 1990s may have begun to reject the lifestyle they came to associate with drug use and criminal activity as they observed older siblings and friends becoming addicted to drugs or getting arrested (Curtis, 1998). The decrease in the relative size of the youth population in the United States also may have contributed to the reduction in crime (Zimring, 2007). Each of these factors likely exerts some influence on crime rates (Cook & Laub, 2002).

Another explanation—always popular in some circles—is that rapid growth in the use of incarceration after 1980 increased the deterrent effect of the justice system. Indeed, the most careful research does suggest that the extent of incarceration is partly associated with changes in crime rates and the scale of the nationwide crime drop. Some estimates suggest that growth of incarceration alone might explain one third of the crime decline at a national level (Levitt, 2004). When the incarceration levels and crime rates of individual states are examined, however, the relationship between incarceration and crime diminishes (Ouimet, 2002; Spelman, 2006).

Some of the more provocative explanations for the overall crime decline include growing police forces, the legalization of abortion in the 1970s, and the broader availability of firearms. Levitt (2004), for example, estimated that an increase in the number of police officers could explain between 10% and 20% of the total crime decline. Other researchers pointed out that, along with the general reduction in crack cocaine use, drug distribution methods in recent years shifted away from large open-air markets (in which dealers sell drugs in public spaces) and toward small-scale dealers selling primarily to people in their immediate social groups (Curtis, 1998). Such a shift would have likely produced a reduction in violence associated with illegal drug markets.

In one of the most controversial lines of inquiry, Levitt (2004) and Donahue and Levitt (2001) argued that legalized abortion accounted for some of the reduction in crime rates. States that legalized abortion prior to the 1973 U.S. Supreme Court ruling in *Roe v. Wade* were the first states to demonstrate reductions in crime rates, and states with the highest rates of abortion demonstrated the largest decreases in crime. Other researchers disputed these findings, of course, showing that crime variations across time and between states are not consistent with the hypothesis that legalized abortion had a significant impact on the criminal behavior of subsequent birth cohorts (Joyce, 2004).

Still other popular explanations for the crime decline have included the role of firearms, with some observers pointing to the fact that crime rates fall with handgun use. In fact, the drop in youth homicides did mirror the steady decline in the rate of handgun homicides, but non-gun homicide rates decreased along with gun-related homicides, thereby reducing the potential weight of this theory (Blumstein & Wallman, 2006; Cook & Laub, 2002).

Finally, some researchers suggest that crime rates fall due to environmental changes, including the expansion and restoration of cities and the growth of racial and ethnic diversity in the U.S. population. Studies show that urban development, the refurbishment of abandoned buildings, and construction of new residences and businesses on empty lots contributed to neighborhood stability and enhanced informal social controls, which may have helped to lower crime rates (Barker, 2010). Similarly, the increasing diversity of the American population may have had an effect on crime trends. Increases in the immigrant populations of metropolitan areas are associated with decreases in violent crime, particularly robberies (Stowell et al., 2009). In large and diverse cities such as New York, Houston, and Miami, the sharp rise in immigrant populations may have counterbalanced the criminogenic factors existing in formerly crime-prone neighborhoods, resulting in lower crime rates overall (Barker, 2010).

The Great American Crime Decline, as Franklin Zimring described it, inspired researchers around the world to generate competing explanations for fluctuating crime trends. Criminologists will likely continue to debate the causes of the decline, but one thing is clear: the fluctuating rate of juvenile crime and youth crime exerts a strong influence on the overall rate of serious and violent crime. The remainder of this chapter explores the extent of this influence.

■ Youth Crime Trends

By the mid-1990s, more than a decade of sharp increases in violent youth crime commanded the attention of the nation's policymakers, news media, and the public. The juvenile justice system was widely criticized and virtually every state in the country was implementing juvenile justice reforms intended to reverse the rising tide of juvenile crime (Butts & Mitchell, 2000). In most cases, the goal of these reforms was to make the juvenile system "tougher" (Butts & Mears, 2001). Of course, the nationwide rise in violent crime was never simply about juvenile crime. Typically, violent crime trends are dominated by the large number of "youth" crimes, or crimes by young people between the ages of 15 and 24. This is just as true about falling crime as it is about periods of increasing crime. Young people have a disproportionate effect on crime trends, but the juvenile justice system is responsible for only some of these youth—often those under age 18, but sometimes under age 17 or even 16. To understand the extent and nature of youth crime trends, researchers must examine data about young adults as well as juveniles.

There are several ways to examine youth crime trends and to identify the contributions of juveniles and older youth to crime in general. The most useful methods rely on analyses of (1) crimes cleared by juvenile arrests, (2) the actual number of juvenile and youth arrests, and (3) per capita rates of arrest for juveniles and older youth.

Crime Clearances

The best source of data about changes in juvenile and youth crime in the United States is the information collected by law enforcement agencies across the country and reported to the Uniform Crime Reporting (UCR) program at the Federal Bureau of Investigation (FBI). Information from the UCR includes the number of various crimes reported to police and the percentage of those crimes "cleared" (or solved) with the arrest of a juvenile—more specifically, the percentage of crimes cleared by the arrest of one or more persons, none of whom is aged 18 or older. Tracking the number of reported crimes cleared by juvenile arrests (juvenile "clearances") is useful for gauging the extent to which juveniles account for the total level of crime, or least that portion of crime coming to the attention of law enforcement.

In general, the juvenile proportion of actual arrests tends to be higher than the juvenile proportion of *crimes cleared* by arrests, in part reflecting the greater likelihood of juveniles to commit crimes in groups (Table 3.1). In 2011, arrests involving juveniles accounted for 13% of all arrests for the four offenses included in the UCR Violent Crime Index (i.e., murder, robbery, aggravated assault, and forcible rape). Thus, adult arrests represented 87% of all arrests for Violent Index crimes. On the other hand, juveniles accounted for just 10% of the Violent Index crimes cleared that year. Similarly, juvenile arrests accounted for 21% of all arrests for Property Crime Index offenses, but these arrests cleared just 15% of serious property crimes. In other words, adults ages 18 and older were involved in 85% of the Property Index offenses cleared by arrest.

The trending pattern in juvenile clearances is an important way to assess the trajectory of youth crime since 1981 (Fig. 3.2). For example, the juvenile proportion of property crime clearances began to fall just as the youth crime decline began in 1994 and it continued to fall nearly continuously through 2011. Between 1995 and 2011, the juvenile proportion of clearances for offenses in the FBI's Property Crime Index dropped from 25% to 15%, suggesting either that the falling rate of property crime among juveniles exceeded the decline among adults or that adult property crimes were actually increasing during this time.

On the other hand, the proportion of violent crimes cleared by the arrest of juveniles appeared to fluctuate between 1981 and 2011, rising from 1987 through 1994, and then falling for several years just as the youth crime decline

Table 3.1   **Juveniles Under Age 18 as a Proportion of Arrests and Crimes Cleared: 2011**

	Youth under age 18 as a percentage of *Arrests*	Youth under age 18 as a percentage of *Crimes Cleared*
Violent Crime Index	13%	10%
Murder	8	4
Forcible rape	14	10
Robbery	23	13
Aggravated assault	11	9
Property Crime Index	21%	15%
Burglary	22	13
Larceny-Theft	21	15
Motor Vehicle Theft	22	12
Arson	46	36

Source: Crime in the United States 2011, Tables 28 and 47. Washington, DC: Federal Bureau of Investigation, U.S. Department of Justice.

appeared. Unlike the clearances of property offenses, the juvenile proportion of violent crime clearances stabilized from 1998 to 2004, suggesting that juvenile violence was falling at approximately the same rate that violence among adults was falling. A short resurgence occurred in 2004 through 2006, but the juvenile proportion of clearances dropped steeply once again from 2006 through 2011. Again, this suggests that after 2006 the number of violent crime arrests involving juveniles was declining at a sharper rate than the number of arrests involving adults. This second crime drop, in other words, may have been largely a youth crime drop.

The pattern can be seen in several of the individual offenses included in the UCR Violent Crime Index (Fig. 3.3). Juvenile murder clearances fell sharply through 2004 but then increased between 2004 and 2006 before

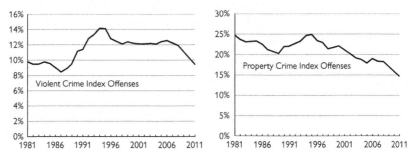

Figure 3.2   **Percentage of FBI Index Crime Clearances Involving Juveniles Under Age 18: 1981–2011.**

Source: *Crime in the United States* (annual) 1981 through 2011. Washington, D.C.: Federal Bureau of Investigation, U.S. Department of Justice.

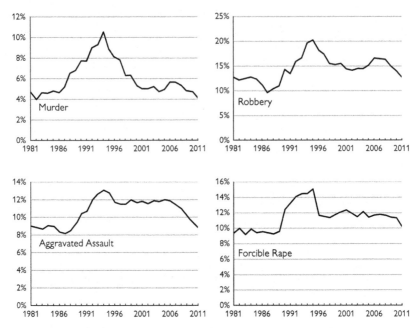

Figure 3.3   Percentage of FBI Violent Crime Index Clearances Involving Juveniles Under Age 18: 1981–2011.

Source: *Crime in the United States* (annual) 1981 through 2011. Washington, D.C.: Federal Bureau of Investigation, U.S. Department of Justice.

plunging again through 2011. The trend in juvenile clearances for aggravated assault was slightly different, remaining essentially unchanged from 1998 through 2006 and then dropping consistently from 2006 through 2011. Thus, aggravated assault arrests involving juveniles were likely falling more steeply than they were among adults ages 18 and older. A similar pattern is apparent in juvenile crime clearances for robbery. Following a temporary rebound between 2004 and 2006, the decline in juvenile clearances for robbery outpaced those of adults. Again, these patterns in violent crime clearances suggest the existence of the second crime decline among juveniles between 2006 and 2011.

Arrests

Analyzing UCR data about the number of arrests involving juveniles and youth is useful for monitoring the relative contribution of young people to the total crime problem. Arrest data are not a precise measure of crime itself, but they are a valid measure of the crime problems handled by police agencies across the country. Arrest data, of course, are not the only information that could be used to analyze trends in juvenile and young adult crime, but data from other sources are geographically inconsistent and unstandardized (i.e., data from courts), available only at the national level and not the state or local level (i.e., victim surveys), or lacking detailed information about the ages of the offenders involved in each crime (i.e., reported crimes and crime clearances). Unlike data about reported crimes and crime clearances, arrest data can be separated into more than two age groups to reveal disparities within the adult population. To explore the offending of more differentiated age groups, such as 18- to 20-year-olds and 21- to 24-year-olds, this chapter next analyzes arrest data directly.

The best way to examine trends in crime by different age groups is to analyze the national arrest estimates created by the Bureau of Justice Statistics (BJS) from the FBI's UCR data. Researchers must rely on the BJS national estimates because, while the FBI has been collecting arrest data from law enforcement agencies across the United States for 80 years, the agency publishes sample-specific data nearly exclusively. In other words, the FBI reports the number of arrests made by those agencies for which it has data each year (often representing about 75% of the U.S. population). The FBI, however, does not adjust these sample-specific arrest figures to represent arrests nationally.

In recent years, national estimates have become more accessible through the efforts of the BJS within the U.S. Department of Justice (Snyder & Mulako-Wangota, 2013). Statistical analysts at BJS create national estimates from the FBI's sample-specific data using a method disseminated more than 20 years ago by Dr. Howard Snyder. The estimation process begins with the single set of national arrest estimates calculated by the FBI each year for each major offense and for all ages combined (traditionally found in Table 29 of the annual report, *Crime in the United States*). To create national arrest estimates for varying age groups and then to calculate per capita arrest rates for those groups, analysts determine the proportion of sample-specific arrests for each offense that involved individuals of various ages. Those proportions are then applied to the overall national estimate for each offense to create national arrest estimates for detailed age groups. Next, the BJS process calculates arrest rates by dividing each national arrest estimate over the appropriate population as indicated by the age-specific population estimates from the U.S. Bureau of the Census.[1]

According to the most recent BJS estimates and other estimates calculated using the BJS method, law enforcement agencies across the United States made an estimated 1.5 million total arrests involving juveniles under age 18 in 2011, down substantially from 2.8 million in 1995 (Fig. 3.4). Another 1.7 million arrests involving youth ages 18 through 20 were reported in 2011, down from 2 million arrests in 1995. Arrests involving youth ages 21 through 24 also dropped slightly, from 2.1 to 1.9 million. Figure 3.4 clearly reveals the second crime decline between 2006 and 2011, and the drop in overall arrests after 2006 is clearly steepest among juveniles under age 18.

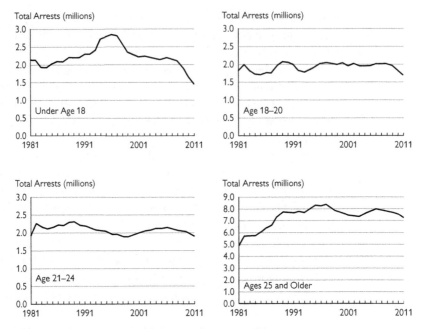

Figure 3.4   **National arrest estimates for all offenses: 1981–2011.**

Source: National estimates of arrests are derived by weighting the sample-specific figures from the Uniform Crime Reports. Estimates for 1981–2010 are from Snyder & Mulako-Wangota (2013). Estimates for 2011 are calculated directly using the same method with figures from the FBI report, *Crime in the United States 2011*.

These figures, of course, represent arrests for *all* offenses, including minor crimes that are not reported consistently across jurisdictions and from year to year, such as disorderly conduct, vandalism, and shoplifting. Examining changes in the total number of arrests for different age groups is not sufficient for a full understanding of the characteristics of the crime decline among young people. What offenses were involved in the millions of youth arrests made in 2011? Were they more serious or more violent than the youth offenses in 1981 or 1995? In addition, some crime fluctuations may be due to changes in the population. How many youth were in the U.S. population in 2011 compared with 1981 and 1995? An examination of youth crime trends is more accurate when it focuses on the per capita rate of arrests rather than the volume of arrests, and when it concentrates on the serious offenses that are more likely to be reported consistently and reliably to the FBI (i.e., the offenses included in the FBI's Crime Index and especially the Violent Crime Index).

Violent Crime Arrest Rates

Criminologists once predicted a relatively constant relationship between age and crime, positing that youth would be always over-represented in arrest

Ages 10–17 as Percent of Total

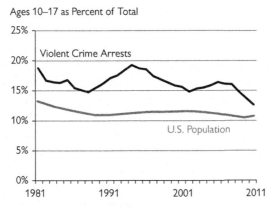

Figure 3.5   **Juvenile Proportion of Violent Crime Arrests and the U.S. Population: 1981–2011.**

Source: National estimates of arrests are derived by weighting the sample-specific figures from the Uniform Crime Reports. Estimates for 1981–2010 are from Snyder & Mulako-Wangota (2013). Estimates for 2011 are calculated directly using the same method with figures from the FBI report, *Crime in the United States 2011*. Population estimates are from the U.S. Bureau of the Census.

statistics (Hirschi & Gottfredson, 1983). In 1981, according to estimates from the U.S. Census Bureau, youths ages 10 to 17 represented 13% of the total population of the United States. If they were arrested at the same rate as everyone else, they would have accounted for 13% of violent crime arrests. Instead, according to the UCR, they accounted for 19% of all arrests for the four offenses included in the Violent Crime Index (Fig. 3.5).

With the onset of the 1990s crime wave and subsequent decline, however, the once-persistent relationship between the juvenile population and the juvenile proportion of violent crime arrests began to change. Between 1985 and 1995, the height of the violent crime wave, the disproportionate representation of juveniles actually increased. In 1995, 10- to 17-year-olds represented just 11% of the U.S. population, but they made up 19% of violent crime arrests. Between 1995 and 2011, the juvenile proportion of the U.S. population changed only slightly, fluctuating between 11% and 12%. As a percentage of all violent crime arrests, however, 10- to 17-year olds fell from 19% to 15% during the first crime decline, or between 1995 and 2004. After rebounding slightly between 2004 and 2006, the percentage dropped again during the second crime decline. By 2011, the juvenile percentage of violent crime arrests was just two points higher than the juvenile percentage of the U.S. population (13% compared with 11%). The first crime decline basically returned the juvenile percentage of violent crime arrests to levels that were similar to those of the early 1980s. The second crime decline brought the percentage lower than ever and very close to the juvenile proportion of the U.S. population as a whole.

Did the trends in arrests of juveniles and older youth bring about the second crime decline? What do youth crime trends look like if we control for the size of the population and analyze arrest rates per capita? If we examine the rate of juvenile arrests for Violent Index offenses, it is clear that juvenile arrests increased between the mid-1980s and mid-1990s and then fell dramatically through 2004, independently of the size of the juvenile population. In fact, the violent crime arrest rate grew 67% between 1981 and 1994, from approximately 300 arrests per 100,000 juveniles ages 10 to 17 to just over 500 arrests per 100,000. It then plummeted 46% to 270 per 100,000 in 2004.

The pattern varied only slightly among the individual offenses that make up the Violent Crime Index. The rate of juvenile murder arrests increased 86% between 1981 and 1994, to a rate of approximately 12 arrests per 100,000 juveniles. Between 1994 and 2004, the murder arrest rate for juveniles dropped to 3.3 per 100,000, which at that time was the lowest level of juvenile murder arrests experienced since 1980. The rate of juvenile arrests for murder actually grew 10% over several years after 2004, reaching 4 per 100,000 in 2007. Then, the rate dropped sharply to a new low: 2.5 arrests per 100,000 10- to 17-year-olds.

Robbery arrest rates followed a similar but more dramatic pattern when compared with murder arrest rates. The rate of juvenile arrests for robbery fell 60% between 1994 and 2004, from 184 to 75 per 100,000 juveniles. Then, between 2004 and 2006, the arrest rate climbed 38%, reaching a rate that once again exceeded 100 arrests for every 100,000 juveniles in the population. The increase stopped, however, and by 2011 the robbery arrest rate had dropped back to 71 per 100,000 juveniles, for the lowest rate recorded since 1981.

The pattern of juvenile arrest rates for aggravated assault differed from the rates of murder and robbery. The arrest rate for aggravated assault, for example, more than doubled between the 1980s and 1990s. After growing from 131 to 286 per 100,000 juveniles between 1981 and 1994, the rate dropped more gradually after 1994. By 2004, the aggravated assault arrest rate (179 per 100,000) still remained substantially higher than it had been in 1981 (132 per 100,000). Yet, the arrest rate continued to fall after 2004 and it did so more consistently than either the murder or robbery arrest rate. The rate reached its all-time low (121.5 per 100,000) in 2011. Because aggravated assaults usually account for more than half of all juvenile arrests for Violent Index offenses, the persistent decline of aggravated assault arrests caused the total violent crime rate for juveniles to depart from the pattern seen in murder and robbery arrests.

When public concerns about violent crime are on the rise, policymakers naturally turn their attention to violent youth crime, and this is certainly appropriate. Violent crime is disproportionately associated with young people, but young in this context means under age 20 or even below age 25. It is not accurate to describe the increases in violent youth crime between the mid-1980s and mid-1990s as a wave of "juvenile" violence (i.e., crime

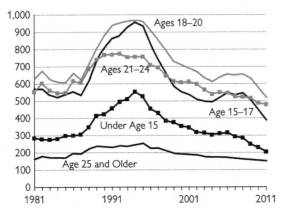

Figure 3.6 **Violent Crime Arrest Rates (per 100,000 population): 1981–2011 Youth Contribution to Violent Crime Decline.**

Source: National estimates of arrests are derived by weighting the sample-specific figures from the Uniform Crime Reports. Estimates for 1981–2010 are from Snyder & Mulako-Wangota (2013). Estimates for 2011 are calculated directly using the same method with figures from the FBI report, *Crime in the United States 2011*. Rates are calculated by dividing arrest estimates over the appropriate population. For juveniles under age 18, the denominator used is the population ages 10–17.

by offenders below age 18). Of all violent crime arrests in 1995, for example, just 18% involved juveniles under age 18, while 27% involved young adults between the ages of 18 and 24.

When youth crime rates are analyzed in more than two age groups, it is clear that violent crime trends are similar for juveniles under age 18 and older youth between age 18 and 24 (Fig. 3.6). The same patterns are seen for all age groups, but considerably more volatility is visible in the violent crime rates of young people. The increases in arrest rates between 1987 and 1994 were striking for young offenders, and the declines in rates after 1994 were strong for all youthful offenders. In every category under age 25, the violent crime arrest rate in 2011 was substantially lower than the rate had been in 1981. For older adults, however, the crime decline largely brought the rate back to where it was in 1981. Moreover, although the short increase in violent crime arrests between 2004 and 2006 was due almost entirely to increases among youth between the ages of 15 and 20, the subsequent drop during the second crime decline of 2006–2011 was also generated by the young. Just how much of both crime declines can be attributed to changing arrest patterns among young offenders?

The previous analysis suggested that recent declines in youth violence—measured by arrests of young people age 24 and younger—were steeper than declines in violent crime among older age groups. The chapter turns next to a related question: how much of the overall violent crime drop in America was due to changes in youth crime? The question can be answered by examining

Table 3.2   **Number of FBI Violent Crime Arrests by Age Group: 1981–2011**

Age at Arrest	1981	1994	2004	2011	Percent Change 1994–2004	Percent Change 2004–2011
14 and Younger	23,400	46,900	29,100	18,500	−38%	−36%
Ages 15–17	67,600	103,300	61,700	49,500	−40%	−20%
Ages 18–20	82,200	102,400	76,900	70,500	−25%	−8%
Ages 21–24	94,700	114,300	90,800	84,200	−21%	−7%
25 and Older	222,500	411,900	328,000	312,000	−20%	−5%
Total	490,500	778,800	586,600	534,700	−25%	−9%

Source: National estimates of arrests are derived by weighting the sample-specific figures from the Uniform Crime Reports. Estimates for 1981–2010 are from Snyder & Mulako-Wangota (2013). Estimates for 2011 are calculated directly using the same method with figures from the FBI report, *Crime in the United States 2011*.

Note: Detail may not add to total due to rounding.

the age composition of the relative increases and decreases in arrests between 1994 and 2004, and between 2004 and 2011.

According to the BJS national estimates, there were 778,800 total arrests for Violent Crime Index offenses in 1994, up 59% overall from 1991 (Table 3.2). Arrests increased for all age groups, and the total amount of the increase was 288,300 (i.e., the difference between 778,800 arrests in 1994 and 459,500 arrests in 1981). When the increase is disaggregated by age group, we see that the number of arrests grew by 100% among juveniles age 14 and younger, and by 53% among 15- to 17-year-olds. The number of arrests grew just 25% among older youth ages 18 to 20, and only 21% among young people between the ages of 21 and 24. Arrests among adults age 25 and older swelled by 85% between 1981 and 1994.

Note, however, that the size of the age groups varies considerably. While arrests doubled among young people below the age of 15, the total number of arrests in that age category was 46,900 in 1994, far smaller than the number of arrests among older juveniles (103,300). When we consider the number of new arrests in 1994 compared with 1981, it is clear that older juveniles ages 15 to 17 contributed 35,700 "new" arrests (103,300 in 1994 vs. 67,600 in 1981) while younger juveniles under age 15 contributed just 23,500 "new" arrests (up from 23,400 in 1981 to 46,900 in 1994). If these age groups are combined into just three categories (juveniles, youth ages 18–24, and adults over age 25), we see that juveniles accounted for 21% of the increase in arrests between 1981 and 1994, while older youth accounted for 14% of total growth, and adults over age 25 represented 66% of the total increase (Fig. 3.7).

In this way, the contribution of each age group to the total increase and decrease in the volume of violent crime arrests can be estimated by calculating the change in arrests for one group and comparing it to the total size of the change for offenders of all ages. The results of this comparison suggest

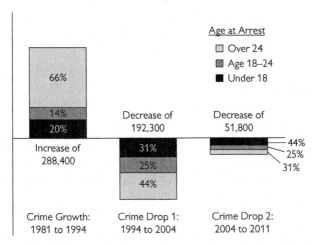

Figure 3.7   Contribution to Change in Violent Crime Arrests: 1981–2011.

Source: National estimates of arrests are derived by weighting the sample-specific figures from the Uniform Crime Reports. Estimates for 1981–2010 are from Snyder & Mulako-Wangota (2013). Estimates for 2011 are calculated directly using the same method with figures from the FBI report, *Crime in the United States 2011*.

that during the first crime decline (or 1994–2004) all juveniles (under age 18) accounted for a combined decline of 59,400 arrests. Because the total change in violent crime arrests between 1994 and 2004 was a drop of 192,200, this suggests that juveniles accounted for 31% of the total decline (i.e., 59,400 divided by 192,200).

Older youth ages 18 to 24, on the other hand, accounted for 25% of the decline because the number of arrests involving 18- to 24-year-olds fell from 216,700 in 1994 to 167,700 in 2004. This decline of 49,000 arrests represented just over 25% of the total decline of 192,200 during that period. Adults ages 25 and older accounted for 44% of the total decrease in arrest volume during the first crime decline of 1994–2004. The total number of arrests involving offenders ages 25 and older fell from 411,900 in 1994 to 328,000 in 2004, for a decrease of 83,900.

Thus, juveniles and older youth combined (all youth under age 24) were responsible for 34% of the increase in violent crime arrests between 1981 and 1994, but they accounted for 56% of the subsequent drop in arrests between 1994 and 2004. The first crime drop was disproportionately attributable to the declining number of arrests involving young people under age 25.

Finally, the analysis confirms that the second crime drop was proportionally even more attributable to the falling number of arrests among young people than was the first crime drop. Violent crime arrests overall fell by nearly 52,000 between 2004 and 2011. Decreases in arrests of adults over age 25 accounted for only 31% of the total crime drop after 2004. Juveniles accounted for 44% of the decline, while older youth ages 18 to 24 accounted for 25% of the total. Together, therefore, juveniles and older youth contributed more than two thirds of the overall decrease in violent crime arrests.

Conclusion

Researchers will likely continue to debate the reasons why violent crime in the United States increased sharply in the 1980s and early 1990s before dropping just as precipitously after the mid-1990s. All researchers will agree, however, that trends in violent crime during the past three decades had much to do with changing rates of youth crime. This chapter examined these trends and analyzed what portion of the overall crime drop might be attributed to juveniles (under age 18) and older youth (ages 18–24). The results demonstrate that while young people helped to generate 20% of the growth in violent crime arrests between 1981 and 1994, they contributed a far more disproportionate share to the crime decline in violence after 1994. Most of the decline in violent crime, in fact, was due to falling arrests among young offenders. Juveniles and older youth together accounted for 56% of the first crime drop between 1994 and 2004, and they represented 69% of the total decline in violent arrests during the second crime drop that continued at least through 2011.

Note

1 Not all of the information in this section comes directly from BJS. At the time this chapter was completed, the BJS had released national estimates only through the year 2010. For our analysis, we calculated estimates for 2011 using the same process employed by BJS. In addition, although the BJS creates arrest rates for juveniles under age 18 with denominators representing *all* children under age 18 (including infants and toddlers), we calculated alternative rates with denominators that included only youth 10–17 years of age.

References

Barker, V. (2010). Explaining the great American crime decline: A review of Blumstein and Wallman, Goldberger and Rosenfeld, and Zimring. *Law & Social Inquiry, 35*(2), 489–516.

Baumer, E. P. (2011). Crime trends. In Tonry, M. (Ed.), *The Oxford handbook of crime and criminal justice* (pp. 26–59). New York: Oxford University Press.

Blumstein, A. (2002). Youth, guns, and violent crime. *The Future of Children, 12*(2), 38–53.

Blumstein, A., & Rosenfeld, R. (2008). Factors contributing to U.S. crime trends. In Goldberger, A., & Rosenfeld, R. (Eds.), *Understanding crime trends: Workshop report* (pp. 13–44). Washington, DC: National Academies Press.

Blumstein, A., & Wallman, J. (2006). The recent rise and fall of American violence. In Blumstein, A., & Wallman, J. (Eds.), *The crime drop in America* (pp. 1–12). New York: Cambridge University Press.

Butts, J. A., & Mears, D. P. (2001). Reviving juvenile justice in a get-tough era. *Youth & Society, 33*(2), 169–198.

Butts, J. A., & Mitchell, O. (2000). Brick by brick: Dismantling the border between juvenile and adult justice. *Criminal Justice 2000,* Volume 2. Washington, DC: National Institute of Justice, U.S. Department of Justice.

Cook, P. J., & Laub, J. H. (2002). After the epidemic: Recent trends in youth violence in the United States. *Crime and Justice, 29,* 1–37.

Curtis, R. (1998). The important transformation of inner-city neighborhoods: Crime, violence, drugs and youth in the 1990s. *Journal of Criminal Law and Criminology, 88*(4), 1233–1276.

Donahue, J., & Levitt, S. D. (2001). The impact of legalized abortion on crime. *Quarterly Journal of Economics, 116*(2), 379–420.

Greenberg, D. F. (2013). Studying New York City's crime decline: Methodological issues. *Justice Quarterly.* DOI:10.1080/07418825.2012.752026 (published online).

Hirschi, T., & Gottfredson, M. (1983). Age and the explanation of crime. *American Journal of Sociology, 89*(3), 552–584.

Joyce, T. (2004). Did legalized abortion lower crime? *Journal of Human Resources, 1,* 1–28.

Lawrence, R., & Hesse, M. (2010). *Juvenile justice: The essentials.* Thousand Oaks, CA: Sage.

Levitt, S. D. (1998). Juvenile crime and punishment. *Journal of Political Economy, 106,* 1156–1185.

Levitt, S. D. (2004). Understanding why crime fell in the 1990s: Four factors that explain the decline and six that do not. *Journal of Economic Perspectives, 18*(1), 163–190.

Ouimet, M. (2002). Explaining the American and Canadian crime "drop" in the 1990s. *Canadian Journal of Criminology, 44,* 33–50.

Snyder, H. N., & Mulako-Wangota, J. (2013). *Arrest data analysis tool.* Washington, DC: Bureau of Justice Statistics, U.S. Department of Justice. [Internet: http://www.bjs.gov/index.cfm?ty=daa).

Spelman, W. (2006). The limited importance of prison expansion. In Blumstein, A., & Wallman, J. (Eds.), *The crime drop in America* (pp. 97–129). New York: Cambridge University Press.

Stowell, J. I., Messner, S. F., McGeever, K. F., & Raffalovich, L. E. (2009). Immigration and the recent violent crime drop in the United States: A pooled, cross-sectional time-series analysis of metropolitan areas. *Criminology, 47*(3), 889–928.

Zimring, F. E. (2007). *The great American crime decline.* New York: Oxford University Press.

4

Theories of Juvenile Crime and Delinquency

Cesar J. Rebellon

■ Introduction

On December 14, 2012, Adam Lanza shot and killed 20 children and six adults at Sandy Hook Elementary School in Connecticut after having previously shot and killed his mother in their home. At the age of 20, he was technically no longer a juvenile, but high-profile tragedies like this one tend to result in a great deal of informal theorizing about what could have led a young individual to engage in a behavior that most of us find hard to fathom. Some may be quick to blame the latest violent videogame, and others may instead blame the absence of a parent from the household. Social scientific theories of juvenile crime and delinquency, however, differ from such assertions in a number of important ways.

First, they are broader and more abstract than such assertions. They do not attempt to pin a particular crime on any one specific source, but suggest one or more underlying patterns of social interaction that, over time, may increase the probability of juvenile crime. Rather than suggesting that a particular videogame is to blame, a social scientific theory may argue that the game in question is merely one particular example of the many ways in which violence is learned in modern society. Rather than suggest that single parenthood is to blame, another theory might argue that a two-parent household is but one source of social control that, when combined with others, might serve to prevent juvenile crime.

Second, social scientific theories of juvenile crime and delinquency do not simply aim to explain why such behavior happens. Rather, the focus of most juvenile crime theories is explaining why there exists variation in juvenile crime and delinquency. Some theories, collectively referred to as *micro-level* theories, attempt to explain why some juveniles engage in more crime than others. Other theories, collectively referred to as *macro-level* theories, attempt to explain why some neighborhoods, states, or even nations tend to have a higher rate of juvenile crime. Perhaps reflecting the dual realities that most juveniles violate the law to some degree and that most law violators are not mentally ill (Moffitt, 1993), social scientific theories focus primarily on explaining variation in typical crimes such as assault, vandalism, theft, robbery, or substance use rather than on the extremely rare mass homicides that capture the lion's share of media attention.

Third, social scientific theories should be empirically testable. Even as they involve abstract concepts like social learning or social control, social scientific theories should simultaneously provide sufficient description of those concepts to guide social scientists in developing metrics with which to rank individuals or geographic regions according to their levels of each concept. Upon the development of such metrics, social scientific theories must further provide clear hypotheses about the ways in which these concepts are related to juvenile crime. They should, for example, describe whether and why those exposed to high levels of social learning or low levels of social control are expected, on average, to be more delinquent. A good social scientific theory is not merely one that seems plausible or well-argued, rather, it is one whose hypotheses have been supported with empirical data.

The current chapter compares and contrasts the hypotheses of the major social scientific theories of juvenile crime and delinquency. It is divided into five major sections, each of which covers one set of related theories. For each set of theories, the chapter describes the major concepts that these theories use to explain variation in juvenile crime across individuals and, where applicable, across geographic regions. Of particular importance, the chapter will further describe the various ways in which social scientists have subjected these theories to empirical scrutiny, describe the current state of the evidence bearing on each theory, and discuss the implications of each theory for effective delinquency prevention.

■ Deterrence Theory

Deterrence theory can be traced to writings of 18th-century Enlightenment scholars such as Cesare Beccaria. These scholars were critical of what they believed to be excessively harsh criminal justice policies, including torture and the death penalty. They were similarly critical of criminal justice policies that were subject to the whims of capricious judges and that, as a result, were often applied inconsistently to different people who had committed similar crimes. They therefore outlined a number of principles that they believed would promote a criminal justice system that could be humane, but simultaneously effective, in deterring criminal behavior. Collectively, these principles remain the general foundation upon which modern deterrence theorists have built their explanation of why juvenile crime happens and why some juveniles are more criminal than others (Beccaria, 1764).

Whereas many in the general public approach juvenile crime by first asking why a given individual might engage in a crime like theft, deterrence theory instead asks why others refrain from committing the same act. In particular, deterrence theory assumes that all people naturally seek pleasure and attempt to minimize pain. Therefore, according to deterrence theory, people steal because they want something they do not have, they assault others because those others have angered them, and they use drugs because drugs make them feel good. From the vantage point of deterrence theory, asking what causes teenagers to commit crime is tantamount to asking what causes teenagers to have sex. Regardless of the particular act in question, deterrence theory conceptualizes major acts of juvenile crime and minor acts of juvenile delinquency as alternative examples of the universal human tendency to maximize pleasure.

Faced with the task of explaining why some youth violate more laws than others, deterrence theory therefore does not suggest that some individuals are substantially more motivated. Rather, it argues that the primary source of variation in delinquency resides in some juveniles' higher levels of restraint against universal motivations. In particular, drawing on the Enlightenment belief that human beings possess free will and the ability to use reason, it suggests that juveniles have the capacity to weigh the costs and benefits of a given behavior before acting. However, because it views the benefits of crime and delinquency as a constant that is shared equally by all people, deterrence theory suggests that the perceived threat of punishment is the primary factor distinguishing the delinquent from the conformist. From a deterrence perspective, the poverty-stricken youth who perceives a high probability of punishment for theft should be less likely to steal than the middle-class youth who perceives a low probability of punishment. Further, deterrence theorists situate the primary source of punishment in the sanctions rendered by formal authorities like the police and juvenile courts. Thus, the fundamental hypothesis of deterrence theory is that a given individual will be deterred from delinquency to the degree that he or she believes such behavior will result in formal sanctions that outweigh its benefits.

According to deterrence theory, three critical characteristics of formal sanctions determine whether they will be effective in persuading youth that the costs of delinquency outweigh the benefits. First, effective punishment must be of high *certainty*. The greater the proportion of offenders in the community that a given youth witnesses getting caught and punished, for example, the greater the youth in question will be subjected to what deterrence theorists call "general" deterrence. Similarly, the greater the proportion of a particular youth's violations that are detected and subjected to formal sanction at the hands of legal authorities, the greater the youth in question will be subjected to what deterrence theorists call "specific" deterrence. Second, deterrence theory asserts that effective punishment in the legal system must be of high *celerity*. Not only is it important to detect and punish as high a proportion of law violations as possible, but, in addition, those punishments should occur as quickly as possible following any given violation. Third, each punishment's *severity* should be proportional to the severity of the violation in question. Violations like homicide, which are strongly disapproved by a high proportion of citizens, should result in more severe formal sanctions than violations like underage drinking, which are strongly disapproved by fewer citizens. Recalling Enlightenment scholars' concern with promoting a system of justice that is humane, however, deterrence theory suggests that no punishment should be more severe than is necessary to slightly outweigh the potential benefits of crime and delinquency.

Whereas the fundamental propositions of deterrence theory outlined above date back to the 18th century, extensive empirical testing of the theory did not begin until the latter half of the 20th century. The empirical testing that has taken place since has yielded mixed support for the theory, with most tests focusing on the relationship between delinquency and perceived certainty of punishment. On one hand, empirical tests consistently find evidence that individuals who *perceive* a higher certainty of being caught and punished for law violations demonstrate significantly lower levels of delinquency than do their counterparts (Piquero & Pogarsky, 2002). On the other hand, some evidence suggests that the actual experience of getting caught for violations is associated with more, rather than less, future delinquency (Pogarsky & Piquero, 2003). Thus, while the consistency of results concerning perceived certainty suggests support for one of deterrence theory's fundamental hypotheses, results concerning the actual experience of punishment suggest a "positive punishment effect" rather than the anticipated deterrence effect.

A number of explanations for the positive punishment effect have been offered over the past decade. One explanation suggests that more delinquent individuals may tend to fall victim to what has alternatively been termed the "gambler's fallacy" or the "resetting effect," whereby individuals mistakenly assume that the probability of getting caught a second time decreases once an individual has been caught the first time (Pogarsky & Piquero, 2003). A second explanation, related to learning and subcultural theories described below, suggests that being caught and sanctioned by legal authorities may demonstrate toughness to delinquent associates, thus increasing one's social standing among other law violators (Anderson, 1999). However, although preliminary research does suggest limited support for these first two explanations of the positive punishment effect, perhaps a simpler explanation stems from a point raised at the outset of this chapter about the need for theorists to provide clear descriptions of how researchers can measure critical concepts. In particular, studies finding the above positive punishment effect have sometimes measured punishment in terms of relatively minor sanctions like being pulled over for traffic violations. Many people who have been pulled over will certainly attest to the physiological anxiety that often accompanies the experience—and, if nothing else, the experience certainly takes time from one's day. Yet suppose that an individual is pulled over, given a warning, and then let go. Does such an experience rightfully reflect a measure of punishment or, instead, does it more appropriately reflect the avoidance of severe punishment like arrest? In such cases, one could reasonably argue that escaping a severe punishment outweighs the experience of a mild punishment, yielding an overall lesson that violations do not tend to meet with severe repercussions. Recent extensions of deterrence theory explicitly predict that avoiding punishment is associated with a higher probability of future crime and delinquency, with preliminary research supporting this notion (Piquero & Pogarsky, 2002). Likewise, some research suggests that although moderately severe punishments like arrest may not *increase* the perceived certainty of further punishment, they likewise do not *decrease* perceived certainty, as might be expected if positive punishment truly reflected a resetting effect (Pogarsky et al., 2005). Thus, it may be the case that the positive punishment effect reflects insufficient theoretical discussion of what qualifies as "punishment" or perhaps a poor fit between the conceptualization of punishment and the empirical measures with which it has been operationalized in the existing literature.

Even if the positive punishment effect reflects nothing more than faulty measurement, there remain several good reasons to question whether deterrence theory alone is capable of providing a complete explanation for why some youth violate more laws than others. First, there is limited research that has examined the relationship between celerity of punishment and future offending, with the existing evidence suggesting that celerity has little effect on delinquency (Nagin & Pogarsky, 2001). Second, the negative association between delinquency and perceived certainty of punishment is relatively weak in comparison to the relationship that delinquency bears with a number of variables derived from alternative theoretical perspectives (Loughran et al., 2012). Third, excessively severe punishments like waiving juveniles to the adult system have been linked to a greater, rather than lower, risk of recidivism (Bishop et al., 1996).

Implications

Although the weight of the evidence suggests that deterrence theory may not provide a complete explanation for why some youth are more likely to violate the law, it nonetheless suggests that deterrence plays at least some role. In particular, the perceived certainty of punishment emerges as a consistent, though not particularly strong, predictor of juvenile crime and delinquency. Those individuals who perceive a higher certainty of being caught and punished tend to be slightly less delinquent than their counterparts. Evidence concerning the speed of punishment remains too limited at this point to draw more than the most tentative of conclusions. Evidence concerning the severity of punishment remains more complicated, with some suggesting that extremely mild or extremely severe forms of punishment may actually entice further offending. In light of such evidence, it would appear that one component of any effort to control juvenile crime and delinquency might reasonably involve making sure that juveniles are aware of the legal consequences for law violations and that law enforcement officials detect and punish law violations as consistently as possible. Further, the existing research provides evidence that punishments should be severe enough that they are not interpreted as punishment avoidance, but not so severe that they expose juveniles to the trauma associated with the adult criminal justice system.

■ Control Theory

Much like deterrence theorists, control theorists conceive of crime and delinquency as natural manifestations of the universal human tendency to seek pleasure and avoid pain. Control theorists therefore share with deterrence theorists the notion that variation in crime must be explained by variation in social constraints against delinquency. However, whereas deterrence theorists situate the primary source of restraint in the effectiveness of punishments rendered by formal authorities like the police and juvenile courts, control theorists situate the primary source of restraint among informal authority figures like parents and neighbors.

Micro Level

At the micro level, Hirschi (1969) argues that there is a higher level of delinquency among those individuals who have weak or broken social bonds to society. Hirschi discusses four social bonds that are related to delinquent activity. First, *Attachment* refers to how much an individual is emotionally invested in the positive appraisals of others. Second, *Commitment* refers to how much an individual has a stake in conforming to conventional norms so as not to risk losing the fruits of past labor or the potential for future success in mainstream society. Third, *Involvement* refers to how much an individual spends time pursuing conventionally approved activities, thus leaving little time for delinquency or crime. And finally, *Belief* refers to how much an individual has internalized negative appraisals of activities that mainstream society condemns. Existing research, including Hirschi's own work, provides evidence that individuals who possess higher levels of these four social bonds tend, on average, to engage in lower levels of delinquency (Agnew, 1991). At the same time, there is less research that explicitly identifies the precise social mechanisms through which these bonds are developed and/or broken, thus making the transition from theory to practice potentially difficult.

However, there is a more recent version of control theory that provides more explicit discussion of the precise types of social stimuli that may effectively promote social control. In their influential book *A General Theory of Crime*, Gottfredson and Hirschi (1990) argue that the first seven or so years of a child's life represent a critical period during which children are amenable to the development of a trait called self-control. According to Gottfredson and Hirschi, children develop self-control to the degree that parents or other informal authorities consistently set rules, monitor behavior, and punish children for violations of those rules. The punishments in question should not be overly harsh; indeed, some research provides compelling evidence that punishments like physical abuse may contribute to more, rather than less, delinquency (Rebellon & Van Gundy, 2005). However, non-abusive punishments are viewed as critical in Gottfredson and Hirschi's self-control theory. Much as deterrence theory argues that formal punishment should be of high certainty after a violation, self-control theory argues that informal punishment must be applied consistently after each rule violation during early childhood. When it is, individuals are said to develop a greater ability to exert self-control. This ability is indicated, among other things, by less impulsivity, less selfishness, a lower tendency to lose one's temper, and a lower tendency to take unwise physical risks. According to self-control theory, delinquency takes place when an individual has failed to develop high self-control and is presented with the opportunity to pursue immediate pleasure at the potential cost of long-term benefit. Rather than studying hard to prepare for a long-term career, the individual with low self-control may seek immediate pleasure via substance use, precocious sexual involvement, or theft of desired property. Rather than resolving interpersonal disputes or conflict via compromise or negotiation, the same individual may instead use violence to deal with his or her frustration.

Social scientists have conducted a tremendous amount of research concerning self-control theory. This research yields strong, but not complete, support for its major hypotheses. Most of this research has examined whether individuals who possess traits like impulsivity and risk-taking, which are indicative of low self-control, also tend to exhibit higher involvement in delinquency and crime. Innumerable studies have found a strong association between such measures of self-control and delinquency, even after controlling statistically for the potential influence of variables derived from alternative theories (Pratt & Cullen, 2000). Further, this correlation appears to exist not only in the United States, whose culture values individualism more so than many others, but in a host of cultures throughout the world (Rebellon et al., 2008). Research examining the relationship between parenting and self-control is somewhat less common, but such research does yield support for the assertion that parents who consistently monitor and sanction inappropriate behavior tend to have children with higher levels of self-control (Unnever et al., 2003). At the same time, despite self-control theory's ardent assertion that variables derived from alternative perspectives are not important in the explanation of juvenile crime, research consistently suggests that they are (Agnew, 2005). Likewise, contrary to self-control theory's predictions, emerging research in the field of neuroscience suggests that self-control is malleable after the first decade of life and that willpower is like a mental muscle that can be developed with "exercise" (Baumeister & Tierney, 2011).

Macro Level

While the above control theories attempt to explain variation in crime across different individuals, social disorganization theory provides an explanation of variation in crime across geographic regions such as neighborhoods. With roots at the University of Chicago in the first half of the 20th century, social disorganization theory began partly as a reaction against the work of 19th-century biological theorists like Lombroso (1876), who situated the causes of crime in "atavistic" defects believed to characterize the criminal's biological constitution. University of Chicago sociologists from Park and Burgess (1925) to Shaw and McKay (1942) agreed, if implicitly, with micro-level control theories, which argue that people share a self-evident and relatively equal motivation for crime. Yet rather than focusing on individual-level explanations for variation in delinquency, such scholars observed that certain neighborhoods tended to exhibit relatively high delinquency rates regardless of the particular individuals who happened to reside within them at any given point in time. This suggested to them that variation in delinquency is not merely a characteristic of particular individuals, but is instead a macro-level phenomenon reflecting some neighborhoods' predispositions for allowing delinquency to flourish. Seeking systematic patterns in the characteristics of such neighborhoods, social disorganization theorists observed that such neighborhoods tended to be characterized by concentrated economic deprivation, a mix of many different ethnic groups (i.e., ethnic heterogeneity), and a tendency for people to move in and move out frequently (i.e., residential mobility). In an effort to explain why such characteristics might be associated with high rates of delinquency, such theorists suggested that these characteristics make it difficult for a neighborhood's constituent individuals to organize collectively for the purpose of informally guarding each other's property and well-being. One can imagine, for example, that neighbors working multiple jobs, speaking different languages, and moving frequently might have a difficult time build informal relationships of trust that provide the foundation for collective guardianship against crime. Rather than guarding each other's property and well-being as a collective social network, individuals in such neighborhoods might therefore be largely on their own, thus increasing the opportunity for delinquent youth to victimize residents.

Empirical research concerning the central tenets of social disorganization theory is very difficult to conduct. In large part, this reflects the need for tests of the theory to include data from individuals nested within many different neighborhoods. Such data are rarely available on a large scale in the United States and, as a result, major tests of social disorganization theory have tended to take place in Great Britain, where such data are more commonly collected by the British government. Using these data, researchers have constructed measures of neighborhood characteristics like concentrated economic deprivation, ethnic heterogeneity, and residential mobility. Likewise, they have constructed measures of social disorganization including the degree to which different neighborhoods are characterized by weak friendship networks, low levels of participation in local organizations, and a high density of unsupervised teenage groups engaging in unstructured socializing. Such data reveal that neighborhoods with the above characteristics do tend to be associated with higher levels of social disorganization, which, in turn, is associated with higher rates of crime and delinquency (Lowenkamp et al., 2003; Sampson & Groves, 1989).

Implications

Whereas deterrence theory's implications for controlling delinquency revolve around effective formal punishment for violations that have taken place, control theories focus on preventing violations via the establishment of informal control. At the micro level, for example, self-control theory suggests that early childhood is a critical period during which parents and other informal authority figures must monitor and sanction inappropriate behavior. Only after experiencing this type of socialization consistently during these formative years does the theory suggest that a child will develop the self-control needed to refrain from severe crime during the teenage years. From the perspective of self-control theory, punishing a teenager who has failed to develop self-control will not necessarily provide effective deterrence because such individuals may be too impulsive to consider the pros and cons of future delinquency in sufficient depth before acting. At the macro level, social disorganization theory suggests that neighborhoods and cities will control their rates of delinquency to the degree that adults form strong friendship networks and actively participate in community organizations. By doing so, a given neighborhood or city is said to be socially organized in such a way as to promote collective efficacy (Sampson et al., 1997) and limit youths' opportunity for the unsupervised activity that may facilitate delinquency (Osgood et al., 1996).

■ Strain Theory

Whereas deterrence and control theories share the fundamental premise that delinquency is simply a manifestation of people's common attempt to maximize immediate pleasure and that people therefore share equal motivation for delinquency, strain theories instead suggest that some individuals or groups experience significantly more motivation than others. From the perspective of strain theory, delinquency is not necessarily a reflection of people's normal pursuit of self-interest but, instead, is a reaction to unusually stressful experiences in the physical or social environment. Much as a balloon can sustain only a certain amount of air pressure before it pops, strain theory suggests that juveniles can withstand only a certain degree of stress before they turn to delinquency as a means of coping.

Micro Level

Classic strain theorists like Albert Cohen (1955) argued that some youth feel greater motivation for delinquency as a result of the trouble that they have achieving what they perceive to be middle-class status in American culture. Such youth may have high aspirations for middle-class status but their parents may not be capable of equipping them with the clothing, etiquette, or knowledge to command middle-class respect from teachers or other informal authority figures. Traditional strain theorists conceptualized strain as the resulting gap between high aspirations for middle-class status and low expectations for achieving it. Further, they suggest that strain varies significantly from one individual to another and that those individuals highest in strain are disproportionately prone to engage in delinquency as a means of dealing with their frustration. Although such strain theories received substantial academic attention in the 1960s, they soon fell from favor, largely because social scientists failed to find strong evidence of the fundamental hypothesis that individuals experiencing a large gap between aspirations and expectations for middle-class success would be more delinquent than their counterparts (Agnew, 1992).

In the 1990s, however, strain theory began a revival that has continued to the present day. This revival was spearheaded by Robert Agnew, who argued that tests of classic strain theories had failed to yield strong empirical support because they conceptualized and measured strain in too narrow a way. According to Agnew's (1992) General Strain Theory (GST), motivation for delinquency does vary from one individual to another, but not primarily on the basis of a gap between economic aspirations and expectations. Agnew argues that aspirations are often idealized and that, as a result, failing to achieve them may often not provoke a high degree of strain. While many would love to win the lottery, for example, low expectations for purchasing the winning ticket may not provoke the type of negative emotion that one might associate with a higher risk for delinquency. Rather, Agnew suggests that a greater amount of strain is likely to result from a gap between expectations and actual outcomes, such as being promised a raise but then failing to receive it, or from the general failure to achieve outcomes that one perceives to be fair. Contrary to earlier versions of strain theory, GST suggests that the outcomes in question need not be economic in nature; rather, they may include a failure to achieve any positively valued outcome that is expected or deemed fair. Agnew goes on to hypothesize that delinquency-inducing strain may result not only from the above failures to achieve positively valued goals, but also from the removal of positively valued outcomes or from the imposition of noxious stimuli like bullying, parental abuse, or other forms of victimization. In all cases, he suggests that strain increases the probability of delinquency because it promotes negative emotions like anger or frustration. At the same time, Agnew (1992) does not argue that strain always results in delinquency, nor does he argue that differences in strain are the only important factors affecting interpersonal variation in delinquency. According to Agnew, some individuals possess greater resources for coping in legitimate ways with strains of the above types. Some, for example, may have access to non-delinquent coping strategies like organized sports or anger-management training that may facilitate the venting of frustration in conventional ways. Others may have access to greater levels of social support from family and friends and, as a result, may have an easier time dealing with their strain without engaging in delinquency.

A great deal of research has examined the empirical validity of GST's primary hypotheses. This research has generally yielded strong, but not complete, support for its predictions. For example, even after controlling statistically for variables derived from alternative theories, numerous studies find evidence that experiencing stressful life events or negative stimuli is associated with delinquency (Agnew, 2006). Some of this research has further explored whether this relationship may simply reflect the possibility that delinquency can increase one's exposure to stressful life circumstances rather than vice versa. Results of such research suggest that a substantial portion of the relationship results from the influence of strain on delinquency rather than vice versa (Hoffmann & Cerbone, 1999). Likewise, research suggests support for the notion that delinquency serves as means of coping with the negative emotion that may result from strain (Brezina, 1996). Moreover, preliminary research finds that failing to achieve a promised promotion is associated with higher levels of anger, which, in turn, is associated with a higher intent to steal (Rebellon et al., 2009). Likewise, preliminary research finds that middle-school and high-school students who perceive greater levels of injustice at the hands of such figures as parents, teachers, and peers are more prone to engage in a wide range of delinquent acts, that this relationship remains even after controlling for critical variables derived from alternative theories, and that the same relationship is largely explained by higher levels of anger among those who perceive unjust treatment (Rebellon et al., 2012). At the same time, research exploring GST's predictions about coping resources and social support generally does not find evidence that these factors serve as buffers against the delinquency-provoking influence of strain (Paternoster & Mazerolle, 1994).

Macro Level

Robert Merton's (1938) essay "Social Structure and Anomie" is often cited as providing the foundation for macro-level strain theories of delinquency. Although he technically did not like applying the term "strain" to his theory of American crime rates (Cullen & Messner, 2007), he argued that the high rate of American crime compared to that of many other industrialized nations reflected an imbalance between the high level of attention that American culture pays to achieving the American Dream and the more modest attention that it pays to achieve it via the ostensibly legitimate channels of hard work and perseverance. Building on Merton's theorizing, more recent scholars like Messner and Rosenfeld (1994) have proposed that there exists an imbalance in the attention that American culture pays to economic versus non-economic social institutions. In their Institutional Anomie Theory (IAT), they suggest that American culture systematically devalues institutions like the family and education, which are forced to accommodate themselves to the needs of economic production. As a result, informal social controls are weaker in American society than they are in many other cultures. Thus, while IAT suggests that there exists important culture varia-tion in the motivation for economic success and that such variation pro-vides one component of the explanation for American crime rates relative to other industrialized nations, IAT simultaneously suggests that the theoreti-cal mechanisms through which this motivation affects crime rates reside in weak informal control at the macro level.

A number of studies have examined the core tenets of both anomie theory generally and IAT specifically. Blau and Blau's (1982) classic study, for example, compares the rates of major crimes like homicide and robbery across standard metropolitan statistical areas (SMSAs) throughout the United States. Their analyses reveal that those SMSAs with higher levels of inequal-ity tend to exhibit significantly higher rates of violence and, further, that inequality is much more strongly related to violence than is poverty per se. In combination with research finding only weak evidence of a link between socioeconomic status and delinquency at the micro level (Tittle & Meier, 1990), Blau and Blau's results suggest that it is not absolute levels of depri-vation that promote delinquency as much as it may be the *relative* levels of deprivation that individuals feel when they compare themselves to those in the wealthier surrounding neighborhoods. More recent research replicates the finding that inequality is related to violence and, in addition, provides partial support for Messner and Rosenfeld's IAT by finding that the relation-ship between inequality and violence is mediated partly by weakness in non-economic institutions like family and education (Maume & Lee, 2003).

Implications

Strain theories at both the micro and macro levels suggest that effective delin-quency control requires paying attention to the various sources of pressure that they believe to propel some individuals and groups into greater delinquency. While eliminating strain altogether is unrealistic, GST suggests that it is impor-tant to prevent exposure to excessive strain like physical abuse. Likewise, given support for GST's assertion that strain affects delinquency by increasing negative emotions, delinquency-control efforts may benefit from the inclusion of an anger-management component. At the macro level, while some degree of inequality is necessary in a free-market economic system, IAT implies that efforts to control violence could benefit from the promotion of norms that value non-economic institutions like family and education.

■ Learning Theory

Whereas control theorists begin with the premise that individuals are born anti-social until socialized and strain theorists with the premise that individuals are prosocial until strained, learning theorists begin with the premise that individuals are not innately prosocial or antisocial. Instead, learning theory asserts that individuals exposed to prosocial role models internalize prosocial values while those exposed to delinquent role models internalize delinquent norms. To the degree that the balance of an individual's internalized norms lean in the direction of deviance, learning theory suggests his or her risk for delinquency increases.

Micro Level

In his seminal statement of Differential Association Theory, Edwin Sutherland (1947) argued that crime, like any form of behavior, is learned via social interaction. According to Sutherland, the greater the proportion of one's social associates who violate the law, the greater the probability that one will adopt a preponderance of attitudes favorable to law violation. In turn, the more favorable one's attitudes to law violation, the greater the probability that one will become a criminal. More recent learning theorists agree with Sutherland's fundamental premise but have elaborated upon his theory by combining it with the general principles of operant psychology. Burgess and Akers (1966), for example, argued that individuals become deviant as a result of associating with deviant peers but remain deviant largely as a function of the degree to which their deviance yields reward. Peers may grant a measure of status, for example, to delinquents in return for providing group resources like alcohol whose procurement requires theft or illegal purchase. Similarly, peers may grant inclusion or positive social attention to delinquents in return for "borrowing" a parent's car without permission to provide group transportation, for demonstrating the bravado or nerve to stand with the group in gang fights, or for simply providing entertainment via their involvement in seemingly irrational hazing rituals (Rebellon, 2006).

Empirical research traditionally yields strong support for social learning theory. Akers and colleagues (1979), for example, used survey data to demonstrate that self-reports of personal alcohol and marijuana use are strongly correlated with measures of peer involvement in the same behaviors, and a multitude of further studies yield similar results even after controlling statistically for variables like self-control (Pratt & Cullen, 2000). At the same time, recent research suggests several caveats. First, while the weight of the evidence continues to suggest that associating with delinquent peers promotes delinquency, the logistical and ethical issues involved in conducting randomized experiments to test criminological theories mean that researchers must rely primarily on correlational methods of empirical research. Such methods make it difficult to establish the temporal ordering that is responsible for the relationship between two variables. Some theorists, for example, acknowledge a strong correlation between personal and peer delinquency but suggest that it reflects the individual's tendency to associate with similar others rather than reflecting those others' effect on the individual's behavior (Glueck & Glueck, 1950). Panel studies have attempted to explore which assertion is more accurate by analyzing data collected from the same individuals at multiple time points.

Such research yields mixed results, with some studies now finding stronger evidence of peer influence (Akers & Lee, 1996) and others finding stronger evidence that individuals tend to associate with similar others (Matsueda & Anderson, 1998).

Second, recalling the importance of measuring concepts accurately, some researchers have questioned whether traditional measures of social learning variables are sufficiently accurate to generate valid findings. For example, traditional studies measure peer delinquency indirectly by asking respondents to estimate how many of their friends they *believe* to have engaged in delinquency. Research, however, finds evidence that individuals tend to "project" their own behavior inaccurately unto others, thus calling into question whether studies using such measures of peer delinquency yield valid results (Jussim & Osgood, 1989). Although the limited existing research using direct measures of peer delinquency continues to suggest that peers influence personal behavior, such research finds the magnitude of peer influence to be substantially smaller than traditional research using indirect measures of peer behavior (Meldrum et al., 2009). Beyond the difficulties associated with measuring peer behavior, research has had difficulty generating complete measures of such concepts as imitation, attitudes, and reinforcement. Among studies that have attempted to measure such concepts, results sometimes yield only modest support for learning theory's speculation about the degree to which such factors are independently associated with personal delinquency or for its speculation that such factors mediate the influence of peer behavior on personal behavior (Akers et al., 1979).

Macro Level

There exist two dominant versions of macro-level learning theory in the current literature. The first dates back to the subcultural theory of Wolfgang and Ferracuti (1967) and suggests that behaviors like violence may flourish within certain subsets of society on the basis of collective norms allowing or promoting such behavior. A recent version of this theory emerged with the work of Elijah Anderson (1999), whose ethnographic research during the 1990s found evidence that violence in the inner-city subculture of Philadelphia revolves largely around establishing and maintaining a degree of respect amid informal interaction in public places. Violations of an individual's respect may take many forms that include staring too long, taking one's property, or insulting one's reputation. Whatever the form of such violations, however, maintaining respect within the subculture of the street requires a youth, particularly a male, to punish the violator publicly, often with violence. In all cases, however, one of Anderson's critical observations remains that there exist informal rules, among delinquents and non-delinquents alike, of how and when violence should be employed. Further, while Anderson finds evidence that well-parented youth in inner-city Philadelphia may be less violent overall, he nonetheless finds compelling evidence that such youth sometimes adopt an aggressive demeanor when the subcultural "code of the street" requires it for the purpose of maintaining respect to prevent the appearance of weakness.

The second major version of macro-level learning theory is Akers' (2009) Theory of Social Structure and Social Learning (SSSL). According to the SSSL model, variables reflecting commonly researched structural correlates of macro-level variation in crime all exert their influence on individuals' relative levels of delinquency by affecting the degree to which those individuals associate with delinquent peers, imitate the delinquency of those peers, adopt a preponderance of attitudes favorable to delinquency, and receive more reinforcement than punishment for their delinquency. The SSSL model divides macro-level variables into several different sets. One set, collectively referred to as "Differential Social Organization," includes such variables as population density and age distribution. A second set, collectively referred to as "Differential Location in the Social Structure," includes such variables as class, gender, and the racial composition of different geographic regions. A third set, collectively referred to as "Theoretically Defined Structural Variables," includes the core variables described in Anomie Theory and Social Disorganization Theory. A final set, collectively referred to as "Differential Social Location," includes membership in small collectives like families. In all cases, these macro-level variables are said to influence individual delinquency via their collective effect on micro-level social learning variables.

While only limited research has examined the empirical validity of the SSSL model, Akers (2009) describes preliminary research supporting his macro-level theory. In particular, such research suggests that certain macro-social contexts expose individuals differentially to the micro-level learning variables that are themselves associated with delinquency. Suppose, for example, that one compares regions of high versus low population density. According to the SSSL model, the former regions might have a higher average rate of delinquency in part because individuals within them are simply more likely to encounter delinquent models in the social environment. So too, other structural variables may differentially expose individuals in different geographic regions to a different ratio of favorable versus unfavorable attitudes toward delinquency or to different levels of physical and social reinforcement for delinquency.

Implications

One of social learning theory's key implications is that controlling delinquency requires preventing exposure to delinquent behavioral role models that promote and reinforce delinquency. Of note, Akers (2009) explicitly argues that the delinquent peers in question need not actively pressure a non-delinquent to exert an influence on his or her behavior. Rather, delinquent associates may affect a youth's behavior simply by modeling deviance in the absence of any explicit pressure. Further, even insofar as delinquency is less strongly related to direct measures of peer delinquency versus perceptions of peer delinquency, Akers (2009) observes that perceptions may themselves have etiological importance as part of the explanation for why some youth are more delinquent than others.

At the same time, two considerations may arguably limit the utility of learning theory, as currently formulated, for controlling delinquency. First, to the degree that personal behavior is more related to perceptions of peer behavior than to actual peer behavior, learning theory provides little guidance as to the origins of such perceptions. Learning theory implies that such perceptions may come from any number of sources, including actual peer delinquency, false rumors about peer delinquency, and media depictions of delinquency in general. However, absent clear hypotheses about which specific sources of such perceptions matter most versus least, it is difficult to test learning theory fully and, in turn, to develop interventions aimed at altering perceptions of peer delinquency. Second, insofar as learning theory implies that effective intervention hinges on preventing reinforcement for delinquency, it has yet to identify systematically what social stimuli are most versus least rewarding to most individuals. Without a clear sense of what stimuli are most commonly rewarding, however, it remains difficult for interventionists to know what types of reinforcement their interventions should use their limited resources to prevent. Nonetheless, learning theory suggests that delinquency might be most usefully controlled by preventing exposure to deviant role models, by preventing youth from believing (whether accurately or inaccurately) that their social associates are engaging in delinquency, and by limiting the degree to which delinquency yields physical or social rewards.

■ Biosocial Theory

Although the dominant theories of delinquency in the current literature remain social psychological and sociological in nature, scholars in these fields have begun in recent decades to embrace interdisciplinary research aimed at combining these theories with biological and psychological perspectives. In part, this reflects growing evidence from the field of behavioral genetics that identical twins are more similar in their delinquency than are fraternal twins, suggesting that a portion of interpersonal variance in delinquency may reflect the interaction of genetic predisposition with the individual's social environment (Rutter et al., 2006). In part, it likewise reflects evidence that such biological variables as testosterone levels, neurophysiological arousal, and neurotransmitter levels are related to interpersonal variation in delinquency (Rowe, 2002). While chapter 6 will discuss these types of issues in greater depth, it is important to note that the emerging mainstream view among criminologists suggests that biological and social factors interact to promote delinquency.

Moffitt's Developmental Taxonomy

One notable example of the compatibility between social and biological theory is provided by Moffitt's (1993) Developmental Taxonomy, which suggests that there exist two distinctive groups of delinquents. The first group comprises what Moffitt calls life-course-persistent (LCP) offenders, who are said to constitute only about 6% of the population and who are said to be primarily male. According to Moffitt's theory, these offenders begin getting into relatively serious trouble at an early age and continue offending well into adulthood. Moffitt argues that an individual is at risk for becoming an LCP offender upon experiencing neuropsychological deficits while *simultaneously* being raised in a disadvantaged household (e.g., a household characterized by such factors as low socioeconomic status and poor parenting). Moffitt refers to the second group of delinquents as adolescence-limited offenders; she believes they constitute, ironically, a *majority* of all youth (with non-offenders technically representing a literally "deviant" minority). Moffitt argues that adolescence-limited offenders tend to violate the law in at least minor ways during adolescence when they begin mimicking the behavior of their LCP counterparts in an effort to assert their autonomy. Moffitt observes that modern youth are experiencing puberty at an earlier age while simultaneously encountering increasing educational and legal barriers to the social status of adulthood. She argues that AL offending is partly a reaction to this "maturity gap." While research concerning Moffitt's theory may currently be somewhat limited, preliminary studies suggest her approach to provide a promising avenue for achieving a fuller understanding of how biological and social forces interact to promote delinquency (Moffitt, 2006).

Implications

Some mistakenly assume that biologically informed delinquency theories provide few avenues for intervention. In truth, however, there exist a number of potential interventions that such theories suggest to be possible. First, even insofar as such traits as impulsivity are partly inherited, the evidence from both sociological and psychological studies described above suggests that individuals can develop and exercise their countervailing ability to exert self-control. Second, many biological variables do not reflect inherited tendencies. Prenatal exposure to maternal cigarette smoking (Brennan et al., 1999) and early childhood exposure to toxins like lead (Narag et al., 2009), for example, have been linked to an increased propensity for delinquency. As such, altering the environment to prevent such exposures may serve as one component of a comprehensive delinquency-prevention strategy. Third, biosocial theories like Moffitt's explicitly argue that biological and social factors often *interact* to promote delinquency. This means that even insofar as genetics predisposes some individuals to a higher risk of delinquency, one may still attempt to prevent youth from experiencing the environmental triggers that turn such predispositions into behavior.

Summary

The present chapter has reviewed the hypotheses of the major theories of juvenile crime and delinquency at both the micro and macro levels. It has further provided an assessment of the degree to which empirical research has supported these assertions. Deterrence and control theories suggest that delinquency simply reflects the natural and universal pursuit of pleasure. Deterrence theory suggests that this pursuit can be constrained by effective punishment at the hands of the juvenile justice system. Control theory suggests it can instead be constrained by proper childhood socialization at the hands of informal authorities like parents and by strong networks of informal social control in which neighbors collectively guard each other's property and well-being. Strain theory suggests that some individuals experience more pressure for coping with negative emotions through delinquency and that societies paying excessive attention to economic versus non-economic institutions may exacerbate such pressure for all youth. Learning theory suggests that individuals engage in greater delinquency to the degree that they are exposed to delinquent role models and internalize a preponderance of attitudes favorable to delinquency, both of which are said to be more likely in certain subcultures or in certain types of neighborhoods. Biosocial theories suggest that a host of biological and psychological variables may combine with the above social forces to increase delinquency.

Given that each of these perspectives has received at least some amount of empirical support, scholars like Agnew (2005) have attempted to combine them into an overarching theory, while scholars like Akers (2009) have suggested that their theory is already general enough to subsume the predictions of the others. Other scholars, however, argue that some theories begin with fundamentally incompatible assumptions about the degree to which motivation varies across individuals or geographic regions, and that such theories therefore are simply incompatible (Gottfredson & Hirschi, 1990). Even insofar as the above perspectives are compatible, however, future research will be necessary to more precisely specify such issues as which particular types of strain are most crime-provoking and which particular types of rewards or punishments are most likely to encourage or discourage delinquency. In the meantime, the research discussed above can serve as a preliminary set of guidelines helping practitioners to organize and make sense of the existing literature concerning why delinquency takes place and why it varies across people and geographic regions.

References

Agnew, R. (1991). A longitudinal test of social control theory and delinquency. *Journal of Research in Crime and Delinquency, 28,* 126–156.

Agnew, R. (1992). Foundation for a general strain theory of crime and delinquency. *Criminology, 30,* 47–87.

Agnew, R. (2005). *Why do criminals offend? A general theory of crime and delinquency.* New York: Oxford University Press.

Agnew, R. (2006). *Pressured into crime: An overview of general strain theory.* Los Angeles, CA:Roxbury.

Akers, R. L. (2009). *Social learning and social structure: A general theory of crime and deviance.* New Brunswick, NJ: Transaction.

Akers, R. L., Krohn, M. D., Lanza-Kaduce, L., & Radosevich, M. (1979). Social learning and deviant behavior: A specific test of a general theory. *American Sociological Review, 44,* 635–655.

Akers, R. L., & Lee, G. (1996). A longitudinal test of social learning theory: Adolescent smoking. *Journal of Drug Issues, 26,* 317–343.

Anderson, E. (1999). *The code of the street: Decency, violence, and the moral life of the inner city.* New York: W. W. Norton & Company.

Baumeister, R. F., & Tierney, J. (2011). *Willpower: Rediscovering the greatest human strength.* New York: Penguin Group.

Beccaria, C. (1764 [2009]). *On crimes and punishments.* Translated by Graeme R. Newman & Pietro Marongiu. New Brunswick, NJ: Transaction.

Bishop, D., Frazier, C. E., Lanza-Kaduce, L., & Winner, L. (1996). The transfer of juveniles to criminal court: Does it make a difference? *Crime & Delinquency, 42,* 171–191.

Blau, J. R., & Blau, P. M. 1982. The cost of inequality—Metropolitan structure and violent crime. *American Sociological Review, 47,* 114–129.

Brennan, P. A., Grekin, E. R., & Mednick, S. A. (1999). Maternal smoking during pregnancy and adult male criminal outcomes. *Archives of General Psychiatry, 56,* 215–219.

Brezina, T. (1996). Adapting to strain: An examination of coping responses. *Criminology, 34,* 39–60.

Burgess, R. L., & Akers, R. L. (1966). A differential association-reinforcement theory of criminal behavior. *Social Problems, 14,* 128–147.

Cohen, A. K. (1955). *Delinquent boys.* Glencoe, IL: Free Press.

Cullen, F. T., & Messner, S. F. (2007). The making of criminology revisited—An oral history of Merton's anomie paradigm. *Theoretical Criminology, 11,* 5–37.

Glueck, S., & Glueck, E. (1950). *Unraveling juvenile delinquency.* Cambridge, MA: Harvard University Press.

Gottfredson, M., & Hirschi, T. (1990). *A general theory of crime.* Stanford, CA: Stanford University Press.

Hirschi, T. (1969). *The causes of delinquency.* Berkeley, CA: University of California Press.

Hoffmann, J. P., & Cerbone, F. G. (1999). Stressful life events and delinquency escalation in early adolescence. *Criminology, 37,* 343–373.

Jussim, L., & Osgood, D. W. (1989). Influence and similarity among friends—An integrative model applied to incarcerated adolescents. *Social Psychology Quarterly, 52,* 98–112.

Lombroso, C. (1876 [2006]). *The criminal man.* Translated by Mary Gibson and Nicole Hahn Rafter. Durham, NC: Duke University Press.

Loughran, T. A., Pogarsky, G., Piquero, A. R., & Paternoster, R. (2012). Re-examining the functional form of the certainty effect in deterrence theory. *Justice Quarterly, 29,* 712–741.

Lowenkamp, C. T., Cullen, F. T., & Pratt, T. C. (2003). Replicating Sampson and Groves's test of social disorganization theory: Revisiting a criminological classic. *Journal of Research in Crime and Delinquency, 40,* 351–373.

Matsueda, R. L., & Anderson, K. (1998). The dynamics of delinquent peers and delinquent behavior. *Criminology, 36,* 269–308.

Maume, M. O., & Lee, M. R. (2003). Social institutions and violence: A sub-national test of institutional anomie theory. *Criminology, 41,* 1137–1172.

Meldrum, R. C., Young, J. T. N., & Weerman, F. M. (2009). Peers, self-control, and crime: Assessing effect size across different measures of delinquent peers. *Journal of Research in Crime and Delinquency, 46,* 353–376.

Merton, R. K. (1938). Social structure and anomie. *American Sociological Review, 3,* 672–682.

Messner, S. F., & Rosenfeld, R. (1994). *Crime and the American dream.* Belmont, CA: Wadsworth.

Moffitt, T. E. (1993). Adolescence-limited and life-course-persistent antisocial behavior: A developmental taxonomy. *Psychological Review, 100,* 674–701.

Moffitt, T. E. (2006). A review of research on the taxonomy of life-course-persistent versus adolescence-limited antisocial behavior. In F. T. Cullen, J. P. Wright, & K. R. Blevins (Eds.), *Taking stock: The status of criminological theories—Advances in criminological theory* (15:277–311). New Brunswick, NJ: Transaction.

Nagin, D. S., & Pogarsky, G. (2001). Integrating celerity, impulsivity, and extra-legal sanction threats into a model of general deterrence: Theory and evidence. *Criminology, 39,* 865–891.

Narag, R. E., Pizarro, J., & Gibbs, C. (2009). Lead exposure and its implications for criminological theory. *Criminal Justice and Behavior, 36,* 954–973.

Osgood, D. W., Wilson, J. K., O'Malley, P. M., Bachman, J. G., & Johnston, L. D. (1996). Routine activities and individual deviant behavior. *American Sociological Review, 61,* 635–655.

Park, R. E., & Burgess, E. W. (1925). *The city: Suggestions for investigation of human behavior in the urban environment.* Chicago, IL: University of Chicago Press.

Paternoster, R., & Mazerolle, P. 1994. General strain theory and delinquency—A replication and extension. *Journal of Research in Crime and Delinquency, 31,* 235–263.

Piquero, A. R., & Pogarsky, G. (2002). Beyond Stafford and Warr's reconceptualization of deterrence: Personal and vicarious experiences, impulsivity, and offending behavior. *Journal of Research in Crime and Delinquency, 39,* 153–186.

Pogarsky, G., & Piquero, A. R. (2003). Can punishment encourage offending? Investigating the "resetting" effect. *Journal of Research in Crime and Delinquency, 40,* 95–120.

Pogarsky, G., Kim, K., & Paternoster, R. (2005). Perceptual change in the National Youth Survey: Lessons for deterrence theory and offender decision-making. *Justice Quarterly, 22,* 1–29.

Pratt, T., & Cullen, F. T. (2000). The empirical status of Gottfredson and Hirschi's general theory of crime: A meta-analysis. *Criminology, 38,* 931–964.

Rebellon, C. J. (2006). Do adolescents engage in delinquency to attract the social attention of peers? An extension and longitudinal test of the social reinforcement hypothesis. *Journal of Research in Crime and Delinquency, 43,* 387–411.

Rebellon, C. J., Manasse, M. E., Van Gundy, K., & Cohn, E. (2012). Perceived injustice and delinquency: A test of General Strain Theory. *Journal of Criminal Justice, 40,* 230–237.

Rebellon, C. J., Piquero, N. L., Piquero, A. R., & Thaxton, S. (2009). Do frustrated economic expectations and objective economic inequity promote crime? A randomized experiment testing Agnew's General Strain Theory. *European Journal of Criminology, 6,* 47–71.

Rebellon, C. J., Straus, M., & Medeiros, R. (2008). Self-control in global perspective: An empirical assessment of Gottfredson and Hirschi's General Theory within and across 32 national settings. *European Journal of Criminology, 5,* 331–361.

Rebellon, C. J., & Van Gundy, K. (2005). Can control theory explain the link between parental physical abuse and delinquency? A longitudinal analysis. *Journal of Research in Crime and Delinquency, 42,* 247–274.

Rowe, D. (2002). *Biology and crime.* Los Angeles, CA: Roxbury Publishing Company.

Rutter, M., Moffitt, T. E., & Caspi, A. (2006). Gene-environment interplay and psychopathology: Multiple varieties but real effects. *Journal of Child Psychology and Psychiatry, 47,* 226–261.

Sampson, R. J., & Groves, W. B. (1989). Community structure and crime—testing social-disorganization theory. *American Journal of Sociology, 94,* 774–802.

Sampson, R. J., Raudenbush, S. W., & Earls, F. (1997). Neighborhoods and violent crime: A multi-level study of collective efficacy. *Science, 377,* 918–924.

Shaw, C. R., & McKay, H. D. (1942). *Juvenile delinquency and urban areas.* Chicago, IL: University of Chicago Press.

Sutherland, E. (1947). *Principles of criminology* (4th ed.). Philadelphia, PA: Lippincott.

Tittle, C. R., & Meier, R. F. (1990). Specifying the SES/delinquency relationship. *Criminology, 28,* 271–299.

Unnever, J. D., Cullen, F. T., & Pratt, T. C. (2003). Parental management, ADHD, and delinquent involvement: Reassessing Gottfredson and Hirschi's general theory. *Justice Quarterly, 20,* 471–500.

Wolfgang, M. E., & Ferracuti, F. (1967). *The subculture of violence.* London: Tavistock Publications.

5 Risk and Protective Factors for Involvement in Juvenile Justice

Implications for Prevention

Traci L. Wike and Caren L. Putzu

■ Introduction

Juvenile delinquency continues to be a serious and costly problem in the United States. Although delinquency caseloads decreased by 20% from 1997 to 2009, the U.S. courts handled 1.5 million juvenile justice cases in 2009 (Knoll & Sickmund, 2012). Early intervention efforts aimed at intervening during an adolescent's initial involvement with the system have been developed to reduce the likelihood that a youth will re-enter the system. However, evidence suggests that early intervention efforts may actually increase the probability that justice-involved youth will re-offend and remain in the system (Gatti, Tremblay, & Vitaro, 2009). Other types of intervention efforts have emphasized addressing factors that contribute to delinquent behavior in order to prevent youth involvement with juvenile justice before it happens. This latter prevention-focused approach utilizes an ecological framework to identify the presence of risk and protective factors that influence the likelihood that a youth will engage in delinquency (Fraser & Terzian, 2005; Hawkins & Weis, 1985; Kirby & Fraser, 1997). *Risk factors* refer to individual and contextual characteristics that increase the risk of developing problems with delinquency. *Protective factors* refer to characteristics that act as buffers to protect against the risk of delinquency (Fraser & Terzian, 2005; Kirby & Fraser, 1997).

Research using a risk and protection approach has contributed much to our understanding of potential pathways to juvenile delinquency. Although no single path to delinquency exists, research shows a positive relationship between risk of juvenile offending and a number of risk factors and risk factor domains, an additive effect (Kirby & Fraser, 1997; Wasserman et al., 2003). Youth with multiple risk factors over the course of their lifetime are more likely to experience a *cumulative risk effect* that increases their risk for delinquency involvement (Kirby & Fraser, 1997). In addition, the interaction of risk factors, a multiplicative effect when several risk factors are present, and the way that certain protective factors may work to offset risk factors are necessary considerations when addressing the problem of juvenile delinquency. Regarding the broad spectrum of risk factors, Coie and colleagues (1993) noted the following: (1) dysfunction has a complicated relationship with risk factors, and rarely is one risk factor associated with a particular disorder; (2) the impact of risk factors may vary with the developmental state of the individual; (3) exposure to multiple risk factors has a cumulative effect; and (4) many disorders share fundamental risk factors. In other words, although some juvenile offenders may share common risk factors, the patterns and particular combination of risk factors vary from juvenile to juvenile. Therefore, efforts aimed at reducing or preventing delinquency necessitate knowledge of relevant risk and protective factors as well as an understanding of the unique and complex relationships between them.

The purpose of this chapter is to provide an overview of the known risk and protective factors related to youth involvement with the juvenile justice system. The first section outlines research identifying salient individual and contextual risk factors for juvenile delinquency across five domains of adolescent development: individual, family, peer, community, and school. Next, we provide characteristics present in these domains that may serve as protective factors for the development of delinquent behavior. Research pertaining to similarities and differences in risk and protective factors based on gender and race or ethnicity is discussed. Finally, we outline some examples of intervention approaches that use a risk and protection framework as a strategy for prevention of juvenile delinquency and involvement with the juvenile justice system and discuss implications for prevention practice. It is important to note that although risk factors are used to predict the likelihood of later offending, many youth with multiple risk factors never commit a delinquent act. Therefore, the presence of a risk factor may increase the probability of offending, but it does not make offending a certainty.

■ Domains of Risk and Protection

From an ecological perspective, child and adolescent development occurs as a result of the complex interplay among individual and contextual influences across the lifespan (Bronfenbrenner, 1979). These areas of influence, or domains, consist of individual, family, peer, community, and school characteristics and experiences. Risk and protective factors may be present in one or more domains and multiple factors may exist within a single domain. Assessing risk and protective factors across these multiple domains offers insight into possible levels of individual vulnerability to delinquency involvement and provides guidance for developing strategies for delinquency prevention.

Individual

Various interpersonal and behavioral characteristics have been linked to juvenile offending. Early antisocial behaviors, such as oppositional rule violation, aggression, theft, physical fighting, and vandalism, have been found to be robust predictors for early-onset delinquency in boys (Parker & Morton, 2009; Wasserman et al., 2003). Aggressive behavior exhibited in early childhood increases the risk of a child following a *life-course-persistent* trajectory of behaviors in adolescence and adulthood, such as violent crime, dating and relationship violence, and various forms of delinquency (Brame, Nagine, & Tremblay, 2001; Moffitt, 1993a; Moffitt & Caspi, 2001; Tremblay et al., 2004). In addition, favorable attitudes and beliefs toward delinquency have been shown to be predictive of juvenile offending (Elliott, 1994).

In addition to antisocial and aggressive behavior, difficulties related to emotional and cognitive development have also been associated with risk for delinquency. In a qualitative study with 24 juvenile male offenders, Simoes, Matos, and Batista-Foguets (2008) found that deficits in decision making were influential factors leading to delinquency involvement. Participants described engaging in delinquency without considering possible consequences, such as getting in trouble. They also expressed gaining pleasure and excitement from their delinquent activities and perceived their activities to be low risk in terms of going to jail (Simoes et al., 2008). Low levels of behavioral inhibition, which includes fearfulness, anxiety, timidity, and shyness, and high levels of behavioral activation, which includes novelty and sensation seeking, impulsivity, hyperactivity, and predatory aggression, increase the risk for antisocial behavior leading to delinquency involvement (Wasserman et al., 2003).

Emotional and cognitive development appears to be associated with a child's ability to control social behavior within the first two years of life. Basic cognitive deficits may also be associated with impaired social cognitive processes, such as language, aggression, oppositional behavior, attention, hyperactivity, and failure to attend to appropriate social cues (e.g., adults' instructions, peers' social initiations). These factors may affect the learning of social rules and play an important role in the development of early delinquency (Moffitt, 1993b). For instance, delayed language development may increase a child's stress level and impede normal socialization (Loeber, Farrington, & Petechuck, 2003). A difficulty in identifying risk factors in young children is the discernment between inappropriate and developmentally normal behaviors. For example, aggression, noncompliance, and lying can be normative for a 2-year-old and contribute to the development of self-identity and self-control. However, more extreme acts of aggression are not a part of the normal development of a preschool child and can act as a precursor to early delinquency. In addition, early emotional deficits can influence the development of aggressive behavior in later years. One study found that aggressive responses to shame were a significant predictor for delinquency, which may signal a lack of coping skills and ability to manage emotions appropriately (Hart, O'Toole, Price-Sharps, & Shaffer, 2007).

Youth living with disabilities or emotional conditions may be at a higher risk of engaging in delinquency (McNamara & Willoughby, 2010; Morris & Morris, 2006). However, risk varies based on type of disability and type of delinquent behavior (Shandra & Hogan, 2012). For example, youth experiencing emotional/mental or behavior problems are more likely to engage in delinquency than those with learning disabilities (Shandra & Hogan, 2012). Although disability status may serve as a risk factor for delinquency, the actual mechanism that links disabilities with delinquency has been more difficult to ascertain.

Another risk factor for youth involvement with delinquency is the use and abuse of substances (Bender, 2010; Simoes et al., 2008). A statewide study of 4,036 high-school students in South Carolina found drug use to be among the most significant predictors of aggression, with youth being almost three times more likely to get into physical fights if they used drugs (McKeown, Jackson, & Vaois, 1998). The involvement with various risky behaviors such as substance abuse increases with age, and it is most likely no coincidence that delinquency peaks in adolescence (Loeber et al., 2003). Some adolescents show delinquent behaviors only at this stage of development, while others start much earlier. Research also shows that individuals who begin earlier are at a greater risk to become serious violent and chronic offenders and, in turn, persist and extend this delinquent trajectory to adulthood (Loeber et al., 2003).

Many youth have experienced significant, negative life events that have been found to be related to a variety of negative psychological outcomes that put them at risk for juvenile delinquency. Experiences ranging from robbery, abuse, victimization, natural disasters, financial hardships, serious illness, and loss of close loved ones have been found to correlate with depression, anxiety, and fear (Fite et al., 2012) as well as delinquency and aggression (Kim, Conger, Elder, & Lorenz, 2003). The relationship between negative life experiences and both internal and external problems is dynamic such that social stress at one point in time increases later adjustment, and maladjustment increases stress in a reciprocal fashion. In other words, the "reciprocal process through which stressful life events and adolescent maladjustment can be thought of as both causes and effects over time" (Kim et al., 2003, p. 139).

Family

Family serves as a primary foundation for a child's life and, as such, can dramatically influence a child's experiences throughout the life course. Several family factors have shown to be influential and predictive of later problems with delinquency in adolescence, including low socioeconomic status, low maternal educational attainment, teenage parenthood, and low parental attachment (Derzon, 2010; Wasserman et al., 2003). Parental attachment refers to the nature of the early relationship between mother and infant and the generalization of that relationship to the child's later relationships with other individuals, including friends and intimate partners. Ainsworth (1989) notes that the experience of attachment should provide security and comfort to a child and provide the ability to move away from that security with the confidence to engage in other activities. In this way, the child develops a positive sense of self and feels competent and valued. However, if this security does not develop, the child may begin to deny the need for attachments. This may manifest as avoiding closeness, intimacy, and dependence on future relationships as well as maximizing cognitive, emotional, and physical distance from others to achieve self-reliance and independence (Mikulincer, Shaver, & Pereg, 2003). Several studies have examined the relationship between parental attachment and delinquency behavior. Low levels of parental attachment have been linked with an increase of internalizing problem behavior such as withdrawal, anxiety, and depression as well as aggressive behavior and delinquency (Buist, Dekovic,

Meeus, & van Aken, 2004). Similarly, early parent–child conflict has been associated with an increased likelihood of early-onset delinquency (Ingoldsby et al., 2006).

Family structure also represents an important risk domain for juvenile delinquency. Factors such as low parental supervision and monitoring, family disruption, child maltreatment, and harsh and punitive parenting practices have been shown to increase the risk for youth involvement in delinquency (Hoeve et al., 2009; Moffitt, 2006; Patterson & Yoerger, 2002). Conversely, increases in family time and parental attachment have been associated with significant decreases in delinquent behavior (Schroeder, Osgood, & Oghia, 2010). However, a family transition from single parents to a blended family or cohabiting family appears to have mixed results. Family transition is beneficial for youth who have a strong relationship with their residential parent prior to the family transition but detrimental to behavioral outcomes for the youth who report poor parental attachment prior to the family transition (Schroeder et al., 2010).

The number of children in a family may also serve as a risk factor for delinquency (Wasserman et al., 2003). One study found that in the case of single parents, the odds of juvenile delinquency increased an additional 35% for each extra person living in the household. For stepparent families, the odds increased 31% (Kierkus & Hewitt, 2009). However, this could be due to difficulties coping with the responsibility of caring for large numbers of children, which may result in decreased supervision as well as decreased parental attachment, or perhaps the family's financial burden increases with size, which also may increase family stress.

An overwhelming number of children are victims of maltreatment, which studies have shown can put youth at an increased risk for subsequent delinquency. It is estimated that 1.5 million children were victims of maltreatment in 2010, and 34% were under the age of 4 (U.S. Department of Health and Human Services, 2011). Among children who experience maltreatment, evidence indicates that the age during the episode or period of maltreatment puts children at a higher risk for delinquency. One study found that adolescents who were physically abused in the first five years of life were almost twice as likely to have been arrested (Lansford et al., 2007). In addition, children who experience multiple types of maltreatment are two times more likely to engage in violent delinquent behavior (Crooks, Scott, Wolfe, Chiodo, & Killip, 2007).

Peers

Studies have provided consistent evidence that involvement with a delinquent peer group increases an individual youth's risk for engaging in delinquency (Cairns, Cairns, Neckerman, Ferguson, & Gariepy, 1989; Dishion, Veronneau, & Myers, 2010; Hawkins, Catalano, & Miller, 1992; Warr & Stafford, 1991). For adolescents ages 12 to 14, the presence of antisocial peers represents a key predictor for juvenile delinquency (Lipsey & Derzon, 1998). From a socialization perspective, the peer domain influences delinquent behavior in an environment in which deviant peers model and reinforce delinquent behaviors (Dishion & Tipsord, 2011). Delinquent youth participating in the study by Simoes and colleagues (2008) indicated that their association with friends involved in delinquency influenced their own decisions to engage in delinquent behavior. Participants stated that these friends, referred to as "bad companies," encouraged them to get involved. Evidence also suggests that having a best friend involved in delinquency predicts self-reported delinquent behavior (Fite et al., 2012; Smith & Ecob, 2013). Fite and colleagues (2012) found that having a delinquent best friend exacerbated the link between neighborhood problems and child delinquency, such that high levels of peer delinquency and neighborhood problems were strongly, positively associated with child delinquency. In contrast, at low levels of best friend delinquency, neighborhood problems were unrelated to child delinquency. The study by Fite and colleagues also reported that the impact of best friend delinquency was also strong enough to overshadow the effects of negative life events in a child's life, such as parental divorce and familial incarceration (Fite et al., 2012).

In addition to presenting the risk for delinquent involvement, certain factors may affect the magnitude of the delinquent peer effect. Evidence suggests that the impact of association with delinquent peers is variable, and the source of this variability likely stems from the youth's susceptibility to that peer influence. Miller (2010) found that being more susceptible to peer influence, regardless of whether the susceptibility was in reference to delinquent or non-delinquent behaviors, was associated with heightened levels of self-reported delinquency. Specifically, the participants who were more likely to conform to their friends' behaviors were more likely to report delinquent involvement (Miller, 2010). Others have suggested that early parent–child conflict and neighborhood disadvantage contribute to the development of delinquent behaviors when children enter school (Ingoldsby & Shaw, 2002). However, the development of deviant peer relationships may be the factor that maintains and even exacerbates early starting delinquent behavior over time (Ingoldsby & Shaw, 2002). Moreover, children may be exposed to violence and conflict early in their lives, but the additional influence of deviant norms and behaviors by their peers reinforces their previous experiences.

Peer rejection also serves as a risk factor for juvenile delinquency. Children who experience rejection from peers and exhibit aggressive behavior often have difficulty maintaining positive friendships and are at higher risk for problems with self-esteem, poor self-concept, externalizing and internalizing problems, academic difficulties, loneliness, substance use, and violent behavior (Dodge et al., 2003; Laird, Jordan, Dodge, Pettit, & Bates, 2001; Morrow, Hubbard, McAuliffe, Rubin, & Dearing, 2006; Parker & Asher, 1993; Putallaz et al., 2007). One study found that peer rejection in third grade predicted increasingly greater antisocial behaviors from sixth grade onward for boys, even when controlling for earlier aggressive behavior (Coie, Terry, Lenox, Lochman, & Hyman, 1995). Rejected children may not feel a strong sense of belonging with their peer group, leading them to engage in more delinquent behavior in an effort to gain approval in their peer group.

Community

The neighborhood environment can exert substantial influence on a child's life. Studies have found that children raised in disadvantaged neighborhoods are more likely to engage in delinquent behavior (De Coster, Heimer, & Wittrock, 2006; Wasserman et al., 2003). However, the mechanism of neighborhood disadvantage and how it affects child development is a little more complex. Neighborhoods with high rates of crime and delinquency may model negative, delinquent behavior for a child (Haynie, Silver, & Teasdale, 2006; Jencks & Mayer, 1990). In other words, a child who often witnesses violence and crime in his or her neighborhood may begin to believe in the efficacy of the use of violence and poor conflict resolution skills to deal with one's problems. Others have taken a developmental perspective and suggest the conceptualization of neighborhood and the amount of contact a young child has is minimal and therefore the community domain may not be a salient factor for a young child. However, as children grow older, their perception of and contact with neighborhood expands, and effects become more direct (Aber, Gephart, Brooks-Gunn, Connell, & Spencer,1997; Ingoldsby & Shaw, 2002).

Adolescents living within high-crime neighborhoods are often subjected to greater risks and feelings of danger, which may lead to feeling a need to protect oneself. This sense of self-protection may then lead to engaging in delinquency (Fite et al., 2012). For example, the National Survey of Children's Exposure to Violence purports that more than one in five 14- to 17-year-olds (22.2%) had witnessed a shooting in the previous year (Finkelhor, Turner, Ormrod, Hamby, & Kracke, 2009). Liberman (2007) found that adolescents' exposure to firearm violence approximately doubled the probability that an adolescent would commit serious violence over the subsequent two years. The findings of this study suggest that the strongest predictor of carrying a concealed gun for adolescents was a perception of safety in the neighborhood (Liberman, 2007).

School

Poor academic performance, specifically in elementary grades, has been linked to later delinquent behavior (Hawkins et al., 2000). In addition, high rates of truancy in elementary and middle school have been linked to increased rates of violent behavior in adolescence (Hawkins et al., 2000; Wasserman et al., 2003). It seems logical that a child who is missing a lot of school would also have poor academic performance; however, some see these factors as a subsequent development of additional domains of risk factors (Loeber & Farrington, 2000). In other words, poor academic performance and truancy may be a manifestation of something much more complex.

School engagement and school bonding, often used interchangeably, have received quite a bit of attention as a potential risk factor. School engagement can be conceptualized as a student's "active participation in school and classroom activities and a concomitant feeling of identification with school" (Finn, 1989, p. 123). Students' related feelings and experiences include attachment, commitment, and a sense of belonging. School bonding has been defined in terms of two primary and interdependent components: "attachment, characterized by close affective relationships with those at school; and commitment, characterized by an investment in school and doing well in school" (Catalano, Haggerty, Oesterle, Fleming, & Hawkins, 2004, p. 252). Several studies have examined school bonding and school engagement and have found that students who are engaged in delinquent behavior have lower perceived levels of school bonding and school engagement (Crooks et al., 2007; Hawkins et al., 2000; Wasserman et al., 2003). One study examined the mediating effects of school engagement in the relationship between maltreatment and delinquency and found that children who were at greater risk of maltreatment were significantly more disengaged at school, and school disengagement predicted higher initial delinquency (Bender, 2012). Considering the tumultuous home environment that is most likely present for maltreated children, it is not surprising that they would have difficulty engaging in their school environments.

School climate and school safety have also been linked to school engagement or bonding. Some school policies, such as zero-tolerance policies, have raised concerns that they may not have the intended consequences the proponents had claimed. Zero-tolerance policies and out-of-school suspension policies were enacted to make schools safer and create a better learning climate. The results of one longitudinal study suggest the frequent use of out-of-school suspension had no measurable positive deterrent or academic benefit to either the students who are suspended or to non-suspended students. In fact, the use of out-of-school suspension with elementary-school and middle-school students predicted future suspensions, poor academic performance, and failing to graduate on time (Mendez, 2003). Another study found that when controlling for various risk factors, students were more likely to engage in violent delinquency if they were attending a school with an "unsafe" climate than if they were attending a school with a "safe" climate (Crooks et al., 2007). For adolescents, schools represent a highly influential environment for social development because of the heightened importance of peer groups during the developmental period of adolescence. As such, individual schools, and their culture and climate, may contribute additional risk and protection for juvenile delinquency.

■ Protective Factors

Acknowledging the presence of risk factors is important to understanding an adolescent's likelihood for engaging in delinquency. However, equal consideration should be given to the contribution of protective factors in reducing the probability of developing problem behaviors associated with risk factors. In line with the ecological perspective, protective factors also exist and interact across multiple domains of an adolescent's life (Kirby & Fraser, 1997). The exact definition of protective factors varies, with some viewing protective factors as the opposite or absence of risk. However, a well-accepted and highly used definition of protective factors is that they are resources that serve as a buffer to interact with or moderate the exposure to risk (Jenson & Fraser, 2006; Kirby & Fraser, 1997).

Although the risk of juvenile offending is dependent on the number of risk factors a youth experiences, the number of protective factors is also highly influential in determining whether or not a youth engages in delinquency (Loeber & Farrington, 2000). Many individuals may experience a high number of risk factors without engaging in delinquent activity due to the presence of protective factors that mitigate the risk. Characteristics in the individual, family, peer, and school domains that act as protective factors for youth include a positive or resilient temperament, sense of self-efficacy, prosocial beliefs, prosocial peer group, social problem-solving skills, parent attachment, commitment to family, and school connectedness and school bonding (Hawkins et al., 1992; Hawkins, Kosterman, Catalano, Hill, & Abbott, 2005; Kirby & Fraser, 1997; Williams, Ayers, & Arthur, 1997).

The peer domain represents an important domain for addressing both risk and protection with youth. While affiliation with antisocial peers can increase the risk for delinquency, affiliation with prosocial peers can provide a protective effect that decreases the risk for delinquency. Likewise, involvement in prosocial activities has been associated with affiliating with more prosocial peers and endorsing more prosocial beliefs (Barry & Wentzel, 2006; Wentzel, Filisetti, & Looney, 2007). Studies have demonstrated that greater prosocial involvement is also associated with lower rates of emotional and behavioral problems, school dropout, and criminal arrests (Dishion, French, & Patterson, 1995; Mahoney, 2000; Rae-Grant, Thomas, Offord, & Boyle, 1989). A study by Kaufmann, Wyman, Forbes-Jones, and Barry (2007) found that prosocial involvement (i.e., participating in structured activities) moderated the positive relationship between antisocial peer affiliations and delinquency.

Research by Zimmerman and Pogarsky (2011) found that family support has a considerable impact on delinquent behaviors. According to the study, an increase of one standard deviation in family support translated to a 13% reduction in externalizing problems such as aggression, and an 18% reduction in offending behaviors (Zimmerman & Pogarsky, 2011). Appropriate parental supervision and positive communication between parents and their children are also important, especially to convey potential outcomes for engaging in delinquent behaviors (Simoes et al., 2008). Families that encourage prosocial behaviors such as helping, sharing, and cooperation help youth build their sense of self-esteem and self-efficacy.

Evidence also suggests that the presence of a supportive and positive non-parental adult can provide a protective effect for youth (Beam, Gil-Rivas, Greenberger, & Chen, 2002). Mentoring is a specific strategy that matches a non-parental adult with a child to spend quality time together where the adult can provide support and guidance, with the aim of helping the child better negotiate life's difficulties. Two aspects of the mentoring relationship determine quality: emotional closeness and amount of time spent together (Whitney, Hendricker, & Offutt, 2011). Keating, Tomishima, Foster, and Alessandri (2002) found that participating in a mentoring program for 6 months resulted in decreased internalizing and externalizing behaviors for youth. However, the evidence that mentoring programs increase positive outcomes for youth is mixed (Bernstein et al., 2009; Wheeler, Keller, & DuBois, 2010). One study found no differences between having no mentor versus having a low-quality mentor on youth's depressed affect and self-esteem, suggesting that the quality of the mentoring relationship is important to the success of this intervention. This same study, however, found no differences in delinquency reporting for youth regardless of the quality of their mentoring relationship (Whitney et al., 2011).

School attachment and bonding may also act as protective factors for youth at risk of juvenile justice involvement. Feelings of belonging and attachment to school have been associated with positive developmental outcomes for youth. For example, a study by Catalano, Haggarty, Oesterle, Fleming, and Hawkins (2004) found that youth who felt more investment in school and experienced closer attachments to those in the school environment were more likely to be academically successful and less likely to exhibit less problematic behaviors, such as substance use, high-risk sexual behavior, and use of violence. See Table 5.1 for a list of domains of risk and protective factors for delinquency.

■ Differences in Risk and Protective Factors by Gender and Race or Ethnicity

Gender

Key risk factors specific to girls' delinquency include trauma and sexual abuse, mental health and substance abuse problems, high-risk sexual behaviors stemming from early puberty, problems with school, and affiliation with deviant peers (Hawkins et al., 2009; Hubbard & Pratt, 2002; Lederman, Dakof, Larrea, & Li, 2004). Although risk and protective factors for juvenile delinquency overlap and may operate similarly for boys and girls, existing evidence suggests

Table 5.1   **Domains of Risk and Protective Factors for Juvenile Delinquency**

Domain	Risk Factors	Protective Factors
Individual	• Aggressive behavior in early childhood • Emotional and cognitive developmental difficulties • Low levels of behavioral inhibition • Use or abuse of substances • Oppositional rule violation • Favorable attitudes toward delinquency	• Positive or resilient temperament • Sense of self-efficacy • Prosocial beliefs • Social problem-solving skills
Family	• Experience of abuse, neglect and maltreatment • Low levels of parental attachment • Low levels of parental supervision • Number of children in a household (for single-parent households) • Low socioeconomic status • Low maternal educational attainment level	• Higher levels of parental attachment • High levels of commitment to family • Supportive family environment • Appropriate levels of parental supervision and involvement • Positive communication between parents and children
Peer	• Involvement with a delinquent peer group • Peer rejection	• Involvement with prosocial peer groups • Positive peer interactions • Prosocial activities
School and Community	• Poor academic performance, especially in early grade levels • High truancy rate, especially in elementary school • Low school engagement/bonding levels • Negative school climate and lack of feelings of safety at school • High neighborhood crime and delinquency rates • Feelings of risk and danger in one's neighborhood • High levels of neighborhood poverty	• Higher levels of school engagement/bonding • Positive school climate and feelings of safety at school • Supportive community members

that gender differences may exist in sensitivity levels to and rates of exposure to some risk and protective factors (Zahn et al., 2010). Due to differing biological, psychological, and socialization experiences, girls and boys may exhibit delinquent behaviors of different types and rates (Moffitt, Caspi, Rutter, & Silva, 2001). Traumatic experiences serve as risk factors for both genders; however, some studies indicate that girls, especially those involved in delinquency, have higher rates of sexual violence trauma than boys and non-delinquent girls (Smith, Leve, & Chamberlain, 2006; Zahn et al., 2010). Delinquent youth, both male and female, have a higher incidence of physical violence than non–justice-involved youth (Leve & Chamberlain, 2004). Also, girls are at higher risk for mental health problems, such as depression and anxiety due to victimization, than boys, who are more likely to receive a diagnosis of ADHD or conduct disorder (Teplin, Abram, McClelland, Dulcan, & Mericle, 2002; Zahn et al., 2010).

In addition, girls and boys may be differentially exposed to various risk factors for delinquency, and therefore, they differ in sensitivity to risks. For example, evidence suggests that girls may experience a greater number of negative life events that increase their sensitivity to certain risks, specifically those related to family and peers that affect their choices to engage in delinquency (Ge, Conger, Lorenz, & Simons, 1994; Zahn et al., 2010). In particular, girls who reach puberty early are at greater risk for delinquency, with parental conflict, exposure to delinquent peers, and romantic relationships with older male adolescents strengthening the relationship between early puberty and delinquent behavior (Haynie, 2003; Zahn et al., 2010).

Race or Ethnicity

Racial and ethnic minorities are disproportionately represented in the criminal and juvenile justice systems (Ewing, Venner, Mead, & Bryan, 2011). African American youth in particular experience greater risk for exposure to violence, poverty, and chronic stress (Deater-Deckard, Dodge, Bates, & Pettit, 1998; Li, Nussbaum, & Richards, 2007). These risk factors often co-occur and create adverse environments that lead to potential involvement with delinquency (Farmer et al., 2004; Li et al., 2007; McLoyd, 1998). In a study by Li and colleagues (2007), poverty, chronic hassles, and exposure to violence predicted externalizing and internalizing behaviors for a sample of urban, African American youth. However, these three risk factors interacted with the protective factors of family support and individual inner confidence to reduce the effects of risk and promote resilience for these youth (Li et al., 2007).

In addition to poverty and chronic stress, another risk factor that may put racial and ethnic minority youth at greater risk for delinquency involvement is racial discrimination. Caldwell, Kohn-Wood, Schmeelk-Cone, Chavous, and Zimmerman (2004) examined the influences of racial discrimination and racial identity on the violent behaviors of 325 African American youth. Results indicated that racial discrimination strongly predicted violent behavior among the sample youth, but positive racial identity buffered the effect of discrimination (Caldwell et al., 2004). Although individual and contextual characteristics that act as risk factors for all youth also apply to racial and ethnic minority youth, positive self-esteem and racial identity have particular implications for these youth in delinquency prevention practice.

■ Examples of Evidence-Based Prevention Programs

Approaching the problem of juvenile delinquency through the lens of risk and protection has resulted in many advances in the development of prevention interventions. A risk and protection perspective implies that the most effective prevention programs should seek to reduce possible risk factors and enhance protective factors in order to reduce the likelihood of juvenile offending. To that end, two types of prevention approaches have been implemented; universal and selective. A third type of strategy, an indicated approach, refers to interventions that target individuals who are considered to be highly at risk due to appearance of early behaviors or symptoms but who have not initiated delinquency. Indicated approaches are also referred to as early interventions (Williams et al., 1997).

Universal prevention programs are designed to be delivered to all individuals in a particular setting, such as a classroom, school, or afterschool setting, regardless of their level of risk. In contrast, selective prevention programs intervene only with youth identified as being at risk for one or more of the outcomes that the intervention seeks to affect. Many youth problems, such as substance use, violence, school failure, and juvenile delinquency, share risk and protective factors. The content of prevention interventions varies based on the specific outcomes programs target and the theoretical base for change underlying the intervention design. However, these programs share a focus on targeting outcomes that involve correlated risk and protective factors leading to problematic behaviors, including juvenile offending.

An example of an evidence-based, school-based intervention aimed at preventing negative youth outcomes, such as involvement in delinquency, is the Seattle Social Development Project (SSDP) (Catalano et al., 2004). Initiated in 1981, SSDP longitudinally examined the developmental pathways to juvenile delinquency and substance use for children and youth. Implemented in a school context, SSDP focused on reducing children's risk for these problem behaviors by promoting protective factors, such as school bonding, prosocial behavior, and social competence (Catalano et al., 2004). Studies evaluating the intervention have shown reduction in externalizing behaviors for boys (Hawkins, van Cleve, & Catalano, 1991), increased social competence ratings by teachers (O'Donnell, Hawkins, Catalano, Abbott, & Day, 1995), reductions in risk for violent behavior, school misbehavior, and alcohol use (Hawkins, Catalano, Kosterman, Abbott, & Hill, 1999), and, at age 21 follow-up, a reduced likelihood of using substances and being court involved (Hawkins et al., 2005).

Like SSDP, the Fast Track Prevention Project aims to reduce the risk factors and strengthen the protective factors for youth to prevent delinquency and other problems. However, Fast Track represents a multicomponent intervention that is implemented in multiple contexts and consists of a classroom curriculum, teacher training, and targeted individual and family activities for higher-risk children (Conduct Problems Prevention Research Group [CPPRG], 1999). Results of the Fast Track intervention include lower levels of serious conduct problems (Greenberg, 1998), lower levels of reported classroom hyperactivity-disruptive behavior and peer nominations of aggression (CPPRG, 1999), lower rates of peer deviance, and lower rates of home and community conduct problems (CPPRG, 2004).

Conclusion and Implications for Prevention Practice

The wealth of evidence supporting the utility of addressing risk and protective factors for the prevention of juvenile delinquency provides a compelling argument for using this evidence in practice with children and youth. Using the ecological framework to identify characteristics that are influential for youth across individual, family, peer, school, and community domains can be useful in guiding current intervention practice. However, it is important to remember that the presence of risk alone does not determine whether or not a youth will exhibit delinquent behaviors or become a juvenile offender. Practitioners working with children and youth to prevent delinquency must consider the number of risks a youth experiences, the type of risks involved, the number and type of domains that provide the risk, the developmental stage of the youth, the youth's gender and race or ethnicity, and, most importantly, the presence of protective factors that work to reduce the likelihood of these risk factors. Determining how to incorporate the existing evidence on what constitutes potential risk and protection for youth into current practice may be useful for guiding individual practitioners as well as knowledge of the existing delinquency prevention programs that provide the strongest evidence of effectiveness.

References

Aber, J. L., Gephart, M., Brooks-Gunn, J., Connell, J., & Spencer, M. B. (1997). Neighborhood, family, and individual processes as they influence child and adolescent outcomes. In J. Brooks-Gunn, G. J. Duncan, & J. L. Aber (Eds.), Neighborhood poverty: Vol. 1. Context and consequences for children (pp. 44–61). New York: Russell Sage Foundation.

Ainsworth, M. D. S. (1989). Attachment beyond infancy. American Psychologist, 44(4), 709–716. doi:10.1037/0003-066X.44.4.709

Barry, C. M., & Wentzel, K. R. (2006). Friend influence on prosocial behavior: The role of motivational factors and friendship characteristics. Developmental Psychology, 42, 153–163.

Beam, M. R., Gil-Rivas, V., Greenberger, E., & Chen, C. (2002). Adolescent problem behavior and depressed mood: Risk and protection within and across social contexts. *Journal of Youth and Adolescence, 31*(5), 343–357. doi:10.1023/A:1015676524482

Bender, K. (2010). Why do some maltreated youth become juvenile offenders? A call for further investigation and adaptation of youth services. *Children and Youth Services Review, 32*, 466–473. doi:10.1016/j.childyouth.2009.10.022

Bender, K. (2012). The mediating effect of school engagement in the relationship between youth maltreatment and juvenile delinquency. *Children and Schools, 34*(1), 37–48. doi:10.1093/cs/cdr001

Bernstein, L., Rappaport, C., Olsho, L., Hunt, D., & Levin, M. (2009). *Impact Evaluation of the U.S. Department of Education's student mentoring program.* Washington, DC: National Center for Education Evaluation and Regional Assistance, Institute of Education Sciences, U.S. Department of Education.

Brame, B., Nagine, D. S., & Tremblay, R. E. (2001). Developmental trajectories of physical aggression from school entry to late adolescence. *Journal of Child Psychology and Psychiatry, 42*, 503–512. Retrieved from http://www.wiley.com/bw/journal.asp?ref=0021-9630

Bronfenbrenner, U. (1979). *The ecology of human development.* Cambridge, MA: Harvard University Press.

Buist, K. L., Dekovic, M., Meeus, W., & van Aken, M. A. G. (2004). The reciprocal relationship between early adolescent attachment and internalizing and externalizing problem behavior. *Journal of Adolescence, 27*, 251–266. doi:10.1016/j.adolescence.2003.11.012

Cairns, R. B., Cairns, B. D., Neckerman, H. J., Ferguson, L. L., & Gariepy, J. L. (1989). Growth and aggression: Childhood to early adolescence. *Developmental Psychology, 25*, 320–330. doi:10.1037/0012-1649.25.2.320

Caldwell, C. H., Kohn-Wood, L. P., Schmeelk-Cone, K., Chavous, T. M., & Zimmerman, M. (2004). Racial discrimination and racial identity as risk or protective factors for violent behaviors in African-American young adults. *American Journal of Community Psychology, 33*, 91–105. doi:10.1023/B:AJCP.0000014321.02367.dd

Catalano, R. F., Haggerty, K. P., Oesterle, S., Fleming, C. B., & Hawkins, J. D. (2004). The importance of bonding on school for health development: Findings from the Social Development Research Group. *Journal of School Health, 74*(7), 252–261. doi:10.1111/j.1746-1561.2004.tb08281.x

Coie, J. D., Terry, R. A., Lenox, K., Lochman, J. E., & Hyman, C. (1995). Childhood peer rejection and aggression as predictors of stable patterns of adolescent disorder. *Development and Psychopathology, 7*, 697–713. Retrieved from http://journals.cambridge.org/action/displayJournal?jid=DPP

Coie, J. D., Watt, N. F., West, S. G., Hawkins, D., Asarnow, J. R., Markman, H. J.,...Long, B. (1993). The science of prevention: A conceptual framework and some directions for a national research program. *American Psychologist, 48*(10), 1013–1022. doi:10.1037/0003-066X.48.10.1013

Conduct Problems Prevention Research Group (1999). Initial impact of the Fast Track prevention trial for conduct problems: II. Classroom effects. *Journal of Consulting and Clinical Psychology, 67*, 648–657. doi:10.1037/0022-006X.67.5.648

Conduct Problems Prevention Research Group (2004). The effects of the Fast Track program and serious problem outcomes at the end of elementary school. *Journal of Clinical Child and Adolescent Psychology, 33*(4), 650–661. doi:10.1207/s15374424jccp3304_1

Crooks, C. V., Scott, K. L., Wolfe, D. A., Chiodo, D., & Killip, S. (2007). Understanding the link between childhood maltreatment and violent delinquency: What do schools have to add? *Child Maltreatment, 12*(3), 269–280. doi:10.1177/1077559507301843

Deater-Deckard, K., Dodge, K. A., Bates, J. E., & Pettit, G. S. (1998). Multiple risk factors in the development of externalizing behavior problems: Group and individual differences

Development and Psychopathology, 10, 469–493. Retrieved from http://journals. cambridge.org/action/displayJournal?jid=DPP

De Coster, S., Heimer, K., & Wittrock, S. M. (2006). Neighborhood disadvantage, social capital, street context, and youth violence. *The Sociological Quarterly, 47*, 723–753. doi:10.1111/j.1533-8525.2006.00064.x

Derzon, J. H. (2010). The correspondence of family features with problem, aggressive, criminal, and violent behavior: A meta-analysis. *Journal of Experimental Criminology, 6*(3), 263–292. doi:10.1007/s11292-010-9098-0

Dishion, T. J., French, D. C., & Patterson, G. R. (1995). The development and ecology of antisocial behavior. In D. Cicchetti & D. J. Cohen (Eds.), *Developmental psychopathology* (Vol. 2, pp. 421–471). New York: Wiley.

Dishion, T. J., Veronneau, M. H., & Myers, M. W., (2010). Cascading peer dynamics underlying the progression from problem behavior to violence in early to late adolescence. *Development and Psychopathology, 22*, 603–619. doi:10.1017/S0954579410000313

Dishion, T. J., & Tipsord, J. M. (2011). Peer contagion in child and adolescent social and emotional development. *Annual Review of Psychology, 62*, 189–214. doi:10.1146/annurev. psych.093008.100412

Dodge, K. A., Lansford, J. E., Burks, V. S., Bates, J. E., Pettit, G. S., Fontaine, R., & Price, J. M. (2003). Peer rejection and social information-processing factors in the development of aggressive behavior problems in children. *Child Development, 74*, 374–393. Retrieved from http://www.wiley.com/bw/journal.asp?ref=0009-3920

Elliott, D. S. (1994). *Youth violence: An overview.* Center for Study and Prevention of Violence. Boulder, University of Colorado. Retrieved from http://www.colorado.edu/cspv/publications/papers/CSPV-008.pdf

Ewing, S. W. F., Venner, K. L., & Mead, H. K., & Bryan, A. D. (2011). Exploring racial/ethnic differences in substance use: A preliminary theory-based investigation with juvenile justice-involved youth. *BMC Pediatrics, 11*, 71–81. doi:10.1186/1471-2431-11-71

Farmer, T. W., Price, L. N., O'Neal, K. K., Leung, M., Goforth, J. B., Cairns, B. D., & Reese, L. E. (2004). Exploring risk in early adolescent African American youth. *American Journal of Community Psychology, 33*, 51–59. doi:10.1023/B:AJCP.0000014318.16652.30

Finkelhor, D., Turner, H., Ormrod, R., Hamby, S., & Kracke, K. (2009, October). *Children's exposure to violence: A comprehensive national survey* (Juvenile Justice Bulletin). Washington, DC: Office of Juvenile Justice and Delinquency Prevention. Retrieved from https://www.ncjrs.gov/pdffiles1/ojjdp/227744.pdf

Finn, J. D. (1989). Withdrawing from school. *Review of Educational Research, 59*(2), 117–142. Retrieved from http://www.jstor.org/stable/1170412

Fite, P., Preddy, T., Vitulano, M., Elkins, S., Grassetti, S., & Wimsatt, A. (2012). Perceived best friend delinquency moderates the link between contextual risk factors and juvenile delinquency. *Journal of Community Psychology, 40*(6), 747–761. doi:10.1002/jcop

Fraser, M. W., & Terzian, M. A. (2005). Risk and resilience in child development: Practice principles and strategies. In G. P. Mallon & P. McCartt Hess (Eds.) *Handbook of children, youth, and family services: Practice, policies, and programs* (pp. 55–71). New York: Columbia University Press.

Gatti, U., Tremblay, R. E., & Vitaro, F. (2009). Iatrogenic effect of juvenile justice. *Journal of Child Psychiatry and Psychology, 50*, 991–998. doi:10.1111/j.1469-7610.2008.02057.x

Ge, X., Conger, R. D., Lorenz, F. O., & Simons, R. L. (1994). Parents' stressful life events and adolescent depressed mood. *Journal of Health and Social Behavior, 35*, 28–44. Retrieved from http://www.jstor.org/stable/2137333

Greenberg, M. T. (1998, August). *Testing developmental theory of antisocial behavior with outcomes from the Fast Track Prevention Project.* Paper presented at the American Psychological Association, Chicago, IL.

Hart, J. L., O'Toole, S. K., Price-Sharps, J. L., & Shaffer, T. W. (2007). The risk and protective factors of violent juvenile offending: An examination of gender differences. *Youth Violence and Juvenile Justice, 5*(4), 367–384. doi:10.1177/1541204006297367

Hawkins, J. D., Catalano, R. F., Kosterman, R., Abbott, R., & Hill, K. G. (1999). Preventing adolescent health-risk behaviors by strengthening protection during childhood. *Archives of Pediatrics and Adolescent Medicine, 153*, 226–234. doi:10.1001/archpedi.153.3.226

Hawkins, J. D., Catalano, R. F., & Miller, J. Y. (1992). Risk and protective factors for alcohol and other drug problems in adolescence and early adulthood: Implication for substance use prevention. *Psychological Bulletin, 112*, 64–105. doi:10.1037/0033-2909.112.1.64

Hawkins, J. D., Herrenkohl, T. I., Farrington, D. P., Brewer, D. P., Catalano, R. F., Harachi, T. W., & Cothern, L. (2000, April). *Predictors of youth violence* (Juvenile Justice Bulletin). Washington, DC: Office of Juvenile Justice and Delinquency Prevention. Retrieved from https://www.ncjrs.gov/pdffiles1/ojjdp/179065.pdf

Hawkins, J. D., Kosterman, R., Catalano, R. F., Hill, K. G., & Abbott, R. D. (2005). Promoting positive adult functioning through social development intervention in childhood: Long-term effect from the Seattle Social Development Project. *Archives of Pediatric and Adolescent Medicine, 159*, 5–31. doi:10.1001/archpedi.159.1.25

Hawkins, J. D., von Cleve, E., & Catalano, R. F. (1991). Reducing early childhood aggression: Results of a primary prevention program. *Journal of the American Academy of Child & Adolescent Psychiatry, 30*, 208–217. Retrieved from http://dx.doi.org/10.1097/00004583-199103000-00008

Hawkins, J. D., & Weis, J. G. (1985). The social development model: An integrated approach to delinquency prevention. *Journal of Primary Prevention, 6*, 73–97. doi:10.1007/BF01325432

Hawkins, S. R., Graham, P. W., Williams, J., & Zahn, M. A. (2009). *Resilient girls: Factors that protect against delinquency.* Office of Juvenile Justice and Delinquency Prevention.

Haynie, D. (2003). Contexts of risk? Explaining the link between girls' pubertal development and their delinquency involvement. *Social Forces, 82,* 355–397. Retrieved from http://www.jstor.org/stable/3598149

Haynie, D., Silver, E., & Teasdale, B. (2006). Neighborhood characteristics, peer networks, and adolescent violence. *Journal of Quantitative Criminology, 22*, 147–169. doi:10.1007/s10940-006-9006-y

Hoeve, M., Dubas, J. S., Eichelsheim, V. I., van der Laan, P. H., Smeenk, W., & Gerris, J. R. M. (2009). The relationship between parenting and delinquency: A meta-analysis. *Journal of Abnormal Child Psychology, 37*(6), 749–775. doi:10.1007/s10802-009-9310-8

Hubbard, D. J., & Pratt, T. C. (2002). A meta-analysis of the predictors of delinquency among girls. *Journal of Offender Rehabilitation, 34*, 1–13. doi:10.1300/J076v34n03_01

Ingoldsby, E. M., & Shaw, D. S. (2002). Neighborhood contextual factors and early-starting antisocial pathways. *Clinical Child and Family Psychology Review, 5*(1), 21–55. doi:1096-4037/02/0300-0021/0

Ingoldsby, E. M., Shaw, D. S., Winslow, E., Schonberg, M., Gilliom, M., & Criss, M. M. (2006). Neighborhood disadvantage, parent-child conflict, neighborhood peer relationships, and early antisocial behavior problem trajectories. *Journal of Abnormal Child Psychology, 34*(3), 303–319. doi:10.1007/s10802-006-9026-y

Jencks, C., & Mayer, S. (1990). The social consequences of growing up in a poor neighborhood. In L. E. Lynn & M. F. H. McGeary (Eds.), *Inner-city poverty in the United States* (pp. 111–186). Washington, DC: National Academy Press.

Jenson, J. M., & Fraser, M. W. (2006). A risk and resilience framework for child, youth, and family policy. In J. M. Jenson & M. W. Fraser (Eds.), *Social policy for children and families: A risk and resilience perspective* (pp. 1–18). Thousand Oaks, CA: Sage.

Kaufmann, D. R., Wyman, P. A., Forbes-Jones, E. L., & Barry, J. (2007). Prosocial involvement and antisocial peer affiliations as predictors of behavior problems in urban adolescents: Main effects and moderating effects. *Journal of Community Psychology, 35*, 417–434. doi:0.1002/jcop.20156

Keating, L. M., Tomishima, M. A., Foster, S., & Alessandri, M. (2002). The effects of a mentoring program on at-risk youth. *Adolescence, 37*(148), 717–735.

Kierkus, C. A., & Hewitt, J. D. (2009). The contextual nature of the family structure/delinquency relationship. *Journal of Criminal Justice, 37*, 123–132. doi:10.1016/j.jcrimjus.2009.02.008

Kim, K. J., Conger, R. D., Elder Jr., G. H., & Lorenz, F. O. (2003). Reciprocal influences between stressful life events and adolescent internalizing and externalizing problems. *Child Development, 74*(1), 127–143. doi:10.1016/j.jcrimjus.2009.02.008

Kirby, L., & Fraser, M. (1997). Risk and resilience in childhood. In M. W. Fraser (Ed.), *Risk and resilience in childhood: An ecological perspective* (pp. 10–33). Washington, DC: NASW Press.

Knoll, C., & Sickmund, M. (2012). Delinquency cases in juvenile court, 2009. *Juvenile offenders and victims, National Report Series*, Office of Juvenile Justice and Delinquency Prevention, US Department of Justice: Washington, DC. Retrieved from http://www.ojjdp.gov/pubs/239081.pdf

Laird, R. D., Jordan, K. Y., Dodge, K. A., Pettit, G. S., & Bates, J. E. (2001). Peer rejection in childhood, involvement with antisocial peers in early adolescence, and the development of externalizing behavior problems. *Development and Psychopathology, 13*, 337–354. Retrieved from http://journals.cambridge.org/action/displayJournal?jid=DPP

Lansford, J. E., Miller-Johnson, S., Berlin, L. J., Dodge, K. A., Bates, J. E., & Pettit, G. S. (2007). Early physical abuse and later violent delinquency: A prospective longitudinal study. *Child Maltreatment, 12*(3), 233–245. doi:10.1177/1077559507301841

Lederman, C. S., Dakof, G. A., Larrea, M. A., & Li, H. (2004). Characteristics of adolescent females in juvenile detention. *International Journal of Law and Psychiatry, 27*, 321–337. doi:10.1016/j.ijlp.2004.03.009

Leve, L. D., & Chamberlain, P. (2004). Female juvenile offenders: Defining an early-onset pathway for delinquency. *Journal of Child and Family Studies, 13*(4), 439–452. doi:1062-1024/04/1200-04390

Liberman, A. (2007). *Adolescents, neighborhoods and violence: Recent findings from the Project on Human Development in Chicago neighborhoods*. Washington, DC: National Institute for Justice.

Li, S. T., Nussbaum, K. M., & Richards, M. H. (2007). Risk and protective factors for urban African-American youth. *American Journal of Community Psychology, 39*, 21–35. doi:10.1007/s10464-007-9088-1

Lipsey, M. W., & Derzon, J. H. (1998). Predictors of violent or serious delinquency in adolescence and early adulthood: A synthesis of longitudinal research. In R. Loeber & D. P. Farrington (Eds.), *Serious and violent juvenile offenders: Risk factors and successful interventions* (pp. 86–105). Thousand Oaks, CA: Sage.

Loeber, R., & Farrington, D. P. (2000). Young children who commit crime: Epidemiology, developmental origins, risk factors, early interventions, and policy implications. *Development and Psychopathology, 12*(4), 737–762. Retrieved from http://journals.cambridge.org/action/displayJournal?jid=DPP

Loeber, R., Farrington, D. P., & Petechuck, D. (2003). Child delinquency: Early intervention and prevention. *Child Delinquency* (May), 3–19. Retrieved from https://www.ncjrs.gov/pdffiles1/ojjdp/186162.pdf

Mahoney, J. L. (2000). School extracurricular activity participation as a moderator in the development of antisocial patterns. *Child Development, 71*, 502–516.

McKeown, R. E., Jackson, K. L., & Vaois, R. F. (1998). The frequency and correlates of violent behaviors in a statewide sample of high school students. *Family and Community Health, 20*, 38–54. Retrieved from http://www.familyandcommunityhealth.com

McLoyd, V. C. (1998). Socioeconomic disadvantage and child development. *American Psychologist, 53*, 185–204. doi:10.1037/0003-066X.53.2.185

McNamara, J. K., & Willoughby, T. (2010). A longitudinal study of risk-taking behavior in adolescents with learning disabilities. *Learning Disabilities Research & Practice, 25*, 11–24. doi:10.1111/j.1540-5826.2009.00297.x

Mendez, L. R. (2003). Predictors of suspension and negative school outcomes: A longitudinal investigation. *New Directions for Youth Development, 99*, 17–33. doi:10.1002/yd.52

Mikulincer, M., Shaver, P. R., & Pereg, D. (2003). Attachment theory and affect regulation: The dynamics, development, and cognitive consequences of attachment-related strategies. *Motivation and Emotion, 27*(2), 77–102. doi:0146-7239/03/0600-0077/0

Miller, H. V. (2010). If your friends jumped off of a bridge, would you do it too? Delinquent peers and susceptibility to peer influence. *Justice Quarterly, 27*(4), 473–491. doi:10.1080/07418820903218974

Moffitt, T. E. (1993a). Adolescent-limited and life-course-persistent antisocial behavior. *Psychological Review, 100*, 674–701. Retrieved from www.apa.org/journals/rev/

Moffitt, T. E. (1993b). The neuropsychology of conduct disorder. *Development and Psychopathology, 5*, 135–151. Retrieved from http://journals.cambridge.org/action/displayJournal?jid=DPP

Moffitt, T. E. (2006). Life-course persistent versus adolescence-limited antisocial behavior. In D. Cicchetti & D. J. Cohen (Eds.), *Developmental psychopathology: Risk, disorder, and adaptation* (vol. 3, pp. 570–598, 2nd ed.). Wiley: New York.

Moffitt, T. E., & Caspi, A. (2001). Childhood predictors differentiate life-course persistent and adolescent-limited antisocial pathways among males and females. *Development and Psychopathology, 13*, 355–375. Retrieved from http://journals.cambridge.org/action/displayJournal?jid=DPP

Moffitt, T. E., Caspi, A., Rutter, M., & Silva, P. A. (2001). *Sex differences in antisocial behavior: Conduct disorder, delinquency, and violence in the Dunedin Longitudinal Study.* New York: Cambridge University Press.

Morris, K. A., & Morris, R. J. (2006). Disability and juvenile delinquency: Issues and trends. *Disability & Society, 21*, 613–627. doi:10.1080/09687590600918339

Morrow, M. T., Hubbard, J. A., McAuliffe, M. D., Rubin, R. M., & Dearing, K. F. (2006). Childhood aggression, depressive symptoms, and peer rejection: The mediational model revisited. *International Journal of Behavioral Development, 30*(3), 240–248. doi:10.1177/0165025406066757

O'Donnell, J. J., Hawkins, D. J., Catalano, R., Abbott, R. D., & Day, E. (1995). Preventing school failure, drug use, and delinquency among low-income children: Long-term intervention in elementary schools. *American Journal of Orthopsychiatry, 65*, 87–100. doi:10.1037/h0079598

Parker, J. G., & Asher, S. R. (1993). Friendship and friendship quality in middle childhood: Links with peer group acceptance and feelings of loneliness and social dissatisfaction. *Developmental Psychology, 29*, 611–621. Retrieved from http://journals.cambridge.org/action/displayJournal?jid=DPP

Parker, J. S., & Morton, T. L. (2009). Distinguishing between early and late onset delinquents: Race, income, verbal intelligence and impulsivity. *North American Journal of Psychology, 11*(2), 273–284. doi:10.1037/0012-1649.29.4.611

Patterson, G. R., & Yoerger, K. (2002). A developmental model for early- and late-onset delinquency. In J. B. Reid, G. R. Patterson, & J. Snyder (Eds.), *Antisocial behavior in children and adolescents: A developmental analysis and model for intervention* (pp. 147–172). Washington, DC: American Psychological Association.

Putallaz, M., Grimes, C. L., Foster, K. J., Kupersmidt, J. B., Coie, J. D., & Dearing, K. (2007). Overt and relational aggression and victimization: Multiple perspectives within the school setting. *Journal of School Psychology, 45*, 523–547. doi:10.1016/j.jsp.2007.05.003

Rae-Grant, N., Thomas, B. H., Offord, D. R., & Boyle, M. H. (1989). Risk, protective factors, and the prevalence of behavioral and emotional disorders in children and adolescents. *Journal of the American Academy of Child and Adolescent Psychiatry, 28*, 262–268.

Schroeder, R. D., Osgood, A. K., & Oghia, M. J. (2010). Family transitions and juvenile delinquency. *Sociological Inquiry, 80*(4), 579–604. doi:10.1111/j.1475-682X.2010.00351.x

Shandra, C. L., & Hogan, D. P. (2012). Delinquency among adolescents with disabilities. *Child Indicator Research, 5*(4), 771–788. doi:10.1007/s12187-012-9135-9

Simoes, C., Matos, M. G., & Batista-Foguet, J. M. (2008). Juvenile delinquency: Analysis of risk and protective factors using quantitative and qualitative methods. *Cognition, Brain, Behavior: An Interdisciplinary Journal, 12*(4), 389–408. Retrieved from http://www. cbbjournal.ro/index.php?option=com_content&task=view&id=391&Itemid=43

Smith, D. J., & Ecob, R. (2013). The influence of friends on teenage offending: How long does it last? *European Journal of Criminology, 10*, 40–58. doi:10.1177/1477370812456345

Smith, D. K., Leve, L. D., & Chamberlain, P. (2006). Adolescent girls' offending and health risking sexual behavior: The predictive role of trauma. *Child Maltreatment, 11*, 346–353. doi:10.1177/1077559506291950

Teplin, L. A., Abram, K. M., McClelland, G. M., Dulcan, M. K., & Mericle, A. A. (2002). Psychiatric disorders in youth in juvenile detention. *Archives of General Psychiatry, 59*, 1133–1143. Retrieved from http://www.ncbi.nlm.nih.gov/pmc/articles/PMC2861992/

Tremblay, R. E., Nagin, D. S., Seguin, J. R., Zoccolillo, M., Zelazo, P. D., Boivan, M.,...Japel, C. (2004). Physical aggression during early childhood: Trajectories and predictors. *Pediatrics, 114*, e43–e50. doi:10.1542/peds.114.1.e43

U.S. Department of Health and Human Services, Administration for Children and Families, Administration on Children, Youth and Families, Children's Bureau. (2011). *Child maltreatment 2010.* Retrieved from www.acf.hhs.gov/programs/cb/stats_research/index. htm#can.

Warr, M., & Stafford, M. (1991). The influence of delinquent peers: What they think or what they do? *Criminology, 29*(4), 851–866. doi:10.1111/j.1745-9125.1991.tb01090.x

Wasserman, G. A., Keenan, K., Tremblay, R. E., Coie, J. D., Herrenkohl, T. I., Loeber, R., & Petechuk, D. (2003). *Risk and protective factors of child delinquency.* Bulletin. Washington, DC: U.S. Department of Justice, Office of Justice Programs, Office of Juvenile Justice and Delinquency Prevention. Retrieved from https://www.ncjrs.gov/pdffiles1/ojjdp/193409. pdf

Wentzel, K. R., Filisetti, L., & Looney, L. (2007). Adolescent prosocial behavior: The role of social processes and contextual cues. *Child Development, 78*, 895–910.

Wheeler, M. E., Keller, T. E., & Dubois, D. L. (2010). Review of three recent randomized trials of school-based mentoring. *Social Policy Report, 24*, 1–27.

Whitney, S. D, Hendricker, E. N. & Offutt, C., A. (2011). Moderating factors of natural mentoring relationships, problem behaviors, and emotional well-being. *Mentoring & Tutoring: Partnership in Learning, 19*(1), 83–105.

Williams, J. H., Ayers, C. D., & Arthur, M. W. (1997). Risk and protective factors in the development of delinquency and conduct disorder. In M. W. Fraser (Ed.), *Risk and resilience in childhood: An ecological perspective* (pp. 140–170). Washington, DC: NASW Press.

Zahn, M., Agnew, R., Fishbein, D., Miller, S., Winn, D-M., Dakoff, G., Kruttschnitt, C.,....Chesney-Lind, M. (2010). *Causes and correlates of girls' delinquency.* Office of Juvenile Justice and Delinquency Prevention. Retrieved from https://www.ncjrs.gov/pdffiles1/ ojjdp/226358.pdf

Zimmerman, G. M., & Pogarsky, G. (2011). The consequences of parental underestimation and overestimation of youth exposure to violence. *Journal of Marriage and Family, 73*(1), 194–208. doi:10.1111/j.1741-3737.2010.00798.x

6

Brain Science and Juvenile Justice

Questions for Policy and Practice

Alexandra Cox

■ Case Examples

Gary Durant

Gary Durant was 17 years old and a high-school junior when he was charged with murder for the gang-related shooting of another young man in the District of Columbia. Although Durant was not the shooter, he was said to be present when the murder took place. Durant was charged as an adult and sent to the DC jail. His lawyer argued that he should be transferred to the city's Family Court system. In her pleadings, she drew from brain science, saying that "juveniles are not little adults," and quoting a psychiatrist from a brain behavior laboratory who said "there is no way to state with any scientific reliability that an individual 17-year-old has a fully matured brain" (Sessions Stepp, 2008). According to the *Washington Post*, the prosecutor in the case said that "The defendant's reliance on scientific journal articles goes too far...Taken to its logical extreme [it] would require the juvenile justice system to include all persons under the age of twenty-six or even twenty-seven" (Sessions Stepp, 2008). Ultimately, Durant was convicted of voluntary manslaughter as an adult and he was sentenced to seven years in prison.

Steven Vasquez

When he was 15 years old, Steven Vasquez was charged with conducting a home invasion robbery and rape of a woman who was a stranger to him. His friend, who was with him at the time of the incident, was also charged with the crime. During pretrial hearings, it was revealed that Steven had been exposed to lead poisoning as a young child and thus suffered from brain damage. Despite that evidence, he was convicted and sentenced, as an adult, under New York's Juvenile Offender statute to two and a half to seven and a half years, and was also subject to the Sex Offender Registration Act (SORA) lifetime reporting requirements. After Steven was released from custody five years later, he had a SORA hearing, in which his appellate attorneys asked for a "downward departure" from his sex offender classification. Under SORA, age is considered an aggravating, not a mitigating, factor in one's classification. His attorneys argued that his brain damage left him vulnerable and in need of social supports and services, and that his high-level sex offender classification would essentially render him homeless and without those supports. Under New York's SORA laws, Level III offenders cannot live within 1,000 feet of a school, which prevented Steven from living with his mother. The District Attorney downplayed Vasquez's claim of brain damage and vulnerability and opposed the move to downward departure (Bayer, 2012). Ultimately, the judge in the case agreed to the downward departure. The court found that "Vasquez needs assistance with such tasks as remembering appointments and navigating the social service system and would not receive that help at Bellevue [men's shelter]". Additionally, the court said that in a homeless shelter Vasquez would be "rendered particularly vulnerable to other residents, exposed to crime and most likely subjected to homelessness, thereby increasing his risk of recidivism. Accordingly, a Level III sex offender designation would be counterproductive and serve no societal benefit" (Caher, 2012). It appeared that while the court took Vasquez's brain damage under consideration, it was ultimately his brain damage, in conjunction with his lack of social supports, that swayed the judge's decision.

■ Introduction

The study of adolescent risk taking has a long and rich history in the fields of sociology, psychology, criminology, and social work. This research has played a role in shaping explanations about and responses to delinquent behavior. Recently, researchers have turned their attention to the task of identifying the etiology of such kinds of behavior in the human brain. While this research is relatively new, scholars have suggested that there are links between adolescent brain development, their risk taking, and their abilities to regulate their emotions (Giedd, 2008; Steinberg, 2012). Thus, this new line of research has become a part of the debate about the laws governing young people's offending (Gruber & Yurgelun-Todd, 2006; Kambam & Thompson, 2009).

Juvenile justice reformers have used the findings of developmental neuroscience to advocate for sentencing and penal reforms, arguing that adolescent risk taking is "hard wired" (Bessant, 2008; Maroney, 2009). Some advocates see this research as offering the incontrovertible proof—in the form of "hard" brain science—that teenagers are more likely than adults to both engage in offending and to grow/age out of it. These advocates argue that adolescents must thus be treated more leniently and given more opportunities for rehabilitation (Maroney, 2009). Some see this science as "better" than the behavioral and social science that has been drawn upon for years in order to justify the differential treatment of young people in the criminal justice system (Bessant & Watts, 2012; Maroney, 2009; McCabe & Castel, 2008; Steinberg, 2012). This is illustrated in the case example of Gary Durant, whose attorney argued, via brain science, that he would receive more opportunities for rehabilitation if he were kept in the juvenile system as opposed to being waived into the adult criminal justice system. As the American Medical Association wrote in their friend of the court brief to the U.S. Supreme Court in a recent case about the juvenile death penalty, "to a degree never before understood, scientists can now demonstrate that adolescents are immature not only to the observer's naked eye, but in the very fibers of their brains" (2004, p. 10).

This chapter raises questions about the value that has come to be placed on neuroscience by the legal, clinical, and advocacy communities working to reform the juvenile justice system. It suggests that the use of brain science raises some ethical and practical challenges for adolescents charged with crimes, and it makes several recommendations for the responsible use of the science, in particular by advocates and practitioners. This chapter is exclusively concerned with the use of neuroscience as a *rhetorical* device. The risk-taking "teen brain" has now become the centerpiece of what has arguably been a century-long effort by progressive advocates to ensure that the justice system treats children as children (Bernard & Kurlychek, 2010; Platt, 1969/1977). This chapter will focus on the most recent strategy to treat children less harshly than adults.

It is arguable that conservative rhetoric about juvenile justice reform has become attenuated in recent years (Bernard & Kurlychek, 2010; Merlo & Benekos, 2010). As states face significant financial crises, the downsizing of juvenile justice systems seems to make fiscal sense to some state and local governments (Butts & Evans, 2011), and the issue is becoming decoupled from its previously politicized connections. In place of conservative and retributivist approaches, contemporary advocacy strategies are arguably focused on offering cost-effective reforms to states and local jurisdictions eager to make budget cuts. There has been a significant move toward the decarceration of juvenile facilities in states across the country, and a corresponding uptick in the use of community-based care for young people charged with nonviolent offenses (D. N. Evans, 2012; Hockenberry, Sickmund, & Sladky, 2011). "Evidence-based practices" have come to fill this void and may help state and local agencies seek to boost their symbolic capital with the public and lawmakers by conveying their investment in technical expertise and efficiency (Phoenix, 2010; Widmer, 2009). These practices include family-based interventions, "multi-systemic" therapies, and cognitive-behavioral programming. However, as Butts (2012) has argued, "evidence-based" practices are undergirded by the values and beliefs of those who fund and support them. It is arguable that "brain science" has been incorporated into this "evidence" base as a way of bolstering and justifying new forms of intervention, such as those aimed at a cognitive-behavioral change.

This chapter aims to help us develop a long-term view with respect to the well-being and outcomes for youth involved in the justice system, particularly youth charged with serious crimes, such as Steven Vasquez, described in the case example above. It does not seek to explain the science of the teenage brain, but rather it is concerned with understanding the role that neuroscience has played in the landscape of juvenile justice reform and practice. It sets this rhetoric in the context of other scholarly literature, raises questions for policymakers and practitioners about its uses, and sheds light on some of the ways that knowledge becomes circulated and used within the juvenile justice context.

■ The Scope of the Problem

Despite the rise in decarceration efforts and community penalties in state-level juvenile justice systems in recent years, the United States remains an outlier among nations in its approach to the punishment of young people, particularly young people charged with serious and violent offenses. Across the country, young people charged with serious offenses face lengthy terms of incarceration, sometimes up to life imprisonment. Addressing this issue has become the task of many recent reforms. While the U.S. Supreme Court recently decided, in *Roper v. Simmons,* that teenagers (up age 18) are ineligible for the death penalty, and in *Graham v. Florida,* that states cannot impose mandatory life without parole in cases of juveniles who have not been convicted of homicide, many states continue to send teenagers to juvenile facilities and prisons for lengthy sentences.

Although debates about the efficacy of youth incarceration have existed since the first prison for young people was constructed in New York in 1825, there is a growing base of research evidence that supports the idea that incarceration is actually *criminogenic* in nature for young people charged with crimes (see, e.g., DeLisi, Hochstetler, Jones-Johnson, Caudill, & Marquart, 2011; Gatti, Tremblay, & Vitaro, 2009; Huizinga & Henry, 2008). Researchers have also found that young people accrue *no* benefit in terms of the prevention of future offending from longer lengths of stay in secure custody settings (Loughran et al., 2009). Some scholars have argued that a young person's ability to successfully develop into adulthood may even be *interrupted* by a period of incarceration or time in residential care (Dmitrieva, Monahan, Cauffman, & Steinberg, 2012; Scott & Steinberg, 2008).

Yet, there remain a number of young people who are serving life sentences or who are doing a significant amount of time in custody in the United States. There are 2,750 juveniles serving life without parole, according to a recent survey on the issue (Campaign for the Fair Sentencing of Youth, 2012). The Sentencing Project found that there were over 6,800 young people serving life sentences (with the possibility of parole) in 2009 (Nellis & King, 2009). Additionally, it is estimated that approximately 250,000 young people under the age of 18 are charged in adult justice systems across the United States each year, just as Steven Vasquez and Gary Durant were (Arya, 2011). It thus remains clear that there is limited "penal moderation" (Bosworth, 2011; Loader, 2009) in use when it comes to the punishment of young people charged with serious crimes in the United States, let alone adults.

■ The Contemporary Role of Developmental Science in Juvenile Justice Reform: A Brief History

In 1978, a 15-year-old named Willie Bosket, who was found guilty of the murder of two subway riders, was given a five-year sentence in New York City's Family Court. This case served as a bellwether for a national trend toward the harsher treatment of juveniles that began in the late 1970s and early 1980s, and arguably led advocates to develop reliance upon neuroscience as a tool in their reform strategies. This case, which was well documented in the public media, caused a public outcry. In fact, in 1978, the New York State legislature, in one of the earliest demonstrations of a tough "law and order" approach to young people, passed the Juvenile Offender law, which required that 13- to 15-year-olds convicted of certain violent felonies would receive adult-level penalties, including and up to life in prison (Butterfield, 1996; Singer, 1996). Steven Vasquez was charged under this law and will have an adult conviction on his record for life.

Subsequently, this new trend grew in part out of the skepticism about rehabilitation and an emerging sense that young people like Willie Bosket should be held accountable for their actions (Scott & Grisso, 1998; Scott & Steinberg, 2008). Thus, during the 1980s and 1990s, states across the country began to adopt harsher penalties against young people charged with crimes, especially serious offenses. In fact, scholars like James Q. Wilson went so far as to invoke ideas about rising youth crime and juvenile "super-predators" to support harsher punishments for juveniles (Feld, 1999; Pickett & Chiricos, 2012). According to those in support of "get tough" approaches to juveniles during this era, young people who committed serious crimes were no less rational or responsible than their adult counterparts, and thus should be held accountable in a retributive system, not a rehabilitative one (Scott & Grisso, 1998).

It was up to juvenile justice reformers to identify a rhetorical strategy to combat these ideologies. Some early approaches drew from existing knowledge about adolescent development (Gardner, 1989; Teitelbaum, 1991), and some legal advocates shifted to more substantive arguments based on the available developmental and behavioral sciences, focusing on reasoning, decision making, attitudes toward risk, and peer influences (Scott & Grisso, 1998). However, as states ratcheted up their responses to young people by passing more and more transfer and certification laws, advocates and reformers faced more serious demands to fight back against the conservative and "tough on crime" logics that steered these initiatives into place, and arguably developed a more organized strategy to infuse legal and policy debates with social and medical science (Buss, 2009).

In recent years, advocates have cited neuroscientific research about the adolescent brain to make a case for the lesser punishment of young people charged with crimes (see, e.g., Bazelon, 2009; Harcourt, 2009; Henning, 2009; Lamm, 2009). Part of this has been a deliberate strategy: as Aronson (2008) documents in his article about the uses of brain science in death penalty litigation, the anti-death penalty community made a strategic effort to bring scholars together from a wide range of fields to discuss the uses of brain science in litigation. The early uses of neuroscience in death penalty advocacy, and in particular in state legislative anti-death penalty lobbying and in the friend of the court briefs for the *Roper v. Simmons* case, arguably opened the door for a broader application of the brain sciences by advocates seeking to make a range of reforms in the juvenile justice system.

Today, almost all of the major liberal and progressive juvenile justice reform organizations in the United States have position papers or websites devoted to the use and effectiveness of "brain science" in juvenile justice reform.[1] Legal defense organizations have convened strategy sessions for attorneys in how to employ neuroscience in the courtroom. In fact, prominent professional organizations such as the American Bar Association, the American Medical Association, the American Academy of Child and Adolescent Psychiatry, and the American Psychological and Psychiatric Associations have adopted position papers on the uses of neuroscience in the area of juvenile justice. These organizations have even gone as far as writing friend of the court briefs on the issue.

Unfortunately, in making their claims, advocates often simplify brain science in order to communicate it to a broader audience. For example, some webinars and conferences are dedicated to demystifying brain science, thus enabling advocates to have a better command of the science for their advocacy work.[2] However, several researchers have stated that this could cause a problem as individuals become enamored of such sciences and make claims about it that sometimes outweigh its realities; this has been termed "brain over-claim syndrome" (Morse, 2006; Rose, 2010).

Within an advocacy context, the "science" of the brain research is often posed in opposition to the assumed "softer" social sciences (Aronson, 2007). For example, the authors of a policy paper on the adolescent brain published by a coalition of juvenile justice reformers employ the term "hard science" in describing this research (Act 4 Juvenile Justice, n.d.). "Science" and "evidence" are terms that are arguably used by advocates to legitimize liberal projects of reform that have often been under attack for representing a "soft" approach to crime.

In short, references to neuroscience are abundant in many to most liberal calls for reforms in the juvenile justice system. This research has been used in a broad range of advocacy strategies, from those aimed at ending the use of the death penalty and life without parole for juveniles, to those seeking to improving conditions of confinement, to decarceration strategies. Notions of the "teen brain" have thus become a kind of catchall rhetorical device. As the National Juvenile Justice Network, a prominent national coalition of juvenile justice advocacy organizations, noted in a policy paper about the issue:

> Juvenile justice advocates have found that this research is nothing short of compelling. It opens doors to legislators' offices who never before thought about progressive juvenile justice reform. It gives advocates and lawyers working on behalf of juveniles scientific proof for their claims that children are different from adults, are capable of change, and need support and opportunities for healthy development—the principles that initially led to the establishment of the juvenile court and juvenile justice system. And, perhaps even more importantly, brain development research provides heretofore reluctant legislators from "tough-on-crime" districts a basis for a shift from punishment of juveniles to rehabilitation. (National Juvenile Justice Network, 2012, p. 3)

In short, the research is seen to be a rhetorical tool that convinces policymakers, conservatives, and liberals alike.

It is not uncommon now to see an image of a brain scan in the literature of juvenile justice reformers, in PowerPoint presentations, at conferences on juvenile justice, or in media publications (see, for example American Bar Association, 2004; MacArthur Foundation Research Network on Adolescent Development and Juvenile Justice, n.d.). In these images, the teenager's "underdeveloped" brain is abstracted from the individual and the context. It is arguable that these scans may lead one to believe that the visual diagrams of a young person's mind are an adequate substitute for more holistic knowledge of these children (Bessant, 2008).[3] Yet, the interpretation of these scans is ultimately a subjective process, involving "informed interpretations" (Aronson, 2007, p. 133; Joyce, 2005). There are also numerous limitations to this research relating to the expense of neuroimaging and the difficulty in using it in research settings. There is also a limited focus of the research on *simulation* rather than "real-life" responses (participants are shown images meant to provoke behaviors or emotions) and a lack of controls for the participants' socioeconomic status or other environmental factors (Sercombe, 2010).

Additionally, *causal* links between brain structure and functioning and risk-taking behaviors have not been established in the existing research, and these links may never be possible to establish, especially because of the complex interrelationships between the brain and the environment (Epstein, 2007). In other words, this is an area of research that is in its infancy and needs to be used and interpreted with caution. As Bessant and Watts (2012) argue, we simply do not have enough data about the brain to be able to say what a normal or typical pattern of brain development may be.

Despite these limitations, there are some strong defenders of the use of this research in the juvenile justice context, among them some of the most respected researchers and advocates in the field (National Research Council, 2012; Steinberg, 2012). This chapter is not an attempt to condemn their position on brain science. Rather, I ask whether the research on the adolescent brain *does* actually help to move juvenile justice system reforms in a more progressive direction, particularly for young men like Gary Durant. I argue here that if we take the long view on this issue, and also begin to interrogate the hegemony of notions of "development" and "risk," there may be some pitfalls to this kind of advocacy. Below I will discuss "normal" and "abnormal" development, as well as what we know might exist as key barriers that court-involved youth face in experiencing well-being. I will then begin to lay out the evidence for a more nuanced approach to thinking about this issue.

■ The Normal and the Abnormal Brain

In this section, I will describe some of the silo effects that exist when advocates exclusively depend upon the literature about the "normal" teenage brain when making claims about juvenile offending without addressing the scholarship on abnormal brain development and offending. I will also seek to contextualize and challenge our notions of appropriate or normal development. For the purposes of clarity, this section will be divided in its focus on so-called "normal" or healthy development and "abnormal" or compromised development, but this is simply an organizing rubric. The words "normal" and "abnormal" are in inverted commas because what I hope will be made clear in this section is the way in which this divide is not as clear as it seems, and that the strategy of speaking to only one form of development or another in trying to advance juvenile justice reform may be a risky one.

Normal or Healthy Development

For some, the research on the adolescent brain arguably acts as evidence for our widely cherished views of adolescence as a time of identity formation and turmoil. Adolescence has been conceptualized as a stage of "becoming" an adult (Kelly, 2000; Lee, 2001) that is filled with the so-called "storm and stress" involved in that process (Griffin, 2001). Adolescents are often constructed to be resistant, risky, in turmoil, and acutely vulnerable and open to the pressures of identity formation by others (Kemshall, 2008; Muncie, 2009). Indeed, discourses of development have come to bolster notions of appropriate adolescent behavior.

Developmental psychologists describe the "inevitable process" of young people's maturation and have advanced theories of learning that depended on children's purported malleability (James, Jenks, & Prout, 1998, pp. 17, 42). Jean Piaget, an influential theorist of children's moral development, argued that "development is a journey away from disorder and failure to discriminate between self and world, toward order and discrimination, a 'transition from chaos to cosmos'" (1955, p. xiii). Piaget's theories can be traced to Enlightenment epistemologies that rely heavily on narratives of progress. Kohlberg (1976), a follower of Piaget, argued in his "cognitive developmental" theory that moral behaviors are related to the development of rational thought. These theories have contributed to the perspective that cognitive skills can be enhanced and developed within individuals, ultimately leading to self-mastery (France, 2000).

These normative perspectives on adolescent development have become influential in cognitive-skills–based treatment interventions for young people charged with crimes, which have become enormously popular in recent years (Lipsey & Wilson, 1998). For cognitive behavioralists "crime [i]s the outcome of insufficiently or unevenly developed rational or cognitive capacities" (Duguid, 2000, p. 183). In a direct sign of the links between these ideas about adolescent development and the program of cognitive change, the Juvenile Justice Committee of the National Academy of Sciences provided research support and evidence for, and a tacit endorsement of, cognitive-behavioral programming in juvenile justice contexts (National Research Council, 2012).

Yet, some have been critical of the Piagetian approach to development and have argued that we should not necessarily take for granted that these developmental stages are universal to all adolescents (Epstein, 2007; James et al., 1998; Sercombe, 2010). Some scholars have argued that the "hegemony of developmental stage monitoring" (James, et al., 1998, p. 19) entrenches a "gold standard" of normal childhood, against which those children who do not follow the normatively prescribed developmental stages are seen as deviant.[4] It is arguable that notions of the "normal" and risky teenaged brain that have been promulgated in the juvenile justice context create the conditions in which we become preoccupied with the *management* of this storm and stress and do not allow us to pause and question whether or not this experience of storm and stress is universal to all teenagers.[5] As Maroney (2011) argues, "taking brain development as the primary metric by which to dole out legal rights and protections... could be understood to threaten juvenile autonomy and to invite discriminatory distinctions between groups according to their relative propensities toward early or late development" (p. 770). In the neuropsychological literature about the adolescent brain, the language that is used to describe the young person's process of development reflects some of these biases: young people are said to be evolving *toward* more rational and developed ways of thinking and away from the more primitive, irrational forms of engagement with others (American Psychological Association, 2004; Sercombe, 2010).

Finally, the stories that advocates tell, via neuroscience, about "normal" and risky teenage engagement in risk-taking behaviors have some key inaccuracies, namely that many, if not all, teenagers do not engage in those behaviors *most* of the time (Bessant & Watts, 2012; Matza, 1964). Thus, the so-called consensus that exists about adolescent behavior is one that we must call into question. As the prominent youth studies scholar John Muncie has argued, the "academic, political and media gaze has for so long been focused on the 'melodramatic' and the 'problematic' that the diversity, variability and complexity of young people's lives have been obscured" (2009, p. 188). Other scholars have found through research with young people that they "have sophisticated value systems and... they are deeply engaged in the emotional and ethical labor involved in constructing their identities and their lives" (Thomson & Holland, 2002, p. 104; see also Holland, Thomson, Henderson, McGrellis, & Sharpe, 2000). Thus, these scholars urge us to explore the complexity of young people's agency.

The Abnormal Brain

In part because of the silos of knowledge that exist in the field of youth development and neuroscience, some advocates who embrace the science about the teenaged brain may have neglected to realize that there is a burgeoning literature in the field of criminology in which the brain of the young person, albeit the "offending" brain, is a primary object of study. In drawing upon the research about the "normal" teenaged brain and its development to argue for less severe sentences for juveniles, advocates may inadvertently open the door for the creation of the social exclusion, or perhaps even the disposability, of young people whose brains—and risk taking—do not conform to our conceptions of normal teenaged development (Giroux, 2009; Young, 1999). These are young people, like Steven Vasquez, whose *brain damage* is said to lead to their offending.

A number of researchers have examined abnormal brain development and its relationship with antisocial behavior and offending (van Goozen, Fairchild, Snoek, & Harold, 2007). The work has been influential in criminological theory and discourse, particularly that oriented around risk factor approaches and developmental criminology (Loeber & Welsh, 2012; Rose, 2010). Researchers have identified low intelligence and poor executive functioning as key risk factors for offending behaviors (Farrington, 2007; Raine et al., 2005; Seguin, Pihl, Harden, Tremblay, & Boulerice, 1995).

Some of these researchers have sought to discover the neurobehavioral correlates of what has been termed "life-course-persistent" offending, a pattern of offending that begins early in life and continues into and beyond adolescence (Moffitt, 1993). Moffitt, who has conducted research about what may distinguish life-course-persistent offenders from "adolescent-limited" offenders, argues that those who engage in persistent antisocial behavior have individual traits that, in interaction with particular social environments, predispose them to offending. Moffitt argues that "actual rates of illegal behavior soar so high during adolescence that participation in delinquency appears to be a normal part of teen life" (1993, p. 675). She claims that the group of young people who persist in their offending after their adolescence is a small one. This group has been described as "intractable" by some (Scott & Steinberg, 2008, p. 16). As some of the most influential scholars on adolescent development and juvenile offending argue, drawing from Moffitt's research:

> The typical delinquent youth does not grow up to be an adult criminal,
> in part because the developmentally linked values and preferences
> driving his criminal choices as a teenager change in predictable ways as
> he matures. (Scott & Steinberg, 2008, p. 54)

While Moffitt's theory about delinquent behavior is not without criticism (Skardhamar, 2009), it remains deeply influential in the field of criminology.

Researchers have theorized that there are neuropsychological correlates of life-course-persistent offending (Raine et al., 2005). They have found some support for the relationship between cognitive impairments and persistent offending for some groups of young people (see, e.g., Donnellan, Ge, & Wenk, 2000; Kratzer & Hodgins, 1999; Piquero & White, 2003). They have concluded that there is a strong relationship between deficits in neuropsychological abilities early in life and an enduring "impulsive behavioral style" (Seguin et al., 1995, p. 614). Researchers have also established a relationship between cognitive impairments and an individual's ability to regulate aggressive behavior (Seguin et al., 1995). Psychiatrists from McGill University and the University of Montreal in Canada have found that what they describe as "a long stable history of physical aggression" in young people is associated with difficulties in executive functions (Seguin et al., 1995, p. 615).

In addition, Moffitt's work on life-course-persistent offending has appeared in the debates about the teenage brain. Her findings about "adolescent-limited" offenders have been embraced by advocates who seek to point out that the vast majority of young people who offend will later stop offending (American Psychological Association, 2004; National Research Council, 2012; Scott & Steinberg, 2008). Her "life-course-persistent" offending model was used by the Criminal Justice Legal Foundation in their *amicus* brief to the U.S. Supreme Court in support of the state of Florida in their arguments against banning life without parole for juveniles (Criminal Justice Legal Foundation, 2009, pp. 17–18). It was also referenced by Justice Thomas in his dissent in *Graham v. Florida,* in which he argued that the case did not involve an "average juvenile" (Maroney, 2011, p. 791). Given the reductionist ways in which this research has been used, Steven Vasquez or Gary Durant could have very easily been identified as "life course persistent" by the prosecutors in their cases.

The legal scholar Emily Buss has argued that, in a legal context, "courts, litigants and scholars will pick and choose among the sources to find the research that supports their own predilections" (2009, p. 36). Similarly, Maroney has argued about brain science that "the same body of data can be read in such a way as to support wildly different outcomes" (2011, p. 792). In addition, Maroney points out the ideas about adolescent brains being malleable and subject to the subjective views of those who hear them:

> …legal decision makers (like all people) filter factual assertions, including scientific ones, through their prior beliefs, values, and commitments. They tend to accept evidence as relevant and plausible where it aligns with implicit views and judgments and to reject it when it does not. (2009, p. 171)

It thus becomes problematic when advocates use the neuroscientific evidence as a legal or political strategy, as it seems that the evidence can be used to accept *or* reject claims for fairness and justice.

Yet, telescoping out, researchers have also acknowledged the strong environmental influences on abnormal brain development. Using Moffitt's framework, researchers also found that the life-course-persistent group had higher rates of exposure to abuse and neglect (Raine et al., 2005, p. 45). Scholars in the fields of child development, public health, and neuroscience have examined the ways in which exposure to environmental, emotional, and physical stressors in early childhood may compromise normal brain development (Gunnar, Herrera, & Hostinar, 2009; National Scientific Council on the Developing Child, 2005, p. 3). Children who are at elevated risk of what has been termed "early life stress" (ELS) are said to have compromised brain development, which affects their working memory and thus their ability to learn and to perform in school (Evans & Schamberg, 2009). Some forms of stress that may affect brain development include but are not limited to exposure to severe and chronic abuse, limited access to buffering social institutions, such as Head Start and early childhood education programs, growing up in families facing economic hardship, or neglect (Glaser, 2000, p. 99). While it is clear from the literature that exposure to ELS does not *cause* problems with brain development, these stressors do have negative and life-long effects (National Scientific Council on the Developing Child, 2005). As Glaser argues, "the early years of life constitute a particularly sensitive period during which chronic stress may lead to dysregulation of the stress system and may compromise brain development" (2000, p. 98). In the case of Steven Vasquez, his impoverished childhood placed him at high risk of the lead poisoning that he was exposed to, which ultimately led him to suffer from grave cognitive delays (Springer & Stephens-Davidowitz, 2012).

Many of the phenomena described above—low-level cognitive functioning, impulsivity, exposure to abuse, trauma, and neglect—have been characterized as "risk factors" for offending (Farrington, 2007). The risk factor approach, prominent in the field of criminology, has also been imported into the world of juvenile justice policy. Risk assessment instruments are now widely used in the courts, to guide bail decision making, in probation reports, and in making sentencing decisions. Many risk assessment tools are used for ostensibly benevolent purposes: the now widely implemented Juvenile Detention Alternatives Initiative, led by the Annie E. Casey Foundation, is aimed in part at using risk assessment instruments to *reduce* the reliance on detention in municipalities (Mendel, 2007). As states and local jurisdictions across the country search for ways to reduce their detention numbers, they are more and more often relying upon risk assessment instruments. Indeed, scholars have pointed to the ever-expanding reliance on actuarial tools to guide many criminal justice decision-making mechanisms—and ideas about risk and offending lie at the center of these investigations (Feeley & Simon, 2006; Kelly, 2000; Kemshall, 2010).

It is arguable that there is a strong possibility that an *abnormally* developed brain could be added to the list of "risk factors" that would ultimately lead to greater, rather than lesser, punishment of young people, or the decision to detain rather than release a young person. Not all uses of risk assessment instruments are aimed at limiting the use of detention: in most cases, "risk" is associated with future dangerousness, which can result in preventive forms of punishment. Walsh (2011) argues there is thus a "dual use dilemma" when it comes to the application of neuroscience: it can be used to expand the freedoms and rights of young people, but also to exercise greater control over them. Thus, the question about the uses of brain science should arguably expand beyond the binary of punishment/treatment and toward a broader question about what the implications of preventive "screen and intervene" programs (Rose, 2010) for youth at risk of criminal conduct may look like, and whether they in fact may have grave consequences for the preservation of human dignity.

Similar relationships between the minds and moralities of young people emerged a century ago, when interventions into the lives of the "feeble-minded" children of the 19th century were aimed at improving their "moral sensibilities" as well as at the prevention of crime. Rose (1989) writes about some of the techniques of differentiation used during this time, such as intelligence testing, which had an ostensibly scientific cast but which ultimately helped to mark out differences of race and class. During the 1980s and 1990s, knowledge about the brain was used to initiate some of the most punitive policies against young people. The biological and genetic depravity of young offenders, who were described as "superpredators" and a "bio-underclass" condemned to living a life of mental deficiency and moral depravity, was highlighted in campaigns to develop these policies (Krauthammer, 1989).[6]

Are there actually ways that research about abnormal brain development may be used in ways that focus less on *expanding* the use of selective punishment and incapacitation and instead on *preventing* the punishment of young people? It is possible that advocates' use of evidence about "normal" brain development creates an opening for the research about "abnormal" brain development to be introduced in the juvenile justice policy arena. This could create a dangerous rhetorical battlefield—particularly in the courts—about what constitutes "science" and "evidence" about adolescence that may ultimately detract from the goal of advancing justice, dignity, and respect for all people who offend.

■ Issues, Questions, and Concerns

As discussed above, the identification of future risk is not only a longstanding preoccupation of developmental researchers, but it has now moved into the area of brain science. Increasingly, the brain's biomarkers have been studied for the existence of psychiatric disorders and other potential abnormalities. For those children who have been identified as having abnormal brain development, whether through the use of brain scanning, the evaluation of the health of their biomarkers, and so on, their life trajectories could be negatively affected by an early assessment of risk (Singh & Rose, 2009). [7] While some supporters of the uses of neuroscience as a means of advancing progressive juvenile justice reforms have argued that the likelihood of entering a world where administering individual brain scans is rare, Nikolas Rose, a leading scholar on the intersection of social science, health, and medicine, has pointed out that "a whole range of new technologies, notably those from behavioral genetics and brain scanning, claim that they can identify the precursors, signs or markers of future riskiness in advance, presymptomatically or asymptomatically—that they can identify a 'susceptible individual'" (2010, p. 80). Thus, in a criminal justice system that is steeped in notions of risk prediction, dangerousness, and the management of responsibility (Garland, 2001), we cannot ignore the reality that courts and practitioners might easily grasp onto new prediction technologies.

By identifying the cause of such offending in brain structure and function as they relate to what behavioral scientists have taught us about adolescent development, advocates perhaps all too easily abandon the multitudinous factors—environmental, political, and economic—that contribute to offending and responses to it (although see National Research Council, 2012). For example, there are some *structural* explanations for offending that raise questions about the over-policing and mass incarceration of communities of color, the relationship between social inequality and punishment, and the so-called "school-to-prison pipeline" (Alexander, 2010; Children's Defense Fund, 2007; Clear, 2007; Pettit & Western, 2004). There are also numerous documented barriers that inhibit the successful reentry of young people from custody to communities, and a vast array of collateral consequences of incarceration that often inhibit successful transitions into communities and into adulthood (Apel & Sweeten, 2010; Farrington, Loeber, & Howell, 2012; Harris, Evans, & Beckett, 2010).

From a policy perspective, the idea of the unruly and risky teenager that is sustained through advocates' use of brain science to lobby for more rehabilitative programs, lesser sentences, and other progressive programs for young people may actually play a role in widening the net of control over young people. We have arguably begun to see the effects of this: more and more states across the country are closing juvenile facilities, but they are also increasing the use of electronic monitoring, home-based interventions, and community corrections programs. For those who argue that young people's riskiness needs to be more effectively controlled in the community, this expansion of alternatives is heralded as a great success. Moreover, participation in community-based care alone does not mean that a young person is free from the stigma of criminal justice system involvement (Cox, 2013).

Concluding Comments

Steinberg, a leading scholar on developmental neuroscience, argues that "brain science should inform the nation's policy discussions when it is relevant, but society should not make policy decisions on the basis of brain science alone" (2012, p. 78). From a practice and advocacy perspective, this means that we should have a more nuanced approach to thinking about youth development in the context of juvenile justice systems. There are some indications of this approach in the field of positive youth justice, which employs a strengths-based approach in working with young people in trouble with the law (Butts, Bazemore, & Meroe, 2010). Knowing what we do about hegemony of normative notions of development, advocates can also actually resist the use of developmental discourses in their work, and instead seek an approach to talking about a justice system that is rooted in *human dignity, ethicality*, and *respect* (Paternoster, Brame, Bachman, & Sherman, 1997).

A growing body of research has pointed to the potential significance of strengths-based work with people who offend that is prospective rather than retrospective (McNeill, 2003), is focused on the development and fulfillment of human potential and building a "good life" (Ward & Brown, 2004), and helps people build human *and* social capital (McNeill, Batchelor, Burnett, & Knox, 2005). This approach in part focuses on building individual "capabilities" (Farrall, Bottoms, & Shapland, 2010) rather than on managing risk.

Advocates and practitioners should also seek to move beyond frameworks of adolescent development that neglect to address young people's moral agency and their profound sense of fairness, which has consequences for their investment in the law (Fagan & Tyler, 2005). Adolescents, especially those charged with crimes, are not naïve about the injustices prevalent and present in the criminal justice system. Their knowledge and capacities about these injustices must be taken into consideration in developing advocacy strategies that seek to combat systemic injustices. Advocates, for example, can engage in clearer critiques of police practices that have arguably led to the fractured relationships that exist between many young people of color and law enforcement (see Brunson, 2007). It is argued here that a system of justice that respects young people's need for respect and fairness also would address their treatment by those in positions of power.

As has been discussed above, adolescent development is not a straightforward pathway out of darkness, risk, and turmoil into rationality and self-control. Adolescents possess human agency, or the capacity for action. As such, if they have offended, even if it is a serious offense, they deserve an opportunity to be treated in a way that recognizes their desire to fully realize their subjective understanding of a "good life" or their full functioning as a human being (Farrall, Bottoms, & Shapland, 2010; Ward & Brown, 2004) so they can fully flourish. Bottoms and colleagues argue that facilitating an individual's desistance from offending requires that we understand the ways that individuals' ability to flourish—particularly those who offend in a persistent manner—is often blocked, particularly among the socially excluded. So many young people who offend—and particularly young offenders—fall into this category. Their capacity to find a job and a partner, and ultimately to be a good citizen, all markers of flourishing, are often blocked by social-structural obstacles (Farrall et al., 2010). An advocacy approach to young people who offend that puts their agency, and ultimately their desire for well-being and dignity, at the center of its aims, rather than the outcome of "self-control" or "rationality," can arguably assist young people who have been negatively impacted by the criminal justice system. This can be seen in the case of Steven Vasquez, when the judge recognized that Steven's survival and well-being depended on access to a safe home and appropriate social supports, not brain development.

▄▄▄▄▄▄▄ Notes

1   See, for example, the websites of the Campaign for the Fair Sentencing of Youth, the Campaign for Youth Justice, the Center for Juvenile Justice Reform, the Coalition for Juvenile Justice, the Equal Justice Initiative, the MacArthur Foundation Research Network, the National Juvenile Justice Network, and New York's Schuyler Center. See also recent policy reports by national organizations that reference the research on neuroscience in arguing for a more therapeutic or lenient approach to young people who commit crimes (Human Rights Watch, 2012; Human Rights Watch & Amnesty International, 2005; Justice Policy Institute, 2010).

2   See, for example, "Incorporating Adolescent Brain & Behavioral Development Science into All Stages of the Criminal Proceeding," in *Age Matters: Strategies for Representing Juveniles in Adult Court* (a webcast training series), by the National Association of Criminal Defense Lawyers, <http://www.nacdl.org/agematterswebinar/>; "Adolescent Brains and Juvenile Justice: New Insights from Neuroscience, Genetics, and Addiction Science," Conference held at Arizona State University Law School, May 2011, <http://lsi.law.asu.edu/adolescentbrains2011/>.

3   Juvenile justice reformers who employ adolescent brain research in their advocacy strategies often point to research that employs functional magnetic resonance imaging (fMRIs) to study adolescent behaviors in context (see, e.g., Act 4 Juvenile Justice, n.d.; National Juvenile Justice Network, 2008). They argue that this research indicates a correlation between brain functioning and teenage risk-taking behaviors. This research involves the application of very new imaging technologies in the study of the brain, and the sample sizes of much of this research are extremely small, thus calling into question its generalizability. For example, in some of the most important recent research involving the use of fMRI, the sample sizes were as follows: 16 adolescents in the work of Ernst et al. (2005), 12 and 13 adolescents in Galvan et al. (2007) and Galvan et al. (2006), 24 adolescents in Hare (2008), 19 adolescents in Somerville et al. (2011), 12 adolescents in Baird et al. (1999), and 15 adolescents in van Leijenhorst et al. (2010).

4   Middle-class parents are said to focus on "maximizing those achieved and preferential traits in their children that can testify to their own cultural `superiority,' such as intelligence (as quantified in school performances), physical beauty (defined in dominant cultural terms), and social skills" (Scheper-Hughes & Stein, 1987, p. 9). Those parents who do not engage in these practices of childrearing, drawn from dominant paradigms of child development, are seen to be putting their children at "risk" of deviance and failure.

5   Questions about management have indeed come to the fore among advocates interested in this issue: as one group, Act 4 Juvenile Justice, asks in their brief on the adolescent brain: "How does one guide an adolescent to cope in a healthy manner with this tumultuous stage of life? How do we hold young offenders accountable and take advantage of every opportunity to positively influence their development? How can and should common delinquency prevention and juvenile justice practices and laws change to incorporate a more sensible approach to addressing the needs of adolescents, while balancing them with community safety needs?" (Act 4 Juvenile Justice, n.d.).

6   During this period, the National Institute of Mental Health funded a Violence Initiative Project that was responsible in part for genetic investigations into the levels of aggression in siblings of juvenile offenders (Rose, 2010, p. 91).

7   Singh and Rose raise some fundamental questions about the uses of biomarkers to predict behavioral problems and psychiatric disorders in children: "will ideas about the identity and the capacity of individuals begin to change? ...how will people feel about themselves given their risk profile, and will others perceive them differently? Will 'risk' and 'potential' eventually dominate ideas of personal identity, health status and opportunity in rigid, coercive or stigmatizing ways? Will these ideas become institutionalized within education, law and policy?" (2009: 204).

References

Act 4 Juvenile Justice (n.d.). *Adolescent brain development and juvenile justice fact sheet.* Washington, DC: Act 4 Juvenile Justice.

Alexander, M. (2010). *The new Jim Crow: Mass incarceration in the age of colorblindness.* New York: The New Press.

American Bar Association (2004). *Adolescence, brain development and legal culpability.* Washington, DC.

American Medical Association (2004). *Brief for amici curiae supporting respondent, Roper v. Simmons, 543 U.S. 551, No. 03-633.* Washington, DC.

American Psychological Association (2004). *Brief for amici curiae supporting respondent, Roper v. Simmons, 543 U.S. 551, No. 03-633.* Washington, DC.

Apel, R., & Sweeten, G. (2010). The impact of incarceration on employment during the transition to adulthood. *Social Problems, 57*(3), 448–479.

Aronson, J. D. (2007). Brain imaging, culpability and the juvenile death penalty. *Psychology, Public Policy, and Law, 13*(2), 115–142.

Arya, N. (2011). *State trends: Legislative victories from 2005 to 2010 removing youth from the adult criminal justice system.* Washington, DC: Campaign for Youth Justice.

Baird, A. A., Gruber, S. A., Fein, D. A., Mass, L. C., Steingard, R. J., Renshaw, P. F., & Yurgelun-Todd, D. A. (1999). Functional magnetic resonance imaging of facial affect recognition in children and adolescents. *Journal of the American Academy of Child & Adolescent Psychiatry, 38*(2), 195–199.

Bayer, M. (2012). *Affirmation in response to defendant's motion for a downward departure pursuant to SORA.*

Bazelon, L. (2009, October 12). The juvenile damned: Sentencing children to life without parole is cruel and unusual. *National Law Journal.*

Bernard, T., & Kurlychek, M. (2010). *The cycle of juvenile justice* (2nd ed.). New York: Oxford University Press.

Bessant, J. (2008). Hard wired for risk: neurological science, 'the adolescent brain' and developmental theory. *Journal of Youth Studies, 11*(3), 349–362.

Bessant, J., & Watts, R. (2012). The mismeasurment of youth: why adolescent brain science is bad science. *Contemporary Social Science, 7*(2), 181–196.

Bosworth, M. (2011). Penal moderation in the United States. *Criminology and Public Policy, 10*(2), 335–343.

Brunson, R. (2007). "Police don't like black people": African-American young men's accumulated police experiences. *Criminology and Public Policy, 6*(1), 71–102.

Buss, E. (2009). What the law should (and should not) learn from child development research. *Hofstra Law Review, 38,* 13–65.

Butterfield, F. (1996). *All God's children: The Bosket family and the American tradition of violence.* New York: Harper Collins.

Butts, J. (2012). What's the evidence for evidence-based practice? *Databits.* New York: John Jay Research and Evaluation Center.

Butts, J., Bazemore, G., & Meroe, A. S. (2010). *Positive youth justice: Framing justice interventions using the concept of positive youth development.* Washington, DC: Coalition for Juvenile Justice.

Butts, J., & Evans, D. N. (2011). *Resolution, reinvestment, and realignment: Three strategies for changing juvenile justice.* New York: John Jay College of Criminal Justice.

Caher, J. (2012). More support for sex offender if risk level reduced, judge says. *New York Law Journal.*

Campaign for the Fair Sentencing of Youth (2012). Stats by State. Retrieved December 13, 2012, from http://www.endjlwop.org/the-issue/stats-by-state/

Children's Defense Fund (2007). *America's cradle to prison pipeline*.

Clear, T. (2007). *Imprisoning communities: How mass incarceration makes disadvantaged neighborhoods worse*. New York: Oxford University Press.

Cox, A. (2013). New visions of social control? Young people's perceptions of community penalties. *Journal of Youth Studies, 16*(1), 135–150.

Criminal Justice Legal Foundation (2009). Brief Amicus Curiae of the Criminal Justice Legal Foundation in Support of Respondents, Graham vs. State of Florida, Sullivan vs. State of Florida Nos. 08-7412 and 08-7621 in the Supreme Court of the United States. California.

DeLisi, M., Hochstetler, A., Jones-Johnson, G., Caudill, J. W., & Marquart, J. W. (2011). The road to murder: the enduring criminogenic effects of juvenile confinement among a sample of adult career criminals. *Youth Violence and Juvenile Justice, 9*(3), 207–221.

Dmitrieva, J., Monahan, K., Cauffman, E., & Steinberg, L. (2012). Arrested development: The effects of incarceration on the development of psychosocial maturity. *Development and Psychopathology, 24*, 1073–1090.

Donnellan, M. B., Ge, X., & Wenk, E. (2000). Cognitive abilities in adolescent-limited and life-course-persistent criminal offenders. *Journal of Abnormal Psychology, 109*(3), 396–402.

Duguid, S. (2000). *Can prisons work? The prisoner as object and subject in modern corrections*. Buffalo: University of Toronto Press.

Epstein, R. (2007). The myth of the teen brain. *Scientific American Mind*, 57–63.

Ernst, M., Nelson, E. E., Jazbec, S., McCLure, E., Monk, C., Leibenluft, E., & Pine, D. (2005). Amygdala and nucleus accumbens in responses to receipt and omission of gains in adults and adolescents. *Neuroimage, 25*(4), 1279–1291.

Evans, D. N. (2012). *Pioneers of youth justice reform: Achieving system change using resolution, reinvestment, and realignment strategies*. New York: John Jay.

Evans, G. W., & Schamberg, M. A. (2009). Childhood poverty, chronic stress, and adult working memory. *Proceedings of the National Academy of Sciences USA, 106*(16), 6545–6549.

Fagan, J., & Tyler, T. (2005). Legal socialization of children and adolescents. *Social Justice Research, 18*(3), 217–240.

Farrall, S., Bottoms, A., & Shapland, J. (2010). Social structures and desistance from crime. *European Journal of Criminology, 7*(6), 546–570.

Farrall, S., Bottoms, A. E., & Shapland, J. (2010). Social structures and desistance from crime. *European Journal of Criminology, 7*(6), 546–570.

Farrington, D. P. (2007). Childhood risk factors and risk focused prevention. In M. Maguire, R. Morgan, & R. Reiner (Eds.), *Oxford handbook of criminology* (4th ed.) (pp. 602–640). Oxford: Oxford University Press.

Farrington, D. P., Loeber, R., & Howell, J. C. (2012). Young adult offenders: the need for more effective legislative options and justice processing. *Criminology and Public Policy, 11*(4), 729–750.

Feeley, M., & Simon, J. (2006). The new penology: notes on the emerging strategy of corrections and its implications. *Criminology, 30*(4), 449–474.

Feld, B. (1999). The transformation of the juvenile court—Part II: Race and the "crackdown" on youth crime. *Minnesota Law Review, 84*, 327–395.

France, A. (2000). Towards a sociological understanding of youth and their risk-taking. *Journal of Youth Studies, 3*(3), 317–331.

Galvan, A., Hare, T., Voss, H., Glover, G., & Casey, B. J. (2007). Risk-taking and the adolescent brain: who is at risk? *Developmental Science, 10*(2), F8–F14.

Galvan, A., Hare, T. A., Parra, C. E., Penn, J., Voss, H., Glover, G., & Casey, B. J. (2006). Earlier development of the accumbens relative to orbitofrontal cortex might underlie risk-taking behavior in adolescents. *Journal of Neuroscience, 26*(25), 6885–6892. doi:10.1523/jneurosci.1062-06.2006

Gardner, M. (1989). Punitive juvenile justice and public trials by jury: Sixth Amendment applications in a post-*McKeiver* world. *Nebraska Law Review, 91*(1).

Garland, D. (2001). *The culture of control.* Oxford: Oxford University Press.

Gatti, U., Tremblay, R. E., & Vitaro, F. (2009). Iatrogenic effect of juvenile justice. *Journal of Child Psychology and Psychiatry, 50*(8), 991–998.

Giedd, J. N. (2008). The teen brain: insights from neuroimaging. *Journal of Adolescent Health, 42*(4), 335–343.

Giroux, H. (2009). *Youth in a suspect society: Democracy or disposability.* New York: Palgrave MacMillan.

Glaser, D. (2000). Child abuse and neglect and the brain—a review. *Journal of Child Psychology & Psychiatry & Allied Disciplines, 41*(1), 97.

Griffin, C. (2001). Imagining new narratives of youth: youth research, the 'new Europe' and global youth culture. *Childhood, 8*(2), 147–166.

Gruber, S. A., & Yurgelun-Todd, D. A. (2006). Neurobiology and the law: a role in juvenile justice? *Ohio State Journal of Criminal Law, 3,* 321–340.

Gunnar, M., Herrera, A., & Hostinar, C. (2009, October 12, 2012). Stress and early brain development. *Encyclopedia on Early Childhood Development.*

Harcourt, B. (2009). Sending children to prison for life. *Los Angeles Times.* Retrieved from http://www.latimes.com/news/opinion/commentary/la-oe-harcourt5-2009oct05,0,3635755.story

Hare, T. A., Tottenham, N., Galvan, A., Voss, H. U., Glover, G. H., & Casey, B. J. (2008). Biological substrates of emotional reactivity and regulation in adolescence during an emotional go-no go task. *Biological Psychiatry, 63*(10), 927–934.

Harris, A., Evans, H., & Beckett, K. (2010). Drawing blood from stones: legal debt and social inequality in the contemporary United States. *American Journal of Sociology, 115*(6), 1753–1799.

Henning, K. (2009, December 14). The case against juvenile life without parole: good policy and good law. Retrieved from http://writ.news.findlaw.com/commentary/20091026_henning.html

Hockenberry, S., Sickmund, M., & Sladky, A. (2011). *Juvenile residential facility census, 2008: Selected findings.* Washington, DC: Office of Juvenile Justice and Delinquency Prevention.

Holland, J., Thomson, R., Henderson, S., McGrellis, S., & Sharpe, S. (2000). Catching on, wising up and learning from your mistakes: Young people's accounts of moral development. *International Journal of Children's Rights, 8,* 271–294.

Huizinga, D., & Henry, K. (2008). The effect of arrest and justice system sanctions on subsequent behavior: findings from longitudinal and other studies. In A. M. Liberman (Ed.), *The long view of crime: A synthesis of longitudinal research* (pp. 220–254). New York: Springer.

Human Rights Watch (2012). *Growing up locked down: Youth in solitary confinement in jails and prisons across the United States.* New York: Human Rights Watch.

Human Rights Watch & Amnesty International (2005). *The rest of their lives: Life without parole for child offenders in the United States.* New York: Human Rights Watch/Amnesty International.

James, A., Jenks, C., & Prout, A. (1998). *Theorizing childhood.* Cambridge: Polity Press.

Joyce, K. (2005). Appealing images: magnetic resonance imaging and the production of authoritative knowledge. *Social Studies of Science, 35*(3), 437–462.

Justice Policy Institute (2010). *Healing invisible wounds: Why investing in trauma-informed care for children makes sense.* Washington, DC: Justice Policy Institute.

Kambam, P., & Thompson, C. (2009). The development of decision-making capacities in children and adolescents: Psychological and neurological perspectives and their implications for juvenile defendants. *Behavioral Sciences & the Law, 27*(2), 173–190.

Kelly, P. (2000). The dangerousness of youth-at-risk: the possibilities of surveillance and intervention in uncertain times. *Journal of Adolescence, 23*, 463–476.

Kemshall, H. (2008). Risks, rights and justice: understanding and responding to youth risk. *Youth Justice, 8*(1), 21–37.

Kemshall, H. (2010). Risk rationalities in contemporary social work policy and practice. *British Journal of Social Work, 40*, 1247–1262.

Kohlberg, L. (1976). Moral stages and moralization: the cognitive developmental approach. In T. Lichona (Ed.), *Moral development and behavior: Theory, research, and social issues* (pp. 31–53). New York: Holt, Rinehart and Winston.

Kratzer, L., & Hodgins, S. (1999). A typology of offenders: A test of Moffitt's theory among males and females from childhood to age 30. *Criminal Behaviour and Mental Health, 9*, 57–73.

Krauthammer, C. (1989, July 6). Children of cocaine. *Washington Post* (p. C7).

Lamm, C. (2009, November 11). Youth offenders deserve a chance for rehabilitation. *Roll Call*.

Lee, N. (2001). *Childhood and society: Growing up in an age of uncertainty*. Buckingham: Open University Press.

Lipsey, M., & Wilson, D. (1998). Effective intervention for serious juvenile offenders. In R. Loeber & D. P. Farrington (Eds.), *Serious and violent juvenile offenders: Risk factors and successful interventions* (pp. 313–346). Thousand Oaks, CA: Sage.

Loader, I. (2009). Ice cream and incarceration: On appetites for security and punishment. *Punishment & Society, 11*, 241–257.

Loeber, R., & Welsh, B. (2012). *The future of criminology*. New York: Oxford University Press.

Loughran, T., Mulvey, E. P., Schubert, C. A., Fagan, J., Piquero, A. R., & Losoya, S. H. (2009). Estimating a dose-response relationship between length of stay and future recidivism in serious juvenile offenders. *Criminology, 47*(3), 699–740.

MacArthur Foundation Research Network on Adolescent Development and Juvenile Justice. (August 3, 2009). *Development and criminal blameworthiness*. [PowerPoint Presentation]. Retrieved from http://www.adjj.org/content/resource_page.php?filter=download

Maroney, T. (2009). The false promise of adolescent brain science in juvenile justice. *Notre Dame Law Review, 85*(1), 89–176.

Maroney, T. (2011). Adolescent brain science after *Graham v. Florida. Notre Dame Law Review, 86*(2), 765–794.

Matza, D. (1964). *Delinquency and drift*. New York: John Wiley and Sons Ltd.

McCabe, D. P., & Castel, A. D. (2008). Seeing is believing: The effect of brain images on judgments of scientific reasoning. *Cognition, 107*(1), 343–352.

McNeill, F. (2003). Desistance-focused probation practice. In W. H. Chui & M. Nellis (Eds.), *Moving probation forward: Evidence, arguments and practice* (pp. 146–162). Harlow, Essex: Pearson Education Limited.

McNeill, F., Batchelor, S., Burnett, R., & Knox, J. (2005). *21st-century social work: Reducing re-offending: Key practice skills*. Glasgow: Glasgow School of Social Work.

Mendel, R. (2007). *Beyond detention: System transformation through juvenile detention reform*. Baltimore, MD: Annie E. Casey Foundation.

Merlo, A. V., & Benekos, P. (2010). Is punitive juvenile justice policy declining in the United States? A critique of emergent initiatives. *Youth Justice, 10*(1), 3–24.

Moffitt, T. (1993). Adolescence-limited and life-course-persistent antisocial behavior: a developmental trajectory. *Psychological Review, 100*(4), 674–701.

Morse, S. (2006). Brain overclaim syndrome and criminal responsibility: a diagnostic note. *Ohio State Journal of Criminal Law, 3*, 397–412.

Muncie, J. (2009). *Youth and crime* (3rd ed.). London: Sage.

National Juvenile Justice Network (2008). *Using adolescent brain research to inform policy: A guide for juvenile justice advocates*. Washington, DC.

National Juvenile Justice Network (2012). *Using adolescent brain research to inform policy: A guide for juvenile justice advocates (updated)*. Washington, DC.

National Research Council (2012). *Reforming juvenile justice: A developmental approach*. Washington, DC: National Academies Approach.

National Scientific Council on the Developing Child (2005). *Excessive stress disrupts the architecture of the developing brain*. Cambridge: Harvard University.

Nellis, A., & King, R. (2009). *No exit: The expanding use of life sentences in America*. Washington, DC: The Sentencing Project.

Paternoster, R., Brame, R., Bachman, R., & Sherman, L. W. (1997). Do fair procedures matter? The effect of procedural justice on spouse assault. *Law and Society Review, 31*(1), 163–204.

Pettit, B., & Western, B. (2004). Mass imprisonment and the life course: race and class inequality in U.S. incarceration. *American Sociological Review, 69*(2), 151–169.

Phoenix, J. (2010). Whose account counts? Politics and research in youth justice. In W. Taylor, R. Earle, & R. Hester (Eds.), *Youth justice handbook: Theory, policy and practice*. Cullompton, Devon: Willan.

Piaget, J. (1955). *The construction of reality in the child*. New York: Basic Books.

Pickett, J., & Chiricos, T. (2012). Controlling other people's children: racialized views of delinquency and whites' punitive attitudes toward juvenile offenders. *Criminology, 50*(3), 673–710.

Piquero, A. R., & White, N. A. (2003). On the relationship between cognitive abilities and life-course-persistent offending among a sample of African Americans: A longitudinal test of Moffitt's hypothesis. *Journal of Criminal Justice, 31*(5), 399–409.

Platt, A. (1969/1977). *The Child Savers: The invention of delinquency*. Chicago: The University of Chicago Press.

Raine, A., Moffitt, T. E., Caspi, A., Loeber, R., Stouthamer-Loeber, M., & Lynam, D. (2005). Neurocognitive impairments in boys on the life-course-persistent antisocial path. *Journal of Abnormal Psychology, 114*(1), 38–49. doi:10.1037/0021-843x.114.1.38

Rose, N. (1989). *Governing the soul: The shaping of the private self*. London: Routledge.

Rose, N. (2010). 'Screen and intervene': governing risky brains. *History of the Human Sciences, 23*(1), 79–105.

Scheper-Hughes, N., & Stein, H. F. (1987). Child abuse and the unconscious in popular American culture. In N. Scheper-Hughes (Ed.), *Child survival: Anthropological perspectives on the treatment and maltreatment of children* (pp. 339–358). Dordrecht: D. Reidel Publishing Company.

Scott, E. S., & Grisso, T. (1998). The evolution of adolescence: a developmental perspective on juvenile justice reform. *Journal of Criminal Law and Criminology, 88*(1), 137–189.

Scott, E. S., & Steinberg, L. (2008). *Rethinking juvenile justice*. Cambridge: Harvard University Press.

Seguin, J. R., Pihl, R. O., Harden, P. W., Tremblay, R. E., & Boulerice, B. (1995). Cognitive and neuropsychological characteristics of physically aggressive boys. *Journal of Abnormal Psychology, 104*(4), 614–624.

Sercombe, H. (2010). The "teen brain" research: critical perspectives. *Youth and Policy, 105*, 71–80.

Sessions Stepp, L. (2008). He's a man, as charged; but should emerging brain science affect courts' handling of young defendants? *Washington Post*.

Singer, S. L. (1996). *Recriminalizing delinquency: Violent crime and juvenile justice*. New York: Cambridge University Press.

Singh, I., & Rose, N. (2009). Biomarkers in psychiatry. *Nature, 460*(9), 202–207.

Skardhamar, T. (2009). Reconsidering the theory on adolescent-limited and life-course persistent anti-social behaviour. *British Journal of Criminology, 49*, 863–878.

Somerville, L. H., Hare, T., & Casey, B. J. (2011). Frontostriatal maturation predicts cognitive control failure to appetitive cues in adolescents. *Journal of Cognitive Neuroscience, 23*(9), 2123–2134.

Springer, A., & Stephens-Davidowitz, L. (2012). *Affirmation: The People of the State of New York v. Steven Vasquez.* Author.

Steinberg, L. (2012). Should the science of adolescent brain development inform public policy? *Issues in Science and Technology,* Spring, 67–78.

Teitelbaum, L. E. (1991). Youth crime and the choice between rules and standards. *Brigham Young University Law Review, 1,* 351.

Thomson, R., & Holland, J. (2002). Young people, social change and the negotiation of moral authority. *Children & Society, 16,* 103–115.

Tough, P. (2012). *How children succeed: Grit, curiosity, and the hidden power of character.* New York: Houghton Mifflin.

van Goozen, S., Fairchild, G., Snoek, H., & Harold, G. (2007). The evidence for a neurobiological model of childhood antisocial behavior. *Psychological Bulletin, 133*(1), 149–182.

Van Leijenhorst, L., Moor, B. G., Op de Macks, Z. à. A., Rombouts, S. A. R. B., Westenberg, P. M., & Crone, E. A. (2010). Adolescent risky decision-making: Neurocognitive development of reward and control regions. *Neuroimage, 51*(1), 345–355.

Walsh, C. (2011). Youth justice and neuroscience: a dual-use dilemma. *British Journal of Criminology, 51,* 21–39.

Ward, T., & Brown, M. (2004). The good lives model and conceptual issues in offender rehabilitation. *Psychology, Crime & Law, 10*(3), 243–257.

Widmer, T. (2009). The contribution of evidence-based policy to the output-oriented legitimacy of the state. *Evidence & Policy, 5*(4), 351–372.

Young, J. (1999). *The exclusive society: Social exclusion, crime and difference in late modernity.* Thousand Oaks, CA: Sage.

Juvenile Justice Processing

7 Police Work with Juveniles

Jeremiah Jaggers, Sarah Young, and Wesley T. Church II

■ Introduction

The police have historically had an uneasy and often contemptuous relationship with juvenile delinquents. In many ways, the role of the police is often contradictory and confusing when dealing with children and adolescents who have violated the law. In addition, the job of the police in managing delinquency is complicated because the age of the person is often unknown until action has been taken. This for police can be dangerous because the need to make split-second decisions can be the difference between life and death.

In the late 19th century the court revolutionized the legal process when dealing with juveniles, but the police had no such revolution: they continued to operate under the same premise they had for years. Although they are not required to have them, today many police departments have juvenile officers; however, few have a dedicated force that deal specifically with juveniles. In fact, police management of juveniles is most often dictated by the courts, legislation, public opinion, and the discretion that is afforded each officer.

The police are typically the first contact that juveniles have with the court system, whether they are victims or delinquents. The importance of this gatekeeper function cannot be overemphasized because it often results in the juvenile being labeled a delinquent, which can have profound and lasting effects.

To protect the community is the core function of any police force, and in dealing with juveniles a police officer must determine what is best for the community. However, unlike specialized juvenile courts and detention, the police have to function atypically when dealing with juveniles because the treatment of delinquents has historically had a social work aspect. Many police departments and officers function in a world that prefers to focus on the justice/punitive aspect of police work; that is to say, getting offenders off the streets, responding to emergencies, and in general keeping us all safe. A situation with a juvenile is often different and complicated simply by the fact that the juvenile is considered a child and, as currently accepted by most in our society, not completely responsible for his or her actions. Society tends to agree that a child's actions could be a result of a broken home, a poor neighborhood environment, a poor school, learning/behavioral issues, or all of the above. Whereas society accepts that an adult is solely responsible for his or her actions, it stipulates that a juvenile is not. The police must deal with some if not all of the major socializing institutions—parents, peers, schools, neighborhoods, churches, etc.—with nearly every juvenile arrest, whether they are equipped to do so or not. It is also important that much of the interaction that the police have with juveniles has to do with public order rather than criminal law enforcement, although they do have to deal with juveniles in that area as well. In this chapter we will use the term *juvenile*, which is a legal term that refers to a person under the age of 18 (in most states). Although this is not a term used in general by society, the law does. Thus, in keeping with this custom, we will use *juvenile* to refer to a child or adolescent involved with the juvenile justice system. We will discuss the history and ambiguous nature of the relationship between law enforcement and juveniles in an attempt to appreciate the fine line that police officers walk between protecting society and dealing with and acting in the best interest of our youth.

■ The History of Police and Juvenile Relations

Policing of juveniles, as with policing of adult offenders, has changed over time and is informed by best practices, social values and norms, and the sociopolitical context of the United States. While eras are marked by significant points of change or development (such as the first juvenile court being established in Illinois in 1899, or the Columbine school shootings in 1999 that led to increased police presence in schools), eras are also marked by a change in values, laws, and the nature of crime itself.

The Colonial Period (1636–1825)

Youth in colonial times were viewed as both the property and purview of their families. Families were responsible for controlling the behavior of their children, and a failure to do so was often met with social shaming. It was common for juveniles to be apprenticed into a variety of trades, and a juvenile who broke the law was remanded back to his family ("his" because juvenile apprentices were almost exclusively male). Punishment for crimes was harsh by modern American standards, including "public whippings, dunkings ... expulsion from the community or even capital punishment" (Bartollas, 2006, p. 17). There was no recognition that juveniles who committed crimes should be treated any differently from adult offenders. This may be a reflection of the demands placed on juveniles and a typical life trajectory of individuals during this time period: juveniles were independent, married, and working at much younger ages than by today's standards.

Post-Colonial, Civil War, and Early Progressive Era (1826–1925)

This era marked a dramatic shift in the thinking about and treatment of juvenile offenders. In the mid- to late nineteenth century families with juvenile offenders were viewed as incapable and unworthy moral providers for their delinquent children. The establishment of "houses of refuge" increased during this time, and such places were viewed as moral institutions that would buffer against the ineptitude and failings of weak-minded parents. Juveniles who offended were remanded to these houses of refuge and were considered wards of the state. The family was viewed as a problem and source of negative behaviors, a shift from viewing the family as a positive and moral social unit for juveniles to learn appropriate social skills. As more youth were being remanded to houses of refuge, it was becoming increasingly clear that these youth were not thriving in these institutions due in large part to harsh, unsanitary, and isolating conditions. There was a push to reform the system to better support juveniles whose families and communities were unable to contain or curb their harmful behaviors (Bartollas, 2006).

The year 1899 marked a shift in juvenile delinquency services and laws, as this was when the first court for juvenile offenders was established. Prior to this, youth age 14 and older were treated as adults in the criminal justice system. The establishment of the court system for juveniles increased the rights of both youth and parents. Juveniles were appointed court advocates who could act in their best interests. The larger Hull House movement, led by Jane Addams, raised awareness that the social environment could have a significant impact on youth and families, and it underscored the importance of social services and positive activities (such as recreation and mentorship) that could be a deterrent to juvenile crime. This resulted in a shift from sole individual blame for moral ineptitude to a view that broader social systems could affect individuals and families in ways that they had little control over (such as poverty and unsanitary living and working conditions) (Springer & Roberts, 2011).

The Great Depression and Early Civil Rights Era (1926–1965)

The widespread and crushing poverty of the Great Depression brought an increased awareness of how broader social systems could affect individuals and families, perhaps reducing the stigma of juvenile crime slightly since so many people were struggling. There was an increased focus in the 1930s and 1940s on explaining reasons for juvenile delinquency, and best knowledge of that time suggested that family dysfunction was largely the cause of delinquent behaviors. The laws of the time reflected this viewpoint, punishing and at times jailing parents whose children exhibited delinquent behaviors. These punishments did not result in significant drops in juvenile delinquency however, and new methods to deal with juvenile delinquency were sought (Schmalleger & Bartollas, 2008; Springer & Roberts, 2011).

Modern Juvenile Justice (1966–Present)

The late 1960s and 1970s were characterized by significant reforms for juvenile justice, including an increased emphasis on juvenile and police interactions. Several high-profile court cases (such as *Kent v. United States*, 1966; *In re Gault*, 1967; and *McKeiver v. Pennsylvania*, 1971) highlighted the disparities in treatment and dispensing of justice for youth. These disparities included lack of due process, lack of qualified court-appointed attorneys and advocates, harsh punishments, and arbitrary sentencing. Community-based programs became increasingly popular, and the idea of "children's rights" gained traction nationally in part due to the Civil Rights movement. The federal Juvenile Justice and Delinquency Prevention Act of 1974 was a significant turning point in juvenile justice law, with a push to deinstitutionalize youth, provide more prevention services, improve jailing conditions, and reduce the number of juveniles jailed who had been abused and neglected as children (Bartollas, 2006).

The crack cocaine epidemic of the 1980s and resulting crime rate increases among adults translated to the juvenile justice system as well. Murders, robberies, and drug-related crimes skyrocketed, and there was a national moral backlash that President Ronald Reagan suggested was due to the breakdown in the American family unit, among other factors (Springer & Roberts, 2011). Juveniles were viewed with suspicion and were considered in need of control, and police were "cracking down" on both juvenile and adult offenders as a means of deterring future crime and getting current crime rates under control. The "get tough" mentality resulted in mandatory minimum sentencing (especially for drug-related crimes), an increase in use of the death penalty for juvenile offenders committing certain crimes, and an increased incarceration rate for juveniles.

The past three decades have meant changes in both the types of crimes being committed and the types of services and proceedings that follow. Youth street gangs, discussed below, are increasing and reflect both the poverty and isolation of youth in some communities. School shootings have resulted in an increased police presence in schools. States continue to have uneven responses to juvenile offenders, with some states responding with tougher penalties and longer sentences for youth and other states trying to expand social services and prevention efforts. Despite the unevenness of the dispensing of juvenile justice, the 2005 Supreme Court decision in *Roper v. Simmons* made it illegal to execute juvenile offenders (Springer & Roberts, 2011).

■ Contemporary Juvenile and Police Contact in Context

Interaction between police officers and juveniles has received waxing and waning attention since the 1970s, when the topic was extensively studied in part because of the waves of youth protest in response to political actions by the United States, namely the Vietnam War.

Juvenile–Police Interaction: Schools

Schools are a common point of interaction between juveniles and police. Increasingly, as explained later in this chapter, schools are relying on school resource officers (SROs) to provide security and stability within the school environment. The number of SROs has increased exponentially following the rash of school shootings following Columbine in 1999 (Stone & Spencer, 2011). While SROs can increase positive interactions between juveniles and police in schools, they can also increase arrest rates of youth for minor behavioral issues and can lead to increased distrust between youth and police.

Police and schools are conscious of wanting to facilitate more positive interactions between police and juveniles in addition to relying on police to respond to safety and crime issues. The Drug Abuse Resistance Education (DARE) program, developed jointly by the Los Angeles Police Department and the Los Angeles school system, is a nationally known school-based intervention. Because drug use and experimentation begin in the teenage years for many people, DARE aimed to reach juveniles as early as possible with accurate information about the health and criminal justice effects of illicit drug use. The program is taught like a class, with a veteran police officer serving as the primary instructor. While the effectiveness of DARE has been both affirmed and challenged, it appears to be widely liked by police, school officials, parents, and youth. The collaborative aspect of DARE, strengthening relationships between schools and police, is often highlighted as a positive aspect of the program. In addition, youth are able to view police officers as a resource (Donnermeyer, 1998; Sigler & Talley, 1995).

Juvenile–Police Interaction: Gangs

In 2009, the National Youth Gang Survey estimated there were 28,100 gangs in the United States and over 731,000 gang members (Gang-related violence . . . , 2011). This number represents an increase in the number of gangs and gang members nationally, despite overall rates of crime decreasing.

Juveniles join gangs for many reasons, including lack of social support, wanting to connect to others, and boredom (Office of Juvenile Justice & Delinquency Prevention, 2010). Police intervention and prevention efforts may prove challenging because officers may be viewed as interested only in arresting gang members, as opposed to truly intervening to stop negative gang activity. In addition, officers may be considered as outsiders and not in touch with youth and/or gang issues, and may be viewed with suspicion due to a history of police brutality in many of the same communities where gangs originate and thrive (Office of Juvenile Justice & Delinquency Prevention, 2010).

Several best practices for police and communities in dealing with gang violence have been identified. The Office of Juvenile Justice and Delinquency Prevention's National Comprehensive Gang Model suggests that "community mobilization, opportunities provision, social interaction, suppression, and organizational change and development" are necessary to prevent and control gang activities locally. This model has been tested in both rural and urban environments (Office of Juvenile Justice & Delinquency Prevention, 2010).

Juvenile Attitudes Toward the Police

Youth are socialized in communities that may not hold police officers in high regard due to a number of social and political factors. Juvenile attitudes toward police vary depending largely based on race, socioeconomic status, gender, and prior interactions with police officers.

Research suggests that African American and Hispanic communities endure excessive force, disproportionate stops and arrests, and an increased police presence and scrutiny within communities. While youth as a group have a more negative view of police than other demographic groups (adults, the elderly), attitudes of White youth, African American youth, and Hispanic youth differ greatly. Positive interactions with police appear to buffer against or neutralize negative attitudes toward police for White youth, but positive interactions with police had little impact on how police were viewed by African American and Hispanic youth (Bartollas, 2006; Jefferis, Butcher, & Hanley, 2011).

Higher police presence in low-income areas is well documented, although the reasons are both altruistic and perhaps less so. The connection between crime rates and income has been well documented; however, the assumption that crime happens more often in low-income areas leads to a cycle of increased police presence and monitoring that naturally increases arrest rates and crime rates. Poor youth of all races have a more negative opinion of police, and this is mirrored in the adult population. The nexus of race and class should not be ignored, as being African American or Hispanic and low income suggests that police brutality is more likely (Messner et al., 2001).

Improving relationships between police officers and juveniles is a complicated task. The number of interactions one has with police appears to negatively influence how police are viewed by youth and adults alike. This may suggest that one best practice is to reduce police contact, reserving such contact to when it is necessary. This may not be feasible in all communities where police contact is a regular occurrence, particularly communities with high crime rates and illicit activities. It does suggest that respect and support, and intentionally reducing harassing behaviors on the part of police officers, are important in all interactions between juveniles and police. Implementing best practices associated with schools and with gangs may additionally curb or neutralize negative attitudes juveniles have toward police. Attitudes about police are formed and often times crystalized as juveniles; negative attitudes toward police in youth likely carry (or worsen) into adulthood (Meyer & Reppucci, 2007).

■ *Miranda* and Juveniles

Juveniles in juvenile court delinquency proceedings do not have all the same constitutional rights afforded to adults by the U.S. Constitution; in fact, prior to the mid-1960s juveniles essentially had no due process rights. However, during the past four decades there has been a greater emphasis on procedural rights in the court, thus affording juveniles more rights in relation to due process while at the same time moving the court further toward a traditional adult court and away from the original rehabilitative structural intent of the juvenile court. The U.S. Supreme Court has recognized that juveniles have many of the constitutional due process rights afforded adult defendants: the right to counsel, the right to notice of the charges against them, the right to confront and cross-examine witnesses, and the right against self-incrimination (*In re Gault*, 387 U.S. 1, 1967). Juveniles also have the right to have the alleged offense proven beyond a reasonable doubt (*In re Winship*, 397 U.S. 358, 368, 1970). Although these court cases were instrumental in the "restructuring" of the juvenile court, it should lead one to ask this: What about protection when dealing with the police? To understand the relationship between juveniles and the police, it is important to understand the impact of U.S. Supreme Court decisions in constraining police behavior in their encounters with citizens. When discussing U.S. Supreme Court decisions affecting juveniles, one will typically read about the cases discussed throughout this book (i.e. *Kent, Gault, Winship*). However, the most important U.S. Supreme court case affecting the rights of juveniles is actually a case involving an adult. In 1966, in *Miranda v. Arizona*, the Supreme Court issued a ruling that has forever changed the interactions between the police and citizens.

On March 13, 1963, Ernesto Miranda was arrested based on circumstantial evidence linking him to the kidnapping and rape of a 17-year-old female 10 days earlier. After two hours of interrogation by police officers, Miranda signed a confession to the rape charge on forms that included him making a statement of full confession that was voluntarily and of his own free will, with no threats, coercion, or promises of immunity, and with full knowledge of his legal rights, and understanding any statement made may be used against him.

However, at no time was Miranda told of his right to counsel, and he was not advised of his right to remain silent or that his statements would be used against him during the interrogation before being presented with the form on which he was asked to write out the confession he had already given orally. At trial, when prosecutors offered Miranda's written confession as evidence, his court-appointed attorney, Alvin Moore, objected that because of these facts, the confession was not truly voluntary and should be excluded. Moore's objection was overruled, and based on this confession and other evidence, Miranda was convicted of rape and kidnapping and sentenced to 20 to 30 years imprisonment on each charge, with sentences to run concurrently. Moore filed Miranda's appeal to the Arizona Supreme Court, claiming that Miranda's confession was not fully voluntary and should not have been admitted into the court proceedings. The Arizona Supreme Court affirmed the trial court's decision to admit the confession (*State of Arizona v. Miranda*, 1965). In affirming, the Arizona

Supreme Court emphasized heavily the fact that Miranda did not specifically request an attorney (*State of Arizona v. Miranda*, 1965).

Miranda's new attorney, John Flynn, appealed the case to the U.S. Supreme Court. He asked the court to decide whether the confession of a poorly educated, mentally ill, and indigent defendant not told of his right to counsel, which Miranda never requested, could be admitted into evidence based on the absence of counsel during the initial confession.

On June 13, 1966, Chief Justice Earl Warren delivered the opinion of the Court, ruling that due to the coercive nature of the custodial interrogation by police (Warren cited several police training manuals that had not been provided in the arguments), no confession could be admissible under the Fifth Amendment self-incrimination clause and Sixth Amendment right to an attorney unless a suspect had been made aware of his or her rights and the suspect had then waived them:

> The person in custody must, prior to interrogation, be clearly informed that he has the right to remain silent, and that anything he says will be used against him in court; he must be clearly informed that he has the right to consult with a lawyer and to have the lawyer with him during interrogation, and that, if he is indigent, a lawyer will be appointed to represent him. (*Miranda v. U.S.*, 1966)

Thus, Miranda's conviction was overturned. The Court also made clear what had to happen if the suspect chose to exercise his or her rights:

> If the individual indicates in any manner, at any time prior to or during questioning, that he wishes to remain silent, the interrogation must cease... If the individual states that he wants an attorney, the interrogation must cease until an attorney is present. At that time, the individual must have an opportunity to confer with the attorney and to have him present during any subsequent questioning. (*Miranda v. U.S.*, 1966)

Thus, the court had now set forth the idea that once an individual was taken into custody, the privilege against self-incrimination is jeopardized and that procedural safeguards must be employed to protect this privilege. This case in turn dramatically altered how the police were now able to deal with not only adult citizens, but juveniles as well.

■ Decision Making and Processing of Juvenile Offenders

Police Discretion with Juveniles

Police discretion is a critical component of police authority. This fundamental power to choose whom to engage and to what degree grants police officers the ability to foster positive community relations and build neighborhoods.

Conversely, police discretion can exacerbate the gaps that exist between the police and the policed.

Police discretion is not well defined in the scholarly literature. One definition offered is official action taken by a criminal justice official based upon that official's judgment about the best course of action (Cole & Smith, 1998). Rather than rely on a singular defining concept, police departments have developed guidelines that help officers to know when discretion is acceptable, and under what circumstances (Kelling, 1999). It is generally accepted that the decision-making process can be influenced by many factors, including value judgments and departmental policies (Cole & Smith, 1998). Regardless, police have great autonomy in making street-level decisions.

Police have considerable autonomy when handling juvenile offenders, including reprimand and release, transportation to a juvenile detention facility, and referral to a juvenile court. While most contact with juvenile offenders is informal, this represents the first contact with the juvenile justice system for juvenile offenders. A 2002 study found that in 76% of juveniles who were taken into custody by the police, nonviolent offenses were the reason. Furthermore, only 23% of all juveniles who came into the juvenile justice system were brought in by police contact; others were brought in by court referrals or through agency contact (Myers, 2002). While most of the juveniles who are arrested for nonviolent offenses are brought in by police, the vast majority of juveniles enter detention through other avenues.

Police discretion with juveniles is likely to be influenced by a number of factors. For example, one study found that while most police interactions with juveniles deal with minor law violations, as the seriousness of the legal consequences increases so does the probability of arrest (Black & Reiss, 1970). Other studies have shown that race and gender play a key role in the use of discretion: police officers are more likely to make an arrest when the juvenile is a racial minority or when the offender is male (Lundman, Sykes, & Clark, 1978; Wolfgang, 1972).

The use of police discretion that favors contact with racial minorities and with males has led some to conclude that the police abuse their power. A 2007 report by Huizinga and colleagues showed that police officers made contact and court referrals for minority juveniles at a significantly higher rate than for White juveniles, and this difference could not be explained by differences in offending behavior. This pattern of disproportionate minority contact through the use of police discretion has led some to label it "racial profiling." Researchers have found that African American adults tend to report more negative encounters with the police and perceive encounters with the police based solely upon race more often than other groups (Lundman & Kaufman, 2003). Not surprisingly, youth who experience negative contact with the police hold negative perceptions about law enforcement (Rusinko, Johnson, & Hornung, 1978), and minority youth are more likely to have a negative view of the police (Hurst & Frank, 2000).

Police–Juvenile Interactions

The one-on-one interaction of police with juvenile offenders is an important factor in how discretion is utilized. The juvenile suspect's attitude has a profound impact on the officer's decision to arrest. Many juveniles often attempt to appeal to their friends' sense of boldness rather than being respectful to police. This means some will push the boundaries of acceptable behavior in the presence of law enforcement, even after being warned to deescalate their behaviors. The presence of other juveniles exacerbates the seriousness of police interactions with juveniles, since many choose the adoration of their peers over obeying orders from law enforcement. This bold attitude will often result in arrest.

Research confirms that deference to the police among juveniles results in fewer arrests and fewer juvenile court referrals (Lundman, Sykes, & Clark, 1978; Piliavin & Briar, 1964). However, police departments vary considerably in how they handle juvenile interactions. Many allow officers to decide which juveniles will be referred and which will be arrested based upon the type and severity of the crime. Others provide specific guidelines for officers to follow (Klein, 1970). This variation in police–juvenile interactions may be a response to external pressures placed upon individual police departments.

Police departments are charged with alleviating crime and responding to the unique demands of the communities in which they are situated. Since there is considerable variability in the demographic makeup of communities, there must also be considerable variability in the problems faced by these communities. Thus, each police department is responding to the demands of its particular community. For example, a neighborhood with a serious youth gang problem may respond with a "get tough" policy that includes more juvenile court referrals and more arrests. In contrast, the police in a community with less juvenile delinquency may choose to employ greater discretion when interacting with juvenile suspects.

As previously mentioned, police interactions with juveniles influence their perceptions of law enforcement, and those perceptions frequently last into adulthood. Many juveniles' only exposure to law enforcement is negative— usually when a friend or family member is contacted by a police officer, and occasionally when they themselves are contacted. Therefore police officers must interact with juveniles in a positive manner whenever possible.

School Resource Officers

Until the 1990s, the presence of uniformed law enforcement in public schools was relatively rare. However, the increase in school violence, especially gun-related violence, led to the implementation of student resource officers (SROs). The SRO is an extension of community policing efforts where the police respond to the unique demands of the community and are seen as a positive, not negative, presence. The National Association of School Resource Officers has developed the "triad model" to describe the SRO's duties, which include incorporating the responsibilities of law enforcement officer, counselor, and educator (Burke, 2001). SROs must maintain law and order in the school, help discipline unruly individuals, and maintain the safety of all students. Additionally, SROs are expected to be good role models, to counsel students on behavior issues, and to instruct them on good citizenship and issues regarding the law (Benigni, 2004).

Despite its intent, SROs have not functioned to increase positive perceptions of police or to decrease juvenile–police interactions: quite the contrary. One study found that students' views on criminal offending and the police were not significantly affected by the presence of an SRO (Jackson, 2002). This result directly contradicts the purpose of having a SRO, which is to decrease crime and change perceptions about police. Further research has demonstrated that the presence of an SRO leads to increased arrests, especially for disorderly conduct, when compared to schools without an SRO (Theriot, 2009).

The presence of uniformed police officers has also been labeled the "criminalization" of school discipline. Where students were once paddled for their indiscretions, they are now referred to juvenile court. Where they were once put in the corner for misbehaving, they are now placed into handcuffs. While this example may seem far-fetched, the presence of SROs increases the arrest and referral rate for both serious (drug and weapons offenses) and non-serious violent crime (Na & Gottfredson, 2011). The increased use of zero-tolerance policies, metal detectors, and SROs indicates a shift from the traditional, discretionary use of school discipline to a reactionary, control approach to school discipline, which is oriented in the law enforcement paradigm.

The use of SROs in public schools, the increased implementation of zero-tolerance policies, and the mingling of education with law enforcement has led to an increase in the structural inequalities already faced by minority youths. School discipline, exclusive of any law enforcement component, is tougher on minority youth than non-minority youth (Mendez & Knoff, 2003; Monroe, 2005). Schools with a greater percentage of Black youths use stronger punitive responses and greater control measures to punish students than schools with fewer Black youths (Welch & Payne, 2010). A 2007 article in the *Chicago Tribune* summarized the issue of disproportionate minority punishment by saying, "There's more at stake than just a few bad marks in a student's school record" (Witt).

■ Juvenile–Police Contact: Dispositions

The doctrine of *parens patriae* was developed during a time when juvenile criminals were brought before judges in the same manner as adult criminals. Without any special consideration for their development, juveniles were often convicted and placed in jails with much older, adult criminals. It wasn't until the turn of the 20th century and the development of a separate juvenile court system, underlined by *parens patriae*, that suspected juvenile offenders were treated separately from adults in the criminal justice system (Pisciotta, 1982). The doctrine of *parens patriae* allows the state to function as the guardian of a minor to protect the public interest and to guard the interests of said minor (Gifis, 2003). This led to the use of a rehabilitative approach with juvenile offenders rather than the punitive approach common in the adult criminal system (Smallheer, 1999–2000).

Parens patriae extends beyond the confines of the courtroom to police contact with juveniles. Still, many contend that, as juvenile crime has become increasingly politicized, the juvenile justice system has shifted away from the doctrine of *parens patriae* toward a doctrine of social control. This is reflected in the increasing number of juvenile court referrals for minor, nonviolent offenses (Puzzanchera, Adams, & Sickmund, 2011) and the increased frequency of juveniles being tried as adults (Hartney, 2006; Young & Gainsborough, 2000). With an emphasis on controlling behavior and reducing criminality, the doctrine of social control shifts back toward punitive responses to juvenile delinquency.

Police who encounter suspected juvenile delinquents must make decisions about how to handle delinquent behavior. There are generally five approaches to handling suspected delinquent behavior: warning and release to the community, formal reprimand, referral and release to a diversion agency, juvenile court referral, or arrest and detention. The following sections will discuss each individually.

Warning and Release

Warning and release to the community is the least severe sanction applied to juveniles, usually applied for minor infractions. Usually, the youth receives a warning from the officer on the street before releasing him or her. The officer may also choose to detain the juvenile for questioning that results in warning and release.

Formal Reprimand

In more severe cases, juveniles may be brought back to the police station by an officer and given a formal reprimand. A formal reprimand for delinquent behavior means that a record of the behavior is made by the police. Furthermore, the juvenile's parents are notified about the behavior and the juvenile is generally released to a parent.

Referral to Diversion Agency

In some cases, the police refer juveniles to a criminal diversion program, which is an intervention tasked with redirecting behavior and reducing delinquency.

Some police departments staff their own diversion programs, such as the Dallas Police Department's First Offender Program. This program helps connect families with community resources to prevent problem behaviors and it intervenes when the juvenile has committed a Class A or B misdemeanor or State Jail Felony to divert the juvenile from jail time, with the intent of reducing repeat offenders (Dallas Police Department, 2012). In other cases, the police may refer the juvenile to a community agency for diversion, such as the YMCA or Big Brothers/Big Sisters.

Repeated study has shown that diversion significantly reduces the incidence of arrest (Wilson & Hoge, 2012). However, a substantial gender bias exists, with more females being referred to diversion programs than males, even while controlling for severity of behavior (Alder, 1984). While females may be the primary recipients of diversion, repeated study has demonstrated it is a cost-effective form of intervention (Patrick & Marsh, 2005; Small, Reynolds, O'Connor, & Cooney, 2005)

Juvenile Court Referral

Referral to juvenile court is a process whereby a police officer issues a citation to the youth in question for having committed an egregious violation of the law or for repeatedly engaging in delinquent behavior. After referral, an intake counselor affiliated with the court decides whether a petition should be filed and the juvenile should appear before the judge.

Evidence has been advanced that the greater incidence of minority juveniles appearing before juvenile court judges is not due to higher minority crime; rather, police make contact with minority juveniles more often and refer them more readily to juvenile court than their non-minority counterparts (Huizinga et al., 2007). In 2009, law enforcement was the primary source of juvenile court referrals, accounting for 83% of all referrals. Table 7.1 illustrates some of the characteristics of referred delinquency cases from 2009.

Table 7.1   **Characteristics of Delinquency Cases Referred, 2009**

Individual Characteristics	
Less than 16 years old	52%
Female	28%
White	64%
Most Serious Offense	
Person	24%
Property	38%
Drugs	11%
Public Order	27%

Table 7.2   **Juvenile Arrest Statistics—Violent Crime and Property Crime, 2009**

Most Serious Offense	Juvenile Arrest	Female	Less than 15 y.o.	White
Murder	9%	7%	9%	40%
Rape	14%	2%	32%	65%
Robbery	25%	10%	18%	31%
Aggravated assault	12%	25%	30%	56%
Burglary	25%	11%	27%	61%
Larceny-theft	24%	45%	28%	65%
Motor-vehicle theft	24%	17%	30%	54%
Arson	44%	13%	59%	77%

Arrest and Detention

The most serious disposition is arrest and detention. A police officer issues a citation to refer a juvenile to juvenile court and, rather than return the youth to his or her parents, takes him or her to a juvenile detention facility. Juveniles are taken to detention when the police officer believes that they are a danger to themselves or to the community, or if they lack supervision. Further assessment is generally conducted by intake workers at the detention facility to decide if the juvenile can be returned to his or her parents or if he or she must stay at the facility. Table 7.2 provides an overview of juvenile arrest statistics for 2009, with data from the Office of Juvenile Justice & Delinquency Prevention.

While the number of White youths arrested is higher, the proportion of minority youth arrested and incarcerated far exceeds the proportion of non-minority youth. Disproportionate minority contact and confinement have been the subject of much intellectual research and debate (Kempf-Leonard, 2007). Early scholarly efforts attempted to isolate the individual factors that increased minority youths' propensity to engage in criminal behavior (Hindelang, 1978). However, later research efforts have demonstrated a systematic bias against minority youth on behalf of law enforcement. Police officers make more contact with minority youths and make more referrals to juvenile court for minority youth, even when the type and severity of offending behavior is accounted for (Huizinga et al., 2007).

Conclusion

The front line of defense in the juvenile justice system's battle against juvenile delinquency continues to be the police. The police are the front-line intermediaries between schools, families, neighborhoods, and juvenile delinquents, and they are still the most common referral source of juveniles to the juvenile justice system.

Historically the police have had an uneasy relationship with juveniles, but through time this has led to greater discretion being used when police come in contact with juveniles accused of delinquent acts. The use of discretion may result in the release in the case of a minor incident, referral, or arrest in the case of more serious offenses.

Police discretion and the responses to juvenile offenders depend largely on the various factors that we have laid out and on state laws and departmental procedures that influence and guide officers' actions. As several studies have indicated, personal bias and predispositions will also play a part in how the police interact and use discretion when confronted with a juvenile delinquent. However, whatever the situation and factors presented, the police have a great deal of discretion with juveniles.

The processing of juveniles continues to be a point of concern and even contention. Should juveniles be treated as adults—photographed, fingerprinted, and interrogated—when they are detained, or should the "non-criminal" ideals of the earlier, pre-1960s juvenile court be applied? Juvenile processing will continue to evolve, and while not completely like the adult system, many jurisdictions are allowing greater police latitude in identification, processing, and recordkeeping for juvenile suspects than any time in the recent past.

One of the areas where we have seen police–juvenile contact changing is in the area of prevention-based programs with at-risk juveniles. Historically police involvement with juveniles has been at the point when the police need to "enforce" the law—that is to say, an incident has occurred and some type of action needs to be taken against the suspect. However, several departments are moving toward a greater emphasis on community involvement, such as youth-focused community policing initiatives and other such types of preventive programs that afford at-risk youth a positive involvement with the police.

If this movement becomes more institutionalized in police departments throughout the country, officers may be able to devote more of their time to delinquency prevention and intervention efforts than in the past. The results could be enormous, as cases involving juveniles may not be seen merely as a nuisance but rather as an integral part of police work that adds to the mission rather than detracting from it.

References

Alder, C. (1984). Gender bias in juvenile diversion. *Crime & Delinquency, 30*(3), 400–414.

Bartollas, C. (2006). *Juvenile delinquency* (7th ed.). Boston: Pearson.

Benigni, M. D. (2004). Need for school resource officers. *FBI Law Enforcement Bulletin, 73*(5), 22–24.

Black, D. J., & Reiss, Jr., A. J. (1970). Police control of juveniles. *American Sociological Review, 35*(1), 63–77.

Burke, S. (2001). The advantages of a school resource officer. *Law and Order, 49*(9), 73–75.

Cole, G. F., & Smith, C. E. (1998). *The American system of criminal justice.* Belmont, CA: Wadsworth.

Dallas Police Department. (2012). First Offender Program. Retrieved from: http://www.dallaspolice.net/divisions/youthoperations/firstOffenderProgram.html

Donnermeyer, J. F. (1998). Educator perceptions of the D.A.R.E. officer. *Journal of Alcohol & Drug Education, 44*(1), 1.

Gang-Related Violence Persists, Despite Large Declines in Overall Crime Rate. (2011). *Criminal Justice Research Review, 13*(2), 23.

Gifis, S. H. (2003). *Law dictionary* (5th ed.). Hauppauge, NY: Barron's Educational Series, Inc.

Hartney, C. (2006). *Youth under age 18 in the adult criminal justice system.* Oakland, CA: National Council on Crime and Delinquency.

Hindelang, M. J. (1978). Race and involvement in common law personal crimes. *American Sociological Review, 43*(February), 93–109.

Huizinga, D., Thornberry, T. P., Knight, K. E., Lovegrove, P., Loeber, R., Hill, K., & Farrington, D. P. (2007). *Disproportionate minority contact in the juvenile justice system: A study of differential minority arrest/referral to court in three cities* (NCJ 219743). Rockville, MD: National Institute of Justice/NCJRS.

Hurst, Y. G., & Frank, J. (2000). How kids view cops: The nature of juvenile attitudes toward the police. *Journal of Criminal Justice, 28*(3), 189–202.

Jackson, A. (2002). Police-school resource officers' and students' perception of the police and offending. *Policing: An International Journal of Police Strategies & Management, 25*(3), 631–650.

Jefferis, E., Butcher, F., & Hanley, D. (2011). Measuring perceptions of police use of force. *Police Practice & Research, 12*(1), 81–96.

Kelling, G. L. (1999). *"Broken windows" and police discretion.* National Institute of Justice Research Report. Retrieved from: https://www.ncjrs.gov/pdffiles1/nij/178259.pdf

Kempf-Leonard, K. (2007). Minority youths and juvenile justice: Disproportionate minority contact after nearly 20 years of reform efforts. *Youth Violence and Juvenile Justice, 5*(1), 71–87.

Klein, M. W. (1970). *Police processing of juvenile offenders: Toward the development of juvenile system rates.* Los Angeles: Public Systems Research Institute, University of Southern California.

Lief, M. S., & Caldwell, H. M. (2006). You have the right to remain silent. *American Heritage, 57*(4), 48–59.

Lundman, R. J., & Kaufman, R. L. (2003). Driving while Black: Effects of race, ethnicity, and gender on citizen self-reports of traffic stops and police actions. *Criminology, 41*(1), 195–220.

Lundman, R. J., Sykes, R. E., & Clark, J. P. (1978). Police control of juveniles: A replication. *Journal of Research in Crime & Delinquency, 15*(1), 74–91.

Mendez, L. M. R., & Knopf, H. M. (2003). Who gets suspended from school and why: A demographic analysis of schools and disciplinary infractions in a large school district. *Education and Treatment of Children, 26*(1), 30–51.

Messner, S. F., Raffalovich, L. E., & McMillan, R. (2001). Economic deprivation and changes in homicide arrest rates for white and black youths, 1967–1998: A national time series analysis. *Criminology, 39*(3), 591–613.

Meyer, J. R., & Reppucci, N. (2007). Police practices and perceptions regarding juvenile interrogation and interrogative suggestibility. *Behavioral Sciences & The Law, 25*(6), 757–780.

Miranda v. Arizona, 384 U.S. 436 (1966).

Monroe, C. R. (2005). Why are "bad boys" always black? Causes of disproportionality in school discipline and recommendations for change. *The Clearing House, 79*(1), 45–50.

Myers, S. (2002). *Police encounters with juvenile suspects: Explaining the use of authority and provision of support. Unpublished doctoral dissertation*, State University of New York, Albany.

Na, C., & Gottfredson, D.C. (2011). Police officers in schools: Effects on school crime and the processing of offending behaviors. *Justice Quarterly*, 1–32.

Office of Juvenile Justice & Delinquency Prevention (2010). *Best practices to address community gang problems: OJJDP's comprehensive gang model.* Washington, DC: National Youth Gang Center.

Patrick, S., & Marsh, R. (2005). Juvenile diversion: Results of a 3-year experimental study. *Criminal Justice Policy Review, 16*(1), 59–73.

Piliavin, I., & Briar, S. (1964). Police encounters with juveniles. *American Journal of Sociology, 70*(2), 206–214.

Pisciotta, A. W. (1982). Saving the children: The promise and practice of parens patriae, 1838–98. *Crime & Delinquency, 28*(3), 410–425.

Puzzanchera, C., & Adams, B. (2011). *Juvenile arrests 2009.* Washington DC: Office of Juvenile Justice and Delinquency Prevention.

Puzzanchera, C. Adams, B., & Hockenberry, S. (2012). *Juvenile court statistics 2009.* Pittsburgh, PA: National Center for Juvenile Justice.

Puzzanchera, C., Adams, B., & Sickmund, M. (2011). *Juvenile court statistics 2008.* Pittsburgh, PA: National Center for Juvenile Justice.

Rusinko, W. T., Johnson, K. W., & Hornung, C. A. (1978). The importance of police contact in the formulation of youths' attitudes toward police. *Journal of Criminal Justice, 6*(1), 53–67.

Schmalleger, F., & Bartollas, C. (2008). *Juvenile delinquency.* Boston: Pearson.

Sigler, T., & Talley, B. (1995). Drug Abuse Resistance Education program effectiveness. *American Journal of Police, 14*(3/4), 111–121.

Small, S. A., Reynolds, A. J., O'Connor, C., & Cooney, S. M. (2005). *What works, Wisconsin: What science tells us about cost-effective programs for juvenile delinquency prevention.* A Report to the Wisconsin Governor's Juvenile Justice Commission and the Wisconsin Office of Justice Assistance, Retrieved from: http://www.uwex.edu/ces/flp/families/whatworkswisconsin.pdf

Smallheer, R. L. (1999–2000). Sentence blending and the promise of rehabilitation: Bringing the juvenile justice system full circle. *Hofstra Law Review, 28,* 259–266.

Springer, D. W., & Roberts, A. R. (2011). *Juvenile justice and delinquency.* Boston: Pearson.

State of Arizona v. Miranda, 401 P.2d 721 (1965).

Stone, W. E., & Spencer, D. J. (2011). Enhancing an active shooter school emergency plan using ambient materials and school resource officers. *Southwest Journal of Criminal Justice, 7*(3), 295–306.

Theriot, M. T. (2009). School resource officers and the criminalization of student behavior. *Journal of Criminal Justice, 37*(3), 280–287.

Welch, K., & Payne, A.A. (2010). Racial threat and punitive school discipline. *Social Problems, 57*(1), 25–48.

Wilson, H. A., & Hoge, R. D. (2012). The effect of youth diversion programs on recidivism: A meta-analytic review. *Criminal Justice and Behavior*, doi:10.1177/0093854812451089

Witt, H. (2007). School discipline tougher on African Americans. *Chicago Tribune,* Sept. 24, 2007. Retrieved from: www.chicagotribune.com/news/nationworld/chi-070924discipline,0,22104.story?coll=chi_tab01_layout

Wolfgang, M. E. (1972). Violent crime in a birth cohort. In J. Susman (Ed.), *Crime and justice,* 1–11. New York: AMS Press, Inc.

Young, M. C., & Gainsborough, J. (2000). *Prosecuting juveniles in adult court: An assessment of trends and consequences.* Report of The Sentencing Project, Washington DC. Retrieved from: http://www.prisonpolicy.org/scans/sp/juvenile.pdf

8

Juveniles' Competence and Procedural Rights in Juvenile Court

Barry C. Feld

■ Introduction

Two competing images of youth influence juvenile justice policies. Policymakers sometimes describe young people as vulnerable children who need special safeguards to protect themselves from their own immaturity. At other times, they characterize youths as mature and responsible and treat them like adults. These competing perceptions of adolescents affect the procedural safeguards extended to them and raise questions about their competence to exercise rights and to participate in the justice system.

Progressive reformers envisioned a juvenile court judge who made dispositions in a child's "best interests." Juvenile courts separated children from adult offenders, treated them rather than punished them, and rejected the procedural safeguards of criminal prosecutions. They maximized judicial discretion to rehabilitate delinquent youths. Because delinquency proceedings focused primarily on a child's background and future welfare rather than the crime alleged, juvenile courts dispensed with formal procedures such as lawyers, juries, and rules of evidence (Feld, 1999; Tanenhaus, 2004).

In 1967, the Supreme Court in *In re Gault* (387 U.S. 1 [1967]) began a "due process revolution" that substantially transformed the juvenile court from a social welfare agency into a more formal, legal institution (Feld, 1984, 1988a, 1999; Scott & Steinberg, 2008). Among other safeguards, *Gault* granted delinquents a right to counsel and the Fifth Amendment privilege against self-incrimination, and initiated a procedural convergence between juvenile and criminal courts. Subsequent decisions further emphasized the criminal aspects of delinquency proceedings. *In re Winship* (397 U.S. 358 [1970]) held that the state must prove delinquency "beyond a reasonable doubt" rather than by the lower "preponderance of the evidence" standard in civil cases. *Breed v. Jones* (421 U.S. 519 [1975]) posited a functional equivalence between delinquency and criminal trials and held that the Fifth Amendment's double jeopardy clause barred criminal re-prosecution of a youth after a judge had adjudicated him or her delinquent. However, *McKeiver v. Pennsylvania* (403 U.S. 528 [1971]) declined to give delinquents all criminal procedural safeguards and denied a constitutional right to a jury trial. Although Progressive reformers viewed young people as immature and irresponsible and rejected procedural safeguards, *Gault* viewed youths as competent to exercise legal rights and to participate in the adversarial system.

Judicial and legislative responses to the Court's due process decisions fostered a procedural and substantive convergence between juvenile and criminal courts. Emphasizing procedural formality shifted juvenile courts' initial focus from assessing a youth's "real needs" to proving he or she committed a crime and made the connection between criminal law violations and sanctions explicit. Procedural safeguards allowed juvenile courts to depart from a purely rehabilitative model and impose more punitive dispositions.

By the end of the 20th century, states had adopted harsh, get-tough policies that equated the crimes of adolescents with those of adults—"adult crime, adult time." In the early 1990s, states revised laws to transfer more and younger juveniles to criminal courts, and to punish more severely delinquents who remained in juvenile courts (Torbet et al., 1996). These changes replaced the view of children as immature and irresponsible with one in which the law regarded them as responsible and adult-like offenders (Feld, 2003b). The increased punitiveness of both the juvenile and criminal justice systems over the past quarter-century raises urgent questions about youths' competence to exercise legal rights.

The John D. and Catherine T. MacArthur Foundation responded to the harsh policies that equated youths and adults and sponsored research to identify developmental differences that bear on youths' ability to exercise legal rights (Scott & Steinberg, 2008). The research reports that by age 16 or 17, adolescents possess cognitive abilities similar to adults, but their judgment and self-control do *not* correspond with those of adults until their 20s. Moreover, younger and mid-adolescent youths exhibit substantial deficits in understanding and competence that affect their ability to exercise or waive *Miranda* rights and the right to counsel and to participate in legal proceedings.

Despite developmental differences between adolescents and adults, the Court and most states do not provide youths with additional procedural safeguards to protect them from their immaturity and vulnerability. Instead, states use adult legal standards to gauge juveniles' competence to stand trial and to waive *Miranda* and the right to counsel. Because developmental immaturity impairs youths' competence to exercise rights, formal legal equality results in practical inequality. By contrast, when states have the option to provide delinquents with procedural safeguards comparable with criminal defendants such as a jury trial, they use less effective juvenile court procedures that provide the state with an advantage and make it easier to convict a youth. Moreover, states then use those procedurally deficient delinquency convictions to enhance criminal sentences and to impose collateral consequences.

This chapter examines research on youths' ability to exercise rights and its implications for juvenile court practice; youths' competence to stand trial; police interrogation of juveniles; access to counsel; and the right to a jury trial. It compares and contrasts juvenile and adult criminal procedures and the "law on the books" versus the "law in action" in juvenile courts. Part I reviews developmental psychological research on adolescents' competence to exercise rights. Part II assays youths' adjudicative competence to stand trial. Part III analyzes juveniles' ability to exercise *Miranda* rights, contrasting the legal standards with psychological research on juveniles' competence, and highlighting their vulnerability in the interrogation room. Part IV examines juveniles' competence to waive the right to counsel and the impact of waiver on delivery of legal services. Part V describes *McKeiver's* denial to juveniles of a constitutional right to a jury trial and analyzes why that makes it easier to convict delinquents than criminals and how states' use of delinquency convictions to enhance criminal sentences compounds that procedural disparity. The chapter concludes with policy recommendations to address juvenile courts' chronic procedural deficiencies.

■ Adolescent Competence and Procedural Justice

Created in response to the get-tough policies, in the mid-1990s the John D. and Catherine T. MacArthur Foundation sponsored a decade-long interdisciplinary network on Adolescent Development and Juvenile Justice (ADJJ) to study juveniles' decision making, judgment, adjudicative competence, and culpability (Scott & Steinberg, 2008; http://www.adjj.org). Research on competence focused on how adolescents think, their decision-making capacities, and how their limitations affect their ability to participate in the justice systems. The ADJJ research reported a disjunction between youths' cognitive abilities and their judgment. Even though adolescents by age 16 exhibit intellectual and cognitive abilities comparable with adults, they do not develop mature judgment, ability to exercise self-control, and competence to make adult-quality decisions until their early 20s.

Children Are Different: Law and Developmental Psychology

In 2005 the Supreme Court in *Roper v. Simmons* (543 U.S. 551) barred states from executing youths for crimes committed prior to 18 years of age. *Roper* concluded that changes in state statutes and jury practices reflected a national consensus against executing juveniles. The justices also conducted an independent proportionality analysis and concluded that youths' immature judgment, susceptibility to negative peer influences, and transitory personality development reduced their culpability and barred the most severe sentence. In 2010, the Court in *Graham v. Florida* (130 S. Ct. 2011) extended *Roper's* diminished responsibility rationale and prohibited states from imposing life without parole (LWOP) sentences on youths convicted of non-homicide offenses. In 2012, the Court in *Miller v. Alabama* (132 S. Ct. 2455) and *Jackson v. Hobbs* used *Roper* and *Graham's* diminished responsibility rationale to bar *mandatory* LWOP sentences for youths convicted of murder. All three decisions affirmed that "children are different" from adults and do not deserve as harsh punishment for their crimes. They rested on the same developmental premises that immature judgment and limited self-control cause youth to act impulsively and without full appreciation of consequences, reduce their culpability, and compromise their competence. Greater susceptibility than adults to social influences also affects youths' understanding of and competence to exercise legal rights.

Developmental psychologists study how children's thinking and behavior change as they mature. The ADJJ research distinguishes between youths' cognitive abilities and their maturity of judgment (www.adjj.org; Feld, 2008; Scott & Steinberg, 2008). By mid-adolescence, most youths can distinguish right from wrong and reason similarly to adults (Scott, 1992; Steinberg & Cauffman, 1999; Scott & Steinberg, 2008). For example, youths and adults make informed consent medical decisions similarly (Morse, 1997). However, the ability to make good choices when provided with complete information in a laboratory differs from the ability to make good decisions under stressful conditions with incomplete information (Cauffman & Steinberg, 1995; Steinberg & Cauffman, 1996; Spear, 2000). Emotions influence youths' decision making, and researchers distinguish between conditions of "cold cognition" and "hot cognition" (Aronson, 2007; Dahl, 2004).

Even though adolescents by about 16 years of age exhibit cognitive abilities comparable with adults, they do not develop mature judgment and self-control until their early 20s (Feld, 2008; Scott, Reppucci, & Woolard, 1995; Scott & Steinberg, 2003). Youths' immature judgment results from differences in risk perception, appreciation of future consequences, capacity for self-management, and experience with autonomy (Morse, 1997; Scott & Steinberg, 2003). Youths' poorer decisions reflect differences in knowledge and experience, short-term versus long-term time perspectives, attitude toward risk, and impulsivity, which are normal features of adolescent development (Morse, 1997; Scott & Grisso, 1997; Scott, Reppucci, & Woolard, 1995; Scott & Steinberg, 2003). A person must be able to think ahead, delay gratification, and restrain impulses to exercise good judgment. Adolescents act more impulsively, fail to consider long-term consequences, and engage in riskier behavior than do adults. To a greater extent than adults, adolescents underestimate risks, use a shorter timeframe in their calculus, and emphasize gains rather than losses (Furby & Beyth-Marom, 1992; Grisso, 2000; Scott, 2000). Adolescents possess less information and consider fewer options than do adults (Scott, 2000). Younger teens act more impulsively than do older adolescents or adults.

Youths' risk perception actually *declines* during mid-adolescence and then gradually increases into adulthood: 16- and 17-year-olds perceive fewer risks than do either younger or older research subjects. They are more present-oriented and discount future consequences. They weigh costs and benefits differently than do adults and apply different subjective values to outcomes to their choices (Scott & Steinberg, 2008). Youths view *not* engaging in risky behaviors differently than do adults (Scott, 1992; Scott & Steinberg, 2003, 2008). They crave excitement and heightened sensations—an adrenaline rush (Scott & Grisso, 1997; Spear, 2000). Risk taking and sensation seeking peak around 16 or 17 years of age—the ages when criminal activity increases—and then decline in adulthood. Feelings of invulnerability and immortality heighten these risk proclivities (Furby & Beyth-Marom, 1992).

Neuroscience: Judgment and Impulse Control

The human brain does not mature until the early 20s, and the differences that social scientists observe in youths' and adults' thinking and behavior reflect these developmental features (Dahl, 2004; Maroney, 2009; Scott & Steinberg, 2008; Sowell et al., 2001; Spear, 2000). Adolescents do not have the physiological capacity to exercise adult judgment or control impulses (Dahl, 2004; Gruber & Yurgelun Todd, 2006). Two neurobiological systems underlie youths' propensity for risky behavior. The prefrontal cortex (PFC) of the brain's frontal lobe is responsible for judgment and impulse control, and the limbic system is responsible for emotional and reward-seeking behavior. The PFC operates as the chief executive officer to control higher-level functions such as reasoning, planning, anticipating consequences, and controlling impulses (Aronson, 2009; Kandel et al., 2000). During adolescence and into the early 20s, increased myelination and synaptic pruning of the PFC improves executive functions and reasoning ability.

The limbic system—the amygdala—controls instinctual behavior, such as the fight-or-flight response (Kandel et al., 2000). Adolescents rely more heavily on the limbic system and less heavily on the PFC than do adults (Scott & Steinberg, 2008). During adolescence, the two systems are out of balance: limbic system activity increases, while the prefrontal regulatory system lags behind. Pleasure-seeking and emotional reward responses develop more rapidly than does the system for self-control and self-regulation (Arrendondo, 2003). Youths' impulsive behavior reflects a gut response rather than sober reflection. The neuroscience helps to explain adolescents' impulsive behavior and susceptibility to social influence.

Adolescents' Competence and Legal Standards

Contemporary delinquency proceedings are much more procedurally formal than those envisioned a century ago. Progressive reformers posited a procedurally informal court that acted in the child's best interests. *Gault* granted delinquents the right to counsel and Fifth Amendment privilege against self-incrimination, made delinquency proceedings more formal and complex, and required youths to make difficult legal decisions. Developmental psychologists question whether juveniles possess the cognitive ability, maturity, and judgment necessary to exercise *Miranda* rights during interrogation and to waive counsel, or even the competence to stand trial. The developmental research reviewed previously—impaired judgment, poor self-control, skewed risk-calculus, and short-term time perspective—convincingly indicates that younger and mid-adolescent youths exhibit substantial deficits in understanding and competence compared with adults. Graham (2010) noted how these characteristics adversely affected juveniles' ability to exercise procedural rights and impaired their defense representation:

> [T]he features that distinguish juveniles from adults also put them at a significant disadvantage in criminal proceedings. Juveniles mistrust adults and have limited understandings of the criminal justice system and the roles of the institutional actors within it. They are less likely than adults to work with their lawyers to aid in their defense. Difficulty in weighing long-term consequences; a corresponding impulsiveness; and reluctance to trust defense counsel seen as part of the adult world a rebellious youth rejects, all can lead to poor decisions by one charged with a juvenile offense. These factors are likely to impair the quality of a juvenile defendant's representation. (p. 2032)

Despite clear developmental differences between youths and adults, the Court and most states do not provide additional procedural safeguards to protect juveniles from their own immaturity and vulnerability. Instead, they use adult standards to gauge juveniles' competence to stand trial and to waive *Miranda* rights and counsel.

Competence to Stand Trial

As juvenile courts have become more formal and punitive, analysts increasingly question juveniles' ability to function in complex legal settings with significant penal consequences. To be competent to stand trial, a defendant must have "sufficient present ability to consult with his lawyer with a reasonable degree of rationale understanding [and have a] rational as well as factual understanding of the proceedings against him" and have the capacity "to assist in preparing his defense," (*Drope v. Missouri*, 420 U.S. 162, 1975; *Dusky v. United States*, 362 U.S. 402, 1960). Legal competence to stand trial hinges on a defendant's ability to understand proceedings; to provide, receive, and understand information from counsel; and to make reasonable choices (Bonnie & Grisso, 2000; Grisso, 2000).

Developmental psychologists contend that adolescents' immaturity produces the same deficits of understanding, impairment of judgment, and inability to assist counsel as does severe mental illness or mental retardation (Grisso, 1997b, 2000; Scott & Grisso, 2005). These developmental limitations adversely affect their ability to understand proceedings and to make rational decisions (Grisso, 1997; Scott & Grisso, 2005). Research on competence reports significant age-related developmental differences in understanding and judgment (Grisso et al., 2003). Most juveniles younger than 13 or 14 years of age exhibited impairments similar to adults with severe mental illnesses and lacked the ability to assist or to participate in their defense (Bonnie & Grisso, 2000; Grisso et al., 2003). A significant proportion of juveniles younger than 16 years of age lacked competence to stand trial, and many older youths exhibited substantial impairments (Grisso et al., 2003). Juveniles with below-average intelligence exhibited greater impairment than did either low-intelligence adults or juveniles with normal intelligence (Grisso et al., 2003). Even formally competent adolescents made poorer decisions than did young adults because they emphasized short-term over long-term outcomes and sought peer approval (Bonnie & Grisso, 2000; Scott & Grisso, 1997; Steinberg & Cauffman, 1999).

About half the states address juveniles' competency to stand trial in statutes, court rules of procedure, or case law and conclude that delinquents have a fundamental right not to be tried while incompetent (Scott & Grisso, 2005). Even after states recognize juveniles' right to a competency determination, they differ over the appropriate standard to apply. Some courts apply the adult competency standard in delinquency and criminal prosecutions because both proceedings may result in a child's loss of liberty. Other jurisdictions opt for a more relaxed competency standard in delinquency than in criminal proceedings, because juvenile hearings are less complex and the consequences less severe than criminal proceedings (Scott & Grisso, 2005).

■ Juveniles and Police Interrogation

The Supreme Court has decided more cases about interrogating youths than any other issue in juvenile justice (Feld, 2013). Although the Court repeatedly cautioned that youthfulness adversely affects juveniles' ability to exercise their *Miranda* rights or make voluntary statements, it has not required special procedures to protect young suspects. Rather, it endorsed the adult waiver standard—"knowing, intelligent, and voluntary"—to gauge juveniles' *Miranda* waivers.

Interrogating Juveniles: "Law on the Books"

In the decades prior to *Miranda*, the Court adopted a protectionist stance and cautioned judges to examine closely how youthfulness affected the voluntariness of confessions (Feld, 1999, 2013). *Haley v. Ohio* (1948) emphasized that a 15-year-old boy's youth and inexperience increased his vulnerability and rendered his confession involuntary. *Gallegos v. Colorado* (1962) found that age was a special circumstance that rendered a 14-year-old boy's confession involuntary. *In re Gault* (1967) reiterated concern that youthfulness affected the reliability of juveniles' statements and granted the privilege against self-incrimination in delinquency proceedings. Although some analysts advocate relaxed procedural safeguards in juvenile courts to foster a rehabilitative or preventive mission (Scott & Grisso, 2005), *Winship* and *Breed* recognized juvenile courts' criminal aspects and *Gault* highlighted their adversarial character.

The Court in *Miranda v. Arizona* (1966) required police to warn suspects of their right to remain silent and to assistance of counsel in order to dispel the coercive pressures of custodial interrogation. *Fare v. Michael C.* (1979) held that the test used to evaluate adults' *Miranda* waivers—"knowing, intelligent, and voluntary" under the totality of the circumstances—governed juveniles' waivers as well. *Fare* reasoned that *Miranda* provided an objective basis to evaluate waivers, denied that youths' developmental differences required special procedural protections, and required children to assert rights clearly. *Miranda* provided that if police question a suspect who is in custody—arrested or "deprived of his freedom of action in any significant way"—they must administer a warning. The Court in *J.D.B. v. North Carolina* (2011) considered "whether the *Miranda* custody analysis includes consideration of a juvenile suspect's age" and reasoned that age was an objective fact that would affect whether a person felt restrained.

Most states use *Fare*'s totality framework for juveniles and adults (Feld, 2013). Trial judges consider characteristics of the offender (age, education, IQ, and prior police contacts) and the context of interrogation (location, methods, and length of questioning) when they evaluate *Miranda* waivers. Appellate courts do not assign controlling weight to any factor, and the totality approach provides no meaningful check on trial judges' discretion (Feld, 2000, 2006a). Judges find valid *Miranda* waivers by children as young as 10 years of age with no prior police contacts, with limited intelligence, and without parental assistance.

About 10 states provide additional safeguards beyond the "totality" approach endorsed by *Fare* (Feld, 2006a, 2006b). They require the presence of a parent or other interested adult at a juvenile's interrogation as a prerequisite to a valid *Miranda* waiver. They presume that most juveniles lack competence to exercise *Miranda* rights and require an adult's assistance. They assume that a parent's presence will enhance juveniles' understanding of their rights, mitigate the dangers of unreliable statements, provide an independent witness of what occurs, and reduce police coercion. As juvenile justice has become more punitive, youths need additional procedural safeguards to achieve functional parity with adult defendants (*State v. Presha* 2000). Moreover, parents are the practical means by which juveniles can secure their *Miranda* right to counsel. Commentators endorse parental presence safeguards, even though reasons exist to question the validity of the assumptions (Feld, 2013).

Juveniles' Ability to Exercise Rights: Developmental Psychology

Developmental and social psychologists question whether juveniles have the cognitive capacity or maturity to make "knowing, intelligent, and voluntary" waivers. The foremost research, by Thomas Grisso, reports that most juveniles simply do not understand a *Miranda* warning well enough to invoke or waive rights in a knowing and intelligent manner (Grisso, 1980, 1981). Juveniles most frequently misunderstood that they had the right to consult with an attorney and to have a lawyer present when police questioned them (Grisso, 1980, 1981), and youths 15 years of age and younger exhibited more limited understanding (Grisso, 1980). Although older juveniles exhibited a level of understanding comparable with adults, substantial minorities of both groups failed to grasp some elements of the standard warning.

Juveniles often fail to appreciate the significance of rights or to understand that they can exercise them without adverse consequences (Grisso, 1997a; Grisso et al., 2003). Lower social status and expectations of obedience to authority make children more vulnerable than adults in the interrogation room. Youths respond more passively and acquiesce more easily to police suggestions. *Fare* requires juveniles to invoke *Miranda* rights clearly and unambiguously, but this expectation conflicts with the normal responses and verbal styles of most youths.

To summarize, developmental psychological research spanning decades consistently indicates that adolescents as a class are at a significant disadvantage in the interrogation room. For youths 15 years of age and younger, these disabilities are clear and substantial. While juveniles 16 and 17 years of age exhibit some degree of impairment, they function comparably with adults. Because of developmental differences, using the same legal framework to judge juveniles' and adults' waivers of rights puts youth at a considerable disadvantage.

Juveniles in the Interrogation Room: "Law in Action"

Four decades after *Miranda*, we still know remarkably little about what actually happens when police interrogate suspects (Feld, 2006a, 2006b, 2013; Leo, 1996). Studies immediately after *Miranda* attempted to gauge whether police complied with the warning requirements and to assess the impact of warnings on rates of confessions and convictions (reviewed in Feld, 2006a, 2006b; Leo, 2008). Richard Leo (1996) has conducted the only empirical research on police interrogation of adults in the United States in the last three decades based on his observations of 116 interrogations in an urban California police department and his review of 60 audio and videotapes of interrogations from two other departments. Barry Feld (2006a, 2006b, 2013) reported the first empirical data of custodial interrogation of juveniles based on analyses of 307 recorded felony interrogations in Minnesota. England's *Police and Criminal Evidence Act 1984* (PACE) requires police to record interrogations, and analysts have coded and analyzed tapes and transcripts of British interrogations, assessed the techniques police employ, and examined how suspects with different personal or psychological characteristics responded (Gudjonsson, 2003). Psychologists have conducted laboratory studies to analyze the psychology of interrogation, to assess how social influences affect susceptible subjects, and to identify the individual characteristics and police practices likely to elicit false confessions (Kassin, 2005; Kassin & Gudjonsson, 2004; Kassin et al., 2010). Studies of false confessions describe how police interrogate some suspects and highlight the vulnerability of younger suspects (Drizin & Leo, 2004; Garrett, 2011; Gross et al., 2005; Tepfer, 2010).

Three decades of research reports that about 80% of adults and 90% of juveniles waive *Miranda* rights (Feld, 2013; Goldstein & Goldstein, 2010; Grisso, 1980; Grisso & Pomicter, 1977; Leo, 2008). The largest empirical study of juvenile interrogations reported that 92.8% of youths waived their *Miranda* rights (Feld, 2013). Juveniles' higher waiver rates may reflect their lack of understanding or inability to invoke *Miranda* effectively. Waivers may reflect prior justice system involvement, and juveniles will have had less experience than adults. Juveniles with one or more prior felony arrests waived their rights at significantly lower rates than did those with fewer or less serious police contacts (Feld, 2013). Several factors likely contribute to more invocation by those with more extensive police contacts. Youths who waived their rights at prior interrogations may have learned the disadvantages of confessing. The time youths spend with lawyers may contribute to greater understanding of rights, and those with prior arrests have had more learning opportunities. Youths questioned previously may have learned to cope with and resist the pressures of interrogation.

Once officers secured a juvenile's *Miranda* waiver, they use the same two-pronged strategy employed with adults to overcome suspects' resistance and to enable them more readily to admit responsibility (Feld, 2013). Maximization techniques intimidate suspects and impress on them the futility of denial, and minimization techniques provide moral justifications or face-saving alternatives to enable them to confess (Feld, 2013; Kassin, 2005; Leo, 2008). Despite youths' heightened susceptibility, police do not incorporate developmental differences into the tactics they employ (Owen-Kostelnik et al., 2006). Techniques designed to manipulate adults—aggressive questioning, presenting false evidence, and leading questions—may create unique dangers when employed with youths (Redlich & Drizin, 2007; Tanenhaus & Drizin, 2003). Police did not report receiving special training to question juveniles (Feld, 2013) and used the same tactics they employed with adults (Feld, 2006b; Leo, 1996). Juveniles responded to those tactics, cooperated or resisted, and provided incriminating evidence at about the same rate as did adults. A majority (58.6%) of juveniles confessed within a few minutes of waiving their *Miranda* rights and did not require prompting by police (Feld, 2013). An additional one third (29.8%) of juveniles provided statements of some evidentiary value—for example, admitting that they served as a lookout during a robbery or participated in a burglary even if they did not personally steal property. Police completed three quarters (77.2%) of interviews in less than 15 minutes and concluded nine in 10 (90.5%) in less than 30 minutes.

In the longest interviews, police questioned three youths (1.1%) for more than one-and-one-half hours.

As noted above, some states require a parent to assist juveniles in the interrogation room (Farber, 2004). However, analysts question whether they can provide practical protection (Feld, 2013; Grisso, 1981; Grisso & Ring, 1979). Parents—as adults—exhibit somewhat greater understanding of *Miranda* than do their children, but both share fundamental misconceptions about police interrogation practices (Woolard et al., 2008). Parents did not provide children with useful legal advice, increased pressure to waive their rights, and urged them to tell the truth (Feld, 2013). Parents may be emotionally upset or angry at their child's arrest, believe that confessing will produce a better outcome, or think that children should respect authority or assume responsibility (Feld, 2013). Juveniles rarely spontaneously request a parent for a variety of reasons: estrangement from their parents, feeling that they cannot provide meaningful assistance, embarrassment or shame about their crime, or hope that their parents will not learn of their arrest (Feld, 2013). If parents are present, police either enlist them as allies in the interrogation or neutralize their presence. Officers tell parents that the role of police is to learn the truth and try to recruit parents as collaborators to learn the truth so as to better enable them to help their child. If parents do attend their child's interrogation, police try to render them as passive observers by seating them behind the child and instructing them not to intervene (Feld, 2013). In the vast majority of interrogations at which parents were present, they did not participate after police advised them of the child's *Miranda* rights, sometimes switched sides to become active allies of the police, and played a protective role in only two (8%) interviews (Feld, 2013).

Research on false confessions underscores the unique vulnerability of younger juveniles (Drizin & Leo, 2004; Garrett, 2011; Gross et al., 2005). Police obtained more than one third (35%) of proven false confessions from suspects younger than 18 (Drizin & Leo, 2004), and younger adolescents are at greater risk to confess falsely than older ones (Tepfer et al., 2010).

Developmental psychologists attribute their overrepresentation among false confessors to reduced cognitive ability, developmental immaturity, and increased susceptibility to manipulation (Bonnie & Grisso, 2000; Redlich et al., 2004). They have fewer life experiences or psychological resources with which to resist the pressures of interrogation (Redlich et al., 2004). Juveniles are more likely than are adults to comply with authority figures, tell police what they think they want to hear, and respond to negative feedback (Gudjonsson, 2003). The stress and anxiety of interrogation intensify their desire to extricate themselves in the short run by waiving and confessing (Goldstein & Goldstein, 2010; Owen-Kostelnik et al., 2006). Impulsive decision making and limited ability to consider long-term consequences heighten their risk. Their immature brains contribute to impulsive behavior and heighten vulnerability (Gruber & Yurglin-Todd, 2006; Maroney, 2009).

Miranda is especially problematic for younger juveniles, who may not understand its words or concepts (Grisso, 1980; Grisso et al., 2003). The Court has recognized youths' vulnerability and distinguished between younger and older youths. Developmental psychologists corroborate their differing abilities. Younger juveniles' incomplete understanding and heightened vulnerability warrant greater assistance—a non-waivable right to counsel—to assure voluntariness of a *Miranda* waiver and statement. The Court in *Haley, Gallegos, Gault, Fare*, and *J.D.B.* excluded statements taken from youths 15 years of age or younger and admitted those obtained from 16- and 17-year-olds. That line closely tracks what psychologists have found about youths' ability to understand the warning and concepts. Policymakers should formally adopt that functional line and provide greater protection for youths 15 and younger. Analysts advocate that juveniles younger than 16 years of age "should be accompanied and advised by a professional advocate, preferably an attorney, trained to serve in this role" (Kassin et al., 2010, p. 28). Juveniles should consult with an attorney, rather than to rely on parents, before they exercise or waive constitutional rights (American Bar Association [ABA], 1980; Bishop & Farber, 2007; Farber, 2004). Requiring a child to consult an attorney ensures an informed and voluntary waiver (Farber, 2004). If youths 15 years of age or younger consult with counsel prior to waiver, it will limit somewhat the police's ability to secure confessions. However, if younger juveniles cannot understand and exercise rights without legal assistance, then to treat them as if they do denies fundamental fairness and enables the state to exploit their vulnerability.

■ Juveniles' Competence to Waive or Plead Guilty

Gault compared a delinquency proceeding to a felony prosecution and granted juveniles the right to counsel. *Gault* relied on the Fourteenth Amendment due process clause rather than the Sixth Amendment, which guarantees criminal defendants' right to counsel (*Gideon v. Wainwright*, 372 U.S. 335, 1961), and did not order automatic appointment of counsel. Instead, *Gault* only required a judge to advise a child and parent of a right to counsel and to have counsel appointed if indigent. *Gault* ruled that juveniles could waive counsel, and most states do not use any special measures to protect delinquents from their own improvident decisions, such as mandatory appointment of counsel (Feld, 1984, 2006a). As with *Miranda* waivers, formal equality produced practical inequality—lawyers represent delinquents at much lower rates than they do adult criminal defendants (Burruss & Kempf-Leonard, 2002; Feld, 1988b, 1993; Harlow, 2000).

Despite statutes and court rules of procedure that apply equally throughout a state, juvenile justice administration varies with urban, suburban, and rural context and produces "justice by geography" (Bray et al., 2005; Burruss & Kempf-Leonard, 2002; Feld, 1991, 1993; Feld & Schaefer, 2010a, 2010b;

Guevara et al., 2008). Lawyers appear more frequently in more formal, bureau-cratized, and due process-oriented urban courts (Burruss & Leonard, 2002; Feld, 1991, 1993). In turn, more formal courts tend to hold more youths in pretrial detention and to sentence them more severely. Rural courts tend to be procedurally less formal and to sentence youths more leniently (Burruss & Kempf-Leonard, 2002; Feld, 1991, 1993). Finally, a lawyer's presence appears to be an aggravating factor when judges sentence delinquents. After con-trolling for legal variables, judges sentence youths who appear with counsel more severely than they do those who appear without an attorney (Burruss & Kempf-Leonard, 2002; Feld, 1988b, 1991; Feld & Schaefer, 2010a). Several factors contribute to this consistent finding: lawyers who appear in juvenile court are incompetent and prejudice their clients' cases; judges predetermine sentences and appoint counsel when they anticipate out-of-home placements; or judges punish delinquents for exercising procedural rights (Feld, 1989, 1993; Feld & Schaefer, 2010a).

Presence of Counsel in Juvenile Courts

When the Court decided *Gault*, lawyers seldom appeared in juvenile courts (Note, 1966). Although states amended their juvenile codes to comply with *Gault*, the "law-in-action" lagged behind changes of the "law-on-the-books." Evaluations of initial compliance with *Gault* found that most judges did not advise juveniles of their rights and the vast majority did not appoint counsel (Canon & Kolson, 1971; Ferster et al., 1971; Lefstein et al., 1969; Stapleton & Teitelbaum, 1972). Studies in several jurisdictions in the 1970s and early 1980s reported that juvenile courts failed to appoint counsel for most juveniles (Aday, 1986; Bortner, 1982; Clarke & Koch, 1980). Research in Minnesota in the mid-1980s reported that most youths appeared with-out counsel (Feld, 1988b, 1989, 1993), that rates of representation varied widely between urban, suburban, and rural counties (Feld, 1991, 1993), and that nearly one third of youths whom judges removed from their homes and about one quarter of those whom they confined in institutions were unrepresented (Feld, 1989, 1993). A decade later, about one quarter of juveniles removed from home were unrepresented despite law reform efforts to eliminate the practice (Feld & Schaefer, 2010a, 2010b). A study of deliv-ery of legal services in six states reported that only three of them appointed counsel for a substantial majority of juveniles (Feld, 1988b). Studies in the 1990s described juvenile court judges' failure to appoint lawyers for many youths who appeared before them (Burruss & Kempf-Leonard, 2002; General Accounting Office [GAO], 1995). In 1995, the GAO confirmed that rates of representation varied widely among and within states and that judges tried and sentenced many unrepresented youths. Research in Missouri found urban, suburban, and rural variation in rates of representa-tion and reported that an attorney's presence increased a youth's likelihood to receive out-of-home placement (Burruss & Kempf-Leonard, 2002). Race, gender, and type of representation influenced sentencing severity in different court settings (Guevara et al., 2008).

In the mid-1990s the ABA published two reports on juveniles' legal needs. The first reported that many children appeared without counsel and that those who represented youth lacked adequate training and often failed to provide effective assistance (ABA, 1993; Bishop & Farber, 2007). The second focused on the quality of defense lawyers and again reported that many youths appeared without counsel, and concluded that many attorneys failed to appreciate the challenges of representing young clients (ABA, 1995). Since the late 1990s, the ABA and the National Juvenile Defender Center have conducted more than a dozen state-by-state assessments of juveniles' access to and quality of counsel. These studies report that many, if not most, juveniles appear without counsel and that lawyers who represent youth often provide substandard assistance because of structural impediments to effective advocacy—heavy caseloads, inadequate resources, and the like (see, e.g., Bookser, 2004; Brooks & Kamine, 2003; Celeste & Puritz, 2001; Puritz & Brooks, 2002; Puritz et al., 2002). Moreover, regardless of how poorly lawyers perform, juvenile and appellate courts cannot correct their own errors (Berkheiser, 2002). Juvenile defenders rarely, if ever, appeal adverse decisions and often lack a record with which to challenge an invalid waiver of counsel or trial errors (Berkheiser, 2002; Bookser, 2004; Crippen, 2000; Harris, 1994; Puritz & Shang, 2000).

Waivers of Counsel and Guilty Pleas in Juvenile Court

Several factors account for why so many youths appear in juvenile courts without counsel. Public-defender legal services may be inadequate or non-existent in non-urban areas (ABA, 1995). Judges may give cursory advisories of the right to counsel, imply that a rights colloquy and waiver are just legal technicalities, and readily find waivers to ease courts' administrative burdens (ABA, 1995; Berkheiser, 2002; Bookser, 2004; Cooper et al., 1998). If judges expect to impose a noncustodial sentence, then they may dispense with counsel (Burruss & Kempf-Leonard, 2002; Feld, 1984, 1989; Lefstein et al., 1969).

The most common explanation why so many juveniles are unrepresented is that they waive counsel (ABA, 1995; Berkheiser, 2002; Cooper et al., 1998; Feld, 1989). As with *Miranda* waivers, judges in most states use the adult standard—knowing, intelligent, and voluntary—to gauge juveniles' waivers of counsel (*Johnson v. Zerbst*, 304 U.S. 458 [1938]; *Fare v. Michael C.*, 442 U.S. 707 [1979]; Berkheiser, 2002). They consider the same factors—age, education, IQ, prior police contacts, or experience with delinquency trials—to decide whether youths understood and voluntarily waived counsel (Feld, 1984, 1989, 2006a). Many juveniles waive counsel without consulting with either a parent or an attorney (Berkheiser, 2002). Although judges are supposed to determine whether a child has the ability to understand and exercise rights and to represent himself or herself (*In re Manuel R.*, 207 A.2d 719 [Conn. 1988]; *In re Christopher H.*, 596 S.E.2d 500 [S.C. App. 2004]), judges frequently failed to give delinquents any counsel advisory, often neglected to create a record, and readily accepted waivers from manifestly incompetent children (Berkheiser, 2002). The research on juveniles' adjudicative competence and exercise of *Miranda* rights reviewed earlier applies equally to their ability to make knowing, intelligent, and voluntary waiver of counsel, or to plead guilty, a much more frequent outcome. Many juveniles simply do not understand the meaning of a *Miranda* warning, counsel advisory, or a plea colloquy and cannot exercise their rights effectively (Grisso, 1980, 1981, 2000). Even youths who understand a *Miranda* warning or a counsel advisory may not appreciate the function or importance of rights (ABA, 1995; Grisso, 1980, 1997a; Grisso et al., 2003). Juveniles' diminished competence and inability to understand legal proceedings and judicial encouragement to waive counsel result in larger proportions of youth without lawyers than criminal defendants (Feld, 1988b; Harlow, 2000). These disabilities become even more consequential for the vast majority of unrepresented juveniles who then plead guilty without understanding or appreciating the consequences.

Like adult criminal defendants, nearly all delinquents plead guilty and proceed to sentencing (Feld, 1993). Because most states deny juveniles the right to a jury trial (*McKeiver v. Pennsylvania*), delinquents have very little plea bargaining leverage (Rosenberg, 1993). Juvenile court judges resist sentencing bargains—allowing prosecutors and defense counsel to restrict their discretion (Sanborn, 1993). Even though pleading guilty is the most critical decision a delinquent makes, states use adult legal standards to evaluate juveniles' competence and ability to enter a plea (Sanborn, 1992, 1993; Singleton, 2007). A valid guilty plea requires a judge to conduct a colloquy on the record in which an offender admits the facts of the offense and establishes that the youth understands the charges and potential consequences (Singleton, 2007). Because appellate courts seldom review juveniles' waivers of counsel (Berkheiser, 2002), scrutiny of pleas made without counsel receive even less judicial attention (Sanborn, 1992, 1993).

Justice by Geography in Juvenile Courts

Most states administer juvenile courts at the county or judicial district level, and justice administration varies with locale (Bray et al., 2005; Burruss & Kempf-Leonard, 2002; Feld, 1991, 1993; Feld & Schaefer, 2010b; GAO, 1995). Urban juvenile courts typically operate in a milieu that provides fewer mechanisms for informal social control, tend to be more formal and due process-oriented, place more youths in pretrial detention, and sentence offenders more severely than do suburban or rural courts (Feld, 1991). No reasons exist to believe that rural youths are more competent than urban juveniles to waive legal rights, but rural judges appoint attorneys for delinquents far less often than do their urban counterparts (Burruss & Kempf-Leonard, 2002; Feld, 1991; Feld & Schaefer, 2010b). For example, attorneys in Minnesota appeared with 63% of urban youths, 55% of suburban juveniles, but only 25% of rural youths (Feld, 1991). State law reform efforts to improve delivery of legal services did not eliminate geographic disparities (Feld & Schaefer, 2010b). Missouri attorneys appeared with 73% of youths in urban courts versus 25% in suburban courts and 18% in rural settings (Burruss & Kempf-Leonard, 2002). The GAO (1995) reported that rural youths were four times as likely to appear without counsel as their urban counterparts). Variability in rates of appointment of counsel more likely reflects differences in courts' policies to appoint attorneys than variations in youths' competence to waive rights.

Counsel as an Aggravating Factor in Sentencing

Historically, juvenile court judges discouraged adversarial representation, and organizational pressures to cooperate impeded effective advocacy (Blumberg, 1967; Bortner, 1982; Clarke & Koch, 1980; Feld, 1984; Stapleton & Teitelbaum, 1972). Lawyers in juvenile courts may disadvantage their clients at sentencing (Bortner, 1982; Burruss & Kempf-Leonard, 2002; Feld, 1988b, 1989; Feld & Schaefer, 2010a). Research that controls for legal variables (e.g., present offense, prior record, and pretrial detention) consistently reports that judges removed from home and incarcerated delinquents who appeared with counsel more frequently than they did unrepresented youths (Bortner, 1982; Burruss & Kempf-Leonard, 2002; Clarke & Koch, 1980; Duffee & Siegel, 1971; Feld, 1989, 1993; Feld & Schaefer, 2010a; Guevara et al., 2004). Law reform efforts to improve delivery of legal services actually increased the aggravating effect of representation on sentences (Feld & Schaefer, 2010a, 2010b).

Why is the presence of counsel an aggravating factor at sentencing? First, juvenile defenders may be incompetent and prejudice their clients' cases (Cooper et al., 1998; Knitzer & Sobie, 1984; Lefstein et al., 1969; Stapleton & Teitelbaum, 1972). Public-defender offices may assign their least capable lawyers or their newest attorneys to juvenile court to gain trial experience (Flicker, 1983; Handler, 1965). Court-appointed lawyers may place a premium on maintaining good relations with judges who assign their cases rather than on vigorously defending their oft-changing clients (Feld, 1989; Flicker, 1983). Most significantly, the conditions under which many defense attorneys work constitute a structural impediment to quality representation (ABA, 1995; Cooper et al., 1998; Jones, 2004). Observations and qualitative assessments in several jurisdictions consistently report adverse working conditions—crushing caseloads, penurious compensation, lack of support services, inexperienced attorneys, and inadequate supervision—that detract from or even preclude effective representation (Brooks & Kamine, 2004; Celeste & Puritz, 2001; Jones, 2004; Puritz & Brooks, 2002; Puritz et al., 2002).

Judges may appoint lawyers when they expect to impose more severe sentences (Aday, 1986; Canon & Kolson, 1971). Court decisions prohibit "incarceration without representation" (*Scott v. Illinois*, 440 U.S. 367 [1979]), and judges' efforts to comply with that requirement may explain the relationship between initial decisions to appoint counsel and subsequent decisions to remove youths from their homes (Feld & Schaefer, 2010a). In most jurisdictions, the same judge presides at a youth's arraignment, detention hearing, adjudication, and disposition and may appoint counsel if he or she anticipates a more severe sentence (Feld, 1984). Because judges appoint counsel at the earliest stages of proceedings—arraignment or detention hearing—why would they expect to incarcerate a youth later? Can an attorney provide an effective defense if the judge has already prejudged the case (Burruss & Kempf-Leonard, 2002; Feld & Schaefer, 2010a; Guevara et al., 2008)?

Finally, judges may sentence delinquents who appear with counsel more severely than those who waive because the lawyer's presence insulates them from appellate reversal (Burruss & Kempf-Leonard, 2002; Duffee & Siegel, 1971; Guevara et al., 2004). Juvenile court judges may sanction youths whose lawyers invoke formal procedures, disrupt routine procedures, or question their discretion in ways similar to the harsher sentences imposed on adults who demand a jury trial rather than plead guilty (Engen & Steen, 2000).

Despite these disturbing findings, youths require and deserve safeguards that only lawyers can effectively invoke to protect against erroneous and punitive state intervention (Feld, 1988a, 1999, 2003b). The direct consequence of delinquency convictions—institutional confinement—and the use of prior convictions to sentence recidivists more harshly, to waive youths to criminal court, and to enhance adult sentences make effective assistance of counsel imperative (Feld, 1988a, 2003a).

■ Right to Jury Trial: Accurate Fact Finding and Collateral Consequences

McKeiver v. Pennsylvania (403 U.S. 528 [1971]) declined to grant delinquents all the procedural safeguards of criminal trials. Although *Duncan v. Louisiana* (391 U.S. 145 [1968]) previously gave adult criminal defendants the right to a jury trial in state criminal proceedings, *McKeiver* (1971, p. 541) insisted that "the juvenile court proceeding has not yet been held to be a 'criminal prosecution,' within the meaning and reach of the Sixth Amendment, and also has not yet been regarded as devoid of criminal aspects merely because it usually has been given the civil label." The plurality reasoned that fundamental fairness in delinquency proceedings emphasized accurate fact finding, which a judge could satisfy as well as a jury. *McKeiver* invoked the imagery of a sympathetic, paternalistic judge, disregarded delinquents' need for protection from state overreaching, and rejected concerns that informality could compromise accurate fact finding (Feld, 2003a; McCord & Spatz-Widom, 2001; Poe-Yamagata & Jones, 2000). The Court feared that jury trials would interfere with juvenile courts' informality, flexibility, and confidentiality, would make juvenile and criminal courts procedurally indistinguishable, and could lead to their elimination (Feld, 2003b).

A few states give juveniles a right to a jury trial as a matter of state law (e.g., Feld, 2003a; *In re L.M.*, 186 P.3e 164 [Kan. 2008]), but the vast majority do not. Significantly, in the decades since *McKeiver*, every state has revised its juvenile code, adopted get-tough provisions, fostered a punitive convergence with criminal courts, and eroded the "rehabilitative" rationale for less effective procedures in delinquency trials (Feld, 1988b; Torbet et al., 1996). Despite these substantial changes in juvenile court jurisprudence and sentencing practices, state courts generally reject juveniles' claims that they should enjoy constitutional right to a jury (see, e.g., *In re D.J.* 817 So. 2d 26 [La. 2002]; *State v. Hezzie R.*, 580 N.W.2d 660 [Wis. 1998]; *In re J.F. and G.G.*, 714 A.2d 467 [Pa. Super. Ct. 1998]).

McKeiver assumed that states do not need juries to assure accurate fact finding. However, juries and judges evaluate testimony and decide cases differently, and the denial of jury trials increases the likelihood that outcomes will differ in delinquency and criminal trials. Although judges and juries agree about defendants' guilt or innocence in about four fifths of criminal cases, when they differ, juries acquit more often than do judges (Greenwood et al., 1983; Kalven & Zeisel, 1966). Fact finding by judges and juries is intrinsically different, because the former may preside over hundreds of cases annually while the latter may hear only one or two cases in a lifetime (Ainsworth, 1991; Kalven & Zeisel, 1966; Saks, 1997). Because judges hear many cases, they sometimes become less meticulous when they weigh evidence, become more casual when they evaluate facts, and apply less stringently the reasonable doubt standard than do jurors (Guggenheim & Hertz, 1998). Judges hear testimony from police and probation officers on a recurring basis and develop settled opinions about their credibility (Feld, 1984; Guggenheim & Hertz, 1998). Similarly, judges may have an opinion about a youth's credibility or character or the merits of the case from hearing earlier charges against him or her or presiding at his or her detention hearing. The informality of delinquency proceedings compounds the differences between a judge's and jury's reasonable doubt and places delinquents at a further disadvantage. When juvenile court judges preside at detention hearings, they receive information about a youth's offense, criminal history, or social circumstances. This non–guilt-related evidence increases the likelihood that a judge will convict and subsequently institutionalize him or her (Feld, 1984). The absence of a jury enables judges to conduct suppression hearings during trial, exposes them to prejudicial information about the youth, and further increases the likelihood of an erroneous conviction (Feld, 1984; Guggenheim & Hertz, 1998). Finally, the absence of a jury enables juvenile courts to adjudicate many juveniles without the assistance of an attorney, which further prejudices the accuracy of fact finding (Cooper et al., 1998; Feld, 1993). It is easier to convict a youth in a juvenile court trial than to convict a person in a criminal proceeding with a jury (Greenwood et al., 1983).

Although juvenile courts historically restricted access to juvenile court records to avoid stigmatizing youths, states' use of delinquency convictions to enhance adult sentences has a long lineage (Feld, 2003a). Many states' and the federal sentencing guidelines include some delinquency convictions in a defendant's criminal history score (Miller, 1995; Packel, 2002). This practice raises troubling questions about the quality of justice delinquents receive. The vast majority of states deny juveniles a right to a jury trial. Most delinquents plead guilty—with or without the assistance of counsel—and those pleas constitute convictions for purposes of subsequent sentence enhancement. As a result, states obtain many delinquency convictions that would not have resulted in criminal convictions or pleas if defendants had received adequate procedural safeguards (Feld, 2003a).

While *McKeiver* found delinquency convictions sufficiently reliable to support juvenile dispositions, they may not be reliable enough to support punitive enhancements of criminal sentence. *Apprendi v. New Jersey* (530 U.S. 466 [2000]) reasoned that a jury must find the facts beyond a reasonable doubt that result in an increased sentence. *Apprendi* exempted the "fact of a prior conviction" from its holding because criminal defendants enjoyed the right to a jury trial in the proceeding that led to that "prior conviction." Because most states deny juveniles a jury, their use of delinquency convictions to enhance adult sentence may not satisfy *Apprendi's* rationale to exempt "the fact of a prior conviction" (Feld, 2003a).

A majority of lower courts have concluded that even without a right to a jury, delinquency convictions are sufficiently reliable to use for criminal sentence enhancements (e.g., *U.S. v. Smalley*, 294 F.3d 1030 [8th Cir. 2002]; *U.S. v. Jones*, 332 F.3d 633 [3d Cir. 2003]; Feld, 2003a). In addition to their direct use, states also use delinquency convictions to impose collateral consequences, such as sex-offender registration and other disabilities. A minority of courts deem delinquency procedures inadequate to allow the use of delinquency convictions to enhance criminal sentences (e.g., *United States v. Tighe*, 266 F.3d 1187 [8th Cir. 2001]; *State v. Brown*, 879 So.2d 1276 [La. 2004]; *State v. Harris*, 118 P.3d 236 [Ore. 2005]). These courts conclude that it is unfair to provide youths with fewer procedural safeguards to rehabilitate them and then to punish them more severely as adults.

Conclusion

Recent developmental psychological and neuroscience research has taught us scientifically much more than we previously knew about how children think and act and how their thought processes differ from those of adults. The research findings reinforce the historic recognition that youths' legal competence is less than that of adults and support the rationale for a separate juvenile justice system (Scott & Steinberg, 2008). The decades since *Gault* have witnessed a procedural as well as substantive convergence between juvenile and criminal courts. The greater procedural formality and adversarial nature of delinquency proceedings reflect juvenile courts' shift in emphasis from rehabilitating offenders to protecting public safety. Despite these changes, most states do not provide delinquents with procedural safeguards that provide formal or functional protections comparable to those of adult criminal defendants (Feld, 2003a). Juveniles waive their *Miranda* rights and right to counsel under a standard—"knowing, intelligent, and voluntary" under the "totality of circumstances"—that is unlikely to discern whether they understand and are competent to exercise the rights they relinquish. The high rate of waiver of counsel is an indictment of the juvenile justice system because assistance of counsel is the prerequisite to the exercise of other procedural safeguards. The denial of jury trials calls into question the validity and reliability of delinquency adjudications, both for initial dispositions and for collateral use such as sentence enhancements (Feld, 2003a). In short, states do not provide juveniles with special procedural safeguards to protect them from their own immaturity and vulnerability, nor do they provide them with the full panoply of criminal procedural safeguards to protect them from punitive state intervention. Instead, juvenile courts ensure that youths continue to "receive the worst of both worlds"—treating juvenile offenders just like adult criminal defendants when formal equality redounds to their disadvantage and providing less effective juvenile court procedures when they provide an advantage to the state.

References

Aday, D. P., Jr. (1986). Court structure, defense attorney use, and juvenile court decisions. *Sociological Quarterly, 27,* 107–119.

Ainsworth, J. E. (1991). Re-imagining childhood and reconstructing the legal order: the case for abolishing the juvenile court. *North Carolina Law Review, 69,* 1083–1133.

American Bar Association (1993). *America's children at risk: A national agenda for legal action.* Washington, DC: American Bar Association Presidential Working Group on the Unmet Needs of Children and their Families.

American Bar Association, Institute of Judicial Administration (1980). *Juvenile justice standards relating to pretrial court proceedings.* Cambridge, MA: Ballinger.

Aronson, J. D. (2007). Brain imaging, culpability and the juvenile death penalty. *Psychology, Public Policy and Law, 13,* 115–142.

Aronson, J. D. (2009). Neuroscience and Juvenile Justice. *Akron Law Review, 42,* 917–929.

Arrendondo, D. E. (2003). Child development, children's mental health and the juvenile justice system. *Stanford Law & Policy Review, 14,* 13–28.

Berkheiser, M. (2002). The fiction of juvenile right to counsel: waiver in the juvenile courts. *Florida Law Review, 54,* 577–686.

Bishop, D. M., & Farber. H. B. (2007). Joining the legal significance of adolescent developmental capacities with the legal rights provided by *In re Gault. Rutgers Law Review, 60,* 125–173.

Blumberg, A. S. (1967). The practice of law as a confidence game: organizational cooptation of a profession. *Law & Society Review, 1,* 15–39.

Bonnie, R., & Grisso, T. (2000). Adjudicative competence and youthful offenders. In T. Grisso & R. G. Schwartz (Eds.), *Youth on trial: A developmental perspective on juvenile courts.* Chicago: University of Chicago Press.

Bookser, S. M. (2004). Making *Gault* meaningful: access to counsel and quality of representation in delinquency proceedings for indigent youth. *Whittier Journal of Child & Family Advocacy, 3,* 297–328.

Bortner, M. A. (1982). *Inside a juvenile court: The tarnished ideal of individualized justice.* New York: New York University Press.

Bray, T., Sample, L. L., & Kempf-Leonard, K. (2005). Justice by geography: racial disparity and juvenile courts. In D. Hawkins & K. Kempf-Leonard (Eds.), *Our children, their children: Confronting racial and ethnic differences in American juvenile justice.* Chicago: University of Chicago Press.

Brooks, K., & Kamine, D. (2003). *Justice cut short: An assessment of access to counsel and quality of representation in delinquency proceedings in Ohio.* Washington, DC: American Bar Association Juvenile Justice Center.

Burruss Jr, G. W., & Kempf-Leonard, K. (2002). The questionable advantage of defense counsel in juvenile court. *Justice Quarterly, 19,* 37–68.

Canon, B. C., & Kolson, K. (1971). Rural compliance with *Gault*: Kentucky, a case study. *Journal of Family Law, 10,* 300–326.

Cauffman, E., & Steinberg, L. (1995). The cognitive and affective influences on adolescent decision-making. *Temple Law Review, 68,* 1763–1789.

Celeste, G., & Puritz, P. (2001). *The children left behind: An assessment of access to counsel and quality of legal presentation in delinquency proceedings in Louisiana.* Washington, DC: American Bar Association Juvenile Justice Center.

Clarke, S. H., & Koch, G. G. (1980). Juvenile court: therapy or crime control, and do lawyers make a difference? *Law & Society Review, 14,* 263–308.

Cooper, N. L., Puritz, P., & Shang, W. (1998). Fulfilling the promise of *In re Gault*: advancing the role of lawyers for children. *Wake Forest Law Review, 33,* 651–679.

Crippen, G. L. (2000). Can the courts fairly account for the diminished competence and culpability of juveniles? A judge's perspective. In T. Grisso & R. Schwartz (Eds.), *Youth on trial: A developmental perspective on juvenile justice* (p. 410). Chicago: University of Chicago Press.

Dahl, R. E. (2004). Adolescent brain development: A period of vulnerabilities and opportunities. *Annals of the New York Academy of Sciences, 1021,* 1–22.

Drizin, S. A., & Leo, R. A. (2004). The problem of false confessions in the post-DNA world. *North Carolina Law Review, 82,* 891–1007.

Duffee, D., & Siegel, L. (1971). The organization man: legal counsel in the juvenile court. *Criminal Law Bulletin, 7,* 544–553.

Engen, R. L., & Steen, S. (2000). The power to punish: discretion and sentencing reform in the War on Drugs. *American Journal of Sociology, 105,* 1357–1395.

Farber, H. B. (2004). The role of the parent/guardian in juvenile custodial interrogations: friend or foe? *American Criminal Law Review, 41,* 1277–1312.

Feld, B. C. (1984). Criminalizing juvenile justice: rules of procedure for the juvenile court. *Minnesota Law Review, 69,* 141–276.

Feld, B. C. (1988a). The juvenile court meets the principle of offense: punishment, treatment, and the difference it makes. *Boston University Law Review, 68,* 821–915.

Feld, B. C. (1988b). *In re Gault* revisited: a cross-state comparison of the right to counsel in juvenile court. *Crime & Delinquency, 34,* 393–424.

Feld, B. C. (1989). The right to counsel in juvenile court: an empirical study of when lawyers appear and the difference they make. *Journal of Criminal Law & Criminology, 79,* 1185–1346.

Feld, B. C. (1991). Justice by geography: urban, suburban, and rural variations in juvenile justice administration. *Journal of Criminal Law & Criminology, 82,* 156–210.

Feld, B. C. (1993). *Justice for children: The right to counsel and the juvenile courts.* Boston: Northeastern University Press.

Feld, B. C. (1999). *Bad kids: Race and the transformation of the juvenile court.* New York: Oxford University Press.

Feld, B. C. (2000). Juveniles' waiver of legal rights: confessions, *Miranda,* and the right to counsel. in T. Grisso & R. Schwartz (Eds.), *Youth on trial: A developmental perspective on Juvejile justice* (pp. 105–138). Chicago: University of Chicago Press.

Feld, B. C. (2003a). The constitutional tension between *Apprendi* and *McKeiver:* Sentence enhancements based on delinquency convictions and the quality of justice in juvenile courts. *Wake Forest Law Review, 38,* 1111–1224.

Feld, B. C. (2003b). Race, politics, and juvenile justice: the Warren Court and the conservative "backlash." *Minnesota Law Review, 87,* 1447–1577.

Feld, B. C. (2006a). Juveniles' competence to exercise Miranda rights: an empirical study of policy and practice. *Minnesota Law Review, 91,* 26–100.

Feld, B. C. (2006b). Police interrogation of juveniles: an empirical study of policy and practice. *Journal of Criminal Law and Criminology, 97,* 219–316.

Feld, B. C. (2008). A slower form of death: implications of *Roper v. Simmons* for juveniles sentenced to life without parole. *Notre Dame Journal of Law, Ethics, & Public Policy, 22,* 9–65.

Feld, B. C. (2013). *Kids, cops, and confessions: Inside the interrogation room.* New York: NYU Press.

Feld, B. C., & Schaefer, S. (2010a). The right to counsel in juvenile court: the conundrum of attorneys as an aggravating factor in dispositions. *Justice Quarterly, 27,* 713–741.

Feld, B. C., & Schaefer, S. (2010b). The right to counsel in juvenile court: law reform to deliver legal services and reduce justice by geography. *Criminology & Public Policy, 9,* 327–356.

Ferster, E. Z., Courtless, T., & Snethen, E. (1971). The juvenile justice system: in search of the role of counsel. *Fordham Law Review, 39,* 375–412.

Flicker, B. (1983). *Providing counsel for accused juveniles.* New York: Institute of Judicial Administration.

Furby, L., & Beyth-Marom, R. (1992). *Risk-taking in adolescence: A decision-making perspective.* Washington, DC: Carnegie Council on Adolescent Development.

Garrett, B. L. (2011). *Convicting the innocent: Where criminal prosecutions go wrong.* Cambridge: Harvard University Press.

General Accounting Office (1995). *Juvenile justice: Representation rates varied as did counsel's impact on court outcomes.* Washington, DC: U.S. General Accounting Office.

Goldstein, A., & Goldstein, N. E. S. (2010). *Evaluating capacity to waive* Miranda *rights.* New York: Oxford University Press.

Greenwood, P. W., Abrahamse, A., & Zimring, F. E. (1983). *Youth crime and juvenile justice in California: A report to the Legislature.* Santa Monica, CA: Rand Corporation.

Grisso, T. (1980). Juveniles' capacities to waive *Miranda* rights: an empirical analysis. *California Law Review, 68,* 1134–1166.

Grisso, T. (1981). *Juveniles' waiver of rights: Legal and psychological competence.* New York: Plenum Press.

Grisso, T. (1997). Juvenile competency to stand trial: questions in an era of punitive reform. *Criminal Justice, 3,* 5–11.

Grisso, T. (2000). What we know about youths' capacities as trial defendants. In T. Grisso & R. G. Schwartz (Eds.), *Youth on trial: A developmental perspective on juvenile justice* (pp. 139–170). Chicago: University of Chicago Press.

Grisso, T., & Pomicter, C. (1977). Interrogation of juveniles: an empirical study of procedures, safeguards and rights waiver. *Law & Human Behavior, 1,* 321–342.

Grisso, T., & Ring, M. (1979). Parents' attitudes toward juveniles' rights in interrogation. *Criminal Justice & Behavior, 6,* 211.

Grisso, T., Steinberg, L., Woolard, J., Cauffman, E., Scott, E., Graham, S., Lexcen, F., & Reppucci, N. D. (2003). Juveniles' competence to stand trial: a comparison of adolescents' and adults' capacities as trial defendants. *Law & Human Behavior, 27,* 333–363.

Gross, S. R., et al. (2005) Exonerations in the United States: 1989 through 2003. *Journal of Criminal Law and Criminology, 95,* 523–560.

Gruber, S. A., & Yurgelun-Todd, D. A. (2006). Neurobiology and the law: a role in juvenile justice. *Ohio State Journal of Criminal Law, 3,* 321–340.

Gudjonsson, G. H. (2003). *The psychology of interrogations and confessions: A handbook.* New York: John Wiley & Sons.

Guevara, L., Spohn, C., & Herz, D. (2004). Race, legal representation and juvenile justice: issues and concerns. *Crime & Delinquency, 50,* 344–371.

Guevara, L., Spohn, C., & Herz, D. (2008). Race, gender, and legal counsel: differential outcomes in two juvenile courts. *Youth Violence and Juvenile Justice, 6,* 83–104.

Guggenheim, M., & Hertz, R. (1998). Reflections on judges, juries, and justice: ensuring the fairness of juvenile delinquency trials. *Wake Forest Law Review, 33,* 553–593.

Handler, J. F. (1965). The juvenile court and the adversary system: problems of form and function. *Wisconsin Law Review,* 7–51.

Harlow, C. W. (2000). *Defense counsel in criminal cases.* Washington, DC: Bureau of Justice Statistics, U.S. Department of Justice.

Harris, D. J. (1994). Due process vs. helping kids in trouble: implementing the right to appeal from adjudications of delinquency in Pennsylvania. *Dickinson Law Review, 98,* 209–235.

John D. and Catherine T. MacArthur Foundation (2012). *Adolescent development and juvenile justice.* Available at www.http//adjj.org

Jones, J. B. (2004). *Access to counsel.* Washington, DC: Office of Juvenile Justice and Delinquency Prevention.

Kalven Jr, H. & Zeisel, H. (1966). *The American jury.* Chicago: University of Chicago Press.

Kandel, E. R., Schwartz, J., & Jessell, T. (2000). *Principles of neuroscience* (4th ed.). New York: McGraw Hill.

Kassin, S. (2005). On the psychology of confessions: does innocence put innocents at risk? *American Psychologist, 60,* 215–228.

Kassin, S., & Gudjonsson G. H. (2004). The psychology of confessions: a review of the literature and issues. *Psychological Sciences in Public Interest, 5,* 33–69.

Kassin, S. M., et al. (2010) Police-induced confessions: risk factors and recommendations. *Law and Human Behavior, 34,* 3–38.

Knitzer, J., & Sobie, M. (1984). *Law guardians in New York State: A study of the legal representation of children.* Albany, NY: New York State Bar Association.

Lefstein, N., Stapleton, V., & Teitelbaum, L. (1969). In search of juvenile justice: *Gault* and its implementation. *Law & Society Review, 3,* 491–562.

Leo, R. A. (1996). Inside the interrogation room. *Journal of Criminal Law & Criminology, 86,* 266–303.

Leo, R. A. (2008). *Police interrogation in America.* Cambridge, MA: Harvard University Press.

Maroney, T. A. (2009). The false promise of adolescent brain science in juvenile justice. *Notre Dame Law Review, 85,* 89–176.

McCord, J., & Spatz-Widom, C. (2001). *Juvenile crime, juvenile justice*. National Research Council, Washington DC: National Academy Press.

Miller, N. (1995). *State laws on prosecutors' and judges' use of juvenile records*. Washington, DC: National Institute of Justice.

Morse, S. J. (1997). Immaturity and irresponsibility. *Journal of Criminal Law & Criminology, 88*, 15–67.

Note. (1966). Juvenile delinquents: the police, state courts and individualized justice. *Harvard Law Review, 79*, 775–810.

Owen-Kostelnik, J., et al. (2006) Testimony and interrogation of minors: assumptions about maturity and morality. *American Psychologist, 61*, 286–304.

Packel, A. K. (2002). Juvenile justice and the punishment of recidivists under California's Three Strikes Law. *California Law Review, 90*, 1157–1202.

Poe-Yamagata, E., & Jones, M. A. (2000). *And justice for some*. Davis, CA: National Council on Crime and Delinquency.

Puritz, P., & Brooks, K. (2002). *Kentucky: Advancing justice: An assessment of access to counsel and quality of representation in delinquency proceedings*. Washington, DC: American Bar Association Juvenile Justice Center.

Puritz, P., Scali, M. A., & Picou, I. (2002). *Virginia: An assessment of access to counsel and quality of representation in delinquency proceedings*. Washington, DC: American Bar Association Juvenile Justice Center.

Puritz, P., & Shang, W. (2000). Juvenile indigent defense: crisis and solutions. *Criminal Justice, 15*, 22–28.

Redlich, A. D., & Drizin, S. (2007). Police interrogation of youth. In C. L. Kessler & L. J. Kraus (Eds.), *The mental health needs of young offenders: Forging paths toward reintegration and rehabilitation* (pp. 61–78). Cambridge, MA: Cambridge University Press.

Redlich, A. D., Silverman, M., Chen, J., & Steiner, H. (2004). The police interrogation of children and adolescents. In G. D. Lassiter (Ed.), *Interrogations, confessions, and entrapment* (pp. 105–125). New York: Springer Science.

Rosenberg, I. M. (1993). Leaving bad enough alone: a response to the juvenile court abolitionists. *Wisconsin Law Review*, 163–188.

Saks, M. J. (1997). What do jury experiments tell us about how juries (should) make decisions? *Southern California Interdisciplinary Law Journal, 6*, 1–53.

Sanborn Jr., J. B. (1992). Pleading guilty in juvenile court: minimal ado about something very important to young defendants. *Justice Quarterly, 9*, 127–149.

Sanborn Jr., J. B. (1993). Philosophical, legal, and systemic aspects of juvenile court plea bargaining. *Crime & Delinquency, 39*, 509–527.

Scott, E. S. (1992). Judgment and reasoning in adolescent decision making. *Villanova Law Review, 37*, 1607–1669.

Scott, E. S. (2000). The legal construction of adolescence. *Hofstra Law Review, 29*, 547–588.

Scott, E. S., & Grisso, T. (1997). The evolution of adolescence: a developmental perspective on juvenile justice reform. *Journal of Criminal Law & Criminology, 88*, 137–189.

Scott, E. S., & Grisso, T. (2005). Developmental incompetence, due process, and juvenile justice policy. *North Carolina Law Review, 83*, 793–846.

Scott, E. S., Reppucci, N. D., & Woolard, J. L. (1995). Evaluating adolescent decision making in legal contexts. *Law & Human Behavior, 19*, 221–244.

Scott, E. S., & Steinberg, L. (2003). Blaming youth. *Texas Law Review, 81*, 799–840.

Scott, E. S., & Steinberg, L. (2008). *Rethinking juvenile justice*. Cambridge, MA: Harvard University Press.

Singleton, L. C. (2007). Say 'pleas': juveniles' competence to enter plea agreements. *Journal of Law & Family Studies, 9*, 439–455.

Sowell, E. R., Thompson, P. M., Tessner, K. D., & Toga, A. W. (2001). Mapping continued brain growth and gray matter density reduction in dorsal frontal cortex: Inverse relationships during postadolescent brain maturation. *Journal of Neuroscience, 21* (22), 8819–8829.

Spear, L. P. (2000). The adolescent brain and age-related behavioral manifestations. *Neuroscience and Biobehavioral Reviews, 24,* 417–463.

Stapleton, V., & Teitelbaum, L. (1972). *In defense of youth: A study of the role of counsel in American juvenile courts.* New York: Russell Sage Foundation.

Steinberg, L., & Cauffman, E. (1996). Maturity of judgment in adolescence: psychosocial factors in adolescent decision making. *Law & Human Behavior, 20,* 249–272.

Steinberg, L., & Cauffman, E. (1999). The elephant in the courtroom: a developmental perspective on the adjudication of youthful offenders. *Virginia Journal of Social Policy & the Law, 6,* 389–417.

Tanenhaus, D. S. (2004). *Juvenile justice in the making.* New York: Oxford University Press.

Tanenhaus, D. S., & Drizin, S. A. (2003). Owing to the extreme youth of the accused: the changing legal response to juvenile homicide. *Journal of Criminal Law & Criminology, 92,* 641–705.

Tepfer, J. A., et al. (2010). Arresting development: convictions of innocent youth. *Rutgers Law Review, 62,* 887–941.

Torbet, P., Gable, R., Hurst IV, H., Montgomery, I., Szymanski, L., & Thomas, D. (1996). *State responses to serious and violent juvenile crime: Research report.* Washington, DC: U.S. Department of Justice, Office of Juvenile Justice and Delinquency Prevention.

Woolard, J. L., Cleary, H., Harvell, S., & Chen, R. (2008). Examining adolescents' and their parents' conceptual and practical knowledge of police interrogation: a family dyad approach. *Journal of Youth & Adolescence, 37,* 685–698.

9

Juvenile Detention

David W. Roush, Michelle Brazeal, and Wesley T. Church II

■ Introduction

Depending on your place in the juvenile justice system, the news is either good or not so good. While there has been a reduction in the number of youth in custody, there is much work to be done to improve conditions of confinement. The public relies on juvenile detention, corrections, and adult facilities to protect the public as well as to safely and humanely care for the youthful offenders placed in their custody. Practitioners are expected to not only monitor those in their care but to provide services designed to equip youth with the skills needed to live peaceful and productive lives. Although a fairly straightforward goal, building and maintaining a successful juvenile confinement program is a very complex process.

■ Fewer Youth in Secure Custody

On any given day in the United States, there are approximately 79,000 juveniles in some form of detention; 89% (approx. 70,000) are being held in secure facilities (Snyder & Sickmund, 2006). Unfortunately, this figure fails to account for youth held as juveniles in adult facilities. Although the specific numbers may vary by source, the truth of the story is that the majority of youth in confinement are held in secure youth and adult facilities. However bleak this may seem, the good news is that the number of youth in custody has sustained a significant and steady decrease. The reduction in the number of youth in detention facilities has had the added benefit of reducing overcrowding. Overcrowded conditions have plagued juvenile detention and corrections facilities for the past two decades. Many of the egregious conditions reported by the press (Twedt, 2001) and the courts (Gest, 2004) can be attributed to the demands placed on operations strained by a need for space that far exceeds capacity. This trend has recently begun to change. Whereas it was once difficult to locate an empty detention bed in jurisdictions nationwide, many facilities are now reducing capacity as the demand for bed space declines.

The changes have spawned a debate between social science researchers (Butts, 2013; Butts & Evans, 2011) and juvenile detention reformers (Annie E. Casey Foundation, 2013) as they attempt to discover what is responsible for the reduction. At the center of the debate is whether the data indicate that the shift in public policy and juvenile justice practice is based on current political and economic considerations or represent the outcomes of reform ideology. One point of view asserts that the diversion of youth to less expensive but equally effective non-secure alternatives has been spurred by enlightened thinking, coupled with economic considerations. The opposing view credits reform ideology and core strategies with generating the aforementioned enlightened thinking and practices. Regardless of the reason, the decline in detention rates can be attributed to an ideology that focuses on understanding that detaining low- and medium-risk youth increases their likelihood of recidivism and the economic realities of strained state and county budgets. In fact, many states have implemented strategies that embrace this new ideology and have begun to move away from detention toward community-based services that focus on identifying local and state-level forces that push low-risk/high-needs youth and status offenders into state juvenile justice systems. For some states the economic realities of a strapped county-level juvenile system has created an incentive for local jurisdictions to commit youth to larger state-funded agencies.

Juvenile justice researchers (Butts & Evans, 2012) have described trends in the youth incarceration data that suggest a nationwide reduction occurring simultaneously with juvenile detention reform. For example, between 2000 and 2008, the number of juveniles in public facilities decreased by 28% (Butts, 2013). Over this same period in Chicago, reforms implemented under the Cook County Juvenile Detention Alternatives Initiative yielded a 33% reduction in the detention population. This is an impressive result when considering the size and complexity of the Cook County juvenile justice system. Thus, these Juvenile Detention Alternatives Initiative reforms were likely the accelerant for the national reduction in youth incarceration rates.

■ The New Normal in Secure Custody

While juvenile detention and corrections practitioners have benefited from the lessening of overcrowding, the news is not all good. Not to be drawn into the debate, but it must be recognized that as the number of juveniles in secure facilities is reduced, the composition of the population changes. Some of the benefits realized by reforms have been offset by the distillation of the population of youth who remain incarcerated, the absence of progress to reduce disproportionate minority confinement (DMC), and the lack of insight and instruction about how practitioners are to adapt conditions of confinement to meet the increased challenges associated with the youth that remain. While no one argues or debates the wisdom of incarcerating only those who are at high risk of reoffending or absconding, the system must be prepared to respond to the needs of the juveniles in their care. Objective screening criteria that use risk factors to determine disposition have led to a higher concentration of confined juveniles with mental health problems, learning disabilities, behavioral disorders, and violent tendencies.

If the reformers claim full credit for the reduction in the detention population, then the practitioner should ask why the reformers have not addressed how the system should respond to the predictable characteristics of youth who need secure detention. In the early stages of reform, discussions about conditions of confinement (Burrell, 1999) made no mention of how changes in the detention population would require facilities to change the way they operate. Similarly, when the reform movement embraced the Justice Policy Institute's

(Holman & Ziedenberg, 2006) thesis on the dangers of detention and the rather silly assertion that detention causes recidivism, there was no discussion that the new and reformed juvenile detention system might cause even greater rates of recidivism. Since the reform strategy intended to remove from secure incarceration those youth with the greatest likelihood of success (or stated differently, least likely to recidivate), then basic math predicts an increase in recidivism rates, even if nothing else changes. It would be better for the reformers to disassociate themselves from recidivism as a detention outcome as it is the wrong metric for assessing the effectiveness of juvenile detention.

While the field celebrates the great work of the reformers in changing incarceration policy, the reality is that those who work in facilities are now expected to produce the same outcomes without additional resources and with a population of youth that is, in most cases, substantially more difficult. Therefore, the difficult job of creating and sustaining acceptable conditions of confinement just got more difficult. And so it should not be a surprise that despite decreases in numbers of youth in custody, the number of crises in facilities seems unaffected by the population reductions.

■ Good Detention Practice

Ambivalence has always existed among practitioners regarding the reformer's agenda. Some have interpreted detention reform to be ideologically driven and based on the belief that all incarceration is bad (Holman & Ziedenberg, 2006; Mendel, 2011). The first practitioner challenge came from Earl Dunlap when he served as the Executive Director of the National Partnership for Juvenile Services. "You cannot have it both ways" was Dunlap's response when the reformers objected to helpful programs and services in detention. Reformers believed that these programs enticed juvenile court judges to place more youth in juvenile detention for the wrong reasons, as was the case in Luzerne County, Pennsylvania, where judges were receiving "kickbacks" for placing youth in detention who did not require secure lockup. Dunlap knew that the reformer's criticisms were initially and justifiably fueled by valid examples of egregious conditions of confinement, but he argued that the responsible detention practitioner implemented programs and services that reformers opposed as the best way to remedy troubling conditions of confinement. Carol Brooks (2012), the current National Partnership for Juvenile Services Executive Director, pushed back even more by telling attendees at the 2012 National Partnership for Juvenile Services Annual Conference that while practitioners are in total agreement that harmful juvenile detention is bad, they reject that all juvenile detention is bad. From the practitioner perspective, there is agreement with the reform principles that secure juvenile detention should be used for only those youth who really need it. Therefore, getting the right youth into detention seems to imply a need for good detention practice.

One of the more enduring practitioner resources has been the *Desktop Guide to Good Juvenile Detention Practices* (Roush, 1996). Starting from the assumption that the detention practitioner provides safe and humane custody to any youth legally ordered into detention, the document follows the CHAPTERS model (Soler et al., 1990). This document is a compendium of practitioner-generated materials about constructive ways to address those legal and case law expectations outlined by CHAPTERS. Ironically, the Youth Law Center, which is a leading advocate for children's rights and safe and humane conditions of confinement, provided the legal rationale for the use of programs as the appropriate means of improving conditions of confinement and avoiding litigation.

One of the best examples of appropriate program usage comes from Oklahoma City. In the face of prolonged and severe crowding, former Oklahoma County (OK) Juvenile Bureau Chief Ray Bitsche reaffirmed his belief that "the best security is built on programs and more programs, people and more people" (Previte, 1997, p. 77). Increased staffing and daily programming were the primary defenses against the negative effects of overcrowding. Until there is evidence to the contrary, the same approach might provide positive outcomes with a more difficult population of detainees.

■ The Continuing Challenge of Disproportionate Minority Incarceration

The reform experience in Cook County Juvenile Temporary Detention Center suggests that disproportionate minority incarceration may increase as detention reforms gain traction. In September 2011, the National Council on Crime and Delinquency issued a report where the significant concern was the racial disproportionality at Juvenile Temporary Detention Center. The report stated that African American youth are arrested at five times the rate of White youth and detained at 46 times the rate. The "rate" referenced in the report is the relative rate index, a new strategy for DMC considerations that replaces the disproportionate representation index. The relative rate index focuses on decision points throughout the process and makes direct comparisons to White youth. The perspective of the Heywood Banks Institute is that the relative rate index understates the social significance of the disparity (Bell & Mariscal, 2011, p. 113), making the resolution of the disproportionality in the Cook County an even higher priority. The report implied that this is the highest relative rate of detention for African Americans known to the National Council on Crime and Delinquency.

The report was careful in its explanation of this level of DMC, stating, "The high level of disparity in Cook County is due largely to the fact that so few white youth enter detention." The U.S. District Court-appointed detention superintendent or Transitional Administrator (TA) challenged this explanation because the DMC efforts were different from the population-reduction strategies that removed as many as 500 youth of color from secure detention. The DMC problem is that the proportion of minorities among the remaining detainees increased from 93% to 99% as of 2012. The significant population reduction diverts attention from the increase in minority detainees and avoids the need to drill down as to why DMC outcomes deteriorated, even considering that the DMC efforts do not have the longevity of the population-reduction strategies. Nonetheless, better explanations are needed than "locking up more White youth."

■ Fear of Liability

Operating a successful secure custody facility is difficult, and it is not something that people do well intuitively. Since there are few appropriate pre-employment training experiences for new juvenile facility administrators, most find themselves unable to solve the daily problems of correctional practice in a manner that consistently insulates them from liability. Post-employment training programs through the National Institute of Corrections focus generally on correctional liability, but access to these excellent training programs is insufficient to meet the demands of practitioners nationwide. Instead of providing clear guidance on secure custody practices, attorneys and other correctional law experts advise juvenile confinement administrators to do the "right" thing. This provides little consolation to administrators who are enmeshed in complex and volatile situations with few issues that are clearly defined. To further complicate the matter, many issues are directly under the control of inexperienced direct care staff who have a poorer understanding of legal issues than the administrator. It can be, in simplest terms, the worst of all possible options. To underestimate the gravity of this problem for facility administrators is to miss entirely an influential factor in contemporary juvenile facility management.

In addition to the *Desktop Guide*, new publications are beginning to provide clearer guidelines for successful detention and correction operations (Heinz, Wise, & Bartollas, 2010). This has helped to lessen the fear of litigation among contemporary administrators. Brodsky (1982) described this fear as having the potential to become an obsession that can paralyze administrative decision making and render an organization ineffective. This debilitating effect increases the probability that the institution will be named in a suit about such operational "hot spots" as institutional violence, abuse, Prison Rape Elimination Act, medical and health care services, pandemic preparedness, and conditions of confinement. For many practitioners, fear of liability has turned them from theory- and research-driven strategies for successful operations to an approach oriented to the avoidance of litigation and liability.

■ External and Internal Change Forces

Brodsky (1982) identifies internal and external forces as change agents for custody practice. Brodsky provides a simple model for understanding two different approaches to improving conditions of confinement. We will use these internal versus external pathways as a frame of reference for understanding or explaining current practice.

Internal factors include enlightened administrators who work to create an environment that is just, humane, and safe. Internal change has the advantage of a greater understanding of both the problem and the corresponding solution(s). However, internal change processes are traditionally very slow and very susceptible to social, political, and economic obstacles. Internally, Brodsky discusses standards and accreditation, but much has changed since his article. For example, the information about what works has increased dramatically, including evidence-based practices, best practices, promising practices, refined theory development, and research.

External factors are represented by the courts, indirectly by the Civil Rights of Institutionalized Persons Act (CRIPA) and other actions through the U.S. Department of Justice (DOJ). Change prompted by the court has the advantage of being more immediate and significantly less sensitive to political and economic obstacles. The greatest downside of court-ordered change is the loss of control experienced by practitioners.

Court action, CRIPA actions, and legislative or policymaker-driven directives, statutes, or mandates are intended to alter the operations of a facility to avoid litigation or reduce the costs associated with liability and litigation. These factors include a range of actions that are generally outside the control of an institution or agency. Some of the best information about problems with conditions in facilities that house juveniles comes from the DOJ's CRIPA investigation findings letters. The common theme is the failure to protect the safety of youth in custody These are linked to (a) an intensification of various types of interpersonal violence; (b) the sexual exploitation of youth by staff and other youth; (c) the absence of usable standards based on best practices and evidence-based evaluations that aid in the creation of conditions of confinement that promote versus threaten resident safety; and (d) the growing crisis in the juvenile justice workforce due to the difficulties of recruiting, selecting, and retaining qualified staff to work with troubled youth. In addition, staffing crises are further exacerbated by a depleted economy resulting in budget cuts that affect development and access to training and technical assistance, technology, and other resources that help to ensure safe and healthy conditions of confinement.

The primary products that emanate from external factors that address improved conditions of confinement are Settlement Agreements (including consent decrees, findings letters, and court orders) and standards (American Correctional Association [ACA] Standards and Juvenile Detention Alternatives

Initiative Self-Inspection Standards). There is considerable overlap with standards as they are sometimes part of the Settlement Agreement or they are adopted to favorably influence the court (external factor). More often they are used by practitioners voluntarily, so they are not an external factor in this regard. We have placed them for the moment in this category as their origins are in response to concerns about liability and litigation.

Recent court decisions, however, combine with the Prison Litigation Reform Act (PLRA) to suggest that the court and the legislative branches are backing away from involvement in prisoners' rights litigation and deferring the definition of acceptable correctional practice to the professional correctional community.

■ The Study of Conditions of Confinement

The seminal research on conditions of confinement is the congressionally mandated Study of Conditions of Confinement (Parent, Leiter, Kennedy, Livens, Wentworth, & Wilcox, 1994), hereafter referred to as "the Study." Prior to the Study, the widely held assumption was that changing or improving a facility's policies and procedures, and the corresponding staff development or staff training on these new policies and procedures, would result in a new practice that would meet standards or other expectations, which came to include compliance with court-ordered reforms. This commonly held belief was a part of the standards and accreditation logic of the ACA.

The Study reviewed multiple variables related to conditions of confinement in over 900 juvenile confinement facilities while simultaneously assessing each institution's compliance with important professional standards. The findings were significant, and they resulted in a substantial realignment, perhaps a paradigm shift, of professional standards and standard evaluations in juvenile confinement facilities. The Study found that there was no coherence or relationship between increased standards compliance and improved conditions of confinement. It debunked the idea that quality policy (policy, procedure, and training) equals quality practice, demonstrating that practice was the essential element in the reform and improvement of the conditions of confinement and that the only way to assess practice was through the development of performance metrics. In other words, there needed to be performance-based outcomes that would indicate the nature and extent of the changes set forth in the policies and procedures. The performance-based recommendations provided a foundation for data-driven decisions as a core element of detention reform.

■ Evidence-Based Practices

The field is enamored with evidence-based practices, despite its general inability to distinguish between evidence-based practices and practices based on evidence. Dr. Del Elliott (1980, 2010), generally considered the foremost authority on evidence-based practices in this area, suggested that an evidence-based practice that changes the social context would have more positive influence on behavior than all of the existing, individual evidence-based practices combined. Changing the social context needs to be the new lens through which improved conditions of confinement are viewed.

Perspectives on How to Change Conditions of Confinement

Whether they originate as part of an external set of decisions or are part of an internal set of decisions by the leadership and staff of an agency or institution, the nature of the actions taken to improve conditions of confinement can be generally grouped into two categories—those that are based on case law and legal perspectives and those that are based on social science theory and research. Granted, this is a false dichotomy because both categories are interactive and substantial advances in one influence the other.

While there are many similarities between case law and social science research in determining the best remedies to protection from harm questions, there are some important differences. Beyond the rigors of how outcomes are determined, the two approaches look at things a little differently, use different languages, and have different fundamental assumptions. Legalistic and attorney-driven efforts to change conditions of confinement do not have the same track record or examples of success as social science interventions. We suggest that to maximize outcomes in improving conditions and operations in juvenile detention, the time has come for practitioners to return to an evidence-based, social science-driven approach. Agee (1981) argued that the sometimes competitive nature of attorneys translates into the desire to "out-lawyer" the opponent at the expense of the best interest of incarcerated youth. When this combines with an attorneys' frequent lack of knowledge about social science findings, it creates what she called the "tyranny of non-experts." We would suggest that part of the reason for these differences in outcomes is due to the subtle differences in approaches. As such, we will refer to the liability-, litigation-, and the case law-oriented perspective as the LLCL approach. We will refer to the theory- and research-driven factors as the social science theory and research perspective (SSTR).

LLCL-driven explanations of conditions of confinement are:

☐   Frequently devoid of a scientific method; use of the adversarial method and rules of evidence does not science or research make. LLCL products may be based on evidence, but may lack the regularities and controls to qualify as evidence-based.

☐   Prone to explain what will lead to trouble or problems; do not explain the interactions between variables or how things work.

- ☐ Normative: they prescribe how people should behave. Using the cognitive principles of the late Dr. Albert Ellis (1962), the use of the word "should" suggests a moral imperative on what to do. Ellis would refer to this as an irrational demand, the outcomes of which would be inappropriate behaviors. Normative easily morphs into a problem-oriented perspective (a deficits model).

SSTR is positive (Monahan & Walker, 1986) and concerned about the way the world is and with no necessary implications for the way the world ought to be. This positive approach should be compared with positivism as a criminological approach or a solutions-oriented philosophy (strengths-based model).

The strategy of LLCL is often based on the premise of what to avoid (what not to do). Of course, the problem was that knowing what not to do was only half of the dilemma. The other half is what to do. Missing from this approach is a social science perspective on what to do. Knowing that you are not supposed to turn right at the light does not tell you whether to turn left or go straight to get to your destination. Nonetheless, knowing not to turn right may keep you from getting lost. Both types of information are needed if juvenile justice practitioners and administrators are to have the information needed to run successful, model programs.

■ Strengths and Weaknesses of Each Approach: Lessons for Practitioners

From these perspectives, we can extract some lessons for practitioners regarding both approaches to improving conditions of confinement.

Liability-, Litigation-, and Case Law-Oriented Perspective (LLCL)

Settlement Agreements—Settlement Agreements and other legal documents resulting from litigation or DOJ actions have had mixed outcomes. More importantly, common problems portend common solutions, and jurisdictions that have responded well to CRIPA involvement (e.g., the Kentucky Department of Juvenile Justice) can serve as models for change (Kelly & Hodgkin, 2002). In general, the positive outcomes experienced by practitioners in terms of improved conditions of confinement have resulted from good interactions between plaintiffs' attorneys, defendants' attorneys, and monitors.

Kentucky Department of Juvenile Justice director Ralph Kelly used the Settlement Agreement as leverage to address systemic problems that had not previously gotten the attention of the governor and legislature. With the

Settlement Agreement came financial resources that enabled Kelly to address deficits in staffing levels, training programs, and physical plants. These were the "what" factors that had to be addressed before remedying the deficits. "How" Kelly went about implementing changes in conditions of confinement became the responsibility of a new, comprehensive, extensive, and theory-based staff development and training program based on social science theory in child and youth care practices (Wells, Minor, Parsons, Morrison, & Angel, 2011). Kelly assembled a group of experts who were largely unknown to most local juvenile justice practitioners but who had extensive experience, knowledge, and teaching abilities regarding programs and daily living strategies grounded in an adolescent development perspective. Thus Kelly was able to use the Settlement Agreement as a way to introduce a new way of thinking about youth in "deep end" custody.

Another example is the successful resolution of the Settlement Agreement between the DOJ and the Georgia Department of Juvenile Justice, which can be attributed to the leadership of Orlando Martinez and Albert Murray, respectively. They used the Settlement Agreement to make substantial changes in the operations of its detention and corrections facilities. At the conclusion of the monitoring experience, two facilities had conditions of confinement that were exemplary. One of the facilities, the Dalton Regional Youth Development Center (detention), under the leadership of Bobby Hughes, received national recognition for its programs and services. Here again, the Settlement Agreement combined with SSTR information to improve programs and services.

Settlement Agreements have also been the source of criticism recently. Cohen (2010) issued a specific and thorough critique of DOJ Settlement Agreements, outlining examples where elements of the Settlement Agreement were (a) not based on what he believed to be an accurate interpretation of case law, (b) overreaching in terms of what could be reasonably required, (c) deviating from the findings of the subject matter experts outlined in the findings letters, and (d) unlikely to produce the intended outcomes if defendants resisted. While his targets were the DOJ Settlement Agreements in Ohio and New York, his article seemed to serve as a blueprint for the actions taken by the State of Ohio in a different yet equally broad, sweeping, overreaching Settlement Agreement in *SH v. Reed* (U.S. District Court, Southern District of Ohio, Eastern Division, Case Number 2:04-CV-1206). Cohen's critique of the DOJ Settlement Agreements was not without merit, even though the DOJ overreaching may have been a misguided attempt to resolve Kehoe's (1981) observation that the complexity of juvenile facility operations exceeds the range of remedies available in Settlement Agreements. Recent Settlement Agreements by DOJ have begun address criticisms, and DOJ continues to solicit input from its subject matter experts and monitors.

PLRA: How to Short-Circuit Reform—In the matter of *SH v. Reed* the consent decree stipulations were, perhaps, the most far-reaching to date in juvenile corrections litigation, especially protection from harm. The SH Settlement

Agreement included 21 monitor-identified topic areas and had as many as 13 subject matter experts at one time participating on the monitoring team. A change in the compliance strategy on the part of the Ohio Department of Youth Services (DYS) followed a change in governors, with a new emphasis on cost reduction efforts. Preliminary estimates were that the costs of the SH Settlement Agreement could exceed $30 million annually, so the vehicle selected by DYS for ending the Settlement Agreement was a PLRA action. As the SH monitoring approached the end of the fourth year, DYS filed a motion to terminate SH under PLRA.

The Ohio Correctional Institution Inspection Committee (Saul et al., 2013) reported that on Jan. 18, 2013, the U.S. District Court approved a comprehensive joint agreement between DYS and plaintiffs' counsel and issued a Consent Order for Partial Termination (with prejudice) that significantly reduced monitoring at DYS facilities and altogether eliminated monitoring in several areas, including regionalization, access to counsel, classification, and use of force, among others. Court monitoring continues in the area of mental health and the DYS special management housing units, where youth with chronic behavior issues, generally involving assaults, are assigned. In fairness, DYS accomplished some improvements worthy of national recognition and emulation, especially in the areas of classification, community transition, dental care, education, grievances, investigations, medical care, overall operations, reception, re-entry, release authority, and supervision of staffing. Yet, several critical issues remained unresolved after the PLRA filing and order, including staffing (recruitment, hiring, training, retention, termination), collective bargaining agreements, mental health services, safety, and gang violence-reduction strategies.

Given the particulars of the Settlement Agreement, a PLRA strategy worked. Therefore, practitioners need to be mindful of the state's option at some point in the monitoring process to play the PLRA card. The strategy proved effective from political and economic perspectives. Using the reduced standard of a "constitutional minimum" as the basis for compliance with Settlement Agreement paragraphs, DYS also used a familiar accreditation strategy by arguing that it was in compliance with the vast majority of Settlement Agreement paragraphs and, therefore, had met the constitutional minimum for compliance on the entire Settlement Agreement (about 90%). This was supported by the impressive successes in other areas. The overly simplistic argument appeared to work without an acknowledgment that Settlement Agreements paragraphs, like the various denominations of paper money, are not of equal value or importance, particularly regarding youth and staff safety.

As a postscript, recent reports indicate deterioration in some of the protection from harm issues that were dismissed as a result of the PLRA initiative. The Ohio Correctional Institution Inspection Committee noted an increase in rates of use of force (Hooks, 2013; Juvenile Justice Information Exchange, 2013), while the *Columbus Dispatch* (Johnson, 2013) reported the findings of a recent Bureau of Justice Statistics survey regarding staff sexual misconduct where three of the four DYS juvenile correctional facilities ranked among the highest 13 offending facilities in the nation. As stated earlier, over time, the positive effects deteriorate, and abuses and scandals reappear; thus, the cycle repeats itself (Breed & Krisberg, 1986).

TA: The U.S. District Court Action in Cook County, IL—In September 2007, the U.S. District Court appointed Earl Dunlap as the TA of the 498-bed Cook County Juvenile Temporary Detention Center in Chicago (c.f., *Jimmy Doe, et al., v. Cook County, et al.*, U. S. District Court, Northern District of Illinois, Eastern Division, No. 99 C 3945). Before the Federal Court's intervention, a long line of experts and a series of superintendents with law enforcement and corrections experience promised change by primarily getting rid of the bad employees. In the most powerful of opinions, the court suspended any state laws, county statutes, and collective bargaining agreements that would hinder or impede Dunlap's systems change efforts (see Order, May 8, 2008, for *Doe v. Cook County* above). In her analysis of the Court's action, Turner (2010) called this "impact litigation" and a tool for social change.

With adequate authority, a court-ordered intervention can effectively change conditions of confinement. Ongoing evaluations and reports to the U.S. District Court note specifically (a) improvements in pre-employment education, (b) increased training of new and veteran staff, (c) development of cohesive teams, (d) the reduction of complexity through the use of the psychology of small wins (Centers within the Center), (e) substantially improved mental health services, (f) improved medical services, (g) expanded community, family, and volunteer involvement, (h) adequate staffing levels, (i) increased skill development programs for youth through daily cognitive-behavioral problem-solving groups, and (j) the creation of an institutional climate or social climate that detained youth evaluate or rate at a level that is above average nationally.

The TA authority also permitted a challenge to the Teamsters, the union representing direct care workers, specifically the termination of employment of an employee with substantiated abuse findings based on excessive force in the workplace. In this regard, the TA had enough authority to be able to address many of the challenges associated with the collective bargaining agreement that have discouraged, frustrated, and postponed the development of a timely and effective disciplinary process to allow administrators to remove what the TA referred to as the dangerous individuals on the staff (Donovan, 2010).

Social Science Theory and Research Perspective (SSTR)

Most Settlement Agreements contain a paragraph that states "consistent with generally accepted professional standards," which the Study has defined as the establishment of performance metrics. Within our generation of practitioners, policymakers, social scientists, and attorneys, the performance metric is an essential component of reform and should be a foundation of usable knowledge and conventional wisdom so that it is the equivalent of a constitutional minimum in any finding by the court.

The National Council of Juvenile and Family Court Judges (Marsh & Campie, 2009) is very clear about the organizing principle that weaves together evidence-based programs, and it is a relevant, understandable, and coherent theory. The unifying theory recommended here is field theory (Bell, 2005; Bell et al., 2001; Flay et al., 2004; Haney, 2006; Lewin, 1951). The social psychological foundation of this conditions improvement-oriented approach is the belief that human behavior is a function of the interaction of the person and the environment, including the immediate social situations or social context mentioned earlier.

Performance-Based Standards

The performance-based standards (PbS) movement in juvenile justice has invigorated the field, causing it to look more carefully at conditions of confinement, quality of care, and accountability (Roush, 2004). The PbS hallmark is its vision statement: "Every juvenile detention and corrections facility in America should be run as if your only child were the next youth to be admitted" (Loughran & Godfrey, 2001). This is the longstanding, "old school," commonly understood, unspoken, solitary guideline reflective of the highest commitment to quality care that sometimes seems to run against the grain of contemporary juvenile corrections. It is the quintessential "bright line" between adult and juvenile perspectives on institutions and the nature of the standards that should guide their operations. It is as close to a perfect vision statement as a youth custody facility can express (Roush, 2004).

The strength of the PbS standards is that they are derived more from social science research than legal or case law analyses. They are based on theory (Logan, 1993), a well-articulated vision and mission, goals, and performance outcomes. They start with the definition of the desired outcome, promote the use of good information to inform daily practice, and allow practitioners to identify their own strengths and weaknesses and to create a self-improvement plan to correct weaknesses (Roush, 2004). Based on the quality of PbS data integrity strategies, the PbS database has moved the field closer to a reliable picture of conditions in juvenile detention and corrections facilities. Data of this quality can be extremely valuable to the practitioner in understanding the dynamics of juvenile facility operations (Kupchik & Snyder, 2009).

Quality Assurance. All of the facilities that experience success in the creation and maintenance of safe and humane conditions of confinement rely on good data to drive essential decisions, especially continuous quality improvement strategies. Evaluations, performance metrics, facility improvement plans, feedback loops, and management information systems are critical parts of a competent quality assurance strategy that safeguards and sustains humane conditions of confinement. Without the data-driven elements of these performance metrics, policy and procedure-driven reform is largely vacuous, signaling to the field that change without measuring "how much" and "how well" counts for very little.

■ Exemplary Programs and Conditions

The juvenile justice field does not do very well at reporting its successes, so there are few resources available to practitioners that serve as a "how to" manual on creating and sustaining safe and humane conditions of confinement and helpful programs. However, experience with a variety of facilities, practitioners, and agencies yields some perspective on what works and where you can find examples of what works. In all of these instances, the facility represents a cohesive approach to the care and custody of youth. There is a clear vision and mission that support a well-defined program philosophy that creates consistency and continuity through the development of a social order or a set of behavioral expectations that apply to both adults and youth. Although collective bargaining agreements are in fervent opposition, not all staff members are created equal, and, as Cook and Ludwig (2006) demonstrated, some are more proficient than others in working with behaviorally challenging youth. Therefore, the facilities described below all have a staff recruitment and development program (staff training) that is effective at increasing each staff member's skill sets to work effectively with youth. We offer the following information not as an exhaustive list or even as a comprehensive list of good conditions of confinement. Instead, it is intended to be an example of what can be accomplished through the application of key principles.

Liability-, Litigation-, and Case Law-Oriented Facilities (LLCL)

The ACA can supply a list of accredited detention and corrections facilities, and the assumption is that these accredited facilities also have good conditions of confinement. The problem has been that accredited facilities have been targets of successful litigation on conditions of confinement issues (Roush, 2009). Even in situations where ACA-accredited facilities have received recognition outside of ACA-sponsored activities, such as the Cuyahoga Hills (OH) Juvenile Correctional Facility and the Dalton (GA) Regional Youth Development Center, these recognitions are largely attributable to program decisions independent of ACA standards according to staff.

The strength of the ACA standards (ACA, 1991a, 1991b) is that they represent the best description of the issues, concerns, factors, and elements required to operate a successful juvenile confinement facility or the best available description of the organizational structure of successful operations. Every conscientious practitioner should have a copy of the standards within easy access. The problem is that this description of "what" does not translate easily or consistently into "how" to operate a facility successfully. Similar to playing a piano, the ACA standards represent all 88 keys in perfect pitch—but unless a student is able to play by ear, the presence of a piano does not teach the student how to make music with it. In part because its origins come from the case law and deficits model (LLCL) (Keve, 1996; Reimer & Sechrest, 1979), ACA standards and accreditation have been able to take practitioners only so far.

The same applies to the Juvenile Detention Alternatives Initiative Self-Assessment Standards (Juvenile Detention Alternatives Initiative, 2011), which have not yet identified a facility that represents good conditions of confinement based on the application of these standards. Again, with an orientation toward the identification of deficits and the creation of remedial actions to eliminate the deficits, the ability to create exemplary conditions of confinement is constrained by the notion that correcting what is wrong makes things right.

An often unstated and frequently overlooked strength of both sets of standards is the education of the uninformed about the factors associated with creating and sustaining satisfactory conditions of confinement. In part, this has always been their appeal to the courts, advocates, and reformers. When litigation or crises finally get the attention of decision makers who have neglected or ignored the proliferation of punitive strategies, these standards serve as a wakeup call regarding the nature and extent of the problems and, subsequently, what needs to be done, independent of the issue of how much and how well those things need to be done. The recent reform efforts have persuaded juvenile justice leaders, judges in particular, to adopt the reform's core principles. The infusion of money and technical assistance into the jurisdiction also helps to change the sometimes recalcitrant leader's perspectives, as well as the excellent job the reformers do in providing "reformed" leaders with national exposure and attention. An effective, well-thought-out, and implemented strategy, indeed.

Social Science Theory and Research Facilities (SSTR)

Missouri is a bellwether example of our time, and any discussions of conditions of confinement must include a review of the Missouri Approach (Mendel, 2003). Missouri is an example of how good social science research has been able to create and sustain good conditions of confinement for so long that these old-school concepts are now viewed as new and innovative. Attributed to the leadership of Mark Steward and now Tim Decker, the Missouri Approach demonstrates the advantages of small, regional facilities; small, normalized living units; a healthy ratio of educated and well-trained staff; an abundance of strengths-based and developmentally appropriate programs and services; high levels of family and community involvement; and active involvement and participation by the youth in his or her treatment program. Simultaneously, facility teams work well in identifying how context, situations, and systems (including family systems) influence behaviors, as Haney (2006; Roush, 2009) recommended. To some degree, the Missouri Approach is a practitioner guide on how to implement programs. The process concepts and principles from the Missouri Approach would likely be successful regardless of the program philosophy.

Cognitive-behavioral interventions (Glick, 2006; Latessa, 2006) have been well documented with numerous positive research outcomes. As such, it is a social science program category that warrants consideration by all practitioners, even those in detention who might mistakenly believe that cognitive-behavioral intervention is only for youth rehabilitation programs. All cognitive-behavioral programs implemented with fidelity are inherently strengths-based. The behavioral aspect of a cognitive-behavioral intervention has its origin in reinforcement theory (Becker, Madsen, Arnold, & Thomas, 1976), which identifies a youth's strengths and then provides reinforcement to expand appropriate behavior. The focus on positive behaviors (strengths) reduces the occurrences of negative behaviors and allows youth to work on expanding strengths (Stumphauzer, 1979).

Berrien County Juvenile Center (MI) has a 16-bed secure detention unit that operates on the cognitive-behavioral principles of Rational Behavior Training. Under the leadership of Rich Dama and Terry Martinek, the behavior management tools include a point system; a levels system; a coupon-based token economy; behavior contracts; and the use of 5-minute, same-area timeouts (Burchard & Tyler, 1965). Restraints and room confinements are rare, and residents help other youth to sustain appropriate behavior. The staff conducts daily problem-solving groups based on Rational Behavior Training principles with the focus on successful adaptation to the detention environment.

The Youth Center of the High Plains (Amarillo, Texas) is a dual-purpose facility, containing secure pre-adjudication detention and post-dispositional residential treatment. Under the leadership of Jane King and Neil Eddins, it represents a good example of sustained best practices. Using the Rational Behavior Training principles described above, it has maintained good conditions of confinement for over two decades. The structure and common expectations for behaviors generate a social order that produces high levels of consistency and safety. Youth are free to practice new and appropriate behaviors while simultaneously engaging in new thinking that will sustain appropriate behaviors upon release. One of the strengths of this facility is its training of new and veteran staff. The training is designed to clarify and simplify some rather complex concepts to the point that they are understandable and usable by both adults and youth in the facility.

The Johnson Youth Center Treatment Unit, Alaska Division of Juvenile Justice, altered the thinking and orientation of staff by focusing programs and services on a strengths-based assessment protocol. It is based on the underlying concepts of Positive Youth Development (Barton & Butts, 2008; Butts, Mayer & Ruth, 2005), which include the following: (1) the focus is on strengths and assets rather than deficits and problems; (2) strengths and assets are usually acquired through positive relationships, especially with prosocial and caring adults; and (3) the development and acquisition of youth assets occurs in multiple contexts and environments. Early results suggested that the adoption of this protocol was the catalyst for an improvement in institutional climate as perceived by both youth and staff (Barton, Mackin, & Fields, 2008). Complaints from youth and parents/guardians as well as behavioral incidents at the facility also declined markedly. The follow-up indicates that the institutional climate remains greatly improved and that recidivism results are encouraging, but the implementation of the practice model could be strengthened (Barton & Mackin, 2012). The Johnson Youth Center Treatment Unit experience offers lessons for other practitioners regarding the potential benefits and challenges of adopting a more strengths-based approach.

Summary

"The reformer is always right about what is wrong and generally wrong about what is right." G. K. Chesterton

Laying responsibility for troubled detention facilities at the feet of today's juvenile offender is tempting but erroneous. The future of juvenile detention will require practitioners to work smarter and more effectively. As the detention population changes, efforts to provide secure, safe, effective conditions of confinement must focus not only on limiting liability and litigation but on social science theory and research. For practitioners, success depends on the ability to move adeptly between these two approaches. Administrators and practitioners must understand what not to do, what to do, and how to do it. We recommended a new approach (Roush, 2009) based on Haney's (2006) elements that (1) individual-centered approaches are self-limiting and doomed to fail over time; (2) strong, helpful programs are needed to counteract the inherently dangerous and negative psychological effects of incarceration; and (3) rehabilitative efforts cannot ignore the situations and social environments that youth will be released to.

Also, important developmental strategies are needed to create state-of-the-art juvenile detention, including (1) clear ethical statements and policies combined with purposeful vision statements to set expectations for staff interactions with youth; (2) programs for adolescents that are developmentally appropriate (Beyer, 2011)—detainees must be viewed differently from adults; (3) new youth workers need proper pre-employment education and training beyond a high-school diploma;

(4) professional standards should include practice guidelines supported by good data to measure performance outcomes; and (5) leadership. We would add to these a renewed priority on strategies to improve programs and conditions that are social science theory- and research-driven and strengths-based.

References

American Correctional Association (1991a). *Standards for juvenile detention facilities* (3rd ed.). Laurel, MD: Author.

American Correctional Association (1991b). *Standards for juvenile training schools* (3rd ed.). Laurel, MD: Author.

Annie E. Casey Foundation (2013, February 25). *Juvenile detention alternatives initiative: 2011 annual results report.* Baltimore: Author.

Barton, W. H., & Butts, J. A. (2008). *Building on strength: Positive youth development in juvenile justice programs.* Chicago: Chapin Hall Center for Children at the University of Chicago. Available from: http://jeffreybutts.files.wordpress.com/2008/08/building.pdf

Barton, W. H., & Mackin, J. R. (2012). Towards a strength-based juvenile correctional facility: Sustainability and effects of an institutional transformation. *Journal of Offender Rehabilitation, 51*(7), 435–452.

Barton, W. H., Mackin, J. R., & Fields, J. (2008). Assessing youth strengths in a residential juvenile correctional program. *Residential Treatment for Children & Youth, 23*(3/4), 11–36.

Becker, W., Madsen, C., Arnold, C., & Thomas. D. (1976). The contingent use of teacher attention and praise in reducing classroom behavior problems. *Journal of Special Education, 1,* 287–307.

Bell, C. (2005). *Seven principles for changing at-risk behavior and cultivating resiliency among youth.* Chicago: Community Mental Health Council.

Bell, C., Gamm, S., Vallas, P., & Jackson, P. (2001). Strategies for the prevention of youth violence in the Chicago Public Schools (pp. 251–272). In M. Shafii & S. Shafii (Eds.), *School violence: Contributing factors, management, and prevention.* Washington, DC: American Psychological Association.

Bell, J., & Mariscal, M. (2011). Race, ethnicity, and ancestry in juvenile justice. In F. T. Sherman & F. H. Jacobs (Eds.), *Juvenile justice: Advancing research, policy, and practice* (pp. 111–130). Hoboken, NJ: John Wiley & Sons, Inc.

Beyer, M. (2011). A developmental view of youth in the juvenile justice system. In F. T. Sherman & F. H. Jacobs (Eds.), *Juvenile justice: Advancing research, policy, and practice* (pp. 3–23). Hoboken, NJ: John Wiley & Sons, Inc.

Breed, A. F., & Krisberg, B. (1986, December). Juvenile corrections: Is there a future? *Corrections Today,* pp. 14–20.

Brodsky, S. (1982). Correctional change and the social scientist: A case study. *Journal of Community Psychology, 10,* 128–132.

Brooks, C. C. (2012, October 22). Opening remarks. The annual conference of the National Partnership for Juvenile Services, Las Vegas, NV.

Burchard, J., & Tyler, V. (1965). The modification of delinquent behavior through operant conditioning. *Behavior Research and Therapy, 2,* 245–250.

Burrell, S. (1999). *Improving conditions of confinement in secure juvenile detention centers* (Pathways to Juvenile Detention Reform #6). Baltimore: Annie E. Casey Foundation, Juvenile Detention Alternatives Initiative.

Butts, J. (2013, March 7). Are we too quick to claim credit for falling juvenile incarceration rates? Juvenile Justice Information Exchange. Available online at: (http://jjie.org/too-quick-claim-credit-for-falling-juvenile-incarceration.), downloaded April 2, 2013.

Butts, J., & Evans, D. (2011, September). *Resolution, reinvestment, and realignment: Three strategies for changing juvenile justice.* New York: John Jay College of Criminal Justice.

Butts, J., Mayer, S., & Ruth, G. (2005, October). *Focusing juvenile justice on positive youth development* (Issue Brief #105). Chicago: Chapin Hall Center for Children.

Cohen, F. (2010, Spring). Overreaching & underachieving: The Justice Department & juvenile facilities. *Criminal Law Bulletin, 46*(2), 1–20.

Cook, P. J., & Ludwig, J. (2006). Assigning youths to minimize total harm. In K. A. Dodge, T. J. Dishion, & J. E. Lansford (Eds.), *Deviant peer influences in programs for youth: Problems and solutions* (pp. 67–89). New York: Guilford Press.

Donovan, L. (2010, October 13). Juvenile jail chief worried about 'dirt bag' workers: Threats made against bosses as layoffs loom. *Chicago Sun Times.* Available online at: http://www.suntimes.com/.

Elliott, D. S. (1980). A repertoire of impact measures. In M. W. Klein & K. S. Teilmann (Eds.), *Handbook of criminal justice evaluation* (pp. 507–544). Thousand Oaks, CA: Sage Publications.

Elliott, D. S. (2010, October 6). Making the case for evidence-based programs. Conference presentation to the Juvenile Detention Alternatives Initiative National Conference, Kansas City, MO.

Ellis, A. (1962). *Reason and emotion in psychotherapy.* New York: Lyle Stuart.

Flay, B. R., Graumlich, S., Segawa, E., Burns, J., & Holliday, M. (2004, April). Effects of 2 prevention programs on high-risk behaviors among African American youth: A randomized trial. *Archives of Pediatric and Adolescent Medicine, 158*, 377–384.

Gest, T. (2004). U.S. Justice Department cuffs juvenile corrections: Federal civil rights attorneys increasingly file charges over conditions. *Youth Today, 13*(10), *1*, 10–11.

Glick, B. (2006). *Cognitive behavioral interventions with at-risk youth.* Kingston, NJ: Civic Research Institute.

Haney, C. (2006). *Reforming punishment: Psychological limits to the pains of imprisonment.* Washington, DC: American Psychological Association.

Heinz, J., Wise, T., & Bartollas, C. (2010). *Successful management of juvenile residential facilities: A performance-based approach.* Alexandria, VA: American Correctional Association.

Holman, B., & Ziedenberg, J. (2006, November). *The dangers of detention: The impact of incarcerating youth in detention and other secure facilities.* Washington, DC: Justice Policy Institute.

Hooks, J. (2013, March). *Circleville Juvenile Correctional Facility.* Columbus: The Correctional Institution Inspection Committee.

Johnson, A. (2013, June 7). Report details sex assault crisis in Ohio's juvenile prisons: Three facilities have rates among 13 highest in the nation. *The Columbus Dispatch.* Available online at: http://www.dispatch.com/content/stories/local/2013/06/06/3.

Juvenile Detention Alternatives Initiative (2011). *Detention facility self-assessment revised guidelines: A practice guide to juvenile detention reform.* Baltimore: A Project of the Annie E. Casey Foundation.

Juvenile Justice Information Exchange (2013, April 22). Report says use of force incidents increasing in Ohio DYS facilities. Mental Health and the Juvenile Justice System: Progress, Problems and Paradoxes. Available online at (https://jjie.org/reportsays-use-of-forceincidents-increasingin-ohio-dys-facilities/)

Kehoe, C. J. (1981). Juvenile justice standards: What's in it for the kids and us? In: *Issues in juvenile corrections.* College Park, MD: American Correctional Association.

Kelly, R. E., & Hodgkin, J. H. (2002, January). Reforming juvenile justice in Kentucky: A report on the Commonwealth of Kentucky's effort to address a federal consent decree on juvenile services. In D. W. Roush (Ed.), *Youth corrections compendium: Resources and reflections on strategic reform* (pp. 93–104). Richmond, KY: National Juvenile Detention Association.

Keve, P. W. (1996). *Measuring excellence: The history of correctional standards & accreditation.* Lanham, MD: American Correctional Association.

Kupchik, A., & Snyder, R. B. (2009, September). The impact of juvenile inmates' perceptions and facility characteristics on victimization in juvenile correctional facilities. *The Prison Journal, 89*(3), 265–285.

Latessa, E. (2006). Effectiveness of cognitive behavioral interventions for youthful offenders— Review of the research. In B. Glick, *Cognitive behavioral interventions with at-risk youth* (Chapter 14). Kingston, NJ: Civic Research Institute.

Lewin, K. (1951). *Field theory in social science.* New York: Harper & Row.

Logan, C. H. (1993, October). Criminal justice performance measures for prisons. In J. J. Dilulio, Jr., & J. Q. Wilson, et al. (Eds.), *Performance measures for the criminal justice system.* Washington, DC: U.S. Department of Justice, Bureau of Justice Statistics—Princeton University Study Group on Criminal Justice Performance Measures.

Loughran, E. J., & Godfrey, K. (2001). *Performance-based standards: A system of continuous improvement.* South Easton, MA: Council of Juvenile Correctional Administrators.

Marsh, S. C., & Campie, P. E. (Spring, 2009). Words and concepts matter: Ten Commandments of social science research. *Rapport: National Juvenile Court Services Association, 13*(2), 8–10.

Mendel, R. (2003). *Small is beautiful: The Missouri Division of Youth Services.* Jefferson City, MO: Missouri Division of Youth Services.

Mendel, R. (2011). *No place for kids: The case for reducing juvenile incarceration.* Baltimore: Annie E. Casey Foundation.

Monahan, J., & Walker, L. (1986, March). Social authority: Obtaining, evaluating, and establishing social science in law. *University of Pennsylvania Law Review, 134,* 447–517.

National Council on Crime and Delinquency (2011, September). *Juvenile detention in Cook County: Future directions.* Oakland: National Council on Crime and Delinquency.

Parent, D., Leiter, V., Kennedy, S., Livens, L., Wentworth, D., & Wilcox, S. (1994, August). *Conditions of confinement: Juvenile detention and correctional facilities* (Research report). Washington, DC: U.S. Department of Justice, Office of Juvenile Justice and Delinquency Prevention.

Previte, M. T. (1997, February). Preventing security crises at youth centers. *Corrections Today,* pp. 76–79.

Reimer, E. G., & Sechrest, D. K. (1979). Writing standards for correctional accreditation. *Federal Probation, 43,* 10–16.

Roush, D. W. (Ed.). (1996, October). *Desktop guide to good juvenile detention practice.* Washington, DC: U. S. Department of Justice, Office of Juvenile Justice and Delinquency Prevention.

Roush, D. W. (2004, Winter). The performance-based standard: Implications for juvenile health care. *Journal of Correctional Health Care, 10,* 499–526.

Roush, D. W. (2009). State-of-the-art juvenile detention: In search of a new normal. In A. R Roberts & D. W. Springer (Eds.), *Juvenile delinquency and juvenile justice: Policies, programs, and practice.* Sudbury, MA: Jones and Bartlett Publishers, Inc.

Saul, J., Furderer, D., Geisler, G., Hooks, J., Jackson, A., & Robison, C. (2013, January 29). *Biennial report to the 130th Ohio General Assembly.* Columbus: The Correctional Institution Inspection Committee.

Snyder, H. N., & Sickmund, M. (2006, March). *Juvenile offenders and victims: 2006 national report.* Washington, DC: U. S. Department of Justice, Office of Juvenile Justice and Delinquency Prevention.

Soler, M. I., Shotton, A., Bell, J., Jameson, E., Shauffer, C. & Warboys, L. (1990). *Representing the child client.* New York: Matthew Bender.

Stumphauzer, J. S. (Ed.). (1979). *Progress in behavior therapy with delinquents.* Springfield, IL: Charles C. Thomas, Publisher.

Turner, L. (2010, August 8). Using impact litigation as a tool for social change: Jimmy Doe: A case study. *The Harvard Civil Rights—Civil Liberties Law Review* (CR-CL). Online: http://harvardcrcl.org/2010/08/10/using-impact-litigation-as-a-tool-for-social-change-jimmy-doe-a-case-study-by-lori-turner, downloaded May 15, 2012.

Twedt, S. (2001, July 15). U.S. detention centers becoming warehouses for mentally ill youth. *Pittsburgh Post-Gazette.* Available at: http://www. post-gazette.com/headlines/20010715surveyJP3.asp.

Wells, J. B., Minor, K. I., Parson, S., Morrison, T., & Angel, E. (2011, December). *Facility youth worker: Training needs assessment and job task analysis project.* Richmond, KY: Commonwealth Research Consulting, Inc.

10 Juvenile Drug Courts, Juvenile Mental Health Courts, and Teen Courts

Matthew L. Hiller and Christine A. Saum

■ Introduction

This chapter discusses specialty juvenile court models developed for young offenders with substance abuse problems (juvenile drug courts) or with mental health disorders (juvenile mental health courts), and for diverting youth with minor offenses from formal juvenile justice processing (teen courts). Because each type of court was developed to address a specific issue, this chapter discusses each type separately. For each specialty court, the specific problem addressed is explained first, followed by a general description of the court. Next, a review of the scientific literature on the court's effectiveness is presented. Finally, key topics identified in the literature are discussed, as are suggestions for future research. A general discussion of the similarities between these courts and remaining concerns about them concludes the chapter.

■ Juvenile Drug Courts

Problem Statement

Juvenile drug courts (JDCs), specialty problem-solving courts for addressing substance abuse problems among youth involved in the juvenile justice system, were first used in the early to mid-1990s as a response to interrelated problems of juvenile substance abuse and the dramatically increasing numbers of youth arrested for drug law violations (Butts & Roman, 2004). For example, Snyder (1997) reports that between 1992 and 1996, arrests of juveniles for drug abuse violations increased 120%. Indeed, the need for JDCs persists nearly 20 years after they were first implemented as youth substance abuse and related delinquency continue to be prominent public safety and public health concerns. For instance, data show more than 180,000 arrests were made in 2008 of juveniles for drug law violations (Puzzanchera, 2009). The National Survey of Drug Use and Health showed that in 2011, 10.1% of youth had used an illegal drug in the past month. This included use in the past month for 3.3% of 12- and 13-year-olds, 9.2% for 14- and 15-year-olds, and 17.1% of 16- and 17-year-olds (SAMHSA, 2012).

Description

JDCs are based on a therapeutic jurisprudence philosophy, so they combine juvenile justice case processing with community-based substance abuse treatment. A team of court actors (e.g., judges, prosecutors, defense attorneys, juvenile probation officers) and community service providers (e.g., substance abuse treatment, alternative schools, mental health treatment) work collaboratively to address the youth's use or abuse of illicit drugs, the presumed cause of his or her delinquent behavior. Most JDCs use a phase structure. Each phase has a prescribed minimum duration and number of court contacts, treatment sessions, urine tests, and other supervision and collateral services. Specific goals (e.g., remain drug-free for 90 days, attend school) must be met to progress to a higher phase. As youth advance in the program, the intensity of services gradually diminishes. Most teams hold a weekly "staffing" to discuss the status of the participants. The team relies on the authority of the judge to assign sanctions (e.g., community service, increased status review hearings) for noncompliant behavior and rewards (e.g., praise, phase advancement) to youth as they work through the JDC. The ultimate reward for graduates usually involves having the charge dropped or expunged from their criminal record.

After their inception in the early 1990s, JDCs proliferated quickly. For example, Cooper (2001) reports that between 1995 and 2000, at least 140 JDCs were established across the nation. As of Dec. 31, 2009, the date for which the most recent data were reported, 476 JDCs were in operation, with programs in 47 of the 50 states (Huddleston & Marlowe, 2011). The first JDC programs were modified adult drug court programs (Bureau of Justice Assistance, 2003; Roman, Butts, & Rebeck, 2004). Belenko and Dembo (2003) note that as the juvenile justice system became more adversarial and punitive, an intervention adapted from the adult system became an important option for providing rehabilitation-focused services to youth and their families.

The need to modify the adult drug court model to address the unique needs and circumstances of juveniles was recognized soon after they were first developed (Belenko & Logan, 2003; Cooper, 2002). Stein, Deberard, and Homan (2013) note that JDC participants can be distinguished from adult drug court participants not only in terms of age, but also in terms of the particularly strong influence that delinquent peers and poorly functioning families have on them. Because of their status as minors, most programs require some involvement of the family, and most youth are highly resistant to treatment because they have not yet accrued negative health and legal consequences from their use and abuse of illicit drugs. Although JDCs still bear some resemblance to adult drug courts in their operational characteristics (e.g., active role for the judge, team collaboration, substance abuse treatment), JDCs now specifically address the special needs and circumstances presented by juvenile offenders. Evidence for this comes from a publication developed by a workgroup of JDC practitioners, researchers, and educators (Bureau of Justice Assistance, 2003). This group developed the 16 strategies outlined in Table 10.1 to represent the set of core components for JDCs. Indeed, developing a program model that explicitly addresses each of these as well as including at least one evidence-based program or practice (e.g., The Seven Challenges Program) is a required condition for receiving federal funding to implement or enhance JDCs (c.f., OJJDP, 2012). Deduced from this, the essential components of a contemporary JDC include (1) assessment of treatment needs; (2) juvenile-specific outpatient or residential substance abuse treatment; (3) frequent cooperation among a team of professionals from the juvenile justice system and community providers; (4) frequent, random drug testing;

Table 10.1   **16 Strategies for Juvenile Drug Treatment Courts**

1. *Collaborative planning.* Engage all stakeholders in creating an interdisciplinary, coordinated, and systemic approach to working with youth and their families.

2. *Teamwork.* Develop and maintain an interdisciplinary, non-adversarial work team.

3. *Clearly defined target population and eligibility criteria.* Define a target population and eligibility criteria that are aligned with the program's goals and objectives.

4. *Judicial involvement and supervision.* Schedule frequent judicial reviews and be sensitive to the effect that court proceedings can have on youth and their families.

5. *Monitoring and evaluation.* Establish a system for program monitoring and evaluation to maintain quality of service, assess program impact, and contribute to knowledge in the field.

6. *Community partnerships.* Build partnerships with community organizations to expand the range of opportunities available to youth and their families.

7. *Comprehensive treatment planning.* Tailor interventions to the complex and varied needs of youth and their families.

8. *Developmentally appropriate services.* Tailor treatment to the developmental needs of adolescents.

9. *Gender-appropriate services.* Design treatment to address the unique needs of each gender.

10. *Cultural competence.* Create policies and procedures that are responsive to cultural differences and train personnel to be culturally competent.

11. *Focus on strengths.* Maintain a focus on the strengths of youth and their families during program planning and in every interaction between the court and those it serves.

12. *Family engagement.* Recognize and engage the family as a valued partner in all components of the program.

13. *Educational linkages.* Coordinate with the school system to ensure that each participant enrolls in and attends an educational program that is appropriate to his or her needs.

14. *Drug testing.* Design drug testing to be frequent, random, and observed. Document testing policies and procedures in writing.

15. *Goal-oriented incentives and sanctions.* Respond to compliance and noncompliance with incentives and sanctions that are designed to reinforce or modify the behavior of youth and their families.

16. *Confidentiality.* Establish a confidentiality policy and procedures that guard the privacy of the youth while allowing the drug court team to access key information.

Source: Bureau of Justice Assistance (2003). *Juvenile drug courts: Strategies in practice* (NCJ Publication No. 197866). Washington, DC: U.S. Department of Justice, Office of Justice Programs.

(5) regular reviews by the JDC team of the youth's behavior in school, treatment, community, and the home; (6) regular, scheduled reviews before the JDC judge; (7) collateral services (e.g., mental health treatment, family therapy); and (8) integration of the family into the court and treatment process.

Current research has documented the implementation of these components through process evaluations of several JDCs (Bryan, Hiller, & Leukefeld,

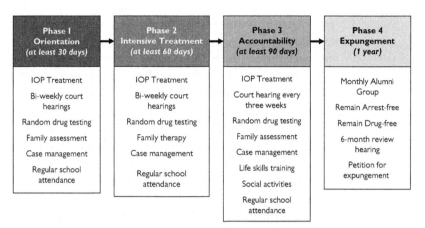

Figure 10.1   **Phase structure of a juvenile drug court in the Mid-Atlantic region of the United States.**

2006; Hiller, Malluche, Bryan, et al., 2010). To provide a concrete case example, data shown in Figures 10.1 and 10.2 are from an unpublished study of a JDC in a large city in the Mid-Atlantic region. Figure 10.1 presents the phase structure of the program and shows the minimum expected duration of each phase as well as the services plan for each. Similar to most JDCs, this program's intensity was greatest in the early phases and least in the last phase. For example, during the first program phase, participants were placed in intensive outpatient substance abuse treatment, attended biweekly status reviews with the JDC judge, completed a family assessment, were subjected to random urine drug tests several times per week, received intensive case management, and

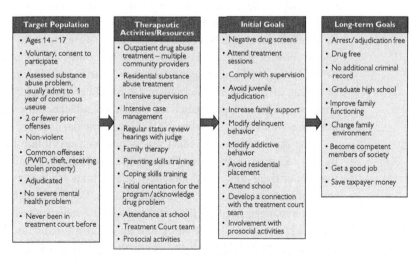

Figure 10.2   **Logic model of a juvenile drug treatment court in the Mid-Atlantic region of the United States.**

were expected to attend school regularly. At the end of Phase 3, participants went through commencement, but they weren't entirely done with the program until the end of Phase 4. This last phase required monthly attendance at an alumni group and a midyear and end-of-year status hearing with the JDC judge. If drug-free and arrest-free during this last year, the participant was eligible for having the charge that led to his or her being in drug court expunged.

Figure 10.2 provides a different perspective of the same program. This logic model presents inputs (target population), throughputs (therapeutic services), and outputs (short- and long-term goals) for the JDC. As shown, the program targeted youth ages 14 to 17 adjudicated for a drug law violation (e.g., possession with intent to deliver) or for substance abuse-related offenses (e.g., theft). Youth assessed with a substance abuse problem and two or fewer prior adjudications were asked to volunteer for the program. Numerous therapeutic activities were provided, including outpatient and/or residential substance abuse treatment. Intensive supervision was provided by not-for-profit community agencies that conducted in-person and phone-based contacts with the individual. Other services included family therapy and parenting skills training for family members. Interestingly, the team felt they were a primary therapeutic resource, a view supported by Stein and colleagues (2013). Initial goals were logically linked to long-term goals and were expected of the participant while in the JDC; these included negative drug screens (an analog for the long-term outcome of remaining drug-free). Other initial goals were to attend treatment, comply with supervision, and attend school. Other long-term goals were to remain arrest-free and improve family functioning.

Effectiveness

Compared to adult drug courts, many fewer studies have examined the effectiveness of JDCs, and the overall methodological quality of this research is poor (Mitchell, Wilson, Eggers, & MacKenzie, 2012). Consequently, findings for the effectiveness of JDCs are mixed, with the preponderance of studies showing better during- and post-program outcomes, particularly for graduates (Carter & Barker, 2011; Shaw & Robinson, 1998). Other studies find that JDC and comparison group participants are similar on substance use and recidivism outcomes (Rodriguez & Webb, 2004; Sloan, Smykla, & Rush, 2004).

The literature on JDC effectiveness has been quantitatively summarized by two recent meta-analyses. The first of these focused broadly on the effectiveness of drug courts and included studies from adult, juvenile, and driving while intoxicated courts (Mitchell, Wilson, Eggers, & MacKenzie, 2012). Data summarized from 34 JDC studies yielded a statistically significant effect for general recidivism, translating into about an 8% reduction for JDCs over comparison groups. Mitchell and colleagues (2012) concluded that JDCs have a small impact on recidivism. In a meta-analysis focused only on JDCs, Stein, Deberard, and Homen (2013) discussed findings from their own unpublished data. They report their meta-analysis of 31 studies showed small but statistically significant effects of JDCs on pre- to post-program recidivism and post-program recidivism. They concluded JDCs reduce recidivism, and the effects were greater for graduates than non-graduates.

Inclusion of evidence-based practices may improve JDC participant outcomes (Belenko & Logan, 2003; McCart, Henggeler, Chapman, & Cunningham, 2012). For example, Henggeler and colleagues (2006) present findings from a randomized trial that added multisystemic therapy and contingency management to juvenile drug court. Compared to treatment as usual (family court services), substance abuse and delinquent behavior were reduced while youth participated in the JDC. Those also receiving multisystemic therapy realized additional reductions in substance abuse behavior, as did youth who got both multisystemic therapy and contingency management. Econometric analyses showed a similar pattern of findings (McCollister, French, Sheidow, et al., 2009).

Key Topics

Other themes emerged in the JDC literature, including high attrition rates, low family support for the youth, high rates of sexual risk and sexually transmitted infections, and the need to understand and test the fidelity and impact of JDC components.

High rates of **program attrition** raise issues of community safety and offender well-being, and these make understanding why youth do not complete the JDC program an important topic of study. From a juvenile justice perspective, early dropout means high-risk individuals are in the community and not receiving care that could mitigate this risk. From the juvenile offender's perspective, premature dropout means he or she is not experiencing the full benefits that treatment might confer (Olver, Stockdale, & Wormith, 2011). High rates of JDC dropout have been noted in several studies (e.g., Applegate & Santana, 2000; Belenko, 1998, 1999, 2001; Cooper, 2001). Stein, Deberard, and Homan (2013) reported the average non-graduation rate for JDCs was 46% across 56 evaluations they examined. Findings showed that non-White participants and boys were less likely to graduate, while age was not related. Participants with less extensive histories of delinquency, those having fewer mental health symptoms, and those with lower addiction severity scores were more likely to graduate. Summarizing their findings, Stein and colleagues (2013, p. 165) noted, "A general conclusion to be drawn from the present review is that adolescents with fewer drug, emotional, and behavioral offense profiles tend to do better…in terms of the likelihood of graduating from programs…"

Given the relationship between family problems and recidivism among juvenile offenders (Cottle, Lee, & Heilbrun, 2001), an important finding reported by several studies is that the level of **family support** is related to outcomes during and after programs for JDC participants (Gilmore, Rodriguez, & Webb, 2005; Salvatore, Henderson, Hiller, et al., 2010). For example, a prospective study of family support on youth performance in JDCs done by Alarid and colleagues (2012) showed participants with greater support were significantly more likely to complete the JDC program and less likely to recidivate after graduation. Unfortunately, JDC judges report that some families are unwilling to recognize the youth's problem and are reluctant to get involved with them in JDC programing (Mericle, Belenko, Festinger, et al., in press). This highlights the need for research focused on engaging family members in JDC.

Youth in the juvenile justice system have high rates of **risky sexual behavior** and are more likely to have sexually transmitted infections (Aalsma, Tong, Wiehe, & Tu, 2010; Dembo, Belenko, Childs, et al., 2009). This also has been found in JDC samples (Ruiz, Stevens, Furhiman, et al., 2009; Tolou-Shams, Houck, Nugent, et al., 2012), making these settings potentially important for interventions targeted at reducing sexually transmitted infections and HIV. Tolou-Shams and colleagues (2011) presented a clinical trial where JDC participants were randomly assigned to five sessions on HIV prevention or on health promotional behavior. Both conditions reduced sexual risk and improved health behaviors, but those in the experimental group did not differ significantly from the control. It was concluded that randomized trials of HIV prevention is feasible in JDC settings and that these interventions may need to be more intensive (Tolou-Shams, Houck, Conrad, et al., 2011).

With respect to **organizational factors**, one of the primary reasons programs fail to achieve their intended impact is because an implementation failure occurs (Rossi, Lipsey, & Freeman, 2004). Studies that have carefully documented the characteristics of more than a single JDC program find a great deal of variation in how they are implemented (Hiller, Malluche, Bryan, et al., 2010). For example, findings from process evaluations of six JDCs showed they varied in many respects, including target population (i.e., age range, eligibility criteria), therapeutic services (e.g., treatment intensity, use of evidence-based practices), structure (e.g., duration, number of phases), and supervision (e.g., frequency of judicial review; Rossman, Butts, Roman, et al., 2004). Although documenting variations in implementation is important, neither study addressed whether the programs studied were implemented well. In fact, none of the studies we reviewed on JDC effectiveness addressed implementation fidelity. The relevance of this to JDC evaluations can be seen in the example of a study of a driving-while-intoxicated court in Rio Hondo, California. Researchers randomly assigned individuals to driving-while-intoxicated court or treatment-as-usual control groups. Findings showed no differences between these groups (MacDonald, Morral, Raymond, & Eibner, 2007). However, as discussed by Marlowe, Festinger, Arabia, and colleagues (2009), closer examination of the program's implementation showed that the services received by both experimental and control groups were virtually identical. Careful documentation of JDC implementation, therefore, is essential to include in future effectiveness studies. Whether a comparison group received the same services as the JDC group, or whether the JDC was implemented with fidelity, can have important implications for study conclusions.

Related to this, additional research is needed to determine whether specific components of the JDC are implemented with fidelity. Again, using an example from the adult drug court literature, specific key components may be poorly implemented. In a field-based observational study of treatment sessions for participants from four drug courts, Taxman and Bouffard (2002) found surprisingly little time was actually spent on treatment. On average, only 22% of sessions included cognitive-behavioral therapy techniques. In fact, much of the time in sessions was devoted to administrative issues, not to clinical tasks and content. Applying this to JDCs, careful monitoring of services fidelity also can inform conclusions about their effectiveness.

Finally, an area of critically needed research relates to whether variations in the intensity of specific key components are related to participant outcomes. For example, research shows that the judge, as a key component, plays an important part in the success of adult drug court participants (e.g., Marlowe, Festinger, Lee, et al., 2006; Saum, Scarpitti, Butzin, et al., 2002), but it is unknown whether this holds true for JDCs, as only one empirical study has been conducted on this issue. Using systematic observations of court sessions, Salvatore, Hiller, Samuelson, and colleagues (2011) found that participants in the same JDC received different amounts of contact with the judge during status hearings (ranging from less than 1–11 minutes, median length 3 minutes). Whether this variation was related to outcomes, however, was not examined. Studies are needed that specifically manipulate the number of appearances before the JDC judge as well as the content and quality of the judge–client interaction to determine whether this is reflected in subsequent outcomes. This is true for other components specified in the 16 strategies (e.g., treatment, urine drug testing, case management): systematic research is needed to identify which components effect positive outcomes and under what conditions (e.g., frequency and intensity of treatment, frequency and randomness of drug testing).

In summary, JDCs were originally adapted from adult drug courts but have evolved to address the unique needs of youth involved in the juvenile justice system. They address clear problems, juvenile delinquency and substance abuse. As a team-based approach to combining treatment and other supportive services with juvenile justice case processing, specific elements of the JDC are directed toward lowering juvenile recidivism rates. However, the effectiveness of JDCs is still under debate in the scientific literature. The general finding is that it does reduce recidivism during and after the program for a small number of its participants. Effectiveness has been increased by including evidence-based practices like multisystemic therapy, and there may be impacts of JDC graduation on preventing later involvement in the adult criminal justice system. Significant issues of concern for practitioners and researchers are the high attrition rates of JDC programs, the effective integration of families into the model, high rates of sexually transmitted infections, and the integrity of the implementation of the program and of its specific components. Studies that systematically manipulate specific program components are needed to determine whether each is associated with outcomes as well as what participant characteristics relate to the impact of these components.

Juvenile Mental Health Courts

Problem Statement

Youth with serious mental health problems often become involved in the juvenile justice system, resulting in higher rates of mental illness in justice settings than the community. For example, Teplin and colleagues (2002) examined the mental health status of a large sample of detained youth (ages 10–18) and found the majority met diagnostic criteria for one or more mental health disorders. Estimates for non-detained juveniles are less, averaging between 20% and 35%, but still higher than community samples (Behnken, Arredondo, & Packman, 2009). Juvenile mental health courts (JMHCs) were developed as a response to this problem as a way of getting seriously mentally ill youth the community-based services they need (Callahan, Cocozza, Steadman, & Tillman, 2012).

Description

Because of their recent introduction to the juvenile justice system, there are relatively few JMHCs. A recently completed national survey identified only 41 in the United States (Callahan, Cocozza, Steadman, & Tillman, 2012), up from the 11 found by Cocozza and Shufelt in 2006. Programs like the Court for Individualized Treatment of Adolescents (Arredondo, Kumli, Soto, et al., 2001) were the first instances of JMHCs, and more than half are in Ohio and California, suggesting "they are not yet a national phenomenon" (Callahan et al., 2012, p. 133).

The JMHC is a specialty problem-solving court that shares many characteristics with its analog in the adult criminal justice system. Both have interdisciplinary teams of professional stakeholders from both the justice and mental health services delivery systems at the core. Focus is placed on connecting participants with mental health treatment and monitoring via probation officers and judicial review, with sanctions used to correct noncompliance and rewards to encourage progress. Like JDCs, team members set aside traditional roles to work in the best interest of the child and his or her family (Arrendondo et al., 2001).

Summarizing data from their survey of JMHCs, Callahan and colleagues (2012) described the common elements among these programs. Structurally, slightly more than half were operated by juvenile courts, 11% by probation, and 17% by juvenile courts and probation. About the same number were pre-adjudication or post-adjudication, with 40% doing both. Nearly two thirds (59%) had a minimum expected duration, usually between 6 and 9 months. Involvement of a parent or guardian was required by 91% of courts. The most common services used were outpatient mental health treatment (71% of programs), family therapy (54%), and case management (43%). Finally, the average number of youth active in the program was 30.

Effectiveness

Although the scientific literature for adult mental health courts suggests they are associated with reductions in general and violent recidivism (Steadman, Redlich, Callahan, et al., 2011), it is unknown whether JMHCs do the same (Callahan et al., 2012). We found only one article that reported outcome data for a JMHC (i.e., Behnken, Arredondo, & Packman, 2009). When graduates were compared on official records data from the 18 months before and 23 months following JMHC admission, findings showed the number of offenses during the follow-up period dropped significantly from an average of 2.98 to 1.14 offenses. Unfortunately data were not presented on the proportion of the graduates who recidivated, and because no comparison group was used, it is unclear whether this reduction is the result of usual juvenile justice practice or the mental health court. Weaker quasi-experimental designs are typical of developing literatures on specialty court effectiveness, and they are important catalysts for future research. Therefore, it is important that further evaluation research using more rigorous designs be conducted to determine whether JMHCs reduce recidivism and improve the care of those with mental health issues.

Key Topics

Co-occurring disorders, in which the youth has multiple major mental health problems concurrently or has both substance abuse and mental health disorders, is a significant issue faced by the juvenile justice system (Abram, Washburn, Teplin et al., 2007). Specific patterns of co-occurring childhood mental health disorders are risk factors for later involvement in the adult criminal justice system (Copeland, Miller-Johnson, Keeler, et al., 2007). However, descriptions of JMHC models suggest that the traditional bifurcation between mental health and substance abuse treatment services systems is maintained. For example, as shown in Figure 10.3, Arredondo and colleagues (2001) chart the path the seriously mentally ill offender takes from detention, to mental

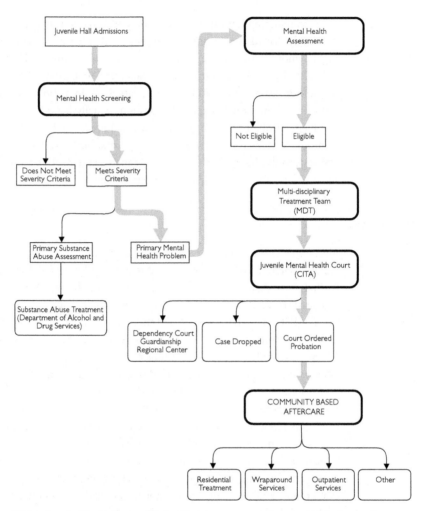

Figure 10.3   Flowchart of juvenile screening, assessment, and processing from the perspective of mental health providers.

Reprinted from Juvenile Mental Health Court: Rationale and Protocols. *Juvenile and Family Court Journal, 52*, (page 10), by D. E. Arredondo, K. Kumli, L. Soto et al., 2001, Hoboken, NJ: John Wiley & Sons, Inc. Copyright 2001 National Council of Juvenile and Family Court Judges. Reprinted with permission.

health screening and assessment, to admission and participation in the JMHC, to community-based aftercare.

During the mental health screening phase, if the youth's primary problem is substance abuse, he or she is referred to the Department of Alcohol and Drug Services for treatment rather than continuing the JMHC eligibility assessment process. This diagram does not indicate what happens to youth who have equally or almost equally severe substance abuse and mental health problems. For these individuals, coordination between both treatment systems is particularly important for providing integrated care (Peters & Hills, 1997). Because many seriously mentally ill youth in the juvenile justice system have a co-occurring substance abuse problem, it seems that the JMHC should adopt an integrated treatment approach for these cases. This is an important area for further study.

The expansion of JMHCs is not without controversy in terms of **unresolved legal issues**, with detractors questioning whether it leads to net widening, whether participation is really voluntary, and whether due process is compromised (Callahan et al., 2012; Cocozza & Shufelt, 2006; Grudzinskas & Clayfield, 2004). Detractors suggest that these programs widen the net by including youth, like status offenders, who normally would not be given much attention by the juvenile justice system. This criticism may be true to some extent because data provided by Callahan and colleagues (2012) indicate that 33% of programs admit youth with status offenses and 63% of courts require youth to admit guilt before being admitted. Related to this are concerns regarding the voluntariness of JMHC participation. Although youth are asked to volunteer to be in the JMHC, two issues arise with this. The first is the extent to which a seriously mentally ill youth can consent/assent to participate in the program. Diminished levels of competency are evident for youth in the juvenile justice system, and this raises questions about whether they truly comprehend for what they are volunteering. The second relates to coercion by alternatives, whereby young offenders with few options and possibly facing lengthy detention chose the "lesser of two evils," when if freely able they might choose not to participate in mental health treatment. Finally, Grudzinskas and Clayfield (2004) raise a concern about whether the procedural safeguards for protecting due process are compromised by the "hands-on judge" and the non-adversarial nature of proceedings. Although everyone may believe that it is in the child's best interests to receive mental health treatment, this might not be the optimal legal decision.

In summary, sharing many similarities with adult mental health courts, JMHCs were developed to address high rates of serious mental illness among juvenile offenders by helping them to get the services they need. With fewer than 50 in operation in the United States, JMHCs have not proliferated as quickly as other problem-solving specialty courts, like JDCs, and thus have not yet reached a national scale. No specific guidelines or models like the 16 strategies for JDCs exist for JMHCs, and there is considerable variation in how these programs are implemented. Because of so few evaluations, the effectiveness of JMHCs is totally unknown. Because many youths have co-occurring mental health and substance abuse problems, an integrated treatment approach should be the norm for programs addressing the problem of serious mental illness among juvenile offenders. Concerns related to net-widening, coercion, and due process require further consideration as this program model continues to evolve.

■ Teen Courts

Problem Statement

A relatively new alternative to the traditional juvenile justice system, teen courts (TCs) are specialty courts designed to solve some of the problems faced by juvenile courts such as case backlog, inefficiency, and high rates of recidivism while providing sanctions for youth without formal proceedings. TCs, sometimes referred to as youth, peer, or student courts, provide an opportunity for young offenders to be sentenced by their adolescent peers rather than by an adult authority figure. TCs aim to deter first-time nonviolent offenders from entering the JJS and to expose them to positive peer role models. Thus, the potential value of the TC model is "peer-driven justice" (Smith & Chonody, 2010) which may offer a more just court experience while encouraging socially appropriate behavior, and in turn, reduce the likelihood of re-offending. By avoiding formal processing in the juvenile justice system, TCs offer youths the opportunity to escape the stigma associated with formal labels and at the same time allow courts to devote scarce resources to more serious offenders. Moreover, TCs provide the opportunity for community adolescents who volunteer to serve as jurors to practice social responsibility and to gain knowledge of and appreciation for the court system (Forgays, DeMilio, & Schuster, 2004).

TCs operate according to restorative justice principles for restoring the offender, the victim, and the community by making the offender accountable for his or her actions and having the offender become involved in the community in a prosocial way. TCs incorporate the ideas of social control and social learning theory by using peers to effect change (Forgays & DeMilio, 2005). These theories emphasize the importance of role models and postulate that youth are most responsive to social sanctions and control from their peers. Moreover, the key components of the TCs experience are admission of guilt publicly before peers, acceptance of a sentence from one's peers, and positive re-engagement with a peer group (Forgays & DeMilio, 2005). The community-based peer jury is believed to be one of the key contributors to the success of TCs.

The first TCs were established in Texas, Illinois, and New York in the 1970s and 1980s (Beck, 1997; Norris et al., 2011). According to the National Association of Youth Courts (2013), there were 78 youth courts in 1994 and over 1,500 as of March 2010. Though approximately one third of TCs hear fewer than 50 cases per year (Butts & Buck, 2000), it has been estimated that TCs handle 100,000 cases each year (Butts, Buck, & Coggeshall, 2002). The rapid growth and popularity of TCs is based on the assumption that a peer-led restorative justice model is an improved alternative to the traditional juvenile justice system or even to that of other less formal options. However, this assumption has not been adequately tested because little research on TCs or the TC model has been conducted (Harrison, Maupin, & Mays, 2001; Minor et al., 1999; Rasmussen, 2004).

Description

TC participants are youths between ages 10 to 18 who have been accused of status offenses or misdemeanor crimes. Rasmussen and Diener (2005) found that the primary referrals to TCs were shoplifting (60%), disorderly conduct (11%), curfew violations (11%), and possession of alcohol (5%). Another study found that referrals included petty theft (65.6%), criminal mischief (10%), and battery (8.9%) (Smith & Chonody, 2010). Few TCs accept youth with previous juvenile justice contact. In a national survey of TCs, Butts and Buck (2000) found that 39% of TCs accept only first-time offenders and 48% indicated they rarely accepted youths with prior arrest records.

Youths who meet eligibility criteria may be referred to TCs by schools, community organizations, police, prosecutors, or other court officials (Fig. 10.4). TCs are operated by agencies that include local governments, police or probation departments, and states' attorney offices (Butts & Buck, 2000). Teen volunteers are recruited and trained in court roles, including juror, judge, and

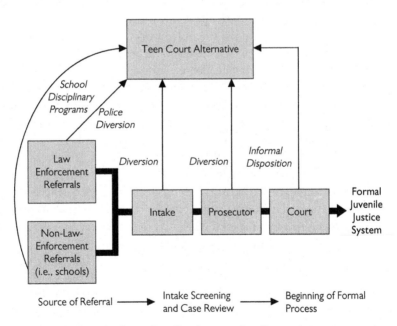

Figure 10.4   Points at which the juvenile offender may be diverted to teen court.

Source: Butts, J. A., & Buck, J. (2000). *Teen courts: A focus on research* (NCJ Publication No. 183472). Washington, D.C.: U.S. Department of Justice, Office of Justice Programs, Office of Juvenile Justice and Delinquency Prevention.

attorney. In some TCs, court personnel are specifically trained in restorative justice principles (Forgays & DeMilio 2005).

TC programs follow one of four general models, but some implement combined models. The National Youth Court Guidelines (Godwin, Heward, & Spina, 2000) describe these four models as adult judge, youth judge, peer jury, and youth tribunal. In the adult judge model, a volunteer attorney or judge serves as the judge for the court, and teens fill all of the remaining court roles. Youth attorneys question defendants and youth jurors determine sanctions. The youth judge model is similar to the adult judge model, but youth volunteers fulfill all roles including that of judge. In the peer jury model, youth do not serve as attorneys; the jurors directly question the offenders and determine sanctions under the supervision of the adult judge. Finally, the tribunal model uses three or four youth judges who question the offender and determine sanctions. A national survey found that 60% of TCs implement the adult judge model, 26% use a teen jury model, 7% a tribunal model, and 7% a youth judge model (Butts & Buck, 2000). Participation is voluntary, and parents must also give consent for their child's participation and agree to attend the hearing and support the offender's sentence completion (Forgays & DeMilio 2005). TCs sessions are typically held in local courthouses but can be held in other locations such as community justice agencies or high schools. The hearing varies according to the model that is employed but has many components of a typical trial. For example, in some TCs, opening and closing statements are given by the youth attorneys who then question the offender, while in other models the peer jurors lead the questioning. At the close of the hearing, jurors deliberate and determine sanctions, but in some TCs the jury makes a recommendation only and the judge may adjust or override the sentence (Beck, 1997; Minor et al., 1999). It is typically not necessary to determine guilt; about 90% of TCs are post-adjudicatory, requiring admission of guilt before entering the TCs (NAYC, 2013). In some TCs, victims can make impact statements describing how the offender's behavior affected them and the judge may address the offender about his or her actions at the conclusion of the hearing (Stickle et al., 2008). Finally, the offender must sign a contract where he or she agrees to complete the assigned sanctions. In some TCs, offenders are monitored by the TC program coordinator; in others, they are supervised by probation officers as they complete their sanctions (Garrison, 2001; Norris, Twill, & Kim, 2011).

The goal of sentencing is to help the teen understand the consequences of his or her actions and to restore the victim and/or the community. Community service is the most common sanction in TCs (Butts & Buck, 2000; Minor et al., 1999) and teens often receive multiple sanctions. For example, Rasmussen and Diener (2005) described the modal sentence in a Midwestern TCs as being 30 hours of community service, serving twice on a future TC jury, an apology and essay (to the victim and/or offender's parents), and a tour of the local jail. Other sanctions include paying restitution or fines and attending education, treatment, or family mediation programs. Programs typically give participants three to six months to complete their sanctions (Beck, 1997; Forgays & DeMilio, 2005; Rasmussen & Diener, 2005). This type of program is considered diversionary because completion may allow the youth to avoid a permanent record. Failure usually results in a referral to juvenile court (Norris et al., 2011).

Most studies show that retention rates for participants are high. For example, in a Maryland study, 85% of the participants completed each component of the process, including successful completion of all assigned sanctions (Stickle et al., 2008). Other studies reveal similar findings, with completion rates ranging from 63.3% in Delaware (Garrison, 2001) to 92% in Washington State (Forgays, 2008), and 95% in Ohio (Norris et al., 2011).

Effectiveness

As TCs proliferate across the nation, so has research on whether they reach their goal of reducing juvenile recidivism. These studies have mixed results: some indicate that TCs "work" to reduce future offending, but others do not show such positive results. For example, in a multisite quasi-experimental study of TCs in four states, findings indicated that recidivism was significantly reduced in two of the states (Butts, Buck, & Coggeshall, 2002). Although not achieving statistical significance, in the third state, findings showed lower recidivism, and recidivism was slightly higher than that of the comparison group in the fourth state. Other studies have found limited to moderate support for TCs' effectiveness, though they used no or relatively weak comparison groups. For example, in New Mexico, researchers found that 25% of the youths recidivated during a four-year follow-up, which was lower than the recidivism rates for other juvenile diversion programs in the county under study (Harrison et al., 2001). A prospective study showed that offenders who reported more serious delinquent behavior at intake reported less delinquency six months after TC compared with those reporting low-level offenses. Other researchers have found generally low post-intervention recidivism rates: 12% in Illinois (Rasmussen, 2004), 15% in Delaware (Garrison, 2001), and 32% in Kentucky (Minor et al., 1999), but these studies did not use comparison groups (Rasmussen & Diener, 2005). Finally, several studies have found TC completers to be less likely to reoffend than non-completers (Forgays & DeMilio, 2005; Harrison et al., 2001; Norris et al., 2011).

Many youth courts deal solely or primarily with first-time offenders, so there is limited research on TC participants who are repeat offenders. One exception to this is a study of 84 Whatcom County TC offenders with at least one prior conviction (Forgays, 2008). Results indicated that for the three years following participation, recidivism was significantly lower for the TC offenders (14%, 12%, and 25% in years 1, 2, and 3, respectively) compared to first-time court diversion offenders (31%, 25%, and 80% in years 1, 2, and 3, respectively).

Other studies are less favorable for concluding that TCs are effective. For example, 635 youth in Greene County (OH) TCs were compared with 186 regular diversion participants. Survival analysis indicated that there were no significant differences in recidivism (Norris, Twill, & Kim, 2011). Moreover, in a randomized controlled study of four TCs in Maryland, researchers found that self-reported delinquency and drug use were higher for TC participants compared with juveniles traditionally processed (Stickle et al., 2008). Further, official records for the 18 months following referral to the TC showed that TC youth recidivated more frequently (32.1%) than did the control group (25.5%). However, this comparison did not reach statistical significance.

Overall, studies have found mixed outcomes on the effectiveness of TCs. When outcomes are positive, peer juries have been credited with promoting rehabilitation as a restorative justice practice. Indeed, as Forgays (2008, p. 483) explained, "judgment by one's peers appears to be an effective deterrent to future crime." On the other hand, several studies have found that TCs have little to no impact or even a detrimental impact on participants. Explanations for this include the focus on low-level offenses, immature youth as participants, over-sanctioning as unfair, the use of ineffective "scared-straight" jail tours as a sanction, and labeling (Norris et al., 2011; Rasmussen & Diener, 2005; Stickle et al., 2008). Although TC is thought to be a less formal and more sensitive process that works to protect youth from the formal labeling associated with the juvenile justice system, it is possible that labeling still occurs, and being embarrassed in front of peers may be especially stigmatizing for youth (Stickle et al., 2008).

Key Topics

Several important themes have emerged in the TC literature. Among these are how TC participants perceive the process and whether it affects their attitudes and beliefs about, and knowledge of, the justice system. The study of the peer jurors' experiences during TC hearings, including how they make decisions during deliberations, is another key area of study.

It is critical to understand the **youth offenders' perceptions** about their involvement in TCs so that programming can be improved to better meet their needs in efforts to produce better outcomes. Interviews with participants in Midwestern TCs assessed satisfaction levels. Findings were that teens had generally positive comments, giving high ratings for procedural justice (perceptions of the fairness of the hearing) and for sentence satisfaction (Rasmussen & Diener, 2005). Participants' perceptions of confidentiality were less positive and fell in the neutral/not sure range. However, none of the participants in a sample from another TC reported that anyone outside of the TC proceedings found out about their hearings (Harrison et al., 2001).

An exit survey completed by Whatcom County TC participants asked about their satisfaction with the TC process (Forgays & DeMilio, 2005). Seventy-three percent of the offenders considered their sentence to be very fair or fair enough, 88% indicted that they understood the court process, 72% rated their court experience as "ok," and 82% would recommend the TC option to a friend. When a second group of participants from this TC was surveyed, they were similarly favorable in their perceptions of the TC experience (Forgays, 2008). Finally, participants in a New Mexico TC reported that the jury was both consistent and reasonable in its sentencing (Harrison et al., 2001).

An important benefit of TCs may be that participants develop better over-all attitudes towards the juvenile justice system and justice officials. In the New Mexico TC, offenders indicated that their views of the law and those working with the system had improved (Harrison et al., 2001). Moreover, participants indicated that the TC made them more trusting of the system and helped them to gain a greater understanding and respect for it. Finally, many volunteered to continue their involvement with the TC beyond their sentence, to act as jurors, advocates, clerks, bailiffs, and advisory board members (Forgays, 2008; Forgays & DeMilio, 2005).

More studies of the key components of teen courts are needed. For example, it is important to know more about the **teen jurors and their delibera-tions** to help us better understand how they process the evidence presented in the court hearing as well as what factors most influence the sanctions they choose to levy on the participant. Some research has been done in this area. For example, a study of 20 TC cases attempted to discern patterns in the questions jurors asked of the offenders (see Beck, 1997). Findings were that jurors asked legal, moral, and lifestyle questions, including topics such as peer pres-sure, getting caught, remorse about the incident, and the likelihood of reof-fending. Though it was assumed that jurors would base sentencing decisions on what they learned during the court hearings, findings showed, despite sig-nificant variation in the types of cases heard, that sanctions varied little (Beck, 1997). In another study, researchers observed 32 TC trials and deliberations and asked teen jurors about their sentencing decisions (Greene & Weber, 2008). They found that deliberations were fairly cursory and that the jurors paid more attention to evidentiary information than to extralegal factors. They also determined that jurors' goals for sentencing were rehabilitative rather than punishment oriented. Moreover, in Forgays, DeMilio, and Schuster's (2004) examination of the Whatcom County TC, they found that adolescents dem-onstrated the ability to follow court procedures and recommended sentences that met restorative justice guidelines. These jurors felt that peer trials were the best way to educate offenders about the impact of their crimes on their victims.

Finally, it is important to study the impact of TCs on the jurors themselves. Researchers surveyed the Whatcom County jurors and found that through their participation, they gained practical knowledge of the judicial system and experienced an increased sense of self-efficacy; jurors felt proud for making an important contribution to their community (Forgays, DeMilio, & Schuster 2004). Because a typical sanction for TC participants is to serve on a future TC jury, it seem like this may be a personally empowering experience, particularly for the former offenders who are a part of the TC workgroup, filling a socially responsible role (Forgays, 2008).

In summary, the main purposes of TCs are to divert youth from formal juvenile justice processing and to reduce future offending behavior. Mixed findings on the effectiveness of these alternative courts indicate a need for more research as these courts continue to proliferate (Stickle et al., 2008). Future research on TCs should include larger sample sizes and/or national samples from diverse TCs, studies that include random assignment to TCs or to other juvenile justice programs and longer follow-up periods to increase the general-izability of findings and to allow for cost–benefit analyses. Also, it is important to examine the effects of the various TC models and the use of various sanc-tions within TCs. Indeed, some researchers have discussed the TC model as being *more* intrusive and *more* formal (note that regular juvenile justice hear-ings don't involve juries) with sanctions that can be *more* severe than those that less serious offenders would receive in the regular juvenile court system (Butts, Buck, & Coggeshall, 2002). Moreover, some believe that TCs are guilty of net-widening (the over-involvement of youth in the juvenile justice system) and think status and other minor offenses should be handled more informally. For instance, some believe that there may be no compelling rehabilitative reason to justify processing lower-level teens in TCs, and researchers suggest that TCs could be more effective by focusing on more problematic juveniles (Rasmussen, 2004; Rasmussen & Diener, 2005). In addition, it is important to understand the role of peer influence on TC participants. For example, it is assumed that letting a peer jury make sentencing recommendations sends a clear message that criminal behavior does not have peer approval (Beck, 1997). However, peer influence is often restricted to negative behaviors, so it would be helpful if we can better identify how peers can change behaviors in constructive ways (Smith & Chonody, 2010). Moreover, the TC movement is still young, and additional research, including more qualitative investigation, is required to establish its efficacy as well as the mechanisms by which TCs may influence their participants. Thus, continued research in these and other areas may be used to inform TC policy and practice.

Conclusion

The three types of specialty courts reviewed in this chapter share a number of features. First, all are attempts to realize the *parens patriae* philosophy that led to the development of juvenile courts in 1899, with each model attempting to work in the best interest of the child. JDCs and JMHCs both do this by connecting youth to appropriate services that address their primary problem of substance abuse or serious mental illness, as well as collateral services to address the other multiple needs and possible causes of the youth's problems, including educational deficits, family dysfunction, and lack of appropriate supervision. TCs and JMHCs also seek to divert offenders from more formal juvenile justice processing. Another similarity between the three specialty court types is that their effectiveness has yet to be firmly established. Generally, findings are mixed for both JDC and TC models, with some studies showing less recidivism, others showing no difference in recidivism, and some showing higher rates of recidivism for participants than comparisons. This can be attributed, in part, to the typically poor research designs used in evaluations of these programs, with many studies lacking or having a poorly selected comparison group, leaving open the possibility that significant internal validity problems were present. Many studies had small samples, limiting statistical power, and most presented recidivism data only for when participants were in the program or used short post-program follow-up intervals. Almost none addressed the key issues of whether the programs diverted youth from deeper involvement in the juvenile justice system or prevented later involvement in the adult criminal justice system. Few studies used randomized designs, but those that did seemed to find small effects in favor of the program. Implementation fidelity is seldom addressed, leaving one to assume that the programs held to their original planning, when it is actually more likely that the programs examined suffered significant implementation problems, resulting in changes that caused them to be unlike the specialty court model they sought to implement. Future studies should overcome these methodological difficulties by using either experimental or strong quasi-experimental designs. Essential will be the careful documentation of what each court does and the determination of which of these "key components" work and for whom.

Despite the above limitations of the scientific literature, all three of these specialty court models are important because they represent attempted innovation as the juvenile justice system has become increasingly punitive, like the adult justice system. JDCs and JMHCs each follow a team-based, problem-solving approach, which Klofas and colleagues (2010) refer to as the "new criminal justice." Members of these teams set aside traditional roles and focus on the common goal of helping the youths, their families, and the community. Each program type emerged for addressing specific juvenile justice problems, including high rates of substance abuse (JDCs) and mental health (JMHCs) problems that significantly exceed those found in the community and diverting youths from formal juvenile justice processing (TCs). And finally, from some practitioners' and researchers' perspectives, these programs represent a return to earlier ideals of rehabilitation rather than punishment and control.

Detractors raise similar concerns for each of these specialty courts. Although these have been addressed in part by JDCs, it is unclear to what extent these concerns hold true for JMHCs and TCs. More work is needed to determine whether these specialty courts widen the net by involving youth who ordinarily would not be so formally processed by the juvenile justice system. Also needed is research on the youths' perceptions of the voluntariness of their participation. It is important to know the extent to which they feel coerced by their limited options to participate and receive services they may not have wanted or sought if free in the community. Finally, legal research needs to explore criticism that the hands-on nature of the judge and the informal, non-adversarial nature of the court hearings subvert procedures intended to ensure due process rights.

In conclusion, the next decade will likely bring significant additions to the scientific and legal literatures for these specialty courts. We hope that the questions regarding the effectiveness of these specialty court models and other key issues will be addressed. Each specialty court model appears to offer the promise of improving youth outcomes, but for now, it is unclear whether they do this. To answer this question, more research using larger samples, stronger comparison groups, and longer follow-up intervals is needed. With additional evidence, perhaps these program models or some of their elements will be found to be useful for improving community safety and offender and family well-being.

References

Aalsma, M. C., Tong, Y., Wiehe, S. E., & Tu, Y. (2010). The impact of delinquency on young adult sexual risk behaviors and sexually transmitted infections. *Journal of Adolescent Health, 46*, 17–24.

Abram, K. M., Washburn, J. J., Teplin, L. A., Emanuel, K. M., Romero, E. G., & McClelland, G. M. (2007). Posttraumatic stress disorder and psychiatric comorbidity among detained youth. *Psychiatric Services, 58*, 1311.

Alarid, L. F., Montemayor, C. D., & Dannhaus, S. (2012). The effect of parental support on juvenile drug court completion and postprogram recidivism. *Youth Violence and Juvenile Justice, 10*, 354–369.

Applegate, B. K., & Santana, S. (2000). Intervening with youthful substance abusers: Preliminary analysis of a juvenile drug court. *The Justice System Journal, 21*, 281–300.

Arredondo, D. E., Kumli, K., Soto, L., Colin, E., Ornellas, J., Davilla, R. J., Edwards, L. P., & Hyman, E. M. (2001). Juvenile mental health court: Rationale and protocols. *Juvenile and Family Court Journal, 52*, 1–19.

Beck, R. J. (1997). Communications in a teen court: Implications for probation. *Federal Probation, 61*, 40–48.

Behnken, M. P., Arredondo, D. E., & Packman, W. L. (2009). Reduction in recidivism in a juvenile mental health court: A pre- and post-treatment outcome study. *Juvenile and Family Court Journal, 60*, 23–44.

Belenko, S. (1998). Research on drug courts: A critical review. *National Drug Court Institute Review, 1*, 1–42.

Belenko, S. (1999). Research on drug courts: A critical review 1999 update. *National Drug Court Institute Review, 2*, 1–58.

Belenko, S. (2001). *Research on drug courts: A critical review 2001 update.* National Drug Court Institute. Alexandria, VA: NDCI.

Belenko, S., & Dembo, R. (2003). Treating adolescent substance abuse problems in the juvenile drug court. *International Journal of Law and Psychiatry, 26*, 87–110.

Belenko, S., & Logan, TK (2003). Delivering more effective treatment to adolescents: Improving the juvenile drug court model. *Journal of Substance Abuse Treatment, 25*, 189–211.

Bryan, V., Hiller, M. L., & Leukefeld, C. G. (2006). A qualitative examination of the juvenile drug court treatment process, *Journal of Social Work Practice in the Addictions, 6*, 91–114.

Bureau of Justice Assistance (2003). *Juvenile drug courts: Strategies in practice* (NCJ Publication No. 197866). Washington, DC: U.S. Department of Justice, Office of Justice Programs, Office of Juvenile Justice and Delinquency Prevention.

Butts, J. A., & Buck, J. (2000). *Teen courts: A focus on research* (NCJ Publication No.183472). Washington, DC: U.S. Department of Justice, Office of Justice Programs, Office of Juvenile Justice and Delinquency Prevention.

Butts, J. A., Buck, J., & Coggeshall, M. B. (2002). *The impact of teen court on young offenders* (NCJ Publication No. 237391). Washington, DC: U.S. Department of Justice, Office of Justice Programs, Office of Juvenile Justice and Delinquency Prevention.

Butts, J. A., & Roman, J. (2004). Drug courts in the juvenile justice system. In J. A. Butts & J. Roman (Eds.), *Juvenile drug courts and teen substance abuse* (pp. 1–25). Washington, DC: Urban Institute Press.

Callahan, L., Cocozza, J., Steadman, H. J., & Tillman, S. (2012). A national survey of U.S. juvenile mental health courts. *Psychiatric Services, 63*, 130–134.

Carter, W. C., & Barker, R. D. (2011). Does completion of juvenile drug court deter adult criminality? *Journal of Social Work Practice in the Addictions, 11*, 181–193.

Cocozza, J. J., & Shufelt, J. L. (2006). *Juvenile mental health courts: An emerging strategy.* Delmar, NY: National Center for Mental Health and Juvenile Justice, Policy Research Associates, Inc.

Cooper, C. (2001). *Juvenile drug court programs* (NCJ Publication No. 184744). Washington, DC: U.S. Department of Justice, Office of Justice Programs, Office of Juvenile Justice and Delinquency Prevention.

Cooper, C. (2002). Juvenile drug treatment courts in the United States: Initial lessons learned and issues being addressed. *Substance Use and Misuse, 37*, 1689–1722.

Copeland, W. E., Miller-Johnson, S., Keeler, G., Angold, A., & Costello, E. J. (2007). Childhood psychiatric disorders and young adult crime: A prospective, population-based survey. *American Journal of Psychiatry, 164*, 1668–1675.

Cottle, C. C., Lee, R. J., & Heilbrun, K. (2001). The prediction of criminal recidivism in juveniles: A meta-analysis. *Criminal Justice and Behavior, 28*, 367–394.

Dembo, R., Belenko, S., Childs, K., Greenbaum, P. E., & Wareham, J. (2009). Gender differences in drug use, sexually transmitted infections, and risky sexual behavior among arrested youths. *Journal of Child and Adolescent Substance Abuse, 19*, 424–446.

Forgays, D. K. (2008). Three years of teen court offender outcomes. *Adolescence, 43*, 473–84.

Forgays, D. K., & DeMilio, L. (2005). Is teen court effective for repeat offenders? A test of the restorative justice approach. *International Journal of Offender Therapy and Comparative Criminology, 49*, 107–118.

Forgays, D. K., DeMilio, L., & Schuster, K. (2004) Teen court: What jurors can tell us about the process. *Juvenile and Family Court Journal, 55*, 25–33.

Garrison, A. H. (2001). An evaluation of a Delaware teen court. *Juvenile and Family Court Journal, 52*, 11–21.

Gilmore, A., Rodriquez, N., & Webb, V. (2005). Substance abuse and drug courts: The role of social bonds in juvenile drug courts. *Youth Violence and Juvenile Justice, 3*, 287–315.

Godwin, T. M., Heward, M. E., & Spina, T. (2000). *National youth court guidelines.* Lexington, KY: American Probation and Parole Association, National Youth Court Center.

Greene, E., & Weber, K. (2008). Teen court jurors' sentencing decisions. *Criminal Justice Review, 33*, 361–378.

Grudzinskas, A. J., & Clayfield, J. C. (2004). Mental health courts and lessons learned in juvenile court. *Journal of the American Academy of Psychiatry and Law, 32*, 223–227.

Harrison, P., Maupin, J. R., & Mays, G. L., (2001). Teen court: An examination of processes and outcomes. *Crime and Delinquency, 47*, 243–264.

Henggeler, S. W., Halliday-Boykins, C. A., Cunningham, P. B., Randall, J., & Shapiro, S. B. (2006). Juvenile drug court: Enhancing outcomes by integrating evidence-based treatments. *Journal of Consulting and Clinical Psychology, 74*, 42–54.

Hiller, M. L., Malluche, D., Bryan, V., DuPont, L., Martin, B., Abensur, R. L., Leukefeld, C. G., & Payne, C. (2010). A multi-site description of juvenile drug courts: Program models and during-program outcomes, *International Journal of Offender Therapy and Comparative Criminology, 54*, 213–235.

Huddleston, W., & Marlowe, D. B. (2011). *Painting the current picture: A national report on drug courts and other problem-solving court programs in the United States.* Alexandria, VA: National Drug Court Institute.

Klofas, J. M., Hipple, N. K., & McGarrell, E. F. (Eds.). (2010). *The new criminal justice: American communities and the changing world of crime control.* New York: Routledge.

MacDonald, J. M., Morral, A. R., Raymond, B., & Eibner, C. (2007). The efficacy of the Rio Hondo DUI Court: A 2-year field experiment. *Evaluation Review, 31*, 4–23.

Marlowe, D. B., Festinger, D. S., Arabia, P.L., Croft, R., Patapis, N. S., & Dugosh, K. L. (2009). A systematic review of DWI court program evaluations. *Drug Court Review, 6*, 1–52.

Marlowe, D. B., Festinger, D. S., Lee, P.A., Dugosh, K. L., & Benasutti, K. M. (2006). Matching judicial supervision to clients' risk status in drug dourt. *Crime and Delinquency, 52*, 52–76.

McCart, M. R., Henggeler, S. W., Chapman, J. E., & Cunningham, P. B. (2012). System-level effects of integrating a promising treatment into juvenile drug courts. *Journal of Substance Abuse Treatment, 43*, 231–243.

McCollister, K. E., French, M. T., Sheidow, A. J., Henggeler, S. W., & Halliday-Boykins, C. A. (2009). Estimating the differential costs of criminal activity for juvenile drug court participants: Challenges and recommendations. *Journal of Behavioral Health Services and Research, 36*, 111–126.

Mericle, A. A., Belenko, S., Festinger, D., Fairfax-Columbo, J., & McCart, M. R. (2013). Staff perspectives on juvenile drug court operations: A multi-site qualitative study. *Criminal Justice Policy Review.*

Minor, K. I., Wells J. B., Soderstrom, I. R., Bingham, R., & Williamson, D. (1999). Sentence completion and recidivism among juveniles referred to teen courts. *Crime and Delinquency, 45*, 467–480.

Mitchell, O., Wilson, D. B., Eggers, A., & MacKenzie, D. L. (2012). Assessing the effectiveness of drug courts on recidivism: A meta-analytic review of traditional and non-traditional drug courts. *Journal of Criminal Justice, 40*, 60–71.

National Association of Youth Courts (2013, April). What is a youth court? Retrieved from http://www.youthcourt.net/?page_id=24.

Norris, M., Twill, S., & Kim, C. (2011). Smells like teen spirit: Evaluating a Midwestern teen court. *Crime & Delinquency, 57*, 199–221.

Office of Juvenile Justice and Delinquency Prevention (OJJDP; 2012). *OJJDP FY 2012: Juvenile drug courts/reclaiming futures* (OMB Publication No. 1121-0329). Washington, DC: U.S. Department of Justice, Office of Justice Programs.

Olver, M. E., Stockdale, K. C., & Wormith, J. M. (2011). A meta-analysis of predictors of offender treatment attrition and its relationship to recidivism. *Journal of Consulting and Clinical Psychology, 79*, 6–21.

Peters, R. H., & Hills, H. A. (1997). *Intervention strategies for offenders with co-occurring disorders: What works?* Delmar, NY: National Gains Center.

Puzzanchera, C. (2009). *Juvenile arrests 2008* (NCJ Publication No. 228479). Washington, DC: U.S. Department of Justice, Office of Justice Programs, Office of Juvenile Justice and Delinquency Prevention.

Rasmussen, A. (2004). Teen court referral, sentencing, and subsequent recidivism: Two proportional hazards models and a little speculation. *Crime & Delinquency, 50*, 615–635.

Rasmussen, A., & Diener, C. I. (2005). A prospective longitudinal study of teen court's impact on offending youths' behavior. *Juvenile and Family Court Journal, 56*, 17–32.

Rodriguez, N., & Webb, V. J. (2004). Multiple measures of juvenile drug court effectiveness: Results of a quasi-experimental design. *Crime and Delinquency, 50*, 292–314.

Roman, J., Butts, J. A., & Rebeck, A. S. (2004). American drug policy and the evolution of drug treatment courts. In J. A. Butts & J. Roman (Eds.), *Juvenile drug courts and teen substance abuse* (pp. 27–54). Washington, DC: Urban Institute Press.

Rossi, P. H., Lipsey, M. W., & Freeman, H. E. (2004). *Evaluation: A systematic approach* (7th ed.). Thousand Oaks, CA: Sage.

Rossman, S. B., Butts, J. A., Roman, J., DeStefano, C., & White, R. (2004). What juvenile drug courts do and how they do it. In J. A. Butts & J. Roman (Eds.). *Juvenile Drug Courts and Teen Substance Abuse* (pp. 55–106). Washington DC: Urban Institute Press.

Ruiz, B. S., Stevens, S. J., Fuhriman, J., Bogart, J. G., & Korchmoras, J. D. (2009). A juvenile drug court model in southern Arizona: Substance abuse, delinquency and sexual risk outcomes by gender and race/ethnicity. *Journal of Offender Rehabilitation, 48*, 416–438.

Salvatore, C., Henderson, J., Hiller, M. L., White, E., & Samuelson, B. (2010). An observational study of team meeting and status hearings in juvenile drug court, *Drug Court Review, 7*, 95–124.

Salvatore, C., Hiller, M. L., Samuelson, B., Henderson, J. S., & White, E., (2011). A systematic observational study of a juvenile drug court judge. *Juvenile and Family Court Journal, 62*, 19–36.

Saum, C., A., Scarpitti, F. R., Butzin, C. A., Perez, V. W., Jennings, D., & Gray, A. (2002). Drug court participants' satisfaction with the treatment and the court experience. *Drug Court Review, 4*, 39–84.

Shaw, M., & Robinson, K. (1998). Summary and analysis of the first juvenile drug court evaluation: The Santa Clara County drug treatment court and the Delaware juvenile drug court diversion program. *Drug Court Review, 1*, 73–85.

Sloan, J. J., Smykla, J. O., & Rush, J. P. (2004). Do juvenile drug court reduce recidivism? Outcomes of drug court and an adolescent substance abuse program. *American Journal of Criminal Justice, 29*, 95–115.

Smith, S., & Chonody, J. M. (2010). Peer-driven justice: Development and validation of the Teen Court Peer Influence Scale. *Research on Social Work Practice, 20*, 283–292.

Snyder, H. M. (1997). *Juvenile arrests 1996* (NCJ Publication No. 167578). Washington, DC: U.S. Department of Justice, Office of Justice Programs, Office of Juvenile Justice and Delinquency Prevention.

Steadman, H. J., Redlich, A., Callahan, L., Robbins, P. C., & Vesselinov, R. (2011). Effect of mental health courts on arrests and jail days: A multi-site study. *Archives of General Psychiatry, 68*, 167–172.

Stein, D. M., Deberard, S., & Homan, K. (2013). Predicting success and failure in juvenile drug treatment court: A meta-analytic review. *Journal of Substance Abuse Treatment, 44*, 159–168.

Stickle, W., Connell, N., Wilson, D., & Gottfredson, D. (2008). An experimental evaluation of teen courts. *Journal of Experimental Criminology, 4*, 137–163.

Substance Abuse and Mental Health Services Administration (SAMHSA, 2012). *Results from the 2011 National Survey on Drug Use and Health: Summary of National Findings*

(NSDUH Series H-44, HHS Publication No. (SMA) 12-4713). Rockville, MD: Substance Abuse and Mental Health Services Administration.

Taxman, F., & Bouffard, J. A. (2002). Treatment inside the drug court: The who, what, where, and how of treatment services. *Substance Use and Misuse, 37,* 1665–1688.

Teplin, L. A., Abram, K. M., McClelland, G., M., Dulcan, M. K., & Mericle, A. A. (2002). Psychiatric disorders in youth in juvenile detention. *Archives of General Psychiatry, 59,* 1133–1143.

Tolou-Shams, M., Houck, C., Conrad, S. M., Taratino, N., Stein, L. A. R., & Brown, L. K. (2011). HIV prevention for juvenile drug court offenders: A randomized controlled trial focusing on affect management. *Journal of Correctional Healthcare, 17,* 226–232.

Tolou-Shams, M., Houck, C. D., Nugent, N., Conrad, S. M., & Reyes, A. (2012). Alcohol use and HIV risk among juvenile drug court offenders. *Journal of Social Work Practice in the Addictions, 12,* 178–188.

Waivers and Transfers of Juveniles to Adult Court

Treating Juveniles like Adult Criminals

Michele Deitch and Neelum Arya

■ Introduction

When youth under the age of 18 commit crimes, they are generally prosecuted and managed by the juvenile justice system. But some criminal acts may result in the youth's transfer to the adult criminal justice system. Such transfers, also called "waivers" or "certification" depending on the state, carry with them a host of serious consequences for youth.

Eleven-year-old Jordan Brown from Pennsylvania may be the country's poster child illustrating the trend of treating youth like adult criminals. A baby-faced fifth-grader, he was charged with killing his father's pregnant girlfriend in 2009. State laws required him to be tried in adult criminal court, despite his youth. If convicted, he faced a mandatory sentence of life without the possibility of parole. He also would have been housed in Pennsylvania's adult prison system. Lawyers were successful in challenging aspects of the law that ultimately resulted in Jordan's transfer back to the juvenile justice system (Juvenile Law Center), but his case remains a shocking reminder that the harshness of the criminal justice system can be applied even to the youngest juvenile offenders in this country.

Trying youth as adults represents a remarkable shift from an almost century-old emphasis on separate and more rehabilitative approaches to dealing with juvenile offenders (Deitch, Barstow, Lukens, & Reyna, 2009). Fears of an epidemic of juvenile crime and so-called "juvenile superpredators" during the 1980s and 1990s fanned public demand for lengthy incarceration for youthful offenders (DiIulio, 1995; Snyder & Sickmund, 2006). The public's mantra became "adult time for adult crime," and legislatures around the country passed new laws to increase the possibility of trying more youth in adult criminal court (Snyder & Sickmund, 2006). This punitive trend collided with an equally strong movement toward harsh sentencing for all offenders. States passed life-without-parole laws, enacted mandatory sentencing policies, and restricted or eliminated parole consideration for many offenses (Deitch et al., 2009). Although these policies were drafted with adult offenders in mind, youth who were transferred into adult criminal court found themselves facing these same sentencing consequences. Today, an estimated 250,000 youth are prosecuted in adult courts every year in the United States, where they are largely subject to the same harsh and often inflexible sanctions as adult offenders (Zeidenberg, 2011).

There are two issues that must be considered separately when analyzing the issue of youth in the adult criminal justice system. First is the issue of whether the juvenile or adult court should hear the case, and the implications of trying a youth in adult criminal court. This carries implications not only for the applicable sentencing laws, but also for courtroom procedures, confidentiality restrictions, and collateral consequences of conviction (Deitch et al., 2009). The second issue has to do with confinement of youth in adult facilities. Many states require youth transferred to adult court to be kept in adult county jails while awaiting trial and in adult prisons if they are convicted. Placing youth in adult facilities places them at great physical risk from adult offenders and denies them the opportunity to participate in the rehabilitative and educational programming typically available in juvenile facilities (Campaign for Youth Justice, 2007; Zeidenberg, 2011).

This chapter begins by explaining how youth get transferred to the adult system, recognizing that states vary widely in their policies in this arena. It goes on to explore the challenges presented by both of the key issues—youth in adult criminal court and youth in adult correctional facilities. Finally, it examines the legal issues raised by the practice of transferring youth to the adult criminal justice system, and more recent trends toward a reversal of these policies.

■ How Youth End Up in the Adult Criminal Justice System

In most states across the country, youth must be 16 to drive; 17 to see R-rated movies; 18 to vote, join the military, or marry without parental consent; and 21 to drink alcohol. These laws indicate a societal understanding that minors are inherently less mature and responsible than adults. Yet, every state also has a way to prosecute a youth as an adult in certain circumstances when he or she commits a crime. In 23 states and jurisdictions there are no statutory minimum age limitations before a youth can be prosecuted as an adult, whereas other states set the lower age limit at 10 or above (Deitch et al., 2009; OJJDP, 2012).

Recent studies reviewing state-specific data have found that many youth who enter the adult system are first-time offenders who have not had the benefit of the juvenile justice system, many are not charged with serious offenses, and the majority of youth receive a sentence of adult probation instead of adult prison (Campaign for Youth Justice & Partnership for Safety and Justice, 2011; Children's Action Alliance, 2010; Children's Law Center, Inc., 2012; Citizens for Juvenile Justice, 2011; Colorado Juvenile Defender Coalition, 2012; Deitch, 2011; JustChildren, 2009; Just Kids Partnership, 2010; Washington Coalition for the Just Treatment of Youth, 2009). These findings run counter to common assumptions that youth transferred to the adult criminal justice system are the "worst of the worst," or that they are chronic, unredeemable offenders.

Mechanisms for Transferring Youth to Adult Criminal Court

The mechanisms and laws allowing youth to be prosecuted in the adult criminal justice system vary widely from state to state, county to county, and even courtroom to courtroom (Fig. 11.1). There are several broad categories of laws

State	Judicial waiver type			Pro-secutorial Discretion	Statu-tory exclu-sion	Age of Juris-diction	Reverse waiver	Once an adult/ always an adult	Blended sentencing	
	Dis-cretionary	Pre-sumptive	Man-datory						Juvenile	Criminal
Number of states	45	15	15	15	29	13	24	34	14	17
Alabama	X				X	18		X		
Alaska	X	X			X	18			X	
Arizona	X			X	X	18	X	X		
Arkansas	X				X	18	X		X	X
California	X	X		X	X	18	X	X		X
Colorado	X	X		X		18	X		X	X
Connecticut			X			18	X		X	
Delaware	X	X			X	18	X	X		
Dist of Columbia	X	X		X		18		X		
Florida	X			X	X	18		X		X
Georgia	X		X	X	X	17	X			
Hawaii	X					18		X		
Idaho	X				X	18		X		X
Illinois	X	X	X		X	17		X	X	X
Indiana	X		X		X	18		X		
Iowa	X				X	18	X	X		X
Kansas	X	X				18		X	X	
Kentucky	X		X			18	X			X
Louisiana	X		X	X	X	17				
Maine	X	X				18		X		
Maryland	X				X	18	X	X		
Massachusetts					X	17			X	X
Michigan	X			X		17		X	X	X
Minnesota	X	X			X	18		X	X	
Mississippi	X				X	18	X	X		
Missouri	X					17		X		X
Montana				X	X	18	X		X	
Nebraska				X		18	X			X
Nevada	X	X			X	18	X	X		
New Hampshire	X	X				17		X		
New Jersey	X	X	X			18				
New Mexico					X	18			X	X

Figure 11.1   Mechanisms for Transferring Youth to the Adult System, 2011

State	Judicial waiver type			Pro-secutorial Discretion	Statutory exclusion	Age of Jurisdiction	Reverse waiver	Once an adult/always an adult	Blended sentencing	
	Discretionary	Presumptive	Mandatory						Juvenile	Criminal
New York					X	16	X			
North Carolina	X		X			16		X		
North Dakota	X	X	X			18		X		
Ohio	X		X			18		X	X	
Oklahoma	X			X	X	18	X	X		X
Oregon	X				X	18	X	X		
Pennsylvania	X	X			X	18	X	X		
Rhode Island	X	X	X			18		X	X	
South Carolina	X		X		X	17				
South Dakota	X				X	18	X	X		
Tennessee	X					18	X	X		
Texas	X					17		X	X	
Utah	X	X			X	18		X		
Vermont	X			X	X	18	X			
Virginia	X		X	X		18	X	X		X
Washington	X				X	18		X		
West Virginia	X		X			18				X
Wisconsin	X				X	17	X	X		X
Wyoming	X			X		18	X			

Adapted from material compiled by P. Griffin for the National Center for Juvenile Justice's State Juvenile Justice Profiles web site. Online. Available at: http://www.ncjj.org/stateprofiles/ Internet citation: OJJDP Statistical Briefing Book. Online. Available: http://ojjdp.gov/ojstatbb/structure_process/qa04115.asp?qaDate=2011. Released on December 17, 2012.

Figure 11.1   (Continued)

allowing the prosecution of youth in adult court. It is important to keep in mind that within these categories, each state's laws often have specific statutory sections with age and offense limitations resulting in a complex web of laws. In other words, how a child can be tried in the adult court in a particular state will vary depending on the type of transfer mechanism, the age of the youth, and the offense charged.

Judicial Waiver

The traditional path to the adult system is known as judicial waiver, and 45 states have judicial waiver statutes (Griffin, Addie, Adams, & Firestine, 2011). Upon request by the prosecutor, a hearing is held in juvenile court where a juvenile court judge makes the decision to transfer a youth's case to adult court after considering several factors. In 1966, the U.S. Supreme Court, in the case of *Kent v. United States*, held that before transferring a youth, juvenile court judges must consider several factors: (1) the seriousness of the alleged offense to the community and whether the protection of the community requires waiver; (2) whether the alleged offense was committed in an aggressive, violent, premeditated, or willful manner; (3) whether the alleged offense was against persons or against property, with greater weight being given to offenses against persons; (4) the prosecutive merit of the complaint and sufficiency of evidence; (5) the desirability of trial and disposition of the entire offense in one court if co-defendants are similarly charged in adult court; (6) the sophistication and maturity of the juvenile; (7) the record and previous history of the juvenile; and (8) the prospects for adequate protection of the public and the likelihood of reasonable rehabilitation of the juvenile (*Kent v. United States*, 1966).

Today most judicial waiver statutes have incorporated these factors for judicial consideration. In addition, some states have judicial waiver statutes with presumptions or mandatory requirements to make it more likely that a youth will be transferred to the adult system (Griffin et al., 2011). Depending on the judge and the quality of legal advocacy, transfer hearings can be either in-depth hearings or short pro forma proceedings.

Prosecutorial Discretion

The prosecutorial discretion transfer mechanism, sometimes referred to as direct file or concurrent jurisdiction, grants prosecutors the choice between filing the case in juvenile or adult court without judicial approval. Fifteen states grant prosecutors full discretion to decide whether certain cases will be tried in the adult system if the child is of a certain age and charged with certain crimes. Unlike judicial waiver statutes, prosecutorial discretion statutes rarely provide any standards or guidance for prosecutors, and there is no hearing or evidentiary record required as the basis of a prosecutor's decision to proceed with the case in adult court (Griffin et al., 2011).

Statutory Exclusion, Age of Jurisdiction, and "Once an Adult/Always an Adult" Laws

Statutory exclusion laws, also known as automatic waiver or legislative waiver provisions, expressly prohibit the juvenile court from hearing certain types of cases. In 29 states, state legislators have decided that youth charged with certain offenses must be prosecuted in the adult system instead of the juvenile system (OJJDP, 2012). In contrast to judges or prosecutors making an individualized decision about a specific youth, state legislators have made the decision about which court a youth should be tried in. For example, many states prohibit children charged with murder from being handled by juvenile courts.

"Age of jurisdiction" laws are a special form of this type of law. While the majority of states have drawn the line at age 18 for their juvenile justice systems (Fig. 11.2), 13 states currently require all youth ages 16 or 17 to be tried in the adult criminal system regardless of how minor the offense (Griffin et al., 2011).

Another version of this type of law is known as a "Once-an-Adult/ Always an Adult" statute; such statutes exist in 34 states. For these laws, the legislature has determined that once a youth has been prosecuted in the adult system the youth may not return to the juvenile court system, even for a minor charge, if the youth has contact with the justice system again (Griffin et al., 2011).

Reverse Waiver and Blended Sentences

Two final types of laws, reverse waivers and blended sentences, are also available in certain states. Some states provide discretion to criminal court judges to send youth back to the juvenile justice system. Reverse waiver laws available in 24 states are similar to judicial waiver statutes except a criminal court

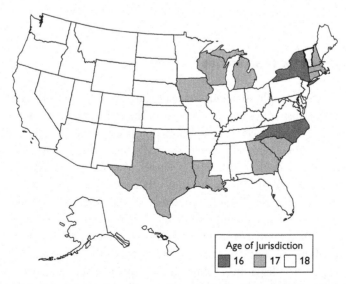

Figure 11.2   **Oldest age for original juvenile court jurisdiction, 2011. Arya, 2011b; reprinted with permission of the Campaign for Youth Justice.**

judge is making the determination to return the youth to the juvenile system. Criminal court judges in 18 states have the power to impose juvenile dispositions rather than adult penalties in certain circumstances through the use of criminal blended sentencing laws. In contrast, juvenile blended sentencing statutes, available in 14 states, allow juvenile court judges to impose adult sentences on youth in the juvenile system. Both types of blended sentences usually have a suspended adult sentence that gets triggered if a youth commits an additional offense, violates the terms of the juvenile sanction, or does not appear to be rehabilitated following the juvenile part of the sentence (Griffin et al., 2011).

■ Scope of the Problem

While transferring youth to the adult criminal justice system may satisfy the public's penchant for more punitive responses to serious juvenile crime, the practice creates tremendous challenges both for youth and for the operations of the criminal justice system. Although prosecuting youth in the adult system results in the labeling of a child as an adult, it does not change the reality that youth come into the adult system with different needs, abilities, and vulnerabilities than adult offenders. These physical, mental, and emotional differences manifest themselves in various ways throughout the trial, sentencing, and punishment phases of criminal cases.

The challenges presented by youth in the adult criminal justice system fall into six discrete areas: racial and ethnic disparities; courtroom procedures; sentencing issues; confinement issues; outcomes; and data collection and analysis. Each of these issues is explored in more detail below.

■ Racial and Ethnic Disparities

Further complicating our understanding of this issue is the fact that racial and ethnic disparities are also evident in the transfer context as they are in other aspects of the juvenile and criminal justice systems. Youth of color are highly over-represented in the adult criminal justice system. (Arya & Augarten, 2008; Arya & Rolnick, 2008; Arya, Villaruel, Villanueva, & Augarten, 2009; Deitch et al., 2009). African-American youth make up 30% of those arrested but only 17% of the overall youth population. At the other extreme end of the system, African-American youth represent 62% of the youth prosecuted in the adult criminal system and are nine times more likely than White youth to receive an adult prison sentence (Arya & Augarten, 2008). Latino and Native youth also experience disparities. Latino children are 43% more likely than White youth to be waived to the adult system and 40% more likely to be admitted to adult prison (Arya et al., 2009). Native youth are 1.5 times more likely to be waived to the adult system and 1.84 times more likely to be admitted to adult prison than White youth (Arya & Rolnick, 2008). Although the federal Juvenile Justice and Delinquency Prevention Act requires that states address racial and ethnic disparities in the justice system, very few jurisdictions have focused on reducing disparities in decisions to transfer cases to the adult system. However, this may be changing. The U.S. Department of Justice (2012) has recently begun to investigate the role of discrimination in the decision to transfer youth to the adult system; the Department has entered into a comprehensive memorandum of understanding with the Juvenile Court of Memphis and Shelby County, Tennessee, after finding that children were routinely deprived of their due process and equal protection rights when being transferred to the adult system. This investigation suggests increasing levels of concerns about racial and ethnic disparity in transfer decisions.

■ Court Processes

The MacArthur Foundation's Network on Adolescent Development and Juvenile Justice has concluded that children "are as poorly prepared to participate in their trials as adults with severe mental illness" (John D. & Catherine T. MacArthur Foundation, 2005, p. 13). Youth are more likely to defer to authority figures such as prosecutors, to be swayed by cross-examination, and to accept plea bargains without being able to grasp the consequences of such legal decisions, and are ill equipped to assist their defense lawyers in preparing for trial or investigation of the case (Deitch et al., 2009). Moreover, few adult criminal court judges have experience trying juveniles, and routine court procedures may be bewildering to youth, whose court-appointed attorneys have little time to explain these courtroom processes to them or their families. Such problems are magnified in cases involving pre-adolescent juveniles (Deitch et al., 2009).

There are collateral consequences associated with trying juveniles in adult court, many of which carry lifetime consequences regardless of the sentence. Adult court proceedings are public and open to the media, which means that the child's criminal history is a matter of public record, even if he or she is ultimately cleared of the crime. Depending on the state involved, those who are convicted may be required to report their convictions on every job, education, or housing application they complete, may suffer a loss of voting privileges, may be barred from federally funded programs and educational grants, may be barred from certain jobs, and may be restricted in where they can live (Deitch et al., 2009).

■ Sentencing Issues

Neuroscience research shows that the frontal lobe of the adolescent brain is not fully developed until age 25, rendering teens far less able than adults to appreciate the long-term consequences of their actions and far more susceptible to their impulses and to peer pressure (Gardner & Steinberg, 2005; Steinberg & Scott, 2003). Adolescent development expert Laurence Steinberg describes the teenage brain as "a car with a good accelerator but a weak brake. With powerful impulses under poor control, the likely result is a crash" (Ritter, 2007, n.p.). These same factors mean that a youth is less culpable than an adult for his or her criminal behavior. Moreover, the fact that their characters and personalities are still changing means that youth are also more responsive to rehabilitative programs than their adult counterparts. Yet the adult criminal justice system, unlike the juvenile justice system, may not be equipped to take account of such differences, especially when mandatory sentences are involved.

In most states, a juvenile prosecuted in adult court is subject to all the same sentencing laws as adult offenders would be, with the exception of the death penalty and some life-without-parole laws. Laws applicable to adult offenders tend to be substantially harsher than those available in the juvenile system. Of particular concern are mandatory sentencing laws that preclude the judge from taking mitigating factors such as the defendant's youth into account and that set a rigid and harsh floor for the applicable penalty for a particular crime. For example, Christopher Pittman, a 12-year-old in South Carolina, was charged with the murder of his grandparents in 2001. Despite his age, a complicated family history, lack of any criminal history, and the possible impact of an antidepressant medication on his actions, the trial court judge was not allowed to consider any of these factors. Instead, Christopher received a mandatory minimum sentence of 30 years without possibility of parole, the lowest possible end of the sentence range for a murder conviction in South Carolina (Deitch et al., 2009). Similarly harsh sentences that take no account of youth have been imposed in countless other cases around the country involving juveniles waived to adult court.

A great deal of national attention has been focused in recent years on the issue of juvenile life without parole (also referred to as JLWOP). Experts have calculated that more than 2,250 individuals around the United States are serving life-without-parole sentences for crimes committed when they were under the age of 18 (Equal Justice Initiative, 2008). Until the U.S. Supreme Court's ruling in *Graham v. Florida* in 2011, JLWOP sentences were even imposed on youth who had committed non-homicide offenses such as sexual assault and burglary (Equal Justice Initiative, 2008; Human Rights Watch & Amnesty International, 2005). In 2012, in the case of *Miller v. Alabama*, the U.S. Supreme Court further declared as unconstitutional mandatory life-without-parole sentences for youth under age 18 who committed homicide crimes.

As a result of these cases, judges must now make an individualized sentencing determination before imposing a life-without-parole sentence on a youth regardless of the crime involved. But courts are wrestling with how to handle sentences that are not technically life-without-parole sentences but are for an unrealistically long term of years—including term-of-years sentences of 50 years or more, or consecutive sentences of 100 years or more (*Bunch v. Smith,* 2012; *People of California v. Caballero,* 2012). Defense attorneys have begun challenging these sentences as violating the spirit of the ruling in *Graham.*

While most media and legal attention has been focused on cases involving juveniles who receive extremely long sentences in the adult system, research reveals that most youth who are transferred to adult court actually receive relatively short sentences or non-prison sanctions. Redding (2010) found that 95% of youth in the custody of the adult system are released before their 25th birthday. National studies reveal that nearly half of youth in adult court are placed on probation or are not convicted, with fewer than 25% receiving a prison sentence (Juszkiewicz, 2007). This is actually not too surprising when we consider that states in which the age of jurisdiction is set below age 18 will always process juveniles in adult court for routine misdemeanors such as shoplifting and possession of drugs, offenses for which probation is a likely outcome. However, recent studies from across the country show this pattern holds true even for transferred youth charged with felony offenses.

A study of Arizona youth found that the overwhelming majority (88%) of youth prosecuted as adults were placed on adult probation, and less than 9% received prison sentences (Children's Action Alliance, 2010). Similarly, a study of youth in Baltimore, Maryland, found that only 10% of youth tried as adults receive adult prison sentences (Just Kids Partnership, 2010). Other state studies show higher rates of adult prison sentencing but still indicate that the majority of youth get placed on probation. In Virginia, 45% of youth convicted as adults received an adult prison sentence. (JustChildren, 2009). Similarly, in Texas, 47% of juveniles transferred by a judge to adult court for a felony offense ultimately received a prison sentence (Deitch, Lipton Galbraith, & Pollock, 2012b). In Colorado, two thirds of youth who are direct-filed in adult court serve time in an adult corrections department (Colorado Juvenile Defender Coalition, 2012). Even when youth receive adult prison sentences, however, their sentences tend to be relatively short, suggesting that many youth could fully serve their sentences in juvenile corrections facilities. For example, studies from Ohio and Washington have found that more than two thirds of youth received adult prison sentences of 5 years or less (Children's Law Center, Inc., 2012; Washington Coalition for the Just Treatment of Youth, 2009), and in Texas nearly 60% of transferred youth serve terms of 10 years or less (Deitch, 2011). Taken together, these state studies suggest two overarching findings. First, youth who are prosecuted in adult criminal court are not "the worst of the worst," and indeed many are charged with less serious offenses than common assumptions may have held. Second, these youth will be coming back to their communities while they are still young, so what happens to them in prison and jail really matters from the standpoint of rehabilitation and public safety.

■ Confinement Issues

In many states, being treated as an adult for criminal justice purposes means that the youth will be confined in adult jails while awaiting trial and in adult prisons if convicted. The Bureau of Justice Statistics reports that in 2009, 7,220 youth under the age of 18 were held in local jails (Minton, 2010) and 2,778 were incarcerated in state-run adult prisons (West, 2010). However, these population figures vary dramatically from state to state, as policies vary widely around the country. Some states require youth to be held in juvenile facilities even if prosecuted and convicted as adults; others allow youth to be housed in juvenile detention facilities before trial, but transfer them to adult prisons if they are convicted; still others require placement in adult facilities at all stages of the process once they are transferred to adult court (Griffin et al., 2011). If confined in adult facilities, youth may well come into contact with adult offenders and may even be housed with them. Contact between youth and adults is sometimes, but not always, restricted by state law or institutional policy (Deitch et al., 2012b; Griffin et al., 2011). Some states have strict sight and sound separation requirements that essentially draw an iron curtain between juveniles and adults, while others make no distinction between transferred juveniles and adult inmates. And federal law that generally requires the separation of juveniles and adults does not apply when transferred youth are involved (Griffin et al., 2011).

Placement of youth in adult facilities presents enormous operational complications for corrections officials, as these youth are a special needs population that is at significant risk when housed with adult offenders. Juveniles are at serious risk of sexual and physical assault, due to their vulnerability. One widely reported estimate is that youth in adult facilities are five times as likely to be raped as their counterparts in juvenile settings (Prison Rape Elimination Act, 2003). They also have vastly higher suicide risks: youth in adult facilities are 36 times more likely to commit suicide than those in juvenile facilities (Campaign for Youth Justice, 2007).

Recognizing these risks and wanting to keep youth safe from adult offenders, correctional administrators often try to house them separately from the adults (Zeidenberg, 2011). Depending on the number of youth in the adult jail or prison, this can be tantamount to placing the youth in solitary confinement. Architectural restrictions and staffing shortages often result in extremely limited out-of-cell opportunities for the youth, since movement in the facility would bring them into contact with adult offenders. As a result, juveniles in adult jails and prisons may have little to no access to educational classes, work opportunities, recreation, or treatment programs, if such programs even exist in the adult facility (Campaign for Youth Justice, 2007; Zeidenberg, 2011). Studies in Colorado, Oregon, Virginia, Texas, and Washington found that the majority of pretrial youth residing in adult jails are kept locked up in their cells 23 hours a day, with virtually no programming (Campaign for Youth Justice &

Partnership for Safety and Justice, 2011; Colorado Juvenile Defender Coalition, n.d.; Deitch et al., 2012b; JustChildren, 2009; Washington Coalition for the Just Treatment of Youth, 2009).

In addition to placing youth in isolation for their own protection and for administrative reasons, correctional staff also may impose solitary confinement as a punitive measure for disciplinary offenses. These placements—involving lockup in a cell for 22 hours per day or more and severely restricted physical and social contact—may last for weeks, months, or even longer. While it is difficult to determine the extent to which young people are being segregated from general-population prisoners and held in solitary confinement in adult jails and prisons, the available data suggest that the practice is widespread (Human Rights Watch & American Civil Liberties Union [ACLU], 2012). Depriving adolescents of social contact, programming, and physical activity comes at severe costs to their mental and physical health. An in-depth study of the issue by Human Rights Watch and the ACLU (2012) found that youth in solitary confinement in adult correctional facilities experienced significant psychological pain and suffering, and that many had cut themselves or had thought of or attempted suicide. Since many of these youth already have traumatic social histories, their treatment in adult correctional facilities may exacerbate their mental illnesses and negative behaviors.

Unlike in juvenile facilities, staff in adult prisons and jails are ill equipped to work with adolescents who are confined in these settings. The staff lack specialized training; there are few if any programs, educational classes, and services geared to the needs of this youthful population; and there is little preparation of the youth for re-entry (Campaign for Youth Justice, 2007). In contrast, juvenile detention facilities and other juvenile residential placements are specifically designed to meet the needs of adolescent offenders. Staff are appropriately trained, and regulations and standards were adopted with the best interests of this population in mind.

Given the significant risks associated with confining youth in adult facilities and the far better alternative of keeping them in juvenile settings, many experts and juvenile corrections professionals have called on policymakers to keep youth under age 18 in juvenile detention facilities even if they are transferred to the adult criminal justice system for prosecution and sentencing purposes (American Bar Association, 2010; American Correctional Association, 2009; American Jail Association, 2008; Campaign for Youth Justice; National Juvenile Detention Association, 1997; National Juvenile Justice Network, 2009). The only objections to such proposals seem to be limited to the additional costs associated with juvenile corrections (due to increased programming and staffing levels) and fears of comingling juveniles charged with serious crimes with lower-level juvenile offenders. However, the juvenile justice system in every state already routinely retains youth charged with very serious and violent offenses. Indeed, one study of Texas youth in the adult system found little difference between those transferred to adult court and those kept in the juvenile system in terms of their offenses and criminal histories (Deitch, 2011).

■ Outcomes

Transferring juveniles to the adult criminal justice system clearly has a negative impact on these youth in terms of the challenges they face navigating adult court procedures and the physical and psychological risks they face if confined in adult facilities. Moreover, their presence in adult court creates complications for justice system personnel, and their placement in adult prisons and jails creates operational burdens for correctional staff. But even beyond these formidable challenges, youth who are transferred to the adult criminal justice system have substantially worse outcomes in terms of recidivism (Bishop, 2000; Redding, 2010). Thus, public safety is compromised by this punitive practice.

In 2007, the Centers for Disease Control Task Force on Community Preventive Services conducted a meta-analysis of all studies assessing outcomes for youth in the adult criminal justice system (Hahn, McGowan, Liberman, Crosby, Fullilove... & Stone, 2007). Overall, the researchers found a 34% increase in recidivism among those juveniles transferred to adult court (Hahn et al., 2007). One study cited by the researchers found a 100% greater risk of violent recidivism among those who spent at least a year in an adult jail or prison compared to those who remain in the juvenile system (Fagan, 1996). The Task Force's conclusion was stark: "[T]ransfer policies have generally resulted in increased arrest for subsequent crimes, including violent crime, among juveniles who were transferred compared with those retained in the juvenile justice system. To the extent that transfer policies are implemented to reduce violent or other criminal behavior, available evidence indicates that they do more harm than good" (Hahn et al., 2007, pp. 1–11). The CDC research team issued an unusual and urgent call to lawmakers to reverse policies that allowed for youth under age 18 to be placed in the adult criminal justice system.

To a large degree, such findings about increased recidivism are not surprising. Youth in the adult criminal justice system receive little rehabilitative programming or education in prisons and jails and may be traumatized by their experiences there, including from extended time spent in solitary confinement. Moreover, they are exposed to adult offenders, who may share with them the skills of their criminal trades (Zeidenberg, 2011). To expect successful outcomes under such circumstances would be the height of optimism.

As mentioned earlier, youth waived to criminal court serve reasonably short sentences, if they receive any prison time at all, and most return to their communities while still in their 20s (Redding, 2010). Thus, the impact of increased recidivism rates should be of significant concern to the communities from which these youth come.

■ Data Challenges

The available national data on youth prosecuted as adults is fragmented and incomplete. The two most important federal agencies collecting and compiling information on this population are the Office of Juvenile Justice and Delinquency Prevention, through a partnership with the National Center on Juvenile Justice, and the Bureau of Justice Statistics (BJS). To begin to remedy this information deficit, BJS has initiated a new study, The Survey of Juveniles Charged as Adults in Criminal Court, to gather information on offender demographics and offense histories, arrest and arraignment mechanisms, transfer mechanisms, and case processing and sentencing outcomes (Griffin et al., 2011).

There are several critical categories of information that currently are not collected or analyzed on a national basis regarding juveniles who are transferred to the adult system. First, very few data systems are able to track youth as they move from arrest to prosecution in adult court to being sentenced as an adult. The only state that currently tracks this information is California. Second, very few states collect demographic characteristics or prior offending information. The lack of this information makes enforcing the federal Juvenile Justice and Delinquency Prevention Act's requirement for states to address racial and ethnic disparities more difficult. Third, most states lack information about how youth who might have contact with the adult system end up back in the juvenile system through reverse waivers or blended sentencing or when charges are dropped in the adult system and they are recharged as a juvenile. Fourth, we do not know what kinds of services or interventions youth who are convicted in adult court might be receiving. Finally, without access to this type of information, it is difficult to determine how these variables may affect recidivism (Griffin et al., 2011; Zeidenberg, 2011).

Data available at the state level are similarly incomplete. Currently, only 13 states publicly report the total number of transfers, and even fewer report offense profiles, demographic characteristics, or details regarding processing and sentencing (Griffin et al., 2011). Even if a state tracks aggregate data about youth in the adult system, state and local agencies are often unable to share information about a specific youth. For example, although Arizona collects a lot of data about youth in the adult system, there is no mechanism or common identifier to track an individual youth through law enforcement records; juvenile and adult court records; juvenile and adult probation files; or detention, jail, and prison files (Children's Action Alliance, 2010).

■ Legal Issues

In the past decade there have been major shifts in the constitutional, statutory, and regulatory approaches to youth in the adult system. The legal landscape is in flux with the changes opening up several new opportunities for lawyers, juvenile justice practitioners, correctional officers, social workers, and advocates to have an impact on the treatment of youthful offenders.

Recent Rulings of the U.S. Supreme Court Addressing Youth

Starting with the 2005 decision, *Roper v. Simmons,* abolishing the death penalty for juveniles, the U.S. Supreme Court began a line of cases ushering in a new jurisprudence for children. The Court's opinions now make clear that the U.S. Constitution requires that criminal sentences and procedures account for the substantial differences between youth and adults.

Relying primarily on research on adolescent development mentioned briefly above, the Supreme Court in *Roper* held that imposing the death penalty on persons who committed crimes before the age of 18 violated the Eighth Amendment's prohibition on cruel and unusual punishment. Five years later, in *Graham v. Florida* (2010), the Court declared that the Eighth Amendment also prohibits life-without-parole sentences for youth convicted of non-homicide offenses.

Roper and *Graham* both rely primarily on three critical differences between youth and adults to justify the special protections for youth. First, youth have a "lack of maturity and underdeveloped sense of responsibility" (*Roper*, 2005, p. 569). Second, youth are particularly "vulnerable or susceptible to negative influences and outside pressures, including peer pressure" (*Graham*, 2010, p. 2026). Third, youth and their characters are "not as well formed" as adults (*Graham*, 2010, p. 2026).

Two additional cases, *J.D.B. v. North Carolina* (2011) and *Miller v. Alabama* (2012), have similarly expanded legal protections for children. In *J.D.B.,* the Court held that under the Fourth Amendment law enforcement must consider a child's age in determining when to advise a youth of his or her *Miranda* rights (i.e., right to be silent, right to a lawyer). Most recently, in *Miller,* the Court had an opportunity to revisit life-without-parole sentences for youth convicted of homicide crimes. The Court did not address the question of whether all life-without-parole sentences imposed on youth violate the Eighth Amendment but rather declared that *mandatory* life-without-parole sentences for youth without individualized consideration are unconstitutional.

These new legal developments are having a ripple effect upon juvenile defense practice. Courts across the country are grappling with how to interpret and implement the new case law. Scholars and advocates are suggesting these cases embody several legal principles that will shape the trajectory of the juvenile justice field in at least three ways. First, youth will be legally recognized as less culpable than adults and should not receive the same punishment or treatment as adults. Second, youth will be entitled to individualized decision making from judges rather than mandatory or automatic blanket policies. Third, given that children have greater potential for reform than adults, the policies and procedures of the justice system will be altered to facilitate the rehabilitation of youth (Arya, 2011a; Guggenheim, 2012; Levick & Tierney, 2012). If the law develops as predicted, there will be expanded roles for lawyers, social workers, psychologists, and other experts to play in making individualized assessments about whether a youth should be transferred to the adult system, the level of culpability on the part of a particular youth and the appropriate sentence to impose, and the youth's potential for rehabilitation.

PREA Standards and Applicability to Youthful Offenders

In a highly unusual bipartisan move, Congress unanimously passed the Prison Rape Elimination Act (PREA) in 2003, creating a Commission to study the issue of sexual assault in correctional facilities and to propose standards to prevent such occurrences (PREA, 2003). After years of study that involved the input of thousands of practitioners, experts, and advocates, the Commission developed its standards and proposed them to the U.S. Attorney General. The Attorney General released final regulations in 2012 that require federal, state, and local adult and juvenile facilities to abide by the PREA standards or risk losing a portion of federal funding (National PREA Resource Center, 2013). While failure to comply with the standards does not create a legal cause of action, violations of the standards would be evidence in a civil rights lawsuit that the agency involved does not comply with best practices in correctional management or take appropriate steps to protect the safety of prisoners.

One of the PREA standards deals explicitly with the protection of youthful offenders in adult prisons and jails (PREA Standards, 2012) and is expected to lead to significant shifts in the way these youth are managed. PREA Standard 115.14 (Youthful Offenders) requires that youth under age 18 be kept sight and sound separated from adult offenders in the parts of prisons and jails used for housing, hygiene activities, and dining. During all other times when there might be incidental contact with adult offenders, there must be direct staff supervision. To accomplish this objective, however, youth should not be placed in isolation nor denied access to programs and services in which the adult offenders participate (PREA Standards, 2012). While many advocates would have preferred a standard that required youth to be removed from adult facilities in accordance with the policy statements of juvenile and adult detention and correctional associations, this standard represents a compromise when state law requires the youth to remain in the adult correctional setting.

Nevertheless, even this standard will be extremely hard for many agencies to meet. As noted earlier, jails in particular may be ill equipped to provide sight and sound separation for youth without placing them in solitary confinement. And states in which the age of juvenile jurisdiction is set below age 18 will have an especially difficult time given the numbers of youth who would have to be managed separately from the rest of the adult population. Because the PREA

Standards are so new, it remains to be seen how compliance with this aspect of the standards will play out around the country, but one possibility is that jurisdictions will find it easier to simply move these youth to juvenile settings both before trial and after conviction rather than to adjust their operational practices or make architectural renovations in the prisons and jails.

■ Trends in State Policies

When state policymakers changed the laws in the 1980s and 1990s to make it easier to prosecute youth in adult court, many believed their efforts would improve public safety and deter future crime. Numerous studies have since concluded that prosecuting youth in adult court is ineffective at deterring crime and reducing recidivism (Redding, 2010; McGowan et al., 2007). In light of this new research, state policymakers have begun to reconsider these laws. In the past decade, nearly half of the states have changed their laws to limit the number of youth prosecuted in adult court and to remove youth from adult facilities (Arya, 2011b; Brown, 2012). These changes are occurring in all regions of the country, spearheaded by state and local officials of both major parties and supported by a bipartisan group of governors. There are four categories of reforms that are taking place across the country.

The first trend is that states and local jurisdictions have changed laws and policies allowing youth to be held in adult jails and prisons. Recognizing the many dangers youth face when incarcerated with adults, several states and local jurisdictions have taken action to remove youth from adult facilities. For example, Texas, Virginia, and Oregon changed the default rules that required youth prosecuted as adults to be housed in adult facilities to a discretionary choice for counties, and Colorado changed the criteria to determine when a youth may be housed in an adult facility (Arya, 2011b; Deitch et al., 2012b). The implementation of PREA is expected to encourage more states and local jurisdictions to remove youth from adult facilities.

The second trend is that states are changing their age of jurisdiction laws, primarily in recognition of the fact that there are better outcomes for youth who remain in the juvenile system. Three states, Connecticut, Illinois, and Mississippi, have recently raised the age of juvenile court jurisdiction so that older youth who previously would be automatically tried as adults are now prosecuted in the juvenile court (Arya, 2011b). There are several reform efforts under way in the remaining states, including high-profile efforts in New York, North Carolina, and Massachusetts, to conform to the nationwide standard of 18 (Citizens for Juvenile Justice, 2011; Deitch, Breeden, & Weingarten, 2012a).

Third, more than a dozen states have changed various aspects of the transfer laws, making it more likely that youth will stay in the juvenile justice system.

Given the diversity of state laws, the legislative modifications are unique to each state. States such as Arizona and Utah have made it easier for youth who were tried as adults to get reverse waiver hearings to allow them to return to the juvenile court. Several states, including Colorado and Nevada, changed the age requirements before youth can be tried as adults. States have also made changes to "once an adult, always an adult" laws. States have also narrowed the types of offenses that require adult court prosecution or have changed the presumptions for adult court prosecution. For example, Illinois removed drug offenders from automatic prosecution in adult court (Arya, 2011b).

Finally, states are rethinking how mandatory sentencing laws affect youth. As noted earlier, youth who are prosecuted and sentenced in the adult criminal justice system are often subject to the same harsh sentencing laws as adults since most states' mandatory sentencing laws do not have statutory exceptions for youth. This means that many states subject youth to harsh mandatory sentencing guidelines without allowing judges to take the child's developmental differences into account. Several states have begun to change their mandatory minimum sentencing laws to take into account the developmental differences between youth and adults, and others are considering such changes. For example, Washington State has eliminated mandatory minimum sentences for youth tried as adults (Arya, 2011b).

Summary and Conclusion

State policymakers changed the laws in the 1980s and 1990s to make it easier to prosecute youth in adult court and sentence youth to harsh mandatory sentences. As a result, nearly 250,000 youth are prosecuted and sentenced as adults each year. Significant consequences follow from placing youth in the adult criminal justice system: they receive adult criminal records, which can cause them to be denied employment and educational opportunities; they can receive extremely long sentences; and they can be at great risk of physical and sexual assault, suicide, or mental health problems if confined in adult facilities.

In recognition of the incompatibility of the adult criminal justice system and the special needs of youth under age 18, a movement to return youth to juvenile court has begun. In the last decade, the courts, legislatures, and justice system officials have begun to demonstrate a recognition that "children are different" when it comes to criminal justice issues. Moreover, many policymakers have been swayed by research showing the poor outcomes for youth in the adult system and the risks this presents for public safety. Policy changes and legal rulings have sought to distinguish juvenile and adult offenders in terms of their sentencing, treatment, programming, and incarceration options and to minimize the risks faced by youth who are transferred to adult court or who are held in adult facilities.

Over 100 years ago, reformers created the first juvenile courts in America in recognition of the special needs of children and youth and a belief in the potential for their rehabilitation. After a couple of recent decades in which those principles seem to have been overlooked, with terrible consequences for the youth involved, present trends seem to suggest that we are in the process of rediscovering the value in having unique court systems, processes, sentencing options, and facilities for adolescent offenders.

References

American Bar Association (2010). Treatment of Prisoners. Standard 23-3.2. *Standards for criminal justice* (3rd ed.). Washington, DC: Author.

American Correctional Association (2009). Position statement: Public correctional policy on youthful offenders transferred to adult criminal jurisdiction. Delegate Assembly, Congress of Correction, Kissimmee, FL: Author. Retrieved from http://www.campaignforyouthjustice.org/documents/natlres/ACA%20-%20Public%20Correctional%20Policy%20on%20Youthful%20Offenders.pdf

American Jail Association (2008). Resolution on juveniles in jails. Originally adopted by Board of Directors on May 22, 1980, revised May 19, 1993, re-affirmed May 3, 2008. Retrieved from http://www.campaignforyouthjustice.org/documents/natlres/AJA%20-%20Juveniles%20in%20Jails.pdf

Arya, N. (2011a). Using *Graham v. Florida* to challenge juvenile transfer laws. *Louisiana Law Review, 71*, 99–155.

Arya, N. (2011b). *State trends: Legislative changes from 2005 to 2010 removing youth from the adult criminal justice system.* Washington, DC: Campaign for Youth Justice.

Arya, N., & Augarten, I. (2008). *Critical condition: African-American youth in the justice system.* Washington, DC: Campaign for Youth Justice.

Arya, N., & Rolnick, A. (2008). *A tangled web of justice: American Indian and Alaska Native youth in federal, state, and tribal justice systems.* Washington, DC: Campaign for Youth Justice.

Arya, N., Villarruel, F., Villanueva, C., & Augarten, I. (2009). *America's invisible children: Latino youth and the failure of justice.* Washington, DC: Campaign for Youth Justice.

Bishop, D. (2000). Juvenile offenders in the adult criminal justice system. *Crime and Justice, 27*, 81–167.

Brown, S. (2012). *Trends in juvenile justice state legislation: 2001–2011.* Denver, CO: National Conference of State Legislatures.

Bunch v. Smith, 685 F.3d 546 (6th Cir. 2012).

Campaign for Youth Justice (2007). *Jailing juveniles: The dangers of incarcerating juveniles in adult jails in America.* Washington, DC: Author. Retrieved from http://www.campaignforyouthjustice.org/Downloads/NationalReportsArticles/CFYJ-Jailing_Juveniles_Report_2007-11-15.pdf

Campaign for Youth Justice (n.d.). http://www.campaignforyouthjustice.org/

Campaign for Youth Justice & Partnership for Safety and Justice (2011). *Misguided measures: The outcomes and impacts of Measure 11 on Oregon's youth.* Washington, DC: Campaign for Youth Justice.

Children's Action Alliance (2010). *Improving public safety by keeping youth out of the adult criminal justice system.* Phoenix, AZ: Author.

Children's Law Center, Inc. (2012). *Falling through the cracks: A new look at Ohio youth in the adult criminal justice system.* Covington, KY: Author.

Citizens for Juvenile Justice (2011). *Minor transgressions, major consequences: A picture of 17-year-olds in the Massachusetts criminal justice system.* Boston, MA: Author.

Colorado Juvenile Defender Coalition (2012). *Re-directing justice: The consequences of prosecuting youth as adults and the need to restore judicial oversight.* Denver, CO: Colorado Juvenile Defender Coalition.

Colorado Juvenile Defender Coalition (n.d.). *Caging children in crisis.* Denver, CO: Colorado Juvenile Defender Coalition.

Deitch, M. (2011). *Juveniles in the adult criminal justice system.* Austin, TX: Lyndon B. Johnson School of Public Affairs. Retrieved from http://www.utexas.edu/lbj/sites/default/files/file/news/juvenilestexas—final.pdf

Deitch, M., Barstow, A., Lukens, L. & Reyna, R. (2009). *From time out to hard time: Young children in the adult criminal justice system.* Austin, TX: Lyndon B. Johnson School of Public Affairs. Retrieved from http://nicic.gov/Library/023876

Deitch, M., Breeden, R., & Weingarten, R. (2012a). Seventeen, going on eighteen: An operational and fiscal analysis of a proposal to raise the age of juvenile jurisdiction in Texas. *American Journal of Criminal Law, 40,* 1–67.

Deitch, M., Lipton Galbraith, A., & Pollock, J. (2012b). *Conditions for certified Juveniles jn Texas county jails.* Austin, TX: Lyndon B. Johnson School of Public Affairs. Retrieved from http://nicic.gov/Library/026403

Dilulio, J. (1995, November 27). The coming of the super-predators. *The Weekly Standard, 1*(11), 23–28.

Equal Justice Initiative (2008). *Cruel and unusual: Sentencing 13- and 14-year-old children to die in prison.* Montgomery, AL: Author. Retrieved from http://www.eji.org/files/Cruel%20 and%20Unusual%202008_0.pdf

Fagan, J. (1996). The comparative impacts of juvenile and criminal court sanctions on adolescent felony offenders. *Law and Policy, 18,* 77–119.

Gardner, M., & Steinberg, L. (2005). Peer influence on risk taking, risk preference and risky decision making in adolescence and adulthood: An experimental study. *Developmental Psychology, 41*(4), 625–635.

Graham v. Florida, 130 S. Ct. 2011 (2010).

Griffin, P., Addie, S., Adams, B. & Firestine, K. (2011). *Trying juveniles as adults: An analysis of state transfer laws and reporting* (OJJDP Bulletin No. 232434). Washington, DC: U.S. Department of Justice.

Guggenheim, M. (2012). *Graham v. Florida* and a juvenile's right to age-appropriate sentencing. *Harvard Civil Rights and Civil Liberties Law Review, 47,* 457–500.

Human Rights Watch & American Civil Liberties Union (2012). *Growing up locked down: Youth in solitary confinement in jails and prisons across the United States.* New York: Author. Retrieved from http://www.hrw.org/reports/2012/10/10/growing-locked-down

Human Rights Watch & Amnesty International (2005). *The rest of their lives: Life without parole for child offenders in the United States.* New York: Author.

J.D.B. v. North Carolina, 131 S. Ct. 2394 (2011).

Just Kids Partnership (2010). *JUST KIDS: Baltimore's youth in the adult criminal justice system.* Baltimore, MD: Author.

JustChildren (2009). *Don't throw away the key: Reevaluating adult time for youth crime in Virginia.* Charlottesville, VA: Author.

Juvenile Law Center (n.d.). *Commonwealth of Pennsylvania v. Jordan Brown.* Retrieved from http://www.jlc.org/legal-docket/commonwealth-pennsylvania-v-jordan-brown

Juszkiewicz, J. (2007). *To punish a few: Too many youth caught in the net of adult prosecution.* Washington, DC: Campaign for Youth Justice. Retrieved from http://www. campaignforyouthjustice.org/documents/to_punish_a_few_final.pdf

Kent v. United States, 383 U.S. 541 (1966).

Levick, M., & Tierney, E. (2012). The United States Supreme Court adopts a reasonable juvenile standard in *J.D.B. v. North Carolina* for purposes of the *Miranda* custody analysis: Can a more reasoned justice system for juveniles be far behind? *Harvard Civil Rights and Civil Liberties Law Review, 47*, 501–527.

Hahn, R., McGowan, A., Lieberman, A., Crosby, A., Fullilove, M.,...Stone, G., Centers for Disease Control Task Force on Community Preventive Services. (2007, November 30). Effects on violence of laws and policies facilitating the transfer of youth from the juvenile to the adult justice system: A report on recommendations of the Task Force on Community Preventive Services. *Morbidity and Mortality Weekly Report 56*(RR09), 1–11.

John D. and Catherine T. MacArthur Foundation (2005, Fall). Juvenile justice: New models for reform. *MacArthur Newsletter, 3.*

McGowan, Angela, et al., Centers for Disease Control Task Force on Community Preventive Services, "Effects on Violence of Laws and Policies Facilitating the Transfer of Youth from the Juvenile to the Adult Justice System: A Report on Recommendations of the Task Force on Community Preventive Services," *MMWR* (November 30, 2007), 7, accessed March 18, 2013, http://www.cdc.gov/mmwr/pdf/rr/rr5609.pdf.

Miller v. Alabama, 132 S. Ct. 2455 (2012).

Minton, T. (2010, June). Jail inmates at midyear 2009—Statistical tables. *Prison and jail inmates at midyear.* Washington, DC: U.S. Department of Justice, Office of Justice Programs, Bureau of Justice Statistics.

National Juvenile Detention Association (1997). *Position statement: Holding juveniles under criminal court jurisdiction in juvenile detention.* Retrieved from http://npjs.org.previewdns.com/wp-content/uploads/2012/12/NJDA-Position-Statement-Jurisdiction.pdf

National Juvenile Justice Network (2009, August). *Policy platform: Conditions of confinement.* Retrieved from http://www.njjn.org/uploads/policy-platforms/Conditions-of-Confinement-Policy-Platform-5-18-12-fin.pdf

National PREA Resource Center (2013). *Frequently asked questions.* Retrieved April 30, 2013, from http://www.prearesourcecenter.org/faq

Office of Juvenile Justice and Delinquency Prevention. (2012). *OJJDP statistical briefing book.* Retrieved from http://www.ojjdp.gov/ojstatbb/structure_process/qa04105.asp?qaDate=2011

People of California v. Caballero, 55 Cal. 4th 262, 282 P.3d 291 (2012).

Prison Rape Elimination Act (2003, September 4). Public Law 108-79.

Prison Rape Elimination Act Prisons and Jail Standards (2012). U.S. Department of Justice Final Rule. 28 C.F.R. 115.14 (Youthful Inmates). Retrieved from http://www.prearesourcecenter.org/sites/default/files/library/prisonsandjailsfinalstandards.pdf

Redding, R. (2010, June). Juvenile transfer laws: An effective deterrent to delinquency?. *Juvenile Justice Bulletin.* Washington, DC: Office of Juvenile Justice and Delinquency Prevention.

Ritter, M. (2007, December 2). Scientists: teen brain still maturing. *Associated Press.* Retrieved from http://www.washingtonpost.com/wp-dyn/content/article/2007/12/02/AR2007120200809_pf.html

Roper v. Simmons, 543 U.S. 551 (2005).

Snyder, H., & Sickmund, M. (2006). *Juvenile offenders and victims: 2006 national report* (NCJ 212906). Washington, DC: Office of Juvenile Justice and Delinquency Prevention.

Steinberg, L., & Scott, E. (2003, December). Less guilty by reason of adolescence. *American Psychologist, 58*(12), 1009–1018.

U.S. Department of Justice Civil Rights Division (2012). *Memorandum of agreement regarding the juvenile court of Memphis and Shelby County.* Retrieved from http://www.justice.gov/crt/about/spl/documents/shelbycountyjuv_agreement_12-17-12.pdf

Washington Coalition for the Just Treatment of Youth (2009). *A reexamination of youth involvement in the adult criminal justice system in Washington: Implications of new findings about juvenile recidivism and adolescent brain development.* Seattle, WA: Author.

West, H. (2010, June). Prison inmates at midyear 2009—Statistical tables. *Prison and jail inmates at Midyear.* Washington, DC: U.S. Department of Justice, Office of Justice Programs, Bureau of Justice Statistics.

Zeidenberg, J. (2011). *You're an adult now: Youth in adult criminal justice systems.* National Institute of Corrections. Washington, DC: U.S. Department of Justice.

School- and
Community-Based Programs

12 Marginalized Students, School Exclusion, and the School-to-Prison Pipeline

Michael P. Krezmien, Peter E. Leone, and Michael G. Wilson

"He who opens a school door, closes a prison."

Victor Hugo

■ Introduction

In recent years, schools have increasingly relied upon school suspensions and expulsions as a response to school disciplinary infractions (Krezmien, Leone, Zablocki, & Wells, 2010). Zero-tolerance policies were designed to improve school safety and prevent future infractions, but evidence suggests that schools actually dedicated greater time and resources to school discipline despite the fact that the suspensions had a negative effect on academic performance (Skiba & Rausch, 2006). At the same time, schools have increasingly referred students directly to the police or to courts (Krezmien et al., 2010), effectively criminalizing school misbehavior. These two co-occurring phenomena have increased the risk of incarceration and represent two different but related paths of the "school-to-prison pipeline."

The terms "school-to-prison pipeline" (American Civil Liberties Union, 2012), "cradle-to-prison pipeline" (Children's Defense Fund, 2012), and "schoolhouse-to-jailhouse track" (Advancement Project, 2005) have been developed to describe the cascade of effects that occur when children are pushed out of schools and into the juvenile justice system. Establishing causal relationships between school misbehavior and subsequent placement in juvenile corrections or prison is difficult (Krezmien et al., 2010). However, sufficient evidence exists to show that in too many schools and too many communities, school discipline policies and inadequate support for students who struggle academically is a serious problem. Evidence shows that Black students, Hispanic students, and students with disabilities are suspended and excluded from schools at a disproportionate rate (Advancement Project, 2005; Fabello et al., 2011; Krezmien, Leone, & Achilles, 2006; Losen et al., 2012; NYCLU, 2011) and that those students are also disproportionately represented in juvenile corrections (Quinn, Rutherford, Leone, Osher, & Poirier, 2005; Snyder & Sickmund, 2006). Rather than contributing to public safety and fiscal responsibility, current school disciplinary policies contribute to disequilibrium between children, their families, and their communities and are a principal component of the school-to-prison pipeline.

Figure 12.1 shows a diagram of two co-occurring pathways from school to prison. Path 1 shows that suspensions and expulsions increasingly place students at risk of becoming incarcerated because they remove students from the positive influences of schools while increasing the opportunities for students to encounter negative influences (negative peers, lack of supervision, drugs and alcohol). This may ultimately lead to criminal misbehavior and subsequent delinquency (Smith, 2011). According to this theory, the more times a

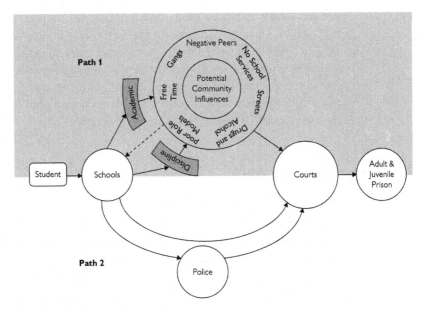

Figure 12.1   Pathways from school to prison.

student is suspended or expelled, the greater the risk of court involvement and subsequent incarceration. While some students receive education services in alternative or specialized settings following their exclusion, children excluded from school have greater opportunity to engage in delinquent and antisocial behavior and are more vulnerable to contact with law enforcement. Path 1 also shows that schools can fail in their support of the educational needs of at-risk youth. Consequently, at-risk students skip school, are retained at high rates, are disengaged from schools and the learning process, and are likely to drop out of school or to leave school without a diploma (Fabello et al., 2011; Wilson & Krezmien, 2007). Path 2 shows a more direct pathway from schools to prisons. Path 2 illustrates schools' referral of students to the police or to the courts, establishing school misbehavior as criminal activity addressed by the legal system rather than through traditional school disciplinary practices (Krezmien et al., 2010). This direct link between schools and the juvenile justice system is a more direct verification of the "pipeline."

The United States leads the world in incarceration, for both adults and juveniles. The United States incarcerates more people than any other country, both in total numbers—one quarter of the world's incarcerated people are in the United States—and per capita (Walmsley, 2011). The United States incarcerates nearly five times as many children per capita as the next highest country. School disciplinary practices, especially the exclusion of students through suspension and expulsion, create conditions in which children fall behind their peers academically and are a great risk of leaving school before graduating from high school (Smith, 2011). Additionally, evidence suggests that a greater percentage of incarcerated youth are referred directly from schools (Krezmien et al., 2010). These two processes represent the basis for the "school-to-prison pipeline." The purpose of this chapter is to examine the evidence associated with the school-to-prison pipeline, to present findings from a study that examines the phenomena from the perspectives of both schools and juvenile corrections, and to present some approaches to stem the flow of children and youth from schools into the juvenile delinquency system.

■ Review of the Literature

To understand the school-to-prison pipeline, it is essential to understand the multiple sources of evidence associated with the pipeline. First, this requires an examination of the school exclusion research. This research demonstrates that students are increasingly suspended and expelled from school and subsequently being placed at risk of delinquency and incarceration. Second, it requires an examination of juvenile delinquency research that directly links school with the courts for school misbehavior that has become increasingly criminalized. Third, it requires an examination of the research that links school exclusions to the research on juvenile delinquency to demonstrate that schools play an active role in pushing students out of school and into the juvenile delinquency system. Removing students from school has consequences not just for the youth involved but also for the larger community. When these students are incarcerated, the community and the government accrue substantial costs associated with arrests, probation, detention, and commitment. When these youth drop out, communities are responsible for substantial costs associated with unemployment and underemployment, as well as the subsequent costs of delinquent behaviors. Research shows that states with higher rates of high-school graduation have lower crime rates and increased benefits to the state economy associated with higher levels of employment (Lochner & Moretti, 2004).

School Exclusion Research

Historically, suspensions and expulsions were reserved for the most serious infractions of the school disciplinary code. While fights and physical aggression are one of the most common reasons for removal from school, a review of school discipline research indicates that the majority of youth are suspended and expelled for nonviolent offenses (Krezmien, Leone, & Achilles, 2006; Fabello et al., 2011; Losen et al., 2012; Skiba & Rausch, 2006). School disciplinary removal serves two important functions for schools: (a) ensure the safety of staff and students and (b) create an environment conducive to learning (Gaustad, 1992). Serious student misconduct, including weapons offenses, drug offenses, and physical attacks, may interfere with these objectives and may require removal from school. However, as stated, the majority of suspensions are for noncriminal violations of rules, such as disruptions, inappropriate language, and unexcused absences (Krezmien, 2012; Losen, Simmons, Staudinger-Poloni, et al., 2003).

Strict enforcement of school rules associated with zero-tolerance policies has resulted in significant overall increases in the national number of suspensions: from about 1.7 million (3.7% of all students) in 1974 to more than 3.3 million (6.8% of all students) in 2006 (Fabello et al., 2011). In addition, several studies have demonstrated persistent overrepresentation of African-American students (Costenbader & Markson, 1998; Raffaele Mendez, Knoff, & Ferron, 2002; Krezmien et al, 2006; Skiba & Peterson, 1997; Zhang et al., 2005) and students with disabilities (Cooley, 1995; Losen, et al., 2012; Skiba, 2002; Zhang et al., 2005) in the suspension rates of schools, school districts, and states. These findings suggest that the increases in rates of school suspension have a disproportionate impact on the students who already have the highest risk for school failure and delinquency. Rather than supporting the most vulnerable children and youth, schools are knowingly or unknowingly pushing them out of schools without the supports necessary for successfully navigating society.

The current policies designed to meet troubling behavior with harsh punishments have been ineffective for reducing or eliminating the behaviors and may indeed exacerbate the problems they are designed to punish (Leone et al., 2003). Nonetheless, zero-tolerance policies continue to dominate public-school disciplinary policies despite an almost complete lack of documentation to support their effectiveness (Skiba & Peterson, 2000). Costenbader and Markson (1998) found that 40% of school suspensions are delivered to repeat offenders, suggesting that suspension is ineffective for those students for whom it is most commonly prescribed. This finding is particularly problematic for special educators who are responsible for promoting prosocial behaviors and eliminating troubling behavior through sustained and systematic behavioral interventions. Exclusionary practices that fail to improve behavior may actually inhibit the effectiveness of special education behavioral programming because they remove students from necessary behavioral and educational services and because they interrupt sustained service delivery. For some students, exclusions may accelerate the course of delinquency by decreasing educational opportunities and increasing occasions to associate with deviant peers, as demonstrated in Path 1 in Figure 12.1.

School exclusions put children at risk for a host of negative social outcomes. This is one of the reasons that the No Child Left Behind Act of 2002 (NCLB) requires suspensions and expulsions to be reported to the federal government and requires the government to use those reports to determine which schools meet the criteria for persistently dangerous schools. Despite high expectations for schools to decrease suspension rates under the mandates of the NCLB, increasing numbers of students continue to be suspended for a host of minor infractions such as truancy, disrespectful behavior, and classroom disruptions. As a result, more students are excluded from school and have an increased likelihood to engage in delinquent activity, experience academic failure, and drop out (Krezmien et al., 2006; Leone et al., 2003; Losen et al., 2003; Skiba & Rausch, 2006). These failures place them at greater risk for involvement with the juvenile justice and the criminal justice systems (Leone, Mayer, Malmgren, & Meisel, 2000). Although public schools are not responsible for the underlying risks associated with negative outcomes, they can ameliorate or exacerbate the vulnerability of children to those negative outcomes (Leone et al., 2003). Based on current school exclusion and dropout data, schools seem to be exacerbating the vulnerability in multiple ways while providing limited or no means for ameliorating them.

A number of researchers have examined the school factors associated with school suspensions to understand the degree to which zero-tolerance policies are affecting students. They have found that numerous school factors, such as poverty, minority representation, low teacher expectations, and school mobility, are linked to high rates of suspension (Christle, Nelson, & Jolivette, 2004; Flannery, 1997; Krezmien, 2007; Skiba et al., 1997). These findings provide some disturbing evidence that schools who serve the most vulnerable children respond the most negatively to student needs. Christle and her colleagues (2004) found that high-suspending schools relied primarily on exclusionary practices to maintain school safety and order, while low-suspending schools utilized school-wide behavioral intervention programs to promote appropriate prosocial behaviors. Flannery (1997) identified several school-level factors related to risk for suspension, including high student/teacher ratios; insufficient curricular and course relevance; weak, inconsistent adult leadership; high suspension rates at schools that have high rates of minority students; and limited academic opportunities for students. Consistent with these findings, Krezmien (2007) found that high student mobility, high percentage of African-American enrollment, poor teacher quality, poverty, and poor student performance on high-stakes assessments were all related to the risk of suspension and the risk of disproportionate suspension of minority students and students with disabilities. Together, these findings indicate that the schools with the greatest number of problems respond the most punitively to school misbehavior, contributing to the school-to-prison pipeline as modeled in Path 1 in Figure 12.1.

■ Criminalization of School Misbehavior and School Referrals to Courts

As greater numbers of students are suspended and expelled from school, schools have also began increasingly to view school misbehavior as a form of delinquency (Krezmien et al., 2010). The passage by Congress of the Gun-Free Schools Act of 1994, following several high-profile school shootings, appears to have redefined the meaning of school misbehavior and responses to it. Among other things, the law required schools to adopt a zero-tolerance policy for weapons and mandated that schools suspend any student who brought a weapon to school for a minimum of 1 year. Schools were also required to report weapons violations to the criminal justice or juvenile justice system. While schools and school systems were free to ignore the mandates of the Gun-Free Schools Act, financial incentives were tied to the legislation so that participating schools that failed to enact zero-tolerance policies did not receive federal support for school safety measures.

In addition to the Gun-Free Schools Act, Title 1 of the Elementary and Secondary Education Act, also known as the No Child Left Behind Act of 2001, pressed school administrators to raise levels of student achievement and held them accountable if they did not (Krezmien et al., 2010). The high-stakes assessments associated with NCLB left little room in schools for student misbehavior. Concurrent with the implementation of this legislation, many administrators interpreted the zero-tolerance polices more broadly than originally intended, suspending students for a wide range of behaviors such as bullying, threatening, using profanity, and using alcohol and tobacco (Hirschfield, 2008; Kupchik, 2009). Many schools have extended the consequences for violating zero-tolerance rules to include longer suspensions and, in some cases, expulsion (Anderson, 2004). Furthermore, some states have mandated suspensions

Table 12.1   Suspensions by Category of Offense, Sample State 1995–2003

| | Suspensions | | | |
	1995	2003	Difference	Percent Change
Suspensions by Category of Offense				
Disrespect	16953	24989	8036	47.4%
Disruption	10098	22910	12812	126.9%
Refusal to Obey	16651	19334	2683	16.1%
Attacks I Threats	25182	43231	18049	71.7%
Weapons	2283	2237	-46	-2.0%
Illicit Substance	4847	4318	-529	-10.9%
Attendance	5184	10869	5685	109.7%
Other Serious	3873	7110	3237	83.6%
Total Suspensions	85071	134998	49927	58.7%
Number of Students Suspended	51082	75521	24439	47.8%
Enrollment	772104	846174	74070	9.6%
Percent of Students Suspended	6.6%	8.9%		

for school disruptions, truancy, and refusal to obey (Krezmien et al., 2006). Table 12.1 displays findings in one state that demonstrate the increases in suspensions for minor misbehavior as zero-tolerance policies were implemented (Krezmien, 2007).

The data displayed in Table 12.1 reveal that zero-tolerance policies were related to substantial increases in total numbers of suspensions and numbers of student suspensions. More importantly, the data show that over the 9 years, there were more than 20,000 additional suspensions for disrespect and classroom disruption and a 110% increase in suspensions for students who skipped school (Attendance). These data reveal a disturbing expansion of disciplinary removal from school, despite evidence that suspensions do not improve student behavior or school safety. In fact, research has shown that high rates of suspension are associated with an increase in disruptive behavior, decreased academic performance, and higher rates of school dropout (Bowditch, 1993; Raffaele-Mendez, as cited in Wald & Losen, 2003; Skiba & Rausch, 2006). Accompanying the increase in the use of suspensions and expulsions is evidence that there has been an increase in the referral of youth to the juvenile courts for school-related behavior in some states (Advancement Project, 2005; Krezmien et al, 2010; Teske, 2012).

During the past two decades there has been a dramatic increase in the number of school suspensions and expulsions in the United States (Advancement Project, 2005; NYCLU, 2011). The most recent data from the National Center on Education Statistics show that from 1999 to 2007, the percentage of all youth in grades 9 to 12 who had ever been suspended increased from 22.0 to 24.5 (U.S. Department of Education, 2011). For minority youth, the rates of suspension were even more striking: suspensions of Black youth increased from 40.9% to 57.0% and of Hispanic youth from 30.1% to 35.5% during this period. In California during the 2009–10 school year, nearly one in five African-American students and one in fourteen Hispanic students were suspended; during the same period only one in 17 White students in California were suspended (Losen et al., 2012). In contrast to the increasing rates of school suspension, evidence from the Institute of Education Sciences and the Bureau of Justice Statistics showed that during a similar period (1995–2009) there was a steady decline in school violence and victimization (Robers, Zhang, Truman, & Snyder, 2012).

Similarly, there has been a decrease in youth crime and a decrease in the number of youth incarcerated for delinquent offenses. However, recent research has also indicated that schools are directly referring a greater percentage of youth to the courts (Krezmien et al., 2010). In all of the literature, marginalized youth (those from diverse backgrounds and those with disabilities) have been disproportionately subject to suspensions, expulsions, and incarcerations. Thus, despite evidence indicating a decline in the frequency and intensity of school discipline problems, the rate at which students are excluded from schools has increased and has increasingly and negatively affected already marginalized youth.

■ Linking Schools and Prisons

One of the most difficult problems in understanding the school-to-prison pipeline is the theoretical nature of the model and a lack of empirical evidence linking school actions to future incarceration. For instance, there are no studies that have been able to track individual students through the theoretical pipeline, so it has not been possible to see that a suspension or expulsion from school leads to a delinquent or criminal act, which in turn results in incarceration in a juvenile or adult corrections facility. Krezmien and colleagues (2010) conducted one of the first studies that demonstrated a direct link between schools and juvenile courts, providing evidence of Path 2 of the school-to-prison pipeline. They examined trends in the number of school referrals directly to the courts in five states and found striking trends in the percentage of court-involved youth who were referred directly by schools.

They found that schools in each of the states represented a greater proportion of referrals to juvenile courts in 2004 than in 1995, and that schools in four of the five states (Arizona, Hawaii, Missouri, and West Virginia) had fairly stable increasing trends in the percentage of referrals (Figs. 12.2 and 12.3).

Krezmien and colleagues attributed increased attention to school misbehavior in the era of accountability as a primary force driving increases in school referral to the courts. They also reported that the reliance on zero-tolerance policies for school misbehavior and the increased use of school resource officers to manage school misbehavior were also related to the increases in school referrals to juvenile courts. The authors expressed a deep concern that schools are utilizing the juvenile justice system to manage problems that were previously considered school disciplinary problems; the data provided verification of the school-to-prison pipeline and Path 2 modeled in Figure 12.1. They

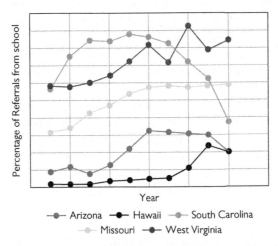

Figure 12.2 **Percentage of all juvenile court referrals originating in schools from 1995 to 2004. (Reprinted from Krezmien et al., 2010, Sage Publications)**

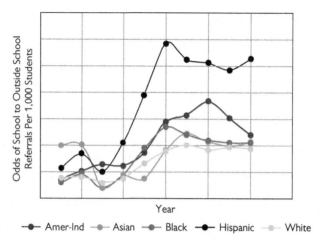

Figure 12.3 **Odds of school to outside-school referrals per 1,000 youths across race for Arizona from 1995 to 2004. (Reprinted from Krezmien et al., 2010, Sage Publications)**

found a variable impact on minority students across the states, but they did find extreme racial disparity in referrals in two of the five states.

■ Examining the Pipeline from the School and Prison Perspective

Wilson and Krezmien (2007) analyzed data that have the potential to provide another perspective on the school-to-prison pipeline by examining the disciplinary experiences of students incarcerated in one of two high-security commitment facilities in one state, as well as the school disciplinary practices of the home schools of the highest percentage of committed youth. The findings provide a unique means of looking at the school-to-prison pipeline from the school perspective as well as from the juvenile justice perspective in a unified analysis.

Table 12.2 displays the suspension and expulsion rates of the males and females incarcerated in the "sample" state. The data were obtained through an exhaustive interview process with each youth, generally within the first week of commitment. The suspension rates of the youth are extraordinary—nearly 10 times the suspension rate in "sample" state's public schools. Furthermore, the nearly identical suspension rates for boys and girls are not consistent with suspension practices in the state or with the school suspension research. While these findings cannot be interpreted as a causal relationship between school disciplinary policies and subsequent incarceration, they do demonstrate clear evidence that incarcerated youth are markedly different from non-incarcerated youth with respect to suspensions. These findings provide a unique means of understanding Path 1 of the school-to-prison pipeline modeled in Figure 12.1.

Table 12.2   **Youth Self-Report of School History of Exclusion, Retention in Grade, and Dropout at the Time of Incarceration in Sample State**

Reports of School History (555 males, 274 females)

	Females	Males
Suspended	84%	85%
Expelled	46%	52%
Retained	55%	64%
Dropped Out	25%	25%

The expulsion rates in Table 12.2 provide further support of Path 1. The expulsion rate for incarcerated youth is perhaps more troubling because of the permanent nature of an expulsion compared to a suspension. During the time these data were collected (2005–2006), less than 0.2% of the public school population in the "sample" state was expelled, indicating that the committed youth were expelled at more than 200 times the rate of typical public-school students. The impact of expulsion is immeasurable, especially within the context of the school-to-prison pipeline model, which theorizes that time out of school is linked with increased opportunities for association with negative peers and settings, contributing to delinquent or criminal behavior. The retention and dropout numbers are also problematic and are related to more insidious mechanisms linked to the school-to-prison pipeline. These findings suggest that schools do not provide adequate services and supports to ensure that at-risk students can achieve academically. Subsequently, students experience continued school failure and become increasingly disengaged from school, eventually dropping out.

The second component of this research was an examination of the characteristics of the incarcerated youths' home schools. Table 12.3 displays some characteristics of 12 home schools of youth incarcerated in the state. These 12 schools represented only 3% of the home schools of incarcerated students but represented 25% of the total population in the juvenile corrections facilities. Consequently, these schools are identified as "feeder schools," schools that have a documented history of pushing youth out of school and feeding them into the juvenile justice system (Wilson & Krezmien, 2007).

Table 12.3 shows that the suspension ratio (the calculation of suspensions to enrollment) is much higher in each of the feeder schools than the state median, with six schools with rates more than twice the state median. Similarly, the percentages of youth who do not meet basic proficiency on the state assessments (MSA) are substantially higher in the feeder schools than the state median. Particularly troubling are the schools in which less than 10% of the students were able to achieve a score of basic proficiency, indicating that these schools are failing to adequately educate the students in a manner that would prepare them to graduate from high school. The percentages

Table 12.3   Characteristics of Schools in Sample State with the Greatest Percentage of Incarcerated Youth

Number		Enrollment	Susp Ratio	%AA	%White	%not Passing State Assessment	Atend Rate	%of teachers not highly qualified	SPED In School	Mobility	FARL
HS 1	14	1983	0.71	92%	3%	89%	88%	69%	11%	25%	25%
HS 2	13	2001	0.67	99%	1%	99%	73%	71%	17 %	33%	489'o
HS 3	14	141	177	49%	46%	75%	86%		20%	10 %	32%
HS 4	17	1936	0.8	71%	19%	97%	81%	75%	16%	29%	66%
HS 5	11	1974	0.48	31%	56%	66%	93%	35%	91%	13%	24%
HS 6	12	1199	0.61	50%	43%	82%	94%	46%	14%	19%	30%
HS 7	11	1201	0.43	20%	76%	78%	92%	43%	13%	17%	30%
HS 8	16	1841	0.31	20%	76%	74%	94%	39%	16%	20%	24%
HS 9	18	1506	0.37	98%	1%	100%	51%	58%	14%	93%	35%
HS 10	11	98	2.01	8%	90%	83%	84%	67%	48%	66%	42%
I-IS 11	11	1387	0.29	18%	74%	76%	89%	36%	14%	23%	35%
HS 12	13	990	0.4	48%	48%	85%	90%	48%	17%	26%	45%
State Median		1075	026	22%	65%	54%	94%	32%	11%	8%	24%

of teachers who are not highly qualified (NHQ) are also high for each of the feeder schools, with five schools having less than half of their teachers highly qualified. The failure of the schools to hire and retain highly qualified teachers also contributes to risk of retention, academic failure, and dropouts in these schools, further increasing the risk for court involvement. Equally troubling are the attendance rates of many of the schools (e.g., HS 9) as well as the mobility rates, which are more than double the state median for all but two of the feeder schools.

The findings from these two components of this study reveal some troubling insights into the school-to-prison pipeline. By looking at the schools in sample state, there is substantial evidence that they are ill equipped or ill prepared to adequately support students through their academic careers. These schools lack qualified teachers and have low attendance rates, which appear to be linked to extremely poor academic outcomes as measured by the high percentages of students who fail to achieve minimal proficiency on state assessments. Subsequently, these students are at high risk for retention and for dropping out. When we examine the students in juvenile corrections, we find co-occurring high rates of retention and dropping out, indicating that these youth have not been adequately supported in their academic endeavors.

While we cannot draw a causal link between the schools and the incarcerated youth, the data make a strong case for the argument that schools that do not adequately support students, particularly struggling students, effectively support a pathway to the juvenile delinquency system, as demonstrated in Path 1 in Figure 12.1.

Additionally, we also found that the schools suspended extremely high percentages of students, with ratios as high as .71 suspensions for every student enrolled. These data indicate that these schools either lack sufficient supports to promote positive school climates or respond to school misbehavior through extreme disciplinary practices. When we look at the characteristics of the incarcerated students, we can see that these students were suspended and expelled at troubling rates. Again, these two sets of data do not confirm the existence of a school-to-prison pipeline through causal modeling, but they represent another strong argument that schools use school disciplinary practices in ways that push students into the juvenile justice system as demonstrated in Path 1 in Figure 12.1.

■ Dismantling the School-to-Prison Pipeline

If schools, school districts, and states are going to respond to the challenges associated with the school-to-prison pipeline they will need to develop and implement broad-based reforms to tackle the complicated risk factors associated with the pipeline. According to our model in Figure 12.1, there are two distinct pathways for the theoretical school-to-prison pipeline. Path 1 represents an indirect model, which purports that a school's disciplinary practices and its failure to adequately support the academic needs of at-risk youth increase a youth's risk of becoming involved in the juvenile delinquency system. That pathway consists of complex factors that "push" students out of school and into the school-to-prison pipeline. While schools have an obligation to respond to disciplinary infractions and maintain order, they can also continue to use inefficient and ineffective practices or choose to respond differently. Interventions to stop or limit Path 1 require schools to implement coordinated and targeted services that include (a) behavior prevention and intervention efforts, (b) academic interventions and supports, and (c) a restorative justice approach to school discipline. Path 2 in our model represents a direct model in which schools directly refer youth to the police or to courts for school misbehavior, essentially criminalizing school misbehavior. Interventions to stop or limit youth moving along Path 2 require schools, school districts, and states to fundamentally revise their disciplinary policies and to adopt restorative justice practices (Teske, 2012) and address the unmet needs of students with disabilities (Tulman & Weck, 2009/10). However, it should be noted that the presence of school resource officers (SROs) and police in schools can promote students' attachment to schools and mitigate school disruption or, conversely, result in increased suspensions and referral of youth to juvenile courts (Kupchik, 2010).

■ Behavior Prevention and Intervention Practices

The development of prosocial responses to student behavior and violations of the disciplinary code is the key to reducing the contribution of schools to the problem of exclusion and incarceration of youth. Recent research has made it increasingly clear that reactive approaches focused on punishment, exclusion, and retribution are ineffective (Skiba, 2002), support the criminalization of minority youth and students with disabilities (Harvard Civil Rights Project, 2000; Zhang, Katsiyannis, & Herbst, 2004), and increase the likelihood of student involvement with the juvenile and criminal systems (Hirschfield, 2008). Given these alarming facts, school systems concerned with order and safety, as well as equity and justice, should look to behavior prevention and intervention measures to address violations of the disciplinary code. A focus on behavior prevention and intervention allows schools to maintain the order and safety necessary to sustain the primary purpose of schooling—teaching and learning—and simultaneously reduces the reactionary tendency to exclude children.

Positive Behavioral Intervention and Support (PBIS) is a behavioral intervention approach focused on altering social contexts to decrease the effectiveness and efficiency of negative behaviors and to increase the likelihood of desired behaviors (Sugai et al., 2000). The PBIS approach adapts many of the inclusionary principles of special education such as individualization, consideration of both the function and context of behaviors, and culturally appropriate interventions based on shared needs of students, families, school actors, and the community. Preliminary evidence suggests PBIS may be effective at reducing the incidence of disciplinary violations (Bradshaw, Reinke, Brown, Bevans, & Leaf, 2008; Lassen, Steele, & Sailor, 2006). A key feature of PBIS is the use of a systems approach to behavioral change (Sugai et al., 2000). Using a systems approach, the focus of change is not merely at the student level but across all systems that potentially influence student behavior. Thus, policies and structures, environments, as well as school actors and families are engaged in the process.

Policies and Structures

Policies and structures can create an administrative context that supports the implementation of positive behavior supports within schools and are necessary for full implementation of PBIS (Bradshaw et al., 2008). Policy and structural approaches may include district-level support for prevention and intervention, systems of response to behavior, systems for monitoring and evaluating prevention and intervention effectiveness, clearly defined behavioral expectations, and implementation across school contexts (e.g., cafeteria, halls, classrooms, parking lot, and buses).

Environments

School and classroom environments play an important role in both learning and behavior (Hallinger & Murphy, 1986; Howard, 2003; Parsons, 2005; Purkey & Smith, 1983; Rolon, 2002; Stewart, 2007). As a result, environmental redesign is a key feature of the PBIS approach. Teachers and administrators should evaluate the physical environment students inhabit (classrooms, cafeteria, buses, etc.) and move through (hallways, social spaces, parking lots, etc.) in and around schools to determine how environmental design may contribute to or mitigate disciplinary problems. For example, schools can identify areas with minimal supervision that create potential sites for disorder in the school and adjust schedules or deploy staff to prevent disorder or bullying in those locations.

Engagement of School and Family Actors

Given the focus on culturally appropriate and participatory interventions in PBIS, engaging all those involved in the process is necessary for full implementation (Sugai et al., 2000). The first component of a comprehensive strategy involves teachers and administrators connecting with students and their families, as recipients of PBIS, to determine their values related to behavior and to jointly develop behavioral expectations as well as other aspects of the intervention. Fundamentally, the behavioral intervention plans designed for the most challenging students should be developed in concert with the family. Whenever possible, these plans should be implemented across the school and home environments, with consistent coordination and communication between school personnel and families. Such an approach would allow the schools and parents to collaborate on interventions that will transform youth behavior and relegate school misbehaviors to an aberrant occurrence as opposed to a behavioral norm.

Academic Interventions and Supports

The second component of a coordinated strategy for limiting youth in Path 1 involves providing engaging, high-quality instruction, specifically targeting struggling learners for ongoing instructional support, individualized programming, and continuous progress monitoring. Because a disproportionate number of youth excluded from school for disciplinary purposes are students eligible for special education, the individualized education plan (IEP) provides a good vehicle to describe both academic and behavioral supports.[1] Given the multifaceted nature of exclusion in schools, no single program or action can be expected to prevent violations of the disciplinary code or exclusion (Gregory, Skiba, & Noguera, 2010). However, providing high-quality and engaging instruction is critical for reducing retention, limiting or eliminating academic failure, reducing disciplinary violations, and postponing or preventing dropping out. Providing engaging instruction in the context of an educational culture fixated on standardized curricula and high-stakes assessments has created substantial tension between the school roles as a place of learning and as a place of order and safety (Amrein-Beardsley, 2009; Horn, 2003). Nevertheless, some support in research suggests that this tension is navigable through the use of effective inclusive schooling principles that meet the needs of all students (Peters & Oliver, 2009).

Considering Path 1 of our model, providing intensive and engaging educational supports, particularly to (a) students at risk for academic failure, (b) students at risk for dropping out of school, and/or (c) students with disabilities, can decrease their risk for truancy, retention, and dropping out, the academic factors directly associated with the school-to-prison pipeline (Smith, 2011). Effective and intensive services that include academic and social supports lead to increased school engagement and school bonding (Krezmien, Shanassa, Wilson, & McLaughlin, 2013). Active engagement in both the academic and social aspects of school can affect a student's likelihood to complete high school and pursue higher education (Fredricks et al., 2004; Rumberger & Arellano, 2007). This effect is even seen in elementary schools-academic engagement in the early school years is predictive of future academic outcomes (Barrington & Hendricks, 1989; Ensminger & Slusarcick, 1992), with significant differences in school engagement between dropouts and graduates identified at an early age (Barrington & Hendricks, 1989). Students who are highly engaged with schools, and who believe that they can complete school and graduate, will be less likely to disengage from schools by skipping school and dropping out.

In addition to intensive academic services and supports, schools can also increase engagement by creating culturally responsive environments. Black and Latino students perceive school environments as more positive when they engage their cultural backgrounds, partner with families, demonstrate cohesion around students' emotional needs, and support academic expectations (Howard, 2003; Parsons, 2005; Rolon, 2002; Stewart, 2007). Addressing these concerns has consistently been associated with higher achievement and lower rates of behavioral problems (Hallinger & Murphy, 1986; Purkey & Smith, 1983). Because school engagement is associated with decreased school failure and dropping out, addressing the academic, social, and cultural concerns may prevent or substantially diminish the likelihood of engaging the school-to-prison pipeline through the academic channel of Path 1 in Figure 12.1.

■ Restorative Justice: Interceding in the School-to-Prison Pipeline

Behavioral prevention and intervention strategies such as PBIS combined with intensive academic supports have the capacity to (a) reduce the frequency and severity of problem behaviors, (b) reduce the likelihood of being suspended, and (c) reduce the risk of disengaging from school. However, even the most culturally appropriate and well-implemented prevention and intervention programs represent only part of the comprehensive response to limiting or preventing a youth from becoming a statistic in the school-to-prison pipeline. Lasting change will require that schools, school districts, and states abandon punitive and ineffective disciplinary policies and adopt rehabilitative and proactive approaches to school misbehavior. While there are a number of alternatives to zero-tolerance practices, none may be as compelling as a restorative justice approach (Umbreit, Coates, & Kalanj, 1994).

Restorative justice is a criminological theoretical framework that requires an offender to take responsibility for his or her actions by engaging the victim to acknowledge and discuss the wrongful act, and by making amends and seeking ways to repair harm and seek constructive solutions. The principal concern of restorative justice practices is on restitution or reparations to the victim of a crime, rather than simply punishment of the accused offender (Wright, 1996; Zehr, 2002). The Center for Restorative Justice (2013) states:

> For communities, restorative justice reinvests citizens with the power to contribute meaningfully to the resolution of community problems; allows citizens to articulate and affirm the moral standards of the community; provides a forum for addressing the underlying conditions which generate harm; and contributes towards the building of safe, thriving and peaceful communities. (para. 8)

This community-based definition applies well to the school discipline model of restorative justice for school misbehavior. It requires schools to treat school misbehavior as a negative occurrence that can become a positive and transformational experience for both the offender and the victim. Contrary to the zero-tolerance approach to school misbehavior, characterized by reactive punitive measures, a restorative justice approach uses models that reduce the likelihood of recurrence of school offenses because they are based on theories of prosocial development and rehabilitation. In the school setting, a restorative justice approach to discipline aligns with the needs of schools to maintain order and safety while maintaining the fundamental purpose of teaching and learning. Zero-tolerance models assume that students who misbehave in school are bad children who need to be punished, while restorative justice models assume that child and adolescent inappropriate behaviors are opportunities for engagement and improvement. Fundamentally, current zero-tolerance policies succeed in pushing students out of schools and increasing the likelihood and intensity of school disengagement. In contrast, restorative justice models are predicated on the belief that children should be in schools, and that schools are environments that protect and teach... especially with respect to appropriate social behaviors.

Summary

The school-to-prison pipeline theory currently lacks the body of empirical research that would allow us to define its causal parameters. However, this chapter has shown that the school-to-prison pipeline is not a hypothetical, esoteric, or heuristic concept tossed about to describe a hypothesized link between the actions of schools and the subsequent involvement of youth in the juvenile or criminal justice systems. Rather, the term accurately reflects the logical effects of actions of school administrators and their school boards to detach bad actors and low performers from their schools. As we have shown, these actions have a disproportional impact on minority youth and students with disabling conditions. The first pathway we have described in this chapter—Path 1—is an indirect route that disconnects youth from school via suspension, expulsion, or educational inadequacies and makes youth vulnerable to delinquent behavior and involvement with the juvenile justice system. The second pathway involves a direct referral of students to law enforcement or the juvenile courts for behaviors that involve violations of the school disciplinary code but frequently do not rise to the level of criminal behavior (Teske, 2012). Schools have the responsibility to educate children and adolescents and prepare them for continuing education, employment, and the responsibilities of citizenship. When actions taken by schools and school systems sever youths' bonds to their schools and peers, they propel youth into the juvenile and criminal justice systems. These actions threaten the fabric of our communities and perpetuate high rates of incarceration and unemployment and the marginalization of a significant segment of our youth.

Note

1 Students eligible for special education and related services who struggle with social behavior are entitled to a functional behavioral assessment (FBA) and, if appropriate, a behavior intervention plan (BIP).

References

Advancement Project (2005). *Education on lockdown: The schoolhouse to jailhouse track.* Washington, DC: Author.

American Civil Liberties Union (2012). http://www.aclu.org/racial-justice/school-prison-pipeline

Amrein-Beardsley, A. (2009). The united, pernicious consequence of "staying the course" on the United States' No Child Left Behind Policy. *International Journal of Education Policy and Leadership, 4*(6), 1–13.

Anderson, C. (2004). Double jeopardy: The modern dilemma for juvenile justice. *University of Pennsylvania Law Review, 3,* 1181–1219.

Barrington, Byron L., & Hendricks, B. (1989) Differentiating characteristics of high school graduates, dropouts, and nongraduates. *Journal of Educational Research, (82)*6, 309–319.

Bowditch, C. (1993). Getting rid of troublemakers: High school disciplinary procedures and the production of dropouts. *Social Problems, 40,* 493–507.

Bradshaw, C. P., Reinke, W. M., Brown, L. D., Bevans, K. B., & Leaf, P. J. (2008). Implementation of school-wide positive behavior interventions and supports (PBIS) in elementary schools: Observations from randomized trials. *Education and Treatment of Children, 31*(1), 1–26.

Center for Restorative Justice (2013). *What is restorative justice?* http://www2.suffolk.edu/research/6953.html

Children's Defense Fund (2012). *Cradle to prison pipeline campaign.* http://www.childrensdefense.org/programs-campaigns/cradle-to-prison-pipeline/

Christle, C., Nelson, C. M., & Jolivette, K. (2004). School characteristics related to the use of suspension. *Education and Treatment of Children, 27*(4), 509–526.

Cooley, S. (1995). *Suspension/expulsion of regular and special education students in Kansas: A report to the Kansas State Board of Education.* Topeka, KS: Kansas State Board of Education.

Costenbader, V., & Markson, S. (1998). School suspension: A study with secondary school students. *Journal of School Psychology, 36,* 59–82.

Kupchik, A. (2010). *Homeroom security: School discipline in an age of fear.* New York: NYU Press.

Ensminger, M., & Slusarcick, A. (1992). Paths to high school graduation or dropout: A longitudinal study of a first grade cohort. *Sociology of Education, 65,* 95–113.

Fabello, T., Thompson, M., Plotkin, M., Carmichael, D., Marchbanks III, M., & Booth, E. (2011). *Breaking schools' rules: A statewide study of how school discipline relates to students' success and juvenile justice involvement.* Council of State Governments Justice Center. Retrieved December 15, 2012, from http://knowledgecenter.csg.org/drupal/system/files/Breaking_School_Rules.pdf

Flannery, D. J. (1997). *School violence: Risk, prevention, intervention, and policy.* (Report No. RR93002016) Retrieved September 27, 2002 from http://eric-web.tc.columbia.edu/monographs/uds109.

Fredricks, J. A., Blumenfeld, P. C., & Paris, A. H. (2004). School engagement: Potential of the concept, state of the evidence. *Review of Educational Research, 74,* 59–109.

Gaustad, J. (1992). *School discipline.* ERIC Digest, No. 78. ERIC Clearinghouse on Educational Management Eugene OR. ERIC Identifier: ED350727. http://www.ericdigests.org/1992-1/school.htm

Gregory, A., Skiba, R. J., & Noguera, P. A. (2010). The achievement gap and the discipline gap: Two sides of the same coin? *Educational Researcher, 39,* 59–68.

Gun-Free Schools Act, Public Law 103-382, 108 Statute 3907, Title 14 (1994).

Hallinger, P., & Murphy, J. F. (1986). The social context of effective schools. *American Journal of Education, 94*(3), 328–355.

Harvard Civil Rights Project and The Advancement Project (2000). *Opportunities suspended: The devastating consequences of zero-tolerance and school discipline policies.* Cambridge, MA: Author.

Hirschfield, P. J. (2008). Preparing for prison? The criminalization of school discipline in the USA. *Theoretical Criminology, 12*(1), 79–101.

Horn, C. (2003). High stakes testing and students: Stopping or perpetuating a cycle of failure? *Theory into Practice, 42*(1), 30–41.

Howard, T. C. (2003)." A tug of war for our minds:" African American high school students' perceptions of their academic identities and college aspirations. *High School Journal, 87*(1), 4–17.

Krezmien, M. P. (2007). *Understanding disproportionate suspensions of minority students and students with disabilities: A multilevel approach.* (Doctoral dissertation). Retrieved from the Digital Repository at the University of Maryland. http://hdl.handle.net/1903/6664

Krezmien, M. P., Leone, P. E., & Achilles, G. M. (2006). Suspension, race, and disability: Analysis of state-wide practices and reporting. *Journal of Emotional and Behavioral Disorders, 14,* 217–226.

Krezmien, M. P., Leone, P. E., Zablocki, M. S., & Wells, C. S. (2010). Juvenile court referrals and the public schools: Nature and extent of the practice in five states. *Journal of Contemporary Criminal Justice, 26,* 273–293.

Krezmien, M. P., Shanassa, E., Wilson, M. G., & McLaughlin, M. (under review). Examining the role of risk for ED in predicting adult educational outcomes. *Education and Treatment of Children.*

Kupchik, A. (2009). Things are tough all over: Race, ethnicity, class and school discipline. *Punishment and Society, 11,* 291–317.

Lassen, S. R., Steele, M. M., & Sailor, W. (2006). The relationship of school-wide positive behavior support to academic achievement in an urban middle school. *Psychology in the Schools, 43*(6), 701–712.

Leone, P. E., Christle, C. A., Nelson, C. M., Skiba, R., Frey, A., & Jolivette, K. (2003). *School failure, race and disability: Promoting positive outcomes, decreasing vulnerability for involvement with the juvenile delinquency system.* College Park, MD: The National Center on Education, Disability and Juvenile Justice.

Leone, P. E., Mayer, M. J., Malmgren, K., & Meisel, S. M. (2000). School violence and disruption: Rhetoric, reality, and reasonable balance. *Focus on Exceptional Children, 33*(1), 1–20.

Lochner, L., & Moretti, E. (2004). The effect of education on crime: Evidence from prison inmates, arrests, and self-reports. *American Economic Review, 94,* 155–189.

Losen, D. J., Simmons, A. B., Staudinger-Poloni, L., Rausch, M. K., & Skiba, R. (May 2003). *Exploring the link between low teacher quality and disciplinary exclusion.* Presented at the Conference on The School to Prison Pipeline sponsored by the Harvard University Civil Rights Project and Northeastern University Institute on Race and Justice. Boston, MA.

Losen, D. J., Martinez, T., & Gilespie, J. (2012). *Suspended in california.* Center for Civil Rights at UCLA, Civil Rights Project/Proyecto Derechos Civiles, Los Angeles. http://civilrightsproject.ucla.edu/resources/projects/center-for-civil-rights-remedies/school-to-prison-folder/summary-reports/suspended-education-in-california/SuspendedEd-final3.pdf

No Child Left Behind (NCLB) Act of 2001, Pub. L. No. 107-110, § 115, Stat. 1425 (2002).

NYCLU (2011). *Education interrupted: The growing use of suspensions in New York City's public schools.* [Available at http://www.nyclu.org/publications/report-education-interrupted-growing-use-of-suspensions-new-york-citys-public-schools

Parsons, E. C. (2005). From caring as a relation to culturally relevant caring: A White teacher's bridge to Black students. *Equity & Excellence in Education, 38*(1), 25–34.

Peters, S., & Oliver, L. A. (2009). Achieving quality and equity through inclusive education in an era of high stakes testing. *Prospects, 39,* 265–279.

Purkey, S. C., & Smith, M. S. (1983). Effective schools: A review. *Elementary School Journal,* 427–452.

Quinn, M. M., Rutherford, R. B., Leone, P. E., Osher, D. M., & Poirier, J. M. (2005). Youth with disabilities in juvenile corrections: A national survey. *Exceptional Children, 71,* 339–345.

Raffaele Mendez, L. M., Knoff, H. M, & Ferron, J. M. (2002). School demographic variables and out of-school suspension rates: A quantitative and qualitative analysis of a large, ethnically diverse school district. *Psychology in the Schools, 39,* 259–277.

Robers, S., Zhang, J., Truman, J., & Snyder, T. D. (2012). *Washington, DC: School crime and safety.* National Center for Education Statistics. [available at http://nces.ed.gov/pubs2012/2012002.pdf]

Rolon, C. A. (2002). Educating Latino students. *Educational Leadership, 60*(4), 40–43.

Rumberger, R. W., & Arellano, B. (2007). *Student and school predictors of high school graduation in California.* California Dropout Research Project at UC Santa Barbara, Policy Brief #5.

Skiba, R. J. (2002). Special education and school discipline: A precarious balance. *Behavior Disorders, 27*(2), 81–97.

Skiba, R. J., & Peterson, R. (2000). School discipline at a crossroads: From zero tolerance to early response. *Exceptional Children, 66*(3), 335–346.

Skiba, R. J., Peterson, R. L., & Williams, T. (1997). Office referrals and suspension: Disciplinary intervention in middle schools. *Education and Treatment of Children, 20,* 295–315.

Skiba, R. J., & Rausch, M. K. (2006). Zero tolerance, suspension, and expulsion: Questions of equity and effectiveness. In C. M. Evertson & C. S. Weinstein (Eds.), *Handbook for classroom management: Research, practice, and contemporary issues* (pp. 1063–1089). Mahwah, NJ: Lawrence Erlbaum Associates.

Snyder, H. N., & Sickmund, M. (2006). *Juvenile offenders and victims: 2006 national report.* Washington, DC: U.S. Department of Justice, Office of Justice Programs, Office of Juvenile Justice and Delinquency Prevention.

Stewart, E. B. (2007). Individual and school structural effects on African American high school students' academic achievement. *High School Journal, 91*(2), 16–34.

Sugai, G., Horner, R. H., Dunlap, G., Heineman, N., Lewis, T. J., Nelson, C. M., Scott, T., Liaupsin, C., Sailor, W., Turnbull, A. P., Turnbull, H. R., Wickham, D., Wilcox, B., & Ruef, M. (2000). *Applying positive behavior support and functional behavioral assessments in schools.* Washington, DC: OSEP Center on Positive Behavioral Interventions and Supports.

Teske, S. C. (2012) Testimony before the Senate Subcommittee on The Constitution, Civil Rights, and Human Rights Subcommittee Hearing on "Ending the School to Prison Pipeline." Available at http://www.judiciary.senate.gov/pdf/12–12-12TeskeTestimony.pdf

Tulman, J. B., & Weck, D. M. (2009/10). Shutting off the school-to-prison pipeline for status offenders with education-related disabilities, *New York Law School Law Review, 54,* 875–907.

Umbreit, M., Coates, R. B., & Kalanj, B. (1994). *Victim meets offender: The importance of restorative justice and mediation.* New York: Criminal Justice Press.

U.S. Department of Education (2011). *Youth indicators 2011, America's youth: Transition to adulthood.* Available at: http://nces.ed.gov/pubs2012/2012026/tables/table_14.asp

Wald, J., & Losen, D. J. (2003) Defining and redirecting a school-to-prison pipeline. *New Directions for Youth Development, 99,* 9–15.

Walmsley, R. (2011). *World prison population list* (9th ed.). University of Essex, UK: International Centre for Prison Studies. Available at: http://www.idcr.org.uk/wp-content/uploads/2010/09/WPPL-9-22.pdf

Wilson, M. G., & Krezmien, M. P. (2007). *School organization and the exclusionary experiences of youth in a state juvenile system: Uncovering juvenile justice feeder-schools?* Paper presented at the Robert B. Rutherford Memorial Teacher Educators of Children with Behavior Disorders Conference. Tempe, AZ.

Wright, M. (1996). *Justice for victims and offenders: A restorative response to crime* (2nd ed.). Winchester, UK: Waterside Press.

Zehr, H. (2002). *The little book of restorative justice.* Intercourse, PA: Good Books.

Zhang, D., Katsiyannis, A., & Herbst, M. (2004). Disciplinary exclusions in special education: A 4-year analysis. *Behavioral Disorders, 29*(4), 337–347.

13 School-Based Delinquency Prevention

Katherine L. Montgomery

■ Case Example

The following is an adapted excerpt from Professor David Dow's (2012) TED Talk presentation entitled *Lessons from Death Row Inmates*. Professor Dow received his masters and J.D. from Yale University, has represented over 100 inmates on death row, and is now a full professor at the University of Houston Law Center. This story is a case about a client with whom he worked for 12 years. (For the full TED Talk presentation, see http://www.ted.com/talks/david_r_dow_lessons_from_death_row_inmates.html.)

■ *My client was a guy named Will. He never knew his father very well, because his father left when his mother was pregnant with him. Will's mom had been diagnosed with paranoid schizophrenia. When Will was 5 years old, she tried to kill him with a butcher knife. She was taken away that evening by authorities and placed in a psychiatric hospital. So, for the next few years, Will lived with his older brother, until his brother committed suicide by shooting himself through the heart. After that, Will bounced around from one family member to another, until he was 9 years old. At the age of 9, he was essentially living on his own. Will eventually joined a gang and committed a number of very serious crimes, including, most seriously of all, a horrible, tragic murder. Will was ultimately executed as punishment for that crime.*

■ *My client, Will, and 80% of the people on death row, had five chapters of their lives that came before the chapter including the death penalty story: prenatal/infancy, early childhood, K–5th grade, 6th–12th grade, and the juvenile justice system. I think of these chapters as points of intervention, places when our society could have intervened in their lives. During these times we could have nudged them off of the path that ultimately led to a consequence that we all, death penalty opponents and death penalty supporters, would agree was a bad result. During each of those five chapters, there were a wide variety of things that society could have done. There were opportunities to intervene in each of these stages.*

■ *We already know that there are a wide variety of interventions that we could be using to prevent a consequence that we can agree is bad. More children will receive these modes of intervention when legislators, policymakers, taxpayers, and citizens agree that that's what we ought to be doing and that's how we should be spending our money. For every $15,000 we spend intervening in the lives of economically and otherwise disadvantaged kids during those earlier chapters, we save $80,000 dollars in crime-related costs down the road.*

■ *I want to tell you about the last conversation I had with Will. It was the day that he was going to be executed. And we were just talking. There was nothing left to do regarding his case, so we just talked about his life. We first talked about his dad, who he hardly knew, and who had died. Then we talked about his mom, who was still alive. And then I said to him, "I know the story. I've read the records. I know that she tried to kill you. But I've always wondered if you actually remembered that, because I don't remember anything from when I was 5 years old. Maybe you just remember somebody telling you?" He looked at me, leaned forward, and he said, "I don't mean any disrespect by this, but when your mama picks up a butcher knife that looks bigger than you are, and chases you through the house, screaming that she's going to kill you, and you have to lock yourself in the bathroom and lean against the door and holler for help until the police get there"—he paused and then said, "that's something you don't forget."*

■ *I hope there's one thing you all won't forget. In the next hour, an average of four homicides will have occurred in the United States. We are going to devote enormous social resources to punishing the people who commit those crimes (and I think that's appropriate because I believe we should punish people who do bad things). But three of those crimes are preventable. If we make the picture bigger, and devote our attention to the earlier chapters in the lives of our nation's youth, then we will never write the first paragraph of their death penalty story.*

■ Scope of the Problem

Unfortunately, Will's childhood is not unique. In fact, the majority of youth who end up in the juvenile justice system have experienced multiple difficulties associated with familial abuse, neglect (National Institute of Justice, 2001), mental health problems (Abrantes, Hoffman, & Anton, 2005), substance use (Tripodi & Springer, 2007), academic failure (Christle, Jolivette, & Nelson, 2005), high levels of victimization (Dembo, Schmeidler, & Childs, 2007), and gang involvement (Gatti, Tremblay, Vitaro, & McDuff, 2005), to name a few. Different from Will's story, the outcome of those who become involved with the juvenile justice system is not always the death penalty, as it is only a small percentage of youth who end up on death row. More common, however, are substantial consequences for both victims and offenders that alter the course of their life trajectory.

An estimated 2 million juveniles are arrested annually for delinquent acts in the United States (Puzzanchera, 2009). The profound impact of this statistic is highlighted when one considers the associated consequences. For example, it is estimated that one attempted robbery translates to $8,000 in estimated emotional damages sustained by the victim (Miller, Cohen, & Wiersema, 1996). The associated fiscal amount related to emotional and financial losses sustained by the victim increases with the severity of the offense: $18,000 for drunk driving, $87,000 for nonfatal sexual or physical assault, and $3 million for a fatal assault. Thus, the consequence of juvenile perpetration on others is great and necessitates prevention of delinquency.

There are also great consequences for the individuals who engage in a delinquent trajectory. Youth who become involved in the juvenile justice system are more likely to drop out of school, become alcohol and drug dependent, parent children at an early age, and become incarcerated as an adult (Greenwood, 2008). Often, these consequences have a cumulative "domino effect," not only in the life of the individual, but also on public health. As an example of one adverse outcome, approximately 7,000 students drop out of school each day in the United States (National Guard Youth Foundation, 2012). It is estimated that the current dropout rates will be responsible for a potential $3 trillion loss to the U.S. economy over the next decade (National Guard Youth Foundation, 2012). There are many factors, though, that are associated with the problem of juvenile delinquency (Hawkins, Catalano, & Miller, 1992). Through understanding the evidence base associated with these factors, school-based delinquency-prevention interventions have been identified.

This chapter will first describe a theoretical lens through which delinquency prevention is viewed. We will then explore research associated with delinquency risk and protective factors that contribute to or prevent the development of involvement with the juvenile justice system. Change in these factors has been found to reduce and prevent delinquency. The most robust literature in the prevention of delinquency is associated with school-based interventions that can change risk and protective factors (Greenwood, 2008). Therefore, this chapter will also offer descriptions of and resources for specific interventions that have been highlighted as evidence-based practices. Finally, this chapter will conclude with a brief section on the clinical issues associated with school-based delinquency prevention.

■ Literature Review

Evidence supporting the prevention of delinquency has grown substantially over the past two decades (Greenwood & Edwards, 2011). The field of juvenile justice has grown from utilizing ineffective and harmful treatments to now recognizing dozens of evidence-based interventions that prevent delinquency (Greenwood, 2008). Juvenile-delinquency prevention is largely informed by research on risk and protective factors (Hawkins, Catalano, & Miller, 1992), and most of the efficacious prevention interventions are delivered in the school setting (Greenwood, 2008). Effective school-based delinquency prevention is supported by a developmental theoretical context.

Theories of School-Based Delinquency Prevention

Researchers working in the area of delinquency prevention have primarily used developmental approaches to inform intervention (c.f., Catalano & Hawkins, 1996; Tremblay & Craig, 1995; Welsh & Farrington, 2009). Delinquency prevention through the lens of a developmental perspective highlights that the most influential periods during which intervention can have the greatest impact with an at-risk youth are childhood and early adolescence (Welsh & Farrington, 2009). Like Professor Dow asserted regarding Will's story, there were a number of opportunities or "chapters" during which Will's trajectory could have been altered. More specifically, Duncan and Magnuson (2004) explain that although change may be possible for some throughout the life course, life trajectories are most likely to be altered with early intervention. They further note:

> Early childhood may provide an unusual window of opportunity
> for interventions because young children are uniquely receptive to
> enriching and supportive environments. . . . As individuals age, they
> gain the independence and ability to shape their environments,
> rendering intervention efforts more complicated and costly.
> (pp. 102–103)

Grounded in a developmental perspective, Richard Hawkins and David Catalano (1996) offered a theoretical delinquency prevention approach known as the Social Development Model. The model incorporates social learning theory, social control theory, and differential association theory and coalesces around school-based developmental changes. They explain that educational transitions (e.g., preschool to elementary, elementary to middle school, and middle school to high school) during development affect behavior. For example, preschoolers may experience difficulty making the transition into the more structured elementary-school environment. Potential behavior problems associated with this transition are likely to be exacerbated by the presence of particular risk factors or by the absence of protective factors. One of the key assumptions of this model is that certain risk and protective factors are more amenable to change during particular developmental periods, and preventive interventions should be designed to intervene at the most appropriate time. This model also assumes that evidence-based practices should be identified and employed that target delinquency risk and protective factors (Hawkins & Catalano, 1996).

Risk and Protective Factors

Delinquency-prevention experts primarily draw from research on risk and protective factors to inform school-based prevention (Welsh & Farrington, 2010. Over the past two decades, researchers have begun to identify factors that either place a youth at risk of becoming delinquent (risk factors) or protect him or her against the risk of becoming involved with the juvenile justice system (protective factors; Hawkins, Catalano, & Miller, 1992). Table 13.1 offers risk and protective factors that have been identified for particular developmental periods. As is reflected in the table, less is known about protective factors, and the evidence on their ability to affect subsequent delinquency is mixed. In a 40-year longitudinal study, Farrington and colleagues (2006) found that

Table 13.1 **Delinquency Risk and Protective Factors**

Domain	Early-Onset Risk Factors	Late-Onset Risk Factors	Protective Factors
Individual	Substance use	Restlessness	Intolerant attitude toward
	Being male	Difficulty concentrating*	deviance
	Aggression*	Risk taking and impulsivity	High IQ
	Hyperactivity	Aggression*	Being female
	Problem (antisocial)	Being male	Positive social
	behavior	Physical violence	orientation
	Exposure to television	Antisocial attitudes, beliefs	Perceived sanctions for
	violence	Crimes against persons	transgressions
	Low IQ	Antisocial behavior	Religiosity
	Antisocial attitudes, beliefs	Low IQ	Resilient temperament
	Dishonesty*	Substance use	Sociability
	Poor cognitive	Low Empathy	
	development		
	Risk-taking behavior		
Family	Low family socioeconomic	Poor parent–child	Warm, supportive
	status/poverty	relationship	relationships with parents
	Antisocial parents	Harsh or lax discipline	or other adults
	Poor parent–child relationship	Poor monitoring,	Parents' positive
	Harsh, lax, or inconsistent	supervision	evaluation of peers
	discipline	Low parental involvement	Parental monitoring
	Divorce	Antisocial parents	
	Separation from parents	Broken home	
	Abusive parents	Low family socioeconomic	
	Neglect	status/poverty	
	Teenage parent	Abusive parents	
	Family criminality	Family conflict*	
	Large family size		
Peer	Weak social ties	Weak social ties	Friends who engage in
	Antisocial peers	Antisocial, delinquent peers	conventional behavior
	Peer rejection	Gang membership	
School	Failure to bond to school	Poor attitude towards school	Commitment to school
	Poor academic	Academic failure	Recognition for
	performance		involvement in
	Low academic aspirations		prosocial activities
Community	Access to weapons	Neighborhood crime, drugs	
	Neighborhood	Neighborhood	
	disadvantage	disorganization	
	Concentration of		
	delinquent groups		

Note: *True for males only.
Source: Adapted from Farrington et al., 2006; Shader, 2004; Wasserman et al., 2003; Office of the Surgeon General, 2001.

the most significant risk factors (present between the ages of 8 and 10) that predicted future delinquent and/or criminal behaviors were family criminality, daring or risk-taking behavior, low school attainment, poverty, and poor parenting. When comparing the primary differences between factors that were associated with participants who were never convicted with those who had a substantial criminal career, they found that the most significant childhood risk factors were having a convicted parent, risk-taking behavior, having a delinquent sibling, having a young mother, low popularity, disrupted family, and large family size (Farrington et al., 2006).

Researchers have also found that the type and the amount of risk factors are important. The results from longitudinal studies investigating antisocial behavior, delinquency, and crime have illustrated that chronic disruptive behavior at an early age is a particularly important risk factor to identify and treat. Not only has it been found to be strongly associated with subsequent delinquency and crime during early childhood, adolescence, and adulthood (Piquero, Farrington, & Blumstein, 2003), but *early chronic disruptive behavior* has also been found to influence other significant domains, such as education, employment, and the quality of relationships (which are also associated with risk factors of delinquency; Moffitt, 1993). Due to the significance of this risk factor, Farrington and Welsh (2007) have asserted that early interventions designed to reduce chronic disruptive behavior should become a policy prescription. The number of risk factors present is important as well. Although the presence of risk factors does not definitively result in a child's involvement with the juvenile justice system, researchers have found that the more risk factors that are present, the greater the likelihood a youth has of becoming delinquent. For example, Herrenkohl and colleagues (2000) found that a 10-year-old with six or more risk factors is 10 times more likely to become a juvenile delinquent than an 18-year-old presenting with one risk factor. Delinquency-prevention researchers have stated that school-based interventions designed to influence multiple risk and protective factors (rather than just one, such as an intervention that targets only substance use reduction outcomes) have a greater likelihood of preventing delinquency. Also, as is described in the following section, schools provide a unique setting in which larger numbers of at-risk youth may be influenced. Therefore, school-based interventions designed to affect multiple risk factors are more favorable options for preventing delinquency.

Evidence-Based Practice and School-Based Delinquency Prevention

As mentioned, some of the most comprehensive and effective interventions designed to prevent delinquency through reducing risk factors and increasing protective factors are school-based programs (Greenwood, 2008). For a long time, schools have been identified as the primary provider of interventions to children (Kratochwill & Shernoff, 2004). The school setting is ideal for delivering delinquency-prevention interventions for several reasons: schools offer the most regular access to delinquency-prone youth throughout important developmental years; they are usually staffed with professionals who desire to see youth succeed; and the community is generally more willing to accept the schools' efforts to socialize their children (Gottfredson, 2001). In addition, schools provide the best way for professionals delivering evidence-based practices to have access to a large number of students (Wilson & Lipsey, 2007).

Most of the evidence-based delinquency-prevention interventions delivered in schools were first developed by researchers outside of the juvenile justice field to address a variety of problematic behaviors such as substance use, academic failure, problematic school behavior, and child abuse (Greenwood, 2008). However, delinquency-prevention researchers drew attention to these programs for their ability to affect delinquency risk factors and thus delinquency prevention (Welsh & Farrington, 2007).

A number of systematic reviews and meta-analyses[1] have recently been published investigating the efficacy of school-based interventions on some factors that place a youth at risk of delinquency (e.g., Farrington & Ttofi, 2009; Foxcroft & Tsertsvadze, 2011; Hahn et al., 2007; Hopfer et al., 2010; Mytton, DiGuiseppi, Gough, Taylor, & Logan, 2006; Stoltz, van Londen, Dekovic, de Castro, & Prinzie, 2012; Wilson, Gottfredson, & Najaka, 2001; Wilson & Lipsey, 2007). Wilson, Gottfredson, and Najaka (2001) investigated the impact of school-based interventions on the prevention of crime, substance use, dropout, and other conduct problems. After reviewing the 165 studies that met their inclusion criteria, they found a number of programs that reduced alcohol and drug use, dropout and nonattendance, and other conduct problems. Specifically, they found that self-control or social competency interventions that used behavioral instructional methods or cognitive-behavioral therapeutic approaches produced primarily positive effects (Wilson, Gottfredson, & Najaka, 2001).

The majority of the other reviews reported on outcomes associated with either aggressive behavior or substance use. For example, Wilson and Lipsey (2007) conducted a meta-analysis on school-based interventions for aggressive and disruptive behavior. They reported on the results of 249 experimental or quasi-experimental design studies conducted around the world and found an overall statistically significant effect with aggressive and disruptive behavior. Additionally, they reported that the majority of school-based interventions were universal (meaning that they were delivered to the whole classroom), and concluded that school-based practitioners could choose from a variety of researcher-implemented interventions. Almost all of the recent reviews reported a positive and significant overall effect size; however, they did not typically report the effects of particular interventions. One of the exceptions to this was a review published by the Cochrane Collaboration (Foxcroft & Tsertsvadze, 2011). They conducted a review on the efficacy of school-based interventions that targeted alcohol misuse among students and reported that the LifeSkills Training program and the Good Behavior Game were considered to be the most effective interventions. These two evidence-based delinquency-prevention interventions, along with a few others, will be described in detail in the next section.

■ Description of Evidence-Based Interventions

The term "evidence-based practice" has become common in the fields of medicine, nursing, policy, psychology, social work, and, importantly, school-based intervention. Gambrill (2001) asserts that it is an approach to practice that offers the very best care available to clients. Through using this approach, benefits associated with cost effectiveness, time efficiency, and lasting positive outcomes are made possible. This approach is fairly new to the field of delinquency. In fact, crime rates soared in the early 1990s (Greenwood & Edwards, 2011), and the most prevalent practices at that time, such as Drug Abuse Resistance and Education (DARE), boot camps, "scared straight," and the "get tough on crime" political agendas, proved to be ineffective and, in some cases, actually increased delinquency (Sherman et al., 1997). Since that time, several practices have been identified as evidence-based practices for preventing delinquency (Farrington & Welsh, 2007; Greenwood, 2008). In addition, cost analyses have estimated that evidence-based practices designed to prevent delinquency can produce savings approximately five to 10 times their original costs (Greenwood & Edwards, 2011). Informed by cost/benefit analyses (e.g., Aos, Lieb, Mayfield, Miller, & Pennucci, 2004), public interest (Nagin, Piquero, Scott, & Steinberg, 2006), as well as other influences, policymakers have made delinquency prevention a priority. Specifically, U.S. scientific commissions on early childhood development and juvenile offending have called for action to make early prevention of juvenile delinquency a top priority (U.S. Department of Health and Human Services, 2001).

In response to the evidence-based practice movement, organizations have developed helpful online tools, reports, and databases for practitioners to identify practices that have been considered to be either promising or effective (Table 13.2). Practices identified on these databases often go through a rigorous review process. In addition, the databases often provide a user-friendly overview of the evidence for readers. For example, SAMHSA's National Registry of Evidence-Based Practices and Programs (NREPP) offers a brief description of the intervention, a review of the outcomes affected by the intervention, a thorough description of the populations who received the intervention, relevant citations of the studies that had been conducted, and a standardized score associated with the quality of the research. The NREPP database also provides a description of how ready the intervention is to be disseminated in real-world settings, costs associated with implementing the program, and contact information for the program developers (see

Table 13.2   **Resources to Identify Evidence-Based Interventions**

Organization	Website
Blueprints for Violence Prevention	http://www.colorado.edu/cspv/blueprints/
The Campbell Collaboration	http://www.campbellcollaboration.org/library.php
Child Trends/ LINKS	http://www.childtrends.org/
The Cochrane Collaboration	http://www.cochrane.org/
Institute of Educational Sciences What Works Clearinghouse	http://ies.ed.gov/ncee/wwc/
Office of Justice Programs	http://crimesolutions.gov/
OJJDP's Model Programs Guide	http://www.ojjdp.gov/mpg/
SAMHSA's National Registry of Evidence-based Practices and Programs	http://www.nrepp.samhsa.gov/

www.nrepp.samhsa.gov). In addition, the Blueprints for Violence Prevention website offers a great tool for readers who are trying to determine the most effective practices to use. The authors explain that just because one agency considers an intervention to be an evidence-based practice does not mean that it actually is. The authors encourage readers to look for interventions that have been identified by several agencies as effective and have achieved high ratings.

It is important to note that these databases are not void of limitations and must be considered through a critical lens (c.f., Montgomery, Kim, & Maynard, under review). For example, Project ALERT is a substance use prevention and intervention program that has been touted as an evidence-based practice. The NREPP database gives it the highest score in readiness for dissemination. However, this score is based on a review of the program that took place in 2006, and since that time, results of randomized control trials have been published that found the Project ALERT intervention either had no impact on student outcomes (Longshore et al., 2006, 2007; Pierre et al., 2005; Ringwalt et al., 2010) or produced negative treatment effects (meaning that students who received the intervention had significantly worse results because of receiving the intervention; Clark et al., 2010). Specifically, 1 year after receiving the intervention, students were more likely to have intentions to smoke cigarettes compared to the control group. Although NREPP still identifies Project ALERT as effective, other databases have made appropriate changes. The Colorado Blueprints for Violence Prevention website, for example, removed Project ALERT in 2009 in response to the new evidence. Because of examples like Project ALERT, practitioners, researchers, and policymakers should consider practices mentioned on these databases carefully. If a particular intervention seems to be an appropriate fit for a practitioner, school, or community, it is important to review the most up-to-date evidence prior to implementation.

Although not comprehensive, the following sections describe some school-based evidence-based programs that target delinquency risk and protective factors. These interventions have a strong research foundation and target multiple factors associated with delinquency. Interventions chosen for this chapter include the Coping Power Program, the Good Behavior Game, LifeSkills Training, Positive Action, Promoting Alternative Thinking Strategies, Safe Dates, and Second Step.

Coping Power Program

The Coping Power Program (Lochman et al., 2009) was designed to address aggression, violence, and delinquency among late-elementary and early-middle-school boys. The program is approximately 16 months in duration and has both child and parent intervention components. Thirty-three 40- to 60-minute group sessions addressing several sociocognitive components are delivered to the students by a school counselor, psychologist, or social worker. The parent component (16 group sessions) is delivered to groups of approximately four to six couples and addresses effective parenting training techniques with at-risk children. Over time, two randomized controlled trials have been conducted on the Coping Power Program and have revealed significantly fewer school problem behaviors, delinquent acts (Lochman & Wells, 2002; Peterson, Hamilton, & Russell, 2009), and learning problems and improved social and adaptive skills (Peterson et al., 2009). Although originally designed for intervention with boys, the Peterson study included girls, suggesting this program is effective for both boys and girls at risk of conduct disorder.

The Good Behavior Game

Developed in the late 1960s, the Good Behavior Game is unique in its simplistic implementation and flexible application. It is one of the oldest school-based prevention intervention programs, with a long history of scientific support. It was first developed to address disruptive classroom behavior in elementary-age students (Barrish, Saunders, & Wolf, 1969). Specifically, it is a classroom-based group contingency behavioral management intervention implemented by elementary school teachers. In the beginning, it is played for short periods of time on select days, but over the course of the year, the teachers increase the length and the frequency of the game. Most students exposed to the Game receive the intervention for one or two academic years in the classroom. Recently, it has been renamed the "PAX Game" due to the negative associations with "good" and "bad" labels that students often internalize. The name "PAX" came from PAXIS Institute, an organization dedicated to the implementation and dissemination of effective programs.

Numerous studies have reported on the effectiveness of the Game with students ranging from first to ninth grades with the intent of altering a number of behaviors: talking out and getting up from their seat (e.g., Barrish, Saunders, & Wolf, 1969; Huber, 1979), disruptive or inappropriate behavior (e.g., Johnson, Turner, & Konarski, 1978; Kellam & Anthony, 1998), inattention (e.g., Phillips & Christie, 1986), aggressive behavior (Huber, 1979), and inappropriate verbalizations, negative comments, and cursing (Salend, Reynolds, & Coyle, 1989). In addition to change in these behaviors at the completion of the intervention, several longitudinal studies have revealed the impact of the Game on a variety of variables over time. For example, Bradshaw and colleagues (2009) followed a cohort of students until age 19 and found higher levels in reading performance, math performance, high-school graduation rates, and rates of college attendance; they were 50% less likely to use special education services. Additional randomized controlled trial longitudinal reports indicated that participants displayed fewer externalizing behavior problems, improvements in positive peer relationships (Witvliet, van Lier, Cuijpers, & Koot, 2009), reduced drug and alcohol dependence disorders, were less likely to smoke and less likely to have antisocial personality disorder (Kellam et al., 2008), and displayed fewer incidents of violent and criminal behavior (Petras et al., 2008), suicidal ideation and suicidal attempts (Wilcox et al., 2008), and aggressive behavior (Kellam et al., 1999) compared to control groups. This fairly inexpensive elementary-age intervention has had a powerful impact on subsequent adolescent behaviors that place them at risk of becoming delinquent.

LifeSkills Training

The LifeSkills Training program is designed to prevent substance use, delinquency, and violence by targeting change in social and psychological risk and protective factors (Botvin, Griffin, & Nichols, 2006). Implemented by teachers in a classroom setting, it has been manualized with age-appropriate material designed for students in elementary, middle, and high schools. Teachers have the option of delivering the one-hour sessions either daily or weekly until the age-appropriate manual is completed.

Multiple randomized controlled trials have been conducted on its effectiveness on a variety of outcome variables. The majority of these studies have been conducted with middle-school students, and researchers found that when receiving this intervention, middle-school students were less likely to begin smoking (e.g., Botvin et al., 1992; Griffin, Botvin, Nichols, & Doyle, 2003), use alcohol (e.g., Griffin et al., 2003; Spoth, Redmond, Trudeau, & Shin, 2002), smoke marijuana (e.g., Spoth et al., 2002), binge drink (e.g., Botvin, Griffin, Diaz, & Ifill-Williams, 2001), use inhalants, engage in polysubstance use (Griffin et al., 2003), engage in verbal or physical violence or delinquency (Botvin, Grffin, & Nichols, 2006), and initiate substance use and were more likely to have refusal intentions (Truedeau, Spoth, Lillehog, Redmond, & Wickrama, 2003). Additionally, for students who received this intervention in middle school, follow-up studies revealed that compared to the control groups, 12th-grade students in the experimental group were less likely to engage in drug or polysubstance use (Botvin, Baker, Dusenbury, Botvin, & Diaz, 1995), use illegal substances (Botvin et al., 2001), and use methamphetamines (Spoth, Clair, Shin, & Redmond, 2006).

Few studies have been conducted investigating the effectiveness of this intervention with elementary-age students. Botvin and colleagues found that among third through sixth graders, the participants were less likely to try smoking, had greater levels of anti-drug attitudes and substance use knowledge, and had higher levels of self-esteem than the control group (Botvin, Griffin, Paul, & Macaulay, 2003). LifeSkills Training has also been credited as being efficacious with minority youth (e.g., Botvin et al., 1992), students with lower socioeconomic status, and youth identified as "high risk" (Griffin et al., 2006).

Positive Action

Positive Action is a school-based prevention program with grade-specific intervention manuals available for kindergarten through 12th grade. Classroom teachers deliver the main intervention component, which targets improving school achievement and attendance, as well as addressing problem behaviors such as substance use, poor classroom behavior, and sexually risky behavior. Positive Action is also designed to improve relationships between the parent(s) and student, family conflict, and family cohesion. Positive Action is a multiyear program, with approximately 140 lessons delivered over the course of one academic year.

Recent research as shown that elementary students who received the intervention were less likely to engage in substance use, violent behavior (Beets et al., 2009; Li et al., 2011), sexually risky activity (Beets et al., 2009), or bullying behavior (Li et al., 2011); were less likely to be suspended; and had significantly higher school attendance and reading and math scores (Snyder, 2010). In addition, the long-term effects of students who participated in this program in elementary school have been reported for both middle- and high-school students (c.f., Flay & Allred, 2003). Middle-school students had higher academic achievement scores, reduced truancy, and reduced disciplinary referrals associated with substance use, violence-related incidents, property crime, and disrespectful and disruptive behaviors. High-school students had higher levels of academic achievement, were more likely to participate in higher education, and were more likely to become employed. Additionally, high-school students had lower dropout rates, fewer in-school suspensions and out-of-school suspensions, less truancy, and fewer disciplinary referrals for substance use, sex-related incidents, falsifying information, and disrespectful and disruptive behaviors (Flay & Allred, 2003). Finally, Lewis and colleagues (in press) most recently reported the results of a randomized control trial of the Positive Action program on the problem behaviors of primarily low-income, minority youth in Chicago. They found that participants were less likely to engage in bullying behaviors or disruptive and violence-related behaviors and had fewer disciplinary referrals and suspensions than those in the control group.

Promoting Alternative Thinking Strategies

Promoting Alternative Thinking Strategies is a school-based prevention program designed for elementary and preschool youth. The elementary intervention is delivered over the course of one academic school year and totals approximately 121 20-minute sessions. this program is delivered three times a week by the teacher in a classroom setting with lessons that include a combination of instruction, modeling, storytelling, role play, discussion, and videos. Recent randomized controlled trials have revealed that participants have significantly reduced levels of aggression (Bierman et al., 2010) and internalizing and externalizing behaviors (Riggs, Greenberg, Kusché, & Pentz, 2006). Studies have also found a significant level of improvement in prosocial behavior, academic engagement (Bierman et al., 2010), emotional knowledge, self-regulation, social interaction, and social skills (Domitrovich, Cortes, & Greenberg, 2007).

Safe Dates

Safe Dates is a school-based program for eighth and ninth graders to prevent partner violence that incorporates both school and community-level activities in intervention (Foshee et al., 1996). School activities encompass the primary prevention components: (1) a peer-performed theater production, (2) a 10-lesson curriculum delivered in the classroom by physical and health education teachers, and (3) a poster contest (Foshee et al., 1998). Community activities (such as a crisis hotline, support group, materials for parents) are offered specifically for adolescents who have been in abusive relationships. Goals in the program, designed for both males and females, include (1) changing adolescent dating violence gender roles and norms, (2) improving peer support and dating conflict skills, (3) increasing help-seeking abilities through community resources, and (4) decreasing both dating abuse and victimization.

The most recent randomized controlled trial offers promising results for dating violence prevention and intervention among adolescents. Foshee and colleagues (2005) conducted a randomized controlled trial with 1,566 primarily White eighth- and ninth-grade students in rural North Carolina schools.

Follow-up data were collected every year for 4 years after the intervention. At each of the follow-up time points, those in the intervention group displayed significantly lower levels of psychological abuse perpetration, physical violence perpetration, and sexual violence perpetration (Foshee et al., 2005).

Second Step

Second Step is a school-based violence-prevention and social skills program. Although this program is newer and has a smaller body of empirical support (Alvarez & Anderson-Ketchmark, 2009), both OJJDP and SAMHSA have highlighted Second Step as efficacious with at-risk youth. Similar to previously described programs, Second Step is delivered by teachers in the classroom. This intervention has been manualized to intervene with students 4 to 14 years of age, and two age-specific curriculums have been developed (preschool through fifth grade and sixth through ninth grade). This 2-year program targets change by teaching socioemotional skills aimed at increasing social competence and reducing impulsive and aggressive behavior through eight to 25 lessons (depending on the grade and year in the program) offered in an academic school year. Specific lessons include developmentally appropriate topics such as anger management, empathy training, and impulse control.

The most recent randomized controlled trial was conducted in the United States and implemented Second Step with at-risk students (Frey, Nolan, Edstrom, & Hirschstein, 2005). This study included 1,253 primarily White second-grade students who remained in the study for approximately 2 years. Moderate levels of attrition and no follow-up data warrant cautious interpretation of the results. That noted, participants displayed significantly lower levels of aggression and less need for adult conflict intervention, and they were more likely to choose positive social goals than those in the control group (Frey et al., 2005). Additional studies have found that participants showed improvement in empathy knowledge, anger management, impulse control (Edwards, Hunt, Meyers, Grogg, & Jarrett, 2005), anxiety symptoms, depressive symptoms (Schick & Cierpka, 2005), social competence, and antisocial behavior (Taub, 2002).

As mentioned, the above list is not comprehensive, and there are over 450 programs that have been identified by at least one organization as potentially evidence-based practices for youth. This list, however, offers examples of programs that have some of the strongest research foundations and address more than one risk and protective factor associated with delinquency prevention in the school setting. Readers are encouraged to use the resources provided in this chapter to identify school-based programs that have a strong foundation in research associated with delinquency-prevention outcomes as well as meet the clinically relevant needs associated with their particular school, region, or state.

■ Clinical Issues

The evidence-based practice movement has had a substantial impact on school-based professionals, and although many positive changes have emerged as a result, clinical issues exist. Of importance are issues associated with implementation (c.f., Aarons, Hurlburt, & Horwitz, 2011). Although studies have shown that particular interventions are effective under the umbrella of well-designed research studies, the same interventions have not always translated as effectively into "real-world" practice settings. Issues associated with necessary training and support, treatment fidelity, access to resources, and sustainability have inhibited the successful translation of these programs into "real-world" practice.

Another issue is associated with teacher delivery. Researchers have begun to highlight that teachers are heavily involved in the delivery of evidence-based programs in the school setting (Franklin, Ryan, Kim, Kelly, & Montgomery, 2012). As seen in the examples above, teachers delivered the majority of the interventions described. However, other macro initiatives have made this difficult. Operating in tandem with the evidence-based practices movement have also been policies associated with the No Child Left Behind Act (NCLB; 2001). A consequence of NCLB for teachers has been the requirement of students achieving particular scores on standardized tests. In some states, teachers have lost their jobs if their students underperformed. Therefore, teachers have had to devote great energy to ensure that their student perform well on the standardized tests, and asking them to use class time to deliver interventions can be a conflicting task. Practitioners looking to implement school-based delinquency-prevention interventions should be aware of the competing macro-level agendas that affect the delivery of effective services.

Adding further evidence that teachers are being encouraged to deliver evidence-based programs in the classroom setting is a three-tier approach to school-based intervention that has gained substantial attention and popularity over the past decade. There are two bodies of literature that incorporate the three-tier approach to intervention: response to intervention and positive behavioral interventions and support. This approach asserts that all students should receive evidence-based tier 1 interventions; students who are still struggling should receive more intensive evidence-based interventions. Tier 1 interventions have been said to meet approximately 85% of student needs, and additional intervention is not needed. This level of intervention is also called universal intervention, which is delivered to all students in a school and classroom setting. Teachers are typically the primary provider of universal, tier 1 services. Approximately 10% to 15% of students are estimated to need tier 2 interventions, where services are delivered in a small group setting. Lastly, tier 3 interventions are considered to be the most intensive, and approximately 1% to 5% of students need this type of intervention. Tier 3 interventions involve services provided to the individual and often involve multimodal intervention (e.g., individual, peer, family, school intervention; National Association of State Directors of Special Education, 2006). Because many states are creating policies associated with the three-tier approach in the school setting (e.g., Institute of Educational Sciences [IES], 2011), and in some cases mandating the use of this approach (e.g., Illinois; IES, 2011), practitioners interested in school-based delinquency prevention may have opportunities to play an important role. As teachers continue to work with limited resources and compromised budgets and salaries, and feel the pressure of competing macro-level agendas to deliver both instructional education and intervention to their students, school-based practitioners may need to offer assistance. For example, they can provide teacher support, training, and resources. In addition, it has been found that principal, staff, and teacher buy-in can be critical in the effective delivery of school-based interventions (McDougal, Graney, Wright, & Ardoin, 2010). So, although schools may have a mandate to use the three-tier approach, its efficacy may be compromised. Practitioners can also play a key role in informing principals and administrators on evidence-based programs designed to meet the needs of their students. The demands placed on schools are arguably greater now than they have ever been before. Practitioners, policymakers, and researchers seeking to prevent delinquency through school-based intervention need to be educated and understand the contexts of these conflicting demands to ensure appropriate delivery of effective services.

Summary and Conclusion

The purpose of this chapter was to describe the evidence associated with school-based delinquency prevention, to describe evidence-based programs that address delinquency risk and protective factors in a school setting, and to highlight the associated clinical issues. Through Will's tragic story and research on youth who become involved in the juvenile justice system, we learned there are a number of problems frequently experienced by delinquent youth. These include, but are not limited to, severe familial neglect and abuse, violence, mental illness, substance use, academic difficulties, and gang activity. Similar to research on the epidemiology of juvenile delinquency, there is a substantial body of overlapping research that highlights the factors that place a child at greater risk of or protect against subsequent delinquency. We also learned that interventions (particularly those that are delivered earlier, in a school setting, and are designed to affect multiple factors) that target change in delinquency risk and protective factors are the most effective at interrupting the delinquent and criminal trajectory. Specifically, several interventions exist that have a strong evidence base and have been shown to affect several identified risk and protective factors: Coping Power Program, the Good Behavior Game, LifeSkills Training, Positive Action, Promoting Alternative Thinking Strategies, Safe Dates, and Second Step. These interventions are described in detail by various federal and private agency websites and databases found in Table 13.2. As urged by using the example of Project ALERT, however, if a particular intervention seems to be an appropriate fit for a practitioner, school, or community, it is important that the most up-to-date evidence is reviewed prior to implementation. Finally, this chapter highlighted that although great strides have been made regarding the use of evidence-based programs in the school setting to reduce juvenile delinquency, many clinical issues associated with implementation and dissemination, teacher support, and conflicting agendas inhibit the successful translation of these programs into "real-world" practice settings.

Delinquency rates have steadily declined over the past two decades (Welsh & Farrington, 2007). These rates are a sharp contrast to the increase in attention to and dissemination of evidence-based programs to prevent delinquency over the same period. This evidence may provide practitioners, policymakers, and researchers hope that effective intervention is occurring in the early "chapters" of children's lives, and fewer "chapters" that involve the juvenile justice system are being written. Although great advancements have been made in the field of school-based delinquency prevention, there is still much more work to be done. It seems appropriate to conclude this chapter with the following quote relevant to delinquency prevention. Brandon Welsh and David Farrington (2007) poignantly concluded an article entitled *Save the Children from a Life of Crime* with the following excerpt:

> The stakes are high. In the United States, crime rates are lower than they have been in more than a generation. An opportunity exists to keep crime rates in check or perhaps to lower them even more. Early prevention is by no means a panacea. But it does represent an integral part of any plan to reduce the nation's crime rate. We believe that the time is right to move beyond rhetoric and to implement a risk-focused, evidence-based national strategy for early prevention. (p. 876)

Note

1 Systematic reviews and meta-analyses have become the gold standard for offering researchers and practitioners an appraisal of the effectiveness of a particular intervention (or group of interventions) with an identified outcome (or group of outcomes). Specifically, the authors use a systematic approach to collect studies that address a particular topic. The final manuscript will offer a detailed description of how effective intervention(s) are with particular outcome(s).

References

Aarons, G. A., Hurlburt, M., Horwitz, S. M. (2011). Advancing a conceptual model of evidence-based practice implementation in public service sectors. *Administrative Policy and Public Health, 38*, 4–23.

Abrantes, A. M., Hoffman, N. G., & Anton, R. (2005). Prevalence of co-occurring disorders among juveniles committed to detention centers. *International Journal of Offender Therapy and Comparative Criminology, 49,* 179–193.

Alvarez, M., & Anderson-Ketchmark, C. (2009). Review of an evidence-based school social work intervention: Second Step. *Children & Schools, 31,* 247–250.

Aos, S., Lieb, R., Mayfield, J., Miller, M., & Pennucci, A. (2004). *Benefits and costs of prevention and early intervention programs for youth.* Olympia, WA: Washington State Institute for Public Policy.

Aos, S., Miller, M., & Drake, E. (2006). *Evidence-based public policy options to reduce future prison construction, criminal justice costs, and crime rates.* Olympia, WA: Washington State Institute for Public Policy.

Barrish, H. H., Saunders, M., & Wolf, M.W. (1969). Good Behavior Game: Effects of individual contingencies for group consequences on disruptive behavior in a classroom. *Journal of Applied Behavior Analysis, 2,* 119–124.

Beets, M. W., Flay, B. R., Vuchinich, S., Snyder, F. J., Acock, A.,...& Durlak, J. A. (2009). Use of a social and character development program to prevent substance use, violent behaviors, and sexual activity among elementary students in Hawai'i. *American Journal of Public Health, 99,* 1438–1445.

Bierman, K. L., Coie, J. D., Dodge, K. A., Greenberg, M. T., Lochman, J. E., McMahon, R. J., & Pinderhughes, E. (2010). The effects of a multiyear universal social–emotional learning program: The role of student and school characteristics. *Journal of Consulting and Clinical Psychology, 78,* 156–168.

Botvin, G. J., Baker, E., Dusenbury, L., Botvin, E. M. & Diaz, T. (1995). Long-term follow-up results of a randomized drug abuse prevention trial in a White middle-class population. *Journal of the American Medical Association, 273,* 1106–1112.

Botvin, G. J., Dusenbury, L., Baker, E., James-Ortiz, S., Botvin, E. M., & Kerner, J. (1992). Smoking prevention among urban minority youth: Assessing effects on outcome and mediating variables. *Health Psychology, 11,* 290–299.

Botvin, G. J., Griffin, K. W., & Nichols, T. R. (2006). Preventing youth violence and delinquency through a universal school-based prevention approach. *Prevention Science, 7,* 403–408.

Botvin, G. J., Griffin, K. W., Paul, E., & Macaulay, A. P. (2003). Preventing tobacco and alcohol use among elementary school students through Life Skills Training. *Journal of Child & Adolescent Substance Abuse, 12,* 1–18.

Bradshaw, C., Zmuda, J., Kellam, S., & Ialongo, N. (2009). Longitudinal impact of two universal preventive interventions in first grade on educational outcomes in high school. *Journal of Educational Psychology, 101*(4), 926–937.

Catalano, R. F. & Hawkins, J. D. (1996). The social development model: A theory of antisocial behavior. In J. D. Hawkins (Ed.), *Delinquency and crime: Current theories* (pp. 149–197). New York: Cambridge University Press.

Christle, C., Jolivette, K., & Nelson, C. (2005). Breaking the school to prison pipeline: Identifying school risk and protective factors for youth delinquency. *Exceptionality, 13,* 69–88.

Clark, H., Ringwalt, C. L., Hanley, S., & Shamblen, S. R. (2010). Project ALERT's effects on adolescents' prodrug beliefs: A replication and extension study. *Health Education & Behavior, 37,* 357–376.

Dembo, R., Schmeidler, J., & Childs, K. (2007). Correlates of male and female juvenile offender abuse experiences. *Journal of Child Sexual Abuse, 16,* 75–94.

Domitrovich, C. E., Cortes, R. C., & Greenberg, M. T. (2007). Improving young children's social and emotional competence: A randomized trial of the preschool 'PATHS' curriculum. *Journal of Primary Prevention, 28*(2), 67–91.

Dow, D. (2012, June). *Lessons from death row inmates.* [Video file]. Retrieved from http://www.ted.com/talks/david_r_dow_lessons_from_death_row_inmates.html

Duncan, G. J., & Magnuson, K. (2004). Individual and parent-based intervention strategies for promoting human capital and positive behavior. In P. L. Chase-Lansdale, K. Kiernan, & R. J. Friedman (Eds.), *Human development across lives and generations: The potential for change* (pp. 93–135). New York: Cambridge University Press.

Edwards, D., Hunt, M. H., Meyers, J., Grogg, K. R., & Jarrett, O. (2005). Acceptability and student outcomes of a violence prevention curriculum. *Journal of Primary Prevention, 26*, 401–418.

Farrington, D. P., Cold, J. W., Harnett, L., Jolliffe, D., Soteriou, N., Turner, R., & West, D. J. (2006). *Criminal careers and life success: New findings from the Cambridge study in delinquent development.* London: Home Office (Research Findings No. 281).

Flay, B. R., & Allred, C. G., (2003). Long-term effects of the Positive Action program. *American Journal of Health Behavior, S1*, S6–S21.

Foshee, V. A., Bauman, K. E., Arriaga, X. B., Helms, R. W., Koch, G. G., & Linder, G. (1998). An evaluation of Safe Dates, an adolescent dating violence prevention program. *American Journal of Public Health, 88*, 45–50.

Foshee, V., Bauman, K., Ennett, S., Suchindran, C., Benefield, T., & Linder, G. (2005). Assessing the effects of the dating violence prevention program "Safe Dates" using random coefficient regression modeling. *Prevention Science: The Official Journal of the Society for Prevention Research, 6*, 245–258.

Foshee, V. A., Linder, G., Bauman, K. E., Langwick, S. A., Arriaga, X. B., Heath, J. L.,...Bangdiwala, S. (1996). The Safe Dates project: Theoretical basis, evaluation design, and selected baseline findings. *American Journal of Preventive Medicine, 12*, 39–47.

Frey, K. S., Nolen, S. B., Edstrom, L. V., & Hirschstein, M. K. (2005). Effects of a school-based social-emotional competence program: Linking children's goals, attributions, and behavior. *Journal of Applied Developmental Psychology, 26*, 171–200.

Franklin, C., Kim, J., Ryan, T. N., Kelly, M., & Montgomery, K.L. (2012). Teacher involvement in school mental health interventions: A systematic review. *Children and Youth Services Review, 34*, 973–982.

Frey, K. S., Nolen, S. B., Van Schoiack Edstrom, L. L., & Hirschstein, M. K. (2005). Effects of a school-based social-emotional competence program: Linking children's goals, attributions, and behavior. *Journal of Applied Developmental Psychology: An International Lifespan Journal, 26*, 171–200.

Farrington, D. P., & Ttofi, M. M. (2009). School-based programs to reduce bulling and victimization. *The Campbell Collaboration, 6*, 1–149.

Foxcroft, D. R., & Tsertsvadze, A. (2011). Universal school-based prevention programs for alcohol misuse in youth people. *The Cochrane Collaboration, 5*, 1–126.

Gatti, U., Tremblay, R., Vitaro, F., & McDuff, P. (2005). Youth gangs, delinquency and drug use: A test of the selection, facilitation, and enhancement hypotheses. *Journal of Child Psychology and Psychiatry, 46*, 1178–1190.

Gottfredson, D. C. (2001). *Schools and delinquency.* New York: Cambridge University Press.

Greenwood, P. W. (2008). Prevention and intervention programs for juvenile offenders. *The Future of Children, 18*, 185–210.

Greenwood, P. W., & Edwards, D. L. (2011). Evidence-based programs for at-risk youth and juvenile offenders: A review of proven prevention and intervention models. In D. W. Springer & A. R. Roberts (Eds.), *Juvenile justice and delinquency* (pp. 369–390). Sudbury, MA: Jones and Bartlett.

Griffin, K. W., Botvin, G. J., & Nichols, T. R. (2006). Effects of a school-based drug abuse prevention program for adolescents on HIV risk behaviors in young adulthood. *Prevention Science, 7*, 103–112.

Griffin, K. W., Botvin, G. J., Nichols, T. R., & Doyle, M. M. (2003). Effectiveness of a universal drug abuse prevention approach for youth at high risk for substance use initiation. *Preventive Medicine, 36*, 1–7.

Hahn, R., Fuqua-Whitley, D., Wethington, H., Lowy, J., Crosby, A., Fullilove, M.,...Dahlberg, L. (2007). Effectiveness of universal school-based programs to prevent violent and aggressive behavior: A systematic review. *American Journal of Preventive Medicine, 33,* 114–129.

Hawkins, J. D., Catalano, R. F., & Miller, J. Y. (1992). Risk and protective factors for alcohol and other drug problems in adolescence and early adulthood: Implications for substance abuse prevention. *Psychological Bulletin, 112,* 64–105.

Herrenkohl, T. I., Maguin, E., Hill, K. G., Hawkins, D. J., Abbott, R. D., & Catalano, R. F. (2000). Developmental risk factors for youth violence. *Journal of Adolescent Health, 26,* 176–186.

Hopfer, D., Shin, Y., Davis, D., Elek, E., Kam, J. A., & Hecht, M. L. (2010). A review of elementary school-based substance use prevention programs: Identifying program attributes. *Journal of Drug Education, 40*(1), 11–36.

Huber, H. (1979). The value of a behavior modification programme, administered in a fourth grade class of a remedial school. *Praxis der Kinderpsychologie und Kinderpsychiatrie, 28,* 73–79.

Institute of Educational Sciences (2011). *State policies and procedures on response to intervention in the Midwest region.* Retrieved from http://ies.ed.gov/ncee/edlabs/regions/midwest/pdf/REL_2011116.pdf.

Johnson, M. R., Turner, P. F., & Konarski, E. A. (1978). The "Good Behavior Game": A systematic replication in two unruly transitional classrooms. *Education and Treatment of Children, 1,* 25–33.

Kellam, S., Brown, C., Poduska, J., Ialongo, N., Wang, W., Toyinbo, P., et al. (2008). Effects of a universal classroom behavior management program in first and second grades on young adult behavioral, psychiatric, and social outcomes. *Drug & Alcohol Dependence, 95,* S5–28.

Kellam, S., Ling, X., Merisca, R., Brown, C., & Ialongo, N. (1999). The effect of the level of aggression in the first grade classroom on the course and malleability of aggressive behavior into middle school: Erratum. *Development and Psychopathology, 11,* 165–185.

Kratochwill, T. R., & Shernoff, E. S. (2004). Evidence-based practice: Promoting evidence-based interventions in school psychology. *School Psychology Review, 33,* 34–48.

Li, K. K., Washburn, I., DuBois, D. L., Vuchinich, S., Ji, P., Brechling, V., Day, J.,...Flay, B.R. (2011). Effects of the *Positive Action* programme on problem behaviors in elementary school students: A matched-pair, randomized control trial in Chicago. *Psychology & Health, 26,* 187–204.

Lochman, J., Boxmeyer, C., Powell, N., Qu, L., Wells, K., & Windle, M. (2009). Dissemination of the Coping Power program: Importance of intensity of counselor training. *Journal of Consulting and Clinical Psychology, 77,* 397–409.

Lochman, J., & Wells, K. (2002). The Coping Power program at the middle-school transition: Universal and indicated prevention effects. *Psychology of Addictive Behaviors, 16,* S40–S54.

Longshore, D., Ellickson, P. L., McCaffrey, D. F., & St. Clair, P. A. (2007). School-based drug prevention among at-risk adolescents: Effects of ALERT Plus. *Health Education & Behavior, 34,* 651–668.

Longshore, D., Ghosh-Dastidar, B., & Ellickson, P. L. (2006). National Youth Anti-Drug Media Campaign and school-based drug prevention: Evidence for a synergistic effect in ALERT Plus. *Addictive Behaviors, 31,* 496–508.

McDougal, J. L., Graney, S. B., Wright, J. A., & Ardoin, S. P. (2010). *A practical guide to implementing effective evidence-based interventions in your school.* Hoboken, New Jersey: Wiley & Sons.

Miller, T., Cohen, M., & Wiersema, B. (1996). *Victims, costs, and consequences: A new look.* Nation Institute of Justice report (njc-155282). Washington, DC: Department of Justice.

Moffitt, T. E. (1993). "Life-course-persistent" and "adolescence-limited" antisocial behavior: A developmental taxonomy. *Psychological Review, 100,* 674–701.

Montgomery, K. L., Kim, J. S., & Maynard, B. (under review). School-based delinquency prevention: A critical review of "evidence-based practices." *Children and Youth Services Review.*

Mytton, J. A., DiGuiseppi, C., Gough, D., Taylor, R. S., & Logan, S. (2006). School-based secondary prevention programs for preventing violence. *The Cochrane Collaboration, 3,* 1–96.

NASDSE (2006). *Response to intervention.* A joint paper by the National Association of state Directors of Special Education and the Council of Administrators of Special Education. Available at: www.nasdse.org/projects.cfm?pageprojectid=23

Nagin, D. S., Piquero, A. R., Scott, E. S., & Steinberg, L. (2006). Public preferences for rehabilitation versus incarceration of juvenile offenders: Evidence from a contingent valuation survey. *Criminology & Public Policy, 5,* 627–652.

National Institute of Justice (2001). *An update on the "cycle of violence."* Retrieved from http://www.nij.gov/pubs-sum/184894.htm.

National Guard Youth Foundation (2012). *Panel discussion on crisis of high school dropouts and cost to our economy—An estimated $3 trillion over the next decade.* Retrieved from http://www.blackradionetwork.com/high_school_dropouts_will_cost_an_estimated_$3_trillion_over_next_decade.

No Child Left Behind Act of 2001, PL. 107-110, 115 Stat. 1425. Jan. 8. 2002.

Peterson, M., Hamilton, E., & Russell, A. (2009). Starting well: Facilitating the middle school transition. *Journal of Applied School Psychology, 25,* 286–304.

Petras, H., Kellam, S., Brown, C., Muthén, B., Ialongo, N., & Poduska, J. (2008). Developmental epidemiological courses leading to antisocial personality disorder and violent and criminal behavior: Effects by young adulthood of a universal preventive intervention in first- and second-grade classrooms. *Drug & Alcohol Dependence, 95,* S45–59.

Phillips, D., & Christie, F. (1986). Behaviour management in a secondary school classroom: Playing the game. *Maladjustment and Therapeutic Education, 4,* 47–53.

Pierre, T. L., Osgood, D., Mincemoyer, C. C., Kaltreider, D., & Kauh, T. J. (2005). Results of an independent evaluation of project ALERT delivered in schools by cooperative extension. *Prevention Science, 6,* 305–317.

Piquero, A. R., Farrington, D. P., & Blumstein, A. (2003). The criminal career paradigm. In M. Tonry (Ed.), *Crime and justice: A review of research,* volume 30. Chicago: University of Chicago Press.

Puzzanchera, C. (2009). *Juvenile arrests in 2007* (NCJ Publication No. 22-5344). Washington, DC: U.S. Department of Justice.

Riggs, N. R., Greenberg, M. T., Kusché, C. A., & Pentz, M. (2006). The mediational role of neurocognition in the behavioral outcomes of a social-emotional prevention program in elementary school students: Effects of the PATHS curriculum. *Prevention Science, 7,* 91–102.

Ringwalt, C. L., Clark, H., Hanley, S., Shamblen, S. R., & Flewelling, R. L. (2010). The effects of project ALERT one year past curriculum completion. *Prevention Science, 11,* 172–184.

Salend, S. J., Reynolds, C. J., & Coyle, E. M. (1989). Individualizing the Good Behavior Game across type and frequency of behavior with emotionally disturbed adolescents. *Behavior Modification, 13,* 108–126.

Schick, A., & Cierpka, M. (2005). Faustlos: Evaluation of a curriculum to prevent violence in elementary schools. *Applied and Preventive Psychology, 11,* 157–165.

Sherman, L. W., Gottfredson, D., MacKenzie, D., Eck, J., Reuter, P., & Bushway, S. (1997). *Preventing crime: What works, what doesn't, what's promising.* Washington, DC: U.S. Department of Justice, Office of Justice Programs.

Snyder, F. J., Flay, B. R., Vuchinich, S., Acock, A., Washburn, I. J., Beets, & Li, K. K. (2010). Impact of a social-emotional and character development program on school-level indicators of academic achievement, absenteeism, and disciplinary outcomes: A matched-pair, cluster randomized, controlled trial. *Journal of Research on Educational Effectiveness, 3*, 26–55.

Spoth, R. L., Clair, S., Shin, C., & Redmond, C. (2006). Long-term effects of universal preventative interventions on methamphetamine use among adolescents. *Archives of Pediatric & Adolescent Medicine, 160*, 876–182.

Spoth, R. L., Redmond, C., Trudeau, L., & Shin, C. (2002). Longitudinal substance initiation outcomes for a universal preventive intervention combining family and school programs. *Psychology of Addictive Behaviors, 16*, 129–134.

Stoltz, S., van Londen, M., Dekovic, M., de Castro, B. O., & Prinzie, P. (2012). Effectiveness of individually delivered indicated school-based interventions on externalizing behavior. *International Journal of Behavioral Development, 36*, 381–388.

Taub, J. (2002). Evaluation of the *Second Step* violence prevention program at a rural elementary school. *School Psychology Review, 31*, 186–200.

Tremblay, R. E. & Craig, W., M. (1995). Developmental crime prevention. *Crime and Justice, 19*, 151–236.

Tripodi, S. J., & Springer, D. W. (2007). Mental health and substance abuse treatment of juvenile delinquents. In A. R. Roberts & D. W. Springer (Eds.), *Social work in juvenile and criminal justice* (3rd ed.) (pp. 151–169). Springfield, IL: Charles C. Thomas.

U. S. Department of Health and Human Services. (2001). *Youth violence: A report of the Surgeon General.* Rockville, MD: U.S. Department of Health and Human Services.

Welsh, B. C., & Farrington, D. P. (2009). Early developmental prevention of delinquency and later offending: Prospects and challenges. *European Journal of Developmental Science, 3*, 247–259.

Welsh, B. C., & Farrington, D. P. (2010). *The future of crime prevention: Developmental and situational strategies.* Washington, DC: U. S. National Institute of Justice.

Wilcox, H., Kellam, S., Brown, C., Poduska, J., Ialongo, N., Wang, W., et al. (2008). The impact of two universal randomized first- and second-grade classroom interventions on young adult suicide ideation and attempts. *Drug & Alcohol Dependence, 95*, 60–73.

Wilson, D. B., Gottfredson, D. C., & Najaka, S. S. (2001). School-based prevention of problem behaviors: A meta-analysis. *Journal of Quantitative Criminology, 17*, 247–272.

Wilson, S. J., & Lipsey, M. W. (2007). School-based interventions for aggressive and disruptive behavior. Update of a meta-analysis. *American Journal of Preventative Medicine, 33*, 130–143.

Witvliet, M., van Lier, P. A., Cuijpers, P., & Koot, H. M. (2009). Testing the links between positive peer relations and externalizing outcomes through a randomized controlled intervention study. *Journal of Consultation and Clinical Psychology, 77*, 905–915.

14 Community-Based Treatment Interventions

Robert Butters

■ Case Example

Maxwell (Max) is a 15-year-old boy who was arrested and booked into the youth detention center for attempted felony assault and possession of a dangerous weapon at school. He has been charged with threatening another youth with a knife. Max is being held in detention awaiting a preliminary hearing. A social worker at the detention center conducted a social history assessment and administered brief mental health and substance abuse screening instruments with Max and his mother. Although Max was initially hesitant to talk with the social worker, once the social worker excused the mother from the interview to complete additional paperwork, Max seemed to relax and was more cooperative during the interview. The social worker was able to gather the following information that was later validated by reviewing collateral reports from the mother, court records, and school.

Max was suspended three times for fighting in elementary school. Max recently changed schools after his mother remarried 4 months ago. He is currently a sophomore in high school and his grades are mostly passing, although his attendance has been spotty since he transferred to this new school. He has been using marijuana and prescription opiates over the last year, with increasing frequency the last few months. This is his first felony charge, although he had a previous theft charge that was dealt with non-judicially when he was 14. Max was living at home with his mother and stepfather prior to this detention. His relationship with his mother and stepfather is reported as stressful and the police have been called to the house twice in the past 6 months to intercede in family arguments. Max is mostly estranged from his biological father, whom his mother divorced when he was 8 years old after years of substance abuse and domestic violence. Max's biological father comes around once or twice a year but is mostly unreliable. Max's mother worries about him being angry all the time and following in his older brother's footsteps—he lives at home when he's not in jail. Max just wants to get out of detention and disputes that he threatened anyone, saying they were just "messing around." However, the school report indicates a history of conflict between Max and other youth.

■ Scope of the Problem

Providing effective treatment for offenders involved in the juvenile justice system is a cornerstone of any effective response to juvenile crime. Fortunately there is a wealth of evidence demonstrating that effective interventions can change most juveniles' criminal trajectories and reduce subsequent criminal activity. Most youthful offenders involved with the courts are criminally unsophisticated and need a relatively low-dosage intervention. However, for youth with more entrenched criminal behaviors or comorbid/co-occurring co-existing mental health and substance abuse disorders treatment must be intensive and longer in duration. In all but the most severe or dangerous cases, youthful offenders should be treated in their communities and preferably while they live at home and continue to attend school.

Community-based treatment of youthful offenders is the subject of this chapter. The chapter is written to provide practical information about community-based treatment options and to highlight research-based interventions and guidelines for evaluating various treatment options.

In 2009 over 1.5 million youth came in contact with the juvenile court. Two thirds of these youth were male, just over one third were minority youth, and over half were under the age of 16 (Puzzanchera & Kang, 2011). Youthful offenders may be referred to the court for a range of offenses including status offenses (curfew, truancy), property crimes, violent crimes, misdemeanors, and felonies. In most jurisdictions, first-time offenders, with minor charges, are processed through a diversionary or non-judicial process and may receive a sanction such as community service or a small fine. On the other hand, repeat offenders or more serious offenders usually appear before a commissioner or a judge and are processed more formally. Upon adjudication these youth may receive a range of sanctions including restitution, a sentence to serve time in a secure facility, and orders to complete treatment services. For the most severe crimes youth are often held in a youth detention center while various assessments are conducted. Sentences for these youth are generally based on not just the circumstances surrounding the crime but intrapersonal, family, and community factors that correlate to dangerousness, amenability to treatment, and likelihood of rehabilitation. In addition, these most serious offenders may be sent to the adult criminal justice system for adjudication or may be placed in residential and/or secure treatment programs.

While the focus of this chapter is community-based treatment, most if not all of the treatment models and best practices are also applicable to more restrictive treatment settings. Unfortunately too many juvenile justice systems continue to over-rely on outdated and ineffective secure residential treatment programs. Of course we need some secure treatment centers for the most serious and violent offenders, and residential treatment centers are essential to stabilize a youth or as an alternative to an unhealthy home environment. But these high-level and high-cost placements should be used only in the most extreme cases, for a limited period of time, and only as part of a continuum of treatment services that include transition back to home and community-based alternatives. The developmental imperative to keep youth in the least restrictive and most naturalistic settings while involved in the juvenile justice system must receive strong consideration in any treatment planning process.

This "wraparound" approach often allows higher-risk youth to remain in community-based settings, thus reducing the use of expensive institutional placements while providing for increased safety, supervision, and improved outcomes. Many jurisdictions are working to improve outcomes by adhering to evidence-based practice guidelines and are demanding more rigorous process and outcome evaluations of youth-serving programs. Even juvenile court judges are using "smart sentencing" practices and have begun to demand that programs who receive referrals to the court adhere to evidence-based principles.

■ Literature Review

Collaboration

Research has demonstrated that the juvenile justice system, while empowered to arrest, prosecute, punish, and even incapacitate offenders, is grossly inadequate to alone address the complex mechanisms that contribute to sustained juvenile offending behavior. Juvenile justice practitioners have begun to embrace models of collaboration, often called "wraparound" services (Pullmann, Kerbs, Koroloff, Veach-White, Gaylor, & Sieler, 2006), multimodal, integrated, or comprehensive models of intervention that involve collaboration between the major systems that a youth encounters, such as mental health, substance abuse services, medical services, child welfare services, and the education system (Cocozza, Skowyra, & Office of Juvenile Justice and Delinquent Prevention, 2000; Hartford, Carey, & Mendonca, 2006; McCarter, Haber, & Kazemi, 2010; Osher, Steadman, & Barr, 2003; Suter & Bruns, 2009; Wilson & Draine, 2006).

True collaboration requires more than just working together or having open lines of communication. Collaboration must include role clarification, clear professional boundaries, an understanding of the collaborators' professional training, and working toward agreed-upon goals. The California Corrections Standards (2011) posits that "the responsibility for the youth in custody . . . is shared among multiple agencies and individuals. Courts, custody, health and mental health staff, substance abuse, school and social services/child welfare personnel all have important roles to play, as do family members and community support providers" (p. i). In response, policymakers have promoted a number of initiatives to improve collaboration through family involvement, by sharing information across service sectors, and by specifically training youth-serving professionals to collaborate in addressing the complex needs of juvenile justice-involved youth (Center for Juvenile Justice Reform, 2008).

In practical terms, effective treatment must address the needs of youth by teaming with professionals outside of our various disciplines. Most juvenile justice practitioners are adept at accessing resources and engaging fellow professionals within their discipline because they speak the same language, have similar goals, and share common ethical guidelines. It is simply easier for social workers to talk with other social workers about a youth and engage them in a treatment team than it is to work effectively with a probation officer, the school principal, or local law enforcement. However, working only within disciplines simply perpetuates the already fragmented and confusing service delivery system and results in less optimal outcomes for youth involved with the courts.

The identification of clear boundaries in service provision is a systemic way that can promote collaboration while still maintaining specialty areas and professional integrity. Skowyra and Cocozza (2007) suggest a mechanism by which the juvenile justice system should take the responsibility for primary care of youth who are detained, but when a youth involved in the system resides in a community setting they suggest that the mental health system assumes the primary treatment responsibility. Skowyra and Cocozza also note that community treatment is generally of higher quality and more cost-effective. While this collaborative model promotes changing the primary responsibility for care depending on where the offender resides, there must be emphasis on transitions between service providers to ensure that youth don't "fall between the cracks" or are exposed to periods of treatment unavailability or of poor supervision as they move between treatment providers.

Regardless of the role and responsibility placed on each system, many researchers stress the importance of high-quality staff who are trained and experienced in the areas of both criminal justice and mental health (Pealer & Latessa, 2004). For example, mental health clinicians who work with offenders should also be trained in criminal justice models and their treatment should use the principles of effective intervention, namely the Risk-Need-Responsivity (RNR) model (Andrews & Bonta, 2010) discussed in detail later in this chapter. Likewise, juvenile justice personnel should be trained in recognizing mental health symptoms, should be aware of the importance of screening and assessment, and should understand the importance of treatment (Lattimore, Broner, Sherman, Frisman, & Shafer, 2003; Walsh & Holt, 1999).

In addition to interdisciplinary collaboration, a comprehensive approach to treatment incorporates various intervention modalities that include supervision, targeted treatment, case management, family support, education, and other services included in a case plan (Baillargeon, Hoge, & Penn, 2010; Martin, Dorken, Wamboldt, & Wootten, 2011; Trupin, Kerns, Walker, DeRobertis, & Stewart, 2011). This comprehensive approach necessitates agency liaisons and information sharing between the criminal justice system and community-based mental health agencies (Osher et al., 2003). It is also crucial to establish linkages through points of contact in the juvenile justice system, especially as youths move between placements. Table 14.1 summarizes Skowyra and Cocozza's (2007) recommendations for effective collaboration between the juvenile justice and mental health systems.

Evidence-Based Interventions with Youthful Offenders

Interdisciplinary collaboration and comprehensive programming models are integral parts of effective interventions for youth involved in the juvenile justice

Table 14.1 **Collaboration between Juvenile Justice System (JJS) and Mental Health System (MHS)**

Collaboration	1. Recognition of mental health issues in juvenile offenders by JJS and MHS
	2. Collaborative and comprehensive planning among JJS and MHS
	3. Inclusion of family members & caregivers in planning process
	4. Identification of joint funding mechanisms
	5. Collaboration at all stages of process (not just beginning or end)
	6. Joint evaluation of programs and services
	7. Cross-training JJS and MHS staff
Identification	1. Systematically screen all youth for mental health issues
	2. Early identification of those in need of emergency services
	3. Access to emergency services for youth needing immediate care
	4. Utilize full mental health assessments as indicated from screenings
	5. Use standardized and validated assessment instruments
	6. Mental health screenings always should be performed in conjunction with risk assessments
	7. Screenings and assessments should always be administered by appropriately trained staff
	8. Protect pretrial mental health information to preserve legal integrity
	9. Routine e-assessment at critical intervention points
	10. Integration of co-occurring substance abuse needs in screenings and assessments
	11. Adaptation of screening and assessment tools for marginalized populations
Diversion	1. Divert youth out of JJS to MHS whenever possible
	2. Standardize procedures to assess appropriateness for diversion
	3. Have effective community-based diversion resources available
	4. Consider diversion at key decision-making points of JJS processing
	5. Regular evaluation to consider mental health needs and community safety
Treatment	1. Employ evidence-based treatments regardless of the setting 2. Shared treatment responsibility for youth between JJS and MHS
	3. Employ qualified mental health professionals in JJS
	4. Involve families in rehabilitation process
	5. Create environments sensitive to the trauma histories of many youth
	6. Increase attention to cultural diversity
	7. Discharge plan collaboratively to ensure continuation of services

Adapted from Skowyra and Cocozza (2007).

system, especially when developing individualized treatment plans based on the unique needs of each youth. The RNR model has emerged as an example of a framework that can guide juvenile justice practitioners to maximize the probability of success while minimizing negative outcomes and utilizing resources efficiently (Andrews & Bonta, 2010; Epperson et al., 2011; Rice & Harris,

1997). A brief overview of the RNR model follows, including implications for treatment.

Andrews and Bonta (2010) identify three core principles that should be used by agencies and practitioners when designing programs and to assist in the development of treatment plans.

The first core principle is the **risk principle**. The risk principle first posits that an individual's probability of risk to engage in future criminal behavior can be predicted. Prediction of risk should be done using actuarial risk measures or instruments that have been validated through research and have demonstrated reasonable levels of validity. This principle also states that the intensity of interventions and treatment should match the level of risk. This means that for low-risk offenders minimal or no intervention is sufficient, while high-risk offenders will require intensive and often extensive services (Andrews & Bonta, 2010). Additionally, higher-risk offenders should be given priority for funding, placement, and treatment over lower-risk offenders. This risk principle makes intuitive sense for most practitioners in the justice system, at least when we consider giving more intensive services to more serious offenders.

The importance of the risk principle can be better understood through discussion of two key concepts, allocation of resources and contagion. Efficient utilization of resources is always an overarching tension in social service agencies. No court, community provider, or agency has extra resources, so efforts must be directed to areas that have the greatest likelihood of success. Therefore, by targeting treatments and titrating dosages according to risk, we maximize our resources (Lowenkamp, Latessa, & Holsinger, 2006).

Among low-risk youth, increased involvement with the juvenile court and related services has a negative effect on overall well-being and recidivism (Rice & Harris, 1997). In addition, when low-risk youth enter a juvenile justice system designed to serve higher-risk offenders, there is a greater likelihood that the high-risk youth will influence the low-risk youth; this is known as the *contagion* effect (Dodge, Dishion, & Landsford, 2006). The result of this contagion is that the younger offenders "learn the craft" of the older offenders and will model and mimic their behavior. Thus, when dealing with low-risk or first-time offenders, diversion programs should always be given first consideration.

The second core principle of the RNR model is the **criminogenic need principle** (Andrews & Bonta, 2010). These criminogenic needs are risk factors that have been demonstrated to increase the probability of recidivism. Andrews and Bonta propose eight major criminogenic risk and need factors that should be the primary focus of any juvenile treatment program: the *Central Eight* (Table 14.2).

Historically, many juvenile justice programs have overemphasized treatment activities that are generally prosocial but are not specifically targeted at the factors that have the strongest relationship with future offending (Andrews & Bonta, 2010). Thus, an essential component of the criminogenic need principle is that correctional interventions must utilize assessment instruments that

Table 14.2 Criminogenic Needs/Risk Factors and Treatment Targets

Criminogenic Need	Treatment Targets
Antisocial Behavior Exploitive, aggressive, or harmful behavior toward others	Increase prosocial behaviors by reinforcing prosocial beliefs supporting a crime-free lifestyle. Develop clear, consistent, and proximate reward and consequence system for addressing behaviors. Teach, model, and reinforce prosocial alternative behaviors, especially in high-risk situations.
Antisocial Personality Pattern Impulsive, sensation seeking, risk-taking, aggressive, manipulative and exploitive	Treatment target: increase self-control and delayed gratification skills, anger and conflict management, problem solving and reinforce prosocial, reciprocal interpersonal interactions
Antisocial Cognition Values, beliefs, feelings, and cognitions that contribute to personal identity that favors and reinforces criminal behavior	Address cognitive distortions and rationalizations that maintain a criminal identity. Build, practice, and reinforce new cognitions and attributions that lead to positive outcomes through cognitive restructuring and cognitive-behavioral therapies.
Antisocial Peers Preferring to associate with pro-criminal peers and isolation from anti-criminal peers and social contexts	Reduce and eliminate association with delinquent peers and increase opportunities for regular association with anti-criminal peers and institutions (school, church, clubs, sports teams, and other structured and supervised activities)
Family Chaotic and poor-quality family relationships that have minimal or no prosocial expectations regarding crime and substance abuse	Increase prosocial communication, nurturance, structure, supervision, and monitoring in the family. Address dysfunctional boundaries and role confusion. Implement behavioral management system that provides for consistent rewards for prosocial family interactions.
School/Work Poor performance and limited engagement with school or work, resulting in dissatisfaction and avoidance of these institutions	Increase school engagement and performance in work and school though remediation of barriers to satisfaction (i.e., Individualized Education Plan, additional job training or alternate job placement). Implement monitoring and behavioral reinforcement program to increase consistent attendance at school and work.
Leisure & Recreation Limited involvement in anti-criminal leisure activities	Expose youth to a variety of prosocial leisure and recreational activities. Increase opportunities for regular involvement in preferred activities and reward milestones in achievement.
Substance Abuse Use and abuse of alcohol, tobacco, or other drugs (ATOD)	Reduce substance use through targeted treatment, increase supervision and reduce access to ATOD, and reduce exposure to ATOD-using peers. Increase capacity to cope with stressors though lifestyle changes like regular exercise, sleep, and nutrition.

Adapted from Andrews and Bonta (2010).

identify criminogenic needs and that the *majority* of the interventions should target these risk factors. Thus, the criminogenic need principle does not preclude these extracurricular activities but *prioritizes* specific criminal treatment targets over interventions that have not been consistently shown to reduce recidivism.

The final core principle set forth by Andrews and Bonta (2010) is the **responsivity principle**. Within this principle both general and specific responsivity are discussed. *General responsivity* is the delivery of an intervention in a manner that matches the learning style and ability of the youth. This means that a program should use methods of delivery that are known to be most effective. According to Andrews and Bonta (2010), "the most powerful influence strategies available are cognitive-behavioral and cognitive social learning," which include "modeling, reinforcement, role playing, skill building, modification of thoughts and emotions through cognitive restructuring, and practicing new, low-risk alternative behaviors over and over again in a variety of high-risk situations until one gets very good at it" (p. 50). Treatment programs targeting reductions in recidivism will be most effective if they employ active, experiential interventions that require both the practitioner and the youth to engage in practice and role play until they have mastered the necessary skills. Understanding the foundations of learning theory and how to master skills is vital when providing effective interventions to youth. An example of an effective group intervention that maximizes general responsivity is presented in Table 14.3.

Specific responsivity instructs programs to tailor treatments to match the individual characteristics of the offender. This may include personality, cognitive style, and cultural characteristics. For example, it would be inappropriate

Table 14.3   Model for Effective Group Treatment

1. Facilitator provides a brief background on target behavior(s)—for example, violence, substance use, family discord (this could be place to use an engaging video clip, other media, or current event).

2. Identify the underlying thoughts, feelings, cognitions associated with the dysfunctional behavior.

3. Identify thoughts that are dysfunctional, cognitive distortions, or misattributions.

4. Explore alternative thoughts/attributions and explore feelings associated with those options.

5. Identify healthy thinking and behavioral alternatives.

6. Facilitator models prosocial thinking and resulting behaviors for group.

7. Youth role play real scenario while being directly observed by facilitator.

8. Facilitator provides positive reinforcement for successes, provides feedback for improvement.

9. Youth continue to practice skill, in increasingly challenging scenarios, until mastered.

10. Youth are provided "homework" to practice skill at home or school and report back to group on successes and challenges.

to put an offender with extreme social anxiety in a large group, or to put an individual with low intelligence or a learning disorder in a group that uses more sophisticated cognitive concepts. Other responsivity factors include mental interpersonal sensitivity, cultural factors, verbal intelligence, cognitive maturity, and level of motivation for treatment. Motivation to change among youth in the justice system is always an important consideration and should be addressed throughout treatment.

Mental health disorders are a specific responsivity factor that should always be considered when treating juveniles. The remediation of mental health problems should not supplant targeted criminogenic treatment, but such problems must be considered a co-occurring condition necessitating treatment adaptation and sometimes targeted treatment so that the juvenile can take full advantage of treatment that reduces the risk of recidivism. Youths with a significant child abuse or trauma history, for instance, may need to have their treatment timing, setting, and techniques adapted so they are not continually triggered and re-experiencing the trauma. Similarly, a highly depressed or anxious youth may need some psychiatric medication to become stable enough to meaningfully engage in treatment. Using collaborative models that facilitate information sharing as well as regular screening and assessment increase the likelihood of detecting and remediating mental health issues early and improving outcomes for youth in the juvenile justice system.

■ Characteristics of Effective Programs

A relatively small number of programs and interventions currently in use by juvenile justice and community-based practitioners have been rigorously evaluated by research. In fact, even interventions that use a "name brand" program and that are extensively studied (Multisystemic Therapy, Multidimensional Treatment Foster Care, Family Functional Therapy, etc.) may not have the same impact shown in the studies due to implementation and fidelity issues.

So a juvenile justice practitioner may well ask: *If no reliable outcome data are available for a program, how I know if that program is effective in reducing recidivism?* Of course, the best answer, empirically, is to design and implement a high-quality evaluation of the program that measures recidivism. The problem with this answer is that experimental research projects are both costly and difficult to implement and, of course, the primary outcome variable of interest, recidivism, requires long follow-up times to truly show treatment effects. Funding and implementing programs while waiting for outcome data, without more proximal indicators of success, can result in wasted resources, ineffective programs, and more crime and victimization.

Most juvenile justice professionals need more immediate information about which programs are likely to reduce recidivism. Fortunately, there are reliable process evaluation models that can provide a more immediate proxy for program

Table 14.4   Elements of Effective Juvenile Justice Programs

Program capacity	Program integrity or the program's ability to deliver effective programming consistently
Leadership and Development	An experienced director or leader who is involved in all aspects of the program, including supervision of staff, improves program quality. Positive and established collaborative relationships with outside agencies.
Staff	Educated and qualified staff who believe in treatment provide majority of programming. Staff should receive ongoing supervision and training.
Quality Assurance	Programs who evaluate both their process and outcomes have better consistency and generally maintain appropriate treatment focus.
Program content	**The degree to which the program adheres to evidence-based principles (Risk-Need-Responsivity [RNR] model)**
Assessment	Programs must assess levels of risk, criminogenic needs, and responsivity factors to more efficiently tailor interventions to offenders. Assessments should be done using validated RNR instruments.
Treatment	Treatment should use primarily social learning, cognitive, and behavioral techniques in treatment. Behavioral reinforcers should be used consistently. Aftercare should be integrated into the treatment program and include family whenever possible.

success. Drawing largely from the literature on "what works" and incorporating RNR principles, the Correctional Program Assessment Inventory and subsequently the Correctional Program Checklist were developed to guide an evidence-based assesment of programs (Lowenkamp, Latessa, & Smith, 2006; Smith, Gendreau, & Swartz, 2009). These evidence-based evaluations use the principles of effective collaboration, the RNR model, and other program factors shown through meta-analysis to reduce criminal recidivism (Lowenkamp, Latessa, & Holsinger, 2006) to provide an indicator of program effectiveness. In fact, alignment with these characteristics has been shown to be correlated with substantial reductions in juvenile recidivism (Pealer & Latessa, 2004). The characteristics of effective programs are grouped into two categories, program capacity and program content. Program **capacity** assesses program leadership, staff characteristics, and quality assurance activities. Program **content** evaluates the assessment and treatment components using the principles of the RNR model. The general principles of effective programs are further summarized in Table 14.4.

■ Clinical or Legal Issues

Working in the juvenile justice system requires specialized knowledge, skills, and values that balance the needs of the youth with the needs of the community. In many cases the treatment needs of youth can appear to conflict with the needs of the community, especially in the areas of safety and justice. For example, youth should be treated in the community whenever possible and the treatment dosage should be adjusted based on the youth's level of risk to reoffend, not the severity of the crime. Therefore most youth should be treated in a less restrictive community setting, where they could commit more crimes, which in turn would lead to additional victims. We could protect against this possibility by keeping the youth incarcerated, but this does little to rehabilitate the youth and may even increase his or her likelihood of reoffending. (Andrews & Bonta, 2010).

Fortunately, juvenile justice professionals can carefully craft recommendations, probation agreements, and service plans that balance the needs of the youth and community *and* yield positive outcomes for both. Therapeutic jurisprudence (Wexler & Winick, 1996) balances the need of the court to administer justice with the juvenile's need for treatment. It provides for justice-related activities such as restitution, accountability, and supervision as adjunctive components of a therapeutic treatment plan. Mental health practitioners who simply advocate for the treatment needs of youth in the juvenile justice system are unlikely to be effective, as are court officials who simply advocate for punitive responses. The former is likely to be dismissed as naïve or "soft," the latter as harsh and short-sighted. Effective work in the justice system necessitates strong collaborative skills and an understanding of the various roles, statutory obligations, and perspectives of the various stakeholders.

The most common ethical dilemma faced by juvenile justice practitioners is finding oneself in a dual role with the youth and/or the court. Clinicians working directly with youth and their families have a wealth of information that is useful to the court as it determines levels of supervision, disposition, and eligibility for programs. Many times treatment providers are placed in ethically tenuous situations as they are asked to provide the court with *therapeutic* progress reports and to comment on *forensic* inquiries regarding risk levels and amenability for treatment.

These therapeutic versus forensic roles should be explicitly identified upfront with the court and the client, and the practitioner should stay strictly within this role at all times (Butters & Vaughan-Eden, 2011). The simplest way to identify this role is to ask: *Who is my client?* For court-employed probation officers and most juvenile justice staff, the answer is typically the court. By definition, this role is generally aligned with determining levels of risk, protecting public safety, supervising offenders, and reporting information back to the court.

Mental health practitioners vary in their role with the court system and must be sure to consider these issues before engaging with a youth in the justice system. Many practitioners are asked to conduct mental health evaluations and risk and needs assessments or to complete presentence reports to inform the court process. In these situations the practitioner generally works for the court and must offer the juvenile and family being assessed a *forensic warning*, advising them that all information being collected will be offered to the court. Alternately, a family counselor working with a youth should clarify that all information disclosed in treatment will be kept confidential (except for mandated reporting requirements). In these cases the counselor should not provide the court with any information about the client unless the appropriate releases of information are signed. Most youth and families involved with the court are happy to sign releases, but it is important to clarify with them that although they may be court-ordered to treatment, the courts cannot force them to waive their rights to privacy and confidentiality of their medical records without due process. Additionally, if the court asks the therapist for forensic information regarding risk or likelihood of reoffending, the counselor should graciously decline, citing ethical limitations.

Too many practitioners in the justice system violate the privacy rights of offenders by sharing information liberally with anyone involved in the case without first considering the impact on the juvenile. As described in the previous section, effective collaboration necessitates clear roles and boundaries when working on multidisciplinary teams. When there are explicitly defined roles, the system can function more efficiently and ethically and achieve the optimal outcomes for youth in the juvenile justice system.

■ Juvenile Treatment Models and Interventions for High-Risk Youth

A number of evidence-based treatment models for high-risk juvenile offenders incorporate the key principles of collaboration and effective interventions that have been shown to be effective in reducing recidivism. This section highlights several of the most promising evidence-based programs for responding to juvenile delinquency.

Multisystemic Therapy

Multisystemic Therapy (MST), developed by Dr. Scott Henggeler and his colleagues at the University of South Carolina is one of several treatment models designed to address the behavioral and delinquency concerns of youth by intervening with the systems in which the youth lives, including the family. MST is a community-based alternative to more restrictive and often costly interventions within the juvenile justice system (Ogden & Hagen, 2006; Schaeffer & Borduin, 2005). Within the MST model, criminogenic needs are targeted by the therapist and family with a typical length of 4 to 6 months. These targets include antisocial behavior, sources of conflict in the family, family relations, peer relations, and school functioning (Littell et al., 2005; Ogden & Hagen, 2006).

Although MST is a relatively costly community-based intervention, at approximately $5,000 per youth (Littell, Popa, & Forsythe, 2005), it typically targets high-risk youth with severe and chronic involvement within the juvenile justice system who would otherwise need residential care. MST is implemented through treatment teams consisting of therapists and crisis caseworkers. MST uses an integrated approach consisting of a combination of approaches from strategic family therapy, structural family therapy, and cognitive-behavioral therapy (Littell, 2004). Additionally, therapists are on call to the family at all times for crisis intervention and parent coaching. Fidelity to the model is monitored through the use of quality assurance tools.

MST is considered many to be one of the most highly evidence-based interventions based on a relatively large number of research studies on the efficacy of the model and a comprehensive intervention framework. A 2011 data report submitted by MST Services reported a 25% to 70% reduction in long-term rates of rearrest, a 47% to 64% reduction in out-of-home placements, marked improvements in family functioning, and a decrease in mental health problems. Alternately, a 2005 systematic review that aggregated eight randomized controlled trials of MST indicate that the evidence regarding the effectiveness of MST is inconclusive (Littell et al., 2005). Nevertheless MST is endorsed as a model program for juvenile offenders by such agencies as Blueprints for Violence Prevention, SAMHSA's National Registry of Evidence-Based Programs and Services, OJJDP Model Program Guide, and Child Trends (Center for the Study and Prevention of Violence, n.d.-c).

Multidimensional Treatment Foster Care

Multidimensional Treatment Foster Care (MTFC) is another evidence-based practice that serves as an alternative to more restrictive and costly residential settings for juvenile delinquents. MTFC posits that a youth's behaviors, attitudes, and emotions are influenced by his or her environment (Smith, 2004). In this case, MTFC is able to influence a juvenile offender through the day-to-day interactions with the MTFC parent in a foster care setting. The main targets of the MTFC model are close supervision, positive adult–youth relationships, and decreased association with delinquent peers (Smith, 2004). In addition Fisher and Chamberlain (2000) report that the model focuses on:

1 Reinforcement of normative and pro-social behaviors
2 Consistent boundaries and immediate sanctions for rule violations
3 Development of positive work and academic skills
4 Parent training
5 Conflict resolution
6 Relationship skills targeted at forming positive bonds with peers and adults

Within the MTFC home, parents provide reinforcement and sanctions through a carefully followed daily behavior management system, which is a point and level system. The behavioral system allows the MTFC parents to structure the youth's environment so that negative behaviors are reduced through consistent sanctions as well as rewarding him or her for prosocial behaviors (Smith, 2004). In addition, the MTFC parents are in daily contact with the MTFC program supervisor for training and guidance. For the MTFC to function fully, diverse team members are needed to provide consistency and individualized treatment (Fisher & Chamberlain, 2000). MTFC treatment teams often consist of probation officers, behavior support specialists, individual therapists, family therapists, medical professionals, case managers, and clinical team supervisors.

The average length for MTFC treatment is 7 months at a cost of approximately $3,900 per month. While MTFC is time-intensive and more costly than typical foster care settings, it is estimated that in the long term using MTFC saved $21,836 to $87,622 per youth (Chamberlain, Leve, & DeGarmo, 2007). Results from MTFC interventions have shown that both boys and girls referred from juvenile justice settings show greater reductions in recidivism than from other group care settings. Lee and Thompson (2008) found that male MTFC youth spent less time in locked settings, had fewer criminal referrals, had fewer delinquent peers, and were more likely to complete treatment and return home than males in other group care settings. MTFC is endorsed as a model program by Blueprints for Violence Prevention, SAMHSA, Office of Juvenile Justice Delinquency Prevention, Office of Justice, and Child Trends (Center for the Study and Prevention of Violence, n.d.-b).

Functional Family Therapy

Functional Family Therapy (FFT) is a short-term family intervention that typically consists of eight to 12 sessions and up to 30 hours of intervention over a period of approximately 3 months. This treatment may be offered in a clinical setting or in the client's home. It consists of three phases: engagement and motivation, behavior change, and generalization (Sexton & Turner, 2010). The engagement and motivation phase focuses on developing alliances, reducing resistance, improving communication, minimizing hopelessness, reducing dropout, developing a family focus, and increasing motivation for change. The behavior change phase includes developing and implementing individual change plans for family members, changing the presenting delinquency behaviors, and building relational skills, including communication and parenting skills. Finally, the generalization phase focuses on maintaining and generalizing the change in the family, preventing relapses, and including appropriate community resources that will help support the change in the family. The average cost of an FFT intervention is approximately $3,750 per youth (Zagar, Busch, & Hughes, 2009).

FFT has shown to be effective in reducing the involvement of youth with other social services, preventing escalation of the presenting problem, preventing younger children in the family from becoming involved in the system of care, and preventing adolescents from entering the adult criminal justice system. FFT has been shown to effectively generalize treatment outcomes across various treatment systems (Center for the Study and Prevention of Violence, n.d.-a). FFT is endorsed as a model program by Blueprints for Violence Prevention, Communities that Care, the Office of Juvenile Justice Delinquency Prevention, and the Office of Justice (Center for the Study and Prevention of Violence, n.d.-a).

Aggression Replacement Training

Aggression Replacement Training (ART) has demonstrated very good outcomes with high-risk juvenile offenders. Originally developed by Arnold Goldstein, the ART model is based on three approaches: **skill streaming** to increase prosocial behaviors, **anger control training** to help manage emotions, and **moral reasoning** exercises to increase prosocial cognitions (Amendola & Oliver, 2010). Skill building, positive and negative reinforcers, and guided group discussions with role plays facilitate the acquisition and reinforcement of skills in the group lessons. Maladaptive anger responses are addressed through a variety of techniques including participation in an anger-inducing role play in which youth recognize triggers, practice anger-reducing techniques and using reminders, practice thinking ahead about consequences, utilize a prosocial alternative to anger, and engage in a self-evaluation of the skills used and their effectiveness. The moral reasoning exercises consider various responses to stories or vignettes and explore the underlying moral and ethical considerations that drive various actions. Through group discussion prosocial values are shaped and reinforced, thus modifying antisocial justifications and cognitions (Glick & Gibbs, 2011). ART is a 30-hour intervention that takes approximately 10 weeks. The groups typically consist of eight to 12 youths and the cost is around $800 per youth for the course of treatment (Barnoski, 2002).

ART has been shown to reduce new felony offenses and reduce recidivism by 28%; however, research does not indicate that it reduces violent felony recidivism (Barnoski, 2002). ART is considered effective by the Office of Juvenile Justice and Delinquency Prevention (Office of Juvenile Justice and Delinquency Prevention, n.d.-a) and the U.S. Department of Education (Amendola & Oliver, 2010).

■ Restorative Justice

Restorative justice for juvenile offenders is a community-based approach to juvenile justice that acknowledges that most low-risk youth are better served in the community and are better served though diversion programs that avoid traditional juvenile justice processing. The Washington State Institute for Public Policy (WSIPP, 2012) found that restorative justice programs (like Victim Offender Mediation [VOM]) were associated with a significant reduction in recidivism and were relatively inexpensive (Lee, Aos, Drake, Pennucci, Miller, & Anderson, 2012). WSIPP calculated that the cost per participant was for VOM $579, for ART $1,510, and for MST $7,370. Further, the report calculated that in nearly all cases, the benefits of all these programs outweigh its costs. Their findings in 2006 led WSIPP to promote restorative justice programs in juvenile courts as "evidence-based investment opportunities available to Washington policymakers" (Aos, Miller, & Drake, 2006, p. 12). Clearly, there are economic benefits of reserving more intensive and expensive justice programs like residential care and MST, FFT, and MTFC for serious, chronic, and high-risk juvenile offenders. Restorative justice programs are evidence-based and cost-effective interventions for low-risk offenders that hold juveniles accountable for their behaviors while offering a more empowering, community-based resolution than traditional juvenile justice programs and should be part of a continuum of interventions in juvenile justice systems.

Restorative Justice Practices

Restorative justice is an alternate way of thinking about justice rather than a specific intervention or program. With dialogue as its central focus, the most common restorative justice practices are VOM, Family Group Conferencing, and Peacemaking Circles. All restorative justice practices have similar attributes, including the participation of victim and offender in a face-to-face dialogue to discuss a particular offense; a third person serves as facilitator, mediator, or circle keeper. When possible all persons participating in the process are prepared in advance so they can learn about the process and ask questions. The encounter allows an opportunity to discuss what happened, the impact that it had, and what needs to happen to repair the harm; ideally, a common understanding is created. These processes can take place at any point in the criminal justice process, from before arrest to after incarceration. For the purposes of low-risk offender diversion, the most promising restorative justice practice is VOM, reviewed in the next section.

VOM

VOM is the oldest and most widely developed, implemented, and empirically validated practice in the restorative justice literature (Bazemore & Umbreit, 1995; Umbreit, 2001; Van Ness & Heetderks, 2002; Zehr, 1990, 2002). Three prominent meta-analyses have been conducted on VOM; all three found reduced recidivism rates for participants (Bradshaw, Roseborough, & Umbreit, 2006; Nugent, Williams, & Umbreit, 2004; Sherman & Strang, 2007).

VOM is a restorative process in which the victim and offender sit down together, in a safe environment with a trained neutral facilitator, to discuss the impact and circumstances of the crime that occurred, as well as options for repairing the harm that was done. Obligations are discussed and outlined between victim and offender; these agreements may entail restitution, restorative community service, formal apologies, and other competency-building activities. VOM is a way to directly hold offenders accountable in a forum that involves victims in the justice process and it often resolves restitution disputes. VOM is always voluntary for all participants.

Victims have an opportunity to tell their story of what happened, ask questions, and obtain meaningful restoration and restitution. Offenders have an opportunity to take direct responsibility for the harm they have done and can act to produce remedy and closure. VOM addresses community well-being by promoting healthy social relationships that deter crime and promote a sense of community connection in youth.

VOM can be an effective diversion from traditional juvenile justice processing and an effective, low-cost intervention for low-risk youth. VOM allows youth to redefine their criminal behaviors as a community harm that they have the power to repair. By facing their victims and other members of the community they learn that they are part of a larger prosocial community and can improve community functioning.

Summary and Conclusion

This chapter on community-based treatment concludes with the disposition, service plan, and treatment programs for the case study on Max. By viewing the case through the information presented here on best practices, ethical and legal considerations, and evidence-based programs, we identify common practices and pitfalls for community practice in the juvenile justice system.

One week after being arrested for assault Max plead not guilty to both charges and was assigned a legal defender and a court probation officer. The probation officer, recognizing the importance of collaboration, tried to schedule a meeting with the social worker, the legal defender, Max, and his mother. Unfortunately, because the collaborative process wasn't institutionalized, the meeting didn't happen for over a month. Max remained in detention during this time, limiting his ability to engage in prosocial activities. Instead, he became friends with several other juveniles also locked in detention.

During the meeting the probation officer shared information about the delinquency charges and the team discussed the options. The legal defender discussed a plea deal in which the attempted assault charge could be dropped and a recommendation would be made for time served, 1 year of probation, court-mandated treatment, and 100 hours of community service. After some discussion the team agreed that this was a good option and the legal defender was able to request a hearing the next week. The social worker presented the social information and results from the mental health and substance screening instruments. The instruments showed that Max likely had a substance abuse problem and displayed some symptoms of depression. Additionally, during a follow-up meeting with the social worker Max disclosed that he had recurrent thoughts of violent images, most often associated with violence between his father and mother.

The social worker recommended that as part of the disposition Max could be ordered to receive counseling to address his issues with substance abuse, anger, trauma, and family issues. Everyone concurred with this recommendation, and because the social worker had developed a trusting relationship with Max the mother asked if she could work with him on these issues. The social worker really liked Max and felt that she could help him, but based on her previous forensic role in the case it would have been inappropriate for her to continue to work with him in a therapeutic role. The social worker declined the request but identified some other practitioners who could provide these services.

One week later at court the judge accepted the plea arrangement and the service plan. The probation officer would supervise Max on probation for a year, monitor his attendance at treatment and behavior at home, and make sure he attended school regularly. Max enrolled in an ART program and started individual and family counseling. He wasn't able to start with any of the therapists recommended by the social worker at detention because of insurance panel restrictions, but he liked his new therapist well enough.

Treatment sessions focused on resolving the trauma associated with witnessing domestic violence and staying sober. The trauma work was very successful, but sobriety was more challenging. It was especially difficult for him to discontinue his marijuana use given that he continued to hang around his older brother and his new friends who used substances regularly. The family counseling was somewhat productive, although his older brother refused to attend the sessions and would often sabotage any progress Max made with his parents. Max graduated from the ART program and exhibited no further anger problems.

School proved to be the biggest challenge for Max. His conviction on the weapons charge resulted in his permanent expulsion from not just his local high school but the entire school district. He initially enrolled in another high school, but taking the bus for an hour each way proved to be too much. Eventually Max enrolled in an alternative high school and was able to attend school with his older brother and his other friends from the detention center. Near the end of his 1-year probation period Max was arrested after a traffic stop for possessing a knife and a bag of prescription pills. Because these charges were both felonies, this was his second weapons charge, and he was on probation, the prosecutor decided to file the charges in adult court. Max now faced up to 10 years in prison.

This case was developed to illustrate a number of key concepts presented in this chapter as well as to emphasize the importance of intervening *early* and *effectively* with juvenile offenders. Max, and others like him, don't have to face charges in the adult system and be subject to long-term incarceration. The case highlights several important concepts.

The probation officer, social worker, mother, Max, and the legal defender did an excellent job in collaboratively developing a plan that included treatment and justice components. Unfortunately, this team approach didn't continue once court was over. The team also didn't include key individuals who could have improved outcomes for Max, specifically a school representative. The inclusion of a school representative as part of the team may have facilitated a discussion of district policies and resulted in a more elegant plea arrangement that would not have prohibited Max from attending school. The social worker did assess a number of Max's treatment needs and did a great job in gathering sensitive information without the parent in the room and in following up later with him to gather more information. Unfortunately her assessment, although probably better than most youth receive in detention, was incomplete and did not identify all of Max's criminogenic needs. For example, the antisocial influence of his brother and other antisocial peers went unaddressed and this factor hindered the success of his substance abuse treatment.

Max was successful in this trauma treatment, but this therapy violated the need principle because it failed to address other criminogenic needs like antisocial peers, family cohesion, and antisocial behaviors. Because of funding issues Max was unable to attend treatment with one of the recommended therapists who had been trained in general mental health therapy and in addressing criminogenic needs. These deficits in the assessment and subsequent counseling program could have been identified by the probation officer if assessed using principles of effective programs.

Because Max's level of risk and need was never assessed, we have no way of knowing if the treatment programs he received were at the appropriate dosage or actually targeted the correct risk factors. It could be that the recommended anger management, substance abuse, trauma treatment, and family counseling were all equally important and necessary. It is also possible that some of the factors were more urgent and needed more targeted intervention, while others, like substance abuse, could have been more effectively targeted by focusing on peer influences.

Community-based treatment of youth involved in the juvenile justice system requires strong skills in interdisciplinary collaboration, knowledge of evidence-based principles and practices, and a thorough understanding of the components of treatment programs that lead to reductions in recidivism. It is neither adequate to simply punish youth into behaving or to simply treat mental health symptoms. Concepts like therapeutic jurisprudence and restorative justice offer frameworks for intervening with youth that balance the needs of the community for safety and justice with the needs of the youth for humane treatment and intervention.

References

Aos, S., Miller, M., & Drake, E. (2006). *Evidence-based public policy options to reduce future prison construction, criminal justice costs, and crime rates.* Olympia, WA: Washington State Institute for Public Policy. Retrieved from http://www.wsipp.wa.gov/rptfiles/06–10-1201.pdf

Amendola, M., & Oliver, R. (2010). Aggression Replacement Training stands the test of time. *Reclaiming Children and Youth, 19*(2), 47–50.

Andrews, D. A., & Bonta, J. (2010). *The psychology of criminal conduct.* Newark, NJ: Anderson Publishing Co.

Baillargeon, J., Hoge, S. K., & Penn, J. V. (2010). Addressing the challenge of community reentry among released inmates with serious mental illness. *American Journal of Community Psychology, 46*(3-4), 361–375. doi:10.1007/s10464-010-9345-6

Barnoski, R. (2002). *Washington State's implementation of Aggression Replacement Training for juvenile offenders: Preliminary findings.* Olympia, WA: Washington State Institute for Public Policy. Retrieved from http://www.wsipp.wa.gov/rptfiles/ART.pdf

Bazemore, G., & Umbreit, M. (1995). Rethinking the sanctioning function in juvenile court: Retributive or restorative responses to youth crime. *Crime & Delinquency, 41*(3), 296–316.

Bradshaw, W., Roseborough, D., & Umbreit, M. (2006). The effect of victim offender mediation on juvenile offender recidivism: A meta-analysis. *Conflict Resolution Quarterly, 24*, 87–98.

Butters, R. P., & Vaughan-Eden, V. (2011). The ethics of practicing forensic social work. *Journal of Forensic Social Work, 1*(1), 61–72.

California Corrections Standards (2011). *Mentally ill juveniles in local custody.* Retrieved from https://www.cdcr.ca.gov/COMIO/docs/Menatlly_Ill_Juveniles_In_Local_Custody.pdf

Center for Juvenile Justice Reform, Georgetown University (2008). *Bridging two worlds: Youth involved in the child welfare and juvenile justice systems: A policy guide for improving outcomes.* Retrieved from http://www.napcwa.org/home/docs/BridgingWorldsPolGuide.pdf

Center for the Study and Prevention of Violence (n.d.-a). *Blueprints for violence prevention program models: Functional Family Therapy.* Retrieved from http://www.colorado.edu/cspv/blueprints/modelprograms/FFT.html

Center for the Study and Prevention of Violence (n.d.-b). *Blueprints for violence prevention program models: Multidimensional Treatment Foster Care.* Retrieved from http://www.colorado.edu/cspv/blueprints/modelprograms/MTFC.html

Center for the Study and Prevention of Violence (n.d.-c). *Blueprints for violence prevention program models: Multisystemic Therapy.* Retrieved from http://www.colorado.edu/cspv/blueprints/modelprograms/MST.htm

Chamberlain, P., Leve, L., & DeGarmo, D. (2007). Multidimensional Treatment Foster Care for girls in the juvenile justice system: 2-year follow-up of a randomized clinical trial. *Journal of Consulting and Clinical Psychology, 75*(1), 187–193.

Cocozza, J. J., Skowyra, K. R., & Office of Juvenile Justice and Delinquent Prevention, W. D. C. (2000). Youth with mental health disorders: Issues and emerging responses. *Juvenile Justice, 7*(1), 3–13.

Dodge, K., Dishion, T., & Landsford, K. (2006). *Deviant peer influences in programs for youth: problems and solutions*. New York: The Guilford Press.

Epperson, M., Wolff, N., Morgan, R. D., Fisher, W. H., Frueh, B. C., & Huening, J. (2011). *The next generation of behavioral health and criminal justice interventions: Improving outcomes by improving interventions*. University of Chicago: Center for Behavioral Health Services and Criminal Justice Research. Retrieved from http://www.cbhs-cjr.rutgers.edu/pdfs/The_next_generation_Monograph_Sept_2011.pdf

Fisher, P., & Chamberlain, P. (2000). Multidimensional Treatment Foster Care: A program for intensive parenting, family support, and skill building. *Journal of Emotional and Behavioral Disorders, 8*(3), 155–164.

Glick, B., & Gibbs, J. (2011). *Aggression Replacement Training: A comprehensive intervention for aggressive youth*. Champaign: Research Press.

Hartford, K., Carey, R., & Mendonca, J. (2006). Pre-arrest diversion of people with mental illness: Literature review and international survey. *Behavioral Sciences & the Law, 24*(6), 845–856. doi:10.1002/bsl.738

Lattimore, P. K., Broner, N., Sherman, R., Frisman, L., & Shafer, M. S. (2003). A comparison of prebooking and postbooking diversion programs for mentally ill substance-using individuals with justice involvement. *Journal of Contemporary Criminal Justice, 19*(1), 30–64. doi:10.1177/1043986202239741

Lee, S., Aos, S., Drake, E., Pennucci, A., Miller, M., & Anderson, L. (2012). *Return on investment: Evidence-based options to improve statewide outcomes, April 2012 update*. Olympia, WA: Washington State Institute for Public Policy. Retrieved from http://www.wsipp.wa.gov/rptfiles/12-04-1201.pdf

Lee, B., & Thompson, R. (2008). Comparing outcomes for youth in treatment foster care and family-style group care. *Child Youth Services Review, 30*(7), 746–757.

Littell, J. (2004). Lessons from a systematic review of effects of Multisystemic Therapy. *Children and Youth Services Review, 27*, 445–463.

Littell, J., Popa, M., & Forsythe, B. (2005). Multisystemic Therapy for social, emotional, and behavioral problems in youth aged 10–17. *The Campbell Collaboration*.

Lowenkamp, C. T., Latessa, E. J., & Holsinger, A. (2006). The risk principle in action: What we have learned from 13,676 offenders and 97 correctional programs. *Crime and Delinquency, 52*(1), 1–17.

Lowenkamp, C. T., Latessa, E. J., & Smith, P. (2006). Does correctional program quality really matter? The impact of adhering to the principles of effective intervention. *Criminology and Public Policy, 5*(3), 575–594.

Martin, M. S., Dorken, S. K., Wamboldt, A. D., & Wootten, S. E. (2011). Stopping the revolving door: A meta-analysis on the effectiveness of interventions for criminally involved individuals with major mental disorders. *Law and Human Behavior*. doi:10.1037/h0093963

McCarter, S. A., Haber, M. G., & Kazemi, D. (2010). Models to guide system reform for at-risk youth. *Child and Youth Care Forum, 39*(6), 465–479. doi:10.1007/s10566-010-9113-7.

MST Services Inc. (n.d.). *Proven results*. Retrieved from http://mstservices.com/index.php/proven-results

Nugent, W., Williams, M., & Umbreit, M. (2004). Participation in victim-offender mediation and the prevalence of subsequent delinquent behavior: A meta-analysis. *Research on Social Work Practice, 14*(6), 408–416.

Office of Juvenile Justice and Delinquency Prevention (n.d.-a). *OJJDP model programs guide: Aggression Replacement Training*. Retrieved from http://www.ojjdp.gov/mpg/Aggression%20Replacement%20Training%20%20174;%20%28ART%20%20174;%29-MPGProgramDetail-292.aspx

Office of Juvenile Justice and Delinquency Prevention (n.d.-b). *Wraparound/Case management.* Retrieved from http://www.ojjdp.gov/mpg/progTypesCaseManagementInt.aspx

Ogden, T., & Hagen, K. (2006). Multisystemic Treatment of serious behaviour problems in youth: Sustainability of effectiveness two years after intake. *Child and Adolescent Mental Health, 11*(3), 142–149.

Osher, F., Steadman, H. J., & Barr, H. (2003). A best practice approach to community reentry from jails for inmates with co-occurring disorders: The APIC model. *Crime & Delinquency, 49*(1), 79–96. doi:10.1177/0011128702239237

Pealer, J., & Latessa, E. J. (2004). Applying the principles of effective intervention to juvenile correctional programs. *Corrections Today,* 26–29.

Pullmann, M. D., Kerbs, J., Koroloff, N., Veach-White, E., Gaylor, R., & Sieler, D. (2006). Juvenile offenders with mental health needs: Reducing recidivism using wraparound. *Crime & Delinquency, 52*(3), 375–397.

Puzzanchera, C., & Kang, W. (2011). *Easy access to juvenile court statistics: 1985–2009.* Online. Available: http://www.ojjdp.gov/ojstatbb/ezajcs/

Rice, M. E., & Harris, G. T. (1997). The treatment of mentally disordered offenders. *Psychology, Public Policy, and Law, 3*(1), 126–183. doi:10.1037/1076-8971.3.1.126

Schaeffer, C., & Borduin, C. (2005). Long-term follow-up to a randomized clinical trial of Multisystemic Therapy with serious and violent juvenile offenders. *Journal of Consulting and Clinical Psychology, 73*(3), 445–453.

Sexton, T., & Turner, C. (2010). The effectiveness of Functional Family Therapy for youth with behavioral problems in a community practice setting. *Journal of Family Psychology, 24*(3), 399–348.

Sherman, L., & Strang, H. (2007). *Restorative justice: The evidence.* London: Smith Institute.

Skowyra, K. R., & Cocozza, J. J. (2007). *Blueprint for change: A comprehensive model for the identification & treatment of youth with mental health needs in contact with the juvenile justice system.* Office of Juvenile Justice and Delinquency Prevention. Online. Retrieved from http://www.ncmhjj.com/Blueprint/pdfs/Blueprint.pdf

Smith, P., Gendreau, P., & Swartz, K., (2009). Validating the principles of effective intervention: A systematic review of the contributions of meta-analysis in the field of corrections. *Victims and Offenders, 4,* 1–22.

Smith, D. (2004). Risk, reinforcement, retention in treatment, and reoffending for boys and girls in Multidimensional Treatment Foster Care. *Journal of Emotional and Behavioral Disorders, 12*(1), 38–48.

Suter, J., & Bruns, E. (2009). Effectiveness of the wraparound process for children with emotional behavioral disorders: A meta-analysis. *Clinical Child and Family Psychology Review, 12,* 336–351.

Trupin, E., Kerns, S. E. U., Walker, S. C., DeRobertis, M. T., & Stewart, D. G. (2011). Family integrated transitions: A promising program for juvenile offenders with co-occurring disorders. *Journal of Child & Adolescent Substance Abuse, 20*(5), 421–436. doi:10.1080/10 67828x.2011.614889

Umbreit, M. (2001). *The handbook of victim offender mediation.* San Francisco: Jossey-Bass.

Van Ness, D., & Heetderks, K. (2002). *Restoring justice* (2nd ed.) Cincinnati, OH: Anderson Publishing Company.

Walsh, J., & Holt, D. (1999). Jail diversion for people with psychiatric disabilities: The sheriffs' perspective. *Psychiatric Rehabilitation Journal, 23*(2), 153–160.

Wexler, D. B., & Winick, B. J. (1996). *Law in a therapeutic key: Developments in therapeutic jurisprudence.* Durham, NC: Carolina Academic Press.

Wilson, A., & Draine, J. (2006). Collaborations between criminal justice and mental health systems for prisoner reentry. *Psychiatric Services (Washington, D.C.), 57*(6), 875–878.

Wraparound Milwaukee (2009). *2009 end of year report.* Retrieved from http://www. milwaukee.gov/ImageLibrary/Groups/cntyHHS/Wraparound/2009WraparoundAnnualR eport.pdf

Zagar, R., Busch, K., & Hughes, J. (2009). Empirical risk factors for delinquency and best treatments: Where do we go from here? *Psychological Reports, 104,* 279–308.

Zehr, H. (1990). *Changing lenses: A new focus for crime and justice.* Scottsdale, PA: Herald Press.

Zehr, H. (2002). *The little book of restorative justice.* Intercourse, PA: Good Books.

15

Neighborhood Street Gangs: Patterns, Activities, and Community-Based Programs

Paul D. Steele

■ Case Example

■ *My name is Carlos T. Ramirez Jr. I was born in El Paso, Texas. My parents are Carlos and Elvia; I've got two younger brothers and a sister. My family was of very low income, trying to survive in the deep poverty conditions of what I call "barrio jumpers." Living from one barrio to the other, trying to climb up the ladder to become a middle-class family, but only finding the same barrio problems and poverty: regardless of the poor barrio, it offered the same old struggles, pain, and miseries....There was no water, no gas, no electricity. I remember having to use a wooden shed restroom outside, taking showers with salt water, pumping water every day from beneath the earth, and living in total darkness, with a flashlight or small petroleum lamp. We had to go miles away for food.*

■ *I became the one to do a lot of the housework, to help my parents out. This is how I learned to do some good cooking as I cooked for my two little brothers (my sister wasn't born yet). After school I washed the dishes, cleaned the house, washed some of the clothes, did the outside house yard work, and helped my neighbors. To us, this was climbing up the ladder from being a poor family to becoming a part of the middle class.*

■ *When I started school, I had friends that came from broken homes or broken families, from single mothers or still living in deep poverty. As children we only saw a struggle of survival. This kind of survival only made me want to defend the poor people, by fighting the middle-class students. I became a real good street fighter, to where when I was in junior high school the high school boys looked up to me.*

■ *I started a low-rider bike club named the Warlords; we stole all the bikes we could from the middle-class children just so the poor kids could fix them up and ride in style. We cruised through other barrios just to show others that the poor kids had something to be proud of, not realizing that it was all achieved through crime. Soon, other poor kids from other barrios started to do the same and would join us in our low-rider bike caravan across the streets of the city.*

■ *People started to know who the Warlords were: we had jackets with our bike club name. Our biggest error was when we started to use graffiti on city walls to promote what some said was a children war: others thought the poor children had declared war on the middle-class or rich children and their families, and even communities. None of us intended for it to be a violent war, nor did we see it that way: we called it survival.*

■ *The violence didn't start till the gangs from the poor side of the city started to call us a threat. Soon it was a hard struggle between our poor low-rider bike club versus other barrio gangs. This kind of encounter forced the Warlords to become a social club; we called it "The Chucos Unides," referring to United Reformers. But the word "Chuco" was now seen as a different term under a gangsta image. So to the barrio gangs we were not united reformers, but united gangstas. We only had intentions to want to help one another or others, especially the poor people, but became involved in the gang barrio warfare.*

■ *Because of my full devotion in responding to gang attacks towards us, I was soon baptized with the nickname of "El Famouso Loco Sir Alcatraz." There was a rumor that, because I had so many enemies and had done a lot of damage everywhere the city, cops planned to not arrest me so I could get killed by another gang. At the age of 13, I was already telling my mother to "start saving money and prepare yourself to bury me before I turn 15."*

■ *"La Vida Loca:"[1] the youth crimes were too many. Arson to a public school, drive-bys, burglaries, robberies, arson on a Catholic church, graffiti wars, drug deals, stealing cars, fights, gang rumbles...we even got accused of flipping a train out of the railroad tracks. These were some of the youth crimes I got accused of or connected to. But one problem existed: no evidence to prove anything on me. These kinds of crime activities earned me power and respect to where on my back, I tattooed the word "Controla" (control) in huge Old English letters to show others that as long as I was alive, and I could go into any barrio, and do my damage and walk away, I was in control.*

■ *I guess the cops got tired of waiting to see someone kill me so, when I was 17 years old, they used another way to try and stop me and I got sent to the prison system for the first time. I arrived as a leader of "The El Paso Tips," that later on would become known as Barrio Azteca or Barrio Aztlan, and become Texas's most wanted prison gang. By the time I was 26 I had been in prison four times, and became an enhanced criminal. At 27 years old I got a habitual in prison for a crime done to me. I got stabbed while asleep in my own prison cell, but because the attackers left the same shank behind, I was charged with possession of a deadly weapon in a penal institution, which carries 2 to 20 years. I was given 40 stacked on my 12 years, making my sentence into 52 years.*

■ *All my life I have asked myself, "Was I truly a sinister criminal that lost control and lost the values, morals, principles and standards that my family, close friends and society tried to teach me?" Or, "Was I only a good gangsta that honestly thought that the crimes I was doing were my best weapon to use in a war of survival against deep poverty, oppression, and racism?" Soon it all gets blended into your criminal life because you are programmed to believe that the gangsta life of force, ignorance and a selfish gangsta pride should be respected or accepted. (Ramirez, 2008)*

What is a street gang? While there are many definitions, a consensus view is that:

> A street gang is any durable, street-oriented youth group whose involvement in illegal activity is part of its group identity. (Klein & Maxson, 2006, p. 4)

A street gang is a group that persists for some time, even if there is significant turnover in its membership. Those who make up the gang are primarily adolescents and young adults who engage in criminal activities and spend a good deal of their time in the community outside of home, work, or school. The social environment in which they live and interact with others strongly influences their criminal behaviors. As shown in Carlos' life, neighborhoods provide a source of personal and group identity, situations that produce crime, and venues in which official and informal efforts to control gangs occur.

■ Scope of the Problem

The proliferation of street gangs has become a source of national concern: the National Youth Gang Center estimated that there were 29,400 gangs in the United States in 2010, with 756,000 members (Egley, 2010). Gangs were traditionally thought of as a problem in only the most impoverished and disorganized inner-city neighborhoods, but they are now a threat in smaller cities, suburban areas, and rural communities (Klein & Maxson, 2006). Gang behavior has grown dramatically between 2002 and 2010 in suburban counties (22%), rural counties (16%), and smaller cities (15%), as well as in larger cities (13%) (Egley, 2010). Their growth has resulted in scores of state and federal agencies investing in research and action programs, thousands of police departments and youth service agencies devising strategies to prevent and intervene with the activities of gang members, hundreds of thousands of crime victims, and widespread fear in areas where gangs are found (Klein & Maxson, 2006). The annual violent death rate for Boston street gang members is estimated at 1% to 2% (Kennedy, Piehl, & Braga, 1996) and is as high as 7% among gang members acting as street-level drug sellers in Chicago (Levitt & Venkatesh, 2000). Even those like Carlos who survive *La Vida Loca* suffer from diminished life outcomes because of their participation in gangs (Klein & Maxson, 2006).

As the number of gangs and gang members increased, so has the seriousness of their criminal offending. No longer are gangs the social groups of the 1920–40s, engaged in petty acts of vandalism and vagrancy in impoverished inner-city neighborhoods (Thrasher, 1927, 1936; Whyte, 1943). Law enforcement agencies report that gang-related homicides increased by 13% in very large cities between 2009 and 2010, and more than half of the homicides in Chicago and Los Angeles in 2010 involved gang members (Egley & Howell, 2012). Much of this violence has been attributed to the propensity of members to possess and use firearms, including high-powered automatic weapons (Bjerregaard & Lizotte, 1995; Braga & Kennedy, 2002; Curry & Decker, 2003; Decker & Van Winkle, 1996; Egley & Howell, 2012; Howell, 1998; Howell & Bilchik, 1995; Huff, 2002; Lizotte, Krohn, Howell, Tobin, & Howard, 2000; Pogrebin, Stretesky, & Unnithan, 2009; Steele, Reeves, & Hare, 2012).

■ Gang Members

Results from the 2009 National Youth Gang Survey (NYGS) indicate that approximately 90% of gang members are males. However, the NYGS relies on official police reports, so differences in police responses to suspected gang members might influence these results. Self-report studies have typically found more female gang members (Bjerregaard & Smith, 1993; Esbensen & Huizinga, 1993; Maxson & Whitlock, 2002; Moore & Hagedorn, 2001), up to as much as 38% of gang members (Esbensen & Winfree, 1998).

Gang offenders, as a group, tend to be relatively young (Curry, Ball, & Fox, 1994; Hill, Howell, Hawkins, & Battin-Pearson, 1999). As reported in the NYGS, most gang members are under 24 years of age. In the mid-1990s, the proportion of gang members who were under 18 years of age was roughly equal to that of adults, but by 2002 juveniles made up only around 30% of gang members. The percentage of juvenile gang members recovered to slightly more than one third of overall gang membership by 2006 (National Gang Center, 2009), and that ratio is sustained in the most recent analysis (National Gang Center, 2011). Gangs in cities and their suburbs have a larger proportion of adult members than gangs in small towns and rural areas, most likely because urban gangs have been established for a longer time (Riedel & Welsh, 2011).

Gangs tend to be racially and ethnically homogeneous groups, and minorities are consistently overrepresented among gang members relative to the general population (Curry, Ball, & Fox, 1994; Esbensen & Huizinga 1993). Slightly less than half of gangs are exclusively or predominantly African American in membership, one third are Hispanic, and about 10% are White (National Gang Center, 2011).

■ Gang Activities

Gang members engage in higher rates of serious violent offending (Battin-Pearson, Thornberry, Hawkins, & Krohn, 1998; Bellair & McNulty, 2009; Gordon et al., 2004; Pogrebin et al., 2009; Steele et al., 2012; Thornberry, Krohn, Lizotte, Smith, & Tobin, 2003) and drug offenses (Egley & Howell, 2012; Gatti, Tremblay, Vitaro, & McDuff, 2005) than non-affiliated youth. They are arrested more frequently (Curry, 2000; Battin-Pearson et al., 1998; Thornberry et al., 2003) and begin their serious offending at an earlier age (Steele et al., 2012).

There are two popular explanations why gang members are more engaged in serious and frequent criminal offending. One explanation is that there is a selection effect: those at the highest risk for offending are attracted to joining a gang. The alternative view is that gangs facilitate criminal activity. Gangs might facilitate crime by making criminal opportunities more available to members, increase access to crime facilitators such as guns and drugs, increase the likelihood of successfully completing crimes by providing willing crime partners, and espouse an ethos of violent retaliation for perceived slights and threats (Anderson, 1990; Katz, 1988; Steele et al., 2012). Criminal activity increases when young people join gangs and decreases when they leave (Klein & Maxson, 2006). Most likely gang selection and enhancement dynamics interact to explain the higher offending rates of gang members, although research studies have reached varied conclusions about the relative influence of each and the conditions under which one is more influential (e.g., Gatti et al., 2005; Gordon et al., 2004; Lacourse, Nagin, Tremblay, Vitaro, & Claes, 2003; Thornberry et al., 2003).

Joining and Leaving Gangs

Several scholars have investigated why young people join gangs. Gangs become more salient in the lives of some youth because of the decline in the influence of families and schools (Bjerregaard & Lizotte, 1995; Blumstein, 1995; Moore, 1991; Vigil, 1988) and because gangs offer companionship, support, and identity (Pogrebin et al., 2009; Thrasher, 1927). Gangs can also provide some protection in high-crime neighborhoods (Decker & Van Winkle, 1996).

Those who are at greatest risk for joining gangs exhibit problem behaviors such as aggressiveness and impulsivity at an early age (Cox, 1996; Craig, Vitaro, Gagnon, & Tremblay, 2002, Esbensen & Deschenes, 1998; Esbensen & Weerman, 2005; Gatti et al., 2005; Jolliffe & Farrington, 2009; Lahey, Gordon, Loeber, Stouthamer-Loeber, & Farrington, 1999; Maxson, Whitlock, & Klein, 1998; Thornberry et al., 2003). They are also likely to have associated with delinquent peers before joining and have come to espouse personal attitudes supportive of delinquent and gang behavior (Bjerregaard & Smith, 1993; Bradshaw, 2005; Branch, 1997; Craig et al., 2002; Eitle et al., 2004; Esbensen & Deschenes, 1998; Esbensen & Weerman, 2005; Esbensen, Winfree, He, & Taylor, 2001; Hill et al., 1999; Lahey et al., 1999; Thornberry et al., 2003). Future gang members are also more likely to have experienced negative life events, including school expulsion and disruption of intimate social relations such as with a parent (Maxson, Whitlock, & Klein, 1998; Thornberry et al., 2003), and to have been raised in homes where they have experienced poor parental supervision (Bradshaw, 2005; Esbensen & Deschenes, 1998; Esbensen & Weerman, 2005; Hill et al., 1999; Thornberry et al., 2003).

Decker and Lauritsen (2002) point out that no systematic study has been completed to explain why members choose to leave a gang. However, descriptive studies generally describe the process of leaving as very difficult since it requires rejecting one's friends (Vigil, 2002). Life course theories indicate that disengaging from criminal groups and lifestyles is an outcome of personal maturation and changing life conditions (Laub & Sampson,

1993). Timing is also an important influence, as either personal victimization or the victimization of a friend can cause a gang member to seriously consider leaving, at least for a period of time (Decker & Lauritsen, 2002; Pyrooz & Decker, 2011).

■ Community Influences on Gangs

> Individual behavior is a product of an interaction between the person and the setting. Most criminological theory pays attention only to the first, asking why certain people might be more criminally inclined or less so. This neglects the second, the important features of each setting that help translate criminal inclinations into action. (Felson & Clarke, 1998, p. 1)

Criminal activity is not randomly distributed but is highly concentrated in crime "hot spots" (Anselin, Cohen, Cook, Gorr, & Tita, 2000; Hipp, Tita, & Greenbaum, 2009; Pierce, Spaar, & Briggs, 1988; Sherman & Eck, 2002; Sherman, Gartin, & Buerger, 1989) and even "micro-locales" within neighborhoods (Steele, 2005, 2006). This is also the case for the presence of gang members and their criminal activities (e.g., Rosenfeld, Bray, & Egley, 1999; Tita, Cohen, & Engberg, 2005).

Community

It is important to define what is meant by "community," since it conveys a range of meanings in the popular and scientific literature. Generally, communities can be defined in cultural and ecological terms. A community could describe a group of people who share particular opinions, attitudes, beliefs, and practices. This sort of cultural definition is helpful in understanding gangs in that shared values promote gang cohesion and become the basis for informal neighborhood adaptation and official reaction to gangs. Alternatively, communities could be defined as a specific territory in a larger locale. This definition is also important in that it can describe political and administrative units and the geographical boundaries for services from programs that serve neighborhoods and individuals.

These definitions are not mutually exclusive; as the pioneers of urban sociology quickly discovered, citizens do not choose their residence and activity space randomly within a larger locale but array themselves in "natural areas" that have emerged through the confluence of ecological, economic, social, and political influences (Park, 1916; Sampson, 2006; Suttles & Suttles, 1972). With the availability of various government data and advanced spatial analytical techniques, it is possible to empirically define natural areas as communities within larger locales. As a consequence, research on social dynamics and the assessment of geographically situated prevention and intervention programs has been increasingly likely to define communities and the activities within them based on a logic of space, street patterns, travel times, and social networks (Grannis, 1998; Laurin, Hare, & Steele, 2012; Sampson, 2006; Steele et al., 2012).

Strategically, anti-gang programs targeting defined gang-ridden neighborhoods are more likely to succeed than those attempting to produce change in a larger geopolitical area. Programs tailored to the conditions of a particular neighborhood, or even a smaller space such as a city block, have the potential to more intensively focus resources, adapt to the immediate cultural environment, and allow for more interaction between gang members, local residents, and those implementing the gang program (Steele, 2005, 2006).

Community Crime Theories

The level of gang activity varies dramatically from place to place, suggesting that community factors have an important influence on gangs. There are a number of explanations of how communities influence crime. Welsh and Holshi (2002) group these explanations into four theories: social disorganization, community disorder, community empowerment, and community regeneration.

The original descriptions of social disorganization theory contend that social order is maintained in a neighborhood primarily through social institutions and informal groups. From this perspective neighborhood poverty, residential mobility, and ethnic heterogeneity erode these mechanisms of social control, and delinquency is the result (Sampson & Lauritsen, 1994; Shaw & McKay, 1942). More contemporary versions of the theory implicate social isolation, the breakdown of families, and the loss of social networks as sources of social disorganization and crime (Sampson, Raudenbush, & Earls, 1997).

Community disorder theory suggests that relatively minor incivilities and disorderly behaviors lead to more serious street crime and urban decay. Disorder begins in the form of loitering, panhandling, and public intoxication, and physical indicators such as abandoned buildings, vandalized public spaces, graffiti, and litter (Skogan, 1990). As decay becomes more significant conventional citizens become more isolated from each other, diminishing their ability to control serious offending and the inroads of gangs into the area (Golub, Johnson, Taylor, & Eterno, 2004; Kelling & Coles, 1997; Wilson & Kelling, 1982).

Community empowerment theory emphasizes the importance of residents in neighborhood management. When citizens become involved in their community, they have a greater stake in its welfare and are willing to take responsibility for its quality of life. Residents develop deeper social networks, satisfaction in their ability to effect change, and a shared sense of mutual concern and collective efficacy (Bennett, 1998), which counteract criminal influences in the neighborhood.

Community regeneration theory argues that stronger social networks alone are not sufficient to reduce crime in poverty-stricken and politically marginalized neighborhoods. Crime prevention also requires sharing government and private-sector resources with economically depressed and socially disorganized neighborhoods. The influx of social and economic capital (Woolcock, 2001) keeps more prosperous residents with conventional values from leaving, creates opportunities for young people to succeed in socially acceptable ways, prevents physical and social decay, and otherwise limits criminal opportunities in which gangs develop (Hope, 1995). Regeneration of the community reduces reliance on traditional intervention and suppression tactics of the criminal justice system and improves the quality of life for residents by strengthening conventional pathways to success (Bennett, 1998; Taub, Taylor, & Dunham, 1984).

In summary, community theories predict that neighborhoods suffering from disorganization and decay are more likely to have higher rates of crime due to physical and social deterioration, impoverishment, and instability that cause the loss of social cohesion and informal social control, and influx of those with criminal intentions. Conversely, neighborhoods prevent crime by strengthening social networks, empowering families, promoting prosocial opportunities, prohibiting delinquent peer groups, and improving community resources and government support.

■ Classifying Community Anti-Gang Programs

Prevention and Intervention

From a public health perspective, anti-gang programs can be classified as primary, secondary, or tertiary prevention. Primary and secondary prevention programs intervene before an undesired condition appears, while the aim of tertiary prevention is to intervene with existing undesired conditions and reduce the chance of their recurrence.

Primary gang-prevention programs are implemented with only the most general criteria for inclusion in the service population. Community-based primary gang-prevention programs run little risk of misidentifying service recipients, since all young people theoretically have at least some chance of becoming gang members, and most neighborhoods have at least some children and adolescents. An example of broadly implemented gang primary prevention is the Gang Resistance Education and Training (GREAT) program, discussed in more detail below.

Secondary gang-prevention programs also intend to prevent undesired gang activities before they occur but use information about the traits and situations of known gang members as a guide to identify others with similar characteristics as service recipients. These traits and situations might be based on the most general descriptions of at-risk individuals, such as just knowing that a child resides in an area where gang behavior is prevalent. On the other hand, some secondary prevention programs have stringent eligibility criteria that consider children's family and social conditions, their psychological state, or their behaviors believed to put them at risk for joining a gang. Primary and secondary prevention programs are often broad in their scope and can affect the lives of children, their parents, and others in the community. While not setting the prevention of gang activity as their objective, they can still substantially reduce it (Greenwood, 2007).

Those who administer anti-gang interventions, or tertiary prevention programs, can confidently identify their service population since they have already engaged in the behaviors that the intervention hopes to prevent in the future. Occasionally gang behavior is reduced by natural social dynamics that promote member attrition (Decker & Lauritsen, 2002), but intervention programs work intentionally to reduce the prevalence of gang activities. While it is generally understood that efforts to prevent "rotten outcomes" are most effective when started early in life (Agnew, 2005; Schorr, 1986) and the most successful approaches deter youth from joining gangs in the first place (Klein & Maxson, 2006), our response to gangs in America is mostly reactive and interventionist in nature.

Composition and Context

Anti-gang programs can also differ based on their assumptions about the makeup of communities. The compositional perspective assumes that communities can be completely understood by knowing the behaviors and characteristics of residents and others who spend time there, their groups, and local institutions (Kirby, 2008). Neighborhood anti-gang programs that develop with this image of a community in mind intervene with the people, on an individual or collective basis, that influence gang members within specific geopolitical units or natural service areas.

The contextual perspective assumes that the actions of those who reside and spend time in a neighborhood are influenced by more than their personal traits and propensities: the structure of the community itself is influential beyond the characteristics of individuals (Kirby, 2008). Criminologists have consistently discovered that the collective characteristics of a neighborhood influence local crime rates beyond the mere aggregation of personal risks for criminal behavior (Bursik & Grasmick, 1993; Hope, 1995; Sampson, 1987). From a contextual perspective, programs that intervene with general community conditions such as poverty, unemployment, family instability, and health-related problems can have an indirect but powerful influence on gang-related delinquency and criminality.

Anti-gang control strategies can address both compositional and contextual influences within neighborhoods. For example, a program could act to mitigate personal risk factors for the youth who compose the potential gang population of a community and also reduce the criminal opportunities available to them. Programs that emphasize person–environment interactions seem to be promising. Wikstrom, in describing his Situated Action Theory, concludes that youth who exhibit high levels of impulsivity are particularly vulnerable to committing delinquent acts in neighborhoods that offer many criminal opportunities (Wikstrom, 2006, 2012; Wikstrom, Oberwittler, Treiber, & Hardie, 2012).

■ Criminals and Crimes

Theory-driven anti-gang programs can also be distinguished by their strategy to either change people or change events. Most theories of crime that consciously or unconsciously form the basis of program interventions are dispositional in nature: they are based on explanations of how offenders differ from non-offenders (Sutherland, 1947). Anti-gang programs grounded in dispositional theories attempt to make gang members or potential gang members be and act like their more conventional peers. On the other hand, there is a growing body of situational crime theories that focus on crime events (Birkbeck & LaFree, 1993). Anti-gang programs that have situational theories as their foundation intend to reduce the prevalence of gang-related criminal events. While dispositional programs might also reduce the occurrence of gang crimes by changing gang members into law-abiding citizens, situational programs strategize to lessen the chances that gang members can complete a crime and avoid detection, thus reducing their motivation to offend. Situational anti-gang programs alter the judgment and actions of potential victims, the environments in which crimes are likely to occur, and the situational influences that precipitate and facilitate criminal action (Clarke, 1992).

■ Anti-Gang Programs

Using the concepts presented in this section, Figure 15.1 presents a classification scheme for anti-gang programs, with examples. Programs can be grouped as (1) preventing or intervening with gangs and gang members, (2) addressing the characteristics of gang members and principal others who compose the community or the community's structural context that facilitates gang activity, and (3) altering the dispositions of gang members or addressing the situational factors that influence the likelihood of gang crimes.

While space does not allow for a discussion of the thousands of anti-gang programs, some that are well known are described and similar programs are

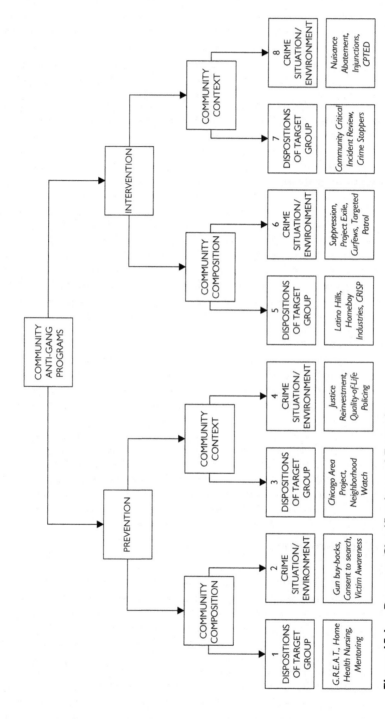

Figure 15.1 Program Classification and Examples.

referenced to illustrate each program category. Operationally, few programs fit neatly into just one of these theoretically generated program categories. Sometimes this is unintentional: programs can suffer from "mission creep" as they set new goals, identify new client needs, lose or receive funding, or are affected by political and community pressures. On the other hand, some programs attempt to integrate several gang-control strategies into a single comprehensive community model. This includes the well-known Office of Juvenile Justice and Delinquency Prevention's Comprehensive Gang Model (Howell & Bilchick, 1995; Mukasey, Sedgwick & Flores, 2007), also known as the "Spergel Model" (Spergel, Wa, & Sosa, 2006). One of the serious problems with comprehensive approaches is to develop effective coordination between many agencies and sub-programs (Klein & Maxson, 2006), but one comprehensive model has been quite successful in reducing gang-related violence: Operation Ceasefire, also known as the Boston Gun Project (Braga, Kennedy, Waring & Piehl, 2001; Kennedy, 1998; Kennedy, Piehl, & Braga, 1996), which used a variety of suppression and intervention strategies to dramatically reduce gang firearm crimes and victimization in its service area.

Prevention Programs that Target Individual Traits and Dispositions

An exemplar prevention program that intends to change the traits and dispositions of juveniles who live in a community is Gang Resistance Education and Training (GREAT). A school-based program that has been provided to a broad range of middle-school students, GREAT deters youth from joining gangs, prevents violent and criminal behavior, and encourages positive relations with police officers. It consists of 13 classroom sessions taught by uniformed police officers and employs a cognitive-behavioral curriculum that teaches responsibility, nonviolent conflict resolution, goal setting, cultural diversity, engaging with prosocial peers, and how one can meet one's social needs without joining a gang. Esbensen, Peterson, Taylor, and Osgood (2012) found that when GREAT was properly implemented, participants were 39% less likely to join a gang than students in a control group, when measured 1 year after the training, and 24% less likely 4 years after the training.

Several programs that support the healthy development of families and their supervision of children have been proven to deter children from joining gangs (Bradshaw, 2005; Esbensen & Weerman, 2005; Gatti et al., 2005; Klein & Maxson, 2006; Maxson & Whitlock, 2002; Thornberry et al., 2003). One of the best-known parent education programs is one reported by Olds, Henderson, Chamberlin, and Tatelbaum (1986) in which nurses provided home visits during the mother's pregnancy and up to 2 years after the child's birth. Nurses give advice concerning the risk of smoking and drinking during pregnancy, fetal and infant nutrition, child development, and childrearing practices. The researchers found that families receiving home nurse visits were less likely to abuse or neglect their children compared to a comparison group of families not receiving home visits. This was particularly evident among poor, unmarried teenage mothers: 19% of non-visited mothers but only 4% of visited mothers were abusive or neglectful. A 15-year follow-up found that children born to lower-class unwed mothers who participated in the nurse home visitation program were only half as likely to have been arrested as children who received no visits (Kitzman et al., 2010; Olds et al., 1998).

Other programs: Big Brothers/Big Sisters (Tierney, Grossman, & Resch, 2000).

Prevention Programs that Target Individual Actions in Crime Situations

Gang members are particularly violent, and many of their acts against others are committed with firearms. One way to reduce gang violence is to reduce gang members' motivation to act violently during confrontations in the community by removing their guns. Gun removal is a particularly controversial issue at a time of mass killings in schools and other public places, and the proliferation of concealed carry permit laws. While proposed laws that would restricting gun ownership have been passed by state or federal legislators, an approach that is popular with the public is gun buybacks. Two of these programs, in St. Louis (Rosenfeld, 1996) and Seattle (Callahan, Rivara, & Koepsell, 1996), have been evaluated to determine their impact on neighborhood violence (Welsh & Holshi, 2002). Depending on the program, residents were given between 6 days and 2 months to turn in guns, in exchange for cash vouchers. None of these programs appeared to be effective in reducing gun violence. Rosenfeld concluded that St. Louis residents owned several other guns and would eventually replace those they turned in. In Seattle, Callahan, Rivara, and Koepsell estimated that only about 1% of guns in the community were actually relinquished, mostly from low-risk groups such as women and the elderly. Kennedy, Piehl, and Braga (1996) conclude that gun buybacks fail because they do not stem the flow of replacement guns into the neighborhood. Still, gun buyback programs are popular and capture media attention, as in the aftermath of the mass school shooting in Newtown, Connecticut.

Another interesting approach to removing guns from the community was the Consent to Search program in St. Louis, which was intended to reduce juvenile firearm possession. In its initial phase, police officers went door to door in high-crime neighborhoods and asked parents for permission to search their home and remove any illegal or unwanted firearms, without legal consequence for them or their children. Consent was granted in almost all cases, and hundreds of guns were seized. Unfortunately, as the program progressed political forces undermined the intent and process of the program, diminishing its success beyond its initial phase (Decker & Rosenfeld, 2004).

Other programs: Awareness programs to avoid burglaries and criminal encounters for potential victims (Bell & Jenkins, 1993; Farrell & Pease, 2001; Pain, 2000).

Prevention Programs that Target Community Resources

One of the best-known programs that attempted to reduce juvenile delinquency by improving the conditions of neighborhood residents is the Chicago Area Project (CAP). The program was first implemented by Clifford Shaw in the 1930s in three neighborhoods, including Russell Square, an impoverished area in South Chicago, where juvenile gangs had proliferated. Much of CAP's work is the development of youth welfare organizations, involving local residents to carry out the work. While implementation strategies vary from neighborhood to neighborhood, CAP has shown that residents of neighborhoods with high rates of crime, delinquency, and gang activity are capable of action in response to the problems of the child residents (Kobrin, 1959). In 1981, a report by the Rand Corporation concluded that the program has been effective in organizing neighborhoods and controlling delinquency (Schlossman & Sedlak, 1983).

Other programs: Neighborhood Watch (Garofalo & McLeod, 1989; Rosenbaum, 1987), Resident Empowerment (Perkins, 1995).

Prevention Programs that Improve the Neighborhood Environment

A newer approach to improving the community context for residents is the justice reinvestment initiative now operating in 12 states. The goal of justice reinvestment is to redirect a small portion of prison budgets to rebuilding human resources and neighborhood infrastructure, including schools, parks, health care facilities, and public spaces (Tucker & Cadora, 2003). The process of justice reinvestment involves (1) analyzing the communities from which incarcerated offenders come and where they will return after prison or jail, (2) developing options for generating savings and increasing public safety, reinvesting the savings in high-crime communities, and (3) measuring the impact of the program (Clear, 2011).

Results of the program have been mixed: when the model is followed, justice reinvestment is successful in reducing crime in high-risk neighborhoods (Council on State Governments, 2013). However, when program administrators deviate from the model, the results are much less successful. In some jurisdictions program administrators have chosen to put the savings into more government programs that do not improve the community infrastructure (Clear, 2011). Rather, efforts to improve the physical characteristics of the neighborhood and provide economic opportunities to reverse economic decay are important to reducing crime (Taylor, 2001).

Other programs: Empowerment Zones (Krupka & Noonan, 2009; Oakley & Tsao, 2006), Quality of Life Policing (Bratton, 1995; Golub et al., 2004).

Intervention Programs that Target Individual Gang Members

Programs that reduce the social cohesion of gangs and encourage gang members to leave the gang have proven to be effective intervention strategies in gang-ridden neighborhoods. For example, the Latino Hills Project in Los Angeles assisted gang members in leaving a gang by providing tutoring, job placement, counseling, and recreation services to gang members on an individual basis. The program has been found to reduce gang member arrest rates and the cohesion of the gang, although the changes were not long-lasting (Klein, 1971). A similar approach is Homeboy Industries, which intervenes with individual members in job training and placement in the Boyle Heights neighborhood of Los Angeles, long known as an area of concentrated gang activity (Boyle, 2010).

An alternative approach is to intervene with gang members to overcome inter-gang violence. The Crisis Intervention Services Project (CRISP) operated for 10 months in a gang-ridden area of Chicago, providing mediation and crisis intervention services. An evaluation of the program reported moderate success in deterring inter-gang incidents, with greater impact on younger gang members (Spergel, 1986). Further, one of the more effective comprehensive anti-gang programs in Chicago incorporated mediation services as a part of its overall approach (Spergel & Grossman, 1997).

One popular yet ineffective program to intervene with gang members on a group basis is the "detached worker program." Social workers counsel gang members in their homes and on the street to re-engage with the conventional aspects of their community. These programs were found to be not only ineffective in Boston (Miller, 1962), but actually counterproductive in that they increased gang cohesiveness and activity in Los Angeles (Klein, 1968). Still, we find detached worker programs operating in several cities (Steele & Guerin, 1996).

Intervention Programs that Reduce Opportunities for Gang Activity

Intervention programs of this type are the most common, and most visible, strategies that criminal justice agencies use for dealing with gang crimes. One way to change the neighborhood social environment and consequent opportunity structure for gang activity is through the use of suppression tactics. Individual and collective gang-suppression programs increase the community tracking of gang members and law enforcement intelligence-gathering activities. Suppression can also involve efforts to enhance the detection and investigation of crimes in gang-ridden neighborhoods, the specialized prosecution of gang members, and imposition of sentencing enhancements for gang members. One strategy for suppressing gang crime is the removal of core gang members from the community. An example of gang member removal is Project Exile, a federal program with enhanced penalties for gun law offenses. Federal penalties for felons in possession of weapons, possession of illegal weapons, and other less common firearm offenses are greater than those in most states, are more likely to result in mandatory prison sentences, and often "exile" offenders to prisons far from their home community, effectively insulating the community from that particular core gang member (Rosenfeld, Fornagno, & Baumer, 2005).

Other suppression programs do not seek the physical removal of gang members but restrict their movements and interactions in the community. For example, juvenile curfew laws were found to reduce gang activity in Dallas (Fritsch, Caeti, & Taylor, 1999), Detroit (Hunt & Weiner, 1977), and Phoenix (LeBoeuf, 1996) and have been found to significantly reduce juvenile crime in scores of larger cities (Klein, 2012).

Other programs: Targeted Patrol (Braga, 2001; McGarrell, Chermak, & Weiss, 2002), Police Saturation (Worrall & Kovandzic, 2010).

Intervention Programs that Improve Community Resources

Programs in this category can be distinguished from prevention programs that target community resources in that the criminal behaviors of gang members can trigger changes in the orientations and dispositions of community members, alter the neighborhood context, and thus reduce gang activity in that area. A program that adopts this approach is the Community Critical Incident Review (CCIR) program. CCIR grew out of the "New Criminal Justice" approach (Klofas, Hipple, & McGarrell, 2010) that integrates crime research and analysis with community action to control crime. While criminal incident reviews have been implemented in various forms in many communities, participants are usually restricted to criminal justice professionals and other experts with the intention of developing strategic and tactical plans to mitigate emerging crime in a specific locale (Klofas et al., 2006), including gang-ridden neighborhoods (Braga, Pierce, McDevitt, Bond, & Cronin, 2008). CCIR is somewhat different in that it engages community residents immediately after a significant crime event has occurred to help in the police investigation by providing suspect and background information. They also are encouraged to cooperate with government agencies and neighborhood groups in implementing targeted crime-prevention activities within narrowly defined areas, such as an apartment complex or a city block (Steele, 2006). CCIR can contribute to other more general community partnerships to improve the community context and reduce crime, such as the Operation Weed and Seed projects that exist throughout the country (Dunworth, Mills, Cordner, & Greene, 1999).

Other programs: Crime Stoppers (Rosenbaum, Lurigio, & Lavrakas, 1989).

Intervention Programs that Block Neighborhood Gang Crime Opportunities

Several situational anti-gang programs attempt to alter the environment in which gang members commit their crimes. The selection of places in need of alteration begins with a spatial analysis of the community to pinpoint locations where gang members commit crimes, congregate, or are likely to encounter rivals. There are scores of environmental approaches to eradicate crime locations.[2] One such program is *nuisance abatement*. In general, this amounts to removing a community "nuisance," by whatever legal means necessary. Some abatement strategies seek to relocate undesirable groups, such as prostitutes (Decker, 1979; O'Connor, 1977), drug dealers, and gang members (Coldren & Higgins, 2003). Civil injunctions filed against gang members have been used, particularly in California, to prohibit gang members from congregating in public, carrying beepers, and drinking in public (Klein & Maxson, 2006; Maxson, Hennigan, & Sloane, 2005), but they have been challenged on constitutionality grounds (Werdegar, 1999).

Another nuisance-abatement approach is to target the owners of properties where gang-related crimes such as drug sales occur. Owners usually cooperate in the removal of gang members and help establish policies to keep them away, either voluntarily or with the threat of civil court suits (Eck & Guerette, 2012b). In extreme cases, when owners are uncooperative, local government can condemn the property and eliminate it as a gang crime location. For example, a rundown motel in a gang-ridden area of Albuquerque had been a location for weekend gang parties where drugs were dealt and consumed, women raped, and weapons made available to juveniles. After repeated attempts to work with the absentee owners, the city condemned the property and demolished it. Also, on the Lower East Side of Manhattan in New York City, a police officer was shot and permanently disabled in a burned-out building that served as a "shooting gallery" for crack addicts. The site was condemned but reopened 12 months later as "La Bodega," a community center where residents could receive drug counseling, social services, and support (Sullivan, Mino, Nelson, & Pope, 2002).

Other programs: Improved street lighting (Farrington & Welsh, 2006), closed-circuit television surveillance (Welsh & Farrington, 2006), street closures (Lasley, 1998), traffic rerouting (Eck, 2002), crime prevention through environmental design (Cozens, Saville, & Hillier, 2005).

Conclusion

Collectively, gang crimes have grown in number and intensity to the point that they pose a significant threat to public safety in many areas of the country. The fact remains, however, that the level of gang participation and activity varies dramatically from place to place, which suggests that community factors have an important impact on gangs. Community crime research has implicated community disorganization and urban decay as criminogenic neighborhood influences. On the other hand, building empowering informal networks and local social institutions and infusing social, financial, and political capital into neighborhoods help to insulate them from the incursions of gangs.

As Abbott points out, understanding of human behavior assumes that "no social fact makes any sense abstracted from its context in social (and often geographic) space and social time. Social facts are *located facts*" (1997, p. 1152, emphasis in the original).

Unfortunately, most gang-prevention and -intervention programs do not take community influences into account (Klein & Maxson, 2006) and assume that any variation in their outcomes between program sites is the result of differences in the characteristics of the clients and staff and the implementation of the program. This chapter briefly identified ways in which the sociocultural and geopolitical characteristics of the community influence the nature of gangs and different programs that attempt to respond to these influences. The anti-gang program classification scheme presented here is based on assumptions of when best to address the problem (prevention or intervention), what to address (people or crimes), and the community's nature (compositional or contextual) and provides at least a glimpse of some programs operating in community environments. Efforts to control gangs in America depend on our ability and willingness to address the problem in the context where we find it.

Notes

1   "The Crazy Life"
2   For a general review of environmental strategies, see Clarke, 1995; Cozens, Saville, & Hillier, 2005; Eck, 2002; Eck & Guerette, 2012a.

References

Abbott, A. (1997). Of time and space: the contemporary relevance of the Chicago School. *Social Forces*, 75, 1149–1182.
Agnew, R. (2005). *Juvenile delinquency: Causes and control* (2nd ed.). Los Angeles: Roxbury.
Anderson, E. (1990). *Streetwise: Race, class and change in an urban community.* Chicago: University of Chicago Press.
Anselin, L., Cohen, J., Cook, D., Gorr, W., & Tita, G. (2000). Spatial analysis of crime. In D. Duffee (Ed.), *Criminal justice volume 4: Measurement and analysis of crime and justice* (pp. 213–262). Washington, DC: U.S. Department of Justice, Office of Justice Programs, National Institute of Justice.

Battin-Pearson, S., Thornberry, T., Hawkins, D., & Krohn, M. (1998). *Gang membership, delinquent peers, and delinquent behavior.* Washington, DC: U.S. Department of Justice, Office of Justice Programs, Office of Juvenile Justice and Delinquency Prevention.

Bell, C., & Jenkins, E. (1993). Community violence and children on Chicago's Southside. *Psychiatry, 56,* 46–54.

Bellair, P., & McNulty, T. (2009). Gang membership, drug selling, and violence in neighborhood context. *Justice Quarterly, 26,* 644–669.

Bennett, T. (1998). Crime prevention. In M. Tonry (Ed.), *The handbook of crime and punishment* (pp. 369–402). New York: Oxford University Press.

Birkbeck, C., & LaFree, G. (1993). The situational analysis of crime and deviance. *Annual Review of Sociology, 19,* 113–137.

Bjerregaard, B., & Lizotte, A. (1995). Gun ownership and gang membership. *Journal of Criminal Law and Criminology, 86,* 37–58.

Bjerregaard, B., & Smith, C. (1993). Gender differences in gang participation, delinquency, and substance use. *Journal of Quantitative Criminology, 9,* 329–355.

Blumstein, A. (1995). Youth violence, guns, and the illicit-drug industry. *Journal of Criminal Law and Criminology, 86,* 10–36.

Boyle, G. (2010). *Tattoos on the heart: The power of boundless compassion.* New York: Free Press.

Bradshaw, P. (2005). Terrors and young teams: Youth gangs and delinquency in Edinburgh. In S. Decker & F. Weerman (Eds.), *European street gangs and troublesome youth groups* (pp. 193–218). Walnut Creek, CA: AltaMira Press.

Braga, A. (2001). The effects of "hotspot" policing on crime. *Annals of the American Academy of Political and Social Science, 578,* 104–125.

Braga, A., & Kennedy, D. (2002). Reducing gang violence in Boston. In W. Reed & S. Decker (Eds.), *Responding to gangs: Evaluation and research* (pp. 265–288). Washington, DC: U.S. Department of Justice, Office of Justice Programs, National Institute of Justice.

Braga, A., Kennedy, D., Waring, E., & Piehl, A. (2001). Problem-oriented policing, deterrence, and youth violence: An evaluation of Boston's Operation Ceasefire. *Journal of Research in Crime and Delinquency, 38,* 195–225.

Braga, A., Pierce, G., McDevitt, J., Bond, B., & Cronin, S. (2008). The strategic prevention of gun violence among gang-involved offenders. *Justice Quarterly, 25,* 132–162.

Branch, C. (1997). *Clinical interventions with gang adolescents and their families.* Boulder, CO: Westview Press.

Bratton, W. (1995). The New York City Police Department's civil enforcement of quality-of-life crimes. *Journal of Law and Policy, 3,* 447–637.

Bursik Jr., R., & Grasmick, H. (1993). Economic deprivation and neighborhood crime rates, 1960–1980. *Law and Society Review, 27,* 263–283.

Callahan, C., Rivara, F., & Koepsell, T. (1996). Money for guns: Evaluation of the Seattle gun buy-back program. In M. Plotkin (Ed.), *Under fire: Gun buy-backs, exchanges, and amnesty programs* (pp. 81–95). Washington, DC: Police Executive Research Forum.

Clarke, R. (1992). *Situational crime prevention: Successful case studies.* Albany, NY: Harrow and Heston.

Clear, T. (2011). A private-sector, incentives-based model for justice reinvestment. *Criminology and Public Policy, 10*(3), 585–608.

Coldren, J., & Higgins, D. (2003). Evaluating nuisance abatement at gang and drug houses in Chicago. In S. Decker (Ed.), *Policing gangs and youth violence.* (pp. 131–166). Belmont, CA: Wadsworth/Thomson Learning.

Council on State Governments. *Lessons from the States: Reducing recidivism and curbing corrections costs through justice reinvestment.* Retrieved from

Cox, R. (1996). An exploration of the demographic and social correlates of criminal behavior among adolescent males. *Journal of Adolescent Health, 19,* 17–24.

Cozens, P., Saville, G., & Hillier, D. (2005). Crime prevention through environmental design (CPTED): a review and modern bibliography. *Property Management, 23*, 328–356.

Craig, W., Vitaro, F., Gagnon, L., & Tremblay, R. (2002). The road to gang membership: Characteristics of male gang and nongang members from ages 10 to 14. *Social Development, 11*, 53–68.

Curry, G. D. (2000). Self-reported gang involvement and officially recorded delinquency. *Criminology, 38*, 1253–1274.

Curry, G. D., Ball, R., & Fox, R. (1994). *Gang crime and law enforcement record keeping. Research in brief.* Washington, DC: US Department of Justice, National Institute of Justice, Office of Justice Programs.

Curry, G.D., & Decker, S. (2003). *Confronting gangs.* Los Angeles: Roxbury.

Decker, J. (1979). *Prostitution: Regulation and control.* Colorado: FB Rothman.

Decker, S., & Lauritsen, J. (2002). Leaving the gang. In C. R. Huff (Ed.), *Gangs in America III* (pp. 51–67). Thousand Oaks: Sage Publications.

Decker, S., & Rosenfeld, R. (2004). *Reducing gun violence: The St. Louis consent-to-search program.* Washington, DC: U.S. Department of Justice, Office of Justice Programs, National Institute of Justice.

Decker, S., & Van Winkle, B. (1996). *Life in the gang: Family, friends, and violence.* Cambridge University Press.

Dunworth, T., Mills, G., Cordner, G., & Greene, J. (1999). *National evaluation of Weed and Seed: Cross-site analysis.* Washington, DC: U.S. Department of Justice, Office of Justice Programs, National Institute of Justice.

Eck, J. (2002). Preventing crime at places. In L. Sherman, D. Farrington, B. Welsh, & D. MacKenzie (Eds.), *Evidence-based crime prevention* (pp. 241–294). New York: Routledge.

Eck, J., & Guerette, R. (2012a). Place-based crime prevention: Theory, evidence, and policy. In B. Welsh & D. Farrington (Eds.), *The Oxford handbook of crime prevention* (pp. 354–383). New York: Oxford University Press.

Eck, J., & Guerette, R. (2012b). "Own the place, own the crime" prevention. In R. Loeber & B. Welsh (Eds.), *The future of criminology* (pp. 166–177). New York: Oxford University Press.

Eitle, D., Gunkel, S., & Van Gundy, K. (2004). Cumulative exposure to stressful life events and male gang membership. *Journal of Criminal Justice, 32*, 95–111.

Esbensen, F. A., & Deschenes, E. (1998). A multisite examination of youth gang membership: Does gender matter? *Criminology, 36*, 799–828.

Esbensen, F. A., & Huizinga, D. (1993). Gangs, drugs, and delinquency in a survey of urban youth. *Criminology, 31*, 565–589.

Esbensen, F. A., Peterson, D., Taylor, T. J., & Osgood, W. (2012). *Is G.R.E.A.T. effective? Does the program prevent gang joining? Results from the national evaluation of G.R.E.A.T.* (Unpublished manuscript). Department of Criminology and Criminal Justice, University of Missouri-St. Louis, St. Louis, Retrieved from http://www.umsl.edu/ccj/pdfs/great/ GREAT Wave 4 Outcome Report

Esbensen, F. A., & Weerman, F. (2005). Youth gangs and troublesome youth groups in the United States and the Netherlands: a cross-national comparison. *European Journal of Criminology, 2*, 5–37.

Esbensen, F. A., & Winfree, L.T. (1998). Race and gender differences between gang and nongang youths: Results from a multisite survey. *Justice Quarterly 15*, 505–526.

Esbensen, F. A., Winfree, L., He, N., & Taylor, T. (2001). Youth gangs and definitional issues: When is a gang a gang, and why does it matter? *Crime & Delinquency, 47*, 105–130.

Egley, A. J. (2010). *Highlights of the 2008 National Youth Gang Survey.* Washington, DC: U.S. Department of Justice, Office of Justice Programs, Office of Juvenile Justice and Delinquency Prevention.

Egley, A. J., & Howell, J. C. (2012). *Highlights of the 2010 National Youth Gang Survey.* Washington, DC: U.S. Department of Justice, Office of Justice Programs, Office of Juvenile Justice and Delinquency Prevention.

Farrell, G., & Pease, K. (2001). *Repeat victimization.* Monsey, NY: Criminal Justice Press.

Farrington, D., & Welsh, B. (2006). Improved street lighting. In B. Welsh & D. Farrington (Eds.), *Preventing crime: What works for children, offenders, victims, and places* (pp. 209–224). New York: Springer.

Felson, M., & Clarke, R. (1998). Opportunity makes the thief. *Police Research Series, Paper, 98.* London: Home Office.

Fritsch, E., Caeti, T., & Taylor R. (1999). Gang suppression through saturation patrol, aggressive curfew, and truancy enforcement: A quasi-experimental test of the Dallas anti-gang initiative. *Crime & Delinquency, 45,* 122–139.

Garofalo, J., & McLeod, M. (1989). The structure and operations of neighborhood watch programs in the United States. *Crime and Delinquency, 35,* 326–344.

Gatti, U., Tremblay, R. E., Vitaro, F., & McDuff, P. (2005). Youth gangs, delinquency and drug use: A test of selection, facilitation and enhancement hypotheses. *Journal of Child Psychology and Psychiatry,* 1178–1190.

Golub, A., Johnson, B., Taylor, A., & Eterno, J. (2004) Does quality-of-life policing widen the net? A partial analysis. *Justice Research and Policy, 6,* 19–42.

Gordon, R., Lahey, B., Kawai, K., Loeber, R., Southhamer-Loeber, M., & Farrington, D. (2004). Antisocial behavior and youth gang membership: selection and socialization. *Criminology, 42,* 55–88.

Grannis, R. (1998). The importance of trivial streets: Residential streets and residential segregation 1. *American Journal of Sociology, 103*(6), 1530–1564.

Greenwood, P. W. (2007). *Changing lives: Delinquency prevention as crime-control policy.* University of Chicago Press.

Hill, K., Howell, J., Hawkins, J., & Battin-Pearson, S. (1999). Childhood risk factors for adolescent gang membership: Results from the Seattle Social Development Project. *Journal of Research in Crime and Delinquency, 36,* 300–322.

Hipp, J., Tita, G., & Greenbaum, R. (2009). Drive-bys and trade-ups: examining the directionality of the crime and residential instability relationship. *Social Forces, 87,* 1778–1812.

Hope, T. (1995). Community crime prevention. In M. Tonry & D. Farrington (Eds.), *Building a safer society: Strategic approaches to crime prevention: Volume 19. Crime and justice: A review of research* (pp. 21–89). Chicago: University of Chicago Press.

Howell, J. (1998). *Youth gangs: An overview.* Washington, DC: U.S. Department of Justice, Office of Justice Programs, Office of Juvenile Justice and Delinquency Prevention.

Howell, J., & Bilchik, S. (1995). *Guide for implementing the comprehensive strategy for serious, violent, and chronic juvenile offenders.* Washington, DC: U.S. Department of Justice, Office of Justice Programs, Office of Juvenile Justice and Delinquency Prevention.

Huff, C. R. (2002). Gangs and public policy: Prevention, intervention, and suppression. In C.R. Huff (Ed.), *Gangs in America III* (pp. 287–294). Thousand Oaks, CA: Sage Publications.

Hunt, A., & Weiner, K. (1977). The impact of a juvenile curfew: Suppression and displacement in patterns of juvenile offenses. *Journal of Police Science and Administration, 5,* 407–412.

Jolliffe, D., & Farrington, D. (2009). A systematic review of the relationship between childhood impulsiveness and later violence. In M. McMurran & R. Howard (Eds.), *Personality, personality disorder and violence: An evidence-based approach* (pp. 41–61). New York: Wiley.

Katz, J. (1988). *Seductions of crime: Moral and sensual attractions in doing evil.* New York: Basic Books.

Kelling, G., & Coles, C. (1997). *Fixing broken windows: Restoring order and reducing crime in our communities.* New York: Simon and Schuster.

Kennedy, D. (1998). Pulling levers: Getting deterrence right. *National Institute of Justice Journal, 236,* 2–8.

Kennedy, D., Piehl, A., & Braga, A. (1996). Youth violence in Boston: Gun markets, serious youth offenders, and a use-reduction strategy. *Law and Contemporary Problems, 59,* 147–183.

Kirby, J. B. (2008). Poor people, poor places and access to health care in the United States. *Social Forces, 87,* 325–355.

Kitzman, H., Olds, D., Cole, R., Hanks, C., Anson, E., Sidora–Arcoleo, K., Luckey, D., Knudtson, M., Henderson, C., & Holmberg, J. (2010). Enduring effects of prenatal and infancy home visiting by nurses on children. *Archives of Pediatrics & Adolescent Medicine, 164,* 412–418.

Klein, M. (1968). Impressions of juvenile gang members. *Adolescence, 3,* 53–78.

Klein, M. (1971). *Street gangs and street workers.* Englewood Cliffs, NJ: Prentice-Hall.

Klein, M. W., & Maxson, C. L. (2006). *Street gang patterns and policies.* Oxford: Oxford University Press.

Klein, P. (2012). The impact of juvenile curfew laws on arrests of youth and adults. *American Law and Economics Review, 14,* 44–67.

Klofas, J., Hipple, N., McDevitt, J., Bynum, T., McGarrell, J., & Decker, S. (2006). *Crime incident reviews: A Project Safe Neighborhood strategic intervention.* Washington, DC: Department of Justice, Office of Justice Programs, National Institute of Justice.

Klofas, J., Hipple, N., & McGarrell, E. (2010). *The new criminal justice: American communities and the changing world of crime control.* New York: Routledge.

Kobrin, S. (1959). The Chicago Area Project—a 25-year assessment. *Annals of the American Academy of Political and Social Science, 322,* 19–29.

Krupka, D., & Noonan, D. (2009). Empowerment zones, neighborhood change and owner-occupied housing. *Regional Science and Urban Economics, 39,* 386–396.

Lacourse, E., Nagin, D., Tremblay, R. E., Vitaro, F., & Claes, M. (2003). Developmental trajectories of boys' delinquent group membership and facilitation of violent behaviors during adolescence. *Development and Psychopathology, 15,* 183–197.

Lahey, B., Gordon, R., Loeber, R., Stouthamer-Loeber, M., & Farrington, D. (1999). Boys who join gangs: A prospective study of predictors of first gang entry. *Journal of Abnormal Child Psychology, 27,* 261–276.

Lasley, J. (1998). *"Designing out" gang homicides and street assaults.* Washington, DC: U.S. Department of Justice, Office of Justice Programs, National Institute of Justice.

Laub, J., & Sampson, R. (1993). Turning points in the life course: Why change matters to the study of crime. *Criminology, 31,* 301–325.

Laurin, M., Hare, T., & Steele, P. (2012). Social ecological factors that determine the locations of gang and non-gang residence, Albuquerque, NM 1996-2006. *Papers of the Applied Geography Conferences, 35,* 366–375.

LeBoeuf, D. (1996). *Curfew, an answer to juvenile delinquency and victimization?* U.S. Department of Justice, Office of Justice Programs, Office of Juvenile Justice and Delinquency Prevention.

Levitt, S., & Venkatesh, S. (2000). An economic analysis of a drug-selling gang's finances. *Quarterly Journal of Economics, 115,* 755–789.

Lizotte, A., Krohn, M., Howell, J., Tobin, K., & Howard, G. (2000). Factors influencing gun carrying among young urban males over the adolescent/young adult life course. *Criminology, 38,* 811–834.

Maxson, C., Hennigan, K., & Sloane, D. (2005). "It's getting crazy out there": Can a civil gang injunction change a community? *Criminology and Public Policy, 4,* 577–605.

Maxson, C., & Whitlock, M. (2002). Joining the gang: gender differences in risk factors for gang membership. In C. Huff (Ed.), *Gangs in America* (3rd ed., pp. 19–35). Thousand Oaks, CA: Sage.

Maxson, C. L., Whitlock, M. L., & Klein, M. W. (1998). Vulnerability to street gang membership: Implications for practice. *Social Service Review, 72,* 70–91.

McGarrell, E. F., Chermak, S. M., & Weiss, A. (2002). *Reducing gun violence: Evaluation of the Indianapolis Police Department's Directed Patrol Project.* US Department of Justice, Office of Justice Programs, National Institute of Justice.

Miller, W. B. (1962). The impact of a 'total-community' delinquency control project. *Social Problems, 10*, 168–191.

Moore, J. W. (1991). *Going down to the barrio: Homeboys and homegirls in change.* Philadelphia: Temple University Press.

Moore, J., & Hagedorn, J. (2001). *Female gangs: A focus on research.* Washington, DC, U.S. Department of Justice, Office of Justice Programs, Office of Juvenile Justice and Delinquency Prevention.

Mukasey, M., Sedgwick, J., & Flores, J. (2007). *Best practices to address community gang problems: OJJDP Comprehensive Gang Model.* Washington, DC: U.S. Department of Justice, Office of Justice Programs, Office of Juvenile Justice and Delinquency Prevention.

National Gang Center (2009). *National Youth Gang Survey analysis.* Retrieved from http://www.nationalgangcenter.gov/Survey-Analysis/.

National Gang Center (2011). *National Youth Gang Survey analysis.* Retrieved from http://www.nationalgangcenter.gov/Survey-Analysis/.

Oakley, D., & Tsao, H-S. (2006). A new way of revitalizing distressed urban communities? Assessing the impact of the federal empowerment zone program. *Journal of Urban Affairs, 28*, 443–471.

O'Connor, P. (1977). Nuisance abatement law as a solution to New York City's problem of illegal sex related businesses in the mid-town area. *Fordham Law Review, 46*, 57–90.

Olds, D., Henderson, C., Chamberlin, R., & Tatelbaum, R. (1986). Preventing child abuse and neglect: a randomized trial of nurse home visitation. *Pediatrics, 78*, 65–78.

Olds, D., Henderson, C., Cole, R., Eckenrode, J., Kitzman, H., Luckey, D., Pettitt, L., Sidora, K., Morris, P., & Powers, J. (1998). Long-term effects of nurse home visitation on children's criminal and antisocial behavior: 15-year follow-up of a randomized controlled trial. *Journal of the American Medical Association, 280*, 1238–1244.

Pain, R. (2000). Place, social relations, and the fear of crime: A review. *Progress in Human Geography, 24*, 365–387.

Park, R. (1916). Suggestions for the investigations of human behavior in the urban environment. *American Journal of Sociology, 20*, 577–612.

Perkins, D. (1995). Speaking truth to power: Empowerment ideology as social intervention and policy. *American Journal of Community Psychology, 23*, 765–794.

Pierce, G. L., Spaar, S., & Briggs, L. R. (1988). *The character of police work: Strategic and tactical implications.* Unpublished paper, Center for Applied Social Research, Northeastern University.

Pogrebin, M. R., Stretesky, P. B., & Unnithan, N. P. (2009). *Guns, violence, and criminal behavior: The offender's perspective.* Boulder, CO: Lynne Riener.

Pyrooz, D., & Decker, S. (2011). Motives and methods for leaving the gang: Understanding the process of gang desistance. *Journal of Criminal Justice, 39*, 417–425.

Ramirez, C. T. (2008, August 12). *Interview with former gang member Carlos T. Ramirez Jr., about the Texas Prison GRAD Program (Gang Renunciation and Disassociation).* Retrieved from http://voices.yahoo.com/interview-former-gang-member-carlos-t-ramirez-1801853.html

Riedel, M., & Welsh, W. (2011). *Criminal violence: Patterns, causes, and prevention.* New York: Oxford University Press.

Rosenbaum, D. P. (1987). The theory and research behind Neighborhood Watch: Is it a sound fear and crime reduction strategy? *Crime & Delinquency, 33*, 103–134.

Rosenbaum, D. P., Lurigio, A. J., & Lavrakas, P. J. (1989). Enhancing citizen participation and solving serious crime: A national evaluation of Crime Stoppers programs. *Crime & Delinquency, 35*, 401–420.

Rosenfeld, R. (1996). Gun buy-backs: Crime control or community mobilization? In M. Plotkin (Ed.), *Under fire: Gun buy-backs, exchanges, and amnesty programs* (pp. 1–28). Washington, DC: Police Executive Research Forum.

Rosenfeld, R., Bray, T., & Egley, A. (1999). Facilitating violence: A comparison of gang-motivated, gang-affiliated, and nongang youth homicides. *Journal of Quantitative Criminology, 15,* 495–516.

Rosenfeld, R, Fornagno, R., & Baumer, E. (2005) Did Cease-fire, Compstat, and Exile reduce homicide? *Criminology and Public Policy, 44,* 419–449.

Sampson, R. J. (1987). Urban black violence: The effect of male joblessness and family disruption. *American Journal of Sociology, 92,* 348–382.

Sampson, R. J. (2006). How does community context matter? Social mechanisms and the explanation of crime. In P. O. Wikstrom & R. Sampson (Eds.), *The explanation of crime: Context, mechanisms, and development* (pp. 31–60). New York: Cambridge University Press.

Sampson, R., & Lauritsen, J. 1994. Violent victimization and offending: Individual-, situational-, and community-level risk factors. In A. Reiss & J. Roth (Eds.), *Understanding and preventing violence: Social influences. Volume 3* (pp. 1–114), National Research Council. Washington, DC: National Academy Press.

Sampson, R., Raudenbush, S., & Earls, F. (1997). Neighborhoods and violent crime: A multilevel study of collective efficacy. *Science, 277,* 918–924.

Schlossman, S., & Sedlak, M. (1983). The Chicago Area Project revisited. *Crime and Delinquency, 29,* 398–462.

Schorr, L. (1986). *Within our reach: Breaking the cycle of disadvantage.* New York: Doubleday.

Shaw, C., & McKay, H. (1942). *Juvenile delinquency and urban areas: A study of rates of delinquents in relation to differential characteristics of local communities in American cities.* Chicago: University of Chicago Press.

Sherman, L., & Eck, J. (2002). Policing for crime prevention. In L. Sherman, D. Farrington, B. Welsh, & D. MacKenzie (Eds.), *Evidence-based crime prevention* (pp. 295–329). New York: Routledge.

Sherman, L., Gartin, P., & Buerger, M. (1989). Hot spots of predatory crime: Routine activities and the criminology of place. *Criminology, 27,* 27–56.

Skogan, W. (1990). *Disorder and decline: Crime and the spiral of decay American neighborhoods.* University of California Press.

Spergel, I. (1986). The violent gang problem in Chicago: A local community approach. *Social Services Review, 60,* 94–129.

Spergel, I., & Grossman, S. (1997). The Little Village Project: A community approach to the gang problem. *Social Work, 42,* 456–470.

Spergel, I., Wa, K., & Sosa, R. (2006). The comprehensive, community-wide gang program model: Success and failure. In J. Short & L. Hughes (Eds.), *Studying youth gangs* (pp. 203–224). Lanham, MD: AltaMira Press.

Steele, P. (2005). The *Westside and Eastside Weed and Seed sites: Social attainment, demographic, and crime characteristics in thirteen contiguous neighborhoods in Albuquerque, New Mexico: Final report.* Washington, DC: Department of Justice, Community Capacity and Development Office.

Steele, P. (2006). *Community Critical Incident Reviews: Modeling a community-oriented policing approach in two Weed and Seed sites: Final report.* Washington, DC: Department of Justice, Community Capacity and Development Office.

Steele, P. D., & Guerin, P. (1996). *Evaluation of the Albuquerque Gang Project.* Santa Fe, NM: New Mexico Children, Youth and Families Department.

Steele, P. D., Reeves, E. B., & Hare, T. S. (August 2012). *Situated violent crime: The influence of gang membership and community factors.* Paper presented at the Annual Meeting of the Society for the Study of Social Problems, Denver, CO.

Sullivan, E., Mino, M., Nelson, K., & Pope, J. (2002). *Families as a resource in recovery from drug abuse: An evaluation of La Bodega de la Familia.* New York: Vera Institute of Justice.

Sutherland, E. H. (1947). *Principles of criminology* (4th ed). Chicago, IL: J. B. Lippincott.

Suttles, G., & Suttles, G. (1972). *The social construction of communities.* Chicago: University of Chicago Press.

Taub, R., Taylor, D., & Dunham, J. (1984). *Paths of neighborhood change: Race and crime in urban America.* Chicago: University of Chicago Press.

Taylor, R. (2001). *Breaking away from broken windows: Baltimore neighborhoods and the nationwide fight against crime, grime, fear, and decline.* Boulder, CO: Westview Press.

Thornberry, T. P., Krohn, M. D., Lizotte, A. J., Smith, C. A., & Tobin, K. (2003). *Gangs and delinquency in developmental perspective.* New York: Cambridge University Press.

Thrasher, F. (1927). *The gang: A study of 1,313 gangs in Chicago.* Chicago: University of Chicago Press.

Thrasher, F. (1936). The Boys' Club and juvenile delinquency. *American Journal of Sociology, 40,* 66–80.

Tierney, J., Grossman, J., & Resch, N. (2000). *Making a difference: An impact study of Big Brothers Big Sisters.* Philadelphia: Public/Private Ventures.

Tita, G., Cohen, J., & Engberg, J. (2005). An ecological study of the location of gang "set space." *Social Problems, 52,* 272–299.

Tucker, S., & Cadora, E. (2003). *Justice reinvestment: to invest in public safety by reallocating justice dollars to refinance education, housing, healthcare, and jobs Ideas for an Open Society, 3.* New York: Open Society Institute,

Vigil, J. D. (1988). *Barrio gangs: Street life and identity in Southern California.* University of Texas Press.

Vigil, J. D. (2002). *A rainbow of gangs: Street cultures in the mega-city.* University of Texas Press.

Welsh, B., & Farrington, D. (2006). Closed-circuit television surveillance. In B. Welsh & D. Farrington (Eds.), *Preventing crime: What works for children, offenders, victims, and places* (pp. 193–208). New York: Springer.

Welsh, B., & Holshi, A. (2002) Communities and crime prevention. In L. Sherman, D. Farrington, B. Welsh, & D. MacKenzie (Eds.), *Evidence-based crime prevention* (pp. 165–197). New York: Routledge.

Werdegar, M. (1999). Enjoining the Constitution: The use of public nuisance abatement injunctions against urban street gangs. *Stanford Law Review,* 409–445.

Whyte, W. (1943). *Street corner society: The social structure of an Italian slum.* Chicago: University of Chicago Press.

Wikstrom, P. O. (2006). Individuals, settings, and acts of crime: situational mechanisms and the explanation of crime. In P. O. Wikstrom & R. Sampson (Eds.), *The explanation of crime: Context, mechanisms, and development* (pp. 61–107). New York: Cambridge University Press.

_____. (2012). Individuals' situational criminal actions: Current knowledge and tomorrow's prospects. In R. Loeber & B. Welsh (Eds.), *The future of criminology* (pp. 55–61). New York: Oxford University Press.

Wikstrom, P. O., Oberwittler, D., Treiber, K., & Hardie, B. (2012). *Breaking rules: The social and situational dynamics of young people's urban crime.* New York: Oxford University Press.

Wilson, J. Q., & Kelling, G. L. (March 1982). Broken windows. *Atlantic Monthly,* 29–38.

Woolcock, M. (2001). The place of social capital in understanding social and economic outcomes. *Canadian Journal of Policy Research, 2,* 11–17.

Worrall, J., & Kovandzic, (2010). Police levels and crime rates: An instrumental variables approach. *Social Science Research, 39,* 506–516.

16 Re-entry and Aftercare

Laura S. Abrams

■ Scope of the Problem

Re-entry and aftercare services can be defined as a set of programs that assist a young person in making a successful transition from a period of secure confinement back into a community setting. These services are primarily designed for youth who have completed a sentence in a correctional setting but may also be relevant for those who have served a relatively shorter amount of time in a detention facility awaiting trial or sentencing. Recognizing that the transition from secure confinement to a community setting is quite challenging, the primary goals of these services are to prevent recidivism by providing support for a young person's educational, vocational, and housing needs as well as to assist with linkages to services, such as the continuation of mental health or substance abuse treatment in the community.

It is difficult to pinpoint exactly how many young people in the United States are eligible for re-entry and aftercare services annually. Researchers have estimated that approximately 100,000 young people in the United States re-enter the community following a placement in a juvenile correctional facility each year (Snyder, 2004). However, this estimate does not include young people who served time in adult jail or others who may have served a lengthy stint of time in juvenile detention (i.e., a short-term placement) while awaiting trial. Another way to consider the scope of the problem is by looking at the number of court-ordered placements each year. According to the Office of Juvenile Justice and Delinquency Prevention, in 2009, juvenile courts in the United States handled an estimated 1.5 million delinquency cases, of which less than a third (488,800) were adjudicated delinquent. Of those found delinquent, 27% (121,176) were mandated to a court-ordered residential placement, which includes locked facilities, wilderness/boot camps, and smaller group home settings. About 85% of these confined young people are young men and 40% are African American (Puzzanchera & Kang, 2011). Thus by most accounts, re-entry and aftercare services have the potential to reach at least 100,000 young people in the United States each year.

As stated, the primary goal of re-entry and aftercare services is to reduce a young person's risk of re-offending upon release. The reason these services are often deemed important is that the majority of young people who spend time in juvenile/adult correctional facilities recidivate into (return to) the juvenile and/or adult criminal justice system within a few years of their release. For example, a longitudinal study of nearly 2,500 high-risk juvenile offenders from a large correctional facility in a Southwestern state found re-arrest rates to be as high as 85% over a 5-year period (Trulson et al., 2005). Similarly, the California Department of Juvenile Justice has reported that 70% of youth paroled from its state-run institutions are re-arrested within 2 years (California Juvenile Justice Reentry Partnership, 2007). Rates of new convictions (a more conservative recidivism measure than new arrests as many arrests do not lead to a conviction) tend to be lower, with eight states (Arkansas, Florida, Georgia, Kentucky, Maryland, North Dakota, Oklahoma, and Virginia) reporting an average 12-month reconviction rate of 33%, accounting for both juvenile and adult system dispositions (Snyder & Sickmund, 2006). While there is no universal definition of "recidivism" (i.e., some states or counties track re-arrests and/or probation violations and others strictly track re-convictions for new crimes) and there are no standard mechanisms for collecting data across states or jurisdictions, many juvenile justice experts contend that high recidivism rates across the board indicate the need for enhanced re-entry and aftercare services (Altschuler & Brash, 2004).

Re-entry services are geared to target and alleviate a set of barriers to healthy community reintegration that often contribute to repeat involvement in crime. For example, youth offenders tend to have histories of educational neglect, learning disabilities, poor academic performance, and school transience (Bullis & Yovanoff, 2002; Coffey & Gemignani, 1994; Moffit, 1990). These cumulative disadvantages in conjunction with the disruptions incurred by spending time in juvenile detention or adult corrections contribute to low rates of GED/high-school diploma attainment. Researchers have estimated that fewer than 20% of formerly incarcerated youth eventually obtain a GED or high-school diploma, compared to 92% of the general population (Osgood, Foster, & Courtney, 2010). High rates of unemployment are strongly related to low levels of educational attainment. For instance, in Bullis and Yovanoff's (2002) longitudinal study of youth offenders released from the Oregon Youth Authority, only 28% of the sample reported employment at 1 year after their release.

In addition to lower educational and vocational attainment, incarcerated youth also tend to have poor outcomes on a range of other indicators of well-being. For example, they have precarious housing situations even when compared to youth with similar socioeconomic backgrounds (Hagan & McCarthy, 2005). Several surveys of homeless shelters for youth have found that more than 30% of the population are formerly incarcerated (Bolas, 2011; Shelton, 2009). Moreover, many young people in the juvenile justice system have diagnosable mental health and substance abuse disorders that may not have been addressed with adequate services during confinement (Grisso, 2004; Koppelman, 2005). In a study of over 1,800 detained youth in Chicago, Teplin and colleagues (2002) found that even when excluding conduct disorder nearly two thirds of males and three quarters of females met the diagnostic criteria for one or more psychiatric disorders, and nearly half of the sample met the criteria for a substance use disorder. These problems are all capable of derailing re-entry stability upon return to the community, particularly when they are left untreated or when continuity of care, including prescription medications, is disrupted.

The community re-entry of youth offenders also entails a host of interpersonal and social challenges. From the perspectives of re-entering youth themselves, qualitative studies have revealed that formerly incarcerated youth often experience numerous social stressors as they adjust to their lives "on the outs." For example, many will struggle to avoid peer influences that they once considered as primary and supportive to them, a process that young people have described as stressful and isolating (Abrams, 2007; Inderbitzen, 2009; Martinez & Abrams, 2013). Family reintegration can also be problematic, as families may either place great pressure on the released young person to "succeed" or, conversely, may contribute to overall criminal influences (Martinez & Abrams, 2013). Moreover, the social stigma associated with having a criminal record, falling behind in school, and being underprepared for the job market can create internal strain, self-doubt, and depression (Sullivan, 1989).

In sum, problems related to re-entry are deep and interrelated, often leading to the need for the provision of services that reach beyond surveillance-only probation activities. These re-entry strategies include several approaches that are reviewed in the next section.

■ Re-entry Interventions and Efficacy

The Individual Approach

The most popular approach to re-entry and aftercare interventions has focused primary attention on the individual adolescent. The research base underlying this individual approach is that certain youth are known to be more "at risk" of re-offending than others, necessitating a carefully planned, case-by-case approach to aftercare planning and support. For example, in determining the risk for re-offending, studies have typically found that males, youth who are first arrested at young ages, those arrested for property offenses, and those with lengthy prior records have increased odds of recidivism (Benda & Tollett, 1999; Myner et al., 1998; Niarhos & Routh, 1992). Additional risk factors for re-offending include psychosocial issues such as substance abuse, poor parental relations, and prior problems in school settings (Dembo, Williams, Schmeidler, Getreu, & Berry, 1991). While some of these factors are "static" (such as demographic characteristics), others may be amenable to change. In attempting to address the individual adolescent, the most common forms of intervention fall into two main categories: case management and mentoring.

In the **case management** approach, a probation officer or a community-based aftercare worker plans and implements an individualized package of services that attempt to ameliorate the risks, address the most pressing needs, and build on the strengths of the young person who is re-entering the community (Justice Policy Institute, 2009). Empirically validated tools such as the Youth Level of Service/Case Management Inventory (YLS/CMI) are often used to perform an initial risk assessment, pinpointing the psychosocial areas, such as school, peers, family, or others, that place the young person most at risk of re-offending (Hoge & Andrews, 2009). Once an empirically validated assessment is administered, the re-entry or aftercare worker will devise a treatment plan to match these major needs and build on the strengths of the youth in his or her re-entry environment. Some of this work can include ongoing meetings with the youth, group aftercare sessions, family work, school liaison work, employment placement, and referrals to other social services. In this type of intervention, the services offered are supportive, flexible, and tailored to individual needs and circumstances (Gies, 2003).

The Office of Juvenile Justice and Delinquency Prevention's *Intensive Aftercare Program* (IAP) is a primary example of an intensive case management intervention. Launched in 1995 in four states (Colorado, Nevada, New Jersey, and Virginia), the IAP was designed to provide individualized treatment during incarceration, a structured transition phase 60 to 90 days prior to release, supportive community resources during the aftercare phase, and varying degrees of surveillance in the community depending on the level of assessed risk (Altschuler & Armstrong, 1994). The IAP included the following essential components (Wiebush et al., 2000):

☐ Risk assessment and classification for establishing eligibility
☐ Individual case planning that incorporates a family and community perspective
☐ A mix of intensive surveillance and enhanced service delivery
☐ A balance of incentives and graduated consequences coupled with the imposition of realistic, enforceable conditions
☐ Service brokerage with community resources and linkage with social networks

Initial process evaluations of the IAP showed promising results (Wiebush et al., 2000). However, outcome studies using both randomized control and quasi-experimental comparison groups found that although the IAP program had high rates of program completion and satisfaction, it did not actually reduce recidivism rates (Frederick & Roy, 2003; Wiebush et al., 2005). In some of the pilot sites, the treatment group actually fared worse than the comparison group. Proposed reasons for the absence of significance included small sample sizes in two of the sites and exposure to some aftercare services among one group of controls (Wiebush et al., 2005).

The IAP results are consistent with other published program evaluations of case management aftercare programs that show modest to no reductions in recidivism, particularly when scholars have examined re-entry periods of 6 months after release or longer (Abrams, Shannon, & Sangalang, 2008; Wells, Minor, Angel, & Stearmen, 2006). In the IAP evaluation and in related studies of case management programs, known risk factors for repeat offending such as age of first arrest, race, and age of release still significantly predicted re-offending above and beyond the services offered (Abrams et al., 2007;

Wiebush et al., 2005; Wells et al., 2006). It appears that intensive aftercare services, delivered primarily by the probation officer, have been unable to break the barriers to healthy community reintegration associated with these other risk factors.

On the more promising side, an exploratory study that examined length of service in a re-entry case management program found that more months of service led to significant reductions in recidivism in the juvenile system (Abrams, Franke, & Terry, 2011). Moreover, additional developments (subsequent to the IAP) have led to models that include a strengths-based approach to re-entry programming (Barton, 2006). This approach, as adopted by the Boys and Girls Club of America's *Targeted Re-entry Initiative* (TRI), works with youth during confinement and upon re-entry in four major ways: community mobilization, recruitment, mainstreaming/programming, and case management (Barton, 2006). While preliminary results of the TRI program in select sites show positive results (Damooei, 2010), the program has not been tested with a rigorous experimental design. Overall, further research is needed to examine whether this newer approach will work, which types of programs better for some youth and not others, and what dosage is needed to counteract some of the more persistent risk factors for recidivism identified in these evaluation studies.

Mentoring is widely used as a prevention and intervention strategy for at-risk youth, including those at risk of trouble with the law, those who have strained parental relationships, and those who are generally struggling academically. In adult–youth mentoring arrangements, mentors provide support and encouragement to their mentees, serve as positive or prosocial role models, and also help their mentees to overcome challenges in school or in other areas of life (Center for Substance Abuse Prevention, 2000). Researchers have found that participation in volunteer or more formal mentoring programs benefits youth in the areas of family relationships, school performance, self-esteem, and other measurable outcomes (Rhodes, Grossman, & Resch, 2000). Applied specifically to re-entry and aftercare, mentoring programs are geared to help the individual offender navigate transition challenges by facilitating a prosocial relationship with a caring adult, providing an additional support system, and offering a positive role model.

Several studies of mentoring programs have produced tentatively promising but mixed results. The Aftercare for Indiana through Mentoring (AIM, 2004) program is an empirically tested program that pairs college students with young people who are housed in a state-run correctional facility. The program was launched in 1995 and the model has currently been adopted in Arkansas and Alaska. Primary researcher and program developer Roger Jarjoura (2003) has found strong evidence of positive outcomes among youth involved in the AIM program. In 1997, youth returning to the Indianapolis area were randomly assigned to one of three conditions: (a) life-skills training while in the institution, (b) life-skills training plus mentoring services before and after release (i.e., the full AIM program), and (c) no AIM services (control condition). After 4 years after release, 43% of youth receiving the full AIM program (i.e., life-skills training and mentoring) were re-incarcerated compared to 50% of life-skills-only participants and 62% of controls (AIM, 2004).

While the AIM program achieved very clear results in regard to recidivism reduction, other studies have found more limited effects of mentoring programs on aftercare outcomes. Using survival analysis, Bouffard and Bergseth's (2008) study of a mentoring re-entry program in a rural Midwestern county found that treatment (n = 63) and control (n = 49) youths did not differ significantly in the amount of time that preceded their time to re-offending. Similarly, Drake and Barnoski's (2006) study of a volunteer mentoring program for returning youth found that although the program reduced initial recidivism rates among the treatment group, these differences dissipated at the 24-month and 36-month follow-up points. In sum, the evidence base suggests that mentoring can lead to some promising benefits, yet these effects may not be sufficient to prevent re-offending in the long run.

Overall, the efficacy of individually oriented programs in reducing recidivism is far from firmly established. Nevertheless, the individual approach is still the most commonly implemented re-entry or aftercare intervention. Based on some of the lessons learned from existing research, the Faith and Service Technical Education Network (FASTEN) lists the following "best practices" for re-entry program development. Practitioners may wish to consider these tips when designing their own program.

Focus your program on the ex-offenders who are most likely to recidivate.
Intervention should be focused on the qualities that are known to place a person at risk to commit crime.
Intervention should be comprehensive; that is, it should treat as many needs of participants as possible.
Teach the participants to recognize and resist antisocial behavior.
Try to discover the learning styles of your program participants and then match them with staff whose teaching styles would best accommodate them.
The program should probably last about 3 to 9 months.
Treatment should come from well-funded programs with committed staff.
Community-based programs are believed to be more effective than institution-based programs.
Involve a researcher when designing and developing your program.
(Quoted from: http://www.urbanministry.org/wiki/best-practices-checklist-ex-offender-reentry-programs)

A useful resource for those interested in mentoring research and practice can be found at the Portland State University, School of Social Work, where Dr. Thomas Keller directs the Center for Interdisciplinary Mentoring Institute (see http://www.pdx.edu/mentoring-research/).

Family Interventions

Another group of re-entry and aftercare programs targets the family system as the site of intervention. A host of family-related factors are associated with delinquent behaviors, such as strained parent–child relationships, inconsistent discipline, neglect, parental substance abuse, violence, sexual abuse, attachment disruption, and inadequate levels of warmth and affection (Underwood, von Dresner, & Phillips, 2006). For these reasons, family-focused interventions operate under the assumption that families may have the greatest influence on the success of young people when they return to the community following a period of confinement.

Family interventions for returning youth offenders, such Multisystemic Therapy (MST), Functional Family Therapy (FFT), and Family Integrated Transitions (FIT), are often delivered by specifically trained therapists when a young person returns home. One of the best-researched family interventions is MST, a home-based intervention that takes approximately 4 months to deliver in collaboration with the family, the offender, and a specially trained family therapist. MST has proved successful in preventing recidivism and promoting family functioning among youth who are at lower levels of involvement with the juvenile justice system (Curtis, Ronan, & Bourdin, 2004) and has been more recently studied as a re-entry intervention. For example, Timmons-Mitchell and colleagues' (2006) experimental study found that youth who did not receive the intervention were 3.2 times more likely to recidivate than the treatment group and, further, that participation in the MST program yielded significant improvements in home functioning, community functioning, and school functioning. There is also evidence that the effects of MST may be longer lasting than more individually oriented interventions. In a randomized clinical trial study, Sawyer and Borduin (2011) evaluated the long-term impact of MST for offenders who ended treatment on average 21.9 years earlier and found that the frequency of misdemeanor offending was five times lower for MST participants. Compared to MST participants, individual-therapy participants were twice as likely to be involved in family-related civil suits during adulthood and four times more likely to recidivate for violent felonies.

Studies of other formalized family interventions have also generally found significant treatment effects. FFT can be defined as:

> ... an empirically grounded, well-documented and highly successful family intervention program for dysfunctional youth. FFT has been applied to a wide range of problem youth and their families in various multi-ethnic, multicultural contexts. Target populations range from at-risk preadolescents to youth with very serious problems such as conduct disorder, violent acting-out, and substance abuse. While FFT

targets youth aged 11–18, younger siblings of referred adolescents often become part of the intervention process. Intervention ranges from, on average, 8 to 12 one-hour sessions for mild cases and up to 30 sessions of direct service for more difficult situations. (Sexton & Alexander, 2003, p. 2)

Drake and colleagues' (2009) meta-analysis of seven independent evaluations of FFT programs found that on average, FFT decreases the likelihood of recidivism for youth offenders from 70% to 57%.

Similar to MST and FFT interventions, another promising program is FIT, which the Washington State juvenile correctional system has implemented and studied. An experimental study comparing 104 youth in the FIT group to 169 control group participants found a recidivism rate of 27% for the FIT group compared to 41% for the controls (Aos, 2004). Moreover, a subsequent study of FIT showed that its participants experienced a 30% reduction in felony-level recidivism specifically (Trupin, Kerns, Walkerm, DeRobertus & Stewart, 2011).

Overall, a review of the empirical literature on family-based re-entry and aftercare indicates that targeting the whole family can yield a greater likelihood of successful re-entry than individual approaches on their own. However, the literature lacks studies of who is most likely to benefit from family interventions or how these might be combined with more individually oriented programs to produce even greater reductions in recidivism.

Considerations in Re-entry Research: Neighborhood Effects

While much of the research on re-entry programs has focused on individual or family-based interventions, a growing body of research has also raised questions about the role of neighborhood factors, such as poverty, unemployment, alcohol outlet density, drug sales, and others in contributing to risk of recidivism risk among youth. These "neighborhood effects" have been found to be correlated with other youth problems, including delinquent behavior. For example, a few key studies found that neighborhood factors such as cohesion and social control predict rates of both self-reported delinquency and documented arrests more significantly than individual characteristics of youth themselves (Elliott et al., 1996; Simka-Fagan & Schwartz, 1986; Wikstrom & Loeber, 2000).

As newer technologies (such as GIS and spatial analysis) and research methods have been increasingly applied to complex and multilayered social problems, a few studies have examined the issue of juvenile re-entry from a neighborhood effects perspective. One cross-sectional study of returning offenders in Los Angeles confirms that youth are indeed released to risky environments. Specifically, the density of returning youth per ZIP code was related to higher unemployment and poverty rates and fewer educational resources compared to communities without high densities of re-entry youth (Abrams & Freisthler, 2010).

While this cross-sectional study affirms general hunches about the conditions of the neighborhoods where young people return following confinement, a handful of studies have attempted to tease apart the contributions of neighborhood factors to recidivism in relation to known individual risks. In one of these studies, Harris and colleagues (2011) examined four explanatory variables for recidivism among a sample of youth in Philadelphia: the background characteristics of the individual, the initial offense that the juvenile committed, social disorganization within his neighborhood, and indicators of delinquency and recidivism near the juvenile's residence. They found evidence of spatial influence on recidivism rates, particularly for drug offenses. Moreover, they concluded, "residing in a high spatial concentration of any particular type of reoffending increases the chance that a delinquent youth will recidivate with that type of offense" (p. 48). Lastly, they found evidence that risk and protective factors may matter for individual youth, but the way that they matter may vary by neighborhood. This research suggests that neighborhood effects may interact with individual factors vis-à-vis some complex social mechanisms that have yet to be articulated or well understood. Moreover, neighborhood factors have not been incorporated into studies of re-entry or aftercare interventions as potentially mediating or moderating the effects of the intervention. The future direction of this spatial research will be important as we continue to learn the components of neighborhoods, even those that are disadvantaged, in reducing the risk of recidivism.

■ Populations Warranting Additional Consideration

Young Women

The presence of young women throughout the juvenile justice system has increased substantially since the 1990s (Snyder & Sickmund, 2006). For example, the number of detained juvenile female offenders increased over 50% between 1991 and 2003, and the number of incarcerated females rose nearly 90% during this same time period (Snyder & Sickmund, 2006). Female offenders currently represent about a quarter of all juvenile arrests, yet they account for 15% of all juveniles in correctional residential placements (Sickmund, Sladky, Kang, & Puzzanchera, 2011). Scholars have debated whether this increase represents changes in policing policies rather than actual changes in young women's levels of criminality (Zahn et al., 2008). Nevertheless, their increased rate of contact with the juvenile justice system has catalyzed policymakers, practitioners, and researchers to focus more attention on this population.

Existing research has not widely studied gender differences in re-entry needs or experiences, yet it has discerned that young women in the juvenile justice system face a unique set of risk factors for delinquency and trouble with the law. For example, several studies have found that young women in the justice system experience significantly higher rates of mental health problems such as depression, anxiety, behavioral disorders, and suicidal ideation than their male counterparts (Cauffman, 2008; Trupin, Abram, Stewart, Beach, & Boesky, 2002). Past histories of sexual abuse, family problems, and low self-esteem are also more common among young women in the justice system compared to young men (Bloom, Owen, Deschenes, & Rosenbaum, 2002; Trupin et al., 2002). These noted differences have contributed to the movement to implement "gender-specific services" in the juvenile justice system, a set of interventions and services that has sought to improve treatment and intervention programs for incarcerated young women and women involved at all levels of the juvenile justice system.

Despite increased attention to the development and implementation of gender-specific programming, little is known about gender differences in the re-entry phase of correctional care. One cross-sectional, exploratory study compared young women to young men in regard to their anticipated aftercare needs and found significant differences in anticipated mental health concerns, willingness to use services, and general re-entry concerns. In particular, young men were more concerned about gang involvement and neighborhood violence, and young women were more inclined to raise concern about locating mental health services. At the same time, minimal gender differences were detected in perceived employment needs and barriers as well as self-efficacy to avoid recidivism (Fields & Abrams, 2010). It is also important to note the interaction between gender and race. For example, in surveys of youth in two Georgia juvenile detention facilities, young African-American women were more likely to have plans to return to school after detention and had the most ambitious career aspirations. They also indicated higher levels of self-efficacy and fewer delinquent activities in comparison to young African-American men. However, the African-American girls experienced more depression and had survived more traumatic events during childhood (Toldson, Woodson, Braithwaite, Holliday, & Rosa, 2010). Thus, while the literature attends to the gender-specific needs of incarcerated female youth, much remains to be discovered about young women's re-entry as well as potential differences within this population based on race, sexuality, childbearing status, and others. In thinking about the specific needs of young women and re-entry, consider the case of Irene (see box).

Several aspects of Irene's story are often (but not always) related to gender, including a history of sexual and family trauma, a patterns of numbing her trauma through drugs and alcohol, and crimes of survival. During her several years of secure confinement, Irene may not have received adequate services for these issues; thus, they may continue to stifle healthy emotional functioning upon her re-entry to society. In addition, because young women often place more importance on relational issues in their process of desistance from crime (Giordano, Cernkovich, & Holland, 2003), it is important to note that Irene's long period of incarceration and lack of reliable family members may cause her to seek support from the wrong type of people, such as those who could lead her back into trouble with the law. Irene's case is also compounded by her absence of family support and having aged out of services for children, so she may need to be more reliant on adult social welfare systems to provide for her basic necessities. All in all, Irene faces many of the typical difficulties associated with re-entry (i.e., lack of a job or economic security) that are compounded by issues more specific to her gender.

■ Young Woman Case Example: Irene

Irene is a strong-willed and bright young woman of South American descent. She was born to a young mother and a substance-abusing father who abandoned the family when Irene was 2 years old. As the only child growing up with just her mother, Irene recounts a family situation filled with physical and emotional abuse, homelessness, poverty, and transience. In one of the houses where she and her mother lived around age 9, she was sexually molested by one of the residents, causing her to become increasingly distrustful of her mother and leading her toward substance abuse to bury her feelings. She started to skip school and to use drugs and alcohol and stayed away from her house, eventually living on the streets and stealing for survival. After a series of arrests for petty crimes, Irene got herself situated with a job and a place to live on her own at age 15. When her fragile situation fell through due to failure to pay the rent, Irene participated in a carjacking involving the use of a weapon. Barely escaping being tried as an adult for a felony-level crime, the judge gave Irene a lengthy sentence in a state juvenile correctional facility; the facility had very few women but offered her vocational training and a chance to complete her high-school diploma. Upon leaving the facility at age 20, Irene had no family members to return to, only $100 in cash, and a bus ticket. Having aged out of most services for minors, Irene is reliant on some of the connections she made during her sentence, including a pastoral mentor, and some of the friends she made within the facility.

As a re-entry case manager for Irene:

☐ What would you consider to be her most pressing re-entry needs?
☐ How would you approach creating a relationship with Irene that she could trust?
☐ What type of plan would you create to facilitate her community reintegration?
☐ How would you help her to develop a positive social support network?

Dual System (Crossover) Youth

There is a significant overlap between youth who are involved with both the child welfare and juvenile justice systems—a population often termed "dual system" or "crossover" youth. For example, Jonson-Reid and Barth (2000) found that 19% of youth incarcerated in California Youth Authority facilities had child abuse cases investigated after age 6, which they consider a conservative estimate of the total number of child welfare-involved youth who become incarcerated as juveniles. Researchers have estimated that the experience of abuse or neglect as a child increases the likelihood of arrest as a juvenile by 59%, as an adult by 28%, and for a violent crime by 30%. Moreover, abused and neglected children tend to be younger at first arrest and have a record of nearly twice as many offenses (Widom & Maxfield, 2001). This information is important because of the finding in the general delinquency literature that shows early onset is associated with an increased variety, seriousness, and duration of problems (Myner et al., 1998).

Re-entry services are especially important for crossover youth as they have higher rates of recidivism. Cusick, Goerge, and Bell (2009) compared Illinois re-entry youth who had not been in the child welfare system with those who had. Dual-involved youth recidivated 51% of the time while those who were not did so at the rate of 42%. In another study in King County, Washington, the recidivism rate for crossover youth was 42% in the first 6 months as compared to 17% for those without involvement with the child welfare system. After 2 years, the rates became 70% and 34% (Halemba & Siegel, 2011). Involvement in the two systems appears to make re-entry even more challenging for the crossover population.

Research on working with crossover youth has found that interventions similar to those used with solely re-entry young people also promote positive outcomes. These include case management, assessments to determine needs and select services, and the need to assist youth so that they make the transition into a stable adulthood. Before releasing crossover youth from confinement, it is important for those in juvenile justice to collaborate with child welfare workers so that services and resources can be coordinated (Altschuler, Stangler, Berkely, & Burton, 2009). This is especially important as youth involved in both systems have specific needs. For example, in one study of young people nearing release in the Los Angeles County probation system, over 75% of crossover youth were classified as transient, meaning they had moved between homes and placements three or more times in their lives. Of those who were not dual-system, only 43% were transient. In addition, 80% of crossover youth had a history of running away, compared to 41% of youths not involved in the child welfare system (Abrams & Fields, 2008). To effectively help young people with re-entry, services need to be appropriately matched with their needs. This is especially important for crossover youth, who can have distinct needs and less family support upon release. Consider, for example, the case of Tyrone (see box), an African-American young man who spent a significant chunk of his adolescent years between the two systems, ultimately winding up in the "dual-system" category.

In Tyrone's case, some of the specific risk factors for his delinquency stem directly from his experience of a difficult journey through the child welfare system: a failed adoption and drifting among group homes and foster care placements. In regard to his re-entry experience, Tyrone is quite vulnerable to recidivism due to his lack of stable housing, a situation that is quite common for youth aging out of foster care as well as those exiting the juvenile justice system (Hagan & McCarthy, 2005). In addition to his housing needs, specific risks for his recidivism would include his daily drug habit, an absence of education and employment readiness, and lack of secure social support. His longing for connections with his biological family members could be helpful but could also lead to a further sense of disappointment. In this sense, Tyrone's case

---

■ Crossover Case Example: Tyrone

Tyrone is an African-American young man with a shy, personable demeanor. Tyrone was adopted as a baby on account of his mother's drug addiction and an absent father. He recalls that his adoptive family provided for his basic needs, but that as the adopted son in the family, he always felt that he was treated as "less than" his siblings. Tyrone struggled with school as a child, but his more concrete troubles began when he started acting out in adolescence with other foster children who were taken into the home. He described sneaking out of the house, experimenting with drugs and alcohol, skipping school, and generally becoming defiant. When he was accused of deliberately starting a fire in the home at age 13, his adoptive parents relinquished him back to the state and he was sent to live in a group home. Not finding any stability or comfort in a group home setting, he then spent his entire adolescent years moving from placement to placement and found himself in and out of juvenile detention for petty crimes such as selling drugs, stealing, and running away. At age 17, he was placed at a probation camp due to a drug possession charge. He was finally released at the age of 18, having aged out of foster care and struggling to find housing. Tyrone has a strong desire to complete his high school diploma or GED, but his daily marijuana habit gets in the way of him achieving his goals. He would like to reconnect with his biological family, but his biological mother is in prison and his three biological siblings are dispersed throughout the area and have not had the experience of growing up together.

As a re-entry case manager for Tyrone:

☐ What services would you assume to be most pressing for him? How could his dual status be used to access specific resources or services?

☐ How would you go about facilitating a trusting relationship with Tyrone, given his history of uncertain and disappointing relationships with adults?

exemplifies some of the complications and particular challenges involved in re-entry for those with a history of involvement with the child welfare system.

Youth with Disabilities

A growing number of advocates have drawn attention to the overrepresentation of youth with physical, learning, developmental, or emotional/mental disabilities who are incarcerated in the juvenile justice system. Published estimates of youth with various disabilities are quite varied due to the definition of disabilities as well as geographical differences between studies. In the most comprehensive and reliable study of this issue to date, Mary Quinn and colleagues (2005) conducted a national survey of juvenile justice administrators and found the following estimates of conditions classified under the Individuals with Disabilities Education Act (IDEA). Among the states reporting their figures (76% states responded to the survey), 33% of the incarcerated youth were classified as having a disability according to IDEA, compared to 8.8% of the general population as indicated by public school data (U.S. Department of Education, 2001). This means that incarcerated youth are four times more likely to have a disability than the general population. Of those noted as having an IDEA disability, the following classifications were found: emotional disability (47.7%), learning disability (38.6%), mental retardation (9.7%), other health impairments (2.9%), and multiple disabilities (0.8%) (Quinn et al., 2005).

Under IDEA, youth with emotional, learning, developmental, or other diagnosed disabilities are entitled to special education and related services while they are under the authority of the juvenile justice system (Burrell & Warboys, 2000). However, scores of critics as well as more in-depth investigations have charged that the needs of youth with disabilities are rarely addressed within the system, resulting in major lawsuits across the county that have even reached the Supreme Court (Office of Juvenile Justice and Delinquency Prevention, n.d). Research on youth with disabilities in regard to re-entry is sparse. Bullis and colleagues' longitudinal study followed over 500 youth offenders after they returned from the Oregon Youth Authority; 59% of them had a classified IDEA disability. At 6 months after release and controlling for a variety of other factors, those who had a disability were 2.8 times more likely to return to the facility than those without a disability and were 2.2 times less likely to be engaged in work or school. These findings illustrate that the presence of a disability is a major risk factor for a failed re-entry process.

Recognizing the need for research on youth with disabilities and re-entry, the National Council on Disabilities (2003, pp. 169–170) recommends the following in considering young people's re-entry and transition needs:

☐ The provisions of IDEA cover all state and local juvenile and criminal adult corrections facilities. Court and administrative decisions have applied IDEA to detention and training schools, jails, and prisons.

☐ Identification of youth with disabilities should be promoted through shared school records and reliance on quality evaluation processes. Local education agencies (LEAs) should assist with identification in situations where short-term facilities have insufficient resources to conduct eligibility evaluations.

☐ Youth with disabilities must be served and educated with non-disabled youth unless the youth's disabilities and individualized education plans (IEPs) cannot be addressed.

☐ Incarcerated youth have due process protections under IDEA that must be observed. Per IDEA, positive behavioral interventions should be integrated with institutional plans, and parents must be included in the IEP process unless a court specifies otherwise.

☐ Eligibility for IDEA services, transitional and interim services and implementation of IDEA, and continuity of IEPs before, during, and after incarceration should be facilitated by schools, LEAs, and the juvenile justice system. IEPs must be provided during lockdowns.

IDEA presents an opportunity to help more incarcerated youth who have disabilities within the system, but only if systems are implementing the law correctly. Currently very little is known about the extent to which the needs of youth with disabilities are being met within the juvenile justice system or upon their re-entry to the community. Clearly more research is needed to assist in advocating for this group who are highly prone to recidivism following their release.

Consider the case of José (see box), which illustrates some of the issues that may arise when working with youth with disabilities in a re-entry capacity.

In José's case, long-term neglect of his learning disability had a major effect on his pattern of delinquency. With multiple school transitions and placements, his disabilities were not diagnosed until he was an adolescent, when he had already drifted from a mainstream school setting and toward negative peer influences. Moreover, cultural factors prevented the parents from being able to advocate for Jose or accept the presence of his diagnoses. From the re-entry perspective, it will be important for Jose to retain his IEP in his new school and remain under the care of a physician for his medication. The social worker would also have to work with the whole family system to accept José's need to follow his transition plans in regard to both his medication and his IEP. José's situation represents how a social worker might also have to invoke the IDEA law to secure continuity of services in an educational setting.

■ **Youth with Disabilities Case Example: José**

José is a Latino young man and a second-generation immigrant from Mexico. Jose began school in kindergarten speaking mostly Spanish, so he was classified as "Limited English Proficient" and placed in a separate classroom. By second grade, his teachers suspected he had attention-deficit/hyperactivity disorder (ADHD) based on his inability to sit still in the classroom and his impulsive behaviors. His parents did not fully understand the possible diagnosis and did not have him assessed or treated. When José was mainstreamed into English classes in fourth grade he was increasingly disruptive, resulting in multiple suspensions and moving schools several times. However, due to his multiple moves and various schools, he was not tested for a behavioral disorder and did not receive any specific services. In middle school, he started to skip school most the time and joined a local gang. His truancy, arrests for "tagging," and defiance at home eventually led to multiple stints in juvenile hall, group homes, and correctional centers beginning at age 14. In one of his group homes José was finally diagnosed with a learning disability and ADHD, resulting in the implementation of an IEP. At age 17, the court allowed José to return home with credits toward a high-school diploma and a prescription for medication to control his impulsivity. His family has welcomed him home but doesn't believe that he has any significant mental health problems.

As a re-entry case manager for José:

☐ What would you consider to be his most pressing needs upon return to his home?
☐ How would you approach working with José's family to keep him on track to graduate from high school?
☐ How would you ensure that his receiving school enforces his IEP?

■ **Summary and Conclusion**

In sum, there is continued widespread consensus among practitioners, policymakers, and criminal justice experts that re-entry services are an important component of success for a young person who is re-entering the community following a correctional stay. Re-entry and aftercare services conform well to the juvenile justice system's overarching goal of rehabilitation. However, existing research has not turned up much support for the efficacy of re-entry services in reducing recidivism. Some of the best-funded experiments, such as the IAP, have not yielded promising results. Family interventions appear to have an evidence base for greater efficacy but often require the assistance of a trained therapist for maximum results (Curtis et al., 2004). There is much more to be learned about re-entry and aftercare interventions, and future research should consider the following types of questions:

☐ Who is most likely to benefit from specific re-entry interventions?
☐ How long (and by whom) should re-entry interventions be delivered?
☐ How can we optimize intervention effects over time?

☐ Is there increased benefit to adding family treatments to an individual case management or mentoring approach?

☐ What is the role of neighborhood effects in producing recidivism outcomes for those involved in re-entry services?

☐ What would a model program look like for young women in the system? For crossover youth? For youth with varying types of disabilities?

With a concerted blend of creativity, rigorous science, and funding, it is likely that re-entry and aftercare services will continue to increase their reach for young people involved in the U.S. juvenile justice system.

References

Abrams, L. S. (2007). From corrections to community: Youth offenders' perceptions of the challenges of transition. *Journal of Offender Rehabilitation, 44*(2/3), 31–53. doi:10.1300/J076v44n02_02

Abrams, L. S., & Fields, D. (2008). *Perceived needs, barriers, and social supports among the youth re-entry population in Los Angeles County.* Los Angeles: UCLA Department of Social Welfare, School of Public Affairs.

Abrams, L. S., & Freisthler, B. (2010). A spatial analysis of risks and resources for re-entry youth in Los Angeles County. *Journal of the Society for Social Work Research, 1*(1), 41–55.

Abrams, L. S., Shannon, S. K. S., & Sangalang. C. (2008). Transition services for incarcerated youth: A mixed-methods evaluation study. *Child and Youth Services Review, 30,* 522–535.

Abrams, L. S., Terry, D., & Franke, T. (2011). Community-based juvenile re-entry services: The effects of service dosage on juvenile and adult recidivism. *Journal of Offender Rehabilitation, 50,* 492–510. doi:10.1080/10509674.2011.596919

Aftercare for Indiana (2004, January). *Aftercare for Indiana through Mentoring (AIM) progress to date.* Retrieved from http://aim.spea.iupui.edu/reentry/latest_research.htm.

Altschuler, D. M., & Armstrong, T. L. (1994). *Intensive aftercare for high-risk juveniles: A community care model.* Washington, DC: Office of Juvenile Justice and Delinquency Prevention, Office of Justice Programs, U.S. Department of Justice.

Altschuler, D. M., & Brash, R. (2004). Adolescent and teenage offenders confronting the challenges and opportunities of reentry. *Youth Violence and Juvenile Justice, 2,* 72–87.

Altschuler, D., Stangler, G., Berkley, K., & Burton, L. (2009). *Supporting youth in transition to adulthood: Lessons learned from child welfare and juvenile justice.* Washington, DC: Center for Juvenile Justice Reform, Georgetown University.

Aos, S. (2004). *Washington State's Family Integrated Transitions program for juvenile offenders: Outcome evaluation and cost-benefit analysis.* Olympia, WA: Washington State Institute for Public Policy. Retrieved from http://www.wsipp.wa.gov/pub.asp?docid=04-12-1201

Barton, W. H. (2006). Incorporating the strengths perspective into intensive juvenile aftercare. *Western Criminology Review 7*(2), 48–61.

Benda, B. B., & Tollett, C. L. (1999). A study of recidivism of serious and persistent offenders among adolescents. *Journal of Criminal Justice, 27*(2), 111–126, doi:10.1016/S0047-2352(98)00051-8

Bloom, B., Owen, B., Deschenes, E., & Rosenbaum, J (2002). Improving juvenile justice for females: A statewide assessment in California. *Crime & Delinquency, 48*(4), 526–552.

Bolas, J. (2011). *State of the city's homeless youth report 2011*. Retrieved from http://www. empirestatecoalition.org/main/pages/escnyc.html

Bouffard, J. A., & Bergseth, K. J. (2008). The impact of reentry services on juvenile offenders' recidivism. *Youth Violence and Juvenile Justice, 6*, 295–318. doi:10.1177/1541204007313384

Bullis, M., & Yovanoff, P. (2002). Those who do not return: Correlates of the work and school engagement of formerly incarcerated youth who remain in the community. *Journal of Emotional and Behavioral Disorders, 10*(2), 66–79. doi:10.1177/10634266020100020101

Bullis, M., Yovanoff, P., Mueller, G., & Havel, E. (2002). Life on the "outs"—examination of the facility-to-community transition of incarcerated youth. *Exceptional Children, 69*, 7–22.

Burrell, S., & Warboys, L. (2000). *Special education and the juvenile justice system*. Washington, DC: Office of Juvenile Justice and Delinquency Prevention.

California Juvenile Justice Reentry Partnership (2007). *California Juvenile Justice Reentry Partnership (CJJRP) aims to improve outcomes for youth*. Retrieved from http://www.cjcj. org/juvenile/justice/california/juvenile/justice/reentry/institute

Cauffman, E. (2008). Bad boys or poor parents: Relations to female juvenile delinquents, *Journal of Research on Adolescence, 18*(4), 699–712.

Center for Substance Abuse Prevention (2002, April). *Mentoring initiatives: An overview of youth mentoring programs*. Washington, DC: Author.

Coffey, O. D., & Gemignani, M. G. (1994). *Effective practices in juvenile correctional education: A study of the literature and research*. Washington, DC: Office of Juvenile Justice and Delinquency Prevention Retrieved from http://eric.ed.gov/ERICDocs/ data/ ericdocs2sql/content_storage_01/0000019b/80/14/61/57.pdf

Cusick, G. R., Goerge, R. M., & Bell, K. C. (2009). *From corrections to community: The juvenile reentry experience as characterized by multiple systems involvement*. Chicago: Chapin Hall Center for Children at the University of Chicago.

Curtis, N. A., Ronan, K., R., & Bourdin, C. A. (2004). Multisystemic treatment: A meta-analysis of outcome studies. *Journal of Family Psychology, 18*(3), 411–419.

Damooei, J. (2010, April). The *evaluation report for targeted reentry program of the Boys and Girls Clubs of Greater Oxnard and Port Hueneme*. Unpublished report: California Lutheran University. Retrieved from: http://www.positiveplace4kids.org/aboutus/Report_TRE_ Program_BGCOGOPH.pdf

Dembo, R., Williams, L., Schmeidler, J., Getreu, A., & Berry, E. (1991). Recidivism among high risk youths: A 2-1/2-year follow-up of a cohort of juvenile detainees. *International Journal of the Addictions, 11*, 1197–1221. Retrieved from http:// informahealthcare.com/doi/ pdfplus/10.3109/10826089109053178

Drake, E. K., Aos, S., & Miller, M. G. (2009). Evidence-based public policy options to reduce crime and criminal justice costs: Implications in Washington state. *Victims and Offenders, 4*, 170–196. doi:10.1080/15564880802612615

Drake, E. K., & Barnowski, R. (2006, July). *Recidivism findings for the juvenile rehabilitation administration mentoring program: Final report*. Olympia, Washington: Washington State Institute for Public Policy. Retrieved from http://www.wsipp.wa.gov/pub. asp?docid=06-07-1202

Elliott, D., Wilson, W. J., Huizinga, D., Sampson, R., Elliott, A., & Rankin, B. (1996). The effects of neighborhood disadvantage on adolescent development. *Journal of Research on Crime and Delinquency, 33*, 389–426. doi:10.1177/0022427896033004002

Fields, D., & Abrams, L. S. (2010). Gender differences in the perceived needs and barriers of youth offenders preparing for community reentry. *Child and Youth Care Forum, 39*, 253–269.

Frederick, B., & Roy, D. (2003, June). *Recidivism among youth released from the youth leadership academy to the city challenge intensive aftercare program*. Research Report from the Office of Justice Systems Analysis. New York: New York State Division of Criminal

Justice Services. Retrieved from http://criminaljustice.state.ny.us/crimnet/ojsa/yla/yla_report.pdf

Gies, S. V. (2003). *Aftercare services.* Washington, DC: U.S. Department of Justice, Office of Justice Programs, Office of Juvenile Justice and Delinquency Prevention.

Giordano, P. C., Cernkovich, S. A., & Holland, D. D. (2003). Changes in friendship relations over the life course: Implications for desistance from crime. *Criminology, 41*(2), 293–328. doi:10.1111/j.1745-9125.2003.tb00989.x

Grisso, T. (2004). *Double jeopardy: Adolescent offenders with mental disorders.* Chicago: University of Chicago.

Hagan, J., & McCarthy, B. (2005). Homeless youth and the perilous passage to adulthood. In D. W. Osgood, E. Michael Foster, C. Flanagan, & G. R. Ruth (Eds.), *On your own without a net: The transition to adulthood for vulnerable populations.* Chicago: University of Chicago.

Halemba, G., & Siegel, G. (2011). *Doorways to delinquency: Multi-system involvement of delinquent youth in King County (Seattle, WA).* Pittsburgh, PA: National Center for Juvenile Justice.

Harris, P., Mennis, J., Obradovic, Z., Izenman, A., & Grunwald. H. (2011). The coaction of neighborhood and individual effects on recidivism. *Cityscape, 13*(3), 33–55.

Hoge, R. D., & Andrews, D. A. (2009). *Youth level of service/case management inventory.* North Tawanada, NY: MHS.

Inderbitzin, M. (2009). Reentry of emerging adults: Adolescent inmates' transition back into the community. *Journal of Adolescent Research, 24*(4), 453–476.

Jarjoura, G. R. (2003). *They all come back: Reflections on a juvenile reentry initiative.* Paper presented at the ACJJ Statewide Conference on Juvenile Justice and Delinquency Prevention. Retrieved from http://aim.spea.iupui.edu/reentry/aftercare%5B1%5D.arkansas.ppt

Jonson-Reid, M., & Barth, R. (2000). From maltreatment report to juvenile incarceration: The role of child welfare services. *Child Abuse and Neglect, 24*, 505–520, doi:10.1016/S0145-2134(00)00107-1

Justice Policy Institute (2009). *The costs of confinement: Why good juvenile justice policies make good fiscal sense.* Washington, DC: Author. Retrieved from http://www.justicepolicy.org/images/upload/09_05_REP_CostsOfConfinement_JJ_PS.pdf

Koppelman, J. (2005). *Mental health and juvenile justice: Moving toward more effective systems of care.* National Health Policy Forum: George Washington University. Issue Brief—No. 805. Retrieved from www.nhpf.org

Martinez, D. P., & Abrams, L. S. (2013). Informal social support among returning young offenders: A meta-synthesis of the literature. *International Journal of Offender Therapy and Comparative Criminology, 57*(2) 169–190.

Myner, J., Santman, J., Cappelletty, G. G., & Perlmutter, B. F. (1998). Variables related to recidivism among juvenile offenders. *International Journal of Offender Therapy and Comparative Criminology, 42*(1), 65–80. doi:10.1177/0306624X9842100

Moffit, T. E. (1990). Juvenile delinquency and attention deficit disorder: Boys' developmental trajectories from ages 3–15. *Child Development, 61*, 610–893 Retrieved from http://www.jstor.org/pss/1130972

National Council on Disability (2003, May). *Addressing the needs of youth with disabilities in the juvenile justice system: The current status of evidence-based research.* Washington, DC: Author.

Niarhos, F. J., & Routh, D. K. (1992). The role of clinical assessment in the juvenile court: Predictors of juvenile dispositions and recidivism. *Journal of Clinical Child Psychology, 21*, 151–159, doi:10.1207/s15374424jccp2102_7

Office of Juvenile Justice and Delinquency Prevention (n.d.). *Educational advocacy for youth with disabilities.* Retrieved from: http://www.ojjdp.gov/pubs/walls/sect-03.html

Osgood, D. W., Foster, E. M., & Courtney, M. E. (2010). Vulnerable populations and the transition to adulthood. *The Future of Children,* 20, 209–229. Retrieved from http://www.princeton.edu/futureofchildren/publications/docs/20_01_10.pdf

Puzzanchera, C., & Kang, W. (2011). *Easy access to juvenile court statistics: 1985–2009.* Available: http://www.ojjdp.gov/ojstatbb/ezajcs/

Quinn, M. M., Rutherford, R., Leone, P., Osher, J., & Poirer, P. (2005). Youth with disabilities in corrections: A national survey. *Exceptional Children,* 71(3), 339–345.

Rhodes, J., Grossman J., & Resch, N. (2000). Agents of change: Pathways through which mentoring relationships influence adolescents' academic adjustment. *Child Development,* 71(6), 1662–1671.

Sawyer, A., & Borduin, C. (2011). Effects of Multi-Systemic Therapy through midlife: A 21.9-year follow-up to a randomized clinical trial with serious and violent offenders. *Journal of Consulting and Clinical Psychology,* 79(5), 643–652. doi:10.1037/a0024862

Sexton, T. L., & Alexander, J. F. (2003). Functional family therapy: A mature clinical model for working with at-risk adolescents and their families. In T. L. Sexton, G. R. Weeks, & M. S. Robbins (Eds.), *Handbook of family therapy: The science and practice of working with families.* New York: Taylor & Francis.

Shelton, E. (2009). Key findings from the 2009 statewide survey. In E. Shelton, J. Heineman, & G. Owen, *Homelessness in Minnesota.* Retrieved from http://www.wilder.org/Wilder-Research/Research-Areas/Homelessness/Pages/default.aspx

Sickmund, M., Sladky, T. J., Kang, W., & Puzzanchera, C. (2011). *Easy access to the census of juveniles in residential placement.* Washington, DC: US Department of Justice, Office of Justice Programs, Office of Juvenile Justice and Delinquency Prevention. http://www.ojjdp.gov/ojstatbb/ezacjrp/

Simka-Fagan, O., & Schwartz, J. (1986). Neighborhood and delinquency: An assessment of contextual effects. *Criminology,* 24, 667–699. Retrieved from http://heinonline.org/HOL/Page?handle=hein.journals/crim24&div=43&g_sent=1

Snyder, H. N. (2004). An empirical portrait of the youth reentry population. *Youth Violence and Juvenile Justice,* 2, 39–55. doi:10.1177/1541204003260046

Snyder, H. N., & Sickmund, M. (2006). *Juvenile offenders and victims: 2006 national report.* Washington, DC: USDOJ, Office of Justice Programs, OJJDP, National Center for Juvenile Justice.

Sullivan, M. L. (1989). *Getting paid: youth crime and work in the inner city.* Ithaca, NY: Cornell University Press.

Teplin, L. A., Abram, K. M., McClelland, G. M., Dulcan, M. K., & Mericle, A. A. (2002). Psychiatric disorders in youth in juvenile detention. *Archives of General Psychiatry,* 59, 1133–1143. Retrieved from http://www.nctsnet.org/nctsn_assets/Articles/104.pdf

Timmons-Mitchell, M. B., Bender, M. A., Kishna, C. C., & Mitchell, C. C. (2006). An independent effectiveness trial of Multi-Systemic Therapy with juvenile justice youth. *Journal of Clinical Child and Adolescent Psychology,* 35, 37–41. doi:10.1207/s15374424jccp3502_6

Toldson, I. A., Woodson, K. M., Braithwaite, R., Holliday, R. C., & Rosa, D. L. (2010). Academic potential among African American adolescents in juvenile detention centers: Implications for reentry to school. *Journal of Offender Rehabilitation,* 49(8), 551–570. doi:http://dx.doi.org/10.1080/10509674.2010.519666

Trulson, C. R., Marquart, J. W., Mullings, J. L., & Caeti, T. J. (2005). In between adolescence and adulthood: Recidivism outcomes of a cohort of state delinquents. *Youth Violence and Juvenile Justice,* 3, 355–387, doi:10.1177/1541204005278802

Trupin, E., Kerns, S., Walker, S., DeRobertis, M., & Stewart, D. (2011). Family Integrated Transitions: A promising program for juvenile offenders with co-occurring disorders. *Journal of Child & Adolescent Substance Abuse,* 20, 421–436.

Trupin, E. W., Stewart, D. G., Beach, B., & Boesky, L. (2002). Effectiveness of a dialectical behaviour therapy program for incarcerated female juvenile offenders. *Child and Adolescent Mental Health, 7*(3), 121–127.

Underwood, L. A., von Dresner, K. S., & Phillips, A. L. (2006). Community treatment programs for juveniles: A best-evidence summary. *International Journal of Behavioral Consultation and Therapy, 2*, 286–304 Retrieved from http://www. eric.ed.gov:80/ERICDocs/data/ ericdocs2sql/content_storage_01/0000019b/ 80/3e/6f/05.pdf

Wells, J. B., Minor, K. I., Angel, E., & Stearman, K. D. (2006). A quasi-experimental evaluation of a shock incarceration and aftercare program for juvenile offenders. *Youth Violence and Juvenile Justice* 2006, 4, 219, doi:10.1177/1541204006290153

Widom, C. S., & Maxfield, M. G. (2001). *An update on the "cycle of violence": Research in Brief.* Washington, DC: U.S. Department of Justice, Office of Justice Programs.

Wiebush, R. G., McNulty, B., & Le, T. (2000, July). *Implementation of the intensive community-based aftercare program.* Washington, DC: U.S. Department of Justice, Office of Juvenile Delinquency and Delinquency Prevention.

Wiebush, R. G., Wagner, D., McNulty, B., & Wang, Y. (2005). *Implementation and outcome evaluation of the Intensive Aftercare Program. Final report* (NCJ Report No. 206177). Washington, DC: National Council on Crime and Delinquency. Retrieved from the U.S. Department of Justice, Office of Justice Programs http://www.ncjrs.gov/pdffiles1/ ojjdp/206177.pdf

Wikstrom, P., & Loeber, R. (2000). Do disadvantaged neighborhoods cause well-adjusted children to become adolescent delinquents? A study of male juvenile serious offending, individual risk and protective factors, and neighborhood context. *Criminology, 37,* 1109–1142.

Zahn, M. A., Brumbaugh, S., Steffensmeier, D., Feld, B. C., Morash, M., et al. (2008). *Girls study group: Understanding and responding to girls' delinquency.* Washington, DC: US Department of Justice, Office of Justice Programs, Office of Juvenile Justice and Delinquency Prevention. Retrieved from: https://www.ncjrs.gov/pdffiles1/ ojjdp/218905.pdf

IV

Evidence-Based Assessment and Treatment with Juvenile Delinquents

17 Risk Assessment with Juvenile Offenders

Henrika McCoy, Joshua P. Mersky, John Leverso,

and Elizabeth A. Bowen

■ Case Example

Dan is a 16-year-old African-American boy who has been arrested for theft. He is not a member of a gang, but he lives in an area where many young men are involved in gangs, and the neighborhood has experienced increasing economic destabilization during the past few years. He lives at home with his biological parents and two younger sisters; his older brother is in his second year of college at a state university located a few hours away. Both of Dan's parents work. His father is a mechanic in an auto shop and his mother is a cashier at a large-box store, but his family does not have health insurance. His mother has been employed at her current job for 3 months but she suffers from chronic back pain, due to a work-related injury a number of years ago, and so it is often difficult for her to maintain regular employment. Dan has attempted to find part-time work to help out his family, but it has been challenging, so, for the past year, he has been regularly stealing food, other items needed for the household, or items that he can easily sell for quick cash to help his family make ends meet. While leaving the large supercenter big-box store not far from his home, Dan is stopped by the security guard. When his backpack is searched the security guard finds milk, lunchmeat, DVDs, batteries, and a number of small electronics. This is the first time that Dan has been arrested, but the items total more than $500, making his crime a Class 3 felony and therefore punishable by up to 5 years in detention. He is subsequently arrested by the local police. His parents are at work and could not be reached to pick him up, so he is held overnight at the local youth detention facility for a hearing to be held the next day.

■ Scope of the Problem

Risk assessments are designed to identify which youth are at the greatest risk of re-offending. Identifying youth who engage in delinquent behavior has been of interest to the legal system since the founding of the juvenile court in 1899 in Cook County, Illinois. The facilitation of this interest has varied widely. When the court was founded, the philosophy was *parens patriae*, "the state must care for those who cannot take care of themselves" (Campbell, 1991, p. 769), which enabled the state to assume a parental role for children not yet at the legal age to care for themselves (Snyder & Sickmund, 2006). However, since that time, a number of circumstances have influenced how youth enter and traverse through the juvenile justice system. In 1967, the Supreme Court decision *In re Gault* moved the court away from *parens patriae* (Feld, 1993), and nationwide jurisdictions followed by changing their system response to youth from rehabilitative to punitive (Gardner, 1997). In addition, due to actual crimes (i.e., school shootings in the 1990s and 2000s), falsehoods (i.e., the predicted rampages of juvenile superpredators), and increased media attention, many erroneously believed that juvenile crime was increasing during the past few decades.

■ Demographics in the Juvenile Justice System: Trends, Race, and Gender

In 1960, there were 1.1 million cases in the juvenile justice system. A subsequent surge began in 1985 and peaked in 1997 with over 1.8 million cases (Puzzanchera, Adams, & Hockenberry, 2012). As of 2009, there were 1.5 million delinquency cases handled in the juvenile justice system, with 52% of those offenses being committed by juveniles younger than age 16 (Puzzanchera et al., 2012).

The juvenile justice system is disproportionately made up of youth of color (Puzzanchera et al., 2012). This disproportionate minority contact has plagued the system for decades and was initially classified as "disproportionate minority confinement" and identified in 1988 by the National Coalition of State Juvenile Justice Advisory Groups (Roscoe & Morton, 1994). The most recent statistics indicate that in 2009, the demographics for the general population were 77% White, 16% Black, 1% Native American, and 5% Asian/Native Hawaiian/Pacific Islander (Puzzanchera & Adams, 2011), while the demographics for youth in the juvenile justice system were 64% White, 34% Black, 1% Native American, and 1% Asian/Native Hawaiian/Pacific Islander (Puzzanchera, Adams, & Hockenberry, 2012). The estimates for the number of Hispanic and Latino youth in the juvenile justice population are difficult to discern from federal reports because the Office for Juvenile Justice and Delinquency Prevention (OJJDP) includes them in the racial category of White (Puzzanchera, Adams, & Sickmund, 2010). However, researchers from other sources have noted that Hispanic and Latino youth are also disproportionately represented in the juvenile justice system when compared to White youth (Villarruel & Walker, 2001). Native American youth are also overrepresented in the juvenile justice system (Hartney, 2008). Their overall population is 1.4%, but their rates of involvement with the system, except for arrests, increase at each level, with the highest at 2.1% for those who are waived to the adult system and 2.3% for those sent to out-of-home placements (Hartney, 2008). In nearly every state, youth of color are significantly more likely than White youth to be treated more harshly in the juvenile justice system, including arrest, detention, prosecution, incarceration, and transfer to adult court, and ultimately more frequent confinement in large public institutions versus private institutions (Bishop, 2005; Hartney, 2008; Models for Change, 2011a; Villarruel & Walker, 2001).

Although not statistically disproportionate when compared to the demographics of the general population, the numbers of girls entering the juvenile justice system is steadily increasing. In 2009, girls accounted for 28% of all cases, with an average increase of 3% each year since 1985 (Puzzanchera et al., 2012). In fact, while the number of cases involving males decreased 24% between 1997 and 2009, the numbers of cases involving females decreased only 1% (Puzzanchera et al., 2012). Finally, across all offenses, the numbers of arrests for girls either increased more or decreased less than the number of arrests for boys (Zahn et al., 2010) and girls are now offending at earlier ages at higher rates (Emeka & Sorenson, 2009).

■ Risk Assessment Utility

The risk assessment process is engaged in during various decision points in the juvenile justice system ranging from arrest to placement. Historically, it was informal and was used at the discretion of individuals who had variable training and knowledge and employed different philosophies and criteria (Glaser, 1987; Grisso, 1998; Wiebush et al., 1995). But in the effort to improve methods of prediction, protection, and prevention, many professionals who work with at-risk youth have come to rely on standardized risk assessment procedures to guide their decisions (Schwalbe, 2007).

The most prominent model for offender rehabilitation is Risk-Needs-Responsivity (RNR). This model relies on risk, need, responsivity, and professional discretion (Andrews, Bonta, & Hoge, 1990; Vincent, Paiva-Salisbury, Cook, Guy, & Perrault, 2012; Ward, Mesler, & Yates, 2007). Offenders are generally delineated into three categories (low-, moderate-, and high-risk) based on their risk factors for violence and aggression (Table 17.1).

Low-risk offenders are viewed as requiring little to no court intervention (Steen, Bond, Bridges, & Kubrin, 2005). Moderate-risk offenders are perceived as vulnerable to reoffending if an appropriate intervention is not implemented (Steen et al., 2005). Those identified as being at most risk of reoffending due to a combination of various risk factors are called high-risk offenders. The risk principle indicates that high-risk offenders are at the greatest risk for reoffending and therefore should receive the most intensive services and monitoring, while low-risk offenders should have minimal intervention or monitoring (Andrews et al., 1990; Vincent et al., 2012; Ward et al., 2007).

The needs principle focuses on criminogenic factors that, if targeted, could possibly alter the chance of recidivism. The principle of responsivity has two components: general and specific (Bonta & Andrews, 2007). General responsivity refers to using influencing behavior through cognitive social learning strategies, whereas specific responsivity is focused on adjusting the cognitive-behavioral intervention to an offender's level of motivation, strengths, personality, learning style, race, and gender. Finally, professional discretion ensures that clinical judgment overrides the aforementioned principles if determined necessary (Andrews et al., 1990; Vincent et al., 2012; Ward et al., 2007).

Risk assessment tools serve many functions and are necessary with the RNR model. As a strategy for decreasing recidivism, they can estimate a

Table 17.1   **Key Risk Factors for Violence and Aggression in Youth**

Historical Factors	Clinical Factors	Contextual Factors
History of violence and delinquency	Substance use problems	Negative peer relations
Early initiation of violence	Mental or behavioral disorder	Gang violence
School problems	Psychopathy	Delinquent peers
Academic failure	Risk taking/impulsivity	Rejected
Low bonding or interest	Behavioral instability	Alienated
Truancy	Affective instability	Poor parental/family management
Frequent school transitions	Risk taking	Poor family management
Victim of maltreatment/abuse	Negative attitudes	Little interaction between youth and parents
Physical abuse	Lack of empathy/remorse	Extreme or inconsistent parental discipline
Sexual abuse	Attitudes that support violence	Lack of personal/social support
Neglect	Hostile attribution bias	Stress & losses
Home/family maladjustment		Contextual crime and violence
Family conflict		Neighborhood crime
Parental criminality		Community disorganization
Low bonding within family		Availability of drugs

Key Risk Factors for Violence and Aggression in Youth. Reprinted from "Assessing violence risk among youth," by R. Borum, 2000, *Journal of Clinical Psychology, 56*(10), p. 1267. Copyright 2000 by John Wiley & Sons, Inc. Reprinted with permission.

juvenile's likelihood of continued involvement in delinquent behavior, including future violence. Risk assessments can also be used to gather information for decision-making purposes such as developing suitable risk management plans so that the most appropriate type of intervention, given a juvenile's level of risk and the number of active risk factors, can be identified (Shepherd, Luebbers, & Dolan 2013). Using such information enables youth to be differentiated by their risk of reoffending and can help to initiate sanctions, including making decisions about adjudication and disposition (Skeem & Monahan, 2011), custodial sentencing, and determination of when those sanctions should be eased or lifted. By identifying the offenders who are most likely to reoffend, public safety can be promoted (Borum, 2000; Wormith & Olver, 2002) and the ability to identify and implement appropriate treatment for youth increases (Wormith & Olver, 2002).

Finally, risk assessments are also used as part of the larger strategy to reduce gender and race disparities in the juvenile justice system (Schwalbe, Fraser, Day, & Cooley, 2006). For example, they can be viewed as part of a larger strategy to increase consistency across sanctioning juveniles, thereby reducing race, ethnicity, and gender disparities and biases in the juvenile justice system (Schwalbe et al., 2006). Mental health and legal professionals frequently use risk assessments to evaluate youth who have been adjudicated or arrested (Vincent et al., 2012) because they allow practitioners to (1) identify and manage youth who are at risk of engaging in offending behavior (Singh, Grann, & Fazel, 2011), (2) estimate the likelihood that a youth will continue to engage in delinquent behavior if an intervention is not utilized, (3) determine the best areas to target with an intervention so as to reduce reoffending, and (4) provide an agency with a standardized method for collecting data (Vincent, Guy, & Grisso, 2012). Valid risk assessments can also inform rehabilitative service plans (Olver, Stockdale, & Wormith, 2009). Assessment data can be used to tailor mental health treatment and other services for juveniles according to their level of need and, in turn, enhance their well-being and reduce the risk of recidivism.

Although most youth who are first-time offenders do not return to the juvenile justice system, four in 10 first-time offenders do recidivate, with repeat offending accounting for the majority of those who engage in delinquent behavior (Barrett, Katsiyannis, & Zhang, 2010). It has been widely demonstrated that recidivism is linked to both static and dynamic (criminogenic) risk factors (Mulder, Brand, Bullens, & van Marle, 2011). While both types of risk factors are indicators of future delinquent behavior, static factors such as prior delinquent behavior or age at first offense cannot improve over time, whereas dynamic risk factors such as peers, mental health needs, or family problems can improve over time (Schwalbe, Fraser, & Day, 2007). It is these criminogenic factors that are often most influential in judicial decisions (Hoge, 2002). The actual severity of reoffending behavior is characterized by the frequency, the type of new offenses, and the amount of harm caused (Mulder et al., 2011).

The format of risk assessments has evolved over time, and in 1954, they were divided for the first time conceptually into whether they used a clinical or actuarial approach (Skeem & Monahan, 2011). Their use has steadily increased since their inception, particularly in response to the Juvenile Justice Delinquency Prevention Act of 1974 (JJDPA; Vincent et al., 2012), and a variety have been created specifically for use with juvenile offenders. They are often delineated into categories, including brief or comprehensive assessments, or according to the decision point at which the assessment is used— pre-adjudication detention, adjudication, disposition, juvenile corrections, or community re-entry. However, in clinical practice, they are often identified by whether the juvenile being assessed is a nonviolent, violent, or sexual offender. In addition, in the literature risk assessments are commonly delineated by generation—first, second, third, or fourth. Following this convention, the following descriptions are reviewed according to generation of development.

First-Generation Risk Assessments

Until the 1970s, assessments remained primarily clinical and were based on the judgments of correctional staff and clinical professionals (Bonta & Andrews, 2007). These first-generation (1G) risk assessments usually unfolded as an unstructured process that was not conducive to gathering, recording, and organizing information, much less facilitating theory development or hypothesis testing. This form of assessment was relied upon, but evidence gradually accumulated that called into question the predictive validity of professional judgment alone. Eventually research revealed that 1G assessments did not perform much better than chance in forecasting recidivism (Andrews, Bonta, & Wormith, 2006).

Second-Generation Risk Assessments

Growing recognition of the limitations of 1G assessments contributed to the emergence of second-generation (2G) risk assessments, which were founded on an actuarial, empirical approach (Bonta & Andrews, 2007; Monahan & Steadman, 1994). Actuarial instruments measure an array of individual and contextual correlates of recidivism, including offense history, psychopathy, antisocial behavior, and substance use count, which are among the more robust individual predictors of reoffending. In addition, 2G assessments often contain an array of family (e.g., criminality, violence), peer (e.g., delinquency, gang involvement), school (e.g., low achievement, dropout), and neighborhood (e.g., crime, social disorganization) factors that are associated with general delinquency and crime (Cottle, Lee, & Heilbrun, 2001; Lipsey & Derzon, 1998; Schwalbe, 2007). Often adapted from adult risk prototypes such as the Salient Factor Score (Hoffman & Beck, 1974), instruments such as the Model Risk Assessment (Howell, 1995) were developed to identify juveniles who are most likely to reoffend (Schwalbe, 2007). Administered to at-risk youth, these tools yield summative risk scores that are positively correlated with reoffending. Meta-analyses have shown conclusively that 2G assessments have acceptable predictive validity and that they are superior to unstructured clinical judgments in predicting juvenile and adult reoffending (Cottle et al., 2001; Grove et al., 2000; Schwalbe, 2007).

Nevertheless, 2G assessments have two significant limitations. First, they are atheoretical (Bonta & Andrews, 2007). They generally measure correlates of recidivism without reference to an underlying etiology of delinquency and crime. This is particularly true of risk assessments used with juveniles that have been adapted from adult risk models without sufficient consideration for the distinctive precursors of youth offending (Olver et al., 2009). Second, 2G instruments typically itemize static risks—that is, they measure dichotomous indicators of prior risk (i.e., yes/no) that are not subject to change over time

(Borum, 2000). Therefore, they are limited in their capacity to inform and evaluate rehabilitative strategies and programs.

Third-Generation Risk Assessments

Given the limitations of 2G instruments, they have largely been replaced by a third generation (3G) of theory-informed assessments that were developed in the late 1970s and early 1980s. Unlike their 2G predecessors, 3G assessments emphasize the measurement of dynamic risks that are sensitive to change. For instance, rather than simply documenting whether an offender has a history of substance use, 3G assessments capture changes in substance use patterns and other associated risks over time (Bonta & Andrews, 2007). Additionally, 3G assessments, like the Level of Service Inventory–Revised (LSI-R; Andrews, Bonta, & Wormith, 2003), created for those 16 years and older, were designed to measure not only risk but also needs that can be addressed through rehabilitative services. As such, 3G risk-need assessments were expected to improve predictions of reoffending as well as case planning and institutional monitoring of service effectiveness (Bonta & Andrews, 2007). Indeed, empirical evidence suggests that 3G assessments have strong psychometric properties and overall outperform 2G assessments, albeit only slightly, in predicting recidivism (Raynor, 2007; Schwalbe, 2007).

Fourth-Generation Risk Assessments

Beginning in the early 2000s and by building on the advances of 3G assessment approaches, a fourth generation (4G) of risk assessments have been released that aim to align assessment data with intervention and monitoring protocols (Andrews et al., 2006). Assessments such as the Level of Service/Case Management Inventory (LS/CMI; Andrews, Bonta, & Wormith, 2004), created for those 16 years old and older, account for a broad range of risks, needs, and protective factors. It also includes information that can be used to match at-risk youth with appropriate intervention strategies. This strategy means that outcomes can be directly linked to the assessment of risk, needs, strengths, and responsivity as well as the reassessment of intermediate outcomes, service plans, and service delivery (Andrews et al., 2006).Yet the key distinction between 3G and 4G assessments is that the latter attempt to combine repeated measurement, information, case management, and rehabilitation into an integrated system that "guides and follows service and supervision from intake through case closure" (Andrews et al., 2006, p. 8). Given their recent emergence, additional empirical data are still needed to ascertain whether the newer 4G assessments improve upon 3G assessments with regard to prediction and clinical utility.

■ Practical Guidelines

In some cases, a particular risk assessment is utilized because it has been mandated by an agency or institutional policy, but in other instances, the evaluator may have the opportunity to select the risk assessment tool. When using risk assessments, the desired outcome is to be able to classify whether the juvenile offender is a low, medium, or high risk (Table 17.2). The level of risk is then used to determine the next steps that should be employed with the offender. Table 17.2 highlights some characteristics that are often associated with each level of risk.

A number of guidelines should be followed when conducting a risk assessment. The checklist in Table 17.3 can be used to assess whether a risk assessment that has been or might be selected is appropriate.

Once the risk assessment has been selected, certain administration guidelines are recommended (Table 17.4).

The following are brief descriptions about six of the most common clinical and actuarial risk assessments that are used with juvenile offenders delineated by population of interest.

Table 17.2   Characteristics Associated with Level of Risk

Risk Level	Yes	No
Low		
The offense committed was out of character.		
The offense was the result of poor decision making.		
The offense was the result of past problems.		
Moderate		
The juvenile needs and is amenable to treatment (i.e., is crying for help, problems are fixable).		
The juvenile needs to be removed from the current environment (i.e., is drifting, the family life is chaotic).		
The juvenile needs to be held accountable.		
High		
The juvenile makes poor lifestyle choices (i.e., criminal lifestyle, does not engage in constructive activities).		
The juvenile displays an egocentric value system (i.e., does not offend easily, does not show concern for others).		
The juvenile is uncooperative or defiant (i.e., there is no desire to change, engages in manipulative behavior).		
The juvenile is out of control (i.e., displays a lack of internal controls, displays a lack of external controls)		

Adapted from Explanations for risk assessments by risk level and race by Steen, S., Bond, C.E.W., Bridges, G., & Kubrin, C. E. in *Our Children, Their Children* (pp. 254), by D. F. Hawkins & K. Kempf-Leonard (Eds.) 2005, Chicago, IL: University of Chicago Press. Copyright 2005 by the University of Chicago Press. Adapted with permission.

Table 17.3   Minimum Standards for Selecting a Risk Assessment—Checklist

Minimum Standard	Yes	No
Is the risk assessment standardized?		
Is the risk assessment replicable?		
Does the risk assessment include empirically supported risk factors?		
Has the risk assessment been shown to have interrater reliability?		
Has the risk assessment demonstrated interrater reliability in multiple studies including those conducted by independent parties?		
Has the risk assessment demonstrated predictive validity in multiple studies, including those conducted by independent researchers?		
Does the risk assessment include criminogenic needs?		
Does the risk assessment include protective factors?		
Does the risk assessment include responsivity factors—dynamic risk factors?		
Does the risk assessment allow the examiner or rater to have discretion when examining idiosyncratic risk factors?		
Is the risk assessment empirically validated?		
Does the risk assessment take into account the changing nature of the developing adolescent?		
Does the risk assessment correlate the changing nature of the developing adolescent to the risk being assessed?		
Is the risk assessment based on actuarial measures of risk?		
Does the risk assessment have a theoretical foundation?		
Does the risk assessment demonstrate predictive validity?		
Is the risk assessment directly relevant to criminal behaviors?		
Does the risk assessment examine multiple domains, including criminal history, antisocial personality, social supports for crime, antisocial attitudes and values, and other domains predictive of criminal behavior?		
Does the risk assessment employ multiple strategies to assess risk and needs?		
Does the risk assessment tools account for the experiences of youth of color?		
Is the language in the risk assessment understood by youths of color?		

Compiled from Bonta, 2002; Catchpole & Gretton, 2003; Vincent, Guy, & Grisso, 2012.

Violent and Nonviolent Behavior Risk Assessment

The **YLS/CMI 2.0** (Youth Level of Service/Case Management Inventory; Hoge & Andrews, 2011) is a semistructured interview that was normed using a sample of over 15,000 boys and girls from the United States. It takes approximately 30 to 40 minutes to complete and is designed to be used with 12- to 18-year-olds. It builds on the original YLS/CMI, which was designed as a combined risk/

Table 17.4   Recommendations for Administering a Risk Assessment—Checklist

Administration Recommendations	Yes	No
Has the risk assessment been implemented as described in the manual?		
Has safety been made a priority?		
Has the context of the assessment been considered?		
Have the implications of the assessment been considered?		
Have you been specific and asked directly about violence?		
Can you conduct a systematic assessment with the data that is relevant?		
Have you considered the base rates and the developmental context?		
Have you considered the developmental context?		
Have you considered the impact of gender?		
Is the assessment individualized?		
Does the assessment focus on situation factors?		
Are you aware of your possible cognitive errors and clinical biases?		
Did you consult with others?		
Is the administration process evidence-based?		
Did you use your professional judgment coupled with multiple sources to carefully and systematically obtain information about the youth and his or her circumstances?		
Did you use one or more standardized, empirically validated risk assessments?		
Do you have a procedure for interpreting the data so that decisions can be made about the youth's future risk and any action needed to respond to the youth can be taken?		

Compiled from Borum, 2000; Vincent, Guy, & Grisso, 2012.

needs assessment and case management tool for predicting reoffending behaviors for males and females. It assists in identifying a youth's strengths, needs, incentives, and barriers. This updated version includes 42 items divided into eight sections: (1) Prior and Current Offenses, (2) Education, (3) Substance Abuse, (4) Family, (5) Personality/Behavior, (6) Peers, (7) Leisure/Recreation, and (8) Attitudes/Orientation. It uses a strengths perspective to focus on a youth's risks and needs and is both culturally and gender informed. The YLS/CMI 2.0 estimates reconviction over a 12-month period, provides a profile of criminogenic needs, addresses factors that might affect treatment responsivity, and is designed to provide users with the opportunity to examine positive attributes of the offender so that strengths can be used when delivering services. The guidelines instruct users to consider gender-specific factors, non-criminogenic needs, and minor risk/need factors, and the assessment items address culturally informed and gender-informed responsivity factors.

The **SAVRY** (Structured Assessment of Violence Risk in Youth; Borum, Bartel, & Forth, 2006) can be used with juveniles age 12 to 18. It was designed to assist in structuring an assessment so that important factors about a youth's level of risk are emphasized. It was not created to be a formal scale or test and therefore has no numerical values or cutoff scores. It takes 10 to 15 minutes to administer and includes 24 items spread over three domains (Historical Risk Factors, Social/Contextual Risk Factors, and Individual/Clinical Factors) that are rated as low, moderate, or high. It also includes six Protective Factor items that are rated as either absent or present. Both proactive and reactive aggression are emphasized, and the risk and protective factors that are included are based on the youth's relationship to other adolescents, not children or adults. The SAVRY uses structured professional judgment; therefore, clinicians use their professional judgment to determine a youth's risk level. Dynamic factors are included in the SAVRY so it can be used when conducting assessments, creating treatment plans, making intervention and supervision plans, and implementing discharge plans.

The **PCL:YV** (Hare Psychopathy Checklist: Youth Version; Forth, Kosson, & Hare, 2003) was adapted from the Hare Psychopathy Checklist -Revised (PCL-R), the most commonly used measure to identify psychopathy in adults. The PCL:YV is a paper-and-pencil format and assesses 20 core characteristics of psychopathy for youth ages 12 to 18. The youth is interviewed face to face for approximately 1.5 to 2 hours, using a semistructured interview, and an expert rater scores the responses on a 3-point Likert scale (0 = absence of a trait, 1 = trait is present sometimes, 2 = trait is consistently present). The scores are totaled and the decisions about a youth should be made based on the score as well as additional collateral information obtained during the affiliated 1-hour interview. The PCL:YV measures affective, interpersonal, and behavioral features and can assist in identifying possible patterns of fighting, bullying, cheating, and other antisocial acts. The PCL:YV has been normed in the United States, the United Kingdom, and Canada with offenders in detention, in inpatient facilities, on probation, arrested and referred for an outpatient evaluation, in the community attending treatment programs, and in open custody.

Sexual Behavior-Specific Risk Assessments

The **ERASOR** (Estimate of Risk Adolescent Sexual Offence Recidivism; Worling & Curwen, 2001) is a single-scale instrument, formatted as a checklist for clinicians to use with adolescents at short-term risk of a sexual reoffense. It includes 25 risk factors, 9 static and 16 dynamic, divided into five categories: (1) Sexual Interests, Attitudes, and Behaviors, (2) Historical Sexual Assaults, (3) Psychosocial Functioning, (4) Family/Environmental Functioning, and (5) Treatment. All of the risk factors are coded as unknown, not present, possibly/partially present, or present. The ERASOR is widely used in the United States and Canada. It is recommended that evaluators collect data from multiple sources, including behavior observation, psychological tests, clinical reviews, and reviews of prior reports and case records. In addition, it is recommended that information is also obtained from those familiar with the offender, such as family members, the victims, the police, and other associated professionals. The manual and coding form for the ERASOR can be obtained for free as a pdf from http://www.erasor.org.

The **J-SOAP-II** (Juvenile Sex Offender Assessment Protocol-II; Prentky & Righthand, 2003) is a revision of the J-SOAP and is designed to be used with 12- to 18-year-old boys who have been adjudicated for sex offenses or have a history of sexual coercive behavior but have not been adjudicated. The assessment is not an actuarial scale, and it includes 28 items matched to four subscales, two static (Sexual Drive/Sexual Preoccupation and Impulsive, Antisocial Behavior) and two dynamic (Clinical/Treatment and Community Adjustment). There are no cutoff scores, and the checklist is designed to support the systematic review of risk factors identified in the literature as associated with criminal and sexual offending. The J-SOAP-II should be used as part of a comprehensive risk assessment, and when possible, it should be scored by two independent clinicians whose scores are then compared. Because risk status can change frequently, some of the scales should be readministered every 6 months, and if there have been known changes in risk, complete reassessments should be completed more frequently.

The **J-SORRAT-II** (Juvenile Sex Offender Recidivism Risk Assessment Tool-II; Epperson, Ralston, Fowers, DeWitt, & Gore, 2006) is an actuarial risk assessment tool designed to provide a risk estimate for sex offense recidivism for juvenile sex offenders between the ages of 12 and 17. The J-SORAT-II was developed using case files from a sample of 636 males between the ages of 11 and 18 who had been adjudicated for a sex offense in Utah. The J-SORRAT-II includes 12 items that are designed to be scored during a file review with a 0 or 1 to indicate whether a risk factor is present or on a 3-point or 4-point scale to indicate varying degrees of the presence of a risk factor (Epperson, Ralston, Fowers, & DeWitt, 2006). The items include behavioral anchors, which reduce the need for the evaluator to interpret the data. It is expected that an evaluator will review the entire file before conducting a review; only official documents from the case file are used, and all items are scored, unless there are insufficient data.

■ Clinical or Legal Issues

Because risk assessments are also used to address race, ethnicity, and gender disparities, they can have particularly significant legal and clinical implications for members of certain vulnerable populations such as youth of color, girls, youth in the child welfare system, and youth with mental health disorders. Predictors of recidivism likely vary by group (Thompson & McGrath, 2012; Vermeiren, Schwab-Stone, Ruchkin, DeClippele, & Deboutte, 2002), but unfortunately, there is also a paucity of research about using risk assessments with those groups.

Youth of Color and Girls

In the research that is available about youth of color and girls, they represent a small fraction of the study participants (Shepherd et al., 2013). In that research, there is also a lack of clarity regarding whether the differences identified between groups are attributable to the accuracy of the risk assessment or other external influences (Schwalbe et al., 2006, 2007). For example, many risk assessments are primarily created and validated using male samples and do not account for variation by gender, even though most boys and girls respond to different thresholds of risk (Emeka & Sorenson, 2009; Schwalbe, 2008). The lack of clarity about this differential validity can lead to potentially harmful outcomes for a youth (Schwalbe et al., 2006), such as inappropriate interventions and responses or overly punitive responses such as restrictive supervision (Emeka & Sorenson, 2009).

Youth of Color

A number of contextual issues should be considered when conducting risk assessments with youth of color. Many youth of color reside in urban areas, and some reside in urban neighborhoods with high concentrations of poverty that place them at a greater risk for engaging in delinquent behavior and having disparate experiences in the justice system (Jargowsky, Desmond, & Crutchfield, 2005; Wright & Thomas, 2003). These disparate experiences in the juvenile justice system include the failure to respond appropriately to mental health needs as well as a lack of culturally appropriate engagement with juvenile offenders.

Youth of color in particular are underserved in mainstream mental health care systems (U.S. Department of Health and Human Services, 2001). Researchers have suggested that those unmet needs can lead to initial and long-term involvement in the juvenile justice system (Becker, Kerig, Lim, & Ezechukwu, 2012; Teplin, 2000). Unfortunately, when youth of color do receive treatment, it is not uncommon for their mental health problems to be inaccurately diagnosed due to cultural differences or other influences (Hicks, 2004; Turner & Kramer, 1995); therefore, the services these youth receive are more likely to be inadequate. African-American youth, for example, are often misdiagnosed or not diagnosed (Fabrega, Ulrich, & Mezzich, 1993; Hubner & Wolfson, 2000). An African-American youth who expresses his or her mental health symptoms aggressively can be perceived as violent, not in need of mental health services, or in need of excessive discipline (i.e., restraints or isolation) for extended periods (Corbit, 2005; Isaacs, 1992).

For Latino youth, it is important that their linguistic and cultural needs are met (Arya, Villarruel,Villaneuva, & Augarten, 2009). The overall Latino population is diverse and their numbers are steadily increasing, with an expected increase in population from 14% in 2005 to 29% in 2050 (Passel & Cohn, 2008). However, according to a report available from the Pew Research Hispanic Center, a significant number of the Latino population, native and foreign-born, are defined as speaking English less than very well (Motel & Patten, 2011). Those statistics indicate that 14% of those between the ages of 5 and 17 fit that criterion; of those over the age of 18, the rates are 41% (Motel & Patten, 2011). This lack of fluency will have a tremendous impact on a youth's or parent's ability to accurately respond to items on a risk assessment.

Native American youth, like other youth of color, disproportionately experience poverty, low levels of educational attainment, and victimization, each of which is a risk factor for becoming involved in the justice system (Hartney, 2008). For many Native American youth, the exposure to those same risk factors may precipitate their involvement in the system. However, once in the system, Native American youth who reside on reservations may experience the system quite differently. The court system is foreign and it can act to separate youths from their culture and family (Seelau, 2012). Utilizing a risk assessment without accounting for a community and familial context that might be different from what has been typically encountered by the person conducting the risk assessment, a lack of access to the family by the court system, and the influence of cultural experiences might lead to inaccurate risk assessment findings.

Finally, risk assessments may fail to identify some strengths and protective factors that are unique to youth of color. Although researchers and service providers have identified protective factors, such as cultural pride and connections to traditional beliefs and practices, as sources of resilience for African-American, Latino, and Native American youth (Cervantes, Ruan, & Dueñas, 2004; Penn, Doll, & Grandgenett, 2008; Williams, 2010), many risk assessments may not recognize the potential impact of these sources of strength. In sum, the intersectionality of race, culture, environment, and mental health status can affect youths' performance on a risk assessment; therefore, their contextual experiences should be considered.

Girls

Some factors increase a girl's risk of delinquency more than a boy's and influence how she enters the system; those factors should be noted during a risk assessment. For example, girls are not as heavily influenced by peer delinquency (Schwalbe, 2008), but early-maturing girls are more likely to engage with older boys who are inclined toward delinquent behavior and thus engage in delinquent behavior themselves (Zahn et al., 2010). It is also hypothesized that the propensity for girls to engage in delinquent behavior increases when the protective bond of a family is weakened by violence, instability, or a lack of parental supervision (Zahn et al., 2010). In addition, although important, antisocial behaviors seem to be less important for girls than boys—more influential are family, a history of abuse, and school (Hubbard & Pratt, 2002).

Like many youth in the juvenile justice system, some girls also have mental health disorders that accompany their delinquent behavior; however, girls are more likely than boys to be depressed or anxious (Zahn et al., 2010). Research suggests that mental health disorders affect girls at even greater rates than boys who are in the juvenile justice system, with the majority of girls having at least one diagnosable mental health disorder (Veysey, 2003). Because girls generally manifest different disorders than boys, their mental health issues are overlooked and not treated or their behaviors related to their mental health disorders are misinterpreted and perceived inaccurately (Veysey, 2003). Trauma also plays an important role, and in particular is extraordinarily relevant for many female juvenile offenders. Many girls in the juvenile justice system have a history of experiencing trauma such as sexual abuse, and often the strategies they use to cope cause them to have contact and conflict with the legal system (Veysey, 2003; Zahn et al., 2010). Sometimes their traumatic experiences can be reignited by contact with officers, such as patdowns or other experiences in facilities, and result in harsh responses (Veysey, 2003). In addition, the aggression that is linked to delinquent behavior can be related to prior experiences of victimization (Zahn et al., 2010). Without receiving treatment that addresses gender-specific and trauma-related experiences, girls are much more likely to engage in delinquent behaviors (Veysey, 2003).

■ Child Welfare and Mental Health

Research examining the use of risk assessments specifically with youth in the child welfare system or those identified as having mental health disorders is nonexistent. This lack of information and the lack of clarity of existing knowledge highlight the need to determine the influence of differences by subgroup (Thompson & McGrath, 2011).

Child Welfare

Many youth are simultaneously involved in the juvenile justice and child welfare systems; these youth are often classified as crossover or dually involved youth (Herz, Lee, Lutz, Stewart, Tuell, & Wiig, 2012). The likelihood of becoming involved in the juvenile justice system increases when youth have experienced neglect and physical abuse and are in the child welfare system (Models for Change, 2011b). In fact, youth who have had such contact are four times more likely than youth who have not had contact to engage in delinquent behavior at an early age (Barrett et al., 2010). Dually involved youth can also find themselves confronted with additional penalties because of their foster care status, such as (1) court systems being reluctant to release them because they are in foster care, (2) finding themselves in a foster family that does not want to become involved in the justice system, or (3) having the court erroneously assume, and make decisions based on that assumption, that the foster family does not want to remain involved (Ryan, Herz, Hernandez, & Marshall, 2007). Crossover youth who move deeper into the juvenile justice system are not likely to have their needs attended to or resolved, needs that can be complex and related to their delinquent behavior coupled with their history of maltreatment (Ryan et al., 2007). These biases against juveniles who are in the child welfare system, as well as their experiences, should be considered during assessment. They are integral and can lead to feelings of rejection and isolation as well as a youth remaining in a secure facility longer than one who resides with his or her biological family. These feelings and experiences have all been shown to increase the potential for recidivism.

Mental Health

At any given time in the juvenile justice system, thousands of youth with psychiatric disorders are temporarily detained in juvenile correctional facilities (Cocozza & Skowyra, 2000; Teplin, 2001). Estimates vary as to exactly how many youth have diagnosable psychiatric disorders, but each report indicates a significant problem. For example, in a study of youth in the Cook County Temporary Juvenile Detention Center, more than one in six incarcerated juveniles were identified as having a major mental health disorder (e.g., affective disorder, psychosis) and associated functional impairments (Teplin, Abram, McClelland, Washburn, & Pikus, 2005). In a three-state study conducted by the National Center for Mental Health and Juvenile Justice and funded by the OJJDP, 70.4% of youth who were detained met the criteria for at least one mental health disorder (Shufelt & Cocozza, 2006). Finally, the results of a 6-month survey conducted in 2003 by the Special Investigations Division of the U.S. House of Representatives (2004) found that of 698 juvenile detention facilities nationwide, 66% reported having youth detained who were waiting to receive external mental health services.

It has been suggested that some juveniles with mental health disorders are remanded to detention facilities due to the failure of the mental health system to meet their needs and not due to criminal behavior (Teplin, 2000). This phenomenon was prompted in the 1990s when many state budgets for public mental health care services were cut and the juvenile justice system became the access point for many to receive mental health services (Chapman, Desai, & Falzer, 2006; Grisso, 2004). Those service cuts led to youth lacking an appropriate setting to meet their needs; thus, many were placed in the juvenile justice system (Teplin, 2000). Unfortunately, such practices have been common, with some local law enforcement agencies classifying their juvenile justice system as a primary referral source for youth with psychiatric disorders (Grisso, 2004).

Having a mental health disorder can increase a youth's potential for recidivism, particularly if access to mental health services remains limited or nonexistent. Untreated mental health problems worsen with juvenile justice involvement (Ford, Chapman, Hawke, & Albert, 2007; Foster, Qaseem, & Connor, 2004), and unmet mental health needs lead to an increased likelihood of subsequent delinquent behaviors (Burns et al., 2003; DePrato & Hammer, 2002). The behaviors associated with untreated mental health disorders can also place a juvenile at greater risk of contact with the criminal justice system and ultimately lead to incarceration (DePrato & Hammer, 2002). For example, a recent report from the National Center for Mental Health and Juvenile Justice (NCMHJJ) indicated that (1) juveniles in the juvenile justice system have higher rates of posttraumatic stress disorder (PTSD) than youth in the general community and (2) many of the PTSD symptoms that occur for youth involved in the system can worsen due to involvement in court hearings and detention (Ford et al., 2007). These rates are significant; trauma that remains unaddressed during a youth's involvement in the juvenile justice system can lead to increasingly risky, retraumatizing, and possibly chronic contact with the juvenile justice system (Ko et al., 2008).

Future Directions

As noted previously, 4G risk assessments generally account for broad risk and protective factors that might contribute to whether a youth reoffends. However, to address the concerns about vulnerable youth, special attention must be paid to the possible influences in their lives that might affect the accuracy of a risk assessment to predict recidivism. It is important to consider the complex circumstances they often experience. By recognizing how these issues can influence the results of a risk assessment, a juvenile's performance on a risk assessment can be contextualized. This makes it even more important that risk assessments be created and tested empirically with the groups that will be assessed (Shepherd et al., 2013); doing so will increase the ability for the risk assessment to be more sensitive to the groups being assessed (Schwalbe et al., 2006). If the information is not obtained, risk assessments may fail to demonstrate validity for vulnerable groups and the disproportionality and biases that exist in the juvenile justice system will persist (Schwalbe et al., 2006).

As risk assessments continue to "morph" and the influences of race, ethnicity, gender, and context are considered, approaches to develop other types of assessments or alter existing ones should be utilized. For example, it is important to ensure that risk assessments demonstrate measurement equivalence; focusing on how culture and gender may influence performance on the completion of screening and assessment tools is a bourgeoning area. This is particularly true in fields such as survey and health care research (see Irwin, Varni, Yeatts, & DeWalt, 2009, or Nápoles-Springer, Santoyo-Olsson, O'Brien, & Stewart, 2006). This focus has recently begun to include examining how race, ethnicity, and gender likely lead to disparate responses on the Massachusetts Youth Screening Instrument version-2, a mental health screening tool used in the juvenile justice systems of 48 states (e.g., Cauffman & MacIntosh, 2006; Jaggers, Young, McKinney, Bolland, & Church, McCoy, 2010). Research has shown that even though this tool is the most commonly used mental health screen, there are clear differences by race and gender that likely affect how youth respond to items and the decisions that are made based on the screening results.

To increase the sensitivity of a risk assessment, one option is to specifically measure the risk factors that are disproportionately experienced by youth of color (Schwalbe et al., 2006). Specific strategies can be employed that can strengthen risk assessments and their ability to assess across race, ethnicity, and gender. The language of the questionnaire and of the person administering the questionnaire must be understood by the youth for the instrument to be effective. For example, as noted previously, youth who speak English as a second language may have difficulty understanding and comprehending the questions in the questionnaire. In addition, youth who understand urban colloquialisms may not clearly understand the Standard English that is used for the assessment. Not accounting for those potential influences can have a negative impact on the decisions made about and the long-term outcomes experienced by a juvenile offender. Finally, for all youth of color, it is essential to incorporate elements that are the foundation of that youth's culture, particularly those that might emphasize family, resilience, or spiritual beliefs. This strategy has been used in prevention models (see Penn, Doll, & Grandgenett, 2008), and replicating it into risk assessment tools, and their interpretation, will allow the process to be strengthened.

Given the increases in the number of girls who have contact with the juvenile justice system, there is a clear need for risk assessments to be able to accurately identify female offenders' level of risk. Thus far, there has been a clear failure to acknowledge the special needs that girls in the juvenile justice system may have (Andrews, Bonta, & Wormith, 2006), but it is necessary in order to identify potential risk factors and ensure proper programming and treatment for this group (Emeka & Sorensen 2009). Extant research has not produced clear recommendations regarding which assessment is best for predicting general recidivism, much less for predicting recidivism of different types or across different contexts and populations. Including a social history focused on gender-specific variables may help to strengthen our understanding of the influence of gender (Emeka & Sorenson, 2009). Ultimately, to assess the risk of reoffending for girls, the impetus for their offending behavior needs to be better understood (Emeka & Sorenson, 2009).

Trauma is a significant factor for many youth in the juvenile justice system. For example, some studies have shown that the girls who are at the greatest risk for becoming involved in the juvenile justice system are those who have experienced symptoms of PTSD, and that risk increases for young and African-American girls (Becker et al., 2012). Unfortunately, the current literature is lacking regarding the impact that traumatic experiences may have on the outcome of a risk assessment. It is possible that a history of trauma can be a risk factor or a risk marker—a precursor to offending behavior (Romaine, Goldstein, Hunt, & DeMatteo, 2011); therefore, risk assessments must incorporate its influence. Incorporating trauma increases the likelihood of it being identified as a part of an intervention strategy; not doing so can lead to a spiral of negative behaviors and experiences, including chronic juvenile and criminal justice system involvement and retraumatization (Ko et al., 2008).

Summary and Conclusion

Risk assessments play an important role in identifying who is at the greatest risk for reoffending. The various iterations of risk assessments have ultimately strengthened their effectiveness. However, efforts clearly need to be made to ensure that risk assessments are valid with vulnerable populations. Risk assessments must be created and tested empirically at the item level and the domain level, and while examining the connection between recidivism and classification, with groups who are comparable to those who will eventually be evaluated (Shepherd et al., 2013; Thompson & McGrath, 2012). The extenuating circumstances and the contextual experiences that affect those youth must be considered. Finally, by including community and environmental variables, we will broaden our understanding of the array of dynamic factors that can influence recidivism (Emeka & Sorenson, 2009).

References

Andrews, D. A., Bonta, J., & Hoge, R. D. (1990). Classification for effective rehabilitation: Rediscovering psychology. *Criminal Justice and Behavior, 17*, 19–52. doi:10.1177/0093854890017001004

Andrews, D. A., Bonta, J., & Wormith, S. J. (2003). *The Level of Service Inventory—Revised (LSI-R)*. Toronto, Ontario, Canada: Multi-Health Systems.

Andrews, D. A., Bonta, J., & Wormith, S. J. (2004). *The Level of Service/Case Management Inventory (LS/CMI)*. Toronto, Ontario, Canada: Multi-Health Systems.

Andrews, D. A., Bonta, J., & Wormith, J. S. (2006). The recent past and near future of risk and/or need assessment. *Crime and Delinquency, 52*(1), 7. doi:10.1177/0011128705281756

Arya, N., Villarruel, F., Villanueva, C., & Augarten, I. (2009). *America's invisible children: Latino youth and the failure of justice*. Washington, DC: National Council of La Raza.

Barrett, D. E., Katsiyannis, A., & Zhang, D. (2010). Predictors, of offense severity, adjudication, incarceration, and repeat referrals for juvenile offenders. *Remedial and Special Education, 31*(4), 261–275. doi:10.1177/0741932509355990

Becker, S. P., Kerig, P. K., Lim, J-Y., & Ezechukwu, R. N. (2012). Predictors of recidivism among delinquent youth: Interrelations among ethnicity, gender, age, mental health problems, and posttraumatic stress, *Journal of Child and Adolescent Trauma, 5*, 145–160. doi:10.1080/19361521.2012.671798

Bishop, D. M. (2005). The role of race and ethnicity in juvenile justice processing. In D. F. Hawkins & K. Kempf-Leonard (Eds.), *Our children, their children* (pp. 23–82). Chicago: University of Chicago Press.

Bonta, J. (2002). Offender risk assessment: Guidelines for selection and use. *Criminal Justice and Behavior, 29*, 355–378. doi:10.1177/0093854802029004002

Bonta, J., & Andrews, D. A. (2007). *Risk-Need-Responsivity Model for offender assessment and rehabilitation.* Ottawa, CA: Her Majesty of the Queen in Right of Canada.

Borum, D. L., Bartel, P., & Forth, A. (2003). *Structured Assessment of Violence Risk in Youth (SAVRY) professional manual.* Lutz, FL: Psychological Assessment Resources.

Borum, R. (2000). Assessing violence risk among youth. *Journal of Clinical Psychology, 56*(10), 1263–1288.

Borum, R., Bartel, P., & Forth, A. (2006). *Structured Assessment of Violence Risk in Youth (SAVRY).* Oxford, UK: Pearson Education.

Burns, B.J., Howell, J.C., Wiig, J.K., Augimeri, L.K., Welsh, B.C., Loeber, R., et al. (2003). *Treatment, services, and intervention programs for child delinquents.* Washington, DC: Office of Juvenile Justice and Delinquency Prevention.

Campbell, H. (1991). *Black's law dictionary* (6th ed.). St. Paul, MN: West.

Catchpole, R. H. & Gretton, H. M. (2003). The predictive validity of risk assessment with violent young offenders. *Criminal Justice and Behavior, 30*(6), 688–708. doi:10.1177/0093854803256455

Cauffman, E., & MacIntosh, R. (2006). A Rasch Differential Item Functioning analysis of the Massachusetts Youth Screening Instrument. *Educational and Psychological Measurement, 66*(3), 502–521. doi:10.1177/0013164405282460

Cervantes, R. C., Ruan, K., & Dueñas, N. (2004). Programa Shortstop: A culturally focused juvenile intervention for Hispanic youth. *Journal of Drug Education, 34*(4), 385–405.

Chapman, J. F., Desai, R. A., & Falzer, P. R., (2006). Mental health service provision in juvenile justice facilities: Pre- and postrelease psychiatric care. *Child and Adolescent Psychiatric Clinics of North America, 15*, 445–458. doi:10.1177/154120400628631

Cocozza, J. J., & Skowyra, K. R. (2000). Youth with mental health disorders: Issues and emerging responses. *Juvenile Justice, 7*(1), 3–13. Washington. DC: US. Department of Justice, Office of Justice Programs, Office of Juvenile Justice and Delinquency Prevention.

Corbit, K. (2005). Inadequate and inappropriate mental health treatment and minority overrepresentation in the juvenile justice system. *Hastings Race and Poverty Law Journal, 3*, 75–93.

Cottle, C. C., Lee, R. J., & Heilbrun, K. (2001). The prediction of criminal recidivism in juveniles a meta-analysis. *Criminal Justice and Behavior, 28*(3), 367–394. doi:10.1177/0093854801028003005

DePrato, D. K., & Hammer, J. H. (2002). Assessment and treatment of juvenile offenders. In D. H. Schetky & E. P. Benedek (Eds.), *Principles and practice of child and adolescent forensic psychiatry* (pp. 267–278). Washington, DC: American Psychiatric Publishing.

Emeka, T. Q., & Sorenson, J. R. (2009). Female juvenile risk: Is there a need for gendered assessment instruments? *Youth Violence and Juvenile Justice, 7*(4), 313–330. doi:10.1177/1541204009334083

Epperson, D. L., Ralston, C. A., Fowers, D., & DeWitt, J. (2006). Appendix C: Juvenile Sexual Offense Recidivism Risk Assessment Tool-II (JSORRAT-II). In D. Prescott (Ed.), *Risk* assessment of youth who have sexually abused: Theory, controversy, and emerging strategies (pp. 223–238). Oklahoma City, OK: Woods N Barnes.

Epperson, D. L., Ralston, C. A., Fowers, D., DeWitt, J., & Gore, K. S. (2006). Actuarial risk assessment with juveniles who offend sexually: Development of the Juvenile Sexual Offense Recidivism Risk Assessment Tool-II (JSORRAT-II). In D. Prescott (Ed.), *Risk assessment of youth who have sexually abused: Theory, controversy, and emerging strategies* (pp. 118–169). Oklahoma City, OK: Woods N Barnes.

Fabrega, Jr. H., Ulrich, R. & Mezzich J. E. (1993). Do Caucasian and Black adolescents differ at psychiatric intake? *Journal of the American Academy of Child and Adolescent Psychiatry 32*(2), 407–413. doi:10.1097/00004583-199303000-00023

Feld, B. (1993). Criminalizing the American juvenile court. *Crime and Justice, 17,* 197–280.

Ford, J. D., Chapman, J. F., Hawke, J., & Albert, D. (2007). *Trauma among youth in the juvenile justice system: Critical issues and new directions.* Delmar, NY: National Center for Mental Health and Juvenile Justice.

Forth, A. E., Kosson, D. S., & Hare, R. D. (2003). *Hare Psychopathy Checklist: Youth Version (PCL:YV).* Toronto, Canada: Multi-Health Systems.

Foster, E. M., Qaseem, A., & Connor T. (2004). Can better mental health services reduce the risk of juvenile justice system involvement? *American Journal of Public Health, 94*(5), 859–865.

Gardner, M. R. (1997). The juvenile court movement. In *Understanding juvenile law* (pp. 179–198). New York: Matthew Bender.

Glaser, D. (1987). Classification for risk. *Crime and Justice, 9,* 249–291.

Grisso, T. (1998). *Forensic evaluation of juveniles.* Sarasota, FL: Professional Resource Press

Grisso, T. (2004). Reasons for concern about mental disorders of adolescent offenders. In *Double jeopardy* (pp. 3–26). Chicago, IL: The University of Chicago Press.

Grove, W. M., Zald, D. H., Lebow, B. S., Snitz, B. E., & Nelson, C. (2000). Clinical versus mechanical prediction: A meta-analysis. *Psychological Assessment, 12*(1), 19–30. doi:10.1037//1040-3590.12.1.19

Hartney, C. (2008). *Native American youth in the juvenile justice system.* Oakland, CA: National Council on Crime and Delinquency.

Herz, D., Lee, P., Lutz, L., Stewart, M., Tuell, J., & Wiig, J. (2012). *Addressing the needs of multi-system youth: Strengthening the connection between child welfare and juvenile justice.* Washington, DC: Center for Juvenile Justice Reform.

Hicks, J. W. (2004). Ethnicity, race, and forensic psychiatry: Are we color blind? *Journal of the American Academy of Psychiatry and Law 32*(1), 21–33.

Hoffman, P. B., & Beck, J. L. (1974). Parole decision-making: A salient factor score. *Journal of Criminal Justice, 2*(3), 195–206.

Hoge, R. D. (2002). Standardized instruments for assessing risk and need in youthful offenders. *Criminal Justice and Behavior, 29,* 380–393. doi:10.1177/009385480202900403

Hoge, R. D., & Andrews, D. A. (2011). *Youth Level of Service/Case Management Inventory 2.0. User's Manual.* North Tonawanda, NY: Multi-Health Systems.

Howell, J. C. (1995). *Guide for implementing the comprehensive strategy for serious, violent, and chronic juvenile offenders.* Washington, DC: Office of Juvenile Justice and Delinquency Prevention.

Hubbard, D. J., & Pratt, T. C. (2002). A meta-analysis of the predictors of delinquency among girls. *Journal of Offender Rehabilitation, 34*(3), 1–13. doi:10.1300/J076v34n03_01

Hubner, J., & Wolfson, J. (2000). *Handle with care: Serving the mental health needs of young offenders.* Washington, DC: Coalition for Juvenile Justice.

Irwin, D. E., Varni, J. W., Yeatts, K., & DeWalt, D. A., (2009). Cognitive interviewing methodology in the development of a pediatric item bank: A Patient Reported Outcomes Measurement Information System (PROMIS) study. *Health and Quality of Life Outcomes, 79*(3). doi:10.1186/1477-7525-7-3

Isaacs, M. R. (1992). Assessing the mental health needs of children and adolescents of color in the juvenile justice system: Overcoming institutionalized perceptions and barriers. In J. Cocozza (Ed.), *Responding to the mental health needs of youth in the juvenile justice system.* (pp. 141–163). Seattle, WA: The National Coalition for the Mentally Ill in the Criminal Justice System.

Jaggers, J., Young, S., McKinney, R., Bolland, K. A., & Church, W. T. (2013). Utilization of the Massachusetts Youth Screening Instrument-2 (MAYSI-2) with a Southern, African American adolescent male population. *Journal of Forensic Social Work, 3*(1), 3–15.

Jargowsky, P. A., Desmond, S. A., & Crutchfield, R. D. (2005). Suburban sprawl, race, and juvenile justice. In D. F. Hawkins & K. Kempf-Leonard (Eds.), *Our children, their children* (pp. 167–201). Chicago, IL: University of Chicago Press.

Ko, S. J., Ford, J. D., Kassam-Adams, N., Berkowitz, S. J., Wilson, C., Wong, M….Layne, C. M. (2008). Creating trauma-informed systems: Child welfare, education, first responders, health care, juvenile justice. *Professional Psychology: Research and Practice, 39*(4), 396–404. doi:10.1037/0735-7028.39.4.396

Lipsey, M. W., & Derzon, J. H. (1998). Predictors of violent or serious delinquency in adolescence and early adulthood: A synthesis of longitudinal research. In R. Loeber & D. P. Farrington (Eds.), *Serious and violent juvenile offenders: Risk factors and successful interventions* (pp. 86–105). Thousand Oaks, CA: Sage.

McCoy, H. (2010). Using cognitive interviewing to explore causes for racial differences on the MAYSI-2. *Crime and Delinquency,* Advance online publication. doi:10.1177/0011128710388922

Models for Change (2011a). *Knowledge brief: Are minority youths treated differently in juvenile probation?* Retrieved May 30, 2012, from http://www.modelsforchange.net/publications/314

Models for Change (2011b). *Knowledge brief: Is there a link between child welfare and disproportionate contact in juvenile justice?* Retrieved May 30, 2012, from http://www.modelsforchange.net/publications/317

Monahan, J., & Steadman, H. J. (1994). Toward a rejuvenation of risk assessment research. In J. Monahan & H. J. Steadman (Eds.), *Violence and mental disorder: Developments in risk assessment* (pp. 1–17). Chicago, IL: University of Chicago Press.

Motel, S., & Patten, E. (2011). *Table 20: Language spoken at home and English-speaking ability by age, race, and ethnicity, 2011. Statistical portrait of Hispanics in the United States, 2011.* Washington, DC: Pew Hispanic Center.

Mulder, E., Brand, E., Bullens, R., & van Marle, H. (2011). Risk factors for overall recidivism and severity of recidivism in serious juvenile offenders. *International Journal of Offender Therapy and Comparative Criminology, 55*(1), 118–135. doi:10.1177/0306624X09356683

Nápoles-Springer, A. M., Santoyo-Olsson, J., O'Brien, H. O., & Stewart, A. L. (2006). Using cognitive interviews to develop surveys in diverse populations, *Medical Care, 44*(11, Suppl 3), S21–S30. doi:10.1097/01.mlr.0000245425.65905.1d

Olver, M. E., Stockdale, K. C., & Wormith, J. S. (2009). Risk assessment with young offenders: A meta-analysis of three assessment measures. *Criminal Justice and Behavior, 36*(4), 329–353. doi:10.1177/0093854809331457

Passel, J. S., & Cohn, D. (2008). *U.S. population projections: 2005–2050.* Washington, DC: Pew Hispanic Center and Social Demographic Trends.

Penn, J., Doll, J., & Grandgenett, N. (2008). Culture as prevention: Assisting high-risk youth in the Omaha Nation. *Wicazo Sa Review, 23*(2), 43–61.

Prentky, R. A., & Righthand, S. (2003). *Juvenile Sex Offender Assessment Protocol II Manual.* Washington, DC: Office of Juvenile Justice and Delinquency Prevention.

Puzzanchera, C., & Adams, B. (2011). *Juvenile arrests 2009* (Report No. NCJ 236477). Washington, DC: U.S. Department of Justice, Office of Justice Programs, Office of Juvenile Justice and Delinquency Prevention.

Puzzanchera, C., Adams, B., & Hockenberry, S. (2012). *Juvenile court statistics 2009*. Pittsburgh, PA: National Center for Juvenile Justice.

Puzzanchera, C., Adams, B., & Sickmund, M. (2010). *Juvenile court statistics 2006–2007*. Pittsburgh, PA: National Center for Juvenile Justice.

Raynor, P. (2007). Risk and need assessment in British probation: the contribution of LSI-R. *Psychology, Crime & Law, 13*(2), 125–138. doi:10.1080/10683160500337592

Romaine, C. L. R., Goldstein N. E. S., Hunt, E., & DeMatteo, D. (2011). Traumatic experiences and juvenile amenability: The role of trauma in forensic evaluations and judicial making. *Child Youth Care Forum, 40*, 363–380. doi:10.1007/s10566-010-9132-4

Roscoe, M., & Morton, R. (1994). *Disproportionate minority confinement*. Washington, DC: U. S. Department of Justice, Office of Justice Programs, Office of Juvenile Justice and Delinquency Prevention.

Ryan, J. P., Herz, D., Hernandez, P. M., & Marshall, J. M. (2007). Maltreatment and delinquency: Investigating child welfare bias in juvenile justice processing. *Children and Youth Services Review, 29*, 1035–1050. doi:10.1016/j.childyouth.2007.04.002

Schwalbe, C. S. (2007). Risk assessment for juvenile justice: A meta-analysis. *Law and Human Behavior, 31*(5), 449–462. doi:10.1007/s 10979-006-9071-7

Schwalbe, C. S. (2008) A meta-analysis of juvenile justice risk assessment instruments. *Criminal Justice and Behavior, 35*(11), 1367–1381. doi:10.1177/0093854808324377

Schwalbe, C. S, Fraser, M. W., & Day, S. H. (2007). Predictive validity of the Joint Risk Matrix with juvenile offenders: A focus on gender and race/ethnicity. *Criminal Justice and Behavior, 34*(3), 348–361. doi:10.1177/0093854806292244

Schwalbe, C. S., Fraser, M. W., Day, S. H., & Cooley, V. (2006). Classifying juvenile offenders according to risk and recidivism: Predictive validity, race/ethnicity, and gender. *Criminal Justice and Behavior, 33*, 305–324. doi:10.1177/0093854806286451.

Seelau, R. (2012). The kids aren't alright: An argument to use the nation building model in the development of native juvenile justice sysrems to combat the effects of failed assimilative policies. *Berkeley Journal of Criminal Law, 171*, 97–148.

Shepherd, S. M., Luebbers, S., & Dolan. M. (2013). Gender and ethnicity in juvenile risk assessment. *Criminal Justice and Behavior, 40*(4), 388–408. doi:10.1177/0093854812456776

Shufelt, J. L., &. Cocozza, J. J. (2006). *Youth with mental health disorders in the juvenile justice system: Results from a multi-date prevalence study*. Delmar, NY: National Center for Mental Health and Juvenile Justice.

Singh, J. P., Grann, M., & Fazel, S. (2011). A comparative study of violence risk assessment tools: A systematic review and metaregression analysis of 68 studies involving 25,980 participants. *Clinical Psychology Review, 31*(3), 499–513. doi:10.1016/j.cpr.2010.11.009

Skeem, J. L., & Monahan, J. (2011). Current directions in violence risk assessment. *Current Directions in Psychological Science, 20*(1), 38–42. doi:10.1177/0963721410397271

Snyder, H. N., & Sickmund, M. (2006). *Juvenile offenders and victims: 2006 national report*. Washington, DC: U. S. Department of Justice, Office of Justice Programs, Office of Juvenile Justice and Delinquency Prevention.

Steen, S., Bond, C. E. W., Bridges, G., & Kubrin, C. E. (2005). Explaining assessments of future risk: Race and attributions of juvenile offenders in presentencing reports. In D. F. Hawkins & K. Kempf-Leonard (Eds.), *Our children, their children* (pp. 245–269). Chicago, IL: University of Chicago Press.

Teplin, L. A. (2000). Juvenile justice and identification of mental health needs. In *U. S. Public Health Service, report of the Surgeon General's conference on children's mental health: A national action agenda*. Washington, DC: Department of Health and Human Services.

Teplin, L. A. (2001). *Assessing alcohol, drug, and mental disorders in juvenile detainees*. Washington, DC: US. Department of Justice, Office of Justice Programs, Office of Juvenile Justice and Delinquency Prevention.

Teplin, L. A., Abram, K. M., McClelland, G. M., Washburn, & Pikus, A. K. (2005) Detecting mental disorder in juvenile detainees: Who receives services. *American Journal of Public Health, 95*(10), 1773–1780.

Thompson, A. P., & McGrath, A. (2012). Subgroup differences and implications for contemporary risk-need assessment with juvenile offenders. *Law and Human Behavior, 36*(4), 345–355. doi:10.1037/h0093930

Turner, C. B., & Kramer, B. M. (1995). Connections between racism and mental health. In C.V. Willie, P. P. Rieker, B. M. Kramer, & B. S. Brown (Eds.), *Mental health, racism, and sexism* (pp. 3–25). Pittsburgh: University of Pittsburgh Press.

U.S. Department of Health and Human Services (2001). *Mental health: Culture, race, and ethnicity—a supplement to mental health: A report of the Surgeon General.* Rockville, MD: U.S. Department of Health and Human Services, Substance Abuse and Mental Health Services Administration, Center for Mental Health Services.

U.S. House of Representatives Committee on Government Reform—Minority Staff Special Investigations Division (2004). *Incarceration of youth who are waiting for community mental health services in the United States.* Washington, DC: Author.

Vermeiren, R., Schwab-Stone, M., Ruchkin, V., De Clippele, A., & Deboutte, D. (2002). Predicting recidivism in delinquent adolescents from psychological and psychiatric assessment. *Comprehensive Psychiatry, 43*(2), 142–149. doi:10.1053/comp.2002.30809

Veysey, B. M. (2003). *Adolescent girls with mental health disorders involved with the juvenile justice system.* Delmar, NY: National Center for Mental health and Juvenile Justice.

Villarruel, F. A., & Walker, N. E. (2001). *¿dónde está la justicia? A call to action on behalf of Latino and Latina youth in the U.S Justice System.* Retrieved from http://www.cclp.org/documents/BBY/Donde.pdf

Vincent, G. M., Guy, L. S., & Grisso, T. (2012). *Risk assessment in juvenile justice: A guidebook for implementation.* Retrieved from Models of Change website: http://www.modelsforchange.net/publications/346

Vincent, G. M., Paiva-Salisbury, M. L., Cooks, N. E., Guy, L. S., & Perrault, R. T. (2012). Impact of risk/needs assessment of juvenile probation officers' decision making: Importance of implementation. *Psychology, Public Policy, and Law, 18*(4), 549–576. doi:10.1037/a0027186

Ward, T., Mesler, J., & Yates, P. M. (2007). Reconstructing the Risk-Need-Responsivity model: A theoretical elaboration and evaluation. *Aggression and Violent Behavior, 12,* 208–228.

Wiebush, R. G., Baird, C., Krisberg, B., & Onek, D. (1995). Risk assessment and classification for serious, violent, and chronic juvenile offenders. In: *A sourcebook: Serious violent & chronic juvenile offenders.* Thousand Oaks, CA: Sage.

Williams, L. (2010). Cultural interventions for reducing violence among young, African American males. In W. E. Johnson, Jr. (Ed.), *Social work with African American males: Health, mental health, and social policy* (pp. 265–291). New York: Oxford University Press.

Worling, J. R., & Curwen, T. (2001). Estimate of Risk of Adolescent Sexual Offense Recidivism (ERASOR; Version 2.0). In M.C. Calder (Ed.), *Juveniles and children who sexually abuse: Frameworks for assessment* (2nd ed., pp. 372–397). Lyme Regis, UK: Russell House.

Wormith, J. S., & Olver, M. E. (2002). Offender treatment attrition and its relationship with risk, responsivity, and recidivism. *Criminal Justice Behavior, 29,* 447–471.

Wright, R., & Thomas, W., Jr. (2003). Disproportionate representation: Communities of color in the domestic violence, juvenile justice, and child welfare systems. *Family Court Journal, 54*(4), 87–95.

Zahn, M., Agnew, R., Fishbein, D., Miller, S., Winn, D.-M., Dakoff, G...Chesney-Lind, M. (2010). *Causes and correlates of girls delinquency* (NCJ Publication No. 226358). Retrieved from Office of Juvenile Justice and Delinquency Prevention website: https://www.ncjrs.gov/pdffiles1/ojjdp/226358.pdf

18

Mental Health and Youth in the Juvenile Justice System: Current Status and Evidence-Informed Future Directions

Cynthia Weaver, Edward Byrnes, and Wesley T. Church II

■ Introduction

Recent trends in juvenile justice offer an opportunity to improve the system response to youth presenting with co-occurring mental health (MH) disorders and delinquent behavior. There was a 13% reduction in the number of juvenile arrests between 2006 and 2009, from 2,195,200 to 1,906,600 (Puzzanchera, Adams, & Kang, 2012). There was also an 11% reduction in the number of formal referrals to juvenile courts between 2006 and 2009, from 927,808 to 823,234 (Sickmund, Sladky, & Kang, 2012). Although this decreasing systemic pressure could provide opportunities for innovation, the case-processing evidence for this same time period suggests little departure from historical practices. Decreases in the number of youth adjudicated, held in detention, and placed out of their homes corresponded with the decreased number of juvenile arrests (14%, 13%, and 14% reductions in numbers, respectively; Sickmund, Sladky, & Kang, 2012); however, the use of probation as a disposition was applied more extensively during this same 4-year timeframe. Sixty-two percent of formally referred juvenile cases had a probation disposition in 2006, and 66% had a probation disposition in 2009 (Sickmund, Sladky, & Kang, 2012).

A probation disposition serves a purpose only if it represents an opportunity for meaningful early intervention with youth and families—otherwise it all too often becomes a vehicle for unnecessary system penetration. This is particularly true for youth offenders living with undiagnosed and/or untreated MH disorders. Even more egregious is the use of probation rather than diversion from the system for first-time youth offenders committing relatively minor offenses who also live with undiagnosed and/or untreated MH disorders. This chapter focuses on the "crisis as opportunity" intersection of juvenile justice and MH system practices for youth living with MH disorders across the spectrum of juvenile justice case processing.

High rates of substance use (SU) and MH disorders among delinquent youth have been well documented in the literature (Abram, Teplin, McClelland, & Dulcan, 2003; Shufelt & Cocozza, 2006; Teplin, Abram, McClelland, Mericle, Dulcan, & Washburn, 2006; Wasserman, McReynolds, Lucas, Fisher, & Santos, 2002; Wasserman, McReynolds, Schwalbe, Keating, & Jones, 2010). Across these studies, MH disorder prevalence rates for incarcerated youth are higher than those among the general population, with depression and anxiety disorders being the most prevalent of the major mental illnesses. Substance abuse, which often presents comorbidly with these major mental illnesses, is the only other disorder with greater prevalence among this population. Researchers have hypothesized that these rates of disorder are not surprising when also considering the social structural/environmental risk factors present in the lives of many delinquent youth that increase stress and adversity (Dohrenwend, 2000; Hawkins, Herrenkohl, Farrington, Brewer, Catalano, & Harachi, 1998). Others note that the criminalization of people living with mental illness has led to an increase in the number of mentally ill people involved in either the juvenile or criminal justice systems (Sentencing Project, 2002; Slate, Johnson, & Buffington-Vollum, 2012). As a result, adult prisons have become the new de facto psychiatric hospitals, and the same may be true for juvenile offenders in secure correctional settings (Sedlak & McPherson, 2010).

Once caught up in the juvenile justice system, SU/MH issues increase in prevalence as youth reoffend and move deeper into the system (Wasserman et al., 2010). It may be that youth with undiagnosed and untreated SU/MH issues are not diverted toward early intervention opportunities, and this contributes to further system penetration (Butts & Evans, 2011). Assessment and treatment protocols informed by recent evidence suggest that diagnostic patterns of disorder can be distinguished across three juvenile justice settings (intake, detention, and secure incarceration), and these deserve consideration in terms of assessment and staff training (Wasserman et al., 2010). The juvenile justice system—in its current incarnation—may not be the ideal milieu for treating SU/MH issues among youth offenders caught up in the system. Nonetheless, when the court partners with other public systems to implement evidence-based treatments within the supervision and monitoring authority of the court, a "crisis as opportunity" intervention point can be navigated. While this intervention point certainly applies to youth on probation, it is also particularly critical for youth offenders living with SU/MH issues re-entering the community from detention or longer-term secure confinement.

■ A Closer Look at Prevalence Rates

Several empirical studies have documented prevalence rates for MH disorders among incarcerated and/or court-involved youth. Prior to 1999, empirical documentation of MH disorders among justice-involved youth was limited. Results could not be compared across sites due to methodological limitations such as limited sample sizes, retrospective chart/record review, biased samples, and measurement problems. More current prevalence studies used standardized assessments that could be compared across sites to document rates of MH disorders among incarcerated youth: for example, either the Massachusetts Youth Screening Instrument (MAYSI) screening instrument (Teplin, Abram, McClelland, Dulcan, & Mericle, 2002) or the Diagnostic Interview Schedule for Children (DISC) assessment instrument (Abram, Teplin, McClelland, & Dulcan, 2003; Shufelt & Cocozza, 2006; Teplin, Abram, McClelland, Mericle, Dulcan, & Washburn, 2006; Wasserman et al., 2002, 2010).

Results of these studies indicated that rates of MH disorders among juvenile justice-involved youth were significantly higher than those found in the general population (Teplin et al., 2006; Wasserman et al., 2002). Two large studies that both used (different versions) of the DISC are the Northwestern Juvenile Project (NJP) in Illinois (Abram et al., 2003; Teplin et al., 2006) and the National Center for Mental Health in Juvenile Justice (NCMHJJ) study in

Louisiana, Texas, and Washington (Schufelt & Cocozza, 2006). NJP documented prevalence rates for over 1,800 detained youth in Cook County, IL, and reported that 60% of males and over 70% of females met the criteria for one or more MH disorders, excluding conduct disorder. Conduct disorder rates for males were 37% and over 40% for females. Rates for depression were 17% for males and over 26% for females. Substance abuse disorder rates were 50% for males and 46% for females. Thirty percent of females met the criteria for an anxiety disorder, as did over 21% of males. Over 56% of females and over 45% of males in the NJP met the criteria for a co-occurring psychiatric disorder (Abram et al., 2003). Excluding conduct disorder, over 33% of females and over 24% of males met the criteria for two or more disorders.

The NCMHJJ study documented prevalence rates among 1,400 youth in more diverse juvenile justice settings—detention, corrections, and community-based programs—in Louisiana, Texas, and Washington using the newer Voice DISC-IV (Schufelt & Cocozza, 2006). Results indicated the following rates for at least one MH disorder after exclusion of common diagnoses: 70% of youth met the criteria for at least one psychiatric disorder after excluding conduct disorder; over 66% met the criteria after excluding SU disorders. Co-occurring rates were reported as follows in the NCMHJJ study: over 60% met the criteria for three or more disorders, with SU the most common co-occurring disorder, followed by mood disorders. Females had higher odds of any disorder compared to males and higher rates of internalizing disorders than males (Teplin et al., 2006; Schufelt & Cocozza, 2006).

A more recent study by Wasserman and colleagues (2010) is one of the more methodologically rigorous prevalence studies to date of SU/MH disorder patterns across juvenile justice settings. The study aggregated diagnostic information for over 9,000 male and female youth obtained using random sampling procedures across 57 juvenile justice sites and three juvenile justice settings (intake, detention, longer-term secure incarceration). The Voice DISC-IV was used to obtain diagnosis-specific prevalence rates (rather than symptoms reported on a screening instrument, such as the Massachusetts Youth Screening Instrument Version 2 [MAYSI-2]). Wasserman and colleagues noted the importance of investigating diagnostic patterns of SU/MH disorders in these three discrete juvenile justice settings as an important tool in modulating assessment and treatment planning within these phases of juvenile justice processing.

In terms of prevalence across these three juvenile justice settings, results indicated that (1) more than half of the study sample met the diagnostic criteria for one or more disorders; (2) over 34% met the criteria for a SU disorder; (3) over 20% met the diagnostic criteria for anxiety disorder; (4) over 27% met the criteria for a disruptive behavior disorder; and (5) over 14% reported at least one lifetime suicide attempt, with over 2% reporting a suicide attempt within the past month (Wasserman et al., 2010). All these prevalence rates increased at statistically significant levels when "deeper-end" juvenile justice settings (detention and secure incarceration) were compared with intake. Youth in detention settings reported the highest odds ratios for affective disorders, anxiety disorders, disruptive behavior disorders, and past-month suicide attempts (compared to intake). Youth in a secure incarceration setting reported the highest rates of SU disorder and lifetime suicide attempts (Wasserman et al., 2003). In terms of gender, female rates for affective and anxiety disorders were double those of males, and female reports of internalizing disorders and disruptive behavior disorders were also significantly higher than males. Youth in detention and secure correctional settings were also more likely to report co-occurring disorders. The authors note that youth in detention, who reported the highest prevalence rates for several disorders, routinely have less access to assessment and treatment services than youth in secure incarceration settings, highlighting the need to improve assessment and treatment planning for youth in detention.

It is useful to estimate the scope of MH disorders at different juvenile justice processing phases in summarizing what these prevalence data indicate. One can describe the high and low prevalence estimates from the studies cited (Abram et al., 2003; Schufelt & Cocozza, 2006; Teplin et al., 2006; Wasserman et al., 2010) and apply them to the number of youth at different levels of juvenile justice system penetration based on U.S. Department of Justice Data (Sickmund et al., 2012). The low estimate for youth in the juvenile justice system meeting the criteria for any major mental illness was 50% and the high estimate was 70%: thus, of the 317,958 youth held in detention during 2009, between 158,979 and 222,571 suffered from a major mental illness (MMI); of the 541,391 who had a probation disposition during 2009, between 270,696 and 378,974 suffered from an MMI; of the 133,797 who were placed out of their homes at disposition, between 66,899 and 93,658 suffered from an MMI. The most severe manifestation of MMI is suicide attempts, and the study by Wasserman and colleagues (2010) reports a 2% rate of youth in the juvenile justice system having attempted suicide during the 30 days prior to participating in the study. Based on counts of youth held in detention, having a probation disposition, or being placed out of their homes at disposition, the estimates of youth having attempted suicide during the past 30 days are 6,359, 10,828, and 2,676, respectively.

When applying this estimation approach to specific major mental disorders one finds that between 54,053 and 82,669 of youth held in detention during 2009 suffered from depression, between 92,036 and 140,762 of youthful probationers, and between 22,745 and 34,787 youth in out-of-home placements. Between 63,592 and 95,387 youth in detention suffered from an anxiety disorder, between 108,278 and 162,417 on probation, and between 26,759 and 40,139 youth in out-of-home placements. Youth with sufficient symptoms and impairment to be diagnosed with an SU disorder included between 108,106 and 158,979 held in detention, between 184,073 and 270,696 probationers, and between 45,491 and 66,899 held in out-of-home placements during 2009.

Between 33% and 60% of youth in the cited studies met the criteria for more than one MMI, which means that during 2009 between 104,926 and 190,775 youth in detention, between 178,659 and 324,835 probationers, and between 44,153 and 80,278 youth in out-of-home placements were likely to be living with co-occurring MH disorders.

As the preceding analysis indicates, the raw numbers of youth involved with the juvenile justice system who are living with mental disorders is staggering. Nonetheless, there is more reason for hope now than ever before. Three areas warranting optimism based on continuing evidence-informed practices include youth-specific assessment instruments, youth-specific MH practices, and innovations in service delivery systems with increasing evidentiary support.

■ Standardized Screening and Assessment for Youth Offenders Living with Mental Illness

The previous discussion of prevalence rates and system penetration make clear the merits of matching screening and assessment protocols to documented patterns of disorder within the three major phases of potential juvenile justice processing (intake, detention, and secure confinement). This of course requires that standardized screening and assessment for SU/MH issues becomes a part of regular juvenile justice processing throughout these stages: as a follow-up to a positive screen at first offender intake, and as a part of standard intake processing for detention and secure confinement. (See Chapter 17 for a more detailed discussion of risk assessment instruments for youth offenders.) Wasserman and her colleagues (2010) note that given the large number of youth in detention with SU/MH issues (compared with youth at intake), use of a standardized assessment rather than a screen would appear to be a more effective response to youth offenders living with mental illness who are detained. This seems particularly relevant given the paucity of MH services available in detention, where confinement is seen as temporary and often lacks any substantive treatment planning.

It is important to understand the state of standardized screening and assessment for MH and SU disorders with adolescents, given the volume of cases processed through the juvenile justice system. Two screening tools, the Global Appraisal of Individual Needs Short Screener (GAIN-SS) (Dennis, Titus, White, & Unsicker, 2008) and the MAYSI-2 (Grisso & Barnum, 2006) will be discussed, as will the DISC (Shaffer, Fisher, & Lucas, 2004) and the GAIN-Initial (GAIN-I; Dennis et al., 2008) for use as a full diagnostic tool.

Screening Instruments

The GAIN-SS (Dennis et al., 2008) is a 20-item instrument derived from the larger GAIN, which includes 123 diagnostic items. The GAIN-SS allows for screening scores and cutpoints on four scales: internalizing, externalizing, SU problems, and crime and violence. The GAIN-SS allows for a general cutpoint score indicating the presence of an MH issue, an SU problem, or a delinquent behavior problem and lower threshold cutpoint scores for each of the four scales. This scoring protocol allows practitioners to identify youth who need further assessment with the GAIN and subsequent appropriate treatment (Dennis, Chan & Funk, 2006).

Dennis and colleagues (2006) reported on the development, reliability, and validity of the GAIN-SS. Using full GAIN data from over 6,000 adolescents, the 20 GAIN-SS items were initially derived from the original GAIN using sensitivity and selectivity analysis, resulting in the selection of five items from each of the four primary scales of the full GAIN instrument. Although the GAIN-SS had slightly lower internal consistency than the GAIN, there was good concurrent validity with the GAIN primary scale scores. Confirmatory factor analysis revealed a very similar structure between the GAIN-SS and the full GAIN. Discriminant validity was also established because the GAIN-SS scales had much higher correlations with the full GAIN primary scales from which they were derived than with the other three primary scales. With good sensitivity established, plotting sensitivity with specificity allowed for GAIN cutpoints to be stated with recommended triage ranges based on these cutpoints. Dennis and colleagues (2006) offer two utilization conclusions about the GAIN-SS: (1) It can serve in the aggregate as a needs assessment and planning tool and (2) it can rapidly identify specific youth who need a more in-depth diagnostic MH assessment.

The MAYSI-2 (Grisso & Barnum, 2006) is a short screening instrument designed to identify potential problems across six domains: (1) alcohol or other drug use; (2) anger and irritability; (3) depression and anxiety; (4) somatic problems; (5) thought disturbances; and (6) traumatic experiences. The MAYSI-2 also screens for immediate suicidal ideation (Grisso & Barnum, 2006). Similar to the Child Behavior Checklist (CBCL) (Achenbach, 1991), the MAYSI-2 is not a diagnostic instrument; rather, it identifies problems for further clinical assessment, although the MAYSI-2 differs from the CBCL in that it includes less than half the number of items of the CBCL, thus reducing the burden on youth completing the instrument. However, two recent studies have documented the possibility of racial bias in the expression and manifestation of psychiatric symptoms using the MAYSI-2 (Jaggers, Young, McKinney, Bolland, & Church, 2013; McCoy, 2011).

The most recent available validity analysis for the MAYSI-2 used data from a largely African-American male sample of 1,192 adolescents who had been held in detention (Archer, Simonds-Bisbee, Spiegel, Handel, & Elkins, 2010). Although racial bias was not directly examined in this study, Archer and colleagues (2010) noted that a study on the same dataset indicated that Caucasian youth were more likely to report MH symptoms on the MAYSI-2 than were youth of other ethnicities. In this study, girls were more likely than boys to endorse MH disorder symptoms, with effect sizes between boys and girls ranging between .13 and .34 on the MAYSI-2 scales. Concurrent and discriminant validity were evaluated using administrative data about social and medical histories for youth, Substance Abuse Subtle Screening Inventory (SASSI) (Miller & Lazowski, 2001) scale scores, and DSM-IV diagnostic criteria. Archer and colleagues (2010) found concurrent validity present, although they used a low threshold criterion correlation for clinically meaningful relationships.

Archer and colleagues (2010) acknowledge that the MAYSI-2 had variable concurrent validity depending on scales and gender and that there was very little previous extant research on this topic. This recent study using a large sample indicates that the MAYSI-2 can be suitable as an initial screening tool, and it was indeed formatted and intended for this purpose. As is true of the GAIN-SS, juvenile justice practitioners must use the MAYSI-2 with the understanding that the results are not diagnostic and are best applied as indicators of where to engage in further assessment of youth MH needs.

Standardized Diagnostic Instruments

The need to use standardized validated assessment instruments that provide a diagnosis is central to matching treatment to condition, as many evidence-based or evidence-supported programs and practices "map onto specific disorders" (Wasserman et al., 2003, p. 754). Two diagnostic instruments, the DISC and the GAIN, are the subjects of review here.

In its most recent version, the DISC is a lay-administered, computer-based diagnostic assessment that assesses more than 30 MH disorders common in children and youth (Voice DISC-IV) (Wasserman, Larkin, Ko, Katz, Cauffman, et al., 2004). "The Voice version of the DISC-IV generates disorders present in the past month" only (Wasserman et al., p. 631), unlike previous interviewer-administered versions of the DISC; however, some diagnoses (such as SU) include questions that ask about impairment across a longer timeframe. The DISC has gone through numerous iterations since its inception nearly three decades ago. Early reports on the DISC focused on discriminant validity (Costello, Edelbrock, & Costello, 1985) and improvements to the original instrument items (Breslau, 1987; Garvey, 1989). This work on the original DISC was concurrent with substantial revisions resulting in the introduction of the revised version, known as the DISC-R. The DISC-R was introduced with a set of reports on interrater and test–retest reliability (Schwab-Stone, Fisher, Piacentini & Shaffer, 1993; Shaffer, Schwab-Stone, Fisher, & Cohen, 1993), concurrent validity (Piacentini, Shaffer, Fisher, & Schwab-Stone, 1993), and diagnostic sensitivity (Fisher, Shaffer, Piacentini, & Lapkin, 1993), documenting development of a stronger instrument for structured diagnostic interviews administered by researchers and clinicians. At this time the DISC was also translated into Spanish and was culturally adapted and field tested in Puerto Rico, including reliability and validity analyses (Bravo, Woodbury-Fariña, Canino, & Rubio-Stipec, 1993).

The DISC went through additional revisions and evaluation for reliability and validity (Jensen, Roper, Fisher, & Piacentini, 1995; Roberts, Solovitz, Chen, & Casat, 1996; Schwab-Stone et al., 1996; Shaffer et al., 2000), including the introduction of the first computer-administered version of the DISC (PC-DISC v.3.0) (Bidaut-Russell, Reich, Cottler, & Robins, 1995). There is currently a version of the DISC that allows a youth to self-administer the interview on a computer in which the items are presented on the screen while an appropriately gentle voice asks the assessment questions through headphones attached to the computer (Voice DISC-IV). Two strengths of the DISC include the ability to arrive at diagnoses and the fact that throughout the iterative development process, careful attention has been paid to both psychometric validity and acceptability to clients and clinicians. Another plus is the fact that the Voice DISC-IV can be administered by lay staff persons, with clinical follow-up based on preliminary diagnoses. The interested reader can find a concise yet comprehensive treatment of the DISC in Shaffer, Fisher, and Lucas (2004).

The GAIN-I (Dennis et al., 2008) is an interviewer-administered instrument that includes 123 diagnostic items that load onto four main scales: (1) the Internal Mental Distress Scale, (2) the Behavior Complexity Scale, (3) the Substance Problem Scale, and (4) the Crime/Violence Scale. These main scales include 15 subscales, and the nine subscales relating to MH and SU include depression symptoms, anxiety symptoms, traumatic distress, homicidal or suicidal thoughts, substance abuse symptoms, substance dependence symptoms, inattentiveness disorders, hyperactivity and impulsivity, and conduct disorder symptoms.

Since its introduction over a decade ago the properties of the GAIN-I have been extensively researched, and this research has clearly and transparently established reliability and construct, concurrent, discriminant and predictive validity (Conrad, Conrad, Dennis, & Riley, 2008a through 2008d). Validation methods have included timeline follow-back methods, urine tests, collateral reports, treatment records, and blind psychiatric diagnosis for concurrent validity. Predictive validity has been established for SU relapse and recidivism to crime (Conrad et al., 2008a through 2008d). The use of real-time data more than administrative records or proxy variables for important MH constructs is a notable methodological strength of studies investigating the validity of the GAIN.

There are two operational advantages of the GAIN-I. One is its validated connection to the GAIN-SS screening instrument, which allows a high level of conceptual clarity when using the short screen for identification and triage of youth at intake and the full GAIN-I with youth identified as needing further assessment at screening. Additionally, since the GAIN-I is administered in an interview by a trained MH professional, the diagnostic results can lead to direct service planning and referral without an additional review by an MH professional.

In this chapter we have presented two diagnostic tools that can be used in juvenile justice settings to assess for MH disorders, both of which have well-established psychometric properties. The Voice DISC and GAIN-I have been validated using blind psychiatric diagnosis and enable systems to use these tools for MH assessment in a way that mitigates assessment costs. More importantly, these tools provide a level of assessment accuracy that can readily assist juvenile justice practitioners in connecting youth to appropriate and evidence-informed treatment.

Context matters in terms of the best "fit"—screening versus assessment. Juvenile justice practitioners in initial intake or short-term settings have screening instruments available to them. Reliability and validity data are available for the MAYSI-2 and the GAIN-SS, with rigorous development and validation data available on the GAIN-SS and its parent instrument, the GAIN. For practical purposes the MAYSI-2 can explicitly screen for thought disorders, while the GAIN-SS can rapidly identify youth with the paradoxical presentation of comorbid internalizing and externalizing disorders. The ability to rapidly screen for internalizing disorders is an advantage of the GAIN-SS, given the high prevalence of depression among juvenile justice populations (Byrnes, Boyle, & Yaffe-Kjosness 2005). On the other hand, practitioners in more long-term settings, or those whose work includes clinical practice within juvenile justice settings, can benefit from using the DISC or GAIN-I to assist them in more precise diagnosis of MH and SU disorders presenting among the youth in their care. It is also encouraging that these instruments are readily available, are easily administered, and require minimal training in their use.

■ Multidisciplinary Treatment Teams and Evidence-Based Service Delivery

New strategies that rely on cross-systems partnerships to treat juvenile offenders living with mental illness draw from the system of care model originally developed for dual-diagnosis clients (Minkoff, 1989). The therapeutic jurisprudence of the court serves as the convening authority through which services are coordinated, implemented, and monitored in this more recent model of care approach for court-involved youth with special needs. Multidisciplinary treatment partnerships form the core of this broad conceptual strategy, and these teams often deploy treatment as well as supervision and monitoring within the juvenile drug court or MH court models. These partnerships require child welfare and MH systems—as well as nonprofit youth-serving providers—to collaborate in the implementation of evidence-based assessment, treatment, and re-entry strategies for youth offenders who are often (or should be) involved in multiple systems, where the juvenile court holds the key to release.

Specialty Courts and Multidisciplinary Teams

Juvenile Drug Courts

Mitchell, Wilson, Eggers, and MacKenzie (2012) conducted a meta-analysis of recidivism among clients of adult and juvenile drug courts. These researchers identified 34 juvenile drug court evaluations that met their inclusion criteria (used an experimental or quasi-experimental design with a comparison group and measured criminal or drug-related recidivism as an outcome). The results of this meta-analysis consistently revealed small effect sizes for juvenile drug courts. On average, juvenile drug court participants had a 43.5% reduction in recidivism. Mitchell and colleagues strongly recommended that in addition to more extensively evaluating juvenile drug court programs, randomized experimental designs be employed more frequently in such evaluations. Although the average effect size for recidivism reductions associated with juvenile drug court participation was small, it was consistently in the desired direction of change, which is a reason for guarded optimism about this service delivery approach. It may behoove future evaluators to examine the possible differential effectiveness of juvenile drug courts with youth who have SU disorders alone compared to those with comorbid presentations, since SU disorders often present comorbidly with MMI. Implementing discrete evidence-based models within the larger juvenile drug court therapeutic jurisprudence framework also deserves exploration.

Juvenile MH Courts

Juvenile MH courts represent another specialty application of the therapeutic jurisprudence model. Cuellar, McReynolds, and Wasserman (2006) reported the results of a quasi-experimental evaluation of the Enhanced Mental Health Services Initiative in Texas, designed to increase diversionary MH services for adults and juveniles. In reporting results for the juvenile diversionary program, the authors noted that the overarching goal of such programs was to "minimize formal court intervention and justice costs, while providing supervision of offending youth and at least a minimal response to the youth's offense" (Cuellar et al., 2006, p. 199), in addition to targeted MH treatment based on diagnosed disorder. Results indicated that implementation of juvenile MH courts that include probation supervision and MH treatment can delay or prevent youth recidivism. Perhaps most importantly, the results of this evaluation showed that over the longer-term outcome analysis (1 year after disposition), "63 fewer arrests occurred per 100 youth served" (p. 209) for youth participating in the juvenile MH court.

New Approaches to Integrated Service Delivery

Specialty courts often implement interventions for special-need youth offenders within a multidisciplinary treatment team structure. It is important to keep in mind that screening, assessment, and treatment practices deployed in correctional, residential, outpatient, or home settings also unfold within one or more juvenile justice processing phases: intake, assessment, diversion, detention, probation, incarceration, re-entry, and/or aftercare. Multiple providers/systems are responsible for implementing discrete aspects of the overall intervention, sometimes concurrently and sometimes sequentially. These roles and assignments are also influenced by the phase of case processing and placement context (detention, incarceration, residential, outpatient).

One recent empirical evaluation reported promising outcomes for a program that implemented three discrete evidence-based treatment models for youth offenders with co-occurring disorders: dialectical behavior therapy, motivational enhancement, and multisystemic therapy (Trupin, Kerns, Walker, DeRobertis, & Stewart, 2011). The quasi-experimental study design evaluated the impact of the Family Integrated Transitions (FIT) program for 105 youth with co-occurring disorders compared with 169 co-occurring youth receiving treatment as usual: both groups were re-entering the community after secure confinement. The FIT model was implemented in two phases: the last 2 to 3 months while still confined, and 4 to 6 months after re-entry into the community, where services were delivered in the home and in the community. The three evidence-based programs were implemented sequentially during incarceration, re-entry, and aftercare, although it is unclear whether there was also a concurrent implementation of evidence-based programs (e.g., during re-entry). Outcome measures included risk of recidivism using Washington State's Initial Security Classification Assessment and actual reoffending rates. Results indicated that FIT participants had significantly lower felony recidivism, although there were no differences in violent felony or misdemeanor reoffending.

Using multidisciplinary teams to deploy sequentially and even consecutively implemented evidence-based treatments within the existing phases of juvenile justice processing provides opportunities for intervention partners to specialize in evidence-based treatments congruent with their organizational cultures and youth care mandates. Further implementation and evaluation of such "combination" models is an important next step in refining treatment models for youth offenders living with mental illness. The sequenced approach of the FIT study (Trupin et al., 2011) is congruent with the overlapping, phase-based intensive aftercare model developed by Altschuler, Armstrong, and McKenzie (1999), where interventions are deployed both sequentially and even congruently (the latter "overlapping" approach taking place during re-entry). Such "next steps" also provide opportunities for dismantling study designs that evaluate the efficacy of evidence-based practices together and separately.

Organizational Capacity

Attention must be paid to organizational mission and culture when assembling cross-systems intervention partnerships. Multidisciplinary treatment teams function most effectively when each partner implements care or supervision components congruent with his or her organizational expertise. Strict fidelity to evaluated implementation procedures is crucial to achieving empirically documented youth outcomes in community-based replication of evidence-based treatments. Such implementation fidelity is crucial but often difficult in the "real-world" settings of multidisciplinary partnerships. It is important to recognize and address these challenges when multiple systems historically dedicated to different, often conflicting processes (treatment and rehabilitation vs. control and punishment) are jointly involved in multidisciplinary partnerships, such as juvenile drug courts or MH courts. Only youth service providers with an organizational culture that can support specific evidence-based treatments should implement such approaches: each system of care partner plays to its strengths in the most effective multidisciplinary partnerships.

■ Evidence-Based Treatment Models for Youth Offenders Living with Mental Illness

Evidence-based models for treatment of justice-involved youth living with mental illness are those that have been demonstrated to be effective through empirical evaluations with diverse juvenile justice populations. Other evidence-informed practices represent promising approaches that still need more rigorous evaluations, such as randomized clinical trials, to be rated as evidence-based models. The summary information for evidence-based and evidence-informed programs and practices relevant to juvenile offenders with SU or MH issues presented in this section comes from SAMHSA's National Registry of Evidence-Based Programs and Practices (NREPP), the Office of Juvenile Justice and Delinquency Prevention (OJJDP) Model Programs Guide, and Blueprints for Healthy Youth Development at the Institute of Behavioral Science, University of Colorado, Boulder. Only programs that included outcomes specific to SU or MH issues for juvenile offenders on these registries have been included. Site-specific quality-of-research ratings are also provided: zero to four for SAMHSA's NREPP and Exemplary (highest) or Effective (second highest out of three rating categories) for the OJJDP Model Programs Guide. Programs listed on the Blueprints site are rated as either Promising or Model programs. Blueprints Model programs meet the additional standards of two high-quality randomized controlled trials or one randomized controlled trial plus one high-quality quasi-experimental evaluation, and outcome impact 12 months after intervention.

Corroborating information is also provided for evidence-based programs and practices listed on the SAMHSA, OJJDP, or Blueprints sites as found in the 2009 McArthur Foundation's "Models for Change: System Reform in Juvenile Justice" report, developed by the National Center for Mental Health and

Juvenile Justice (NCMHJJ), in collaboration with the Louisiana Supreme Court Drug Court Office. "Identification and Treatment of Youth with Mental Health Needs in Contact with the Juvenile Justice System" (Skowyra & Cocozza, 2006) is another valuable resource for promising approaches being used in specific jurisdictions that informed information provided in this chapter.

Evidence-Based Practice in Correctional Settings

The Adolescent Coping with Depression Course (CWD-A) is a cognitive-behavioral therapy group intervention that has been used with youth in detention and correctional settings. CWD-A is categorized as an evidence-based program on SAMHSA's NREPP and as a Promising program by Blueprints. Symptoms associated with adolescent depression are targeted, such as anxiety and irrational thinking. The intervention is deployed in mixed-gender groups of 10 over an 8-week period, using 16 2-hour sessions. Outcome measures include self-reported, parent-reported, and clinician-rated depression symptoms using the Schedule for Affective Disorders and Schizophrenia for School-Aged Children (K-SADS-E) (Rohde, Clarke, Mace, Jorgensen, & Seeley, 2004). Out of a highest rating of 4.0, the NREPP ranks the Quality of Research Ratings by Criteria for CWD-A as 3.7 for Recovery from Depression, 3.7 for Self-Reported Symptoms of Depression, 3.8 for Interviewer-Rated Symptoms of Depression, and 3.6 for Psychosocial Level of Functioning. It has been noted elsewhere that in the correctional milieu MH screening may often miss an internalizing disorder like depression (Wasserman et al., 2003), particularly among incarcerated female juveniles, who have higher prevalence rates for internalizing disorders than their male counterparts (Wasserman et al., 2012).

Although the youth in the CWD-A group experienced a significant decrease in depressive symptoms compared to the control group at the end of treatment, it is worthwhile to note that in the study by Rohde and colleagues (2004), the groups did not exhibit significant differences in their conduct disorder symptoms after treatment or during follow-up. Additionally, initial significant group differences in depression were not observed during the 6- and 12-month follow-up periods. These findings could indicate that comorbid internalizing and externalizing disorders, such as depression with conduct disorder, have a highly nuanced etiology and presentation requiring further basic and applied research to better understand the nature of this paradoxical presentation. This is particularly important within the juvenile justice context, as depression is the most prevalent single MMI among youth offenders, many of whom present with comorbid conduct disorder.

The Mendota Juvenile Treatment Center Program (MJTCP) implements intensive treatment for violent male adolescent offenders with MH disorders in a secure incarceration setting in Wisconsin. MJTCP is categorized as an evidence-based program by SAMHSA's NREPP, where the Quality of Research Ratings by Criteria rates the program as follows on a 4.0 scale: 3.0 for the outcome Violent Recidivism, 2.7 for Behavioral Compliance, and 2.9 for Absence of Security-Based Sanctions. The MJTCP is also listed as an Exemplary model program in the OJJDP Model Programs Guide.

MJTCP has been replicated in other Wisconsin sites as well as one Oregon site. A unique feature of the program is the co-location of a specialized correctional facility on the grounds of a state MH facility (Caldwell, McCormick, Umstead, & Van Rybroek, 2007). The overall treatment model is guided by a decompression strategy, where therapeutic as well as correctional staff consistently respond to defiant behavior through de-escalation rather than punishment. The graduated sanctions and incentives component of the program uses the Today-Tomorrow behavioral point reward system. The cognitive-behavioral treatment approach of Aggression Replacement Training is also used for skills building in emotional regulation. Professional staff includes a multidisciplinary team approach, including a psychiatrist, psychologist, and social workers.

Evidence-Based Practice in Residential Settings

Dialectical Behavior Therapy (DBT) has been used in inpatient and outpatient settings and is beginning to be used in some correctional settings (Croysdale & Drerup, 2008; Trupin, 2011). DBT was originally developed as a cognitive-behavioral-plus-meditative practice intervention for borderline personality disorder (Linehan, 1993). An adaptive version of DBT targets the "emotional regulation, anger, impulse control, and moodiness" (Trupin et al., 2011, p. 423) often experienced by youth offenders with co-occurring disorders. DBT is categorized as an evidence-based program on SAMHSA's NREPP. Out of a highest rating of 4.0, the NREPP ranks the Quality of Research Ratings by Criteria for DBT as 3.7 for the outcome Suicide Attempts, 3.3 for Non-suicidal Self-Injury, 3.4 for Psychosocial Adjustment, 3.4 for Treatment Retention, 3.3 for Drug Use, and 3.2 for Symptoms of Eating Disorders.

Motivational Enhancement Therapy (MET) (Miller, 1992) is an adapted version of Motivational Interviewing that focuses on helping clients explore and move forward with their readiness to change substance-abusing behaviors and attitudes. MET is categorized as an evidence-based program on SAMHSA's NREPP. According to NREPP, MET has been used in inpatient, residential, outpatient, and school settings but only empirically evaluated for older youth. Out of a highest rating of 4.0, the NREPP ranks the Quality of Research Ratings by Criteria for MET as 3.5 for the outcome Substance Use, 3.3 for Alcohol Consumption, 3.5 for Drinking Intensity, 2.6 for Marijuana Use, and 2.7 for Marijuana Problems.

Multidimensional Treatment Foster Care (MTFC) is a residential treatment model for delinquent youth exhibiting antisocial behavior and youth with serious MH problems who are at risk for psychiatric hospitalization. Youth are placed in a therapeutic family setting for 6 to 9 months with foster parents trained in MTFC. Biological parents also receive family therapy and parent education during this out-of-home placement time. The MTFC treatment team works with youth and biological parents to prepare for re-entry/unification and includes a family therapist, an individual therapist, a parent skills trainer, and a caseworker. MTFC is listed as a Model program on the Blueprints for Healthy Youth Development site. MTFC is also listed as an evidence-based practice on SAMHSA's NREPP, where the Quality of Research Ratings by Criteria are as follows on a 4.0 scale: Days in Locked Settings 3.1, Substance Use 2.8, Criminal and Delinquent Activities 3.1, Homework Completion and School Attendance 2.8, and Pregnancy Rates 3.1. MTFC is also categorized as an Exemplary program on the OJJDP Model Program Guide.

Evidence-Based Practice in Outpatient Settings

Trauma Focused Cognitive Behavioral Therapy (TF-CBT) is another evidence-based treatment model that maps onto a specific MH disorder (PTSD) or emotional disturbance. The TF-CBT treatment model initially focuses on individual sessions with youth and adult caregivers and expands to include joint youth and caregiver sessions for a total of 12 to 16 sessions. TF-CBT is recommended by the NCMHJJ (Cohen, Deblinger, Mannarino, & Steer, 2004) as part of an integrated juvenile drug court model for use with co-occurring disorders. TF-CBT is also included on SAMHSA's NREPP. Originally developed to address child sexual abuse trauma, TF-CBT has been adapted to address a broader array of child and adolescent traumatic experiences: for example, witnessing intimate partner violence, neighborhood violence, and removal from family prior to foster care placement. Out of a highest rating of 4.0, the NREPP ranks the Quality of Research Ratings by Criteria for TF-CBT as 3.8 for the outcome Child Behavior Problems, 3.6 for Child Symptoms of PTSD, 3.8 for Child Depression, 3.7 for Child Feelings of Shame, and 3.7 for Parental Emotional Reaction to Child's Experience of Sexual Abuse. NREPP reports the intervention has been empirically evaluated with ages ranging from early childhood through adult.

Evidence-Based Practice in Home-Based Settings

Functional Family Therapy (FFT) is a systematic, evidence-based, manual-driven, family-based treatment program that is successful in treating a wide range of problems affecting youth (including drug use and abuse, conduct disorder, MH concerns, truancy, and related family problems) and their families in a wide range of multiethnic, multicultural, and geographic contexts (Alexander & Sexton, 2002; Sexton, 2010). As a prevention program, FFT is effective in diverting youth away from entering the MH and justice systems (Alexander, Robbins, & Sexton, 2000). As a treatment program, FFT works within clinical and home settings focusing on specific and high-risk youth in justice and MH settings.

In both applications FFT is short term, generally ranging on average from eight to 12 sessions for mild cases, and up to 30 hours of direct service for more difficult cases. In most treatment systems FFT sessions are spread over a 3- to 6-month period, and intervention targets youth populations between the ages of 11 and 18, although younger siblings of referred adolescents are also regularly involved. FFT consists of three specific and distinct phases of clinical intervention: (1) engagement and motivation, (2) behavior change, and (3) generalization. Together, they provide a "map" that details specific goals and strategies for each phase of change and is intended to guide the family psychologist through the often intense, emotional, and conflicted interactions presented by the family (Sexton, 2010). Each of the three phases of FFT has specific therapeutic goals and therapist skills that, when used competently, maximize the likelihood of goal completion. FFT is rated as a Model program on the Blueprints list of programs and an Effective program on the OJJDP Model Programs Guide.

Specialized versions of MST have been developed for specific youth problems (and system contexts). MST for Juvenile Offenders (Schaeffer & Bourduin, 2005) and MST with Psychiatric Supports (MST-Psychiatric) (Huey, Henggeler, Rowland, Halliday-Boykins, Cunningham, et al., 2004) have been evaluated. Across the original and specialized models, MST uses an ecological treatment approach to target risk factors in the home, school, and community and among peers that contribute to youth antisocial behavior, while also strengthening protective factors. MST treatment duration is generally 4 months. Therapist/family contacts occur multiple times weekly, based on family need. SAMHSA's NREPP rates two specialized versions of MST as evidence-based practices. With a highest rating of 4.0, the Quality of Research Ratings for these two versions of MST on the NREPP site are as follows: (1) for MST-Psychiatric—Mental Health Symptoms 3.5, Family Relations 3.3, School Attendance 3.1, Suicide Attempts 3.3, and Days in Out-of-home Placement 3.0 and (2) for MST for Juvenile Offenders—Post-treatment Arrest Rates 2.9, Long-term Arrest Rates 3.0, Long-term Incarceration Rates 3.1, Self-reported Criminal Activity 3.2, Alcohol and Drug Use 2.0, Perceived Family Functioning 3.0, and; Peer Aggression 3.1. The original MST model is rated as a Model program on the Blueprints site as well as an Exemplary model on the OJJDP Model Programs Guide.

A lively debate in the scholarly literature continues regarding the effectiveness of MST. A systematic review (Littell, Popa, & Forsythe, 2005; Littell, Campbell, Green, & Toews, 2009) identified eight published randomized controlled trials on MST that met the following criteria: subjects were between 10 and 17 years old, random assignment to conditions, and MST was provided by MST-licensed programs. The researchers noted that all but one of these eight studies were conducted by persons who were developers of MST or institutionally associated with them. Additionally, methodological concerns were identified with randomization procedures, appropriateness of some outcome measures, differing lengths of follow-up periods, and differing reported sample sizes within individual studies.

MST effect sizes were small among the three studies in the systematic review (Littell et al., 2005, 2009) that included some measure of psychiatric symptoms or internalizing and externalizing behaviors as outcome measures (program completer youth self-report data using the SCL-90-R or GSI-BSI). This is relevant to the current chapter, as we focus narrowly on treating youth offenders living with MH disorders. Only one of the studies in the systematic review of MST included psychiatric hospitalizations as the control condition and subsequent hospitalizations as an outcome measure. Those results indicated that although youth in the MST group had fewer psychiatric hospitalizations than the control group, the difference between the groups at the 1-year follow-up point was small, with 48% of MST youth and 47% of hospitalized youth experiencing any type of out-of-home placement.

At its most implementation-relevant essence, the systematic review by Littell and colleagues (2005, 2009) and subsequent rebuttals/discussion in the scholarly literature (Henggeler, Schoenwald, Swenson, & Borduin, 2006; Ogden & Hagen, 2006) highlight an ongoing and valuable debate in the evidence-based practice implementation community: efficacy versus effectiveness. The efficacy of a model is the extent to which positive outcomes are achieved under *optimal* conditions, whereas the effectiveness of a model documents the extent to which positive outcomes are achieved under *"real-world"* conditions (Society for Prevention Research). In the case of MST, discussions of this issue revolve around optimal conditions as operationalized by intensive "hands-on" supervision from model developers, compared with "real-world" implementation without such rigorous (and costly) supervision. Across *all* EBP models or approaches, this issue of efficacy versus effectiveness relates directly to the replication and "take-up" of evidence-based practice in the public and nonprofit sectors that serve children, youth, and families. It is important to continue to investigate these two different aspects of evidence-based practice implementation as we refine our knowledge of "what works."

■ Medication Management Use and Effectiveness

Although a majority of juvenile justice practitioners have their training in applied social sciences rather than in medicine, psychiatric treatment is part of the MH services array and requires inclusion in any discussion of MH and juvenile delinquency. Camilla Lyons and colleagues (2011) reported on patterns of psychotropic medication use in juvenile justice settings with a largely Latino male sample of 632 youth who were admitted to juvenile justice facilities for long-term confinement. Of these youth 68 (11%) had psychotropic medications prescribed for them within 30 days of being admitted to a facility. Youth were assessed for MH disorders using the Voice-DISC. Although the authors did not provide descriptive statistics about youth diagnoses, they did report that approximately one quarter of the sample met the criteria for mood, anxiety, or attention-deficit disorders. The results of this study indicate that most of the youth were prescribed antidepressant medications either alone or in combination with other medications, with an antipsychotic or another antidepressant being the most common combination of medications. Results also included the finding that youth who met MH disorder criteria were twice as likely to be prescribed medications as those who were not, and that youth presenting with co-occurring disorders were considerably more likely to receive medications than those with only one disorder. Additionally, approximately one fifth of youth who were diagnosed with disorders warranting medication had medications prescribed for them.

Emerging knowledge about psychotropic medications with co-occurring disorders among youth indicates that the somewhat paradoxical combination of internalizing and externalizing disorders may be amenable to pharmacotherapy. In a recently reported randomized controlled trial, Jacobs and colleagues (2010) engaged 439 adolescents enrolled in the Treatment for Adolescents with Depression study in four treatment conditions: (1) cognitive-behavioral therapy alone (CBT); (2) fluoxetine alone (FLX); (3) CBT and FLX combined (FLX), and (4) a placebo pill control condition (PBO). All participants met DSM-IV criteria for Major Depressive Disorder, and depression was also assessed using the Children's Depression Rating Scale–Revised (CDRS–R) (Poznanski & Mokros, 1996). Oppositionality was assessed using the Conners' Parent Rating Scale–Revised (CPRS–R) (Conners, Wells, Parker, Sitarenios, Diamond, & Powell, 1997). The four groups did not significantly differ on the outcome measures, demographic variables, or characteristics of their current depressive episode. At the end of treatment the FLX and COMB groups significantly differed from the PBO group on reductions in oppositionality whereas the CBT group did not differ from the PBO group, and the FLX and COMB groups did not significantly differ from each other. Additionally, the FLX and COMB groups both had significant reductions in oppositionality in comparison to the CBT group. Additional analysis revealed that among participants whose depression went into remission at the end of treatment, all of the active treatments, FLX, CBT, and COMB, displayed significant reductions in oppositionality in comparison to the PBO control group, but among adolescents whose depression was not in remission the CBT group did not significantly differ from the PBO control group in reduced oppositionality.

These results indicate that changes in depression and oppositionality can be interactive and that pharmacotherapy can be an effective treatment for comorbid internalizing and externalizing disorders. These two studies stand in support of prospective research designs to investigate this issue. The prospective TADS data allowed for a more complete analysis of results, causal inference, and understanding of interaction effects, which are essential for progress in improving services for youth with comorbid MH disorders and juvenile justice system involvement. Additionally, the results of the study by Jacobs and colleagues (2010) offer hope for effectively treating the paradoxical combination of simultaneous internalizing and externalizing disorders through a multimodal interdisciplinary approach.

■ Current Status and Future Directions

The sheer number of youth in the juvenile justice system presenting with MH disorders is daunting. Among the detention population alone, the idea of effectively identifying and treating over 100,000 youth annually living with more than one major mental illness can seem staggering to practitioners and policymakers. The extent of MH screening, assessment, and treatment required to respond to the broader constellation of MH disorders present in the lives of juvenile offenders is even more daunting. This aspect of the practice landscape alone should motivate those of us charged with serving youth offenders living with MH disorders to use the best available evidence-informed tools at our disposal to meet the challenge. Embedding this level of evidence-informed response into day-to-day juvenile justice practice requires a commitment to identify and serve this often-neglected population across the system: intake staff; juvenile judges who make critical decisions regarding diversion, probation, or incarceration; probation officers who have the opportunity to make critical referrals for services; administrators who allocate resources; and policymakers who appropriate those resources. Cross-systems partners who provide services to court-involved youth living with MH disorders must also commit to using the best available evidence to develop their capacity to implement evidence-based and/or evidence-informed practices for this population.

Evidence-based screening and assessment tools are available and need to become embedded in day-to-day juvenile justice practice. The availability of reliable and valid screening instruments such as the MAYSI-2 and the GAIN-SS enable intake-level staff members at each phase of juvenile justice processing to rapidly identify youth who may need more in-depth clinical assessment. Both instruments allow lay staff to be trained in their use in a relatively efficient manner. The validated cutpoints of the GAIN-SS can also serve a triage function for systems that are particularly strained by limited resources. Youth who are identified at screening for further assessment can engage in a computer-based self-administered version of the Voice-DISC or GAIN-I. These results can be reviewed by a smaller pool of staff members with advanced education and training in MH assessment and diagnosis, setting the stage for appropriate in-house or referred professional treatment services, depending on the delivery systems available at the local level.

Although evidence-informed practices are available for youth presenting with major MH or SU disorders, outcome research reveals that the comorbidity of internalizing and externalizing disorders can be challenging to treat effectively (Rohde, Clarke, Mace, Jorgensen, & Seeley, 2004). This lack of evidence-informed treatment for the paradoxical presentation of internalizing and externalizing disorders is particularly relevant to youth living with mental illness who are caught up in the juvenile justice system. The evidence-based Adolescent Coping with Depression Course (CWD-A) was used with fidelity in the randomized controlled trial by Rohde and his colleagues, but even though initial reductions in depressive symptoms were observed, these gains were not maintained during the follow-up period for youth with comorbid conduct disorder. On the other hand, when a combination of pharmacotherapy with fluoxetine and cognitive-behavioral therapy was evaluated with youth who presented with oppositionality and depression in a randomized controlled trial by Jacobs and her colleagues (2010), this combined treatment was effective in significantly reducing both the internalizing and externalizing symptoms of youth. What appears to be needed for unraveling the paradoxical presentation of both internalizing and externalizing disorders is more concurrent theoretical and clinical outcome research on the application of modified evidence-based program with justice-involved youth with this comorbid clinical presentation.

As we noted earlier in this chapter, Wasserman and colleagues (2010) called attention to the importance of investigating patterns of MH disorder across phases of juvenile justice processing: intake, detention, and secure incarceration. The fact that prevalence rates for MH disorders increased at statistically significant levels the further youth moved into the juvenile justice system highlights the need for MH screening and assessment earlier rather than later in system processing. It is important to note that such an early response approach must include a pathway to diversion (with outpatient treatment), particularly for first-time youth offenders living with mental illness who have not engaged in severe felony-level offending; otherwise, such early identification and intervention can have the unintended consequence of moving youth into unnecessary juvenile justice system penetration—a situation with iatrogenic effects (Gatti, Tremblay, & Viatro, 2009).

The evidence-based practice (Gambrill, 1997) movement represents a milestone for the helping professions and encourages practitioners to move away from rigid theoretical or ideological orientations toward applying the best research evidence with a goodness of fit for individual clients, while also evaluating outcomes at the case level. This movement encourages a technical eclecticism that is rooted in outcome evidence about treatment efficacy and effectiveness. Although technical eclecticism has been in the practice conversation for many years, such as in Arnold Lazarus' Multimodal Therapy (Lazarus, 1989), many evidence-based interventions are rooted in theories of development, psychopathology, and behavior change, and indeed many social and behavioral science educators adhere, sometimes ideologically, to specific theories or perspectives about professional practice and pass such adherence on to subsequent generations of practitioners. Theoretical eclecticism is articulated in the Integrative Model of Psychotherapy (Prochaska & DiClemente, 1982) as engaging in evidence-informed practices that best fit clients' characteristics, and is therefore congruous with the evidence-based practice process.

Finally, "take-up" of evidence-based programs, particularly by the public systems that serve youth and the nonprofit providers who contract with those systems, will be influenced by ongoing research to disentangle issues related to efficacy versus effectiveness. As noted earlier in this chapter, efficacy relates to implementing evidence-based programs under optimal conditions, and effectiveness relates to implementing them in "real-world" treatment settings. "Next steps" research that seeks to dismantle the essential components of evidence-based practice as well as moderating client and treatment context variables that influence long-term outcomes resonates across the evidence-based practice spectrum, including its implementation with youth offenders living with mental illness.

References

Abram, K. M., Teplin, L. A., McClelland, G. M., & Dulcan, M. K. (2003). Comorbid psychiatric disorders in youth in juvenile detention. *Archives of General Psychiatry, 60,* 1097–1108.

Achenbach, T. M. (1991). *Manual for the Youth Self-Report and 1991 Profile.* Burlington, VT: University of Vermont Department of Psychiatry.

Alexander, J. F., & Sexton, T. L. (2002). *Functional Family Therapy: A model for treating high-risk, acting-out youth.* Wiley Series in Couples and Family Dynamics and Treatment, Comprehensive Handbook of Psychotherapy Volume IV: Integrative/Eclectic (H. J. Lebow, Ed.). New York: John Wiley.

Altschuler, D. M., Armstrong, T. L, & MacKenzie, D. L. (1999). Reintegration, supervised release, and intensive aftercare. *Bulletin.* Washington, DC: Office of Juvenile Justice and Delinquency Prevention, Office of Justice Programs, U.S. Department of Justice.

Archer, R. P., Simonds-Bisbee, E. C., Spiegel, D. R., Handel, R. W., & Elkins, D. E. (2010). Validity of the Massachusetts Youth Screening Instrument-2 (MAYSI-2) scales in juvenile justice settings. *Journal of Personality Assessment, 92*(4), 337–348.

Bidaut-Russell, M., Reich, W., Cottler, L. B., & Robins, L. N. (1995). The Diagnostic Interview Schedule for Children (PC-DISC v.3.0): Parents and adolescents suggest reasons for expecting discrepant answers. *Journal of Abnormal Child Psychology, 23*(5), 641–659.

Bravo, M., Woodbury-Fariña, M., Canino, G. J., & Rubio-Stipec, M. (1993). The Spanish translation and cultural adaptation of the Diagnostic Interview Schedule for Children (DISC) in Puerto Rico. *Culture, Medicine and Psychiatry, 17*(3), 329–344.

Breslau, N. (1987). Inquiring about the bizarre: False positives in Diagnostic Interview Schedule for Children (DISC) ascertainment of obsessions, compulsions, and psychotic symptoms. *Journal of the American Academy of Child and Adolescent Psychiatry, 26*(5), 639–644.

Butts, J. A., & Evans, D. N. (2011). *Resolution, reinvestment, and realignment: Three strategies for changing juvenile justice.* New York: Research and Evaluation Center, John Jay College of Criminal Justice, City University of New York.

Byrnes, E. C., Boyle, S. W., & Yaffe-Kjosness, J. Y. (2005). Enhancing interventions with delinquent youth: The case for specifically treating depression in juvenile justice populations. In L. A. Rapp-Paglicci (Ed.), *Juvenile offenders and mental illness: I know why the caged bird cries* (pp. 49–72). Binghamton, NY: The Haworth Press Inc.

Caldwell, M. F., McCormick, D. J., Umstead, D., & Van Rybroek, G. J. (2007). Evidence of treatment progress and therapeutic outcomes among adolescent with psychopathic features. *Criminal Justice and Behavior, 34*(5), 571–587.

Cohen, J. A., Deblinger, E., Mannarino, A. P., & Steer, R. A. (2004). A multisite, randomized controlled trial for children with sexual abuse-related PTSD symptoms. *Journal of the American Academy of Child and Adolescent Psychiatry, 43*(4), 393–402.

Conners, K., Wells, K., Parker, J., Sitarenios, G., Diamond, J., & Powell, J. (1997). A new self-report scale for assessment of adolescent psychopathology: Factor structure, reliability, validity, and diagnostic sensitivity. *Journal of Abnormal Child Psychology, 25*, 487–497.

Conrad, K. J., Conrad, K. M., Dennis, M. L., & Riley, B. B. (2008a). *GAIN working papers: Rasch analysis of the behavioral complexity scale.* Chicago, IL: Chestnut Health Systems.

Conrad, K. J., Conrad, K. M., Dennis, M. L., & Riley, B. B. (2008b). *GAIN working papers: Rasch analysis of the internal mental distress scale.* Chicago, IL: Chestnut Health Systems.

Conrad, K. J., Conrad, K. M., Dennis, M. L., & Riley, B. B. (2008c). *GAIN working papers: Rasch analysis of the substance problem scale.* Chicago, IL: Chestnut Health Systems.

Conrad, K. J., Conrad, K. M., Dennis, M. L., & Riley, B. B. (2008d). *GAIN working papers: Rasch analysis of the crime and violence scale.* Chicago, IL: Chestnut Health Systems.

Costello, E. J., Edelbrock, C. S., & Costello, A. J. (1985). Validity of the NIMH Diagnostic Interview Schedule for Children: A comparison between psychiatric and pediatric referrals. *Journal of Abnormal Child Psychology, 13*(4), 579–595.

Cuellar, A. E., McReynolds, L. S., & Wasserman, G. A. (2006). A cure for crime: Can mental health treatment diversion reduce crime among youth? *Journal of Policy Analysis and Management, 25*(1), 197–214.

Dennis, M. L., Chan, Y. F., & Funk, R. R. (2006). Development and validation of the GAIN Short Screener (GSS) for internalizing, externalizing and substance use disorders and crime/violence problems among adolescents and adults. *American Journal on Addictions, 15*, 80–91.

Dennis, M. L., Titus, J. C., & White, M. (2008). *Global Appraisal of Individual Needs (GAIN): Administration guide for the GAIN and related measures* (5th ed.). Bloomington, IL: Chestnut Health Systems.

Dohrenwend, B. P. (2000). The role of adversity and stress in psychopathology: Some evidence and its implications for theory and research. *Journal of Health and Social Behavior, 41*, 1–19.

Fisher, P. W., Shaffer, D., Piacentini, J., & Lapkin, J. (1993). Sensitivity of the Diagnostic Interview Schedule for Children, 2nd edition (DISC-2.1) for specific diagnoses of children and adolescents. *Journal of the American Academy of Child and Adolescent Psychiatry, 32*(3), 666–673.

Gambrill, E. (1997). *Social work practice: A critical thinker's guide.* New York: Oxford University Press.

Garvey, S. A. (1989). Development and testing of alternative items for the Diagnostic Interview Schedule for Children. *Dissertation Abstracts International, 50*(5-B), 2151.

Gatti, U., Tremblay, R., & Vitaro, F. (2009). Iatrogenic effect of juvenile justice. *Journal of Child Psychology and Psychiatry, 50*, 991–998. doi:10.1111/j.1469-7610.2008.02057.x

Grisso, T., & Barnum, R. (2006). *Massachusetts Youth Screening Instrument-Version 2: User's manual and technical report* (Rev. ed.). Sarasota, FL: Professional Resource Press.

Hawkins, J. D., Herrenkohl, T., Farrington, D. P., Brewer, D. D., Catalano, R. F., & Harachi, T. (1998). A review of predictors of youth violence. In R. Loeber & D. P. Farrington (Eds.), *Serious and violent juvenile offenders: Risk factors and successful interventions* (pp. 106–146). Thousand Oaks, CA: Sage.

Henggeler, S. W., Schoenwald, S. K., & Swenson, C. C. (2006). Letter to the editor: Methodological critique and meta-analysis as Trojan horse. *Children and Youth Services Review, 28*, 447–457.

Huey, S. J., Henggeler, S. W., Rowland, M. D., Halliday-Boykins, C. A., Cunningham, P. B., Pickrel, S. G., & Edwards, J. (2004). Multisystemic therapy effects on attempted suicide by youth presenting psychiatric emergencies. *Journal of the American Academy of Child and Adolescent Psychiatry, 43*(2), 183–190.

Jacobs, R. H., Becker-Weidman, E. G., Reinecke, M. A., Jordan, N., Silva, S. G., Rohde, P., & March, J. S. (2010). Treating depression and oppositional behavior in adolescents. *Journal of Clinical Child and Adolescent Psychology, 39*(4), 559–567.

Jaggers, J., Young, S., McKinney, R., Bolland, K. A., & Church, W. T. (2013). Utilization of the Massachusetts Youth Screening Instrument-2 (MAYSI-2) with a Southern, African American adolescent male population. *Journal of Forensic Social Work, 3*(1), 3–15.

Jensen, P., Roper, M., Fisher, P., & Piacentini, J. (1995). Test-retest reliability of the Diagnostic Interview Schedule for Children (DISC 2.1): Parent, child, and combined algorithms. *Archives of General Psychiatry, 52*(1), 61–71.

Lazarus, A. A. (1989). *The practice of multimodal therapy: Systematic, comprehensive, and effective psychotherapy.* Baltimore, MD: Johns Hopkins University Press.

Linehan, M. M. (1993). *Cognitive-behavioral treatment of borderline personality disorder.* New York: Guilford Press.

Littell, J. H., Campbell, M., Green, S. & Toews, B. (2009). Multisystemic therapy for social, emotional, and behavioral developmental model of risk and promotive factors, in R. Loeber, N. W. Slot, P. H. Van der Laan and M. Hoeve (Eds.) *Tomorrow's criminals: The development of child delinquency and effective interventions* (pp. 133–161). Farnham: Ashgate.

Littell J., Popa, M., & Forsythe, B. (2005). Multisystemic therapy for social, emotional, and behavioral problems in youth aged 10-17. *The Cochrane Library.*

Lyons, C. L., Wasserman, G. A., Olfson, M., McReynolds, L. S., Musabegovic, H., & Keating, J. M. (2011). Psychotropic medication patterns among youth in juvenile justice. *Administration and Policy in Mental Health and Mental Health Services Research, 38*, Published Online.

McCoy, H. (2011). A path analysis of factors influencing racial differences on the MAYSI-2. *Journal of Offender Rehabilitation, 50*(3), 119–141.

Miller, F. G., & Lazowski, L. E. (2001). *The Adolescent Substance Abuse Subtle Screening Inventory-A2 (SASSI-A2) manual.* Springville, IN: SASSI Institute.

Miller, W. R. (1992). *Motivational enhancement therapy manual: A clinical research guide for therapists treating individuals with alcohol abuse and dependence.* National Institute on Alcohol Abuse and Alcoholism. U.S. Dept. of Health and Human Services, Public Health Service, Alcohol, Drug Abuse, and Mental Health Administration, National Institute on Alcohol Abuse and Alcoholism.

Minkoff, K. (1989). An integrated treatment model for dual diagnosis of psychosis and addiction. *Hospital and Community Psychiatry, 40,* 1031–1036.

Mitchell, O., Wilson, D. B., Eggers, A., & MacKenzie, D. L. (2012). Drug courts' effects on criminal offending for juveniles and adults. *Campbell Systematic Reviews 2012:4.* doi:10.4073/csr.2012.4

Ogden, T., & Hagen, K. A. (2006). Does MST work? Comments on a systematic review and meta-analysis of MST. *Nordic Social Work, 26,* 222–223.

Piacentini, J., Shaffer, D., Fisher, P. W., & Schwab-Stone, M. (1993). The Diagnostic Interview Schedule for Children—Revised Version (DISC—R): III. Concurrent criterion validity. *Journal of the American Academy of Child & Adolescent Psychiatry, 32*(3), 658–665.

Poznanski, E. O., & Mokros, H. B. (1996). *Children's Depression Rating Scale, Revised.* Los Angeles: Western Psychological Services.

Prochaska, J. O., & DiClemente, C. C. (1982). Transtheoretical therapy: Toward a more integrative model of change. *Psychotherapy: Theory, Research & Practice, 19*(3), 276–288.

Puzzanchera, C., Adams, B., & Kang, W. (2012). *Easy access to FBI arrest statistics 1994–2009.* Available at: http://www.ojjdp.gov/ojstatbb/ezaucr/

Roberts, R. E., Solovitz, B. L., Chen, Y. W., & Casat, C. (1996). Retest stability of DSM-III-R diagnoses among adolescents using the Diagnostic Interview Schedule for Children (DISC-2.1C). *Journal of Abnormal Child Psychology, 24*(3), 349–362.

Rohde, P., Clarke, G. N., Mace, D. E., Jorgensen, J. S., & Seeley, J. R. (2004). An efficacy/effectiveness study of cognitive-behavioral treatment for adolescents with comorbid major depression and conduct disorder. *Journal of the American Academy of Child and Adolescent Psychiatry, 43*(6), 660–668.

Schwab-Stone, M., Fisher, P.W., Piacentini, J., & Shaffer, D. (1993). The Diagnostic Interview Schedule for Children—Revised version (DISC—R): II. Test-retest reliability. *Journal of the American Academy of Child and Adolescent Psychiatry, 32*(3), 651–657.

Schwab-Stone, M. E., Shaffer, D., Dulcan, M. K., & Jensen, P. S. (1996). Criterion validity of the NIMH Diagnostic Interview Schedule for Children Version 2.3 (DISC-2.3). *Journal of the American Academy of Child and Adolescent Psychiatry, 35*(7), 878–888.

Sedlak, A. J., & McPherson, K. S. (2010). *Youth's needs and services: Findings from the Survey of Youth in Residential Placement* (NCJ 227728). Washington, DC: Office of Juvenile Justice Delinquency Prevention.

Sentencing Project (2002). *Mentally ill offenders in the criminal justice system: An analysis and prescription.* Washington, DC. Retrieved from http://www.sentencingproject.org/doc/publications/sl_mentallyilloffenders.pdf

Sexton, T. (2010). *Functional family therapy in clinical practice: An evidence based treatment model for working with troubled adolescents.* New York, NY: Routledge.

Schaeffer, C. M., & Borduin, C. M. (2005). Long-term follow-up to a randomized clinical trial of Multisystemic Therapy with serious and violent juvenile offenders. *Journal of Consulting and Clinical Psychology, 73*(3), 445–453.

Shaffer, D., Fisher, P., & Lucas, C. (2004). The Diagnostic Interview Schedule for Children (DISC). In M. J. Hilsenroth & D. L. Segal (Ed.), *Comprehensive handbook of psychological assessment, Vol. 2: Personality assessment* (pp. 256–270). Hoboken, NJ: John Wiley & Sons Inc.

Shaffer, D., Fisher, P., Lucas, C. P., Dulcan, M. K., & Schwab-Stone, M. E. (2000). NIMH Diagnostic Interview Schedule for Children Version IV (NIMH DISC-IV): Description, differences from previous versions, and reliability of some common diagnoses. *Journal of the American Academy of Child and Adolescent Psychiatry, 39*(1), 28–38.

Shaffer, D., Schwab-Stone, M., Fisher, P.W., & Cohen, P. (1993). The Diagnostic Interview Schedule for Children—Revised version (DISC—R): I. Preparation, field testing, inter-rater reliability, and acceptability. *Journal of the American Academy of Child and Adolescent Psychiatry, 32*(3), 643–650.

Shufelt, J. L., & Cocozza, J. J. (2006). *Youth with mental health disorders in the juvenile justice system: Results from a multi-state prevalence study.* Delmar, NY: National Center for Mental Health and Juvenile Justice.

Sickmund, M., Sladky, A., & Kang, W. (2012). *Easy access to juvenile court statistics: 1985–2009.* Available at: http://www.ojjdp.gov/ojstatbb/ezajcs/

Skowyra, K., & Cocozza, J. P. (2006). *A Blueprint for Change: Improving the system response to youth with mental health needs involved with the juvenile justice system.* Delmar, NY: National Center for Mental Health and Juvenile Justice.

Slate, R., Johnson, W. W., & Buffington-Vollum, J. (2013). *Criminalization of mental illness: Crisis and opportunity for the justice system.* Durham, NC: Carolina Academic Press.

Society for Prevention Research. *Standards of evidence: Criteria for efficacy, effectiveness and dissemination.* Online: http://www.preventionresearch.org/StandardsofEvidencebook.pdf.

Teplin, L. A., Abram, K. M., McClelland, G. M., Dulcan, M. K., & Mericle, A. A. (2002). Psychiatric disorders in youth in juvenile detention. *Archives of General Psychiatry, 59,* 1133–1143.

Trupin, E. J., Kerns, S. E., Walker, S. C., DeRobertis, M. T., & Stewart, D. G. (2011). Family Integrated Transitions: A promising program for juvenile offenders with co-occurring disorders. *Journal of Child and Adolescent Substance Abuse, 20*, 421–436.

Wasserman, G. A., Jensen, P. S., Ko, S. J., Cocozza, J., Trupin, E., Angold, A., et al. (2003). Mental health assessments in juvenile justice: Report on the consensus conference. *Journal of the American Academy of Child and Adolescent Psychiatry, 42*, 752–761.

Wasserman, G. A., McReynolds, L. S., Ko, S. J, Katz, L. M., Cauffman,, E., Haxton, W., et al. (2004). Screening for emergent risk and service needs among incarcerated youth: Comparing MAYSI-2 and Voice DISC-IV. *Journal of the American Academy of Child and Adolescent Psychiatry, 43*(5), 629–639.

Wasserman, G. A., McReynolds, L. S., Lucas, C. P., Fisher, P., & Santos, L. (2002). The voice DISC-IV with incarcerated male youth; prevalence of disorder. *Journal of the American Academy of Child and Adolescent Psychiatry, 41*, 314–321.

Wasserman, G. A., McReynolds, L. S., Musabegovic, H., Whited, A., Keating, J. M., & Huo, Y. (2012). Evaluating Project Connect: Improving juvenile probationers' mental health and substance use service access. *Administration and Policy in Mental Health, 36*, 393–405.

Wasserman, G. A., McReynolds, L. S., Schwalbe, C. S., Keating, J. M., & Jones, S. A. (2010). Psychiatric disorder, comorbidity, and suicidal behavior in juvenile justice youth. *Criminal Justice and Behavior, 37*, 1361–1376.

19 Family-Based Interventions for Juvenile Offenders

Stephanie C. Kennedy and Stephen J. Tripodi

■ Case Examples

■ *Henry:*

Henry is slumped in a wooden chair at the courthouse, wearing a suit that's a few sizes too large for his slight frame. His mother sits next to him, nervously encouraging him to sit up straight, pay attention, and behave himself. His three younger siblings whisper and giggle to each other as they leaf through old children's magazines in the back corner of the room. At 14 years old, this is Henry's third time being seen in juvenile court. He received probation for petty theft at age 12 and spent 30 days in an adolescent psychiatric unit last year after setting fires in his housing complex. This time, however, he's charged with possession of a controlled substance with intent to distribute. His mother is terrified that Henry will be sent to a residential facility in another county, or even worse tried as an adult and face prison time.

Just over a year ago, Henry met his biological father for the first time. His father had just been released from a 12-year prison sentence for felony drug trafficking. Since their first meeting, Henry has been spending more and more time at his father's apartment and with his father's friends. Henry's mother suspected that this new relationship would only lead to more trouble for Henry, but she felt powerless to keep them apart. Between her two jobs, three younger children, and Henry's explosive anger, it seemed easier to let him spend time away from her home.

Henry has been attending a second-chance school for 2 years, where he is an average student. He was expelled from public school for aggressive behavior and bullying. At his old school, Henry was diagnosed with oppositional defiant disorder and attention-deficit disorder by a school psychologist. His mother struggled to afford the prescribed medications and eventually stopped them because she felt they only increased Henry's agitation. At his new school, Henry's teacher suspects that he may have dyslexia and has ordered additional assessments. Unfortunately, when his teacher broached the subject at a recent parent–teacher conference, Henry exploded with anger, screaming at her for accusing him of "being stupid." His teacher tried unsuccessfully to calm him down and explain that having dyslexia did not make him stupid. Henry stormed out, not returning to his mother's house or to school for several weeks. Overwhelmed and unsure of what to do next, Henry's mother is desperate for change. She knows that things cannot continue as they are and does not want to see Henry follow the same path as his father.

■ *Nikole:*

Nikole sits alone on a bench outside the courthouse waiting until her family social worker arrives. She's been charged with misdemeanor assault and violation of probation after getting into a fistfight with a group of girls at school. This was the third fight Nikole had been in this term, and although her principal is empathetic to her situation, he had no choice but to write an incident report. Nikole is in the tenth grade and is an academically gifted student but struggles to control her anger. Nikole is currently living with an aunt after a violent altercation with her father 6 months ago. Unfortunately, her aunt is moving out of state for work, which means that Nikole will likely be placed in a residential group home. Nikole feels overwhelmed and out of options. Her social worker is concerned that unless something changes, Nikole will run away again, and she fears that this time, Nikole will be gone for good.

The social worker suspects domestic abuse in Nikole's home, although two investigations in the past 5 years have failed to substantiate such claims. Nikole's parents admit to using harsh punishment techniques out of exhaustion and exasperation because nothing they've tried thus far has succeeded in reducing the daily verbal and physical conflicts between Nikole and other members of the family. Nikole is shutdown emotionally and completely isolated, save for a positive relationship with her aunt and with an after-school music teacher. She feels betrayed and abandoned by her aunt's choice to move away and has shared several poems and journal entries with her social worker referencing suicide. Nikole and her parents have expressed a desire for change, although they all agree that living apart, at least for now, is the right way forward.

■ Scope of the Problem

Between 1980 and 1996, more juveniles were arrested than at any other time in American history (Howell, 2008). Adolescent arrest rates increased so dramatically, in fact, that by 1996 over 9,000 juveniles were arrested for every 100,000 adolescents, compared to approximately 6,500 arrests per 100,000 adolescents in 1980 (Stahl, 2001). Fortunately, beginning in 1997 this trend began to reverse. Since that time, juvenile arrest rates have consistently decreased, with the most dramatic decreases occurring from 1996 to 1999 and 2007 to 2010 (Office of Juvenile Justice and Delinquency Prevention [OJJDP], 2012). By 2010, the juvenile arrest rate was 4,857 for every 100,000 adolescents, marking a 24% reduction since 1980 and a 43% reduction since 1996 (Howell, 2008; OJJDP, 2012; Sickmund, 2009). The decline in juvenile arrests since 1996 is encouraging; however, adolescent criminal behavior continues to affect a shocking number of families throughout the United States. To contextualize these findings, the OJJDP reports that there were close to 2 million juvenile arrests in 2010 alone. Unfortunately, the consequences of juvenile crime extend far beyond the offender and their family—victims and their loved ones, witnesses, and taxpayers are among those affected, directly or indirectly, by juvenile delinquency.

Although the total number of juvenile arrests has decreased significantly in the past several decades, the percentage of girls arrested has increased dramatically. Female juvenile offenders constituted 20% of the juvenile offender population in 1989 but now represent approximately 35% of all juvenile arrests (Zahn et al., 2010). Even more shocking, adolescent females are increasingly being arrested for committing violent crimes. Violent offenses committed by females increased from 10% in 1980 to approximately 35% in 2009 (Henggeler & Sheidow, 2012; Zahn et al., 2010).

Henggeler and Sheidow (2012) identify several risk factors for juvenile delinquency, including individual-level characteristics such as attitudes and cognitions, family-level factors such as poor family dynamics and improper attachment to parents or guardians, and macro-level influences such as poverty and neighborhood crime (Howell, 2008; Loeber, Burke, & Pardini, 2009). Gottfredson and Hirschi (1990) assert that emotional attachment, active parenting, and clear communication are important protective factors against the development of juvenile behavior problems. Additionally, they note that parents who consistently monitor their children's behaviors, rewarding positive behavior and providing consequences for negative behavior, increase their child's self-control and subsequently decrease the chances of delinquent behavior. Parental attitudes toward delinquent behavior have also been identified as powerful determinants of an adolescent's involvement in the criminal justice system (Fagan, Van Horn, Antaramian, & Hawkins, 2011; Gottfredson & Hirschi, 1990; Kumpfer & Alvarado, 2003). Specifically, clear and consistent communication of a parent's expectation of compliant behavior protects against juvenile delinquency (Fagan et al., 2011; Gottfredson & Hirschi, 1990), while more relaxed parental attitudes toward delinquent behaviors increase involvement in the juvenile justice system (Kumpfer & Alvarado, 2003).

The powerful influence of family-level factors (e.g., family conflict, poor communication) on juvenile delinquency has led to the development and testing of family-based interventions for youth involved in the juvenile justice system. Youth who receive family-based interventions show significant reductions in substance use and re-arrest when compared to youth who receive probation or other community-based interventions (Bender, Tripodi, Sarteschi, & Vaughn, 2011; Tripodi & Bender, 2011; Tripodi, Bender, Litschge, & Vaughn, 2010. Although a multitude of interventions are currently being used with juveniles across the country, this chapter discusses the three family-based interventions for juvenile offenders with the most empirical support: Multisystemic Therapy, Functional Family Therapy, and Multidimensional Treatment Foster Care.

■ Literature Review

In the past 30 years, a variety of family-based intervention programs have been developed, implemented, and tested with a juvenile justice population. Interventions that address the family system have demonstrated some of the most promising outcomes for juvenile offenders, including long-term declines in recidivism (Henggeler & Schoenwald, 2011). An exhaustive review of the myriad family therapy interventions used with this population is beyond the scope of this chapter. Therefore, we will focus on the three family therapy interventions which have been endorsed as empirically supported interventions and best practices for juvenile offenders by the OJJDP (www.ojjdp.gov) and the Blueprints for Violence Prevention series (Elliott, 1998). All three treatment models have been tested using rigorous experimental designs with a variety of serious and violent juvenile offenders and have long-term follow-up recidivism data available.

Multisystemic Therapy

Multisystemic Therapy (MST; Henggeler, Schoenwald, Borduin, Rowland, & Cunningham, 2009) is a home-based, short-term, intensive, manualized intervention designed for families of youth ages 12 to 17 with serious psychosocial and behavioral problems. Originally designed for youth displaying antisocial behavior, MST has been used to address drug and alcohol misuse, violence, maltreatment in the home, and juvenile delinquency (Borduin, Schaeffer, & Heiblum, 2009; Henggeler, Melton, Brondino, Scherer, & Hanley, 1997; Randall & Cunningham, 2003; Sawyer & Borduin, 2011). MST uses a family preservation service delivery model, aiming to divert affected youth from residential or institutional care (whether in jails, psychiatric hospitals, or foster homes), with the goal of keeping them at home, in school, and out of trouble (Henggeler et al., 2009). Figure 19.1 is a visual depiction of the MST logic model, including key program components, targets, and outcomes.

MST is regarded as an empirically supported intervention for youth and families in the criminal/juvenile justice, mental health, and child welfare systems. Henggeler and Schoenwald (2011) assert that to date, there are 21 published outcome studies of MST using samples drawn from serious juvenile offenders and their families. The literature on MST spans several decades and includes a wealth of randomized controlled trials with a variety of juvenile populations (e.g., Borduin et al., 1995, 2009; Henggeler, Cunningham, Pickrel, Schoenwald, & Brondino, 1996; Randall & Cunningham, 2003; Timmons-Mitchell, Bender, Kishna, & Mitchell, 2006). These studies suggest that MST participants show significant reductions in out-of-home placements and problematic behaviors—ranging from antisocial behaviors (Borduin et al., 1995; Timmons-Mitchell et al., 2006) to substance misuse (Henggeler et al., 1991; Randall & Cunningham, 2003)—as well as improved family communication (Borduin et al., 2009) and peer relationships (Huey, Henggeler, Brondino, & Pickrel, 2000). In studies using samples drawn from youth already involved with the criminal justice system, long-term outcomes support the effectiveness of MST in reducing re-arrests when compared to probation services or other community-based treatments

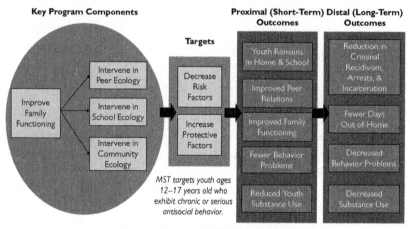

Developed in collaboration with MST Services, January 2011

Figure 19.1   **Multisystemic Therapy logic model. (Reprinted with permission from the Penn State EPISCenter website: http://www.episcenter.psu.edu/ebp/ multisystemic)**

(Borduin et al., 1995; Sawyer & Borduin, 2011; Schaeffer & Borduin, 2005; Timmons-Mitchell et al., 2006).

Additionally, MST has been evaluated for use with juvenile sex offenders, regarded as one of the hardest-to-reach juvenile offender populations. Borduin and colleagues (2009) conducted a randomized controlled trial with 48 juvenile offenders who had been arrested for a serious sexual offense (i.e., rape/ sexual assault or molestation of younger children). At 9 years after treatment, official court records were accessed for all participants. Youth who received the MST intervention recidivated at significantly decreased rates (29.2%) than youth in the alternative treatment group (75%). MST youth were also significantly less likely to have been re-arrested for a sexual offense (8.3% vs. 45.8%). When comparing recidivists in the two groups, survival analyses indicate that MST youth lasted longer in the community than their alternative treatment counterparts without being re-arrested.

Taken together, the findings of these studies provide support for the hypothesis that MST is an effective intervention for juvenile offenders and their families, regardless of the severity or type of crime committed. Perhaps of greater social importance, youth who receive the MST intervention are less likely to be re-arrested for misdemeanor, felony, or civil charges than youth who receive other community treatments as long as 21 years after initial delivery of the intervention (Borduin et al., 1995, 2009; Sawyer & Borduin, 2011; Schaeffer & Borduin, 2005; Timmons-Mitchell et al., 2006).

Functional Family Therapy

Like MST, Functional Family Therapy (FFT; Alexander & Parsons, 1982) is a family-based, short-term, intensive, manualized intervention designed for families of youth ages 11 to 18 with serious psychosocial and behavioral problems. FFT targets youth engaged in or at risk of engaging in delinquent or activities, violence, substance use, or behavioral issues like conduct or oppositional defiant disorder. Unlike MST, however, FFT is delivered in a variety of settings, including the home, school, and community, by a wide range of trained professionals, including social workers, probation officers, and other mental health providers (Haas, Alexander, & Mas, 1988). FFT has been tested and shown to be equally effective in reducing recidivism and increasing positive outcomes for youth from diverse racial, cultural, and ethnic backgrounds (Flicker, Turner, Waldron, Brody, & Ozechowski, 2008). Figure 19.2 is a visual depiction of the FFT logic model, including phases of treatment, targets, and outcomes.

Over a dozen FFT clinical trials have been published on such outcomes as youth antisocial behavior, substance misuse, and a range of criminal behaviors including status, violent, and sex offenses (e.g., Barton, 1985; Gordon, Graves, & Arbuthnot, 1995; Sexton & Turner, 2011). In a review of the literature, Alexander and colleagues (2000) report that youth who received the FFT intervention were significantly less likely to recidivate than youth who received no treatment or probation services. In fact, their analyses show that recidivism was

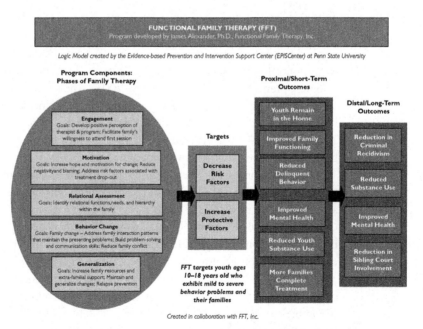

Figure 19.2 **Functional Family Therapy logic model. (Reprinted with permission from the Penn State EPISCenter website: http://www.episcenter.psu.edu/ebp/familytherapy)**

reduced between 26% and 73% among samples of serious youth offenders. Like MST, the positive protective effects of the FFT intervention appear to be stable over time, with 5-year follow-up data demonstrating significant reductions in re-arrests of FFT participants when compared to their counterparts in other treatment conditions (Gordon, Arbuthnot, Gustafson, & McGreen, 1988). Unique to FFT, however, are the observed protective effects of the intervention on the younger siblings of the targeted youth (Alexander et al., 2000; Klein, Alexander, & Parsons, 1977). Klein and colleagues (1977) followed the court involvement of the siblings of the delinquent youth in a clinical trial of FFT 40 months after treatment. They report that 20% of siblings in the FFT condition had court contact during the follow-up period compared to 40% of siblings in the control group and roughly 60% of siblings in alternative treatment conditions. Additionally, Erickson (2008) found FFT to be effective with felony juvenile sex offenders. Results indicate that FFT was equally effective at preventing recidivism for sexual offenses in the 24-month follow-up compared to alternative treatment. Taken together, the majority of FFT evaluations demonstrate decreases in objective problem behavior for youths who receive the FFT intervention (Henggeler & Sheidow, 2012).

Multidimensional Treatment Foster Care

Unlike MST and FFT, which work with youth while they reside with their biological parents, Multidimensional Treatment Foster Care (MTFC; Chamberlain, 2003) provides a therapeutic foster care alternative to incarceration or residential care facilities. MTFC is indicated for youth aged 12 to 17 who have not had success with other in-home or out-of-home treatment modalities or who cannot for emotional or behavioral reasons be maintained in the home (Moore, Sprengelmeyer, & Chamberlain, 2001). The program has been tested and demonstrated to have positive outcomes with youth referred from juvenile justice, child welfare, and mental health settings (Fisher & Chamberlain, 2000). Figure 19.3 is a visual depiction of the MTFC logic model, including goals, key program components, targets, and outcomes.

Seven outcome trials, including five using random assignment to conditions, have tested the effectiveness of MTFC with youth in the United States and Western Europe (e.g., Chamberlain, Leve, & DeGarmo, 2007; Leve & Chamberlain, 2007; Smith, Chamberlain, & Eddy, 2010). Trials comparing youth randomly assigned to receive MTFC versus youth placed in group care settings consistently show significant reductions in re-arrests and re-incarcerations, substance misuse, days in locked settings, and caregiver and self-reported rates of delinquency over a 12- to 18-month follow-up period (Chamberlain et al., 2007; Chamberlain & Reid, 1998; Eddy, Whaley, & Chamberlain, 2004; Leve, Chamberlain, & Reid, 2005).

One of the unique features of the MTFC research base is a detailed exploration of outcomes for juvenile justice girls involved in randomized trials of

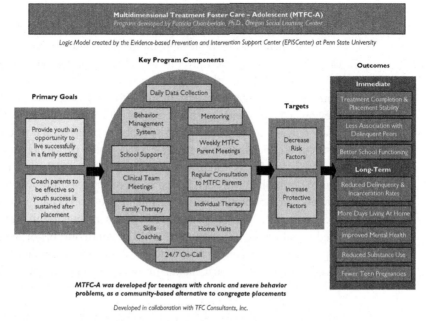

Figure 19.3   Multidimensional Treatment Foster Care logic model. (Reprinted with permission from the Penn State EPISCenter website: http://www. episcenter.psu.edu/ebp/multidimensional)

MTFC. Chamberlain and colleagues (2007) report 24-month follow-up recidivism data for 81 girls randomly assigned to receive either MTFC (n = 37) or group care (n = 44). The significant reductions in re-arrests and days spent in a locked facility reported by MTFC girls at 1 year (Leve et al., 2005) were maintained and exceeded at 24 months when compared to the group care girls. Additional analyses suggest that girls in the MTFC condition were significantly more likely to attend school than their group care counterparts at 12 months after randomization (Leve & Chamberlain, 2007).

The literature suggests that MTFC is an effective intervention for reducing recidivism for juvenile offenders who require out-of-home placement. The positive effects of treatment are maintained as long as 2 years after initial placement for boys and girls. MTFC appears to be an especially potent treatment program for adolescent girls, helping them to avoid further criminal behavior, stay enrolled and active in school, and delay pregnancy (Kerr et al., 2009).

■ Clinical and Legal Issues

Mental health professionals face several challenges when recommending intensive family therapy interventions for juvenile offenders: (1) advocating for the youth to be placed on probation in the least restrictive environment, (2) addressing recidivism if and when it occurs, and (3) confidentiality.

First, mental health professionals often face serious ethical and legal obstacles when trying to divert juvenile offenders from incarceration or residential care. As noted above, the youth who have been found to benefit the most from intensive family interventions like MST, FFT, or MTFC have had multiple previous contacts with the court system. For youth like Henry and Nikole, many judges will see an escalation in problem behavior and recommend more restriction rather than less. In some areas, court personnel are aware of the potential benefits of intensive family treatment models and consider each youth's applicability for such programs. In other areas, however, family therapy is a less common feature of the juvenile justice sentencing process (Henggeler & Schoenwald, 2011). In these circumstances, mental health professionals will need to solicit the full commitment of the youth and his or her family to an appropriate treatment modality before meeting with the judge. Integral to this process is the professional's familiarity with the literature on empirically supported interventions, the populations they serve, and the types of outcomes that have been reported for participants.

Second, mental health professionals face myriad ethical dilemmas when working with juvenile offenders. The intensive family therapies described in this chapter all aim to alter dysfunctional patterns of behavior between the youth and his or her family, school, and community. Family therapy must be seen as a process rather than a magic bullet. In most cases, youth involved in the juvenile justice system experience a complicated constellation of challenges. Therefore, replacing antisocial behaviors with age-appropriate prosocial behaviors takes time and practice. The literature suggests that approximately a third of the youth who receive MST, FFT, or MTFC will recidivate within 12 to 24 months of placement (Chamberlain et al., 2007; Sawyer & Borduin, 2011; Sexton & Turner, 2011). When youth are formally re-arrested or receive informal school referrals for truancy or fighting during the intervention period, the worker must weigh the potential benefits of continued participation in the program versus the potential risks to the larger community.

Confidentiality is the most common ethical dilemma faced by professionals in the field. Issues concerning confidentiality and the duty to report are heightened for workers conducting intensive family therapy with youth and all of the key players in the youth's lives. Probation officers, school administrators, and other interested parties frequently request detailed information about the youth and his or her progress. For youth like Henry and Nikole, violence and alcohol or drug use are common features of their relationships. If, for example, Henry discloses to his mental health professional that he used marijuana, she must evaluate her legal mandate to report this probation violation in the context of damaging the trust and therapeutic alliance she has been working so hard to nurture. There are, of course, no easy answers to such dilemmas. As ethical dilemmas emerge, professionals must decide the best way forward based on treatment gains achieved thus far, the health and safety of all key players, and the potential consequences for the youth if certain information is shared with the judge.

■ Description of Intervention

Henry

At the court date, Henry and his family were sentenced to receive family therapy after Henry's mother, Barbara, told the judge that his behavior had been getting much worse since his father was released from prison the year before. Henry was also sentenced to 12 months of probation. A few weeks later, a social worker named Jane came to the house and met with Henry, Barbara, and his younger siblings. She explained that she worked with a team who provided FFT, an intensive family therapy treatment program that has been shown to improve family communication and youth behavior and to significantly reduce re-arrest rates for as long as 5 years. To achieve the goals of positive behavior change and reduced recidivism, Jane told them that FFT employs a strengths-based, family systems theoretical framework and asserts that the youth's acting-out behaviors serve a key function within the family (Sexton & Alexander, 2002). Therefore, FFT therapists like Jane believe that Henry's problem behavior is merely the visible symptom of an underlying family-based problem. Jane said that she was interested in the relationships in the home, and with the other key players and systems in their lives, like teachers, employers, and friends. Improving communication and reducing conflict at home, Jane explained, was the most effective way to change Henry's behavior.

Jane explained that the FFT intervention typically consists of eight to 30 one-hour sessions delivered over a 3- to 6-month period, which allowed for flexibility in how often they would meet together. Henry and Barbara agreed to meet with Jane twice a week for the next several weeks. As Barbara was overwhelmed with work, home, and childcare duties, they decided to meet at the family home for convenience. They also agreed that Jane could talk to Henry's teacher and father and access Henry's academic records and psychological evaluations. Because FFT has been shown to have lasting and positive effects on the siblings of targeted youth, Jane suggested that Henry's younger siblings be incorporated into therapy sessions when feasible and developmentally appropriate.

The FFT intervention is implemented in five phases: engagement, motivation, relational assessment, behavior change, and generalization. In the early phases of treatment, Jane struggled to engage and motivate Henry and Barbara in the FFT process. Henry and Barbara attended every session, but their patterns of communication were strained and full of negativity and conflict. Henry sat at the kitchen table with his arms crossed, answering questions with as few words as possible. Jane attempted to forge a thera-peutic alliance by reframing, modeling positive communication, and consis-tently highlighting Henry's strengths of determination and resourcefulness and Barbara's family loyalty and hard work. Although Jane had left messages for Henry's biological father inviting him to attend any sessions, he had not yet made an appearance. When Jane asked about Henry's biological father, Barbara waved her hand dismissively and referred to him as "stupid" and a "deadbeat dad."

In their fourth session, Jane recounted the recent conversations she'd had with Henry's teacher and school psychologist. Jane said that both his teacher and psychologist speculated that dyslexia might be influencing Henry's lack of attention and negative behavior in class. Jane watched Henry become increasingly agitated as she spoke and she asked him what he was feeling. Henry shrugged his shoulders. Jane asked Henry to tell them what dyslexia was and he told them that it meant that he couldn't read, which wasn't true. Jane started to explain what dyslexia actually was, when Henry began to shout and bang on the table with his fists. Henry screamed at Barbara that he wasn't stupid like his dad. Barbara stared at him, confused. Henry said he'd never heard anything about his father until the day they met, and now she just calls him stupid because he can't read. Jane reframed Henry's anger as an expression of pain and loss. Henry said he was angry because he wasn't given an opportunity to have a relationship with his father and he never felt like it was okay to even ask questions about him. Now that his father was out of prison, Henry felt like his mother was jealous of their relationship.

Barbara began to cry and admitted that yes, she was jealous. She explained that she was angry with Henry's father, because she'd had to sacrifice spending time with her children to earn a living. Then, after leav-ing her while she was pregnant and contributing nothing to the family for years, Henry's father was able to create a relationship with Henry, even if it was a relationship based on bad behavior. She apologized to Henry for the name-calling and said she only thought Henry's father was stupid because he had the relationship with Henry that she wanted, and he was ruining that relationship by getting Henry involved with drugs. She said she hadn't known that Henry's father wasn't able to read and regardless, her own grand-parents couldn't read, and she considered them to be some of the smartest people she had ever known.

Henry softened as she spoke. After a silence, he said that he understood the material his teacher presented in class until she started writing on the board, and then everything became very difficult to follow. Jane explained dyslexia and how Henry's experience matched up with her understanding of the dis-order. She asked if Henry would be willing to have an assessment and he said yes. Jane asked Henry how he felt about what his mother had said. Henry said that he spent time at his father's house because he felt like his mother didn't want him around—that she loved the younger kids more than she loved him. Barbara hugged and kissed him and said she was so sorry that he felt that way and that she loved him very much, but she felt like she always managed to say or do things that made him angry. Henry told them that things at his father's house were getting out of control, that his father wanted him to sell drugs in the neighborhood and carry a handgun. Henry said he wanted his father to like him, but he was scared.

In the next session, the whole family gathered around the kitchen table and together, they set achievable goals for each individual and the family system as a whole. Henry would enroll in anger management classes and talk to his teacher about assessment for dyslexia. He promised to abstain from drugs and to try to spend time with his father away from his father's apartment and friends. Barbara would attend a parenting class at the local community center and together, she and Henry would work on positive communication. The three younger children volunteered to help more with housework and suggested that they have a "family fun night" at least once a week. Jane reminded the family that she could be reached by phone at any time and they planned to meet again in two weeks.

At the next meeting, the family seemed calmer and happier. Henry reported that he'd started anger management and completed several learning assessments at school. Barbara found a parenting class that worked with her schedule and noted that she and Henry had been really working on positive communication and openness. The younger kids said they loved family fun night because they'd all played charades and eaten pizza. Henry said he had used drugs twice in the past two weeks while at his father's apartment. Jane thanked him for his honesty. Henry said that his father wouldn't meet him anywhere else and that he'd felt pressured to participate. As a group, they discussed how it felt to be the only person putting effort into a relationship. Henry admitted that his father had given him drugs to sell and a handgun. He said that he was scared and although he didn't want to disappoint his father, he didn't want to go to prison either. Jane asked Henry what he wanted to do. Henry looked around the table at his mother and his younger siblings and said that he thought he should call the police.

Both Jane and Barbara applauded Henry for making a tough, adult decision. Jane explained what would happen when Henry talked to the police and together they discussed how to handle potential reactions from his father. Jane said she would go with Henry and Barbara to the police station and that Henry would have to be honest about his drug use. She offered to talk to the judge and explain all of the extenuating circumstances. She felt certain that once the judge knew the full context of the situation, Henry would not face charges for violation of probation.

Over the next several months, Henry and his family continued to make and maintain positive changes. Henry reported his father's activity to the police and turned over the drugs and handgun as evidence. He admitted to using drugs at his father's apartment and selling drugs for his father in the past. The police raided the apartment and found drugs, cash, underage girls, and several dozen automatic weapons, all of which had the serial numbers filed off. Henry's father was arrested, tried, and sentenced to life in prison. After Jane spoke to the judge, the judge agreed not to violate Henry's probation if he would submit to weekly drug testing. Henry agreed and consistently tested negative for drugs from that point forward.

At school, Henry was diagnosed with dyslexia and started working daily with a tutor. His teacher told Jane that Henry's reading comprehension was already improving and that he was calmer and seemed better able to focus in class. The principal noted that Henry had not been cited for any disciplinary infractions and that his attendance had improved dramatically.

Henry told Jane that he had learned a lot from the anger management classes. He had even made a few friends there and said he felt less and less like fighting every day.

Barbara noted that she and Henry had a much calmer and easier relationship. They made a point to spend time together without the younger children, talking about the events of the past and what they planned for the future. Through the parenting class, Barbara found out that she qualified for an educational grant and started taking classes at the local community college toward a paralegal degree. Additionally, applications for Medicaid and Temporary Assistance for Needy Families (TANF) were both approved. This allowed Barbara to quit one of her jobs, to focus on school, and to spend more time at home. The younger children said that they were much happier at home because no one yelled anymore. They loved family fun night and enjoyed telling Jane how their mom even drove a go-kart.

In their final sessions, Jane worked with the family to strategize how to continue all of the positive changes they had made thus far. Jane reflected on how far they had come since their first meeting, highlighting the strengths and successes of each family member. She commended Henry for dramatically improving his grades and school attendance, making friends, and generally enjoying life. And, she noted that Barbara had become so skilled at negotiating bureaucracy and engaging with larger community systems that she would certainly make an excellent paralegal.

Over the next several years, the family maintained the gains made during treatment. Henry visited his father in prison on several occasions but eventually stopped when he came to the conclusion that his father didn't actually care about him as a person. After graduating from high school, Henry enrolled in a counseling program at the community college and has plans to work with juvenile offenders after graduation. Barbara completed her paralegal degree and took a job at a law firm with excellent pay and full benefits for her family. Neither Henry nor his younger siblings had any further contact with the criminal justice system.

Nikole

Julie, the family social worker, explained Nikole's complicated living situation and risk factors to the judge at her most recent court date. She strongly advocated for Nikole to be enrolled in a MTFC program in lieu of being sent to a group home or juvenile detention facility. Julie argued that Nikole's history of running away, her antisocial and aggressive behavior, and her inability to be safely maintained in her family's home made her an ideal candidate for MTFC. She also highlighted Nikole's strong academics, her participation in the music program, and her successful placement with her aunt as further evidence of Nikole's fit for MTFC. Julie told the judge that she had space available for Nikole and could place her in an MTFC home that very day.

Prior to the court date, Julie had explained the basic structure of the MTFC intervention to Nikole and her parents, including risks, benefits, and confidentiality. Julie told them that Nikole would be placed in an MTFC home for 6 to 9 months with specially trained MTFC parents who would be closely monitored by the treatment team (Fisher & Chamberlain, 2000). A case manager, Julie explained, heads the treatment team and would be responsible for making daily phone contact and conducting weekly group meetings with MTFC parents and coordinating the activities of individual and group therapists, skills trainers, a foster parent recruiter/trainer, and other program staff (Chamberlain, 2003). Nikole's MTFC parents would provide daily behavior status reports to monitor Nikole's progress and preserve treatment fidelity. While Nikole was living with her new MTFC parents, Julie noted, her biological parents would receive parenting skills and behavior training education to ensure that the gains Nikole made in treatment would be maintained once she returned home (Fisher & Chamberlain, 2000). As a MTFC family therapist, Julie explained that she would be a member of the treatment team and would maintain close contact with Nikole, her parents, and her MTFC parents.

Julie explained the four key goals of the program: to provide a consistent reinforcing and mentoring environment where academic and positive learning skills can be developed; to provide explicit and supportive daily structure, with well-specified consequences (e.g., use of the point system to earn/lose privileges); to closely supervise Nikole's activities and whereabouts; and to help replace deviant peer associations with prosocial peer relationships (Fisher & Chamberlain, 2000). Julie noted that these goals would be achieved through individual therapy sessions, the maintenance of a positive and predictable home environment, the interruption of coercive family processes, academic support and skill building, and mentoring on the development of positive peer relationships (Chamberlain, 2003; Fisher & Chamberlain, 2000; Smith, 2004).

At the hearing, the judge sentenced Nikole to 12 months of probation and mandated her to receive MTFC. Julie introduced Nikole to her MTFC parents later that day and helped her settle in to her new home. The MTFC case manager, Ellen, met Nikole, Julie, Nikole's parents, and her MTFC parents that evening and together they discussed short-term and long-term goals and the strategies to be used to achieve those goals. The point system was explained to Nikole, who was informed that her movements would be restricted and that she would be closely monitored for the first three weeks of her placement. Nikole was pleased to hear that she would attend the same school and be able to continue to participate in the after-school music program. After the first few weeks, she could use weekly points to earn privileges for the upcoming week. These privileges might include time with friends or other independent activities. The goal of the point system, it was explained, was for her to be rewarded for behaving well. However, verbal abuse or physical fighting, having a surly attitude, or not meeting academic goals would result in her losing points, and therefore losing privileges.

In the first 3 months of her placement, Nikole was thriving. She had adjusted to her new home and routine, even though she now had to share bedroom and bathroom space with her MTFC parents' other children. Her MTFC parents checked on her behavior at school and reported her daily activities to Ellen. Nikole began to attend and even enjoy an anger management class in her community. In supported meetings every weekend, Nikole and her mother were learning how to communicate more effectively and how to express frustration and disappointment without blame or anger. Nikole had even made a few friends and started dating a boy from her school. Nikole's relationship with her father was still tense and combative—he rarely showed up to the weekly meetings and seemed sullen and put-out when he did. Nikole's aunt had moved out of state and wrote encouraging letters every week, telling Nikole how proud she was of her progress. Her MTFC parents highlighted Nikole's strengths and accomplishments, taking every opportunity to celebrate the gains she was making in school and at home.

In her fourth month of placement, Nikole's father lost his job and began drinking excessively. He came to her MTFC parents' home one evening and became verbally abusive and physically violent, breaking Nikole's nose before he could be removed from the premises. The police were called and an incident report was filed, but formal charges were never pursued. Nikole's mother refused to acknowledge her husband's drinking and his problematic behavior in any of the subsequent meetings with Nikole and the treatment team. After that night, Nikole began sneaking out of the house to be with her boyfriend and picking fights with her MTFC parents, their children, and other kids at school. Her MTFC parents put her back on restriction, but she ran away early in her fifth month of placement and was gone for a total of three weeks.

At 2 o'clock in the morning, Nikole called her MTFC parents from a payphone in another city, crying that she was sorry and she was in trouble. She begged them to come get her. Ellen, Julie, Nikole's mother, and her MTFC parents drove several hours to pick her up. When they arrived, Nikole was hiding behind a dumpster in an alley. She told them that she had lied about her age and was working at a local diner. That night, two men attacked her as she walked to a friend's house where she sometimes slept. They had stolen her tip money and broken her wrist before she'd been able to run away and hide.

The women brought Nikole to a local hospital, where her wrist was reset and casted. On the drive home, Nikole admitted that her father had been verbally and physically abusing both her and her mother for years. She said she fought at school when girls saw her bruises and made fun of her in the locker room. She said she was scared for her mother's life. Together, the group made a plan to move forward. Nikole would return to her MTFC parents' house and begin again. Nikole's mother would meet with a lawyer and a victim advocate from a local women's domestic violence shelter. Julie would inform child services about the abuse. Nikole's strength, independence, courage, and resilience were praised throughout the conversation, even though the group agreed that her choice to run away was not a good one. Nikole was surprised to find that talking about the abuse made her feel better and less angry and she pledged to work on more open communication about her feelings.

Nikole spent another 6 months at her MTFC parents' house, growing stronger academically and emotionally. Her mother went to a domestic violence shelter, began intensive therapy, and eventually filed for divorce. At the end of summer school, Nikole and her mother decided to move out of state together, renting an apartment close to her aunt.

Summary and Conclusion

Juvenile offenders present a unique challenge to the profession. Youth in the criminal justice system often display a variety of problem behaviors (e.g., antisocial behavior, substance misuse, violence and aggression) and have not achieved success in more traditional approaches to youth behavior change (e.g., probation, residential care, incarceration). Family-based interventions for juvenile offenders have shown the greatest potential for reducing recidivism and increasing prosocial behavior, especially when compared to no treatment, probation, and incarceration (Henggeler & Schoenwald, 2011). The primary strength of the three treatment modalities reviewed in this chapter is the consideration of the youth in his or her full social context. MST, FFT, and MTFC all enlist the participation of the affected youth, at least one committed parent, additional family members, neighbors, peers, school personnel, and community members in the change process and help each key player to identify how his or her interactions with community systems may maintain or exacerbate problems. By virtue of working within the family system, MST, FFT, and MTFC team members are able to provide therapeutic support in tandem with needed concrete resources (e.g., housing, employment) and overcome key barriers to accessing care for this difficult-to-reach population.

The goal of the juvenile justice system—to deter youth from committing future crimes—is supported by the empirically supported interventions described above.

Employing a public health perspective, MST, FFT, and MTFC aim to positively alter the relationships that juvenile offenders and their families have with each other, with community systems, and with the general public. The public health benefits demonstrated in randomized trials of MST, FFT, and MTFC are decreased recidivism, decreased out-of-home placement, and cost savings (Henggeler & Schoenwald, 2011). Unfortunately, however, research suggests that only a small minority of juvenile offenders (approximately 5%) receive empirically supported interventions like MST, FFT, or MTFC (Greenwood, 2008). Those working in the juvenile justice system must remain up to date on empirically supported interventions tested and proven to improve outcomes for juvenile offenders and their families. Using both common sense and best practices, juvenile justice workers are well positioned to enhance the health and well-being of the youth, families, and communities they serve.

References

Alexander, J. F., & Parsons, B. V. (1982). *Functional family therapy: Principles and procedures.* Carmel, CA: Brooks/Cole.

Alexander, J. F., Pugh, C., Parsons, B. V., Sexton, T., Barton, C., Bonomo, J.,...& Waldron, H. (2000). Functional family therapy. In D. S. Elliott (series ed.), *Blueprints for violence prevention,* Book 3. Center for the Study and Prevention of Violence, Institute of Behavioral Science, University of Colorado, Boulder, CO.

Barton, C. (1985). Generalizing treatment effects of functional family therapy: Three replications. *American Journal of Family Therapy, 13*(3), 16–26.

Bender, K., Tripodi, S. J., Sarteschi, C., & Vaughn, M. G. (2011). A meta-analysis of interventions to reduce adolescent cannabis use. *Research on Social Work Practice, 21,* 153–164.

Borduin, C. M., Mann, B. J., Cone, L. T., Henggeler, S. W., Fucci, B. R., Blaske, D. M., & Williams, R. A. (1995). Multisystemic treatment of serious juvenile offenders: Long-term prevention of criminality and violence. *Journal of Consulting and Clinical Psychology, 63,* 569–578. doi:10.1037/0022-006X.63.4.569

Borduin, C. M., Schaeffer, C. M., & Heiblum, N. (2009). A randomized clinical trial of multisystemic therapy with juvenile sexual offenders: Effects on youth social ecology and criminal activity. *Journal of Consulting and Clinical Psychology, 77*(1), 26–37. doi:http://dx.doi.org/10.1037/a0013035

Chamberlain, P. (2003). *Treating chronic juvenile offenders: Advances made through the Oregon multidimensional treatment foster care model.* Washington, DC: American Psychological Association.

Chamberlain, P., Leve, L. D., & DeGarmo, D. S. (2007). Multidimensional treatment foster care for girls in the juvenile justice system: 2-year follow-up of a randomized clinical trial. *Journal of Consulting and Clinical Psychology, 75*(1), 187–193.

Chamberlain, P., & Reid, J. (1998). Comparison of two community alternatives to incarceration for chronic juvenile offenders. *Journal of Consulting and Clinical Psychology, 6,* 624–633.

Eddy, J. M., Whaley, R. B., & Chamberlain, P. (2004). The prevention of violent behavior by chronic and serious male juvenile offenders: A 2-year follow-up of a randomized clinical trial. *Journal of Emotional and Behavioral Disorders, 12,* 2–8.

Elliott, D. S. (1998). *Blueprints for violence prevention* (Series Ed.). *University of Colorado, Center for the Study and Prevention of Violence.* Boulder, CO: Blueprints Publications.

Erickson, C. J. (2008). *The effectiveness of functional family therapy in the treatment of juvenile sexual offenders.* (Doctoral dissertation). Retrieved from ProQuest Dissertations and Theses. (2009-99080-195)

Fagan, A. A., Van Horn, M. L., Antaramian, A., & Dawkins, J. D. (2011). How do families matter? Age and gender differences in family influences on delinquency and drug use. *Youth Violence and Juvenile Justice, 9,* 150–170.

Fisher, P. A., & Chamberlain, P. (2000). Multidimensional treatment foster care: A program for intensive parenting, family support, and skill building. *Journal of Emotional and Behavioral Disorders, 8*(3), 155–164.

Flicker, S. M., Turner, C. W., Waldron, H. B., Brody, J. L., & Ozechowski, T. J. (2008). Ethnic background, therapeutic alliance, and treatment retention in functional family therapy with adolescents who abuse substances. *Journal of Family Psychology, 22*(1), 167–170.

Gordon, D. A., Arbuthnot, J., Gustafson, K. E., & McGreen, P. (1988). Home-based behavioral-systems family therapy with disadvantaged juvenile delinquents. *American Journal of Family Therapy, 16*(3), 243–255. doi:http://dx.doi.org/10.1080/01926188808250729

Gordon, D. A., Graves, K., & Arbuthnot, J. (1995). The effect of functional family therapy for delinquents on adult criminal behavior. *Criminal Justice and Behavior, 22*(1), 60–73.

Gottfredson, M. R., & Hirschi, T. (1990). *A general theory of crime.* Stanford, CA: Stanford University Press.

Greenwood, P. (2008). Prevention and intervention programs for juvenile offenders: The benefits of evidence-based practice. *The Future of Children, 18,* 11–36. doi:10.1353/foc.0.0018

Haas, L. J., Alexander, J. F., & Mas, C. H. (1988). *Functional family therapy: Basic concepts and training program.* Guilford Press, New York, NY.

Henggeler, S. W., Borduin, C. M., Melton, G. B., & Mann, B. J., Smith, L. A.,...Fucci, B. R. (1991). Effects of multisystemic therapy on drug use and abuse in serious juvenile offenders: A progress report from two outcome studies. *Family Dynamics of Addiction Quarterly, 1*(3), 40–51.

Henggeler, S. W., Melton, G. B., Brondino, M. J., Scherer, D. G., & Hanley, J. H. (1997). Multisystemic therapy with violent and chronic juvenile offenders and their families: The role of treatment fidelity in successful dissemination. *Journal of Consulting and Clinical Psychology, 65*(5), 821–833.

Henggeler, S. W., Cunningham, P. B., Pickrel, S. G., Schoenwald, S. K., & Brondino, M. J. (1996). Multisystemic therapy: An effective violence prevention approach for serious juvenile offenders. *Journal of Adolescence, 19,* 47–61.

Henggeler, S. W., & Schoenwald, S. K. (2011). *Evidence-based interventions for juvenile offenders and juvenile justice policies that support them.* (Social policy report, Vol. 25, No. 1). Ann Arbor, MI: Society for Research in Child Development.

Henggeler, S. W., Schoenwald, S. K., Borduin, C. M., Rowland, M. D., & Cunningham, P. B. (2009). *Multisystemic therapy for antisocial behavior in children and adolescents* (2nd ed.). New York: Guilford Press.

Henggeler, S. W., & Sheidow, A. J. (2012). Empirically supported family-based treatments for conduct disorder and delinquency in adolescents. *Journal of Marital and Family Therapy, 38*(1), 30–58. doi:http://dx.doi.org/10.1111/j.1752-0606.2011.00244.x

Howell, J. C. (2008). *Preventing and reducing juvenile delinquency: A comprehensive framework.* Portland, OR: Sage.

Huey, S. J., Henggeler, S. W., Brondino, M. J., & Pickrel, S. G. (2000). Mechanisms of change in multisystemic therapy: Reducing delinquent behavior through therapist adherence and improved family and peer functioning. *Journal of Consulting and Clinical Psychology, 68*(3), 451–467.

Kerr, D. C. R., Leve, L. D., & Chamberlain, P. (2009). Pregnancy rates among juvenile justice girls in two randomized controlled trials of multidimensional treatment foster care. *Journal of Consulting and Clinical Psychology, 77*(3), 588–593. doi:http://dx.doi.org/10.1037/a0015289

Klein, N. C., Alexander, J. F., & Parsons, B. V. (1977). Impact of family systems intervention on recidivism and sibling delinquency: A model of primary prevention and program evaluation. *Journal of Consulting and Clinical Psychology, 45*(3), 469–474.

Kumpfer, K. L., & Alvarado, R. (2003). Family-strengthening approaches for the prevention of youth problem behaviors. *American Psychologist, 58,* 457–465.

Leve, L. D., & Chamberlain, P. (2007). A randomized evaluation of multidimensional treatment foster care: Effects on school attendance and homework completion in juvenile justice girls. *Research on Social Work Practice, 17*(6), 657–663.

Leve, L. D., Chamberlain, P., & Reid, J. B. (2005). Intervention outcomes for girls referred from juvenile justice: Effects on delinquency. *Journal of Consulting and Clinical Psychology, 73,* 1181–1185.

Loeber, R., Burke, J. D., & Pardini, D. A. (2009). Development and etiology of disruptive and delinquent behavior. *Annual Review of Clinical Psychology, 5,* 291–310.

Moore, K. J., Sprengelmeyer, P. G., & Chamberlain, P. (2001). Community-based treatment for adjudicated delinquents: The Oregon Social Learning Center's 'Monitor' multidimensional treatment foster care program. *Residential Treatment for Children and Youth, 18*(3), 87–97.

Office of Juvenile Justice and Delinquency Prevention (2012). *Statistical briefing book: Law enforcement and juvenile crime.* Retrieved from http://www.ojjdp.gov/ojstatbb/crime/JAR_Display.asp?ID=qa05200

Randall, J., & Cunningham, P. B. (2003). Multisystemic therapy: A treatment for violent substance-abusing and substance-dependent juvenile offenders. *Addictive Behaviors, 28*(9), 1731–1739.

Sawyer, A. M., & Borduin, C. M. (2011). Effects of multisystemic therapy through midlife: A 21.9-year follow-up to a randomized clinical trial with serious and violent juvenile offenders. *Journal of Consulting and Clinical Psychology, 79*(5), 643–652.

Schaeffer, C. M., & Borduin, C. M. (2005). Long-term follow-up to a randomized clinical trial of multisystemic therapy with serious and violent juvenile offenders. *Journal of Consulting and Clinical Psychology, 73*(3), 445–453. doi:http://dx.doi.org/10.1037/0022-006X.73.3.445

Sexton, T., & Turner, C. W. (2011). The effectiveness of functional family therapy for youth with behavioral problems in a community practice setting. *Couple and Family Psychology: Research and Practice, 1,* 3–15. doi:http://dx.doi.org/10.1037/2160-4096.1.S.3

Sexton, T. L., & Alexander, J. F. (2002). Functional Family Therapy: An empirically supported, family-based intervention model for at-risk adolescents and their families. In F. Kaslow (Ed.), *Comprehensive handbook of psychotherapy: Volume 2, Cognitive-behavioral approaches* (pp. 177–140). New York: Wiley.

Sickmund, M. (2009). *Delinquency cases in juvenile court, 2005* (NCJ Publication No. 224538). Washington DC: U.S. Department of Justice, Office of Justice Programs, Office of Juvenile Justice and Delinquency Prevention.

Smith, D. K., Chamberlain, P., & Eddy, M. J. (2010). Preliminary support for multidimensional treatment foster care in reducing substance use in delinquent boys. *Journal of Child & Adolescent Substance Abuse, 19*(4), 343–358.

Smith, K. D. (2004). Risk, reinforcement, retention in treatment, and reoffending for boys and girls in multidimensional treatment foster care. *Journal of Emotional and Behavioral Disorders, 12*(1), 38–48.

Stahl, A. L. (2001). *Delinquency cases in juvenile courts, 1998* (Publication NO. FS-200131). Washington DC: U.S. Department of Justice, Office of Justice Programs, Office of Juvenile Justice and Delinquency Prevention.

Timmons-Mitchell, J., Bender, M. B., Kishna, M. A., & Mitchell, C. C. (2006). An independent effectiveness trial of multisystemic therapy with juvenile justice youth. *Journal of Clinical Child and Adolescent Psychology, 35*(2), 227–236.

Tripodi, S. J., & Bender, K. (2011). Substance abuse treatment for juvenile offenders: A review of experimental and quasi-experimental research. *Journal of Criminal Justice, 39*, 246–252.

Tripodi, S. J., Bender, K., Litschge, C., & Vaughn, M. G. (2010). Interventions for reducing adolescent alcohol abuse: A meta-analytic review. *Archives of Pediatrics & Adolescent Medicine, 164*, 85–91.

Zahn, M. A., Agnew, R., Fishbein, D., Miller, S., Winn, D. M., Dakoff, G.,...& Chesney-Lind, M. (2010). *Causes and correlates of girls' delinquency* (NCJ 226358). Washington DC: U.S. Department of Justice, Office of Justice Programs, Office of Juvenile Justice and Delinquency Prevention.

V

Special Issues and Populations

20 Homelessness and Juvenile Justice

Sarah Young, Jeremiah Jaggers, and David E. Pollio

■ Introduction

The number of runaway and homeless youth in the United States is estimated to be between 1.7 and 2.8 million per year, although exact numbers are difficult to determine because of variability of definitions for homelessness (Edidin, Ganim, Hunter & Karnik, 2012; Reeg, Grisham, & Shepard, 2002). In terms of the literature, research on this population generally is described using the term "runaway" for individuals under the age of 18 and "young adult homeless" between ages 18 and 25. The difficulty in sampling homeless youth, especially the most vulnerable within this population that are not connected to services, likely means that numbers are even higher than best estimates. The causes and consequences of homelessness on youth are complex, and various circumstances provide a pipeline into the juvenile justice system. Running away from home, curfew violations, and being truant from school are status offenses that criminalize behavior as a function of age. Additionally, "street" youth (and their behaviors) may be more highly visible and may catch the attention of law enforcement (Chapple, Johnson, & Whitbeck, 2004). Finally, these youth are more likely to experience victimization, to engage in survival activities (both legal and illegal), and to abuse substances compared to their non-homeless peers (Bryan, Schmiege, & Magnan, 2012). These behaviors, many of them used for survival, bring youth to the attention of law enforcement and the judicial system. In turn, youthful offenders are likely to experience homelessness (Toro, Dworsky, & Fowler, 2007). Homeless youth are at higher risk for juvenile justice system involvement for quality-of-life issues such as panhandling and loitering (Bernstein & Foster, 2008). The Substance Abuse and Mental Health Services Administration reports that, in 1996, 18% of homeless people reported having been in juvenile detention (2011). Given the likelihood that homeless youth will experience contact with the juvenile justice system, they must also contend with aging out of the system. The intersections between homelessness, engaging in illegal or risky behaviors, and interactions with police mean that helping professionals are still learning how best to support these youth.

Homelessness, in addition to being a juvenile justice issue, is also a public health issue. Many of the public health consequences of homelessness have their own feedback loop back into the juvenile justice system. For example, homeless youth experience higher rates of substance use and are at risk for sexual exploitation, prostitution, and victimization, all issues that may have legal implications (Chen, Thrane, Whitbeck, Hoyt, & Johnson, 2007; Thompson, Zittel-Palamara, & Forehand, 2005). Homeless youth have a higher prevalence of specific mental health issues (such as psychosis) and have lower school attainment rates compared to their non-homeless peers, both issues that increase interaction with the criminal justice system over the course of an individual's life (Edidin et al., 2012).

This chapter will provide reasons why youth homelessness is a juvenile justice issue. Specific criminal behaviors and offenses that affect the homeless youth population will be discussed. Theories that are commonly used to explain behaviors, motivations, and causes and consequences of youth homelessness will be explored. Finally, subpopulations and special issues will broaden how we think about youth homelessness, with special attention given to current and future service implications.

Variations in what constitutes "homeless" are rampant in the literature and vary from those using a single night of runaway services to more standard definitions including a set number of days without stable residence. Conceptually, the runaway population has been broken down based on reasons for leaving— whether they ran away or were thrown out. For the sake of clarity in this chapter, we will use the term "homeless youth" as a default and use more specific labels appropriate to the constructs and literature being discussed.

■ Origins of Youth Homelessness

Homeless youth are more likely to come from dysfunctional families with episodes of physical, sexual, and/or substance abuse (Edidin et al., 2012). Conceptually, research has suggested that youth initially run away from home for two reasons. "Runaway homeless" youth do not have permission of parents or guardians in leaving home, while "throwaway" youth are expelled from home by their parents or guardians and do not have permission to return (Zide & Cherry, 1992). "Throwaway" youth have been found to have longer shelter stays (due, in large part, to being expelled by parents or guardians), have higher suicidal ideation, and have higher levels of hopelessness (Teare, Furst, Peterson, & Authier, 1992) than runaway homeless youth. Thompson, Safyer, and Pollio (2001) examined national runaway homeless shelter data and found that throwaway youth were more likely than their runaway youth peers to have contact with the juvenile justice system, to be expelled from school, and to have been incarcerated.

Substance Abuse Challenges

Homeless youth are at risk along multiple dimensions. Research demonstrates a higher prevalence of cigarette, alcohol, and marijuana use among homeless youth when compared to their non-homeless peers (Thompson et al., 2005; Whitbeck, Hoyt, & Bao, 2000). Among youth who smoke, homeless youth smoke more cigarettes on average than their non-homeless peers (Ensign & Santelli, 1998; Thompson et al., 2005). Marijuana use among homeless youth is estimated to be three times higher than non-homeless peers (Forst & Crim, 1994; Thompson et al., 2005). Not surprisingly, substance use (particularly illegal substance use) is often attributed as a coping response to the stressors that homeless youth face (Thompson et al., 2005); however, at the same time it increases the odds of interaction with the juvenile and criminal justice system for these youth.

Mental Health Challenges

The prevalence of certain mental health challenges has been found to be higher within the homeless youth population when compared to non-homeless peers, with two thirds of the sample in one particular study estimated to meet the criteria of at least one DSM disorder (Ginzler et al., 2000). Conduct disorder, depression, and dysthymia rates were estimated at between 50% and 73% within this population (Ayerst, 1999; Booth & Zhang, 1997). Higher rates of psychosis, posttraumatic stress disorder, and anxiety are also reported when compared to non-homeless youth (Edidin et al., 2012). One in three homeless youth report suicide attempts, and this was heavily associated with sexual and physical abuse experienced prior to running away or becoming homeless (Greene & Ringwalt, 1996). Homeless female youth are more likely to attempt suicide if they have been sexually abused compared to their male peers (Tyler, Hoyt, & Whitbeck, 2000). It is clear that while homeless youth are vulnerable along multiple dimensions, homeless youth with a history of abuse are particularly vulnerable. The intersection of childhood physical and sexual abuse and later homelessness or runaway behavior has both prevention and treatment implications.

Challenges with Sampling and Determining Prevalence Data

Developing prevalence rates for a population can be challenging, but capturing this data for homeless youth has a host of unique complications. First and foremost, the transient nature of many homeless youth makes multiple measures across time difficult. While a variety of population-based data is available (see Whitbeck & Hoyt, 1999; data accessed from the Runaway Homeless Youth Management Information System [RHY-MIS]; Rice, Tulbert, Cederbaum, Adhikari, & Milburn, 2012), one of the challenges is that youth sampled in these studies were recruited through services such as shelters. These data may oversample from those most connected to and most stabilized by services and may be missing some of the most isolated and vulnerable of the population. Similarly, while the statewide and national Youth Risk Behavior Survey does ask about transience and homelessness, it is administered through school systems, with which many homeless youth are no longer connected (Corliss, Goodenow, Nichols, & Austin, 2011). The concern is that while science is being produced at a high quality, we must be careful not to overgeneralize too much since science is limited by the challenges presented in sampling this population.

■ Criminal Behaviors and Involvement in the Criminal Justice System

While homelessness for youth provides a pathway into the juvenile justice system, it is important to assess exactly what crimes these youth commit, what factors influence those crimes being committed, and how often homeless youth are committing certain crimes. While the challenges of sampling this population have already been discussed, it is worth noting that juvenile justice data (once a crime has been committed or alleged) don't always include data on homelessness. Despite the challenges in sampling and data collection, this section will discuss rates of arrests, the types of crimes that homeless youth often commit, and the link between victimization and the juvenile justice system.

Prevalence and Rates of Arrests

Prevalence data on arrest rates for homeless youth are difficult to obtain and there is scarce research in this area. Many of the data are self-reported, and early data (Hagan & McCarthy, 1992) point to homeless and runaway youth committing more crimes per person than their non-homeless peers. Common offenses committed by this population are theft, assault, prostitution, drug use and sale, and robbery (Whitbeck et al., 1999). Arrest rates appear to be both gendered and closely connected to the types of crimes committed. For example, homeless boys and men appear to be arrested more often, but this may be a direct result in their increased participation in more serious and more violent crimes such as assault and robbery (Horowitz & Pottieger, 1991; Uggen & Kruttschnitt, 1998). Attempts to survive homelessness, find food, and earn income may lead homeless youth to participate in panhandling and "dumpster diving," both behaviors that are legal but make youth visible to law enforcement (Chapple et al., 2004). While these behaviors do not constitute crimes, they do increase the interaction between youth and law enforcement, possibly paving the way into the juvenile justice system (Chapple et al., 2004).

Status Offenses

Status offenses, or statutes that apply to one category of people (usually minors), by their very nature affect homeless youth and often bring these youth into contact with the juvenile justice system. Being charged with a status offense can lead to the youth also being adjudicated as a Child in Need of Supervision (CHINS), a Person in Need of Supervision (PINS), or other acronyms depending on the state, linking the youth to probation departments, case management services, and additional supports (Schmalleger &

Bartollas, 2008). When the requirements of a CHINS or a PINS are not met, the youth may be placed in foster care or juvenile detention or may need to be adjudicated.

Due to the chaotic nature of homelessness, many of these youth are unable or unwilling to maintain regular attendance at school (Edidin et al., 2012). With truancy from school being a status offense, it serves both as a gateway into the juvenile justice system and also a potential spot to intervene with youth and families in an attempt to prevent further interaction with the system (Bartollas, 2006). Likewise, many states and municipalities categorize the act of running away as a status offense. CHINS or PINS classification allows for needed service delivery with less stigma than a criminal justice intervention alone (Bartollas, 2006).

When communities are devoid of services for homeless youth, status offenses serve to criminalize homelessness for youth when such youth may not have the power to correct the situation. Smoking, alcohol consumption, and curfew laws are other common status offenses that affect homeless youth. Because such youth are often visible and their behaviors are public, this brings them to the attention of law enforcement (Edidin et al., 2012). Thus, law enforcement and the juvenile justice system may lack the necessary training and services to deal effectively with the precipitating causes of the status offense and the overarching homelessness, creating a cycle of arrests, adjudication, and releases that don't serve the individual needs of the homeless youth.

Victimization

While youth who are homeless are likely to have experienced victimization prior to becoming homeless, they are also likely to experience victimization as a result of their homelessness. Homelessness can produce a combustible mix of interactions with dangerous, aggressive, and predatory associates as well as invisibility of the needs of this population as a result of their transience and social isolation. A lack of job skills or difficulties in appropriate socialization may lead to youth dealing drugs or committing other types of crime as a means of survival (Whitbeck et al., 1999). Limited choices for safe and legal employment force these youth into dangerous situations with dangerous people, increasing their experiences of being victims of violence (Whitbeck et al., 1999). Youth may pursue sex work, which can be voluntary (if the youth is at an age where he or she can legally consent to sexual activity) or forced (Annitto, 2011). Many engage in sex work as a survival behavior, to earn money or in exchange for food, drugs, or shelter. Homeless youths' transience and disconnection make them easy prey for sex traffickers. Sex work, especially when combined with drug abuse, increases health risks for such infections as HIV, syphilis, herpes, trichomoniasis, and other various sexually transmitted infections (STIs; Gangamma, Slesnick, Toviessi, & Serovich, 2008). Advocates for this population suggest that although homeless youth may appear hardened and criminal in behavior and attitude, the issue of child prostitution should be considered a child welfare issue and not a juvenile justice issue (Mitchell, Finkelhor, & Wolak, 2010).

■ Special Issues

Social and Peer Networks

Research on homelessness in general has long assumed that homeless individuals are socially isolated and that relationships outside the homeless population generally disappear over time (Solarz & Bogat, 1990). More recently, research on the adult homeless population has questioned this assumption, moving from a simple understanding of the population as isolated to one with a more complex conceptualization that suggests that individual social networks do not completely attenuate among their housed social networks, and those that do disappear are replaced by other relationships among their homeless compatriots (Eyrich, Pollio, & North, 2003). Social support among the general adult homeless population further demonstrates that different subgroups have distinct patterns of social supports and that social network members tend to share patterns of risky behaviors (Eyrich et al., 2003; Polgar, North, & Pollio, 2009). Recent research on young-adult homeless populations has similarly affirmed the importance of social networks and identified the critical nature of these relationships on risk behaviors associated with juvenile justice involvement.

Discussing social networks and their impact on individual risk behaviors requires distinguishing between the peer network and its place within the larger social network. Peer networks are those individuals who are viewed as directly connected to other individuals through either affinity or shared space. Methodologically, peers are generally identified directly by other members of their peer networks (Rice, Barman-Adhikari, Milburn, & Monro, 2012). Peer networks can be very integrated (all members are connected directly) or dispersed (multiple individual links with ties to specific individuals). Social networks include all the individuals within an environment, generally a spatial location such as a neighborhood. Social networks include multiple peer networks, as well as unconnected individuals.

Understanding the influence of peer and social networks includes a number of key dimensions, including length of time homeless, location of network (inside or outside of the homeless population), and shared risk factors among homeless peer networks. In terms of length of time homeless, research has indicated that young adults who have recently entered into homelessness maintain their contact with friends at home and supportive family members, while who have been homeless for a longer time tend to rely more on their peers (Rice, Barman-Adhikari, Milburn, & Monro, 2012). Because length of time homeless and number of runaway episodes are associated with identification with runaway culture and negative behaviors, including increased juvenile system involvement (Thompson & Pollio, 2006), it appears reasonable to suggest that over time young-adult homeless move to more "street-involved" peer networks with shared norms and behaviors.

Research examining the composition of peer networks appears to support this explanation. Connections with supportive family members and peers from the original home are associated with positive help-seeking behaviors (Rice, Milburn, & Rotheram-Borus, 2007; Rice, Stein, & Milburn, 2008). Conversely, greater peer support from other young-adult homeless is associated with a greater likelihood of survival behaviors (e.g., panhandling, prostitution) (Ferguson, Bender, Thompson, Xie, & Pollio, 2011). Individuals within these high-risk peer networks also tend to show higher levels of a variety of risk behaviors, including drug use and HIV risk behaviors (Kipke, Montgomery, Simon, & Iverson, 1997a; Rice, Milburn, Rotheram-Borus, et al., 2005; Tyler et al., 2000). In examining the composition of peer networks, Johnson, Whitbeck, and Hoyt (2005) show that peer networks also vary considerably based on demographic characteristics, such as gender, race, and age.

Rice and colleagues (2012) have examined the interrelationships between social networks, peer networks, and risk behaviors in a drop-in center sample in Los Angeles. They found that the social network consisted of a core of interconnected peer networks, surrounded by a number of freestanding peer networks, and a number of individuals without peer networks. The core of the social network generally consisted of individuals with longer periods of homelessness and higher levels of risk behaviors. Although the cross-sectional nature of the data does not allow them to examine it directly, they speculate about a process through which those on the periphery (who are shorter-term homeless), if they remain homeless, gradually become embedded in the core with an attendant increase in risk behaviors. This process appears to fit well with previous findings reported about the association between time homeless and risk behaviors.

Transience

An area that has relevance understanding behaviors leading to juvenile justice involvement specifically, and for homelessness in runaway youth and homeless young adults more generally, is transience. In discussing transience in this population, the literature includes two interrelated concepts—differences between homeless populations across locations and actual movement itself. For the latter concept, transience has been discussed as a number of different moves, distance traveled, and comparisons between low- and high-transience groups.

Although national policy response has assumed a certain homogeneity to the runaway homeless population and created service models that are consistent across populations (Karabanow & Clement, 2004), data from these national programs (provided through variation iterations of the RHY-MIS) have demonstrated considerable differences in populations across the various federal regions (Pollio, Thompson, & North, 2000; Thompson, Maguin, & Pollio, 2003; Thompson, 2004) on both demographic and risk factors. Regional differences include substance use, length of runaway experiences, and rates of reported abuse (Thompson et al., 2003).

Homeless populations have also been found to differ distinctly across cities (Bender, Thompson, et al., 2007; Ferguson, Jun, Bender, Thompson, & Pollio, 2010) and even between neighborhoods within cities (Witkin, Milburn, Rotheram-Borus, Batterham, May, & Brooks, 2005). In a multi-city study of transience, different cities were found to have distinct populations of young-adult homeless (Ferguson, Bender, Thompson, Maccio, Xie, & Pollio, 2011), including very distinct demographic and risk behavior differences. For example, youth in Austin, TX, were found to have experienced homelessness for longer periods of time, had a greater likelihood of substance use, and were more transient, while youth in St. Louis, MO, had shorter periods of homelessness, were less likely to use substances, and were likely to still be in their birth city. Demographically, youth in Austin were more likely to be Caucasian and older, youth in St. Louis were more likely to be African American and younger, while youth in Los Angeles, CA, were more likely to be Hispanic (Bender, Thompson, Pollio, & Sterzing, 2010; Ferguson et al., 2010). Differences have also been found in similarly sampled groups in New York and Los Angeles (Pollio, Batey, Ferguson, Bender, & Thompson, 2013).

In thinking about the differences between the cities, the populations appear to be quite different in their social construction of being homeless, and that transience is a factor in creating these different groups (Bender et al., 2007, 2010; Ferguson et al., 2010). Austin might perhaps be characterized as a city where the young-adult homeless are more likely to be characterized by the term "street youth." In its use here, the social relationships potentially are built around the shared experience of drug use, with many of the individuals present being experienced in homelessness. St. Louis, by contrast, might best be characterized by a greater focus on "neighborhood" homelessness. Young-adult homeless in St Louis appear to be more likely to remain affiliated with the social networks with which they are familiar and to be more stable in their relationships with others in their geospatial environment. While it is not possible to do more than speculate on the causality of these social constructions, it is extremely interesting to note that the populations reflect the public perceptions of the cities—Austin with its business slogan of "Keep Austin weird" and St. Louis with its reputation for family focus and neighborhood affiliations. It appears possible that the young-adult homeless populations in other locations also attract (or keep) populations reflective of the city's public perception.

Similar to the research on specific locations, transience appears to be associated with differences in young-adult homeless risk behaviors related to juvenile justice and other system involvement. Greater transience has been associated with increased use of street survival behaviors (e.g., panhandling and prostitution: Ferguson et al., 2011), likelihood of arrest (Ferguson et al., in press), HIV risk behaviors (German, Davey, & Latkin, 2007), trauma and PTSD (Bender et al., 2010), and unprotected sex (Weir, Bard, O'Brien, Casciato, & Stark, 2007). The findings on transience also appear to support the concept that a city such as Austin attracts populations who are both more likely to have relocated and travel greater distances to associate with others perceived as similar. This finding echoes social comparison theory and group dynamics (Cartwright & Zander, 1968), which argues that individuals compare themselves to and are members of groups with others who are perceived as similar to themselves. Young-adult homeless appear to be willing and able to migrate to be with populations they believe to be similar to themselves and perhaps more accepting of their choices.

In summing up the literature on social networks and transience, it is clear that these two constructs are functionally overlapping. Individuals with greater length of time homeless and greater transience and more embedded within social networks are more likely to be substance using/abusing and are more likely to be involved in the juvenile justice system. Further, individuals who are longer-term homeless are more likely to be transient and seek others who are socially comparable to form peer networks.

Technology

One of the most interesting new areas of research for this population is in the area of technology. Research on the general population has suggested that use of technology is positively associated with socioeconomic status—the "digital divide"—and that technology use is limited among lower socioeconomic populations (Drori & Jang, 2003). The construct has been generally assumed to be applicable to young-adult homeless and runaway populations, given their limited economic means and increased likelihood of educational dropout (Thompson, Jun, Bender, Ferguson, & Pollio, 2010; Thompson & Pollio, 2006). Recent evidence, however, has questioned this assumption.

In terms of accessing technology, research has found rates of consistent access of the Internet ranging from more than 75% in one study of young-adult homeless in Los Angeles and New York City (Guadagno, Muscanell, & Pollio, 2013) to over 90% in a study of a similar population in Denver and Los Angeles (Pollio, Batey, Ferguson, Bender, & Thompson, 2013). Further, approximately half of young-adult homeless report technology use daily (Pollio et al., in press). Ongoing research has suggested that this use represents a significant activity in the life of this population. In an unpublished focus group study of young adults in Los Angeles and New York City, individuals across multiple groups affirmed the central nature of technology such as texting and online social networks in their daily activities. In more than one group, individuals reported that they prioritized funding their cell phone plans above purchasing food (Pollio, Jaggers, Hudson, & McClendon, unpublished manuscript). Further, across multiple focus groups individuals demonstrated a sophisticated and complex understanding of the technology itself, including detailing means to circumvent agency barriers to accessing social network sites.

Given the previously noted findings about the social networks and transience of this population, it might be expected that communication and technology use might be limited to other members of this population, and that certain subgroups might be less likely to use technology than others (e.g., persons with mental illness). Neither of these assumptions has proven to be true. In fact, when asked about with whom they communicated, young adults consistently listed family members and non-homeless friends (Pollio et al., in press), along with their homeless friends and acquaintances. Further, analyses examining subgroup differences found basically no changes in rates of technology use between subgroups, including groups with mental illness or substance use disorders, and across multiple demographic categories. Similar to the previous discussion of transience, some differences in type of technology use were noted between West and East Coast samples (use of Facebook vs. MySpace: Guadagno, Muscanell, & Pollio, 2013), but in general, the conclusion about general use is that technology use is extremely high, and this conclusion generalizes across all runaway and young-adult populations studied to date.

The consistently high use reported in initial inquiries (Pollio et al., 2013) has led to research questioning the validity of the digital divide construct for the young-adult homeless, and by extension, in the general population. To address that question, a sample of young-adult homeless was compared to a similarly aged sample of college undergraduates at a large, public university (Guadagno et al., 2013). In comparing rates and type of social network technology use between the two groups, findings indicated that overall similarities were far greater than differences. Perhaps the only important difference between the two samples was that the young-adult homeless population was more likely to use technology for communication, while undergraduates were more likely to use technology for recreational purposes. This suggests that young-adult homeless are more likely to use technology for instrumental purposes (e.g., finding employment or locating resources) along with high rates of recreational use. Based on the results of the study, the authors added to other recent literature questioning the "digital divide" construct for young adults in general (Jones, Johnson-Yale, & Pérez, 2009) and for homeless young adults in particular.

One finding from the comparison that did emerge was differences between males and females in the young-adult homeless sample. Young-adult women reported being less likely to use social networks to contact friends and also less likely to post public messages. This finding is in opposition to general population (Weiser, 2000) and college studies (Muscanell & Guadagno, 2012), which find that women are more likely to use technology and social networks for personal communication. Research on the acceptability of technology as a means to reach social networks (Rice et al., 2012) suggested the acceptability of using social networks to reach young-adult homeless populations and also found that the close connections among women may be advantageous for using technology to access populations.

Lesbian, Gay, Bisexual, Transgender, and Queer Youth

Lesbian, gay, bisexual, transgender, and queer (LGBTQ) youth are a notable subpopulation represented within the broader homeless young-adult population, with unique needs, challenges, and strengths. Between 20% and 40% of homeless youth identify as LGBTQ, a disproportionate number when compared to the estimated 2% to 10% of the overall population (Corliss, Goodenow, Nichols, & Austin, 2011; Ray, 2006). While data on homeless youth in general can be difficult to obtain, gathering meaningful data about LGBTQ youth who are also homeless can be much more complicated. Survey instruments and other data-collection techniques often see these issues as separate, and it is rare to find meaningful data asking both about being LGBTQ and about being homeless for young adults (Corliss et al., 2011). While we want to know much more than we do about this population, the data gathered thus far suggest that LGBTQ homeless youth are a vulnerable population nested within an already vulnerable homeless young-adult population.

The reasons LGBTQ youth become homeless are varied, and research is split in terms of finding themes. Some research suggests that LGBTQ youth leave home or are rendered homeless for very similar reasons compared to their heterosexual and gender-conforming peers (Cochran et al., 2002). While wanting more autonomy and avoiding family conflicts were reasons both LGBTQ and heterosexual/gender-conforming youth gave for becoming homeless, this same study suggests that LGBTQ youth leave home more often than their non-LGBTQ homeless peers (Cochran et al., 2002). Other research suggests that LGBTQ youth have unique challenges and life narratives that render them homeless. If LGBTQ youth disclose their LGBTQ identity to parents or guardians, they risk physical harm that may occur as a reaction to disclosing their identity. LGBTQ youth may run away from home because they are afraid of physical or emotional abuse, they may run from home because they cannot be accepted as an LGBTQ person, or they may be rendered homeless because their parents or guardians may kick them out (Edidin et al., 2012; Ray, 2006). In addition to family discord, LGBTQ youth may face unsafe and/or hostile school environments due to discrimination (Corliss et al., 2011). A breakdown in school attendance due to discrimination may increase the number of status offenses a LGBTQ youth commits, providing a pathway into the juvenile justice system.

When LGBTQ youth are homeless, they are increasingly at risk of negative health and mental health outcomes compared to their non-LGBTQ peers. LGBTQ youth use most drugs more frequently (apart from marijuana) compared to non-LGBTQ youth and are more likely to use a wider variety of substances on a regular basis, and lesbians and bisexual women appear to be disproportionately at risk for substance abuse (Cochran et al., 2002; Corliss et al., 2011). LGBTQ homeless youth have reported higher rates of certain mental health challenges, including depression, suicidal ideation and attempts, and psychosis (Ginzler et al., 2000; McCaskill, Toro, & Wolfe, 1998). While both groups report leaving home due to sexual abuse by parents or guardians, LGBTQ youth report it as a main reason for running away twice as frequently as non-LGBTQ homeless peers (Corliss et al., 2011). Higher rates of physical abuse as a driving force for youth homelessness are reported in this population as well (Corliss et al., 2011).

■ Services and Interventions

Little work has been done to provide targeted services and interventions for homeless youth in the juvenile justice system. Even though homeless youth experience high rates of abuse (Keeshin & Campbell, 2011), high prevalence of mental illness and substance use (Edidin et al., 2012), and a greater number of encounters with the juvenile justice system (Ferguson et al., 2012), few juvenile justice interventions have been developed for this population. The following is a brief overview of some of the available services and interventions for homeless youth in the juvenile justice system, including a discussion of aging out of the juvenile justice system. It should be noted that the services and interventions discussed are not targeted specifically at homeless youth in the juvenile justice system but are widely used and available nonetheless.

As indicated earlier, homelessness places youth at greater risk for encounters with the juvenile justice system (Ferguson et al., 2012). The greater the number of individual and social factors contributing to the juvenile's entry into the juvenile justice system the longer the involvement with the juvenile justice system (Maschi et al., 2008). The provision of services for homeless youth is therefore essential, since many who enter into the juvenile justice system will exit and remain homeless (U.S. Department of Health & Human Services, 2005).

Runaway Shelters

Runaway shelters are a major type of service offered to homeless youth. These shelters typically offer emergency, short-term services to youth who have run away or are living on the street. These shelters typically focus their efforts on family reunification, though this is not always the case (Slesnick et al., 2009). Research has shown that youth using runaway shelters had reduced days on the run, fewer school and employment problems (Pollio et al., 2006; Thompson et al., 2002), and reduced behavioral and emotional problems (Barber et al., 2005). It does appear that the effect is relatively short and that shorter shelter stays might be as effective as longer stays (Pollio et al., 2006).

Youth Drop-in Centers

Youth drop-in centers offer another venue for services. Many homeless youth are street-dwelling and prefer not to use shelters. Drop-in centers provide services such as food, clothing, showers, and laundry (Joniak, 2005) without having to stay, as with a runaway shelter. Nationally, there are currently fewer than 50 youth drop-in centers but more than 4,000 adult drop-in centers. Therefore, research on the efficacy of drop-in centers is scant. Early research indicates that drop-in centers provide a safe environment where homeless youth can build trust with staff (Slesnick et al., 2008a) and possibly reduce homelessness (Slesnick et al., 2008b).

Transitional Living Program

The Family and Youth Services Bureau provides grants to agencies to establish transitional living programs for homeless youth, age 16 to 21. These programs are set up to help homeless youth make the transition to functioning adults and to prevent adult homelessness. As such, they are required to offer a litany of services including mental health care, social and vocational skills education, and stable housing (Family and Youth Services Bureau, 2012). Other than these requirements, agencies are given latitude in how they wish to establish their program (Giffords, Alonso, & Bell, 2007). One study points to length of stay as a key component for youths' success (Nolan, 2006). However, there remains a paucity of research on the efficacy of transitional living programs.

■ Interventions for the Population

Interventions for homeless youth work to reduce high-risk behaviors that generally contribute to maintaining homelessness. Such interventions include case management, vocational training, substance abuse treatment, and sexual health interventions.

Case Management

Case management is employed across a broad array of homeless services with a broad array of clientele. Intensive case management programs work to improve outcomes of homeless adolescents, most often focusing on mental health. Case management services, while employed commonly among community mental health providers, are considered essential among homeless service providers (Sosin & Durkin, 2007). One study of case management services among homeless youth found that services increased quality of life and decreased aggression and behavioral problems (Wagner et al., 1994).

Vocational Training

Similar to case management, vocational training provides skills necessary for social functioning but is focused on employment and career skills. The National Coalition for the Homeless estimates that only 44% of all homeless people are employed (2009). Vocational skills training attempts to overcome the many barriers to employment that homeless youth experience. These barriers include social and vocational skills, stress management, education, and practical matters (contact information, résumé, and clothing) (Long, Rio, & Rosen, 2007). While few studies have been done to examine the effectiveness of vocational training for homeless youth, Ferguson and Xie (2008) found that vocational training improves overall life satisfaction, though career information was not reported.

Substance Abuse Interventions

The causes and consequences of homelessness can be difficult to untangle, and this is especially true with substance abuse. Substance use and abuse rates are higher among homeless youth than among those who are in a stable housing environment (Edidin et al., 2012; Greene, Ennett, & Ringwalt, 1997; Kipke, Montgomery, Simon, Unger, & Johnson, 1997b). However, whether substance use and abuse is a cause or consequence of homelessness among youth is not always clear. Interventions using family-based therapy have been shown effective in reducing substance use among youth residing in shelters (Slesnick & Prestopnik, 2005, 2009). Many have argued for less intensive intervention strategies for street-dwelling youth (Baer, Peterson, & Wells, 2004; Peterson et al., 2006). However, less intensive interventions have not proved as favorable as more intense interventions (Slesnick et al., 2009) like the community reinforcement approach (Godley et al., 2001).

Sexual Health Interventions

The prevalence of STIs among homeless populations far exceeds that of housed individuals (Allen et al., 1994). This is often attributed to the high-risk sexual behaviors engaged in by homeless individuals (Johnson et al., 1996). Among shelter youth, providing access to condoms decreases high-risk sexual behaviors among both males and females (Rotheram-Borus et al., 2003). Results were less promising among street-dwelling youth. Three different interventions were examined at drop-in centers: (1) a peer-education intervention (Booth, Zhang, & Kwiatkowski, 1999), (2) a program that offered counseling, case management, and STI testing (Tenner et al., 1998), and (3) a group-based intervention. None of the three was able to improve behavioral outcomes.

Interventions for LGBTQ Youth

Understanding the nature of what causes homelessness for LGBTQ youth is key to wrapping appropriate services around the youth and developing treatment options. If the driving reason behind an LGBTQ youth leaving home is that the family is not affirming of the youth being LGBTQ, family acceptance work (including family therapy, referrals to support groups for families with similar dynamics, and supportive education) may reconnect the youth with family supports. When family acceptance and family reunification might not be possible, mentorship and acceptance among service providers of the LGBTQ youth may make a marked difference in decreasing risky behaviors such as high-risk sex, prostitution, and drug abuse (Ray, 2006). If service providers assess every youth by asking about sexual orientation and gender identity, this marks the service provider and agency as LGBTQ competent and affirming. Some narratives from LGBTQ homeless youth report further marginalization in shelters and other homeless services (Cochran et al., 2002). Best practices suggest that transgender youth should be allowed to identify as the gender of their choosing, and should be delivered services based on this self-identification. Ultimately, reconnecting youth with family, strengthening family relationships, and providing accepting and competent services for youth who cannot be reconnected with family may decrease interaction with the juvenile justice system. These relationships have decreased substance abuse rates, illegal behavior, and survival sex, all behaviors that increase interactions with the juvenile justice system (Stein, Milburn, Zane, & Rotheram-Borus, 2009).

Conclusion and Future Directions

The findings on social networks have distinct implications for service use. Previous research on service use and social group membership in the general population has suggested the importance of access to entire networks (Pollio, 1999). Members of peer networks in community settings were found to have lower rates of service involvement than individuals with peer networks already service involved. Because social groups tend to share patterns of risk behaviors (Baron, 2008; McCarthy,

Hagen, & Martin, 2002; Rice, Barman-Adhikari, Milburn, & Monro, 2012; Wenzel, Tucker, Golinelli, Green, & Zhou, 2010), it would appear an optimal strategy to provide services to entire peer networks. Another possibility would be to use peers already with social networks as recruitment nodes, accessing entire peer networks or even across the broader connections by having these individuals recruit others with whom they have personal relationships.

The argument that recruiting within social networks is an optimal strategy for accessing this population also resonates with service implications around transience research. Although federal policy has been based on homogeneity of service needs, the research clearly indicates the need for tailoring service models to the various different populations at different locations. In areas with more marginalized populations with higher levels of risk factors, there is an increased need for addiction services and a greater need to access established peer networks. In areas where populations have generally stayed in their neighborhoods or cities of origins, there is an increased potential for family-level interventions.

Another implication from the transience research suggests the potential for outreach based on geospatial constructs. For example, outreach might take place in geospatial locations, such as parks where peer networks with similar service needs congregate. This concept overlaps with the implications of recruiting within peer and social networks. A second service implication emerges from the migration constructs. It appears likely that there are established routes leading to locations that attract similar populations. Outreach at locations along these routes might have the potential for reaching individuals before they embed within high-risk networks.

Another promising direction for providing services to peer and social networks is through the high levels of technology use in the young-adult homeless population. Increasing evidence indicates the potential for technology to provide interventions to this difficult-to-reach population. Beyond the documented high levels of usage for this population, research has indicated the potential for online interventions to this population regarding HIV-AIDS behaviors, such as increased condom use (Rice, 2010) and AIDS knowledge (Young & Rice, 2011). Rice and colleagues have documented the possibility of using social network technology to provide services to young-adult homeless populations (Rice, Tulbert, Cederbaum, Adhikari, & Milburn, 2012). This combination of accessing social networks, accessing individuals across spatial locations, and delivering services directly to a population that has been well documented to be reluctant to engage in treatment represents an extremely promising direction for future service delivery and development.

References

Allen, D. M., Lehman, S. J., Green, T. A., Lindergren, M. L., et al. (1994). HIV infection among homeless adults and runaway youth, United States, 1989–1992. AIDS, 8(11), 1593–1598.

Annitto, M. (2011). Consent, coercion, and compassion: Emerging legal responses to the commercial sexual exploitation of minors. *Yale Law & Policy Review, 30*(1), 1–70.

Ayerst, S. (1999). Depression and stress in street youth. *Adolescence, 34*(135), 567–575.

Baer, J. S., Peterson, P. L., & Wells, E. A. (2004). Rationale and design of a brief substance use intervention for homeless adolescents. *Addiction Research and Theory, 12,* 317–334.

Barber, C. C., Fonagy, P., Fultz, J., Simulinas, M., & Yates, M. (2005). Homeless near a thousand homes: Outcomes of homeless youth in a crisis shelter. *American Journal of Orthopsychiatry. 75,* 347–355.

Baron, S. W. (2008). Street youth, unemployment, and crime: Is it that simple? Using General Strain Theory to untangle the relationship. *Canadian Journal of Criminology and Criminal Justice/La Revue Canadienne de Criminologie et de Justice Pénale, 50*(4), 399–434.

Bartollas, C. (2006). *Juvenile delinquency* (7th ed.). Boston: Pearson.

Bender, K., Ferguson, K. M., Thompson, S. J., Komlo, C., & Pollio, D. E. (2010). Factors associated with trauma and posttraumatic stress disorder among homeless youth in three U.S. cities: The importance of transience. *Journal of Traumatic Stress, 23*(1), 161–168.

Bender, K., Thompson, S. J., McManus, H., Lantry, J., & Flynn, P. M. (2007). Capacity for survival: Exploring strengths of homeless street youth. *Child and Youth Care Forum, 36*(1), 25–42.

Bender, K., Thompson, S. J., Pollio, D. E., & Sterzing, P. (2010). Comparison of social estrangement among young adults who are homeless in St. Louis, Missouri and Austin, Texas. *Journal of Human Behavior in the Social Environment, 20*(3). 193–217.

Bernstein, N., & Foster, L. (2008). *Voices from the street: A survey of homeless youth by their peers.* Retrieved from: http://www.library.ca.gov/crb/08/08-004.pdf

Booth, R., & Zhang, Y. (1997). Conduct disorder and HIV risk behaviors among runaway and homeless adolescents. *Drug and Alcohol Dependence, 48,* 69–76.

Booth, R. E., Zhang, Y., & Kwiatkowski, C. F. (1999). The challenge of changing drug and sex risk behaviors of runaway and homeless adolescents. *Child Abuse & Neglect, 23,* 1295–1306.

Bryan, A. D., Schmiege, S. J., & Magnan, R. E. (2012). Marijuana use and risky sexual behavior among high-risk adolescents: Trajectories, risk factors, and event-level relationships. *Developmental Psychology, 48*(5), 1429–1442.

Cartwright, D., & Zander, A. (1968). *Group dynamics: Research and theory* (3rd ed.). New York: Harper & Row.

Chapple, C. L., Johnson, K. D., & Whitbeck, L. B. (2004). Gender and arrest among homeless and runaway youth: An analysis of background, family, and situational factors. *Youth Violence and Juvenile Justice, 2*(2), 129–147.

Chen, X., Thrane, L., Whitbeck, L., Hoyt D., & Johnson, K. (2007). Onset of conduct disorder, use of delinquent subsistence strategies, and street victimization among homeless and runaway adolescents in the midwest. *Journal of Interpersonal Violence, 22*(9), 1156–1184.

Cochran, B. N., Stewart, A. J., Ginzler, J. A., & Cauce, A. M. (2002). Challenges faced by homeless sexual minorities: Comparison of gay, lesbian, bisexual, and transgender homeless adolescents with their heterosexual counterparts. *American Journal of Public Health, 92*(5), 773–777.

Corliss, H. L., Goodenow, C. S., Nichols, L., & Austin, S. (2011). High burden of homelessness among sexual-minority adolescents: Findings from a representative Massachusetts high school sample. *American Journal of Public Health, 101*(9), 1683–1689.

Drori, G. S., & Jang, Y. S. (2003). The global digital divide: A sociological assessment of trends and causes. *Social Science Computer Review, 21,* 144–161.

Edidin, J. P., Ganim, Z., Hunter, S. J., & Karnik, N. S. (2012). The mental and physical health of homeless youth: A literature review. *Child Psychiatry & Human Development, 43*(3), 354–375.

Ensign, J., & Santelli, J. (1998). Health status and service use: Comparison of adolescents at a school-based health clinic with homeless adolescents. *Archives of Pediatric Adolescent Medicine, 152*, 20–24.

Eyrich, K. M., Pollio, D. E., & North, C. S. (2003). A comparison of alienation and replacement theories of social support in homelessness. *Social Work Research, 27*(4). 222–231.

Families and Youth Services Bureau (2012). *Transitional living program fact sheet.* Retrieved from: http://www.acf.hhs.gov/programs/fysb/resource/tlp-fact-sheet

Ferguson, K. M., Bender, K., Thompson, S. J., Maccio, E. M., Xie, B., & Pollio, D. (2011). Social control correlates of arrest behaviors among homeless youth in five U.S. cities. *Violence and Victims, 26*(5), 648–668.

Ferguson, K. M., Bender, K., Thompson, S. J., Xie, B., & Pollio, D. (2012). Exploration of arrest activity among homeless young adults in four U.S. cities. *Social Work Research, 36*(3), 233–238.

Ferguson, K., Bender, K., Thompson, S., Xie, B., & Pollio, D. (2011). Correlates of street-survival behaviors in homeless young adults in four U.S. cities. *American Journal of Orthopsychiatry, 81*(3), 401–409.

Ferguson, K., Bender, K., Thompson, S., Xie, B., & Pollio, D. (2012). Exploration of arrest activity among homeless young adults in four U.S. cities. *Social Work Research, 36*(3), 233–238.

Ferguson, K., Jun, J., Bender, K., Thompson, S., & Pollio, D. E. (2010). A comparison of addiction and transience among street youth: Los Angeles, California, Austin, Texas, and St. Louis, Missouri. *Community Mental Health Journal, 46*. 296–307.

Ferguson, K. M., & Xie, B. (2008). Feasibility study of the Social Enterprise Intervention with homeless youth. *Social Work Practice, 18*(1), 5–19.

Forst, M. L., & Crim, D. (1994). A substance abuse profile of delinquent and homeless youths. *Journal of Drug Education, 24*, 219–231.

Gangamma, R., Slesnick, N., Toviessi, P., & Serovich, J. (2008). Comparison of HIV risks among gay, lesbian, bisexual and heterosexual homeless youth. *Journal of Youth & Adolescence, 37*, 456–464.

German, D., Davey, M. A., & Latkin, C. A. (2007). Residential transience and HIV risk behaviors among injection drug users. *AIDS and Behavior, 11*(S2), 21–30.

Giffords, E. D., Alonso, C., & Bell, R. (2007). A transitional living program for homeless adolescents: A case study. *Child & Youth Care Forum, 36*(4), 141–151.

Ginzler, J., Cauce, A., Paradise, M., Embry, L., Morgan, C., Lohr, Y., & Theofelis, J. (2000). The characteristics and mental health of homeless adolescents: Age and gender differences. *Journal of Emotional and Behavioral Disorders, 8*(4), 230–239.

Godley, S. H., Meyers, R. J., Smith, J. E., Karvinen, T., Titus, J. C., Godley, M. D., et al. (2001). *The adolescent community reinforcement approach for adolescent cannabis users.* DHHS Publication No. (SMA) 01–3489. Retrieved from: http://kap.samhsa.gov/products/manuals/cyt/pdfs/cyt4_07.pdf

Greene, J. M., Ennett, S. T., & Ringwalt, C. L. (1997). Substance use among runaway and homeless youth in three national samples. *American Journal of Public Health, 87*(2), 229–235.

Greene, J. M., & Ringwalt, C. L. (1996). Youth and familial substance use's association with suicide attempts among runaway and homeless youth. *Substance Use and Misuse, 31*(8), 1041–1058.

Guadagno, R. E., Muscanell, N., & Pollio, D. E. (2013). Re-thinking the digital divide: A comparison of social network use between college students and young adult homeless. *Computers in Human Behavior, 29*(1), 86–89.

Hagan, J., & McCarthy, B. (1992). Street life and delinquency. *British Journal of Sociology, 43*(3), 533–561.

Horowitz R., & Pottieger, A. E. (1991). Gender bias in juvenile justice handling of seriously crime-involved youths. *Journal of Research in Crime and Delinquency, 28*(1), 75–100.

Johnson, T. P., Aschkenasy, J. R., Herbers, M. R., & Gillenwater, S. A. (1996). Self-reported risk factors for AIDS among homeless youth. *AIDS Education and Prevention, 8*(4), 308–322.

Johnson, K. D., Whitbeck, L. B., & Hoyt, D. (2005). Predictors of social network composition among homeless and runaway adolescents. *Journal of Adolescence, 28*(2), 231–248.

Jones, S., Johnson-Yale, C., & Pérez, S. (2009). U.S. college students' Internet use: Race, gender and digital divides. *Journal of Computer-Mediated Communication, 14*, 244–264.

Joniak, E. A. (2005). Exclusionary practices and the delegitimization of client voice: How staff create, sustain, and escalate conflict in a drop-in center for street kids. *American Behavioral Scientist. 48*, 961–988.

Karabanow, J., & Clement, P. (2004). Interventions with street youth: A commentary on the practice-based research literature. *Brief Treatment and Crisis Intervention, 4*(1), 93–108.

Keeshin, B. R., & Campbell, K. (2011). Screening homeless youth for histories of abuse: Prevalence, enduring effects, and interest in treatment. *Child Abuse & Neglect, 35*, 401–407.

Kipke, M. D., Montgomery, S. B., Simon, T. R., & Iverson, E. F. (1997a). Substance abuse disorders among runaway and homeless youth. *Substance Abuse and Misuse, 32*(7-8), 969–986.

Kipke, M., Montgomery, S., Simon, T., Unger, J., & Johnson, C. (1997b). Homeless youth: drug use patterns and HIV risk profiles according to peer group affiliation. *AIDS & Behavior, 1*(4), 247–259.

Long, D., Rio, J., & Rosen, J. (2007). *Employment and income supports for homeless people.* Paper presented at National Symposium on Homelessness Research held on March 1-2, 2007.

Maschi, T., Hatcher, S. S., Schwalbe, C. S., & Rosato, N. S. (2008). Mapping the social service pathways of youth to and through the juvenile justice system: A comprehensive review. *Children and Youth Services Review, 30*(12), 1376–1385.

McCarthy, B., Hagan, J., & Martin, M. J. (2002). In and out of harm's way: Violent victimization and the social capital of fictive street families. *Criminology, 40*(4), 831–866.

McCaskill, P. A., Toro, P. A., & Wolfe, S. M. (1998). Homeless and matched housed adolescents: a comparative study of psychopathology. *Journal of Clinical Child Psychology, 27*(3), 306–319.

Mitchell, K. J., Finkelhor, D. D., & Wolak, J. J. (2010). Conceptualizing juvenile prostitution as child maltreatment: Findings from the national juvenile prostitution study. *Child Maltreatment, 15*(1), 18–36.

Muscanell, N. L., & Guadagno, R. E. (2012). Make new friends or keep the old: Gender and personality differences in social networking use. *Computers in Human Behavior, 28*, 107–112.

National Coalition for the Homeless (2009). *Employment and homelessness.* Retrieved from: http://www.nationalhomeless.org/factsheets/employment.html

Nolan, T. C. (2006). Outcomes for a transitional living program serving LGBTQ youth in New York City. *Child Welfare, 85*(2), 385–406.

Peterson, P. L., Baer, J. S., Wells, E. A., Ginzler, J. A., & Garrett, S. B. (2006). Short-term effects of a brief motivational intervention to reduce alcohol and drug risk among homeless adolescents. *Psychology of Addictive Behaviors, 20*, 254–264.

Polgar, M. F., North, C. S., & Pollio, D. E. (2009). Parenting adults who become homeless: Variations in stress and social support. *American Journal of Orthopsychiatry, 79*(3), 357–365.

Pollio, D. E. (1999). Group membership as a predictor of service use-related behaviors for persons on the streets. *Research on Social Work Practice, 9*(5), 575–592.

Pollio, D. E., Batey, D. S., Ferguson, K., Bender, K., & Thompson, S. (2013). Technology use among emerging adult homeless in two U.S. cities. *Social Work, 58*(2), 173–175.

Pollio, D. E., Jaggers, J., Hudson, A., & McClendon, J. B. *How young adult homeless use technology: A qualitative study of technology use.* Unpublished manuscript.

Pollio, D. E., Thompson, S. J., & North, C. S. (2000). Agency-based tracking of difficult-to-follow populations: Runaway and homeless youth programs in St. Louis, Missouri. *Community Mental Health Journal, 36*(3), 247–258.

Pollio, D. E., Thompson, S. J., Tobias, L., Reid, D., & Spitznagel, E. (2006). Longitudinal outcomes for youth receiving runaway/homeless shelter services. *Journal of Youth and Adolescence. 35,* 859–866.

Ray, N. (2006). *Lesbian, gay, bisexual and transgender youth: an epidemic of homeless.* National Gay and Lesbian Task Force Policy Institute and the National Coalition for the Homeless, New York.

Reeg, B., Grisham, C., & Shepard, A. (2002). *Families on the edge: Homeless young parents and their welfare experiences. A survey of homeless youth and service.* Washington, DC: Center for Law and Social Policy.

Rice, E. (2010). The positive role of social networks and social networking technology in the condom-using behaviors of homeless young people. *Public Health Reports, 125*(4), 588.

Rice, E., Barman-Adhikari, A., Milburn, N. G., & Monro, W. (2012). Position-specific HIV risk in a large network of homeless youths. *American Journal of Public Health, 102*(1), 141–147.

Rice, E., Milburn, N., & Rotheram-Borus, M. (2007). Pro-social and problematic social network influences on HIV/AIDS risk behaviours among newly homeless youth in Los Angeles. *AIDS Care, 19,* 697–704.

Rice, E., Milburn, N. G., Rotheram-Borus, M. J., et al. (2005). The effects of peer group network properties on drug use among homeless youth. *American Behavioral Scientist, 48,* 1102.

Rice, E., Stein, J. A., & Milburn, N. (2008). Countervailing social network influences on problem behaviors among homeless youth. *Journal of Adolescence, 31,* 625–639.

Rice, E., Tulbert, E., Cederbaum, J., Adhikari, A. B., & Milburn, N. G. (2012). Mobilizing homeless youth for HIV prevention: a social network analysis of the acceptability of a face-to-face and online social networking intervention. *Health Education Research, 27*(2), 226–236.

Rotheram-Borus, M. J., Song, J., Gwadz, M., Lee, M., Van Rossem, R., & Koopman, C. (2003). Reductions in HIV risk among runaway youth. *Prevention Science, 4,* 173–187.

Sampson, R. J., & Laub, J. H. (2003). Life-course desisters? Trajectories of crime among delinquent boys followed to age 70. *Criminology, 41*(3), 301–340.

Schmalleger, F., & Bartollas, C. (2008). *Juvenile delinquency.* Boston: Pearson.

Slesnick, N., Bartle-Haring, S., Dashora, P., Kang, M., &, Aukward, E. (2008a). Predictors of homelessness among street living youth. *Journal of Youth and Adolescence. 37,* 465–474.

Slesnick, N., Dashora, P., Letcher, A., Erdem, G., & Serovich, J. (2009). A review of services and interventions for runaway and homeless youth: Moving forward. *Children & Youth Services Review, 31*(7), 732–742.

Slesnick, N., Kang, M., Bonomi, A. E., & Prestopnik, J. L. (2008b). Six- and twelve-month outcomes among homeless youth accessing therapy and case management services through an urban drop-in center. *Health Services Research. 43,* 211–229.

Slesnick, N., & Prestopnik, J. L. (2005). Ecologically based family therapy outcome with substance-abusing runaway adolescents. *Journal of Adolescence, 28,* 277–298.

Slesnick, N., & Prestopnik, J. L. (2009). Comparison of family therapy outcome with alcohol-abusing, runaway adolescents. *Journal of Marital & Family Therapy, 35*(3), 255–277.

Solarz, A., & Bogat, A. G. (1990). When social support fails: The homeless. *Journal of Community Psychology, 18*(1), 79–96.

Sosin, M., & Durkin, E. (2007). Perceptions about services and dropout from a substance abuse case management program. *Journal of Community Psychology, 35*(5), 583–602.

Substance Abuse and Mental Health Services Administration (2011). *Current statistics on the prevalence and characteristics of people experiencing homelessness in the United States.* Retrieved from: http://homeless.samhsa.gov/ResourceFiles/hrc_factsheet.pdf

Teare, J. F., Furst, D. W., Peterson, R. W., & Authier, K. (1992). Family reunification following shelter placement: Child, family, and program correlates. *American Journal of Orthopsychiatry, 62.* 142–146.

Tenner, A. D., Trevithick, L. A., Wagner, V., & Burch, R. (1998). Seattle Youth Care's prevention, intervention, and education program: A model of care for HIV- positive, homeless, and at-risk youth. *Journal of Adolescent Health, 23,* 96–106.

Thompson, S. J. (2004). Risk/protective factors associated with substance use among runaway/homeless youth utilizing emergency shelter services nationwide. *Substance Abuse, 25*(3), 13–26.

Thompson, S., Jun, J., Bender, K., Ferguson, K. M., & Pollio, D. E. (2010). Estrangement factors associated with addiction to alcohol and drugs among homeless youth in three U.S. cities. *Evaluation and Program Planning, 33*(4), 418–427.

Thompson, S. J., Maguin, E., & Pollio, D. E. (2003). National and regional differences among runaway youth using federally funded crisis shelters. *Journal of Social Service Research, 30*(1), 1–17.

Thompson, S. J., & Pollio, D. E. (2006). Identifying the role of institutional disaffiliation, psychological dysfunction, identification with runaway culture, and human capital in adolescent runaway episodes. *Social Work Research, 30*(4), 245–252.

Thompson, S. J., Pollio, D. E., Constantine, J., Reid, D., & Nebbitt, V. (2002). Short-term outcomes for youths receiving runaway homeless shelter services. *Research on Social Work Practice, 12*(5), 589–603.

Thompson, S. J., Safyer, A. W., & Pollio, D. E. (2001). Differences and predictors of family reunification among subgroups of runaway youths using shelter services. *Social Work Research, 25*(3), 163–172.

Thompson, S. J., Zittel-Palmara, K. M., & Forehand, G. (2005). Risk factors for cigarette, alcohol, and marijuana use among runaway youth utilizing two services sectors. *Journal of Child and Adolescent Substance Abuse, 15*(1), 17–36.

Toro, P., Dworsky, A., & Fowler, P. (2007). *Homeless youth in the United States: Recent research findings and intervention approaches.* Paper presented at the 2007 National Symposium on Homelessness Research. Retrieved from: http://aspe.hhs.gov/hsp/homelessness/symposium07/toro/index.htm

Tyler, K. A., Hoyt, D. R., & Whitbeck, L. B. (2000). The effects of early sexual abuse on later sexual victimization among female homeless and runaway adolescents. *Journal of Interpersonal Violence, 15,* 235.

Uggen, C., & Kruttschnitt, C. (1998). Crime in the breaking: Gender differences in desistance. *Law and Society Review, 32*(2).

U.S. Department of Health and Human Services. (2005). *Promising strategies to end youth homelessness: Report to Congress.* Retrieved from: http://www.acf.hhs.gov/programs/fysb/content/docs/reporttocongress_youthhomelessness.pdf

Wagner, V., Sy, J., Weeden, K., Blanchard, T., Cauce, A. M., Morgan, C. J., Moore, E., Wurzbacher, K., & Tomlin, S. (1994). Effectiveness of intensive case management for homeless adolescents: Results of a 3-month follow-up. *Journal of Emotional and Behavioral Disorders, 2*(4), 219–227.

Weir, B. W., Bard, R. S., O'Brien, K., Casciato, C. J., & Stark, M. J. (2007). Uncovering patterns of HIV risk through multiple housing measures. *AIDS and Behavior, 11*(S2), 31–44.

Weiser, E. (2000). Gender differences in Internet use patterns and Internet application preferences: A two-sample comparison. *CyberPsychology & Behavior, 4,* 167–178.

Wenzel, S., Tucker, J., Golinelli, D., Green, H., & Zhou, A. (2010). Personal network correlates of alcohol, cigarette, and marijuana use among homeless youth. *Drug & Alcohol Dependence, 112*(1), 140–149.

Whitbeck, L., & Hoyt, D. R. (1999). *Nowhere to grow: Homeless and runaway adolescents and their families.* New York: Aldine de Gruyter.

Whitbeck, L. B., Hoyt, D. R., & Bao, W-N. (2000). Depressive symptoms and co-occurring depressive symptoms, substance abuse, and conduct problems among runaway and homeless adolescents. *Child Development, 71*(3), 721–732.

Witkin, A. L., Milburn, N. G., Rotheram-Borus, M. J., Batterham, P., May, S., & Brooks, R. (2005). Finding homeless youth: Patterns based on geographical area and number of homeless episodes. *Youth & Society, 37*(1), 62–84.

Young, S., & Rice, E. (2011). Online social networking technologies, HIV knowledge, and sexual risk and testing behaviors among homeless youth. *AIDS & Behavior, 15*(2), 253–260.

Zide, M. R., & Cherry, A. L. (1992). A typology of runaway youths: An empirically based definition. *Child and Adolescent Social Work Journal, 9,* 155–168.

21

Disproportionate Minority Contact (DMC) in the U.S. Juvenile Justice System

Susan A. McCarter

■ Introduction and Scope: Minority Overrepresentation

Overrepresentation of individuals occurs when the number of persons present in a certain category exceeds the number of those persons typically represented in the general population. This phenomenon is also referred to as disproportionality in that the classification may reflect a figure that is not proportionate to the general population (Vallas, 2009). Neither of these terms, however, is inherently evaluative, and judgment about overrepresentation depends on the goals or desired outcomes of the individual or organization examining this phenomenon.

Within the juvenile justice system, the mission of the Office of Juvenile Justice and Delinquency Prevention (OJJDP) is to provide "national leadership, coordination, and resources to prevent and respond to juvenile delinquency and victimization." OJJDP is guided by the Juvenile Justice and Delinquency Prevention (JJDPA) of 1974[1] (P.L. 93-415, 42 U.S.C. 5601 et seq.), which maintains four core protections: (1) deinstitutionalization of status offenders—requiring that status offenders not be detained either in juvenile or adult facilities, (2) "sight and sound" separation—requiring that adult jails or lockups work to keep juveniles separated from adult prisoners, (3) jail removal—requiring that youth not be placed in adult jails or lockups except under very limited circumstances (added in 1980), and (4) disproportionate minority confinement—requiring states to address the issue of overrepresentation of youth of color in the justice system (added in 1992). The stated purpose of the disproportionate minority confinement core requirement is "to ensure equal and fair treatment for every youth in the juvenile justice system, regardless of race and ethnicity."

Youth of color, however, are overrepresented in the U.S. juvenile justice system (Bishop, Leiber, & Johnson, 2010; Kempf-Leonard, 2007; Leiber & Rodriguez, 2011) and at every decision point within the system (Hartney & Vuong, 2009; Leiber, 2002; Puzzanchera & Adams, 2008). In 2009, the U.S. juvenile general population (under 18) totaled almost 75 million and of those youth, 78% were classified as White, 16% Black, 5% Asian/Native Hawaiian/Other Pacific Islander, and 1% American Indian/Alaska Native. That same year, the juvenile courts processed more than 1.5 million delinquency cases and of those cases, 64% were for White youth, 34% Black youth, 1% Asian youth, and 1% American Indian youth (www.ojjdp.gov/ojstabb/ezapop/).

In 2009, most of the drug offense cases involved White youth (75%), whereas person offense cases involved the largest proportion of Black youth (41%) (Fig. 21.1).

During that same year, OJJDP also reports that "the rate at which Black youth were referred to the juvenile court for a delinquency offense was more than 150% greater than the rate for White youth" (Knoll & Sickmund, 2012). Similarly, the National Council on Crime and Delinquency notes that the proportion of White youth transferred to adult court is 75% of their proportion in

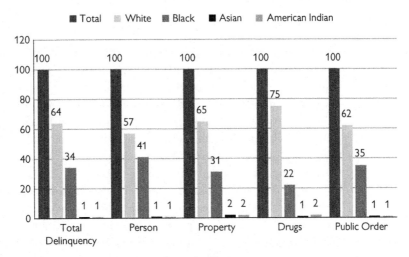

Figure 21.1   **2009 Juvenile Delinquency Cases by Race.**

Source: Knoll, C., & Sickmund, M. (2012). *Delinquency Cases in Juvenile Court, 2009.* National Center for Juvenile Justice Office of Juvenile Justice and Delinquency Prevention, NCJ 239081. Online. Available: http://www.ojjdp.gov/ojstatbb/

the general population, while African American youth are transferred at 200% of their proportion in the general population (Hartney & Vuong, 2009).

Juvenile justice research acknowledges differences in crime commission by race, but most scholars concur that variation in juvenile justice processing and outcomes cannot be attributed to differential offending or legal factors alone (Bishop, 2005; Huizinga, Thornberry, Knight, & Lovegrove, 2007; McCarter, 2009a; Pope & Leiber, 2005). Alex Piquero writes:

> Differences both in processing and in offending are almost surely involved [in minority overrepresentation in the juvenile justice system], and determining their relative importance would probably have little effect on policy or practice. What may be more valuable, instead, would be to understand *how* differences in processing and in offending contribute to minority overrepresentation. (2008, pp. 60–61)

■ Legal Issues/Policy Response to Minority Overrepresentation

In 1988, as part of the reauthorization of the JJDPA, the law was amended, requiring that states address disproportionate minority confinement. The reauthorization stipulated that disproportionate minority confinement was indicated if the proportion of youth detained or confined in secure detention facilities, secure correctional facilities, jails, and lockups who are members of minority groups are overrepresented when compared to their numbers in the general population (Public Law 93-415, Section 223 [a][23]).

Few states, however, took action to reduce minority overrepresentation. So, Congress amended the JJDPA again in 1992 and elevated disproportionate minority confinement to a core requirement, attaching Formula Grants' allocations to states' compliance with the disproportionate minority confinement requirement (Title II, Part B). A fourth amendment modified the act again in 2002 and changed the language from disproportionate minority "confinement" to disproportionate minority "contact." Some scholars believe this change in language had little effect, since the overall goal continues to be the equitable treatment of all youth (Leiber & Rodriguez, 2011), whereas others point to two potential important effects of this change (McCarter, 2011). Firstly, it serves to broaden the examination of disproportionate minority confinement from solely at the final and most severe sanction/decision point within the juvenile system to instead include all juvenile justice system decision points. (The nine decision points generally considered for assessing disproportionate minority contact are arrest, referral, diversion, detention, petition/charges filed, adjudicated delinquent, probation, secure confinement, and transfer.) Secondly, it distributes the intervention efforts from focusing just on programming for youth and their families to potentially including policy and systemic responses as well (McCarter, 2011). The DMC Technical Assistance Manual (2009, 4th ed., p. Intro 2) suggests that changing the language from "confinement" to "contact" "reaffirms the fact that DMC is the result of a number of complex decisions and events and that only through a comprehensive, balanced, and multidisciplinary approach can the states and localities reduce DMC." Hereafter, the acronym "DMC" will refer to disproportionate minority contact.

OJJDP suggests that for states to be found in compliance with the DMC requirement, they must participate in five sustained efforts: (1) identification—catalog the extent to which DMC exists, (2) assessment/diagnosis—evaluate the reasons for DMC, if it exists, (3) intervention—develop an intervention plan to address the identified reasons, (4) evaluation—assess the effectiveness of strategies to address DMC, and (5) monitoring—track DMC trends over time (DMC Technical Assistance Manual, 2009; Pope, Lovell, & Hsia, 2002). See Figure 21.2.

Finally, policy responses to DMC have also come in the way of precedent-setting civil rights lawsuits. As was evident in states' responses to the DMC core requirement, local jurisdictions exhibit varied levels of DMC and support for DMC reduction. Yet, until recently, no one ever cited the unconstitutionality of this or sued a jurisdiction because of it. In the past 4 years, the Civil Rights Division of the U.S. Justice Department has filed two separate lawsuits against local jurisdictions for unconstitutional treatment of youth within their juvenile justice systems (http://www.justice.gov/crt/). The first was a lawsuit against the Juvenile Court of Memphis and Shelby County, in which the Justice Department suggested that it had reasonable cause to believe that this juvenile court failed to protect the rights of children appearing before it on delinquency matters by failing to (1) provide constitutionally required due

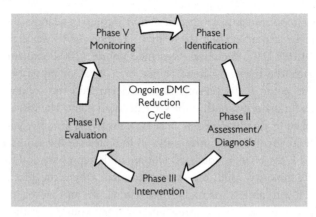

Figure 21.2   Phases for Ongoing DMC Reduction.

process, (2) administer justice in a nondiscriminatory manner, and (3) provide reasonably safe conditions of confinement. The investigation was opened in August 2009 and conducted pursuant to the Violent Crime Control and Law Enforcement Act of 1994 and Title VI of the Civil Rights Act of 1964. Findings were released on April 26, 2012, and included the allegation that the court's administration of juvenile justice discriminates against African-American children.

In the second case, the Justice Department's Civil Rights Division contended that the Meridian Police Department, Lauderdale County Youth Court, and the State of Mississippi's Division of Youth Services engaged in a pattern of practice of unlawful conduct through which they routinely and systematically arrested and incarcerated children, including for minor school rule infractions, without even the most basic procedural safeguards, which is in violation of the Fourth, Fifth, and Fourteenth Amendments and the constitutional rights of these children. The lawsuit was filed on October 24, 2012, seeking declaratory, injunctive, and equitable relief. The complaint also alleged that the county officials contributed to a school-to-prison pipeline whereby children have been systematically incarcerated for committing minor offenses, including school disciplinary infractions (http://www.justice.gov/crt/).

■ Measuring DMC

Initial measures of DMC used a representation index to calculate minority over-representation or the percentage of youth of a particular race as compared with their percentage in the general population. The representation index method was then replaced by a disproportionate representation index, which provided context within the juvenile justice decision points for the disproportionality (DMC Technical Assistance Manual, 2009). Yet this measure did not evaluate the disproportionality of a specific minority group in relation to a non-minority group. To accomplish this, the relative rate index (RRI) was created.

OJJDP's DMC Technical Assistance Manual (2009) explains that the RRI compares the relative volume or rate of activity for minority youth at each decision point in the juvenile justice system with the volume of that same activity for majority youth at the same decision point. The RRI is a single figure calculated by dividing the rate of activity involving minority youth by the rate of activity involving majority youth. If the rates are the same, the RRI = 1. If the RRI is less than 1, youth of color are underrepresented; if the RRI is more than 1, minority youth are overrepresented. Often, the first decision point assessed with an RRI matrix is arrest/referral. So, an example of an RRI could be the comparison of the arrest rate for Black youth with the arrest rate for White youth. By dividing their counts of delinquency arrests in 2009 by the 10- to-17-year-old population in that same year, one would calculate that the White arrest rate was 44.5 arrests for every 1,000 White youth aged 10 to 17 in the U.S. population and the Black arrest rate was 99.1. The RRI for this arrest example would be the Black rate divided by the White rate, yielding an RRI of 2.2.

To calculate DMC nationwide, OJJDP includes arrest estimates from the Bureau of Justice Statistics. These figures are based on data reported to the FBI's Uniform Crime Reporting Program and include the annual number of delinquency arrests for persons aged 10 to 18 who are White/Caucasian, Black/African American, American Indian/Alaskan Native, or Asian/Native Hawaiian/Other Pacific Islander (Table 21.1).

These data are limited in that they do not allow for comparison by ethnic identity. (Population estimates are provided by the Centers for Disease Control and Prevention, available at http://www.ojjdp.gov/ojstatbb/ezapop/).

Still, reviewing the 2009 arrest rate RRI example shows an RRI of 2.2, which means that the arrest rate for Black youth in 2009 was more than double the White rate, documenting disproportionality at arrest (Table 21.2). Does this suggest that the arrest process is racially biased? Not necessarily; there are many legal and extralegal factors that contribute to disproportionality, and they all should be empirically evaluated. The RRI can identify the disproportionality of one group to another (with some limitations), but it cannot explain the source or cause of the overrepresentation.

To receive full funding through the Formula Grants program, states must demonstrate their compliance with the DMC core requirement. This means identifying the extent to which DMC exists in their jurisdiction, assessing the reasons for DMC (if it exists), developing and implementing delinquency prevention and system improvement strategies (if DMC exists), and evaluating and monitoring the improvement strategies' effectiveness. These steps are outlined in the states' 3-year plan, to which OJJDP requires annual updates to maintain compliance and funding.

Table 21.1   **2009 Case Processing Summary Rates for Delinquency Offenses**

Rate	All	White	Minority	Black	AIAN	AHPI
Juvenile arrests per 1,000 persons in population	52.1	44.5	78.0	99.1	46.3	15.3
Cases referred per 100 juvenile arrests	88.5	84.9	95.5	95.5	105.6	88.5
Cases diverted per 100 cases referred	26.6	29.4	21.8	21.6	21.5	25.2
Cases detained per 100 cases referred	21.1	18.4	26.0	26.3	23.5	21.2
Cases petitioned per 100 cases referred	54.7	51.6	60.2	60.2	60.4	58.5
Cases adjudicated per 100 cases petitioned	59.4	61.2	56.6	55.9	68.6	60.6
Probation cases per 100 adjudicated cases	59.6	62.0	55.7	54.9	60.9	67.7
Placement cases per 100 adjudicated cases	27.4	25.3	30.8	31.2	29.1	23.1
Cases judicially waived per 100 cases petitioned	0.9	0.9	1.0	1.0	1.6	0.5

AIAN, American Indian or Alaskan Native; AHPI, Asian, Hawaiian, or Pacific Islander.

Source: Puzzanchera, C., & Adams, B. (2012). *National Disproportionate Minority Contact Databook.* Developed by the National Center for Juvenile Justice for the Office of Juvenile Justice and Delinquency Prevention. Available online: http://www.ojjdp.gov/ojstatbb/dmcdb/

Table 21.2   **2009 Case Processing Summary: Rates by Decision Points Relative Rate Indices for Delinquency Offenses**

Relative Rates	Minority	Black	AIAN	AHPI
Arrest rate	1.8	2.2	1.0	0.3
Referral rate	1.1	1.1	1.2	1.0
Diversion rate	0.7	0.7	0.7	0.9
Detention rate	1.4	1.4	1.3	1.2
Petitioned rate	1.2	1.2	1.2	1.1
Adjudicated rate	0.9	0.9	1.1	1.0
Probation rate	0.9	0.9	1.0	1.1
Placement rate	1.2	1.2	1.2	0.9
Waiver rate	1.1	1.1	1.8	0.5

All RRIs are relative to whites.

AIAN, American Indian or Alaskan Native; AHPI, Asian, Hawaiian, or Pacific Islander.

Source: Puzzanchera, C., & Adams, B. (2012). *National Disproportionate Minority Contact Databook.* Developed by the National.

Center for Juvenile Justice for the Office of Juvenile Justice and Delinquency Prevention. Online. Available: http://www.ojjdp.gov/ojstatbb/dmcdb/

■ Factors Contributing to DMC Micro, Mezzo, and Macro Issues

Work with court-involved youth often focuses on the risk and protective factors that contribute to or protect one from juvenile delinquency, such as psychological, biological, familial, social, and educational factors. Echoing the reconceptualization of "disproportionate minority confinement" to "contact," practice in juvenile justice has now begun to explore structural/political, racial/cultural, and even spiritual factors that may also affect minority overrepresentation at micro, mezzo, and macro levels (McCarter, 2009b). Consider these themes and their potential for risk and resiliency for adolescents. What follows is a sample of the recent studies examining these factors.

Psychological Factors

Simões, Matos, and Batista-Foguet (2008) conducted structural equation modeling with data from 300 juvenile offenders and then focus groups with 24 incarcerated boys aged 11 to 18. The psychological themes that emerged from their study were cognitive—positive expectations from risk behaviors, positive attitudes toward delinquency, low risk perception for punishment, decision-making skills deficit; behavioral—substance use, risk behaviors as ways to spend leisure time; and personality-driven—sensation seeking (p. 401).

Biological Factors

Age has been found to affect processing and outcomes in the juvenile justice system in that often older juveniles may come with more extensive records and may be viewed as more dangerous or threatening; thus, they often receive more severe punishments (Leiber & Mack, 2003). Moreover, the ages of jurisdiction and related policies vary considerably by state; for example, the age of majority in North Carolina is 15, in Illinois it is 16, and in California it is 17 (McCarter & Bridges, 2011). Similarly, recent findings regarding brain development suggest that adolescent decision making is neurobiologically different than that of adults (Johnson, Blum, & Giedd, 2009). This type of research was cited to support the Supreme Court's *Roper v. Simmons* decision (543 U.S. 551, 2005), which contends that culpability is affected by understanding, maturity, and decision-making ability.

Familial Factors

Some studies point to single-parent households with lower family incomes and less supervision as risk factors for contributing to DMC (Amato, 2000;

494

Eitle, 2006). Others suggest that there may be a reaction effect from the system to the young person based on his/her family—for instance, OJJDP's listing of "decision-making factors" as a potential DMC contributing mechanism, stating that "juvenile justice decision makers respond differently to youth from an intact two-parent family setting than to youth from a single-parent home" (Leiber & Mack, 2003; OJJDP's DMC Contributing Mechanisms).

Social Factors

Peer attitudes, attitude transference, and peer delinquent behavior all affect adolescents' self-reports of delinquency according to a study by Megens and Weerman (2011). Their research also adds that the attitudes of friends may influence delinquency even more so than the actual delinquent behavior on the part of one's peers (p. 437). OJJDP includes "living in disorganized neighborhoods" as a social factor that may disproportionately affect minority youth and put them at greater risk of system involvement (OJJDP's DMC Contributing Mechanisms).

Educational Factors

Christle, Jolivette, and Nelson's study (2005) found that the majority of court-involved adolescents had experienced educational challenges such as academic failures, lack of connection to school, and dropout risk but that school-level factors can also act as protective factors against further school problems as well as juvenile delinquency. They point to supportive school leadership, dedicated and collegial staff, standardized behavior management techniques, and effective scholastic instruction as educational factors that can minimize the potential risks of juvenile delinquency (2005, p. 69).

Structural/Political Factors

Since *A Call for Justice* was published in 1995, several states have examined their access to counsel and the quality of their legal representation in delinquency proceedings. The American Bar Association and the Mid-Atlantic Juvenile Defender Center partnered with several law and research groups to study Virginia's representation in juvenile court in 2002 (Puritz, Scali, & Picou, 2002). One of their key findings indicated that youth of color are disparately treated in the Commonwealth; some of the reasons offered were biased police patrol, lack of parental empowerment, and access to resources (including satisfactory counsel). The assessment identified significant gaps in indigent defense practices and suggested that the system, as it is currently structured, has a "disproportionate impact on poor and minority children" (Puritz et al., p. 1).

Racial/Cultural Factors

Various racial and cultural factors can contribute to both risk and resiliency. Smokowski, David-Ferdon, and Stroupe (2009) examined the intersection of acculturation and violence for Latino, Asian/Pacific Islander, and American Indian/Alaska Native adolescents and identified racial/cultural factors with both risk and protective elements; e.g., greater adolescent assimilation corresponded to increased risk factors for youth violence whereas ethnic identity and involvement were seen as cultural assets against youth violence (p. 215). OJJDP's DMC Contributing Mechanisms include the element of differential treatment. Differential treatment is explained by this statement, "Minority youth are processed differently based on intentional or unintentional bias. Intentional bias is overt and operates on stereotypes and assumptions. Unintentional bias is typically indirect and operates through legitimate criteria but disadvantages minority youth."

Spiritual Factors

One factor that is relatively unstudied is religiosity/spirituality. Using the 2008 National Survey on Drug Use and Health's sample of 17,705 adolescents, researchers investigated the relationships between latent religiosity classes and substance use, violence, and delinquency (Salas-Wright, Vaughn, Hodge, & Perron, 2012). They found that participation in the religiously devoted classes was associated with a decreased likelihood of substance use behaviors, fighting, and theft (p. 1560).

In addition to the myriad of factors that can contribute to DMC, once minority overrepresentation occurs, there is often a cumulative effect (Pope et al., 2002), or what the DMC Technical Assistance Manual (2009) refers to as an "amplification phenomenon." Piquero (2008) attests that "the racial differences that begin with juvenile involvement in crime become larger as youth make their way through the different stages of the juvenile justice system... At each stage of the system, minority representation grows larger and at a faster rate than that of whites" (p. 60). Detained youth were found to be twice as likely to be adjudicated delinquent as youth who were not detained prior to adjudication (Wu, Cernkovich, & Dunn, 1997), and although minorities represented 29% of cases sent to intake, youth of color represented 44% of the cases sent to youth prisons/waived to adult court (Bishop & Frazier, 1996). And, as noted previously, studies have found that minority overrepresentation occurs at each decision point within the juvenile justice system, from arrest to secure confinement/transfer (Leiber, 2002; NCCD, 2007).

■ Themes to Address DMC

Based on decades of study, the OJJDP's DMC "lessons learned" (DMC Technical Assistance Manual, 2009) and juvenile justice advocates' recommendations

(Juvenile Justice and Delinquency Prevention Coalition, 2008) suggest four prominent themes to address DMC:

1 Create systems to collect local data at every point of contact for youth in the juvenile justice system (disaggregated by variables such as race, ethnicity, offense, etc.)

2 Sustain DMC reduction efforts with support from the top as well from the informed public, strong collaborative partnerships across agencies, and a coordinating body to oversee the efforts

3 Use multipronged interventions with measurable objectives and outcomes

4 Conduct program evaluation and progress reports regularly and report these findings publicly

Create Systems to Collect Local Data at Every Point of Contact for Youth

The true extent of DMC may be masked by the lack of consistency in data collection across states (Leiber & Rodriguez, 2011). Data collection strategies should include statewide systems that track individuals from first contact with law enforcement through each decision point, link legal variables with extralegal variables, and disaggregate data by both race and ethnicity. In 2007, Kimberly Kempf-Leonard wrote,

> After nearly 20 years of the federally supported DMC initiative in juvenile justice, levels of minority overrepresentation remain uncomfortably high in most states and at the national level... First, we must understand what characteristics of minority status merit attention... Second, we need to apply uniform definitions to youths' offending and assessments of their personal needs... only with these two improvements... is it then possible to assess the role of juvenile justice decisions in differential treatment. (pp. 82–83)

Level of discretion and review/appeal protocol at the various decision points have also been found to affect processing and outcomes (Leiber Bishop, & Chamlin, 2011; Piquero, 2008). The first point of contact is usually with law enforcement, school officials, intake personnel, or social services practitioners, and these officials are often afforded higher levels of discretion with less scrutiny than personnel at other stages. And, as noted earlier, once youth enter the system, the effects of racial and ethnic disparities accumulate as they move through the justice system.

Moreover, one elementary component that hampers many juvenile jurisdictions is the fact that ethnic identity is either not captured at all or youth are forced to choose between race and ethnicity (e.g., Circle one: Black, White, Hispanic, Asian, or "Other"). Villarruel and colleagues (2002) suggest that when Latino/a youth are classified as White, the extent of ethnic overrepresentation cannot be assessed accurately. Similarly, some practitioners argue that data collection should include primary language, language spoken at home, English language proficiency of youth and his/her family, and so forth, such that culturally and linguistically sensitive services can be provided (Mauer & King, 2007).

Given the growing percentage of Latino/a youth in the United States and the demonstrated cumulative effect of DMC on youth of color, establishing accurate and consistent definitions of minority status including ethnic identity is important. Whereas DMC may have originally been considered a Black/White issue, similar effects are being experienced at disproportionate rates for youth of other races and ethnic groups. For example, Latino/a youth are 4% more likely to be petitioned, 16% more likely to be adjudicated delinquent, 28% more likely to be detained, and 41% more likely to receive an out-of-home placement than are White youth—as evidenced in Table 21.3. Similar to the experience of African-American youth, the greatest disparity is evident at the harshest disposition for juveniles, transfer to adult court: Latino/a youth are 43% more likely than Whites to be transferred to the adult system and

Table 21.3 **2010 Placement Status Counts for Youth Aged 13 to 17 by Race/Ethnicity**

Count	White	Black	Hispanic	American Indian	Asian	Pacific Islander	Total
Detained: Await juvenile court adjudication	135	49	147	30	10	12	383
Detained: Adjudicated-await disposition	42	17	42	5	0	1	107
Detained: Adjudicated-await placement	119	68	124	5	0	2	318
Detained: Await transfer hearing	1	0	0	0	0	0	1
Detained: Await criminal court hearing	5	4	47	0	3	0	59
Committed: Adjudicated, placed here	3,661	5,214	2,578	277	72	47	11,849
Committed: Convicted, criminal court	78	273	234	3	8	1	597
Diversion	3	1	1	7	0	0	12
Total	4,044	5,626	3,173	327	93	63	13,326

Source: Sickmund, M., Sladky, T. J., Kang, W., & Puzzanchera, C. (2011). *Easy Access to the Census of Juveniles in Residential Placement.* Available: http://www.ojjdp.gov/ojstatbb/ezacjrp/

40% more likely to be admitted to adult prison (Arya, Villarruel, Villanueva, & Augarten, 2009). Finally, juvenile justice data tracking does not include changes in U.S. demographic and immigration patterns, and data for non-Black minority youth (e.g., Latinos/as, Native Americans, Asian Americans) are "virtually non-existent" in FBI-reported data as well as self-report studies of crime and delinquency (Piquero, 2008).

Sustain DMC Reduction Efforts

Soler and Garry (2009) recommend establishing a steering committee that includes key stakeholders from the juvenile justice system (e.g., chief judge from juvenile court, police captain, senior public defender, senior prosecutor/District Attorney, and chief court counselor). They suggest that these stakeholders are essential in ensuring that committee decisions are implemented and that these high-level leaders attest to the priority and importance of DMC reduction across systems and agencies. The steering committee should also include nontraditional stakeholders (e.g., child/parent advocates, directors of community organizations, civil rights leaders, educators, practitioners) as well as youth (and their families) who are currently or have recently been in the system. Cook County, IL (South Suburbs), has an example of a successful DMC workgroup that includes these various stakeholders. Soler and Garry conclude:

> Community representatives often understand the program and service delivery needs of youth, families, and communities in greater context. Reductions in overrepresentation cannot be sustained without an infrastructure of effective community-based detention alternatives, diversion, and other programs to address and prevent youth involvement in the criminal justice system. (p. 5)

Use Multipronged Interventions with Measurable Objectives and Outcomes

Moving beyond identification and assessment/diagnosis and into intervention and evaluation will improve the assessment of the role of juvenile justice decisions in differential treatment. Leiber and Rodriguez (2011) note three trends in addressing minority overrepresentation: direct service provision, training and technical assistance, and broader system change. Juvenile justice practitioners are involved with all three. First, direct service provision would include presentence reports, intake assessments, mental health and substance abuse counseling, various intervention and therapy programs, probation and parole services, and corrections. Second, training and technical assistance would include cultural sensitivity/humility, research and data expertise (including how to construct and use RRIs), social programming techniques, program evaluation, and so forth. Finally, broader system change could be achieved through policy analysis, advocacy, and law-making/policy-setting for offenders, victims, and their families. Kempf-Leonard states, "scholars now recognize the need to apply useful ecological perspectives to understand local conditions that put minority youths at a differential risk" (2007, p. 82).

Leiber and Rodriguez (2011) further contend that "it is imperative that both differential offending and system issues be part of the conversation on the implementation of the DMC mandate" (p. 118). Huizinga and colleagues (2007) conducted a study with youth in Pittsburgh, Rochester, and Seattle and found clear evidence of DMC at each site; DMC could not be explained by variations in the offending behaviors of different racial groups, and it was reduced by considering the combined effect of a number of additional risk factors. Practitioners can work to bolster the protective factors while minimizing the risk factors and potentially mitigate the effects of extralegal variables.

The James D. and Catherine T. MacArthur Foundation created the Models for Change program, which:

> supports a network of government and court officials, legal advocates, educators, community leaders, and families working together to ensure that kids who make mistakes are held accountable and treated fairly throughout the juvenile justice process. [They] provide research-based tools and techniques to make juvenile justice more fair, effective, rational and developmentally-appropriate. (www.modelsforchange.net/about/index.html, paragraph #1)

The Models for Change reform initiative began with juvenile justice reform in four states and now is working on mental health services, juvenile indigent defense, and ethnic disparities in 12 additional states. One particular project in Pennsylvania seeks to reduce racial and ethnic disparities by working to incorporate data into decision making, improve data, implement objective screening tools, develop alternatives to detention and out-of-home placement, create graduated responses for youth on probation, practice with linguistic and cultural competence, and strengthen youth–police relationships (Shoenberg, 2012). Their results are encouraging. In Berks County, PA, the efforts were able to reduce the use of detention 60% from 2007 to 2011 such that on average, 16 fewer Latino youth and 5 fewer African-American youth were in detention on any given day. Use of out-of-home placement was also reduced 67% between 2007 and 2012 from 339 placements per year to 111, saving the county approximately $2 million per year. From this project, practitioners strongly suggest involving nontraditional and diverse stakeholders, creating methods of regular data collection and analysis, funding the dissemination of findings and results, and finally remembering that change takes time, courage, leadership, and sustained commitment (Shoenberg, 2012).

Conduct Program Evaluation/Progress Reports Regularly and Report These Findings Publicly

Reauthorization of the JJDPA is an opportunity to strengthen accountability for and evaluation of DMC reduction efforts. Currently, the JJDPA language instructs states to address DMC by sustaining five efforts: (1) identify the extent to which DMC exists, (2) assess the reasons for DMC (if it exists), (3) develop an intervention plan to address these identified reasons, (4) evaluate the effectiveness of strategies to address DMC, and (5) monitor DMC trends over time (Pope et al., 2002). States are in various stages within these five phases (Leiber, 2002), and few have demonstrated ongoing and sustained efforts (Leiber & Rodriguez, 2011). Regarding phases 4 (evaluation) and 5 (monitoring), Leiber and Rodriguez (2011) argue that even though it has been 20 years since the DMC mandate was implemented, few evaluations of DMC reduction strategies have been conducted, and overall there has been a "lack of systematic evaluation of the success of specific initiatives across multiple jurisdictions" (p. 114).

Some states certainly need additional training and resources to address DMC and be compliant with this core protection. Learning to adopt best practices bolsters states' abilities to differentiate and replicate effective juvenile justice programming, and training, coupled with incentive grants, may encourage states to evaluate and implement best practices in juvenile justice reform and collect outcome data on program effectiveness. In addition to supporting and evaluating states' compliance with JJDPA core protections, greater transparency and accountability would therefore be achieved by making states' reports publicly available. The OJJDP administration should be required to investigate and report issues of noncompliance—at the very least, this might prevent future civil rights investigation and litigation. Schoenberg (2012) states that in jurisdictions that have successfully instituted policy and practice changes, fairness and equity are now a lasting part of the agency and court culture.

In sum, OJJDP recognizes that "DMC is the result of a number of complex decisions and events and that only through a comprehensive, balanced, and multi-disciplinary approach can the states and localities reduce DMC" (DMC Technical Assistance Manual, 2009, p. 2). Cabaniss, Frabutt, Kendrick, and Arbuckle (2007) contend that despite the emotionally charged tenor of race and social injustice, some communities are able to transcend the defensiveness and divisiveness by examining data and decision point maps that clearly delineate the extent of the problem. This requires a deeper examination than can be provided by RRIs. Finally, Bishop (2005) suggests that "understanding the intervening mechanisms is essential if we are to replace 'stab in the dark' efforts to reduce disproportionate minority confinement with strategic changes in policy and practice that hold more promise for success" (p. 24).

■ Case Example

■ *This is a true detention story relayed without identifying case details by a North Carolina juvenile court judge who, affected by this incident and others, now serves on the Race Matters for Juvenile Justice Steering Committee, www.rmjj.org.*

I was presiding in Juvenile Delinquency Court conducting Detention and First Appearance Hearings. In North Carolina, all juveniles charged with felony offenses must come to Court immediately after being charged to be apprised of their charges and legal rights, to inform their parents of expectations for guardians in juvenile court, and to determine whether they should be detained or released to their parents. Depending on the severity of the offense and the juveniles' past delinquency history they may or may not already be detained. That determination is made based on recommendations from arresting officers and juvenile court counselors (JCCs) at the time the youth is charged. If the JCC believes the juvenile meets the criteria for detention and is a danger to the community s/he seeks a secured custody order from a judge, which then allows the juvenile to be arrested and detained pending his/her first appearance. On this particular day, there were a number of juveniles on the first appearance docket with a wide variety of charges—some were already in detention while others remained home with their families. I began plowing through my cases.

About midway through my afternoon hearings, I called the first of two co-defendants charged with armed robbery. The juvenile came in what I sometimes call "door number 2," meaning the bailiffs brought him into the courtroom from a holding cell. The juvenile was in shackles and had been in custody since he was charged a day earlier. Frankly, I expected him to be in detention, since armed robberies are among the most serious offenses we see in juvenile court. Almost all juveniles charged with this offense are detained at their first appearance. Many remain in detention until their cases are adjudicated and disposed. Others are released at some point prior to adjudication, with very restrictive conditions of release. For example, the young person might be placed on house arrest with an electronic monitor or released on a very strict supervision plan called the ATD or alternative to detention program. As expected, the young man came into court with the deputies, while his family filed into the courtroom from the lobby. He had a huge number of family members and friends supporting him, many more than I usually see. His parents were present, along with aunts, uncles, and grandparents. In addition, his youth pastor was there to speak on the juvenile's behalf. It turns out that the juvenile and his co-defendant "planned," and I use that term loosely, the crime after watching *Oceans 11* or some other heist movie. At any rate, they decided they would conduct their own heist at a local fast-food restaurant. They entered with matching "Scream" Halloween masks on their faces, each of them carrying handguns. Well, they turned out to be pellet guns, but they looked like real weapons. It turns out that they were horrible criminals. Both were caught almost immediately and charged. Co-defendant 1, I will call him "John," had no delinquent record, was an average student at school, had never been suspended from or expelled from school, had a tremendous family support system, and was extremely active in positive activities in his church. In balancing safety to the community with the strengths of the juvenile and the many positive supports in his life, I recommended an assessment to determine if ATD or other conditions would be appropriate and scheduled a detention hearing four days later. I fully anticipated that the juvenile would be deemed appropriate for our ATD program and released at his next hearing.

Following John's hearing, I called in his co-defendant, who I will refer to as "Sam." When I called in the case, again a huge contingent of family and supporters came into Court on behalf of Sam. Rather than a pastor, a coach from the juvenile's school appeared to attest to his good character. Meanwhile, my bailiff stood in the courtroom next to the holding cell door. After a few moments, I reminded him that we needed the youth to be brought into the courtroom from the holding cell. He said, "Judge, we don't have any more juveniles in the back. I think that's the young man you want right there." With that he pointed to a young man in the courtroom, who had come in with the rest of the family. His lawyer agreed that this was "Sam" and ushered him to the defendant's table. The remainder of the hearing was much the same. I found out that Sam had no delinquent record, was an average student at school, had never been suspended or expelled from school, had a tremendous family support system, and was extremely active in positive activities with his sports team. I also found out that Sam and John had been best friends since first grade, that they lived one street over from one another, and that their families were also friendly with one another. Oddly, no one in my courtroom (defense attorneys, DAs, JCCs, or anyone else) raised the elephant in the room, namely that John was in detention and Sam was home with his family. So I asked what led to this difference and couldn't find any factor, save one. Besides their very similar backgrounds, both had weapons during the robbery, both participated actively during the crime, and both planned their heist together. The fact that the reader, along with everyone in every audience to whom I've relayed this story, knows that the difference involves race, and that John is African-American and Sam is White, pretty much sums up how implicit bias continues to play a role in our justice system. From my knowledge of those involved I do not believe that in this case there was any intention to treat these two young men differently, but implicit bias is insidious and leads to many disparities within our juvenile justice system.

Note

1   The JJDPA was last reauthorized in 2002. In 2009 it was presented again for reauthorization through Senate Bills 3155 and 678, but as of this printing it has yet to be reauthorized.

References

Amato, P. R. (2000). The consequences of divorce for adults and children. *Journal of Marriage and the Family, 62*(4), 1269–1287.

Arya, N., Villarruel, F., Villanueva, C., & Augarten, I. (2009, May). *America's invisible children: Latino youth and the failure of justice.* Washington, DC: Campaign for Youth Justice.

Bishop, D. (2005). The role of race and ethnicity in juvenile justice processing. In D. Hawkins & K. K. Leonard (Eds.), *Our children, their children: Confronting racial and ethnic differences in American Juvenile Justice* (pp. 23–82). Chicago, IL: The University of Chicago Press.

Bishop, D., & Frazier, C. (1996). Race effects in juvenile justice decision-making: Findings of a statewide analysis. *Journal of Criminal Law and Criminology, 86*, 392–413.

Bishop, D., Leiber, M., & Johnson, J. (2010). Contexts of decision making in the juvenile justice system: An organizational approach to understanding minority overrepresentation. *Journal of Youth Violence & Juvenile Justice, 8*(3), 213–233. doi:10:1177/1541204009361177

Cabaniss, E. R., Frabutt, J. M., Kendrick, M. H., & Arbuckle, M. B. (2007). Reducing disproportionate minority contact in the juvenile justice system: Promising practices. *Aggression and Violent Behavior, 12*, 393–401. doi:10.1016/j.avb.2006.09.004.

Christle, C. A., Jolivette, K., & Nelson, C. M. (2005). Breaking the school to prison pipeline: Identifying school risk and protective factors for youth delinquency. *Exceptionality, 13*(2), 69–88.

DMC Technical Assistance Manual (2009, July). *Disproportionate minority contact: Technical assistance manual* (4th ed.). U.S. Department of Justice, Office of Justice Programs, Office of Juvenile Justice and Delinquency Prevention. Available online: www.ncjrs.gov/html/ojjdp/dmc_ta_manual/

Eitle, D. (2006). Parental gender, single-parent families, and delinquency: Exploring the moderating influence of race/ethnicity. *Social Science Research, 35*(3), 727–748.

Hartney, C., & Vuong, L. (2009). *Created equal: Racial and ethnic disparities in the U.S. Criminal Justice System.* Oakland, CA: National Council on Crime & Delinquency.

Huizinga, D., Thornberry, T., Knight, K., & Lovegrove, P. (2007). *Disproportionate minority contact in the juvenile justice system: A study of differential minority arrest/referral to court in three cities.* U.S. Department of Justice, Document No. 219743.

Johnson, S., Blum, R., & Giedd, J. (2009). Adolescent maturity and the brain: The promise and pitfalls of neuroscience research in adolescent health policy. *Journal of Adolescent Health, 45*(3), 216–221. doi:10.1016/j.jadohealth.2009.05.016

Juvenile Justice and Delinquency Prevention Coalition (2008). *Juvenile Justice and Delinquency Prevention Act (JJDPA) recommendations and background.* Act 4 Juvenile Justice. www.act4jj.org

Kempf-Leonard, K. (2007). Minority youths and juvenile justice: Disproportionate minority contact after nearly 20 years of reform efforts. *Youth Violence and Juvenile Justice, 5*(1), 71–87.

Knoll, C., & Sickmund, M. (2012). *Delinquency cases in juvenile court, 2009.* National Center for Juvenile Justice Office of Juvenile Justice and Delinquency Prevention, NCJ 239081. Available online: http://www.ojjdp.gov/ojstatbb/

Leiber, M. J. (2002). Disproportionate minority confinement (DMC) of youth: An analysis of state and federal efforts to address the issue. *Crime & Delinquency, 48*(1), 3–45.

Leiber, M., Bishop, D., & Chamlin, M. B. (2011). Juvenile justice decision-making before and after the implementation of the Disproportionate Minority Contact (DMC) Mandate. *Justice Quarterly, 28*(3), 460–492. doi:10.1080/07418825.2010.516005

Leiber, M., & Mack, K. (2003). Race, age, and juvenile justice processing. *Journal of Crime & Justice, 25*(2), 23–47.

Leiber, M., & Rodriguez, N. (2011). The implementation of the disproportionate minority confinement/contact (DMC) mandate: A failure or success? *Race and Justice, 1*(1), 103–124. doi:10.1177/2153368710377614

Mauer, M., & King, R. S. (2007). *Uneven justice: State rates of incarceration by race and ethnicity.* Washington, DC: The Sentencing Project, 2007.

McCarter, S. A. (2009a). Legal and extralegal factors affecting minority overrepresentation in Virginia's juvenile justice system: A mixed method study. *Child and Adolescent Social Work Journal, 26*(6), 533–534. doi:10.1007/s10560-009-0185-x

McCarter, S. A. (2009b). *Micro, mezzo, and macro implications of minority overrepresentation in juvenile justice: A social work perspective.* Paper presented at the Thirteenth Annual Conference of the Society for Social Work Research, New Orleans, LA.

McCarter, S. A. (2011). Disproportionate minority contact in the American juvenile justice system: Where are we after 20 years, a philosophy shift, and three amendments? *Journal of Forensic Social Work, 1*(1), 96–107. doi:10.1080/1936928x.2011.541217

McCarter, S. A., & Bridges, J. B. (2011). Determining the age of jurisdiction for adolescents: The policy debate. *Journal of Policy Practice, 10*(3), 168–184. doi:10.1080/155887/42.2011.582805

Megens, K. C. I. M., & Weerman, F. M. (2011). The social transmission of delinquency: Effects of peer attitudes and behavior revisited. *Journal of Research in Crime and Delinquency, 49*(3), 420–443. doi:10.1177/0022427811408432.

Models for Change. www.modelsforchange.net

Piquero, A. (2008). Disproportionate minority contact. *The Future of Children, 18*, 60–61.

Pope, C. E., & Leiber, M. (2005). Disproportionate minority contact (DMC): The federal initiative. In D. Hawkins & K. Kempf-Leonard (Eds.), *Our children, their children: Confronting racial and ethnic differences in American juvenile justice* (pp. 351–389). Chicago, IL: The University of Chicago Press.

Pope, C. E., Lovell, R., & Hsia, H. (2002). *Disproportionate minority confinement: A review of the research literature from 1989 to 2001.* Washington, DC: U.S. Department of Justice, Office of Juvenile Justice and Delinquency Prevention.

Public Law 93-415, Section 223 [a][23], Juvenile Justice and Delinquency Prevention Act of 1974.

Puritz, P., Scali, M. A., & Picou, I. (2002). *An assessment of access to counsel and quality of representation in delinquency proceedings.* The American Bar Association Juvenile Justice Center & Mid-Atlantic Juvenile Defender Center.

Puzzanchera, C., & Adams, B. (2008). *National disproportionate minority contact databook.* Developed by the National Center for Juvenile Justice for the Office of Juvenile Justice and Delinquency Prevention. Online. Available: http://www.ojjdp.gov/ojstatbb/dmcdb/

Puzzanchera, C., & Adams, B. (2012). *National disproportionate minority contact databook.* Developed by the National Center for Juvenile Justice for the Office of Juvenile Justice and Delinquency Prevention. Online. Available: http://www.ojjdp.gov/ojstatbb/dmcdb/

Puzzanchera, C., Adams, B., & Hockenberry, S. (2012). *Juvenile court statistics 2009.* Pittsburgh, PA: National Center for Juvenile Justice.

Roper v. Simmons (2005). 543 U.S. 551, 1125 W. 3d 397.

Salas-Wright, C. P., Vaughn, M. G., Hodge, D. R., & Perron, B. E. (2012). Religiosity profiles of American youth in relation to substance use, violence, and delinquency. *Journal of Youth & Adolescence, 41*, 1560–1575. doi:10.1007/s10964-012-9761-z.

Schoenberg, D. (2012, December). *Innovation brief: Reducing racial and ethnic disparities in Pennsylvania.* Models for Change. Available: www.modelsforchange.net

Sickmund, M., Sladky, T. J., Kang, W., & Puzzanchera, C. (2011). *Easy access to the census of juveniles in r* Available: http://www.ojjdp.gov/ojstatbb/ezacjrp/

Simões, C., Matos, M. G., & Batista-Foguet, J. M. (2008). Juvenile delinquency: Analysis of risk and protective factors using quantitative and qualitative methods. *Cognition, Brain, & Behavior: An Interdisciplinary Journal, 13*(4), 389–408.

Smokowski, P., David-Ferdon, C., & Stroupe, N. (2009). Acculturation and violence in minority adolescents: A review of the empirical literature. *Journal of Primary Prevention, 30*(3–4), 215–263. doi:10.1007/s10935-009-0173-0

Soler, M., & Garry, L. M. (2009). *Reducing disproportionate minority contact: Preparation at the local level.* Washington, DC: U.S. Department of Justice, Office of Juvenile Justice and Delinquency Prevention.

Vallas, R. (2009). The disproportionality problem: The overrepresentation of Black students in special education and recommendations for reform. *Virginia Journal of Social Policy & the Law, 17*(1), 181–208.

Villarruel, F. A., Walker, N. E., Minifee, P., Rivera-Vasquez, O., Peterson, S., & Perry, K. (2002). *¿Donde esta la justicia? A call to action on behalf of Latino and Latina youth in the U.S. justice system.* East Lansing, MI: Institute for Children, Youth, and Families, Michigan State University. NCJ 196500. http://www.ncjrs.gov/App/Publications/abstract.aspx?ID=196500

Wu, B., Cernkovich, S., & Dunn, C. S. (1997). Assessing the effects of race and class on juvenile justice processing in Ohio. *Journal of Criminal Justice, 25,* 265–277.

22 The Wayward Girl in the 21st Century: Female Pathways to Delinquency

Lisa Pasko, Scott K. Okamoto, and Meda Chesney-Lind

The objectives of this chapter are as follows:

- ☐ Describe the history and current state of girls' offending and their consequent growth and involvement in courts and corrections
- ☐ Develop feminist criminological theories to female delinquency
- ☐ Demonstrate how girls' law-breaking and justice experiences are rooted in the social conditions of their lives and in the "gendered" expectations of law enforcement agencies
- ☐ Critically examine girls' violence and aggression
- ☐ Summarize needed directions in gender-based juvenile justice initiatives

Historically research on delinquency and the juvenile justice system has mostly focused on male offenders. Gender was rarely explicitly and candidly examined, and consequently girls were often forgotten or relegated to a footnote. Critiquing mainstream criminology for the repeated omission of girls as offenders and victims, early feminist criminologists began conducting empirical studies of the female juvenile offender and demonstrated that explanations of their criminal activities were often riddled with unfounded assumptions and stereotypes (Belknap, 2007; Chesney-Lind & Pasko, 2013). Currently, a growing body of research has kept gender in the foreground of criminological analysis, as many studies have explicated the life experiences, backgrounds, and environments associated with female offending (see Chesney-Lind & Pasko, 2013; Miller, 2008). Further studies have also explored the historical status of girls in the justice system as well as their contemporary growth in correctional populations (Pasko, 2010). In addition, other recent scholarship has insisted on blurring the dichotomies of "girls as victims" and "girls as offenders" and, instead, has conceptualized their offending as ultimately linked to previous victimization experiences (Belknap, 2007; Bloom et al., 2004; Britton, 2000; Chesney-Lind & Pasko, 2013; Daly, 1994).

This chapter highlights girls' experiences inside and outside the justice system. First, it reviews both historically and contemporarily the judicial response as well as the scope of girls' law violations, along with the reasons and justifications for girls' commitment to reformatories and detention facilities. Second, it explicates feminist theoretical explanations for girls' delinquency, underscoring the "pathways perspective" and showing how girls' offenses are inextricably linked to their prior victimization experiences. Third, this chapter takes a critical examination of girls' violence and animates how changes in school and law enforcement policies have affected girls' arrest rates for assault. Lastly, this chapter ends with policy and programming recommendations and future directions.

■ Introduction

In the early years of the juvenile justice system, adolescent offenders were viewed as "little adults," often receiving punishments commensurate with those of older lawbreakers. By the late 1800s, increases in immigration, urbanization, poverty, and industrial jobs launched societal concerns and a subsequent larger Progressive movement—a Child Savers movement—that aimed to "save" poor, delinquent children from themselves and their morally neglected surroundings (Champion, 2001; Platt, 1977). With *ex parte Crouse* (1839), the Pennsylvania Supreme Court elaborated the doctrine of *parens patriae*, establishing that the state has authority to remove children from improperly supervised households and that the state has the responsibility to care for those who are legally incapable of caring for themselves. By the early 1900s, the first juvenile courts (or family courts as they are now known in many states) were established in Chicago, Denver, and San Francisco. Because incarceration with adult offenders did not seem to deter these youth from criminal behavior, social reformists also founded separate correctional institutions for juvenile offenders (Chesney-Lind & Pasko, 2013). Called Houses of Refuge, these reform schools' primary goal was to provide discipline and education to incorrigible youth who lacked desirable character (Platt, 1977).

Despite the fact that boys represented the overwhelming majority of criminally involved youth, girls were not exempt from the control and authority of the juvenile court and reform schools. With a specific focus on the "wayward girl," the Child Savers movement provided an opportunity to patrol the puritanical boundaries of sexuality. Particularly concerned with prostitution, promiscuity, and the "fallen," rescue homes, homes for unwed mothers, and girls' reformatories served the multiple functions of teaching domestic skills and "impressing acceptable moral attitudes and religious devotion, providing prenatal and natal care and containing girls' sexuality and venereal disease" (Knupfer, 2001, p. 90). Studies of early family court activity revealed that virtually all the girls who appeared in these courts were charged for "immorality" or "waywardness." For example, "in Honolulu during 1929 to 1930, over half of the girls referred to court were charged with immorality, which meant evidence of sexual intercourse" (Chesney-Lind & Pasko, 2013, p. 57). Whereas the first juvenile court originally defined "delinquent" as those under 16 who had violated a city ordinance or law, when the definition was applied to girls, the court included "up to the age of eighteen when activities included incorrigibility (beyond parental control), associations with lascivious or immoral persons, vagrancy, frequent attendance at pool halls or saloons, immoral conduct, and use of indecent language" (Knupfer, 2001, p. 81). Ultimately, many of the activities of the Child Savers and early juvenile courts revolved around policing the behavior of working-class and immigrant girls to prevent their straying from a "moral" path.

Throughout the years, girls with minor law violations but "serious" moral infractions have repeatedly populated the juvenile justice system. For example, Brenzel (1983) writes that in late 1800s in Lancaster, Massachusetts, girls were sentenced to reform school in order "to punish petty larceny; to supply a home; to affect moral salvation; to prevent further lewd acts; and to provide protection from physical abuse." In addition, Brenzel points out that "In every case, the need to alleviate some form of deprivation was apparent" (p. 130). Knupfer (2001) found similar themes in her analysis of the early juvenile court in Chicago. Between 1904 and 1927, 60% to 70% of delinquent girls placed on probation or in institutions were first-time offenders, and virtually all of them were brought in on charges of incorrigibility. Undeniably, judges more frequently institutionalized girls than boys for sexual delinquency or immorality, considering it a "more dangerous" sex offense (Pasko, 2008a). Embedded in these deliberations was a dichotomous image of girls—one of a victim or an errant, yet essentially good, girl and another of a "sexualized demon" who was a danger not just to herself but to the larger society (Knupfer, 2001). Additionally, nearly all girls who had sex with more than one partner were institutionalized, and nearly 70% of them were victims of incest.

An examination of judicial sentiments and sentencing practices of girls throughout the mid-20th century demonstrates few changes in the system. In 1940, girls in Los Angeles were overwhelmingly referred to family court for status offenses (78%), such as running away from home, truancy, curfew violations, or "general unruliness at home." Nearly half of the status offenders were charged directly with sexual misconduct, although most were found to have not engaged in any form of prostitution and it was often with a single partner (Odem & Schlossman, 1991). In 1956, according to the President's Commission on Law Enforcement and the Administration of Justice, half of the girls petitioned to the juvenile court were appearing for status offenses, as compared with only one fifth of the boys (Jolly, 1979). In 1970, large numbers of girls in New Jersey were committed to training schools for "their own protection" and as a means of preventing pregnancy (Chesney-Lind & Pasko, 2013). Lastly, Andrews and Cohn (1974) found in 1972 that judges in New York had continued concerns about girls' morality, as did their personal and stereotypical opinions of girls as sexual manipulators and troublemakers. Consequently, girls, in comparison to their male counterparts, were sentenced more harshly for status offenses and, despite the absence of serious law violations, were as likely as boys to be institutionalized.

By the late 1970s, correctional reformers, concerned about abuse of the status offense category by juvenile courts (though not necessarily about girls), were instrumental in urging the U.S. Congress to pass the Juvenile Justice and Delinquency Prevention Act of 1974 (JJDPA). This legislation required that states receiving federal delinquency prevention money begin to divert and deinstitutionalize their status offenders. Despite erratic enforcement of this provision and considerable resistance from juvenile court judges, girls were the clear beneficiaries of the reform. Incarceration of young women in training schools and detention centers across the country fell dramatically in the decades since its passage, which is in distinct contrast to patterns found early in the century. However, recent years (mid-1990s to current day) have seen a steady increase in girls' arrests, petitions to juvenile court, and commitments.

While girls' offenses continue to be fairly minor, they are now conspicuous at every level of the justice system.

Modern Juvenile Justice: Girls Inside and Outside the System

The pattern of arresting, adjudicating, and institutionalizing girls for minor offenses, status offenses, and sexual misconduct continues today in the juvenile justice system. Under a paternalistic ideology, police, courts, and other juvenile justice players (probation officers, as a primary example) exercise the repeated need to "protect their daughters, usually from sexual experimentation and other dangers on the streets" (Chesney-Lind & Sheldon 2004, p. 171). Indeed, the majority of girls' arrests and referrals to juvenile court continue to be for status (namely, running away and truancy) and low-level property offenses (larceny theft), while the judicial focus on girls' sexuality, along with the bifurcated image of the good girl versus promiscuous female juvenile offender remains static. For example, in 2011, less than a third of girls' arrests were for Part I offenses (murder, forcible rape, robbery, aggravated assault, burglary, larceny, motor vehicle theft, and arson), and of these Part I arrests, 83% were for larceny/theft. Indeed, low-level theft, low-level assault, and curfew violations made up nearly half of all girls' arrests (Federal Bureau of Investigation, 2012). Yet girls continue to be an ever-increasing portion of the overall juvenile justice system. In 1975, girls represented 15% of all juvenile arrests; in 1990, they represented 19%; by 2012, they were nearly 32% (Federal Bureau of Investigation, 2007; Steffensmeier, 1993).

Juvenile court data also suggest a similar trend. Whereas boys represent the majority of cases handled by juvenile courts, girls in the 21st century represent over one quarter of all delinquency cases, nearly a 100% increase over the past 20 years (Office of Juvenile Justice and Delinquency Prevention, 2006). Increases in female caseloads as well as the proportion of girls' cases petitioned to juvenile court have outpaced boys. Over the past 20 years, the number of girls formally adjudicated as delinquent doubled; the number of boys formally adjudicated as delinquent grew by only 33% (Puzzanchera & Kang, 2011).

Girls have also become an increasing proportion of juveniles in custody, with one out of seven youth in residential placements now female (Sickmund et al., 2011). Girls being detained for "violent" offenses were far more likely than boys to be held on "other person" offenses like simple assault (as opposed to more serious, Index violent offenses like aggravated assault, robbery, and murder). One fifth of the girls but less than 10% of the boys in residential placement were held for these minor forms of violence (Sickmund et al., 2011).

Girls are also disproportionately more likely to be admitted to training schools or group homes, whereas boys are more likely to receive day treatment (Chesney-Lind & Sheldon, 2004). Some of the increase in public facilities is due to changes in health care policies. As more health management organizations deny coverage for residential behavioral programs and long-term mental health treatment, more parents seek the juvenile justice system (and, consequently, public commitments) as a means of handling their "unruly" daughters (Chesney-Lind & Pasko, 2013).

"Bootstrapping" Status Offenses

Judges have long engaged in efforts like "violation of a valid court order" or issuing contempt citations to "bootstrap" status offenders into categories that permit their detention. They thereby circumvent the deinstitutionalization component of the JJDPA (Costello & Worthington, 1981). These judicial maneuvers clearly disadvantage girls. For example, Bishop and Frazier (1992) reviewed 162,012 cases referred to juvenile justice intake units in Florida during 1985–87. The researchers found only a weak pattern of discrimination against female status offenders compared to the treatment of male status offenders. However, when they examined the impact of contempt citations, the pattern changed markedly: they found that female offenders referred for contempt were more likely than females referred for other criminal-type offenses to be petitioned to court, and were substantially more likely to be petitioned to court than males referred for contempt. Moreover, the girls were far more likely than boys to be sentenced to detention. Specifically, the typical female offender in their study had a probability of incarceration of 4.3%, which increased to 29.9% if she were held in contempt. Such a pattern was not observed among the males in the study. The authors concluded:

> The traditional double standard is still operative. Clearly neither the cultural changes associated with the feminist movement nor the legal changes illustrated in the JJDP Act's mandate to deinstitutionalize status offenders have brought about equality under the law for young men and women. (p. 1186)

Essentially, once girls were released on probation in the 1990s, they were more likely than boys to return to detention, usually for a technical violation of the conditions of their probation. A study by the American Bar Association and the National Bar Association (2001) found that not only were girls more likely than boys to be detained, but they were also more likely "to be sent back to detention after release. Although girls' rates of recidivism are lower than those of boys, the use of contempt proceedings and probation and parole violations make it more likely that, without committing a new crime, girls will return to detention" (p. 20). Data from four sites (Chicago, Portland, Santa Cruz, and Albuquerque) participating in the Juvenile Detention Alternative Initiative, funded through the Annie E. Casey Foundation, found a gender gap in detention. It has been reported that girls are more likely than boys to be returned to detention (often numerous times). More to the point, a significant proportion of girls' detentions involved technical violations rather than new offenses. Across the Juvenile Detention Alternative Initiative sites, 53% of the girls returned to detention were placed there for "warrant, probation or parole violation, or program failure" compared to only 41% of the boys. The pattern became even more marked on subsequent detentions, when 66% of the girls returning a second time (but only 47% of the boys) were returned for these technical violations (Sherman, 2005).

Much the same pattern has been observed in Canada, where well over a quarter of all the girls (27.3%) brought to youth courts in 1995–96 were charged with "failure to comply" compared to only 5.7% in 1980 (Reitsma-Street, 1999). In fact, the situation could well be worse for Canadian girls than their U.S. counterparts, with Canadian courts increasing the rate of incarceration of female youth at a significant and alarming rate. As an example, the number of girls placed in "secure custody" increased in just the space of four years (1991–95) by an alarming 55%. This increase was virtually all explained by the incarceration of girls for "administrative" offenses (like violating the conditions of probation or being held in contempt of court) and other violations of court rules rather than criminal acts (DeKeseredy, 1999).

Race, Ethnicity, and Girl Offenders

The up-charging, "bootstrapping," and increased detention of "unruly" girls have particularly harsh effects for girls of color. Specifically, previous research has noted a racialized, two-track system of juvenile justice—white girls are more likely to be placed in mental hospitals and private facilities, while girls of color are detained and institutionalized in public ones. In a study of investigation reports from one area office in Los Angeles, Miller (1994) examined the impact of race and ethnicity on the processing of girls' cases during 1992–93. Reviewing the characteristics of the girls in Miller's group revealed the role played by color in the current juvenile justice system. Latinas made up the largest proportion of the population (43%), followed by White girls (34%) and African-American girls (23%) (Miller, 1994). Predictably, girls of color were more likely to be from low-income homes, but this was especially true of African-American girls (53.2% were from families who were part of the Aid to Families with Dependent Children (AFDC) federal assistance program, compared to 23% of White girls and 21% of Hispanic girls). Most importantly, Miller found that White girls were significantly more likely to be recommended for treatment rather than a "detention-oriented" placement than either African-American or Latina girls. In fact, 75% of the White girls were recommended for a treatment-oriented facility compared to 34.6% of the Latinas and only 20% of the African-American girls (Miller, 1994).

Studying a portion of the probation officers' reports in detail, Miller (1994) found key differences in the ways that girls' behaviors were described, reflecting what she called "racialized gender expectations." In particular, African-American girls' behavior was often framed as products of "inappropriate 'lifestyle' choices," while White girls' behavior was described as a result of low self-esteem, being easily influenced, and the result of "abandonment." Latina girls, Miller found, received "dichotomized" treatment, with some receiving the more paternalistic care White girls received, while others received the more traditional punitive treatment (particularly if they committed "masculine" offenses like car theft).

Robinson (1990) examined girls under "protective supervision" for status offenses (Children in Need of Supervsion, or CHINS) and in the juvenile justice system (Department of Youth Services, or DYS) for delinquency violations in Massachusetts and clearly documented racialized patterns of juvenile justice. Her social welfare sample (N = 15) was 74% white/non-Hispanic and her juvenile justice system sample (N = 15) was 53% Black or Hispanic. Her interviews, though, document the remarkable similarities of the girls' backgrounds and problems. As an example, 80% of the girls committed to DYS reported being sexually abused compared to 73% of the girls "receiving services as a child in need of supervision (CHINS)" (p. 311). The difference between these girls was in the offenses for which they were charged—all the girls receiving services were charged with traditional status offenses (chiefly running away and truancy), while the girls committed to DYS were charged with criminal offenses. However, her interviews reveal clear evidence of bootstrapping—attaching more serious charges to simple status offenses—such as the 16-year-old girl who was committed to DYS for "unauthorized use of a motor vehicle." In this instance, Beverly, who was Black, had "stolen" her mother's car for three hours to go shopping with a friend. Previous to this conviction, according to Robinson's interview, she had been a "CHINS" for "running away from home repeatedly." Beverly told Robinson that her mother had been "advised by the DYS social worker to press charges for unauthorized use of a motor vehicle so that Beverly could be sent to secure detention whenever she was caught on the run" (p. 202).

Indeed, Pasko and Lopez's research (in progress) on justice attitudes toward Latina offenders also underscored this bifurcated, racialized path. In their interviews of probation officers, judges, case managers, and other juvenile court and correctional decision makers, the authors show that Latina girls' growing visibility in the juvenile justice system (60% increase between 1999 and 2005) can be explained partially by the negative assumptions about them by decision makers. Believing them to be engaged in at-risk and delinquent behavior even without evidence of such choices, decision makers referred to Latina girls as sexually promiscuous "hoochie mamas," gang-involved, resistant to programming, silent, distrustful, and manipulative. Some of these views also extended to Latina girls' families. While some of the juvenile justice workers in the study recognized that both girls and their families might feel less trustful and less willing to participate as a result of fear of deportation, transportation issues, language barriers, and unfamiliarity with the system, others attributed this "reticence" as an unwillingness to change (on the part of the girls) and disinvestment in their daughters' best interests (on the part of parents).

The Girl Offender: Difficult, Manipulative, and Out of Sight

Once in the system, girls encounter conditions designed for boys, where youth workers perceive girls as challenging, demanding, and "difficult to work with," given workers' lack of training in addressing and identifying girls' needs (Bloom et al., 2002; Dohrn, 2004; Gaarder & Belknap, 2002; Hoyt & Scherer, 1998; Lanctot, Ayotte, Turcotte, & Besnard, 2012; Okamoto, Kulis, Helm, Edwards, & Giroux, 2010). With a focus on their physical appearance and sexuality, the characterization of girls in the courtroom and in their case files regularly obscures girls' agency and deems them to be manipulative, hysterical, and verbally abusive (Alder, 1997; Bloom et al., 2002; Bond-Maupin et al., 2002; Goodkind, 2005; Rosenbaum & Chesney-Lind, 1994). Accordingly, Kempf-Leonard and Sample's (2000) survey of juvenile court judges found that "deceitful, manipulative actions" led to more punitive case processing for girls, but not for boys.

Consistent with these findings, Gaarder and colleagues' study (2004) of 174 girls' case files and 14 interviews with probation officers in Arizona found that stereotypical images of girls outweighed any realities. Once again, girls in their study were labeled as "sexually promiscuous, untrustworthy, trashy, needy, whiny, manipulative, and irresponsible," while connections to their life histories and contexts were lost. Girls' character flaws were conceived as negative internal attributes and independent certainties, divorced from their victimization experiences and current needs. Although probation officers and court psychologists seemed sympathetic to girls' plights, girls were still blamed for their troubles and "their pasts that were catching up to" them (p. 558).

Pasko's (2006) study resulted in similar findings as well. Probation officers deemed girls as trustworthy and believable in their capacity to change and accept responsibility if they conformed to emphasized feminine codes for good girl behavior: small, pretty, quiet, agreeable, friendly, prim, and deferent. If they did not conform, they were constructed as the bad girl, the manipulative and emotional sexual abuse victim, or the (bisexual) wannabe boy, whose sexual practices were in need of surveillance and external control. Essentially, the girls who were "difficult" were indicted not just for resisting the rules of law and requirements of probation, but for resisting codes and norms for acceptable feminine behavior and appearance.

Furthermore, Shorter, Schaffner, Schick, and Frappier (1996) examined the situation of girls in the California juvenile justice system and concluded that the girls in their system were "out of sight, out of mind" (p. 1). Specifically, girls would languish in detention centers waiting for placement, while the boys were released or more speedily put in to their secure or non-secure placement. As a result, 60% of the girls were detained for more than seven days, compared to only 6% of the boys. In addition, Acoca (1998) interviewed 200 girls in county juvenile detention centers in California and reported "specific forms of abuse" experienced by girls including "consistent use by staff of foul and demeaning language, inappropriate touching, pushing and hitting, isolation, and deprivation of clean clothing" (p. 6). Most disturbing, the study found that some strip searches of girls were conducted in the presence of male officers, underscoring the inherent problem of adult male staff supervising adolescent female detainees (Acoca, 1998). Beyond emotional and psychological abuse, sexual abuse is not uncommon in such settings. In Ohio, for example, a 15-year-old girl was sexually assaulted by a deputy jailer after having been placed in an adult jail for a minor infraction (Ziedenberg & Schiraldi, 1997). In addition, due to the isolation and abuse in these settings, girls are at great risk for depression, suicidal ideation and attempts, and self-harm/injury (see Pasko, 2006, 2010).

■ Feminist Criminology and Girl's Delinquency

Feminist criminology addresses the androcentric bias in the major theories of criminal behavior and challenges the masculinist nature of the field (Britton, 2000; Smart, 1976). On the ground, feminist criminology has worked to dispel myths and stereotypes about girls and women, has highlighted the importance of taking victimization seriously, and has worked to improve programming options and to create alternative conditions of confinement for female prisoners (Carlen, 1990). In theory and in research, feminist criminology has brought visibility to girls' crime and has made theorizing gender front and center.

Feminist criminology uses a critical consideration of girls' and women's structural positions in a gender and racially stratified society to understand their behavior (Chesney-Lind & Pasko, 2013; Potter, 2006; Smart, 1976). It explores the dynamics of girls' and women's lives and shows the relationships between their problems and their law violations (Belknap, 2007; Bloom et al., 2003). It recognizes that while girls and women live in the same communities as boys and men, their lives are dramatically shaped by gender (Chesney-Lind & Pasko, 2013). Its approach requires a deep understanding of the strategies female offenders use to negotiate and resist patriarchy and how these strategies can determine what crimes they commit. Essentially, feminist theories of delinquency account for the myriad ways that *gender matters* (Belknap, 2007; Smart,

1976). Feminist criminology not only challenges scholars to understand how and why girls and women break the law; it also requires scholars to acquire a critical understanding of the ways the justice system responds to the female offender.

Early theories and assumptions about the role of gender in the justice system typically viewed girls' and women's treatment as "chivalrous," relative to male offenders, because they were considered more innocent, weaker, and less responsible for their crimes (Belknap, 2007; Pollock-Byrne, 1990). However, feminist criminological studies have revealed that females, in comparison with males, are usually treated more harshly in the earlier stages of the processing system and chivalry is less likely for serious offenses (Belknap 2007; Chesney-Lind & Pasko, 2013). Current feminist criminological theory has also documented the varying forms of discrimination and harsh punishment that sexual-minority females (lesbian, bisexual, transgender, questioning, queer, and inter-sexed youth) as well as girls of color face (Chesney-Lind & Pasko, 2013; Pasko, 2010) and has underscored the extent that female offenders of color are processed more harshly than are White offenders in all stages of the juvenile justice systems (Chesney-Lind & Pasko, 2013; see also Shaffner, 2006). This inclusion of a critical discussion about gender and its intersections with other forms of inequality and marginalization has led to current theoretical developments in multicultural and Black feminist criminology (see Pasko, 2010; Potter, 2006).

Indeed, feminist criminological theory requires scholars to systematically link girls' victimization with their offending patterns and involvement with the justice system (Daly & Chesney-Lind, 1988). It requires scholars to investigate the *blurred boundaries* between experiencing victimization and committing criminal law violations (Belknap, 2007). With an expounded understanding of these boundaries, one of the major theoretical developments in contemporary feminist criminological theory is the pathways perspective (Belknap, 2007; Bloom et al., 2003; Chesney-Lind & Pasko, 2013).

Pathways Perspective

Similar to the life-course perspective, this approach attempts to determine which life experiences, particularly childhood ones, place girls and women on a path toward offending. Such significant pathways factors include witnessing domestic violence, experiencing fragmented families, having chemically dependent and/or criminally involved parents, and enduring sexual and physical abuse (Bloom et al., 2003; Chesney-Lind & Pasko, 2013; Shaffner, 2006). The pathways perspective explains how troubled parents and family disruption often cause girls to become their families' main caretakers and peacekeepers. The impact from the combination of stressful responsibilities and childhood trauma then leads girls to run away (their escape strategy), which increases their exposure to criminal opportunities, drug use, and further sexual victimization on the streets (Belknap, 2007; Bloom et al., 2003; Chesney-Lind & Pasko, 2013; Lloyd, 2012). Studies of girls on the streets or in court populations have consistently validated these assertions, showing high rates of both sexual and physical abuse.

In particular, feminist criminologists of the pathways perspective have focused on the effects of sexual victimization. They have demonstrated how such abuse affects girls' ability to form the attachment bonds needed to deter delinquency and antisocial behavior and increases the likelihood of problematic substance addiction, self-injury, unhealthy attachments to older men, eating disorders, delinquent peer groups, and risky lifestyles (Belknap, 2007; Bloom et al., 2003; Chesney-Lind & Pasko, 2013; Gaarder & Belknap, 2002). Not surprisingly, female offenders, in comparison to their noncriminal counterparts, have higher rates of posttraumatic stress disorders, anxiety disorders, depression, and suicide attempts (Chesney-Lind & Pasko, 2013). All of these processes have the potential to drive abused girls deeper and deeper into the justice system. Once in the justice system, girls often perceive removal from their homes (such as detention or residential placements) as punishment for their family life. Despite the courts' language of care and protection, girls often feel responsible for the abuse, anger, fragmentation of the family, and consequent perceived family resentment. Removal from their homes intensifies those feelings (Holzinger, 2004).

The pathways perspective has also shown how neighborhood and school environments can further atmospheres of alienation for many female offenders, as court-involved girls and women have often witnessed and/or experienced violence outside the home (Belknap, 2007; Bloom et al., 2003; Liljeberg et al., 2010; Ness, 2010; Shaffner, 2006). They also have high rates of truancy, suspensions for nonattendance, and overall low school attachment. For example, in their study of girls transferred to adult court, Gaarder and Belknap (2002) found that many girls felt bored by the material they were supposed to be learning in school and believed that it did not relate to their interests or their lives. Rather than providing a support system, schools seemed unequipped to deal with the multiple problems these girls faced. In addition, girls in their study reported that the struggles of navigating dangerous communities played an important and early role in their lives. They had to develop coping and survival strategies (using and selling drugs, engaging in prostitution, knowing how and when to fight) to manage their perilous surroundings both inside and outside their homes and schools.

■ Theorizing Girls' Violence: A Critical Examination

With reference to what might be called girls' "nontraditional" delinquency, it must be recognized that girls' capacity for aggression and violence has historically been ignored, trivialized, or denied, yet it has always existed. For this reason, self-report data, particularly from the 1970s and 1980s, have always shown higher involvement of girls in assaultive behavior than official statistics would indicate. As an example, Canter (1976) reported a male versus female, self-reported delinquency ratio of 3.4:1 for minor assault and 3.5:1 for serious assault. At that time, arrest statistics showed much greater male participation in aggravated assault (5.6:1, Federal Bureau of Investigation, 1980) and simple assault (3.8:1, Canter, 1982). By the turn of the 20th century, arrest statistics showed a 3.54:1 ratio for "aggravated assault" and a 2.25:1 ratio for "other assaults" (Federal Bureau of Investigation, 1999). Taken together, these numbers suggest the gap is closing between what girls have always done (and reported, when asked anonymously) and arrest statistics, rather than a course change in girls' participation in serious violence. In other words, the apparent percolating growth in girls' arrests for assault has more to do with official policy changes in how girls are handled, rather than a dramatic rise in violence among girls.

Detailed comparisons drawn from supplemental homicide reports from unpublished FBI data in the 1980s and 1990s also hint at the central, rather than peripheral, way in which gender has colored and differentiated girls' and boys' violence. In a study of these FBI data on the characteristics of girls' and boys' homicides between 1984 and 1993, Loper and Cornell (1996) found that girls accounted for "proportionately fewer homicides in 1993 (6%) than in 1984 (14%)" (p. 324). They found that, in comparison to boys' homicides, girls who killed were more likely to use a knife than a gun and to murder someone as a result of conflict (rather than in the commission of a crime). Girls were also more likely than boys to murder family members (32%) and very young victims (24% of their victims were under the age of 3 compared to 1% of the boys' victims). When involved in a peer homicide, girls were more likely than boys to have killed as a result of an interpersonal conflict and were more likely to kill alone, while boys were more likely to kill with an accomplice. Loper and Cornell concluded that "the stereotype of girls becoming gun-toting robbers was not supported" and "the dramatic increase in gun-related homicides . . . applies to boys but not girls" (p. 332).

To further support this notion, other research on trends in self-report data of youthful involvement in violent offenses also fails to show the now-dramatic changes in official statistics. Specifically, a matched sample of "high-risk" youth (aged 13–17) surveyed in the 1977 National Youth Study and the 1989 Denver Youth Survey revealed significant *decreases* in girls' involvement in felony assaults, minor assaults, and possession of hard drugs, and no change in a wide range of other delinquent behaviors—including felony theft, minor theft, and index delinquency (Huizinga, 1997). Indeed, looking at most recent self-report data, the Youth Risk Behavior Surveillance System (YRBSS) data showed, in 1999, 27.35% of girls reported being in a physical fight in the previous year; in 2009, a decade later, the figure had fallen to 22.9% (Centers for Disease Control and Prevention, 2000 and 2010).

The psychological literature on aggression that considers forms of aggression other than physical aggression (or violence) is also relevant here. On the whole, this literature generally reflects that, while males are more likely than females to be physically aggressive, differences begin to even out when verbal aggression is considered (yelling, insulting, teasing; Bjorkqvist & Niemela, 1992; Phillips, 2003). Further, girls in adolescence may be more likely than boys to use "indirect aggression," such as gossip, telling bad or false stories, or telling secrets (Bjorkqvist, Osterman, & Kaukiainen, 1992; Phillips, 2003). When this broad definition of "aggression" is utilized, only about 5% of the variance in aggression is explained by gender (Bjorkqvist & Niemela, 1992). It is important to note, though, that one generally does not get arrested for rumor spreading or other forms of "covert" aggression; it is direct aggression—particularly physical aggression—that produces criminal justice consequences. For that reason, it is important to chart out the contexts that produce violence in girls (see Irwin & Chesney-Lind, 2010, and Morash & Chesney-Lind, 2008, for a further discussion of these issues). And, indeed, there is a gender difference here as well: when girls do use physical violence, they are far more likely to fight with a parent or sibling, whereas boys are more likely to fight with friends or strangers.

Those who study aggression in young children and young adults also note that girls' aggression is usually within the home or among their female peers at school; in previous decades, it was likely to be less often reported to authorities or taken seriously (Bjorkqvist & Niemela, 1992; Owens et al., 2000; Phillips, 2003). Phillips' (2003) study of young women in South London found that the majority of them desired higher status and power within their social hierarchies and frequently used verbal aggression and physical dominance to achieve such goals. Girls used aggressive behavior not only to intimidate and abuse girls lower in the "pecking order" but also as a way of settling disputes resulting from failed friendships. For those girls who used physical violence, fighting became a way of enhancing or defending their status while avoiding or assuaging threats to their reputation. For those girls victimized, school became an alienating factor in their lives, riddled with fear and constant truancies.

Girls' behavior, including violence, needs to be put in its patriarchal context, as Artz (1998) has done in her analysis of girls' violence in Canada. She noted that girls who reported problems with violence reported significantly greater rates of victimization and abuse than their nonviolent counterparts, and that girls who were violent reported greater fear of sexual assault, especially from their boyfriends. Specifically, 20% of violent girls stated they were physically abused at home compared to 10% of violent males and 6.3% of nonviolent girls. Patterns for sexual abuse were even starker: roughly one out of four of the violent girls had been sexually abused compared to one in ten of the nonviolent girls (Artz, 1998). Follow-up interviews with a small group of violent girls found that they had learned at home that "might makes right" and engaged in "horizontal violence" directed at other powerless girls (often with boys as the audience). Certainly, these findings provide little ammunition for those who would contend that the "new" violent girl is a product of any form of "emancipation" (as is often hinted at in media accounts). Histories of physical and sexual abuse, then, may be a theme in girls' physical aggression just as it is in their runaway behavior.

It is also important to note that aggressive and violent girls, ironically, often commit the "ideology of familial patriarchy... [which] supports the abuse of women who violate the ideals of male power and control over women" (DeKeseredy, 2000, p. 46). This ideology is acted out by those males and females who insist upon women being obedient, respectful, loyal, dependent, and sexually accessible and sexually faithful to males. Artz (1998) builds upon that point by suggesting that violent girls more often than not "buy in" to these beliefs and "police" other girls' behaviors, thus serving to preserve the status quo, including their own continued oppression.

Such themes are particularly pronounced among girls who have the most serious delinquent problems. Artz, Blais, and Nicholson (2000), in their study of girls in custody in British Columbia, Canada, found that the majority of girls were also male-focused, expressed hostility to other girls, and wanted very much to have boyfriends—always making sure that they had at least one, both in and out of jail. One girl strongly identified with the boys and saw herself as "one of the guys," also admitting that she had "always wanted to be a boy." Only one girl spoke little about boys—at 18 years of age she was the oldest girl in the center. All the girls used derogatory terms to describe other girls, and when they spoke about girls, their words reflected views of females as "other." Many girls saw other girls as threats, particularly if they were pretty or "didn't know their place" (i.e., thought they were better than other girls). A "pretty" girl, or a girl that the boys pay attention to, was a primary target for girl-to-girl victimization because she had the potential to unseat those who occupied the top rung on the "pretty power hierarchy" (Artz, Blais, & Nicholson, 2000). An "ugly" or "dirty" girl (a girl designated a slut) was also a primary target for girl-to-girl victimization because she "deserved" to be beaten for her unappealing looks and for her "unacceptable" behavior. Most of these girls regarded their victims as "responsible" for the violence that they committed, since they were acting as "sluts," "total bitches," or "assholes."

In short, both girls' and women's victimization as well as girls' violence toward other girls are really twin products of a system of sexual inequality and of one that valorizes male violence as agency and has girls growing up "seeing themselves through the eyes of males" (Artz, 1998, p. 204). Indeed, Schaffner's research (2006, 2007) has also shown how girls' victimization experiences and exposure to violence in the home and in the community often precede their own use of violence. Her interviews with young women in detention centers across the United States consistently revealed "an undeniable connection between their having been harmed earlier in their lives and later court involvement, often for violent offending" (2007, p. 1231). In fact, many girls in her study found that their emotional conditions went unnoticed by parents and justice professionals and the psychological impact of their abuse went undiagnosed by mental health professionals. Instead, girls' coping strategies—such as risky sexual behavior, self-harm, drug use, and eating disorders—were often regarded by the court as evidence of their inability to take responsibility for their actions and of their propensity to be manipulative, hysterical, and in need of protection (see also Gaarder, Rodriguez, & Zatz, 2004).

In Pasko and Dwight's (2010) research that included an examination of girl-advocate probation officers, interviewees felt that the anger, alienation, and fear experienced by sexually abused girls led to violent actions against their mothers, less powerful family members, and other girls in general. Coupled with fewer social and mental health resources to prevent and intervene in domestic problems, interviewees felt that when such girls are made to be the primary caretakers of younger children in the household and have limited freedom to leave their volatile environments, their anger intensifies and results in explosive episodes, occasionally at school. Certainly, these studies provide little ammunition for those who would contend that the "new" violent girl is a product of any form of "emancipation" or of girls' new-found "equal opportunity" into the social worlds of crime and violence (for such arguments, see Garbarino, 2006; Gora, 1982; Prothrow-Stith & Spivak, 2005).

Indeed, further explanations for the uptick in girls' arrests for assault show very little evidence that girls are becoming more violent. Relabeling of behaviors that were once categorized as status offenses (non-criminal offenses like "runaway" and "person in need of supervision") into violent offenses cannot be ruled out in explanations of arrest rate shifts, nor can changes in police practices with reference to domestic violence (Pasko & Chesney-Lind, 2011). A review of over 2,000 cases of girls referred to Maryland's juvenile justice system for "person-to-person" offenses revealed that virtually all of these offenses (97.9%) involved "other" or "simple" assault. Additional examination of these records revealed that about half were "family centered" and involved such activities as "a girl hitting her mother and her mother subsequently pressing charges" (Mayer, 1994).

In reality, when exploring the increases in the arrests of girls for "other assault," it is likely that changes in enforcement practices have dramatically narrowed the gender gap. As noted in the above examples, a clear contribution has come from increasing arrests of girls and women for domestic violence. A California study showed this quite clearly and found that the female share of these arrests increased from 6% in 1988 to 16.5% in 1998 (Bureau of Criminal Information and Analysis, 1999). African-American girls and women had arrest rates roughly three times that of white girls and women in 1998: 149.6 compared to 46.4 (Bureau of Criminal Information and Analysis, 1999). In addition, the relabeling of girls' arguments with parents from status to assault is a form of "bootstrapping" and has also facilitated the incarceration of girls (notably, girls of color) in detention facilities and training schools—something that would not be possible if the girl were arrested for non-criminal status offenses. As Feld's analysis (2009) of girls' arrests for person offenses points out, "the incarceration of larger numbers and proportions of girls for simple assaults suggests a process of relabeling other status-like conduct, such as incorrigibility, to obtain access to secure placement facilities" (p. 260).

Conclusion

What is apparent from the literature on responding to girls' delinquency and violence presented in this chapter is that the systems designed to serve our youth have failed girls. As Luke (2008) points out:

> girls whose use of violence leads to their involvement with the juvenile justice system often come from what the social welfare field calls "multi-problem" families and communities and by the time these girls reach adolescence, they have often been failed by multiple systems that are designed to protect their welfare. (p. 44)

Consequently, schools and other welfare and health service systems need revision and repair to adequately address girls' lives and needs. Yet many recommendations remain focused on identifying, punishing, and, sometimes, eliminating the "violent" and/or delinquent girls; recommendations often refuse to address the problems of these multiple failing systems.

In 1992, as part of the reauthorization of the 1974 JJDPA, new language was added by Congress that required all states applying for federal Formula Grants dollars to examine their juvenile justice systems and ascertain problems in their provisions of services to female juvenile offenders. States were required to examine "gender-specific services for the prevention and treatment of juvenile delinquency, including the types of such services available and the need for such services for females; and a plan for providing needed gender-specific services for the prevention and treatment of juvenile delinquency" (Office of Juvenile Justice and Delinquency Prevention, 1998). Although the quality of such an inquiry varied from state to state, the new language did mark the first time that Congress used the JJDPA as a way of underscoring and focusing on female juvenile offenders. For many individual states, it also represented the first time an organized effort was made to concentrate and scrutinize on services given to adolescent females, with the results leading to better girl offender programming in some jurisdictions.

Despite the increased attention, much is still unknown with regard to specific skills or techniques in working with girls. Indeed, of the 392 girls' programs reviewed by the Office of Juvenile Justice and Delinquency Prevention's Girls Study Group in 2005, only 28 did gender analysis and only six targeted girls in the juvenile justice system.

A lack of programs for girls has, among other things, resulted in dramatic increases in both the detention and incarceration of girls. In short, we are discussing the need for programming for girls in a crisis atmosphere, since the relabeling of girls' behavior as violence threatens to undo some 30 years of deinstitutionalization efforts. Additionally, the content of gender-specific (or girl-sensitive) programs formed within the juvenile justice system requires special vigilance, since the family court has a long history of sexism, particularly in the area of policing girls' sexuality. In fact, the one area where the General Accounting Office found evidence of gender difference was the focus on girls' sexuality. In addition to a fairly routine focus on girls' ability to get pregnant or be pregnant, the researchers reported that institutions that served girls exclusively included testing for sexually transmitted diseases while "at similar male-only facilities operated by the same organizations, such testing was not done unless requested by the males" (General Accounting Office, 1995, 5.2.3). As Kempf-Leonard (1998) has cautioned, the juvenile justice system's long history of paternalism and sexism makes it a problematic site for gender-specific services. Certainly, the existence of such "services" should not be used as justification for incarcerating girls, and girl-specific programming should never be an excuse to return to the "good old days" of girl's institutions where working-class girls were trained in the womanly arts.

The major challenge to those seeking to address the needs of girls within the juvenile justice system remains the demonization of many girls, particularly girls of color, coupled with a considerable invisibility of these young women in the actual programming that either seeks to prevent or intervene in delinquent behavior. The short-lived Congressional focus in the 1990s on girls has unfortunately been followed by a major retreat from such initiatives. Not only that, Congress is apparently encouraging the recriminalization of status offenses, which suggests that without powerful, local advocacy, the nation could again see large numbers of young girls incarcerated "for their own protection." A girl-centered response to this backlash and continued pressure on the juvenile justice system to address girls' pathways to juvenile court and corrections are essential. Much more, not less, work needs to be done to support the fundamental needs of girls on the margin.

Questions

I   What have been girls' historical and contemporary experiences with juvenile court and corrections?

2 Using feminist perspectives to understanding girls' delinquency, how do female juvenile offenders differ from their male counterparts? What is the pathways perspective to understanding girls' delinquency?

3 What is the nature and scope of girls' violence and aggression?

4 What needs to be done to improve intervention services for girl offenders?

References

Acoca, L. (1998). Investing in girls: A 21th century challenge. *Juvenile Justice, 6*(1) 3–13.

Alder, C. (1997, March). *'Passionate and willful' girls: Confronting practices.* Paper presented to the Annual Meeting of Academy of Criminal Justices Sciences. Louisville, Kentucky.

Alder, C., & Hunter, N. (1999). *Not worse, just different? Working with young women in the juvenile justice system.* Melbourne, Australia: The University of Melbourne, Criminology Department.

American Bar Association and the National Bar Association (2001). *Justice by gender: The lack of appropriate prevention, diversion and treatment alternatives for girls in the justice system.* Washington, DC: American Bar Association.

Andrews, R., & Cohn, A. (1974). Ungovernability: The unjustifiable jurisdiction. *Yale Law Journal, 83,* 1383–1409.

Artz, S. (1997). *Sex, power and the violent school girl.* Toronto: Trifolium Books.

Belgrave, F. Z. (2002). Relational theory and cultural enhancement interventions for African American adolescent girls. *Public Health Reports, 117*(suppl. 1), S76–S81.

Belknap, J. (2007). *The invisible woman* (2nd ed.). Belmont: Wadsworth.

Belknap, J., Dunn, M., & Holsinger, K. (1997). *Moving toward juvenile justice and youth-serving systems that address the distinct experience of the adolescent female.* Cincinnati, OH: Gender Specific Services Work Group.

Bergen, H., Martin, G., Richardson, A., Allison, S., & Roeger, L. (2004). Sexual abuse, antisocial behaviour and substance use: Gender differences in young community adolescents. *Australian and New Zealand Journal of Psychiatry, 38,* 34–41.

Bishop, D., & Frazier, C. (1992). Gender bias in the juvenile justice system: Implications of the JJDP Act. *Journal of Criminal Law and Criminology, 82*(4), 1162–1186.

Bjorkqvist, K., & Niemela, P. (Eds.). (1992). New trends in the study of female aggression. In *Of mice and women: Aspects of female aggression.* San Diego: Academic Press.

Bloom, B., & Campbell, R. (1998). Literature and policy review. In B. Owen & B. Bloom (Eds.), *Modeling gender-specific services in juvenile justice: Policy and program recommendations* (pp. 1–96). Sacramento: Office of Criminal Justice Planning.

Bloom, B., Owen, B., Deschenes, E. P., & Rosenbaum, J. (2002). Improving juvenile justice for females: A statewide assessment for California. *Crime and Delinquency, 48,* 526–552.

Bloom, B., Owen, B., & Covington, S. (2004). Women offenders and the gendered effects of public policy. *Review of Policy Research, 21,* 31–48.

Bond-Maupin, L., Maupin, J., & Leisenring, A. (2002). Girls' delinquency and the justice implications of intake workers' perspectives. *Women and Criminal Justice, 13,* 51–77.

Boyle, P. (1999, July/August). Youth advocates gear up to fight over the fine points. *Youth Today,* 46–47.

Brenzel, B. (1983). *Daughters of the state.* Cambridge, MA: MIT Press.

Britton, D. (2000). Feminism in criminology: Engendering the outlaw. *Annals AAPSS, 571,* 57–76.

Brody, G., Conger, R., Gibbons, F. X., Ge, X., McBride Murry, V., Gerrard, M., & Simons, R. (2001). The influence of neighborhood disadvantage, collective socialization, and parenting on African American children's affiliation with delinquent peers. *Child Development, 72*, 1231–1246.

Brooks-Gunn, J., Duncan, G. J., Klebanov, P. K., & Sealand, N. (1993). Do neighborhoods influence children and adolescent development? *American Journal of Sociology, 99*, 353–395.

Budnick, K. J., & Shields-Fletcher, E. (1998). *What about girls?* (OJJDP Publication No. 84). Washington, DC: U.S. Department of Justice.

Bureau of Criminal Information and Analysis (1999). *Report on arrests for domestic violence in California, 1998.* Sacramento: State of California, Criminal Justice Statistics Center.

Canter, R. J. (1982). Sex differences in self-report delinquency. *Criminology, 20*, 373–393.

Champion, D. (2001). *The juvenile justice system.* Upper Saddle River, NJ: Prentice Hall.

Chesney-Lind, M. (1988). Girls in jail. *Crime and Delinquency, 34*(2), 150–168.

Chesney-Lind, M. (1996) Media misogyny: Demonizing 'violent' girls and women. In J Ferrel & N. Websdale (Eds.), *Making trouble: Cultural representations of crime, deviance, and control* (pp. 115–141). New York: Aldine.

Chesney-Lind, M., & Freitas, K. (1999). *Working with girls: Exploring practitioner issues, experiences and feelings* (Rep. No. 403). Honolulu, HI: University of Hawaii at Mänoa, Social Science Research Institute.

Chesney-Lind, M., & Paramore, V. (2001). Are girls getting more violent? Exploring juvenile robbery trends. *Journal of Contemporary Criminal Justice, 17*(2), 142–146.

Chesney-Lind, M., & Pasko, L. (2013). *The female offender: Girls, women and crime* (3rd ed.). Thousand Oaks: Sage.

Chesney-Lind, M., & Shelden, R. G. (2004). *Girls, delinquency, and juvenile justice* (2nd ed.). Belmont, CA: Wadsworth.

Costello, J. C., & Worthington, N. L. (1981). Incarcerating status offenders: Attempts to circumvent the Juvenile Justice and Delinquency Prevention Act. *Harvard Civil Rights-Civil Liberties Law Review, 16*, 41–81.

Daly, K. (1994). *Gender, crime, and punishment.* New Haven, CT: Yale University Press.

DeKeseredy, W. (1999). *Women, crime and the Canadian criminal justice system.* Cincinnati: Anderson.

Dohrn, B. (2004). All ellas: Girls locked up. *Feminist Studies, 30*, 302–324.

Federal Bureau of Investigation (1999). *Crime in the United States 1998.* Washington, DC: Government Printing Office.

Federal Bureau of Investigation (2007). *Crime in the United States 2006.* Washington, DC: Government Printing Office.

Federal Bureau of Investigation (2012). *Crime in the United States, 2012.* Washington, DC: Government Printing Office.

Feld, B. (2009). Violent girls or relabeled status offenders: An alternative explanation of the data. *Crime and Delinquency, 55*, 241–265.

Gaarder, E., & Belknap, J. (2002). Tenuous borders: Girls transferred to adult court. *Criminology, 40*, 481–517.

Gaarder, E., Rodriguez, N., & Zatz, M. (2004). Criers, liars, and manipulators: Probation officers' views of girls. *Justice Quarterly, 21*, 547–578.

Girls Incorporated (1996). *Prevention and parity: Girls in juvenile justice.* Indianapolis: Girls Incorporated National Resource Center.

Goodkind, S. (2005). Gender-specific services in the juvenile justice system: A critical examination. *Affilia: Journal of Women and Social Work, 20*, 52–70.

Hoyt, S., & Scherer, D. (1998). Female delinquency: Misunderstood by the juvenile justice system, neglected by social science. *Law and Human Behavior, 22*, 81–107.

Huizinga, D. (1997). *Over-time changes in delinquency and drug-use: The 1970's to the 1990's.* University of Colorado: Research Brief.

Izzo, R., & Ross, R. R. (1990). Meta-analysis of rehabilitation programs for juvenile delinquents. *Criminal Justice and Behavior, 17*(1), 134–142.

Jolly, M. (1979). Young, female and outside the law: A call for justice for the girl "delinquent." In Crown, R., & McCarthy, G. (Eds.), *Teenage women in the juvenile justice system: Changing values* (pp. 97–103). Tucson, AZ: New Directions for Young Women.

Kellam, S., Ling, G., Merisca, R., Brown, C., & Ialongo, M. (1998). The effect of the level of aggression on first grade classroom on the course of malleability of aggressive behavior in middle school. *Development and Psychopathology, 10,* 165–85.

Kempf-Leonard, K. (1998). *Disparity based on sex: Is gender-specific treatment warranted?* University of Missouri-St. Louis. Unpublished paper.

Kempf-Leonard, K., & Sample, L. (2000). Disparity based on sex: Is gender-specific treatment warranted? *Justice Quarterly, 7,* 89–128.

Knupfer, A. (2001). *Reform and resistance: Gender, delinquency, and America's first juvenile court.* New York: Routledge.

Lanctot, N., Ayotte, M. H., Turcotte, M., & Besnard, T. (2012). Youth care workers' views on the challenges of working with girls: An analysis of the mediating influences of practitioner gender and prior experience with girls. *Children & Youth Services Review, 34,* 2240–2246.

Liu, R. (2004). The conditional effects of gender and delinquency on the relationship between emotional distress and suicidal ideation or attempt among youth. *Journal of Adolescent Research, 19,* 698–715.

Long, P., Forehand, R., Wierson, M., & Morgan, A. (1994). Does parent training with young noncompliant children have long-term effects? *Behaviour Research and Therapy, 32*(1), 101–107.

Loper, A. B., & Cornell, D. G. (1996). Homicide by girls. *Journal of Child and Family Studies, 5,* 321–333.

Mayer, J. (1994, July). *Girls in the Maryland juvenile justice system: Findings of the female population taskforce.* Presentation to the Gender-Specific Services Training, Minneapolis, Minnesota.

Margolin, G., & Davis, E. (2000). The effects of family and community violence on children. *Annual Review of Psychology, 51,* 445–479.

McCormack, A., Janus, M. D., & Burgess, A. W. (1986). Runaway youths and sexual victimization: Gender differences in an adolescent runaway population. *Child Abuse and Neglect, 10,* 387–395.

McKnight, L., & Loper, A. (2002). The effect of risk and resilience factors on the prediction of delinquency in adolescent girls. *Social Psychology International, 23,* 186–198.

Miller, J. (1994). Race, gender and juvenile justice: An examination of disposition decision-making for delinquent girls. In M. D. Schwartz & D. Milovanovic (Eds.), *The intersection of race, gender and class in criminology.* New York: Garland Press.

Miller, J. (2001). *One of the guys: Girls, gangs, and gender.* New York: Oxford University Press.

Ness, C. (2004). Why girls fight: Female youth violence in the inner city. *Annals AAPSS, 565,* 32–48.

Odem, M., & Schlossman, S. (1991). Guardians of virtue: The juvenile court and female delinquency cases in early 20th century Los Angeles. *Crime and Delinquency, 37,* 186–203.

Odem, M. E. (1996). *Delinquent daughters.* Chapel Hill: University of North Carolina Press.

Office of Juvenile Justice and Delinquency Prevention (1998, October). *Guiding principles for promising female programming [On-line].* Available: www.ojjdp.ncjrs.org/pubs/principles/contents.html

Office of Juvenile Justice and Delinquency Prevention (2006). *Juvenile offenders and victims: 2006 national report.* Washington, DC: OJJDP.

Okamoto, S. K. (2000). *Development and validation of the Youth Practitioner Fear Survey (YPFS)*. Unpublished doctoral dissertation, University of Hawaii at Manoa.

Okamoto, S. K., Kulis, S., Helm, S., Edwards, C. & Giroux, D. (2010). Gender differences in drug offers of rural Hawaiian youths: A mixed methods analysis. *Affilia, 25*, 291–306.

Okamoto, S. K., Helm, S., McClain, L. L., Pel, S., Hayashida, J. K. P., & Hill, A. P. (2013). Gender differences in preferred drug resistance strategies of rural Hawaiian youth. *Affilia, 28*(2), 140–152.

Owens, L. Slee, P., & Shute, R. (2000). It hurts a hell of a lot…the effect of indirect aggression on teenage girls. *School Psychology International, 21*(4), 359–376.

Pasko, L. (2006). *The gendered nature of juvenile justice and delinquency in Hawaii*. Unpublished dissertation, University of Hawaii at Manoa.

Pasko, L. (2008). The wayward girl revisited: Understanding the gendered nature of juvenile justice and delinquency. *Sociology Compass, 2,* 1–16.

Pasko, L. (2010). Damaged daughters: The history of girls' sexuality and the juvenile justice system. *Journal of Criminal Law and Criminology, 100*(3), 1099–1130.

Phillips, C. (2003). Who's who in the pecking order? Aggression and 'normal violence' in the lives of boys and girls. *British Journal of Criminology, 43*, 710–728.

Platt, A. (1977). *The Child Savers*. Chicago: The University of Chicago Press.

Poe-Yamagata, E., & Butts, J. A. (1995). *Female offenders in the juvenile justice system*. Pittsburgh: National Center for Juvenile Justice.

Puzzanchera, C., & Kang, W. (2011). *Easy access to juvenile court statistics: 1985–2009*. Online. Available: http://www.ojjdp.gov/ojstatbb/ezajcs/

Reitsma-Street, M. (1999). Justice for Canadian girls. *Canadian Journal of Criminology, 41*(4), 335–363.

Robinson, R. (1990). *Violations of girlhood: A qualitative study of female delinquents and children in need of services in Massachusetts*. Unpublished doctoral dissertation, Brandeis University.

Rosenbaum, J., & Chesney-Lind, M. (1994). Appearance and delinquency: A research note. *Crime and Delinquency, 40*, 250–61.

Schaffner, L. (2007). *Girls in trouble with the law*. New York: Rutgers.

Schiraldi, V., & Soler, M. (1998). *The will of the people? The public's opinion of the Violent and Repeat Juvenile Offender Act of 1997*. Washington, DC: Justice Policy Institute and Youth Law Center.

Shearin, E. N., & Linehan, M. M. (1994). Dialectical behavior therapy for borderline personality disorder: Theoretical and empirical foundations. *Acta Psychiatrica Scandinavica, 89*(Suppl. 379), 61–68.

Sherman, F. (2005). *Detention reform and girls: Challenges and solutions*. Baltimore: Annie E. Casey Foundation.

Sickmund, M., Sladky, T. J., Kang, W., & Puzzanchera, C. (2011). *Easy access to the census of juveniles in residential placement*. Online. Available: http://www.ojjdp.gov/ojstatbb/ezacjrp/

Shorter, A. D., Schaffner, L., Shick, S., & Frappier, N. S. (1996). *Out of sight, out of mind: The plight of girls in the San Francisco juvenile justice system*. San Francisco: Center for Juvenile and Criminal Justice.

Steffensmeier, D. (1993). National trends in female arrests, 1960–1990: Assessment and recommendations for research. *Journal of Quantitative Criminology, 9*, 415.

Steffensmeier, D. J., & Steffensmeier, R. H. (1980). Trends in female delinquency: An examination of arrest, juvenile court, self-report, and field data. *Criminology, 18*, 62–85.

Strauss, D. (2011). Promise and problems: Aggression in male led preadolescent girls group treatment. *Clinical Social Work Journal, 39*(3), 270–278.

Ullman, S. (2004). Sexual assault victimization and suicidal behavior in women: A review of the literature. *Aggression and Violent Behavior, 9*, 331–351.

Wasserman, G. A., Keenan, K., Tremblay, R. E., Coie, J. D., Herrenkohl, T. I., Loeber, R., & Petechuk, D. (2003). *Risk and protective factors of child delinquency.* Washington, DC: Office of Juvenile Justice and Delinquency Prevention.

Youth Risk Behavior Surveillance Survey (YRBSS) (2012). *National trends in youth behavior.* Atlanta: Centers for Disease Control.

Ziedenberg, J., & Schiraldi, V. (1997). *The risk juveniles face when they are incarcerated with adults. Policy report.* Washington, DC: Justice Policy Institute.

23 Juvenile Sex Offenders: History, Policies, and Assessment

Megan Schlegel

■ Introduction

There are no exact figures for how many juveniles are arrested or incarcerated for all sexual offenses in the United States. It is difficult to obtain this type of estimate, as each state defines and adjudicates these crimes differently, thus making it difficult to ascertain exact numbers. However, according to the 2002 report from the Federal Bureau of Investigation's (FBI) Uniform Crime Reports (UCR) there were 2,814 juveniles arrested for forcible rape in that year. Comparatively, in 2011, there were 1,735 juveniles arrested for forcible rape, representing a 38.3% decrease in arrests when compared to 2002 (FBI, 2011). Despite this decline, during this same decade, five new pieces of federal sexual offender legislation were passed, each more punitive and comprehensive than the next, aimed specifically at juveniles. In addition, there were countless pieces of legislation aimed at this same population passed at the state level (Terry & Ackerman, 2009). There is an inherent contradiction when the number of arrests for a crime are decreasing but the number of pieces of legislation involving this same crime is increasing at an exponential rate.

Classification

Similar to the discussion of the prevalence of the juvenile sex offender (JSO), it is complicated to pinpoint who is classified as a juvenile offender across the United States, as many states have different ages at which children are considered adults (ranging from age 15 to 18 years). Broadly, the term "juvenile sex offender" includes any individual under the age of 17 who has been convicted in a juvenile court of a sexual crime (Barbaree & Marshall, 2006). However, juveniles who are tried in adult or criminal courts for sexual offenses can also be included in this group if they were under the age of 17 at the time of the crime. Many states have no lower age limit for JSOs, but among those that do, North Carolina is the lowest, at age 6. Every state has an upper age limit, and the highest (used by most) is age 17 (Gibson & Vandiver, 2008).

Policy Significance

The current JSO policies are fairly broad and all-encompassing in an effort to protect public safety; unfortunately, these policies are also quite expensive to implement and may actually serve to decrease public safety by allocating funding to treatment for JSOs who do not need treatment and removing money from budgets for policing and surveillance. Accurate risk assessment (see Chapter 17) of juveniles who do present a future risk for reoffense, either sexual or nonsexual, could inform public policy in a durable and meaningful manner and have beneficial implications for offenders, for the criminal justice system, and for the community. If empirical research provided a means of identifying which factors are traditional risk factors for JSOs to reoffend and then targeted services and policies to the individuals who are determined to be at a high risk for reoffending, legislators would be able to reduce the amount of wide-sweeping policies that serve to detain and treat all JSOs as a homogenous population, even those who receive no benefit from these services.

In terms of policy evaluations, the results provide clear directions for future policies for JSOs. Letourneau, Bandyopadhyay, Sinha, and Armstrong (2009b) suggest that registration guidelines should be based on risk factors, not offenses, and the duration of registration should reflect the individual's developmental age. Another area of significance for policy is the idea that current JSO policies, particularly those regarding public registration, are imposing adult sanctions on juveniles who are without the benefits of due process that adults subject to these same sanctions receive (Caldwell, Ziemke, & Vitacco, 2008). Finally, several studies suggest that the public registration of juveniles should be eliminated, which in turn calls into question the permanency of such polices for juveniles (Caldwell et al., 2008; Letourneau, Bandyopadhyay, Sinha, & Armstrong, 2009a; Trivits & Reppucci, 2002).

Although it is imperative to remain up to date on current policy, it is also critical to understand the history of the particular area of public policy in the United States. The juvenile justice system has a long history, at times coinciding with the adult criminal justice system while at other times taking a strong divergence. As these policies bridge the two systems closer together, this chapter also contains some discussion of adult sex offenders and policies aimed at these offenders, as the juvenile policies often have an adult counterpart. This inclusion is intended to provide a more detailed exposition of JSO legislation in the United States.

■ History of Sexual Offender Legislation in the United States

The majority of scholars begin their analysis of sex offender legislation with the 1930s. As with many current sex offender laws, emotionally charged cases of child sexual abuse instigated stricter sexual offense legislation in the United States in the 1930s (Terry & Ackerman, 2009). Most scholars cite the case of Albert Fish, who was rumored to have tortured and killed over 100 children across the United States, as the case that provided the impetus for stricter legislation regarding the prosecution and incarceration of sexual offenders (Taylor, 2004). Throughout the late 1930s to the 1950s, many states implemented policies to incapacitate sexual offenders by sending them to mental hospitals. Michigan was the first state to do so, and soon 28 other states followed; these policies were based upon the prevailing thought at that time that all sexually based offenses were due to psychological disturbances in the brain and therefore would best be treated at a mental institution.

Offenders were sent to an institution until they were "cured" or were no longer considered a danger to society (Terry & Ackerman, 2009). Sexual offenses were broadly categorized at this point, and one could be placed in a mental institution for anything from peeping and lewd acts to sexual molestation (Terry & Ackerman, 2009). Unfortunately, "dangerousness" was a difficult concept to measure and was also subject to cultural influences (e.g., at that time, homosexual men were considered "dangerous" and therefore subject to imprisonment), so many offenders were imprisoned indefinitely, until the cultural norms shifted. Homosexuality is one such example; the American Psychiatric Association listed "homosexuality" as a sexual deviation in the Diagnostic and Statistical Manual of Mental Disorders until 1973, and it was not until 1992 that the World Health Organization removed homosexuality from its list of diseases (Terry & Ackerman, 2009).

By the late 1940s, many scholars were beginning to question the use of civil commitment for all sexual offenders. Tappan (1950) produced a comprehensive report depicting the inaccuracies regarding sexual offenders that were currently reflected in the laws. He argued that the costs for civil commitment were too onerous for the taxpayers and the practice of committing men without due process set up a dangerous situation for civil rights (Tappan, 1950). In the 1970s and 1980s, cultural norms shifted yet again and the focus shifted to sexual victimization; this was mainly related to the rise of feminist researchers and focused predominantly on sexual abuse occurring within the home, rather than offenses committed by strangers (Terry & Ackerman, 2009).

Current Sexual Offender Legislation in the United States

In the early 1990s, a new wave of legislation drastically changed the perception of sex offenders in the United States. Washington was the first state to implement specific laws intended to promote public safety and prevent sexually based offenses against children. Two specific cases led to this new legislation, both involving offenders who had previously been released from prison after having served sentences for sexual crimes and giving statements that indicated they would harm other children if released (Terry & Ackerman, 2009). Washington, as well as the majority of other states in the United States, had finite sentences for sexual acts; legislators pushed for more comprehensive legislation to ensure public safety from sexual offenders. These laws were largely a reaction to the two previously mentioned heinous cases of sexual abuse and molestation against children in Washington; the subsequent laws were named for the children who were killed by sexual offenders and thus started a sequence of "memorial laws" for sexual offenses, or laws named for the children who were sexually assaulted and killed (Terry & Ackerman, 2009). The first act passed in Washington, which would later be replicated in other states and at the federal level, was entitled the Community Protection Act of 1990. The act dealt specifically with

14 provisions for ensuring community safety once a sex offender was released from prison back into the community (Terry & Ackerman, 2009).

In 1994, the Jacob Wetterling Crimes Against Children and Sexually Violent Offender Registration Act was passed, requiring sexual violent offenders and offenders who committed crimes against children to register with law enforcement agencies (Robbers, 2009). This federal act required each state to create a registry for offenders convicted of sexual offenses against children (Robbers, 2009). The Wetterling Act was amended in 1996 by the passage of Megan's Law, which required states to establish a statewide system for registering and tracking registered sexual offenders, and this system must be available to the public. The Jacob Wetterling Act and Megan's Law were both federal policies that were to be implemented on the state level; if states failed to comply with these acts, they were subject to losing 10% of their funding under the Edward Byrne Memorial State and Local Law Enforcement Assistance grant program (Sample & Bray, 2006). Also in 1996, the federal government passed the Pam Lychner Sexual Offender Tracking and Identification Act, establishing a national database of sex offenders with the FBI (Terry & Ackerman, 2009). Several states adopted their own measures in attempts to ensure public safety. One example is Florida's Jimmy Ryce Involuntary Civil Commitment for Sexually Violent Predators Treatment and Care Act, which provided for the long-term civil commitment of sexual offenders who are assessed to be at a high risk for recidivism (Terry & Ackerman, 2009). Many other states implemented similar legislation.

In 2000, the federal government passed the Campus Sex Crimes Act, which requires sexual offenders to provide information about the higher-education institutions that they attend or where they are employed, in an effort to reduce the number of sexual assaults on college campuses (Terry & Ackerman, 2009). In addition to the memorial laws, there were broader measures of federal legislation enacted to protect children, as well as to investigate and prosecute sexual offenders. The PROTECT Act of 2003 created a national Amber Alert system, lifted the statute of limitations on sexual abuse charges, authorized supervised release programs for sexual offenders after release from prison, and increased various other penalties for criminal and sexual offenses against children (Terry & Ackerman, 2009). In 2005, the Jessica Lunsford Act was passed in Florida, increasing the supervision of sexual offenders on the state registry, requiring the fingerprinting of all school employees, and increasing the penalties for crimes against minors. Similar to many of the aforementioned memorial laws, similar legislation was passed in many other states after Florida implemented these policies (Terry & Ackerman, 2009).

The Sex Offender Registration and Notification Act

The most recent legislative act, the Sex Offender Registration and Notification Act (SORNA), Title I of the Adam Walsh Child Protection and Safety Act of 2006, is the most punitive and comprehensive piece of sexual offender legislation ever passed. The law was passed by the federal government and requires each state to implement legislation including the following provisions: (1) DNA samples are required of all sex offender registrants, (2) all JSOs are required to register on the public registry, and offenders over the age of 14 who were convicted of certain offenses are subject to community notification upon their release into the community (Terry & Ackerman, 2009), (3) juveniles convicted of a sexual offense are required to register for a minimum of 10 years (Letourneau et al., 2009b), (4) failure to register was made into a felony offense, punishable by up to 10 years in prison, (5) state registries must include information on all three tiers of offenders (previously only the high-risk offenders had their information posted), (6) Tier 3 offenders must register for life and register in person with law enforcement agencies every 3 months, and (7) Tier 2 and Tier 1 offenders are required to register for 25 years (registration in person with law enforcement every 6 months) and 15 years (registration in person with law enforcement every 12 months), respectively (Terry & Ackerman, 2009). The Adam Walsh Act was passed quickly by Congress but has not been implemented in most states (Dickson, 2009). The act was passed in 2006 and originally gave states 3 years to comply with the new portions of the law, or risk losing federal funding. It is critical to note that the legislation provided no additional funding to implement these policies. However, as this newest act was quite far-reaching in its scope and required massive overhauls to the current systems, Attorney General Eric Holder granted the states a 1-year extension in June 2009 when it was clear that not one state was ready to comply with the act (Dickson, 2009). However, when the national administration changed in 2008 with the election of President Obama, the leadership of the Office of Sex Offender Sentencing, Monitoring, Apprehending, Registering, and Tracking (SMART) changed, and states who submitted documentation for compliance with SORNA seemed to be judged very differently (e.g., many states submitted packages that were markedly different than other states and diverged significantly from the original requirements of SORNA) and were deemed in compliance. As of December 2012, the following states/territories are in compliance with SORNA: Alabama, Commonwealth of the Northern Mariana Islands, Delaware, Florida, Guam, Kansas, Louisiana, Maryland, Michigan, Mississippi, Missouri, Nevada, Ohio, Pennsylvania, South Carolina, South Dakota, Tennessee, U.S. Virgin Islands, and Wyoming (U.S. Department of Justice, 2012).

Final Thoughts on Sex Offender Legislation

The pervasive theme in these recent legislative acts is that without some sort of intervention or public surveillance, sex offenders will never stop committing sex crimes (Sample & Bray, 2003). This legislation reflects a growing public concern that JSOs recidivate at a much higher rate than any other type of juvenile offender and, as such, should be subject to additional sanctions (Vitacco, Caldwell, Ryba, Malesky, & Kurus, 2009). Laws that specifically target JSOs and mandate punitive sanctions after release into the community are based on the assumption that JSOs differ in critical and durable ways from other juvenile delinquents (Caldwell, 2007). These public policies have often been based on inaccurate or incomplete information on the risk of juvenile sexual recidivism (Letourneau & Miner, 2005; Zimring, 2004).

■ Review of Empirical Evidence of JSO Legislation and Recidivism

Over the past two decades, there has been an increasing focus on the occurrence of sexual offenses committed by adolescents. These statistics have contributed to a new discourse that adolescent sexual offending is quickly approaching epidemic proportions. Conversely, other studies suggest that adolescent sexual offending increased sharply from the late 1980s to 1994 and experienced an equally sharp decrease from 1994 to 2000 (Letourneau & Miner, 2005). Similarly, Franklin Zimring (2004), a professor of law at University of California-Berkeley and a renowned expert on adolescent sexual offender policy, indicated that juvenile sex offense rates from the 1970s through 2000 can be characterized more by stability than by change in either direction. Despite the differing viewpoints on the actual prevalence of adolescent sexual offending in the United States in the past two decades, there has been a surge of legislation regarding JSOs.

This legislation reflects a growing public concern that JSOs recidivate at a much higher rate than any other type of juvenile offender and, as such, should be subject to additional sanctions (Vitacco et al., 2009). One method of assessing recidivism risk is to use the battery of risk assessment measures and tools specifically geared toward JSOs.

Rationale for Creating Risk Assessment Tools for JSOs

Assessing a JSO's level of risk for recidivism occurs at various stages in the adjudication process. At the earliest, the individual's risk for future criminality may inform whether a juvenile is transferred to adult court (*Kent v. United States*, 1966) or whether the individual is allowed to remain in the juvenile system. After the individual is adjudicated, the judge may use the results from the risk assessment and a review of the individual's file to help inform his or her decision about whether the JSO should be detained in a secure facility or placed on probation (Prentky & Righthand, 2003).

The majority of sexual offenders are referred for some type of psychosocial treatment, and treatment providers need risk assessment results to determine the level and type of treatment a juvenile requires (Prentky & Righthand, 2003). Finally, JSOs who receive probation, or who are paroled from a detention center, are assessed for risk, and these results determine the level of sanctions and surveillance to which the JSO is subjected. For example, JSOs who are deemed to be a significant risk to public safety are subjected to community notification statutes that include, but are not limited to, postcards delivered to neighbors about the arrival of a sex offender in their neighborhood, notifying officials at their school and/or workplace, and having their name displayed on a public registry online (Caldwell, 2002; Trivits & Reppucci, 2002). Additionally, JSOs who are deemed to be at a high risk for sexual reoffense may be subjected to residency restrictions; essentially, these individuals may be forced to live outside a certain perimeter of schools, daycare centers, and public parks (Trivits & Reppucci, 2002). As these individuals are likely still living with a parent or guardian, these residency restrictions may force an entire family to move to comply with the law. Finally, in studies of adult sex offenders, it is evident that many began their sexual offending at an early stage, so an accurate assessment of which JSOs are likely to reoffend, and placing them in appropriate treatment, may serve to avoid creating numerous new victims and a life of crime for the offender (Hanson & Bussiere, 1998; Hunter, 1999).

While there are many reasons listed above for the creation of risk assessments to ascertain high-risk individuals, it is equally important to identify which JSOs are at lower risk and to determine appropriate placements for these individuals. Lower-risk JSOs can be treated effectively and safely in the community and do not need to be removed from home and school during critical developmental periods without due cause (Martinez, Flores, & Rosenfeld, 2007). Additionally, the costs to monitor an individual and subject him to community notification statutes are quite high and are passed on to the taxpayers; therefore, resources must be devoted to the individuals who are at the highest risk, and less costly, both financially and emotionally, supervision must be provided to the individuals who are at a low risk for offending. It is clear that accurate risk assessment tools can serve a vital purpose for the field, but it is not yet clear if any of the risk assessment tools currently used can accurately predict recidivism risk, either sexual or nonsexual.

■ Risk Assessment Tools for JSOs

Currently, the field of adolescent sex offending has "no single instrument or combination of instruments that has demonstrated adequate predictive power for conducting sex offender risk evaluations" (Vitacco et al., 2009, p. 934). To identify which elements should likely be included on assessment tools, it is useful to examine what elements should be examined to determine risk. Several studies suggested that assessments of risk must include measurements of functioning in the following areas: intellectual and neuropsychological, personality and psychopathological, social and behavioral, sexual, history of victimization, and substance usage (Collie & Ward, 2007; Veneziano & Veneziano, 2002). These factors are all referred to as "dynamic" factors in that they are constantly changing in an individual. Additionally, most studies suggest that risk assessments must include static factors such as offense history, victim characteristics, age at index (first) offense, and many others (Collie & Ward, 2007; Elkovitch, Viljoen, Scalora, & Ullman, 2008; Hiscox, Witt, & Haran, 2007; Veneziano & Veneziano, 2002). Most assessment tools rely almost exclusively on static factors, as these measures can be completed with a file review and are therefore more cost-effective and efficient. However, some researchers have concluded that it is imperative to include dynamic factors, particularly substance abuse and treatment response, to accurately assess an individual's risk at a specific point in time (Janus & Prentky, 2004; Martinez et al., 2007). Finally, research has also suggested that the same factors that predict general recidivism do not predict sexual recidivism (Langstrom & Grann, 2000); consequently, new assessment tools had to be created for JSOs, as they are believed to be different from other juvenile delinquents in critical and durable ways (Caldwell, 2007). A review of the assessment tools currently being used will provide insight into areas where the tools provide meaningful results and areas where future research is needed.

Juvenile Sex Offender Assessment Protocol II (J-SOAP-II)

Perhaps the most often studied risk assessment tool for JSOs in its original version, the J-SOAP-II was created as a revision to the original J-SOAP (Prentky, 2006). Multiple principal component and factor analyses were conducted on the J-SOAP and revealed a four-factor structure rather than the original three-factor solution theorized by Prentky, Harris, Frizzell, and Righthand (2000); the tool was therefore restructured into four subscales and named the J-SOAP-II (Prentky, 2006).

The tool was normed upon 96 male youths in a detention facility. The intended population for use is 12- to 18-year-old JSOs, and specifically for juveniles who used sexually coercive behavior. Additionally, the tool was developed to predict general delinquency for JSOs. The tool comprises 28 items, rated on a 3-point scale (3 = present, 2 = partially present, and 0 = absent/unknown). Higher scores on the measure indicate a greater risk for reoffense. Scores are summed, but there are currently no empirically informed cutoff scores for clinical use; the tool is currently intended to be used as a structured clinical guide. The opinions of clinicians that result in the use of this type of tool are referred to as empirically informed clinical judgments, or instrument-informed clinical judgments. When there are no clear cutoff scores, risk factors should be assessed in conjunction with clinical judgment to determine risk level (Elkovitch et al., 2008). The 28 items represent four subscales: two assess static factors and two assess dynamic factors. The two subscales that examine static factors are Sexual Drive/Pre-occupation and Impulsive/Anti-social Behavior. The scales that assess dynamic factors are Intervention and Community Stability.

As the tool, in its revised version, is fairly new, few studies have examined its psychometric properties. Parks and Bard (2006) found preliminary support for its concurrent validity, construct validity, and interrater reliability. Righthand and colleagues. (2005) reported a Cronbach's alpha measure of internal consistency scores for each of the scales on a preliminary version of the revised tool: .64, .88, .95, and .80 for scales 1 through 4, respectively. These scores suggest the scales have fairly high internal consistency. Additionally, many studies have examined the predictive validity, and subsequently the clinical utility, of the J-SOAP-II. Viljoen and coworkers (2008) found that the total score on the J-SOAP-II predicted nonsexual violent recidivism but not sexual recidivism. Similarly, Prentky (2006) found that tool can predict sexual violence but cannot distinguish between risk for sexual offense and risk for general criminal reoffense; essentially, while the tool may have some predictive ability for recidivism, it cannot distinguish which JSOs will commit a new nonsexual offense versus those who will commit a new sexual offense. Further support was found in Caldwell and Dickinson's (2009) study; as hypothesized by the authors, higher risk scores were associated with higher levels of reoffending.

An additional study by Martinez and colleagues (2007) reviewed the use of the tool with Hispanic and African-American adolescent males, a population upon which the tool was frequently utilized, but one that was not included in the original study. The researchers found acceptable interrater reliability for the tool (.70). Internal consistency for the tool was also found to be good ($\alpha = .87$). To assess the predictive validity for the tool, Martinez and colleagues (2007) studied whether the total score of the J-SOAP-II was significantly associated with two binary outcome variables (e.g., presence of a new offense or absence of a new offense). Assessed by Spearman correlation coefficients, the researchers found that the tool had adequate predictive utility: any reoffense $r(60) = .34$, $p = .008$; sexual reoffense, $r(60) = .31$, $p = .017$. Finally, the predictive accuracy was assessed and they found a moderate level of predictive accuracy for the J-SOAP-II total score with any reoffense and sexual reoffense (Martinez et al., 2007). Perhaps the most significant aspect of their study, in addition to the inclusion of minority youth in the sample, is that the dynamic subscales were more predictive than the static subscales, providing further support for the idea that dynamic risk factors should be included in other empirical assessment tools.

While most of the studies included in this review supported the use of the J-SOAP-II in the assessment of sexual and general recidivism in JSOs, Elkovitch and colleagues (2008) found that the tool did not predict sexual violence recidivism. Although the results of this study are contradicted by various other studies, it is still important for clinicians, judges, and any other relevant personnel to consider in selecting which tool is best for their purposes. While the J-SOAP-II has received preliminary support, more extensive testing with a broader population would be extremely beneficial to ascertain whether this tool can be used on all JSOs, and if not, which populations should be assessed using different tools.

Juvenile Sex Offense Recidivism Risk Assessment Tool–II (J-SORRAT-II)

The J-SORRAT-II was created by Epperson, Ralston, Fowers, DeWitt, and Gore (2005). The scale was normed upon 636 male youths who had been adjudicated for a sex offense and is intended for use in JSOs who were 12 to 18 years old at the time of their index (first) offense. The scale is quite brief, only 12 items. The items are scored on a 0 (not present) or 1 (present) scale, or 3- or 4-point scales; the variances in the possible points for each item account for varying degrees of severity within the risk factor being assessed (Epperson et al., 2005). The scale is not organized into subscales and focuses solely on static factors by excluding all assessment of dynamic factors (Viljoen et al., 2008).

In the original study for the J-SORRAT-II, Epperson and colleagues (2005) examined the predictive validity, computing a coefficient of .89 for predicting the likelihood of sexual recidivism as a juvenile and .79 for predicting the likelihood of sexual recidivism as a juvenile OR adult. However, Viljoen and colleagues (2008) noted that this study did not use an independent sample for the predictive validity tests (e.g., the researchers used the same sample upon which the tool was originally created), likely inflating the predictive validity of the tool.

Conversely, in Viljoen and colleagues' (2008) comparison study of several risk assessment tools, the researchers assessed the psychometric properties of the J-SORRAT-II and found that interrater reliability for the scale, assessed by intraclass correlation coefficient (ICC), was quite high, at .89. In terms of predictive validity, they found that it did not predict sexual aggression or nonsexual aggression. In terms of postdischarge offenses, it did not predict reoffending of any type (Viljoen et al., 2008). In light of these results, it does not appear that the J-SORRAT-II is a very effective tool for predicting recidivism, either sexual or nonsexual, in JSOs.

Estimate of Risk of Adolescent Sex Offense Recidivism (ERASOR)

The ERASOR was originally created by Worling and Curwen (2000) to evaluate the recidivism risk for JSOs who attended specialized treatment at a facility in Canada. Their original sample consisted of 58 offenders (53 males and 5 females) who underwent at least 12 months of treatment, with a comparison group of 90 offenders (86 males and 4 females) who refused treatment, who dropped out of treatment, or who received only an initial assessment with no follow-up treatment (Worling & Curwen, 2000). This is noteworthy because this is one of the first tools to assess JSOs after treatment, and it is imperative to study the attrition rates and consider this in examining recidivism data.

The intended population for use with the ERASOR is JSOs who are 12 to 18 years old and who have previously committed a sexual assault. The scale comprises 25 items and is intended for use as a structured assessment guide, to be considered in conjunction with clinical judgment and extensive file review to ascertain accurate risk. The items are rated on a 3-point scale—present, partially present, or not present/unknown. There are five scales, assessing various areas of functioning: Sexual Interests/Attitudes/Behaviors, Historical Sexual Assaults, Psychosocial Functioning, Family/Environmental Functioning, Treatment and Other Factors (not assessed above). The first scale, Sexual Interests/Attitudes/ Behaviors, measures historical factors by examining the JSO's file and rating the nine items on these static factors. The remaining four scales comprise 16 dynamic risk factors. A noteworthy feature of this tool is that it is intended for short-term risk assessment (1 year at most) and should not be used to evaluate long-term risk (Worling, 2004). This reflects the dynamic nature of the majority of items on the tool and the recognition that adolescents can change drastically in a year and tools must be readministered to reflect these changes. Additionally, as the tool was created to measure whether a treatment group had a differing recidivism risk versus a comparison group, the authors clearly had a vested stake in ascertaining whether the treatment made any difference; therefore, they used dynamic factors that most accurately assess any changes in the individual.

Few studies have examined the properties of this tool, but the few in existence provide preliminary support for its use (Worling, 2004; Worling & Curwen, 2000; Worling, Litteljohn, & Bookalam, 2010). Interrater reliability for the overall risk assessment, assessed by ICC, was very high at .92; the ICCs for the individual risk factors were somewhat lower, but all but one of the 25 were above .60, indicating acceptable interrater agreement (Worling, 2004). The internal consistency for the scale was adequate, at .75, $F(24, 3216) = 35.48$, $p < .001$. Additionally, the researcher examined the item-total correlations, or the measure of the contribution that each item makes to the overall score, and found that 21 of the 25 items made an adequate contribution (Worling, 2004). Worling (2004) also assessed the predictive validity of the ERASOR using ROC analyses; the AUC was .72 for the total ERASOR score, indicating the tool may be of some assistance in assessing an individual's level of risk. Finally, Worling (2004) also examined whether the scores on the dynamic factors changed from before to after treatment: scores were reduced, indicating that treatment was effective at reducing some criminogenic behaviors and the tool was able to pick up these changes. Similar to the other tools discussed above, more research is needed to support the use of the ERASOR in JSOers, but the preliminary evidence suggests it may be efficacious at assessing risk.

Juvenile Risk Assessment Scale (JRAS)

The JRAS is a modified version of the adult Registrant Risk Assessment Scale (RRAS), which was created in New Jersey to place adult offenders into risk tiers after the passage of Megan's Law required it (Hiscox et al., 2007). After Megan's Law mandated the placement of sex offenders on three tiers according to risk, the New Jersey Supreme Court tasked the Attorney General's office with creating a tool to measure the risk for each offender. The RRAS was the result of a compilation of other risk assessment tools, research input, and input from a myriad of other sources (Hiscox et al., 2007). The JRAS is a slightly modified version of the adult tool; a committee voted to alter the age ranges for victims, to change the length of time since last offense, and to add a variable, sex of victim. These changes all were made to reflect changes in the research regarding the recidivism risk for juvenile offenders (Hiscox et al., 2007).

The JRAS comprises 13 items that reflect three sub-areas of assessment (sex offense history, antisocial behavior, environmental characteristics). The tool was originally tested on 231 male offenders, 11 to 19 years old, and adjudicated for a sex offense. The population included roughly equal numbers of Caucasians and African Americans. The creators also used a comparison group in their original test (Hiscox et al., 2007).

At the time of this review, there was only one published study found reviewing the JRAS, by Hiscox, Witt, and Haran (2007). The JRAS had adequate internal consistency (.66). The correlations between JRAS score and recidivism revealed that the JRAS scores did not correlate with sexual recidivism or nonsexual recidivism. In recognition that low base rates typically depress correlation coefficients, the researchers used ROC analyses, which are traditionally not as affected by low base rates, to determine that sexual recidivism was moderately predicted by JRAS tier (AUC = .656) (Hiscox et al., 2007). They also conducted a classification efficiency analysis, revealing that JRAS scores were insufficient at .66 (Hiscox et al., 2007). Of particular concern for judges, attorneys, clinicians, and any other professionals who use the JRAS to assess juveniles is that the chances of false positives/negatives from scores on the JRAS are high, which presents potential concerns regarding its clinical utility. Finally, it is critical to note that the RRAS has not yet been the subject of a predictive validity study (Hiscox et al., 2007). More research on the use of the JRAS, particularly focusing on its predictive validity and internal consistency, should be conducted to ensure that it is efficacious for continued use in JSO classification in New Jersey and elsewhere.

Multiplex Empirically Guided Inventory of Ecological Aggregates for Assessing Sexually Abusive Adolescents and Children (MEGA)

The MEGA was created by Miccio-Fonseca in 2009 to assess changes in risk, as it is intended to be administered every 6 months (Miccio-Fonseca, 2009). This is one of the only assessment tools that was created with the recognition that risk levels should change, particularly after undergoing treatment, and therefore risk assessments should capture these changes (Miccio-Fonseca, 2009). The tool is intended for use in youth under the age of 19 to assess risk for sexually abusive behavior and/or sexual improprieties. The tool comprises 76 items, organized into seven aggregates to assess different domains of functioning: neuropsychological, family lovemap, antisocial, sexual incident, coercion, stratagem, and relationship (predatory) (Miccio-Fonseca, 2009). The tool can be completed in a case file review, but a clinical interview can be included when needed.

As the tool is fairly new, the only study examining its psychometric properties was published by its author. The scales had good internal consistency reliability, but they were highly correlated with each other, indicating they lacked discriminant validity (e.g., the scales were highly correlated with one another because they were measuring the same concepts). The author also conducted a principal components analysis, which produced a four-factor solution. The author then conducted a cluster analysis with four scales: risk, protective risk, estrangement, and persistent sexual deviancy (Miccio-Fonseca, 2009). As there is only one study on the tool, completed by its creator, more research is certainly necessary to establish if it can be used to determine recidivism risk.

Advantages of Risk Assessment Tools

The preceding review of empirical assessment tools exemplifies the efficacy and the concerns in using these tools in JSOs. As evidenced, there are several tools that have more empirical evidence supporting their use and several that should no longer be used based on the evidence presented. Overall, there are several benefits of risk assessment tools for juveniles.

Tools that can adequately predict recidivism, either general or sexual, help to ensure appropriate placement for high-risk youth by informing decisions for placement and treatment in secure facilities. Conversely, by correctly identifying lower-risk adolescents, the tools allow some individuals to stay within their home, community, and school, which has been shown to reduce chances of recidivism, if properly supported, and reduces the burden on taxpayers for paying to detain youth who do not need a secure facility (Martinez et al., 2007).

These tools can also help identify which youth need treatment, and at what level. By correctly placing juveniles in need of treatment in the appropriate level of services and using other services for juveniles who do not need treatment, this again reduces the burden on taxpayers and provides the most appropriate services to the youth who are in need. The majority of the research on treatment for JSOs shows its effectiveness (Fanniff & Becker, 2006; Worling & Curwen, 2000; Worling et al., 2010), further reinforcing that matching juveniles with the correct treatment is paramount to reducing recidivism in this population. Finally, the results from the empirical studies of these tools inform judicial proceedings far better than clinical judgment and are therefore critical to use in court settings (for a complete review of this topic, see Janus & Prentky, 2004).

The recidivism rate for JSOs is approximately 10% averaged across studies (Trivits & Reppucci, 2002), so if assessments are not conducted and accurately detect which individuals are at a higher risk, potentially punitive policies will be applied equally to all JSOs. Relying solely on current policies means there is a 90% chance for a false positive, and therefore a 90% chance that resources will be used on a child who will not benefit from extensive services—and this may divert money from JSOs who need the treatment (Trivits & Reppucci, 2002). False positives are unacceptable in light of the negative consequences associated with a high-risk finding and potential adjudication on lifetime public registries (Vitacco et al., 2009). Conversely, false negatives allow individuals to be released into the community and threaten public safety. Ultimately, it is up to policymakers to decide whether they would rather threaten public safety by allowing more offenders back into the community, or if they would rather violate the rights of the accused offenders who may not be a risk to their communities.

Disadvantages of Risk Assessment Tools

As evidenced in the sexual recidivism section above, the base rates for sexual recidivism in JSOs are quite low, which makes it fairly difficult to predict risk accurately, regardless of which tool is used (Prentky et al., 2000). Additionally, adolescents are rapidly changing in their development, social environments, and even familial relationships, which complicates prediction research.

Perhaps the critique of risk assessment tools that is most often cited is that they typically only involve static or historical factors and fail to account for dynamic factors (Martinez et al., 2007). The reasons for this are predominantly financial (e.g., it is cheaper to conduct a file review than to conduct a clinical interview and assess change). Although these fiscal concerns are important, it should be more important to assess juveniles correctly so that treatment, detention, and parole resources can be used in the most effective means possible. Additionally, as cited above, many studies support the efficacy of treatments for JSOs, but tools assessing only static factors do not detect any changes in individuals following treatment. As treatment is often mandated and is paid for by taxpayers, it seems imperative that tools assess whether the treatment made any changes.

As the majority of these tools can be completed either by file review or self-report, it is important to note concerns related to self-report measures. It has been reported that if JSOs with conduct disorder take self-report scales, their self-centeredness and irresponsibility are diametrically opposed to a self-report scale (Kennedy, Licht, & Caminez, 2004). Thus, as it stands to reason that since many JSOs have conduct disorder, the use of assessment tools may be virtually useless in predicting their risk. Another critique of all self-report measures is that they are subject to social desirability bias, impression management, and deception: JSOs may use deceptive techniques and other types of impression management more than the general juvenile population, which diminishes the efficacy of risk assessment tools in this population (Collie & Ward, 2007; Gress, 2005).

Finally, Vitacco and colleagues (2009) found that "research does not support the use of any of the specialized risk assessment instruments for the task of predicting sexual recidivism in adolescents" (p. 934). As stated above, "the field of adolescent sex offending has no single instrument or combination of instruments that has demonstrated adequate predictive power for conducting sex offender risk evaluations" (Vitacco et al., 2009, p. 934). This suggests that despite the increasing availability of tools designed to specifically assess recidivism in JSOs, there is not yet one tool that can accurately predict risk, which could have disastrous consequences for public safety, the JSOs themselves, and the criminal and juvenile justice systems. Although many of these tools are widely used, further research must be conducted to determine which tools, if any, should still be used; if none has adequate predictive power, a new tool must be created.

Final Thoughts on Risk Assessment Tools

This review included the myriad of assessment tools currently available to assess recidivism risk, both sexual and nonsexual, in JSOs. As evidenced, there are several tools that provide promising results and several others that, according to the empirical research, should no longer be used to assess JSOs without being drastically changed. There are several common themes of factors to be assessed and item construction that seemed to predict recidivism well in the risk assessment tools.

Dynamic factors appeared to predict recidivism significantly better than static factors, particularly in minority populations. Along these same lines, tools assessing dynamic factors also reflected positive changes an individual made after court-mandated treatment, thus providing more evidence that dynamic factors must be included. Similarly, tools that incorporated a clinical interview, even a brief interview, in addition to a file review produced the most predictive results. Although this is more time-consuming and therefore more expensive, tools must be constructed with the intention of being completed via a file review and a brief interview.

As the review of recidivism data suggested, JSOs have a much higher likelihood of reoffending with a nonsexual crime than with a sexual crime. Several of the tools appeared to produce more efficacious results with sexual recidivism, whereas others had greater predictive validity related to non-sexual recidivism. For this reason, criminal justice professionals and clinicians may prefer to use multiple tools in their assessment of JSOs to get an accurate idea of their likelihood of both sexual and nonsexual recidivism. Clearly, individuals who are likely to reoffend sexually only could then be assigned to an appropriate course of treatment, while the individuals who are likely to reoffend in a nonsexual crime could receive psychosocial education appropriate to their criminogenic risks. In addition to treatment decisions, this could provide support for judges' decisions regarding detention, parole, and transfer to adult court. If this technique were used, the classification and treatment of JSOs could be more efficient and ideally would produce much lower recidivism statistics.

The J-SOAP-II, the J-SORRAT-II, and the ERASOR have been researched more often than any of the other tools presented. Results from these studies provide conflicting results, suggesting that more research must be done in this area to assist clinicians and criminal justice professionals in selecting the most appropriate tool to inform their decisions.

■ Policy Implications

The policy implications are clear: if criminal justice professionals have access to risk assessment tools that accurately predict both sexual and nonsexual recidivism, legislators would be able to reduce the amount of wide-sweeping policies that serve to detain and treat all JSOs as a homogenous population, even those who will receive no benefit from these services. In the case of detention, these policies will likely serve to increase their chances of committing future offenses, as research has shown that individuals who have been placed in a detention facility are far more likely to return to a facility than those offenders who were allowed to remain in their own community. The current policies are fairly broad and all-encompassing in an effort to protect public safety; unfortunately, these policies are also quite expensive and may actually serve to decrease public safety by allocating funding to treatment for JSOs who do not need treatment, and removing money from budgets for policing and surveillance. Accurate risk assessment could inform public policy in a durable and meaningful manner and could have beneficial implications for offenders, for the criminal justice system, and for the community.

In terms of the policy evaluations, the results provide clear directions for future policies for JSOs. Letourneau, Bandyopadhyay, Sinha, and Armstrong (2009a) suggest that registration guidelines should be based on risk factors, not offenses, and the duration of registration should reflect the individual's developmental age. The public registration of juveniles should be eliminated, and therefore the permanency of such polices for juveniles could be eliminated. Several other studies echo this sentiment (Caldwell et al., 2008; Letourneau et al., 2009b; Trivits & Reppucci, 2002).

Caldwell, Ziemke, and Vitacco (2008) noted that SORNA imposes adult sanctions (e.g., public registry) on juveniles who are without the benefits of due process that adults subject to these same sanctions receive. This is related to the larger issue of the public registration of juveniles being contrary to the primary aims of the juvenile justice system—and in fact serving to render those goals obsolete.

Conclusion

This issue is the most concerning regarding JSO legislation: virtually every aspect of it is focused on the aims of the adult criminal justice system and ignores centuries of work in the juvenile justice system. Increasing punitive focus, public registration, permanency of statutes, and failure to recognize the differences between adults and children are all encompassed in these new policies. These policies bring to the forefront an argument about the legitimacy of the juvenile justice system for modern-day policies. Legislators in many states and at the national level are suggesting, with their votes, that they believe modern society no longer has a place for the juvenile system. Further rigorous empirical research and presentation of the results of these studies to legislators is imperative to preserve the integrity of the juvenile justice system; without further research with similar results to the aforementioned studies in this review, the juvenile justice system may cease to be relevant for JSOs, despite data from developmental, legal, and medical scholars that juveniles are inherently different than adults.

References

Barbaree, H. E., & Marshall, W. L. (2006). An introduction to the juvenile sex offender: Terms, concepts, and definitions. In H. E. Barbaree & W. L. Marshall (Eds.), The juvenile sex offender (pp. 1–18). New York: The Guilford Press.

Bureau of Justice (2001). National Archive of Criminal Justice data. Retrieved November 1, 2010 http://www.icpsr.umich.edu/NACJD/bjs_pubs.html

Caldwell, M. F. (2002). What we do not know about juvenile sex offense recidivism risk. Child Maltreatment, 7(4), 291–302.

Caldwell, M. F. (2007). Sexual offense adjudication and sexual recidivism among juvenile offenders. Sex Abuse, 19, 107–113.

Caldwell, M. F., & Dickinson, C. (2009). Sex offender registration and recidivism risk in juvenile sex offenders. Behavioral Sciences and the Law, 27, 941–956. doi:10.1002/bsl.907

Caldwell, M. F., Ziemke, M. H., & Vitacco, M. J. (2008). An examination of the Sex Offender Registration and Notification Act as applied to juveniles: Evaluating the ability to predict sexual recidivism. *Psychology, Public Policy, and Law, 14*(2), 89–114. doi:10.1037/a0013241

Center for Sex Offender Management (2010). *The comprehensive assessment protocol: A systemwide review of adult and juvenile sex offender management strategies.* Retrieved October 29, 2010, from http://www.csom.org/pubs/cap/index.html

Collie, R. M., & Ward, T. (2007). Current empirical assessment methods for adolescents and children who sexually abuse others. *Journal of Human Behavior in the Social Environment, 16*(4). doi:10.1080/10911350802081634

Dickson, C. (2009). Federal sex offender registry rules would create a curious exception to the juvenile justice secrecy model. *The News Media & The Law, 33*(3), 7.

Elkovitch, N., Viljoen, J. L., Scalora, M. J., & Ullman, D. (2008). Assessing risk of reoffending in adolescents who have committed a sexual offense: The accuracy of clinical judgments after completion of risk assessment instruments. *Behavioral Sciences and the Law, 26,* 511–528. doi:10.1002/bsl.832

Epperson, D. L., Ralston, C. A., Fowers, D., DeWitt, J., & Gore, K. S. (2005). Actuarial risk assessment with juveniles who offend sexually: Development of the Juvenile Sexual Offense Recidivism Risk Assessment Tool-II (JSORRAT-II). In D. S. Prescott (Ed.), *Risk assessment of youth who have sexually abused: Theory, controversy, and emerging strategies.* Oklahoma City, OK: Woods 'N' Barnes.

Fanniff, A. M., & Becker, J. V. (2006). Specialized assessment and treatment of adolescent sex offenders. *Aggression and Violent Behavior, 11,* 265–282. doi:10.1016/j.avb.205.08.003

Federal Bureau of Investigation (2006). *Crime in the United States 2005.* Washington, DC: U.S. Department of Justice. Retrieved from.

Federal Bureau of Investigation (2010). *Ten-year arrest trends, totals, 2001–2010.* Retrieved February 4, 2012, from http://www.fbi.gov/about-us/cjis/ucr/crime-in-the-u.s/2010/crime-in-the-u.s.-2010/tables/10tbl32.xls

Federal Bureau of Investigation (2011). *Ten-year arrest trends, totals, 2002–2011.* Retrieved April 27, 2013, from http://www.fbi.gov/about-us/cjis/ucr/crime-in-the-u.s/2011/crime-in-the-u.s.-2011/tables/table-32.

Gibson, C., & Vandiver, D. M. (2008). *Juvenile sex offenders: What the public needs to know.* Westport, CT: Praeger Publishers.

Gress, C. L. Z. (2005). Viewing time measures and sexual interest: Another piece of the puzzle. *Journal of Sexual Aggression, 11*(2), 117–125. doi:10.1080/13552600500063666

Hanson, R. K., & Bussiere, M. T. (1998). Predicting relapse: A meta-analysis of sexual offender recidivism studies. *Journal of Consulting and Clinical Psychology, 66,* 348–362.

Hiscox, S. P., Witt, P. H., & Haran, S. J. (2007). Juvenile Risk Assessment Scale (JRAS): A predictive validity study. *Journal of Psychiatry & Law, 35,* 503–539.

Hunter, J. (1999). *Understanding juvenile sexual offending behavior: Emerging research, treatment approaches, and management practices.* Washington, DC: Center for Sex Offender Management.

Janus, E. S., & Prentky, R. A. (2004). Forensic use of actuarial risk assessment: How a developing science can enhance accuracy and accountability. *Federal Sentencing Reporter, 16*(3), 176–181.

Kennedy, W. A., Licht, M. H., & Caminez, M. (2004). False positives among adolescent sex offenders: Concurrent and predictive validity of the Millon Adolescent Clinical Inventory. *Journal of Offender Rehabilitation, 39*(4), 1–13. doi:10.1300/J076v39n04_01

Kent v. United States, 383 U.S. 541 (1966).

Langstrom, N., & Grann, M. (2000). Risk for criminal recidivism among young sex offenders. *Journal of Interpersonal Violence, 15*(8), 855–871.

Laws, D. R., Hanson, R. K., Osborn, C. A., & Greenbaum, P. E. (2000). Classification of child molesters by plethysmographic assessment of sexual arousal and a self-report measure of sexual preference. *Journal of Interpersonal Violence, 15,* 1297–1312.

Letourneau, E., Bandyopadhyay, D., Sinha, D., & Armstrong, K. S. (2009a). Effects of sex offender registration policies on juvenile justice decision making. *Sexual Abuse: A Journal of Research & Treatment, 21*(2), 149–165.

Letourneau, E., Bandyopadhyay, D., Sinha, D., & Armstrong, K. S. (2009b). The influence of sex offender registration on juvenile sexual recidivism. *Criminal Justice Policy Review, 20*(2), 136–153.

Letourneau, E., & Miner, M. H. (2005). Juvenile sex offenders: A case against the legal and clinical status quo. *Sexual Abuse: A Journal of Research & Treatment, 17,* 293–312. doi:10.1007/s11194-005-5059-y

Martinez, R., Flores, J., & Rosenfeld, B. (2007). Validity of the Juvenile Sex Offender Assessment Protocol-II (J-SOAP-II) in a sample of urban minority youth. *Criminal Justice and Behavior, 34*(10), 1284–1295. doi:10.1177/009.3854807301791

Miccio-Fonseca, L. C. (2009). MEGA: A new paradigm in protocol assessing sexually abusive children and adolescents. *Journal of Child & Adolescent Trauma, 2,* 124–141. doi:10.1080/19361520902922434

Parks, G. A., & Bard, D. E. (2006). Risk factors for adolescent sex offender recidivism: Evaluation of predictive factors and comparison of three groups based upon victim type. *Sexual Abuse: A Journal of Research & Treatment, 18,* 319–342.

Prentky, R. (2006). Risk management of sexually abusive youth: A follow-up study. Retrieved October 15, 2010, from National Institute of Justice/NCJRS http://ncjrs.gov/pdffiles1/nij/grants/214261.pdf

Prentky, R., Harris, B., Frizzell, K., & Righthand, S. (2000). An actuarial procedure for assessing risk with juvenile sex offenders. *Sexual Abuse: A Journal of Research & Treatment, 12*(2), 71–93.

Prentky, R., & Righthand, S. (2003). *Juvenile Sex Offender Assessment Protocol (JSOAP): Manual.* Bridgewater, MA: Justice Resource Center.

Robbers, M. L. (2009). Lifers on the outside: Sex offenders and disintegrative shaming. *International Journal of Offender Therapy and Comparative Criminology, 53*(1), 1–22.

Sample, L. L., & Bray, T. M. (2003). Are sex offenders dangerous? *Criminology and Public Policy, 3*(1), 59–82.

Sample, L. L., & Bray, T. M. (2006). Are sex offenders different? An examination of rearrest patterns. *Criminal Justice Policy Review, 17*(1), 83–102.

Tappan, P. W. (1950). *The habitual sex offender: Report and recommendation of the Commission on the Habitual Sex Offender.* Trenton: Commission on the Habitual Sex Offender.

Taylor, T. (2004). Albert Fish: The life & crimes of one of America's most deranged killers. *Dead men do tell tales.* Retrieved January 31, 2011, from http://www.prairieghosts.com/fish.html

Terry, K. J., & Ackerman, A. R. (2009). A brief history of major sex offender laws. In R. G. Wright (Ed.), *Sex offender laws: Failed policies, new directions* (pp. 65–98). New York: Springer Publishing Company.

Trivits, L. C., & Reppucci, N. D. (2002). Application of Megan's Law to juveniles. *American Psychologist, 57*(9), 690–704. doi:10.1037/0003-066X.57.9.690

U.S. Department of Justice (2010). *Office of Sex Offender Sentencing, Monitoring, Apprehending, Registering, and Tracking.* Retrieved from http://www.ojp.usdoj.gov/smart/index.htm.

U. S. Department of Justice (2012). *Office of Sex Offender Sentencing, Monitoring, Apprehending, Registering, and Tracking.* Retrieved from http://www.ojp.usdoj.gov/smart/index.htm.

Veneziano, C., & Veneziano, L. (2002). Adolescent sex offenders: A review of the literature. *Trauma, Violence, & Abuse, 3*(4), 247–260. doi:10.1177/152483802237329

Viljoen, J. L., Scalora, M., Cuadra, L., Bader, S., Chavez, V., Ullman, D., et al. (2008). Assessing risk for violence in adolescents who have sexually offended: A comparison on the J-SOAP-II, J-SORRAT-II, and SAVRY. *Criminal Justice and Behavior, 35*(1), 5–23. doi:10.1177/0093854807307521

Vitacco, M. J., Caldwell, M. F., Ryba, N. L., Malesky, A., & Kurus, S. J. (2009). Assessing risk in adolescent sexual offenders: Recommendations for clinical practice. *Behavioral Sciences and the Law, 27,* 929–940.

Worling, J. R. (2004). The Estimate of Risk of Adolescent Sexual Offense Recidivism (ERASOR): Preliminary psychometric data. *Sexual Abuse: A Journal of Research & Treatment, 16*(3), 235–254.

Worling, J. R., & Curwen, T. (2000). Adolescent sexual offender recidivism: Success of specialized treatment and implications for risk prediction. *Child Abuse & Neglect, 24*(7), 965–982.

Worling, J. R., Litteljohn, A., & Bookalam, D. (2010). 20-year prospective follow-up study of specialized treatment for adolescents who offended sexually. *Behavioral Sciences & the Law, 28,* 46–57. doi:10.1002/bsl.912

Zimring, F. E. (2004). *An American travesty: legal responses to adolescent sexual offending.* Chicago: The University of Chicago Press.

24 Serious, Chronic, and Violent Offenders

Bryanna Hahn Fox, Wesley G. Jennings, and Alex R. Piquero

■ Scope of the Problem

In 1991, juveniles were responsible for one in five violent crimes reported to the National Crime Victimization Survey in the United States (Federal Bureau of Investigation, 1992). By 2011, that number decreased to 12% of all reported violent crimes, or one in eight, being committed by a juvenile offender (Federal Bureau of Investigation, 2012). While these figures represent a decline in the youth violence, with a few exceptions (Loeber & Farrington, 2012; Zahn, 2009) there has also been a decrease in the amount of criminological research dedicated to understanding the most serious juvenile offenders. This chapter reviews the main research findings on serious, chronic, and violent (SCV) juvenile offenders, synthesizes key findings concerning the risk factors, interventions, and possible prevention regarding SCV juvenile offenders, and concludes with suggestions for future theoretical, empirical, and policy-relevant research.

■ Literature Review

Juvenile offenders are generally classified into three types, based upon the type and rate of offenses they commit. The largest group, nonviolent offenders, make up one quarter to half of all juvenile offenders who do not commit violent criminal acts (Thornberry et al., 1995). The remaining two categories are involved in violence (e.g., homicide, rape, robbery, aggravated assault, and kidnapping) but differ to the degree in which they commit violent acts. Nonchronic violent offenders, who commit violence at a low frequency during childhood and adolescence, were shown to make up 36% to 43% of juveniles in the Office of Juvenile Justice and Delinquency Prevention (OJJDP)-sponsored Denver and Rochester longitudinal studies (Thornberry et al., 1995). Despite being the smallest (in proportion) of the three types, SCV juvenile offenders[1] commit violence with the greatest frequency and account for the vast majority of all serious violent juvenile offenses (Thornberry et al., 1995). Although these classifications are based solely on offense frequency and offense type, they serve as an important heuristic in delineating the different types of juvenile offenders, and most importantly, help to identify the unique risk factors, developmental features, and interventions related to offenders in each of the categories.

While SCV offenders were known to be responsible for a disproportionate amount of violent offenses, the number of SCV offenders was shown to have risen at a staggering rate between 1987 and 1994 (Loeber & Farrington, 2000). In two of the three Causes and Correlates Studies supported by OJJDP in Denver and Pittsburgh, it was observed that 10% of 11- to 12-year-olds had a prior police contact as a result of their delinquent or criminal behavior (Espiritu et al., 2001; Loeber & Farrington, 2000). In 1995, OJJDP commissioned a

Study Group on Serious and Violent Juvenile Offenders to learn more about SCV offenders and how best to treat or prevent juveniles at risk of committing serious violence. Comprising 16 criminologists and 23 co-authors led by Rolf Loeber and David Farrington, the Study Group reviewed and conducted research on young violent offenders for 2 years to highlight the key risk factors and developmental features of SCV offenders and ultimately gave credence to applying a risk-factor prevention model in criminological research (Farrington et al., 2012; Loeber & Farrington, 2000). Through the Study Group's findings, as well as additional longitudinal research on adolescent samples in Denver, Pittsburgh, and Rochester, and a growing body of research on SCV offenders over the past 20 years, there has been a substantial increase in knowledge on the causes, correlates, and prevention strategies for SCV juvenile behavior. This chapter now turns toward a review of the key studies and findings on each of these topics, with the intent to highlight the unanswered questions that should be addressed in future research.

■ Developmental Origins of SCV Offenders

In Loeber and Farrington's (1998a) summary of the Study Group's research and findings, several important conclusions were drawn regarding the risk factors and developmental origins of SCV offenders. In particular, Loeber and Farrington noted that several key behavioral, psychological, social, familial, individual, and biological factors were related to a significant risk of becoming an SCV juvenile offender. These risk factors, and the supporting research, are reviewed and discussed in the sections that follow.

Behavioral and Psychological Risk Factors

SCV offenders often show many conduct problems during childhood, which tend to increase in severity and frequency as the children age (Loeber & Farrington, 1998a). While the typical problem behaviors of SCV children are noncriminal in nature, committing serious delinquent or criminal acts at an early age is one of the strongest predictors of a future chronic violent offender

---

■ **Uniform Crime Reports Facts on Violent Juvenile Offenders**

☐ 1.1 million juveniles were arrested in the United States in 2011.

☐ Almost 17% of juvenile arrests were for violent crimes.

☐ Juveniles committed 12% of all violent crimes.

☐ Murders committed by juveniles decreased by 13% since 2001, but there was an 11% increase in armed robberies during the same time.

during adolescence and adulthood (see Farrington, 1998; Piquero et al., 2003; Piquero, Hawkins, & Kazemian, 2012). Specifically, children who commit crimes or serious delinquent offenses before age 12 were shown to have a two to three times greater risk of becoming an SCV offender at age 17 than children who had a later onset (Loeber & Farrington, 2000). And of children who began their delinquency at age 9 or younger, 37% were later found to be classified as SCV offenders, compared to 17% of children whose age of criminal onset was at age 12 or older (Thornberry et al., 1995). Also, SCV youths have been shown to exhibit many co-occurring behavioral and psychological problems during childhood, including aggression, risk taking, hyperactivity, impulsiveness, low intelligence, and low school attainment (Farrington, 1998). Of these, the strongest predictor of future youth violence was repeatedly shown to be physical aggression as reported by teachers, parents, peers, or the children themselves (Haapasalo & Tremblay, 1994; Patterson et al., 1992; Tremblay et al., 1994). Farrington's analysis of the Cambridge Study of Delinquent Development, a longitudinal follow-up of 411 boys in south London, showed that over 20% of the most aggressive boys at ages 8 to 10 were convicted of a violent offense by age 32, though less than 10% of the less aggressive boys went on to commit a violent offense (Farrington, 1991). In Orebro, Sweden, a study of 1,000 youth showed that 66% of boys with high aggressiveness scores at ages 10 and 13 had arrests for violence by age 26, which is more than double the violence rate for the boys scoring lower on aggression in childhood (Stattin & Magnusson, 1989, p. 714). After reviewing 16 surveys on men's self-reported aggression and violence taken over 21 years, Olweus (1979) reported an average stability coefficient (correlation) of .68 between aggression and violence. The relationship between childhood aggression and juvenile violence in males was replicated in six longitudinal studies, taking place in five countries, spanning three continents, with research consistently showing that aggression and antisocial behavior usually predates the onset of serious delinquency by several years (Loeber & Stouthamer-Loeber, 1998). Aggression has also been shown to be such a strong predictor of violence that Laub and Lauritsen (1993) concluded, "the stability of aggressive behavior patterns throughout the life course is one of the most consistently documented patterns found in longitudinal research" (p. 239).

In addition to high levels of aggression, impulsivity, hyperactivity, and risk taking also strongly relate to future youth violence. In the Dunedin Birth Cohort Study, impulsiveness in boys aged 3 to 5 predicted convictions for violence up to age 18, compared to those with nonviolent or no convictions (Henry et al., 1996). The Copenhagen Perinatal Project showed similar results, with hyperactivity (e.g., restlessness, poor concentration) at ages 11 to 13 predicting arrests for violence up to age 22 (Brennan et al., 1993). In fact, more than half of the boys in the Copenhagen Perinatal Project with both hyperactivity and mothers with serious delivery complications were arrested for violence, while only 10% of the remaining boys had such arrests. The Cambridge Study showed that risk-taking behavior at ages 8 to 10 predicted both self-reports and convictions for violence at older ages (Farrington, 1998). Interestingly, nervousness and anxiety were found to negatively relate to violence, making these among the first "protective" factors against becoming a SCV offender (Caspi et al., 1994, p. 180). A meta-analysis by Lipsey and Derzon (1998) corroborated that low IQ, low school achievement, hyperactivity, impulsivity, and risk taking were key predictors of serious and violent criminal behavior during childhood, adolescence, and early adulthood (p. 97).

Intelligence and school achievement were shown in several studies to relate to an increased likelihood of chronic and violent criminal behavior. In the Philadelphia Biosocial Project, low verbal and performance IQ at ages 4 and 7, along with low vocabulary, math, language, spelling, and comprehension standardized test scores at ages 13 to 14, correlated with increased arrests for violence at age 22 (Denno, 1990). This was also observed in London, where low nonverbal IQ at ages 8 to 10 predicted later violence, and low school achievement at age 10 predicted increased future violence in Pittsburgh (Loeber & Farrington, 1998). A notable finding emerged from the Project Metropolitan study of 12,000 boys in Copenhagen, where it was found that low IQ at age 12 had a .94 correlation to violence at ages 15 and 22 (Hogh & Wolf, 1983).

While these are important and compelling results, there are still many questions left unanswered regarding the behavioral and psychological risk factors of becoming an SCV offender. For instance, although it is clear that early onset, aggression, impulsivity, low intelligence, high risk taking, and other developmental issues are related to an increased risk of becoming an SCV offender, it is unclear why only some children with these behavioral and psychological issues become SCV offenders, under what conditions the relationships exists, and for which children in particular this relationship holds true (Loeber & Farrington, 2000).

Social Risk Factors

Before the work of the Study Group was conducted, it had already been established that various social factors such as peer delinquency and low socioeconomic status have an impact on an individual's likelihood of criminal and deviant behavior (Bandura, 1973; Burgess & Akers, 1966). However, it was unknown the extent to which these factors played a role in the chronic and violent criminal behavior of juveniles, and what other social factors may influence these behaviors as well. Thus, the Study Group examined the impact of a host of social factors on SCV behavior in juveniles using a variety of longitudinal studies from countries around the world. It was concluded that several social factors strongly predict youth violence, including having delinquent friends, gang membership, peer rejection, poor school and social bonds, low socioeconomic status, and urban home location (Loeber &

■ **Behavioral and Psychological Factors**

☐ Early onset of deviant or criminal behaviors
☐ Exhibiting aggressive behaviors in childhood and adolescence
☐ Impulsiveness, hyperactivity, and risk taking in childhood
☐ Low intelligence levels
☐ Poor school achievement

Farrington, 1998a). The Study Group also found that these factors not only differed in their influence on future violence, they also varied in importance with age.

For instance, associating with delinquent peers was a very strong predictor overall of serious violent offending in the Rochester Youth Development Study (Thornberry et al., 1995), and additional research using data from the National Youth Survey showed that peer delinquency was the most proximal influence on SCV offending (Elliott, 1994). However, there were important caveats that are relevant. For one, in Lipsey and Derzon's (1998) meta-analysis, it was shown that peer delinquency predicted youth violence at ages 12 to 14, but not ages 6 to 11 (p. 97). Further, Elliott and Menard (1996) showed that delinquent peer bonding predicted delinquency but also that delinquency predicted delinquent peer bonding. As a result, there was much left to untangle regarding the relationship between having delinquent friends and delinquent involvement, as well as why the influence of peer delinquency changes with age.

One activity that was uniformly found to raise the risk of juvenile violence was gang membership and gang association. Youths who join gangs are more frequently involved in serious violence than those who are not gang members (Loeber & Farrington, 1998b). In the Denver Youth Study, juvenile gang members committed 80% of all serious violent crime recorded for the entire sample, while the remaining high-risk youths committed just 20% of the total offenses. It was also found that gang members, who are a small fraction of the total juvenile population, were shown to commit the vast majority of delinquent and criminal acts for the age group. Specifically, approximately 30% of the sample in the Rochester Youth Development Study was involved in a local gang, but that group accounted for almost 80% of the serious and violent crimes on record (Thornberry et al., 1995). In Denver, this figure was even more pronounced, as 18% of boys and 9% of girls were reported gang members, and gang members committed 85% of the entire sample's serious violent offenses (Thornberry et al., 2004). Gang membership was also shown to be a strong predictor of violent behavior, even when prior violence, delinquent peers, family socioeconomic status, school commitment, parental supervision, and negative life events were controlled for (Battin-Pearson et al., 1998). Gang

■ **Social Risk Factors**

☐ Associating with peers committing criminal or deviant acts
☐ Associating with violent or aggressive peers
☐ Gang membership
☐ Poor school and social bonds
☐ Peer rejection in grade school
☐ Living in an urban location
☐ Poor, disorganized, and low social control neighborhoods
☐ Low socioeconomic status of the family

membership has also been shown to be significantly related to violent victimization (Gibson et al., 2009, 2012; Gover et al., 2009). Because of the widespread attention given to gangs and their criminal acts, and because gangs are among the strongest forms of peer influence on offending (Howell, 1998), the Study Group recommended gang prevention as a method of decreasing serious violence among juveniles.

School- and community-related risk factors for SCV offenders were not well established at the time the Study Group began their work, although a few studies examining various school influences on antisocial behavior have generally shown that poor academic performance and weak bonds to school are related to various conduct problems, as well as the onset, frequency, and seriousness of delinquency in children (Brewer et al., 1995; Hawkins et al., 1998; Maguin & Loeber, 1996). More research on school-related risk factors was recommended (see Gottfredson, 2001).

An associated social risk factor for SCV offending is peer rejection. After controlling for prior antisocial behavior, results from the Oregon Youth Study showed that peer rejection in fourth grade significantly predicted deviant behavior in children up to 2 years later (Patterson & Bank, 1989). Peer rejection was thought to provoke a child rejected from conventional peer groups to associate with deviant peers or even join a gang (Patterson et al., 1991).

Several community-related social factors have been shown to increase the likelihood of SCV offending, such as living in urban areas, neighborhoods with high poverty levels, poor social controls, and high levels of crime, as well as a low socioeconomic status for a child's family and/or community. In general, children, particularly boys, raised in urban areas are more likely to be violent than children living in rural locations (Farrington, 1998). Using data from the National Youth Survey, Elliott and colleagues (1989) found that the robbery and assault rate was substantially higher among urban youth compared to their rural and suburban counterparts (p. 46). There have been several important relationships uncovered using within-city analyses, as it has been shown that there is a greater incidence of violence for juveniles living in high-crime areas than similar children living in urban, but low-crime, neighborhoods in both Rochester and Pittsburgh (Loeber & Farrington, 1998a; Thornberry et al., 1995, p. 227). Similarly, living in neighborhoods with weak social controls, where delinquent or criminal activity goes unreported or even unnoticed, puts youth in the neighborhood at higher risk of future violence (Sampson et al., 1997), as does living in the poorest neighborhoods of cities (Bursik & Grasmick, 1993; Loeber & Wikstrom, 1993). Juveniles in more disadvantaged neighborhoods have been shown to offend more and have a higher likelihood of committing more serious offenses than children in locations with a higher socioeconomic status. This was found to be true in Seattle (Catalano & Hawkins, 1996), Pittsburgh (Wikstrom & Loeber, 2000), and London (Loeber & Farrington, 1998a).

The impact of low socioeconomic social status extends beyond the neighborhood to the family level as well, with results from the National Youth Survey suggesting that assault and robbery is twice as likely among "lower-class youth" as compared to those from the middle class (Elliott et al., 1989, p. 38). In government-funded public housing in Pittsburgh, nearly 70% of 19-year-olds and 41% of 13-year-olds were found to be SCV offenders. Similar relationships between low socioeconomic status and youth violence were found in Stockholm (Wikstrom, 1985), Copenhagen (Hogh & Wolf, 1983), London (Loeber & Farrington, 1998), and Dunedin (Henry et al., 1996). In fact, the only social risk factor measured in the London and Pittsburgh studies that emerged as a strong and significant predictor of youth violence was family dependence on welfare benefits (Loeber & Farrington, 1998). Despite this strong and consistent association between socioeconomic status and violence (Lipsey & Derzon, 1998), the causal mechanisms underlying the relationship were not well understood by the Study Group (Stouthamer-Loeber et al., 2002).

Familial Risk Factors

The Study Group also found that several family factors, including poor parental supervision, low parental attachment, harsh discipline, child abuse and maltreatment, and coming from a single-parent household, were all shown to predict future violence for children (Loeber & Farrington, 1998a). In the Cambridge-Somerville Youth Study, violent offenders were less likely than nonviolent offenders to have experienced strong parental supervision, parents' affection, and good discipline (McCord, 1996, p. 150). Poor parental supervision and attachment were also significant predictors of self-reported violence in two additional studies: the Rochester Youth Development Study (Thornberry et al., 1995) and the Chicago Youth Development Study (Gorman-Smith et al. 1996). Poor parental supervision predicted official violence for boys in London, and harsh maternal discipline predicted violence in both London and

Pittsburgh. Parental conflict and a broken family predicted violence in both cities (Loeber & Farrington, 1998a). Harsh punishment at age 8 was also found to predict arrests for violence up to age 30 for a sample of nearly 900 boys in New York State (Eron et al., 1991). In the Cambridge-Somerville Study, McCord (1997) found that physical punishment significantly predicted children's future violence, especially if combined with low parental warmth and affection.

On a similar note, child delinquents were shown to disproportionately be victims of child abuse and maltreatment (Loeber & Farrington, 2000). In the Rochester Youth Development Study, maltreated children under age 12 were significantly more likely to commit violence between ages 14 and 18, independent of gender, ethnicity, socioeconomic status, and family structure (Smith & Thornberry, 1995, p. 463). In fact, the most famous study of child abuse in the United States showed that the odds for child abuse predicting juvenile violence was 2.0 (Maxfield & Widom, 1996, p. 393). However, it should be noted that a retrospective case-control study in North Carolina contradicts these results, as the relationship between child abuse and future violence was shown to disappear once variables such as age, gender, and race were controlled for (Zingraff et al., 1993). A meta-analysis conducted of all relevant research on parent–child relations and future juvenile violence showed that measures of parental attitude, supervision, discipline, and child abuse were all significant predictors of serious and violent offending, though child abuse was a relatively weak predictor compared to parenting style (Lipsey & Derzon, 1998, p. 97).

Parents may also have a more indirect influence on their child's behavior, as research has found that children raised in a single-parent household in the Pittsburgh Youth Development Study and the British National Survey of Health and Development were found to have higher rates of official and self-reported violence than children in two-parent homes (Loeber & Farrington, 1998a; Wadsworth, 1978), and living in a single-parent household at age 13 significantly predicted violent convictions up to age 18 in the Dunedin study (Henry et al., 1996). Furthermore, children living with parents who have a criminal record were significantly more likely to commit official and self-reported violence in the Cambridge Study, as well as the Cambridge-Somerville Study in Boston (Loeber & Farrington, 1998a).

■ Family- and Parenting-Related Risk Factors

☐ Poor parental supervision
☐ Low parental attachment during childhood
☐ Harsh or punitive discipline
☐ Child abuse or maltreatment
☐ Coming from a single-parent household

Individual and Biological Risk Factors

Although individual and biological risk factors are often thought to be some of the most supported and clear-cut predictors of SCV offending among juveniles, the intersection of race, gender, biology, and youth offending was a highly ambiguous terrain. While one of the few criminological facts is that males generally commit crime at higher rates than females, it is unclear whether this relationship applies during childhood as well. And while over three times as many boys were referred to juvenile court than girls in 1997 (Loeber et al., 2003), this difference in offending rates actually represented a closing of the gap between genders, as female rates of juvenile offending rose nearly 70% between 1988 and 1997, while official rates for boys increased only 26% (Snyder, 2001). More recent analyses of gender differences continue to show some gap narrowing for certain offenses (Jennings, 2011; Zahn, 2009). Research on aggression in early childhood suggests that the prevalence of indirect aggression is nearly equal for both genders, and perhaps even slightly higher for females (Offord et al., 1996; Piquero et al., 2012).

It remains unclear why boys would show an earlier onset of delinquency than girls (Kempf-Leonard et al., 2001; Snyder, 2001) and why the proportion of boys who commit serious violence, such as assault and robbery, prior to age 13 nearly triples the proportion of girls (Espiritu et al., 2001). So, while official data show that females are underrepresented in arrests for serious and violent offenses with respect to their proportion of the population, the gap between genders is less pronounced in self-reported data, and females actually commit more status offenses during childhood than boys (Loeber et al., 2003). The Study Group noted that more (self-reported) research be conducted to understand the relationship between gender and SCV offending.

Similarly unclear is the impact of race on the risk of committing violence for juveniles. It is true that arrest rates for African-American boys were higher than the rate for White males in 1997 when the Study Group concluded its work, particularly for serious and violent offenses (Kempf-Leonard et al., 2001). However, once racial differences in offending rates are examined in the context of social or neighborhood factors, a different picture emerges with respect to race. For instance, the variance in offending rates by race disappeared in Pittsburgh once controls for neighborhood status were included (Peeples & Loeber, 1994). The Study Group examined this issue further by conducting new analyses on the 1958 Philadelphia Birth Cohort and found that an early onset was the only strong and significant predictor of chronic violence, even when race and gender were included (Kempf-Leonard et al., 2001; Loeber & Farrington, 2000). Still, it is clear that more research is needed to understand the underlying mechanisms behind racial differences in offending (Cohen et al., 2010; Piquero, 2008), an observation that the Study Group strongly recommended in all future research on juvenile delinquency.

While biological research in criminology has only recently advanced to the point of examining genetic and neurological risk factors for crime (Beaver & Wright, 2005), studies have been conducted on the impact of physiology, neurotransmitters, hormones, and birth complications on the risk of violent youth offending. In particular, fearlessness theory, which held that a low heart rate indicates low autonomic arousal and increased risk-taking behavior, was proposed and tested using participants' resting pulse rates in several longitudinal studies (Raine, 1993). In the British National Survey of Health and Development, 5,300 children born in England, Wales, or Scotland had their heart rates measured at age 11, and those with a low heart rate were significantly more likely to have convictions for violent or sexual offenses at age 21 (Wadsworth, 1976). In fact, over 80% of violent offenders in the study had below-average heart rates (Wadsworth, 1976). Similar results were found in Montreal, where low heart rate was significantly correlated with bullying and fighting at age 11 (Kindlon et al., 1995), and in the Cambridge Study, where twice as many boys with low resting heart rates were convicted for violence as compared to boys with average or above-average heart rates (Farrington, 1997). Overall, one of the most replicated findings is that chronic and violent youth tend to have low resting heart rates, supporting the fearlessness theory of juvenile violence (Raine, 1993).

Researchers have also hypothesized that certain neurotransmitters, such as serotonin, may influence the propensity toward violence, as low serotonin levels in the brain have previously been linked to higher levels of aggression (Farrington, 1998). The impact of serotonin on youth violence was investigated by Moffitt and colleagues (1997), and the results showed that those who scored highly on self-reported violence at age 21 also had high blood serotonin levels, indicating low serotonin levels in the brain. Moreover, the relationship between serotonin levels and violence remained even after controlling for the subjects' intelligence, socioeconomic status, drug and alcohol use, and other variables.

Testosterone is another facilitator of aggression (Archer, 1991; Rubin, 1987; Turner, 1994), although very little research was conducted on its impact on juvenile violence at the time of the Study Group's report. Most studies evaluating the link between testosterone and aggression have measured verbal aggression rather than physical violence (Olweus, 1986), and those that did examine the relationship were largely inconclusive. For instance, in the Montreal Longitudinal-Experimental Study, fighting and bullying were associated with low testosterone levels at age 13 but with high testosterone levels at age 16 (Tremblay et al., 1997). Taken together with research suggesting that male prisoners incarcerated for violent crimes tend to have higher testosterone levels than nonviolent offenders and the general population (Archer, 1991; Rubin, 1987), it is possible that high levels of testosterone may be relevant as a significant predictor of youth violence only after puberty (Farrington, 1998).

■ **Possible Biological Risk Factors**

☐ Low resting heart rate, indicating low autonomic arousal
☐ Low levels of serotonin in the brain
☐ High levels of testosterone
☐ Complications during delivery, indicating neurological damage

---

Additional research on the link between testosterone and violence in juveniles is needed to test this hypothesis.

Finally, maternal complications during delivery were thought to be a potential risk factor for SCV offenders, as these complications may lead to neurological damage that increases aggression and risk of violence (Farrington, 1998). In Copenhagen, data from the Danish Perinatal Study indicate that 80% of violent offenders scored in the high range of delivery complications, compared with only 30% of nonviolent offenders and 47% of the general population (Kandel & Mednick, 1991). However, support for the causal underpinnings of pregnancy and delivery complications on future violence was mixed, as delivery complications predicted arrests for violence up to age 22, but pregnancy complications did not significantly predict violence at any age (Kandel & Mednick, 1991). Furthermore, in the Cambridge Study and the Philadelphia Biosocial Project, neither pregnancy nor delivery complications predicted arrests or self-reported violence among participants (Denno, 1990; Farrington, 1998).

It is possible, though, that pregnancy or delivery complications predict violence only when coupled with other factors, as the only other study to link delivery complications to violence showed a much higher risk of future violence when a parent had a history of psychiatric illness (Brennan et al., 1993; see also Piquero & Tibbetts, 1999). As a father's psychiatric disorder would have no impact on the neurological damage of a child during delivery, the underlying causes for these relationships are in need of greater understanding. Furthermore, as each of the biological risk factors for chronic youth violence included in the Study Group's report, with the exception of low resting heart rate, had mixed support, was not largely replicated, or was tested on very small samples (e.g., only 50 boys were included in the Montreal Longitudinal-Experimental Study's biological analyses), it was strongly recommended that replication and additional research using large samples, more biological factors, and the inclusion of more social and psychological factors be conducted (Raine et al., 1997).

Many of these and other recommendations for research made by the Study Group were acted upon by a variety of researchers since the report's publication. The results of these studies on SCV offenders, the meta-analyses reviewing decades of work from around the world, and the newest risk factors shown to relate to chronic youth violence are all discussed below.

■ Recent Research on Risk Factors for SCV Offending

The research conducted and reviewed by the Study Group produced several significant and informative findings, many of which have been re-examined and replicated in later studies. In almost all cases, the Study Group's conclusions have been supported by additional research, meta-analyses, and systematic reviews of the body of existent research (Farrington et al., 2012). For instance, Jolliffe and Farrington (2009) conducted a systematic review of all relevant studies to date, which showed that high impulsivity during childhood significantly predicted later violence. A follow-up analysis of the Cambridge Study revealed that the best predictors of future serious and chronic delinquent behavior (measured using the Antisocial Personality Scale) were having a convicted parent, a nervous or depressed mother, harsh discipline, parental conflict, a large family, high child neuroticism, and low school attainment for the child (Loeber & Farrington, 2000). Further analyses of the Cambridge data showed that risk taking, hyperactivity, dishonesty, low nonverbal IQ, low school attainment, low family income, poor housing, large family size, harsh parental discipline, poor supervision, parental conflict, a young mother, a convicted parent, a disrupted family, and troublesome behavior of boys at ages 8 to 10 predicted youth violence at ages 15 to 18, with the increased odds of boys with these risk factors committing violence ranging from 1.8 to 4.7 over boys without these risk factors (Farrington, 2002). Most recently, Farrington and colleagues (2013) performed an analysis on the Cambridge males who exhibited the most early childhood risk factors, and they reported that the most at-risk males had the greatest number of adolescent convictions and adult convictions compared with the males who did not evince such high risk. These most at-risk males were disproportionately concentrated in the high-rate adolescent-peaked and high-rate chronic-offending trajectories in conviction records searched between ages 10 and 56.

Finally, additional analysis of the Pittsburgh Youth Study data by Loeber and colleagues (2005) found that the strongest childhood predictors of violence up to age 30 were having criminal onset before age 10, low family socioeconomic status, living in a disadvantaged neighborhood, family receiving welfare benefits, poor parental supervision, harsh punishment, delinquent peers, gang membership, poor school performance, and physical aggression toward others. Newly identified risk factors include a teenage mother, two or more caretaker changes prior to age 10, maternal cigarette or alcohol use during pregnancy, cruelty and callous/unemotional behavior toward others, low expectations of being caught, drug use or sales, and carrying or using a weapon (Loeber et al., 2005). However, using the predominately African-American Philadelphia sample of the National Collaborative Perinatal Project, Piquero (2000) found that after controlling for a host of family and child development variables (including IQ, birth weight, family socioeconomic status, school achievement, disciplinary problems, neurological abnormalities, biosocial interaction, offense frequency, and more), the strongest predictor of whether a child would engage in violence by age 18 was offending frequency, though low IQ was also a weaker, yet significant, predictor. Still, these recent findings show that many of the behavioral, psychological, social, and familial factors identified by the Study Group have been supported and replicated by additional research. Of course, more studies are needed to further untangle the mechanism underlying these findings in order to continue specifying key relationships and identifying more risk factors for youth violence.

There has been some research on individual and biological factors; for the most part, the results also support the findings from the Study Group. Moffitt and her colleagues (2001) published one of the most comprehensive studies of gender effects on antisocial behavior using data from the Dunedin Study. Their analyses showed that men were consistently more antisocial than women through age 21, albeit with two notable exceptions. First, males and females were roughly equal in terms of the number of drug- and alcohol-related offenses that they committed. Second, males and females were most similar in their antisocial behavior during middle adolescence. These authors also found that males tend to commit more serious offenses than females, and even the most criminally active females offended at a rate much lower than the chronic offending males. Also, in the Rochester Youth Development Study, Thornberry and colleagues (2003) found that gang membership was nearly identical for boys and girls between ages 14 and 18. These results support the Study Group's conclusion that the gender gap for offending is very narrow during childhood and adolescence but widens substantially during adulthood.

Similarly, an analysis of the race and gender composition for violence and homicide in the 2008 Uniform Crime Reports by Rosenfeld and colleagues showed that males made up the vast majority of offenders arrested for all violent offenses, and African Americans, who made up 13% of the population in 2008, committed between a third and half of all types of violent crimes (Rosenfeld et al., 2012). Of the limited number of other studies examining the racial composition of violence, it is often found that African Americans are overrepresented and have a higher and earlier prevalence peak than Whites in violent offending (Piquero, Jennings, & Barnes, 2012). One study that examined the racial gap in violence found that over 60% of the disparity in violent offending was explained by individual impulsivity, verbal and reading ability, marriage and immigration status, neighborhood context, and length of residence (Sampson et al., 2005).

While these figures confirm the Study Group's original research, racial differences in violent offending remain long ignored and not well understood (see Jennings et al., 2010; Maldonado-Molina et al., 2009; Piquero & Brame, 2008)—with even fewer studies examining the issue of race in terms of juvenile offending (Bonnie et al., 2012), and research on the rapidly growing population of Hispanics in the United States is almost nonexistent in juvenile criminal career research (Piquero, Jennings & Barnes, 2012). Each of these needs further research attention.

Another area that was largely underresearched in 1998 was the impact of biological factors on violent behavior, though this topic has received far more coverage than the issue of race and gender since the report's publication. Specifically, a number of studies have expanded on the biologically informed work of Raine, Moffitt, and Caspi to examine the role that genes play in the origins of violent behavior (Barnes et al., 2011; Beaver et al., 2010; Caspi et al., 2002; Guo et al., 2008). This recent line of biosocial research, based largely upon genetically informed data using monozygotic twin pairs, has shown that genes have a much greater influence on chronic and serious offenders than those who commit less serious offenses only during adolescence (Barnes et al., 2011).

As chronic offenders are the most likely to commit violent offenses, there is reason to believe genes may be a significant predictor of violence in a juvenile sample as well. Additional research has also examined the influence of neurology and brain structure on criminal behavior (Raine, 2008; Raine et al., 2005) and has found links between deficits in the frontal lobes of the brain, which control executive functions such as attention, concentration, abstract reasoning, planning, self-awareness, and inhibition of inappropriate or impulsive behaviors (Moffitt & Henry, 1991), and many predictors of SCV offending such as increased impulsivity, hyperactivity, low intelligence, and low school achievement. More research should aim to identify and further specify the links between genes, neurology, biology, and chronic violence.

Another interesting area of research has been the exploration of generational period factors and their impact on the propensity for violence within certain juvenile cohorts. In a very interesting study, Fabio and colleagues (2006) simultaneously assessed the impact of age, cohort, time period, and a variety of risk factors on longitudinal changes of violence within the Pittsburgh Youth Study participants. Results of the multilevel analysis showed that the oldest cohort, who grew up largely in the 1990s, showed higher levels of violence at each age compared to younger cohorts, even

---

■ New Research on Risk Factors

☐ Along with social risk factors, genes may play a role in violence, but precise mechanisms remain unidentified.

☐ Neurological deficits may be responsible for an increase in certain risk factors that relate to higher rates of violence.

☐ Period effects may have an impact on an entire group or generation's level of violence, even when controlling for other critical risk factors.

when controlling for several individual, social, familial, and developmental risk factors, as well as rates of gun carrying, drug dealing, and gang membership in the city for each period (Fabio et al., 2006). This finding indicates that the period effect (i.e., changing social factors) may have an impact on the entire cohort's level of violence above and beyond the risk factors held constant in all cohorts (Fabio et al., 2006). It also shows that known societal risk factors, such as the onset of crack cocaine and higher gang membership rates, which occurred in higher concentrations for certain cohorts, are not able to explain the differences in the greater and longer violent careers for some cohorts compared to others. While the increase in risk factors may have resulted in more individuals participating in high-risk or violent activities, the increase by itself could not account for differences in violence between cohorts (Fabio et al., 2006).

Another important discovery in Fabio and colleagues' study is that the shape of the age–crime curve may shift depending upon generational membership, as their analysis showed that the oldest cohort took an extra 3 years to drop to the level of violence of the youngest cohort at age 19 (Fabio et al., 2006). A similar occurrence took place in the Freiburg Cohort Study, as people born in the years 1970, 1973, 1975, and 1978 all showed slightly different shapes of age–crime curves in terms of prevalence and desistence of offending (Grundies, 2000). It is possible that changes in the age–crime curve result when a cohort of high-risk individuals intersects with high-risk period effects, leading to more crime or a later desistence of offending, thereby altering the age–crime curve (Fabio et al., 2006, p. 158). This would have a major impact on criminological theory, particularly in Developmental and Life-Course Criminology, as models would need to account for individual, social, and period factors in order to more fully explain and predict violent criminal behavior (Fabio et al., 2006).

■ Prevention and Interventions for SCV Offenders

As research on the age–crime curve and chronic violent offenders consistently shows that individuals with early onset, a proclivity to commit violence, particularly at young ages, and a host of serious risk factors for crime and delinquency are all markers of long-term offending from childhood through adulthood (Piquero et al., 2003), there is a salient advantage in terms of policy and prevention by focusing research on SCV offenders (Loeber & Farrington, 2000). To the extent that researchers can accurately and reliably identify the SCV offenders at a young age, before multiple crimes and violent offenses have been committed, there is ample opportunity to prevent the crimes by intervening early in the life course. While this may seem easier than intervening for other populations, particularly given the robust array of risk factors that were previously discussed, in actuality, the task of identifying and properly intervening with SCV offenders is more difficult than it appears (Piquero, Jennings, & Barnes, 2012). Although growing up in a poor neighborhood, attending a bad school, living in a broken home with an emotionally detached parent, receiving harsh discipline, and being highly impulsive and hyperactive would statistically place a child at high risk of becoming a SCV offender, according to evidence presented throughout this chapter, it does not mean that all children who grow up in bad neighborhoods, go to bad schools, have a single and detached parent, receive harsh punishments, and are impulsive and hyperactive go on to commit SCV offenses. To be clear: These factors put a child at greater risk of becoming an SCV offender, but they are in no way deterministic. Thus, it is very difficult to predict with absolute accuracy which specific children exhibiting these risk factors will go on to become SCV offenders (Loeber et al., 2003).

There have been several prevention programs designed to apply to all children who have certain critical risk factors, with the goal of preventing harmful behaviors from occurring in the children who would otherwise go on to commit chronic violence. As for the other participants, a successful prevention program would at least do no harm but would preferably still help them deal with the issues that originally put them at risk for SCV offending. For the prevention programs to be most beneficial to participants, the

---

■ Summary of Risk Factors for SCV Offending by Age

- ☐ Pregnancy to toddler years
  - ☐ Smoking and drinking during pregnancy
  - ☐ Delivery complications
  - ☐ Poor parenting skills
  - ☐ Emotionally detached mother
- ☐ Toddler years to mid-childhood
  - ☐ Aggressive behavior
  - ☐ Antisocial behavior, including hyperactivity, risk seeking, and a lack of empathy
  - ☐ Harsh discipline, maltreatment, and abuse by parents
  - ☐ Erratic parenting behaviors
- ☐ Late childhood to teenage years
  - ☐ Poor academic achievement and negative attitude toward school
  - ☐ Peer rejection
  - ☐ Associating with delinquent peers
  - ☐ Living in a disadvantaged neighborhood
  - ☐ Attending a bad school
  - ☐ Poor parental supervision
  - ☐ Early onset of criminal or delinquent behaviors
  - ☐ Substance use and sexual activity

target groups and material covered vary according to which risk factors are most prevalent at each age group (Farrington & Welsh, 2007). For instance, during pregnancy through toddlerhood, the strongest risk factors for future violence are maternal smoking and/or drinking during pregnancy, delivery complications, poor parenting skills, and an emotionally detached mother (Loeber et al., 2003). Therefore, the most successful prevention programs during pregnancy through toddlerhood focus on educating and supporting parents on the mother's behavior during pregnancy, parent–child interactions, and parenting skills during the early childhood years (Piquero et al., 2009; Wasserman et al., 2000). These programs are often provided through the hospital or the mother's physician and target poor families in disadvantaged neighborhoods. For instance, the Elmira Prenatal/Early Infancy Project sent nurses to the homes of unmarried pregnant woman with low socioeconomic status, with the goal of educating and aiding the women through their pregnancy up until the child was 2 years old (Olds et al., 1998). Results of a 13-year follow-up showed that the nurse visits had a positive impact on the behavior of the 15-year-old children, as there was a decrease in substance use, sexual activity, runaways, arrests, and convictions for delinquent or criminal behavior, as compared to the children of similar women who did not receive the visits (Olds et al., 1998). A recent meta-analysis of early family/parent training programs by Piquero and colleagues (2009) provided strong evidence that these programs improve child outcomes. Unfortunately, early intervention programs usually do not cover techniques for parents to reduce antisocial behavior in later years, and the programs tend not to be standardized and are difficult to generalize or take to large scale. Long-term follow-ups on these programs have been limited, but reviews generally show positive benefits in terms of level of care for the child and the child's future health (Piquero et al., 2009; Wasserman et al., 2000).

During the preschool years, the most significant risk factors for future violence and serious delinquency are aggression, hyperactivity, risk taking, sensation seeking, a lack of empathy on behalf of the child, harsh discipline, erratic parenting, and maltreatment and abuse by the child's parents (Loeber et al., 2003). Prevention programs during the preschool years tend to target the child's behavior but often do not include any training for parents (Wasserman et al., 2000). Nevertheless, the preschool-age prevention programs have been generally successful in long-term follow-ups, as they have shown positive effects on the antisocial behaviors of participating children (Wasserman et al., 2000). In particular, the High/Scope Perry Preschool Project focused on encouraging prosocial behaviors for 3- and 4-year-olds at risk for school failure, with a long-term program evaluation indicating that the program participants showed multiple prosocial functioning benefits as well as half the lifetime arrests, as compared to the control group children in the study (Schweinhart et al., 1993). Still, additional follow-ups of standardized prevention programs are necessary.

The number of risk factors for SCV offending quickly increases when children are approximately 6 years old, and in some children, the onset of delinquency will begin to take place shortly thereafter. The main risk factors for violence during late childhood and the early teens include poor academic achievement, negative attitude toward school, peer rejection, delinquent peer association, early onset of delinquent behavior, living in a disadvantaged neighborhood, attending a bad school, having poor parental supervision, and early onset of substance use or sexual activity (Loeber & Farrington, 1998b; Loeber et al., 2003). The wide variety of risk factors makes the design and implementation of prevention programs during the later childhood and teenage years more complicated, particularly because most programs are school-based only (Wasserman et al., 2000). This means that families are not involved in the programs, and the programs tend to deal only with the school-related risk factors.

However, one program that has received a great deal of attention and a wealth of support in the program evaluation literature is Multisystemic Therapy (MST). MST is unique as it is an intensive family- and community-centered treatment, with therapists coming to a child's home and various community locations, including school, to focus on an individualized and flexible agenda of individual (e.g., cognitive) and social (i.e., family, peer, school) risk factors that are known to be associated with adolescent antisocial behavior (Schaeffer & Borduin, 2005). When MST was applied to a sample of violent and chronic juvenile offenders at "imminent risk of incarceration," Henggeler and colleagues (1992) found that the rate of incarceration for the treated group decreased by 64% in 59 weeks, and the survival rate (percentage of youths not rearrested) was doubled by a 2.4-year follow-up. Furthermore, family cohesion improved and aggression decreased for youths who received MST (Henggeler et al., 1992). A recent study showed that MST still had a lasting impact up to 16 years later, when participants were an average of 29 years old, with MST participants showing 54% fewer arrests and a 50% versus 81% recidivism rate when compared to control group participants (Schaeffer & Borduin, 2005). To date, MST is the only treatment program[2] able to demonstrate short- and long-term effects with SCV juvenile offenders (Borduin et al., 1995; Henggeler et al., 1992, 1993).

While MST is the most successful prevention program in terms of providing both short- and long-term effects for participants, there are several other promising interventions that were recommended by the Study Group after demonstrating either short- or long-term success in reducing future criminal and antisocial behavior among participants. Among the most promising were mentoring programs, comprehensive community interventions, classroom and behavior management programs, social competence promotion curriculums, conflict resolution and violence prevention curriculums, bullying prevention, afterschool recreation programs, and multicomponent classroom-based prevention programs (Loeber & Farrington, 1998a).

Summary and Conclusions

Despite the body of knowledge accumulated on the developmental origins and risk factors for youth violence, there is no single approach that may prevent or correct SCV offending in juveniles. However, preventive and remedial interventions that focus on known risk factors, and on knowledge of the behavioral development of juveniles, are the most effective and promising "single-pronged" options available (Loeber & Farrington, 1998a). Specifically, interventions that educate and aid mothers during pregnancy and their child's infancy, address antisocial behaviors to children in preschool, and teach prosocial skills and problem-solving techniques in adolescence are among the most successful for reducing problematic behaviors in children. Unfortunately, there is limited evidence available to show that the changes in behavior resulting from these prevention programs will endure over time. Instead, a comprehensive, individualized, family- and community-based intervention, such as MST, seems to hold the most promise, and recent research confirms the MST program's success in changing the behavior of violent youth both in the short term and in the long term.

Taken together, these findings suggest that SCV offending interventions should focus on changing both the conditions and institutions that influence offending in the individual, family, school, and community (Farrington, 2002). In other words, future youth violence prevention programs should aim to be more of an ongoing care model and should aim to address the multiple major risk factors of SCV behavior that arise at various periods between birth and adolescence. The development of a long-term prevention program addressing multiple risk factors and problematic environments is the most promising way forward to prevent chronic violent juvenile offending. Still, many policymakers are concerned that such a comprehensive and ongoing program would be extremely costly and therefore unlikely to be enacted during a period of constrained economic resources. However, it is important to consider the difference in costs between an intensive prevention program, such as MST, and correctional incarceration. In 1992, the average cost per day for a juvenile correctional facility was $105.27 (Camp & Camp, 1993), while a 15-week MST program during the same year averaged only $31.43 per day (Tate et al., 1995). In addition to the initial cost savings of over $3 for every $1 invested in a comprehensive preventive approach, there are additional savings when recidivism rates, court costs, and impact on victims are considered. For these reasons, there is actual empirical support for the old adage that "an ounce of prevention is worth a pound of cure."

Still, there is much more to learn regarding the development and risk factors for SCV juvenile behavior, as well as the comprehensive prevention and intervention programs aimed at disrupting the developmental and environmental pathways for violence over the lifespan. Future research will require the use of even more longitudinal samples—especially those that follow subjects in late middle adulthood in order to assess long-term prediction and long-term effects—and the examination of more possible correlates and causes of SCV behavior. Long-term evaluations of promising prevention programs are also needed to determine if more sophisticated and intensive programs yield positive results in terms of preventing youth violence in both the short term and long term. This is particularly important when programs may be evaluated using more precise methodologies and refined designs, allowing more meaningful and reliable conclusions on their effectiveness.

Notes

1   Some scholars refer to this group as "serious violent offenders," as limitations and difficulties associated with juvenile court referrals, arrest reports, and self-reported offending may prevent a reliable definition of chronic offending to be reached (Loeber & Farrington, 1998a, p. 2).
2   Research has examined the impact of social skills training (e.g., Aggression Replacement Training) and problem-solving skills training (e.g., The Viewpoints Training Program) on adolescent violent and antisocial behavior, and both have showed promising short-term effects on the level of criminal and antisocial behaviors in the program participants. However, neither program showed significant long-term differences in criminal and antisocial behavior between treatment and control groups in randomized controlled trial evaluations (Tate et al., 1995).

References

Archer, J. (1991). The influence of testosterone on human aggression. *British Journal of Psychology, 82,* 1–28.

Bandura, A. (1973). *Aggression: A social learning analysis.* Englewood Cliffs, NJ: Prentice-Hall.

Barnes, J. C., Beaver, K. M., & Boutwell, B. B. (2011). Examining the genetic underpinnings to Moffitt's developmental taxonomy: A behavioral genetic analysis. *Criminology, 49,* 923–954.

Battin-Pearson, S. R., Thornberry, T. P., Hawkins, J. D., & Krohn, M. D. (1998). Gang membership, delinquent peers, and delinquent behavior. *Juvenile Justice Bulletin, Youth Gang Series.* Washington, DC: US Department of Justice, Office of Juvenile Justice and Delinquency Prevention.

Beaver, K. M., Vaughn, M. G., DeLisi, M., & Higgins, G. E. (2010). The biosocial correlates of neuropsychological deficits: Results from the National Longitudinal Study of Adolescent Health. *International Journal of Offender Therapy and Comparative Criminology, 54,* 878–894.

Beaver, K. M., & Wright, J. P. (2005). Biosocial development and delinquency involvement. *Youth Violence and Juvenile Justice, 3,* 168–192.

Bonnie, R. J., Johnson, R. L., Chemers, B. M., & Schuck, J. (Eds.). (2012). *Reforming juvenile justice: A developmental approach.* Washington, DC: The National Academies Press.

Borduin, C. M., Mann, B. J., Cone, L., Henggeler, S. W., Fucci, B. R., Blaske, D. M., & Williams, R. A. (1995). Multisystemic treatment of serious juvenile offenders: Long-term prevention of criminality and violence. *Journal of Consulting and Clinical Psychology, 63,* 569–578.

Brennan, P. A., Mednick, B. R., & Mednick, S. A. (1993). Parental psychopathology, congenital factors, and violence. In S. Hodgins (Ed.), *Mental disorder and crime* (pp. 244–261). Newbury Park, CA: Sage.

Brewer, D. D., Hawkins, J. D., Catalano, R. F., & Neckerman, H. J. (1995). Preventing serious, violent, and chronic juvenile offending: A review of evaluations of selected strategies in childhood, adolescence, and the community. In J. C. Howell, B. Krisberg, J. D. Hawkins, & J. J. Wilson (Eds.), *Sourcebook on serious, violent, and chronic juvenile offenders* (pp. 61–141). Thousand Oaks, CA: Sage.

Burgess, R., & Akers, A. (1966). A differential association-reinforcement theory of criminal behavior. *Social Problems, 14*, 363–383.

Bursik, R.J., & Grasmick, H.G. (1993). *Neighborhoods and crime: The dimensions of effective community control.* New York: Lexington Books.

Camp, C., & Camp, G. (1993). *The corrections yearbook.* Criminal Justice Institute.

Caspi, A., McClay, J., Moffitt, T. E., Mill, J., Martin, J., Craig, I., Taylor, A., & Poulton, R. (2002). Role of genotype in the cycle of violence in maltreated children. *Science, 297*, 851–854.

Caspi, A., Moffitt, T. E., Silva, P.A., Stouthamer- Loeber, M., Krueger, R. F., & Schmutte, P. S. (1994). Are some people crime-prone? Replications of the personality-crime relationship across countries, genders, races, and methods. *Criminology, 32*, 163–195.

Catalano, R. F., & Hawkins, J. D. (1996). The social development model: A theory of antisocial behavior. In J. D. Hawkins (Ed.), *Delinquency and crime: Current theories* (pp. 149–197). New York: Cambridge University Press.

Cohen, M., Piquero, A. R., & Jennings, W. G. (2010). Monetary costs of gender and ethnicity disaggregated group-based offending. *American Journal of Criminal Justice, 35*, 159–172.

Denno, D. W. (1990). *Biology and violence: From birth to adulthood.* Cambridge: Cambridge University Press.

Elliott, D. S. (1994). Serious violent offenders: onset, developmental course, and termination. *Criminology, 32*, 1–21.

Elliott, D. S., Huizinga, D., & Menard, S. (1989). *Multiple problem youth: Delinquency, substance use, and mental health problems.* New York: Springer-Verlag.

Elliott, D. S., & Menard, S. (1996). Delinquent friends and delinquent behavior: temporal and development patterns. In J. D. Hawkins (Ed.), *Delinquency and crime: Current theories* (pp. 28–67). Cambridge: Cambridge University Press.

Eron, L. D., Huesmann, L. R., & Zelli, A. (1991). The role of parental variables in the learning of aggression. In D. J. Pepler & K. H. Rubin (eds.), *The development and treatment of childhood aggression* (pp. 169–188). Hillsdale, NJ: Erlbaum.

Espiritu, R. C., Huizinga, D., Crawford, A., & Loeber, R. (2001). Epidemiology of self-reported delinquency. In R. Loeber & D. P. Farrington (Eds.), *Child delinquents: Development, intervention, and service needs* (pp. 47–66). Thousand Oaks, CA: Sage.

Fabio, A., Loeber, R., Balasubramani, G. K., Roth, J., Fu, W., & Farrington, D. P. (2006). Why some generations are more violent than others: Assessment of age, period, and cohort effects. *American Journal of Epidemiology, 164*, 151–160.

Farrington, D. P. (1991). Childhood aggression and adult violence: Early precursors and later life outcomes. In D. J. Pepler & K. H. Rubin (eds.), *The development and treatment of childhood aggression* (pp. 5–29). Hillsdale, NJ: Erlbaum.

Farrington, D. P. (1997). The relationship between low resting heart rate and violence. In A. Raine, P.A. Brennan, D. P. Farrington, & S. A. Mednick (Eds.), *Biosocial bases of violence* (pp. 89–105). New York: Plenum.

Farrington, D. P. (1998). Causes, and correlates of male youth violence. In M. Tonry (Ed.), *Crime and justice, Vol. 24* (pp. 421–475). Chicago: University of Chicago Press.

Farrington, D. P. (2002). Multiple risk factors for multiple problem violent boys. In R. R. Corrado, R. Roesch, S. D. Hart, & J. K. Gierowski (Eds.), *Multi-problem violent youth: A foundation for comparative research on needs, interventions and outcomes* (pp. 23–34). Amsterdam: IOS Press.

Farrington, D. P., Loeber, R., & Ttofi, M. M. (2012). Risk and protective factors for offending. In B. Welsh & D. P. Farrington (Eds.), *Oxford handbook of crime prevention* (pp. 46–69). Oxford: Oxford University Press.

Farrington, D. P., Piquero, A. R., & Jennings, W. G. (2013). *Offending from childhood to late middle age: Recent results from the Cambridge Study in Delinquent Development.* New York: Springer.

Farrington, D. P., & Welsh, B. C. (2007). *Saving children from a life of crime.* New York: Oxford University Press.

Federal Bureau of Investigation (1992). *Crime in the United States, 1991.* Washington, DC: U.S. Government Printing Office.

Federal Bureau of Investigation (2012). *Crime in the United States, 2011.* Washington, DC: U.S. Government Printing Office.

Gibson, C., Miller, J. M., Jennings, W. G., Swatt, M., & Gover, A. (2009). Using propensity score matching to understand the relationship between gang membership and violent victimization: A research note. *Justice Quarterly, 26,* 625–643.

Gibson, C., Swatt, M., Miller, J. M., Jennings, W. G., & Gover, A. (2012). The causal relationship between gang joining and violent victimization: A critical review and directions for future research. *Journal of Criminal Justice, 40,* 490–501.

Gorman-Smith, D., Tolan, P. H., Zelli, A., & Huesmann, L. R. (1996). The relation of family functioning to violence among inner-city minority youths. *Journal of Family Psychology, 10,* 115–129.

Gottfredson, D. C. (2001). *Schools and delinquency.* New York: Cambridge University Press.

Gover, A. R., Jennings, W. G., & Tewksbury, R. (2009). Adolescent male and female gang members' experiences of violent victimization, dating violence, and sexual assault. *American Journal of Criminal Justice, 34,* 103–115.

Grundies, V. (2000). *The effect of period on the age-crime curve: A log-linear analysis of crime rates estimated by a study of four cohorts.* Frieburg, Germany: Max Planck Institute for Foreign and International Criminal Law.

Guo, G., Ou, X.-M., Roettger, M., & Shih, J. C. (2008). The VNTR 2 repeat in *MAOA* and delinquent behavior in adolescence and young adulthood: associations and *MAOA* promoter activity. *European Journal of Human Genetics, 16,* 626–634.

Haapasalo, J., & Tremblay, R. E. (1994). Physically aggressive boys from ages 6 to 12: Family background, parenting behavior, and prediction of delinquency. *Journal of Consulting and Clinical Psychology, 62,* 1044–1052.

Hawkins, J. D., Herrenkohl, T. I., Farrington, D. P., Brewer, D., Catalano, R. F., & Harachi, T. W. (1998). A review of predictors of youth violence. In R. Loeber & D. P. Farrington (Eds.), *Serious and violent juvenile offenders: Risk factors and successful interventions* (pp. 106–146). Thousand Oaks, CA: Sage.

Henggeler, S. W., Melton, G. B., & Smith, L. A. (1992). Family preservation using Multisystemic Therapy: An effective alternative to incarcerating serious juvenile offenders. *Journal of Consulting and Clinical Psychology, 60,* 821–833.

Henggeler, S. W., Melton, G. B., Smith, L. A., Schoenwald, S. K., & Hanley, J. H. (1993). Family preservation using Multisystemic Treatment: Long-term follow-up to a clinical trial with serious juvenile offenders. *Journal of Child and Family Studies, 2,* 283–293.

Henry, B., Caspi, A., Moffitt, T. E., & Silva, P. A. (1996). Temperamental and familial predictors of violent and nonviolent criminal convictions: age 3 to age 18. *Developmental Psychology, 32,* 614–623.

Hogh, E., & Wolf, P. (1983). Violent crime in a birth cohort: Copenhagen, 1953–1977. In K. T. van Dusen & S. A. Mednick (Eds.), *Prospective studies of crime and delinquency* (pp. 249–267). Boston: Kluwer-Nijhoff.

Howell, J. C. (1998). Youth gangs: An overview. *Juvenile Justice Bulletin.* Washington, DC: US Department of Justice, Office of Justice Programs, Office of Juvenile Justice and Delinquency Prevention.

Jennings, W. G. (2011). Sex disaggregated trajectories of status offenders: Does CINS/FINS status prevent male and female youth from becoming labeled delinquent? *American Journal of Criminal Justice, 36,* 177–187.

Jennings, W. G., Maldonado-Molina, M., Piquero, A. R., Odgers, C., Bird, H., & Canino, G. (2010). Sex differences in trajectories of offending among Puerto Rican youth. *Crime & Delinquency, 56,* 327–357.

Jolliffe, D., & Farrington, D.P. (2009). A systematic review of the relationship between childhood impulsiveness and later violence. In M. McMurran & R. C. Howard (Eds.), *Personality, personality disorder, and violence* (pp. 40–61). New York: Wiley.

Kandel, E., & Mednick, S. A. (1991). Perinatal complications predict violent offending. *Criminology, 29,* 519–529.

Kempf-Leonard, K., Chesney-Lind, M., & Hawkins, J. D. (2001). Ethnicity and gender issues. In R. Loeber & D. P. Farrington (Eds.), *Child delinquents: Development, intervention, and service needs* (pp. 247–269). Thousand Oaks, CA: Sage.

Kindlon, D. J., Tremblay, R. E., Mezzacappa, E., Earls, F., Laurent, D., & Schaal, B. (1995). Longitudinal patterns of heart rate and fighting behavior in 9- through 12-year-old boys. *Journal of the American Academy of Child and Adolescent Psychiatry, 34,* 371–77.

Laub, J. H., & Lauritsen, J. L. (1993). Violent criminal behavior over the life course: A review of the longitudinal and comparative research. *Violence and Victims, 8,* 235–252.

Lipsey, M. W., & Derzon, J. H. (1998). Predictors of violent or serious delinquency in adolescence and early adulthood: A synthesis of longitudinal research. In R. Loeber & D. P. Farrington (Eds.), *Serious and violent juvenile offenders: Risk factors and successful interventions* (pp. 86–105). Thousand Oaks, CA: Sage.

Loeber, R., & Farrington, D. P. (Eds.). (1998a). *Serious and violent juvenile offenders: Risk factors and successful interventions.* Thousand Oaks, CA: Sage.

Loeber, R., & Farrington, D. P. (1998b). Never too early, never too late: Risk factors and successful interventions with serious and violent juvenile offenders. *Studies on Crime and Crime Prevention, 7,* 7–30.

Loeber, R., & Farrington, D. P. (2000). Young children who commit crime: Epidemiology, developmental origins, risk factors, early interventions, and policy implications. *Development and Psychopathology, 12,* 737–762.

Loeber, R., & Farrington, D. P. (Eds.). (2012). *From juvenile delinquency to adult crime: Criminal careers, justice policy, and prevention.* New York: Oxford University Press.

Loeber, R., Farrington, D. P., & Petechuk, D. (2003). Child delinquency: Early intervention and prevention. *Juvenile Justice Bulletin.* Washington, D.C.: US Office of Juvenile Justice and Delinquency Prevention.

Loeber, R., Farrington, D. P., Stouthamer-Loeber, M., Moffitt, T. E., Caspi, A., White, H. R., Wei, E. H., & Beyers, J. M. (2003). The development of male offending: Key findings from fourteen years of the Pittsburgh Youth Study. In T. P. Thornberry & M. D. Krohn (Eds.), *Taking stock of delinquency: An overview of findings from contemporary longitudinal studies* (pp. 93–136). New York: Kluwer/Plenum.

Loeber, R., Pardini, D., Homish, D., Wei, E. H., Crawford, A. M., Farrington, D. P., et al. (2005). The prediction of violence and homicide in young men. *Journal of Consulting and Clinical Psychology, 73,* 1074–1088.

Loeber, R., & Stouthamer-Loeber, M. (1998). Development of juvenile aggression and violence: Some common misconceptions and controversies. *American Psychologist, 53,* 242–259.

Loeber, R., & Wikstrom, P.-O. (1993). Individual pathways to crime in different types of neighborhood. In D. P. Farrington, R. J. Sampson, & P.-O. Wikstrom (Eds.), *Integrating individual and ecological aspects of crime* (pp. 169–204). Stockholm: National Council for Crime Prevention.

Maguin, E., & Loeber, R. (1996). Academic performance and delinquency. In M. Tonry (Ed.), *Crime and justice, Vol. 20* (pp. 145–264). Chicago: University of Chicago Press.

Maldonado-Molina, M. M., Piquero, A. R., Jennings, W.G., Bird, H., & Canino, G. (2009). Trajectories of delinquency among Puerto Rican children and adolescents at two sites. *Journal of Research in Crime & Delinquency, 46,* 144–181.

Maxfield, M. G., & Widom, C. S. (1996). The cycle of violence revisited 6 years later. *Archives of Pediatrics and Adolescent Medicine, 150,* 390–395.

McCord, J. (1977). A comparative study of two generations of Native Americans. In R. F. Meier (ed.), *Theory in criminology: Contemporary views* (pp. 83–92). Beverly Hills, CA: Sage.

McCord, J. (1996). Family as crucible for violence: Comment on Gorman-Smith et al. (1996). *Journal of Family Psychology, 10,* 147–152.

Moffitt, T. E., Caspi, A., Fawcett, P., Brammer, G. L., Raleigh, M., Yuwiler, A., & Silva, P. (1997). Whole blood serotonin and family background relate to male violence. In A. Raine, P. A. Brennan, D. P. Farrington, & S. A. Mednick (Eds.), *Biosocial bases of violence* (pp. 231–249). New York: Plenum.

Moffitt, T. E., Caspi, A., Rutter, M., & Silva, P.A. (2001). *Sex differences in antisocial behaviour: Conduct disorder, delinquency, and violence in the Dunedin Longitudinal Study.* Cambridge: Cambridge University Press.

Moffitt, T. E., & Henry, B. (1991). Neuropsychological studies of juvenile delinquency and juvenile violence. In J. S. Milner (Ed.), *Neuropsychology of aggression* (pp. 131–146). Boston: Kluwer.

Offord, D. R., Lipman, E. L., & Duku, E. K. (1996). Epidemiology of problem behavior up to age 12. In R. Loeber & D. P. Farrington (Eds.), *Child delinquents: Development, interventions, and service needs* (pp. 95–116). Thousand Oaks, CA: Sage.

Olds, D. L., Henderson, C. R., Cole, R., Eckenrode, J., Kitzman, H., Luckey, D., Pettitt, L., Sidora, K., Morris, P., & Powers, J. (1998). Long-term effects of nurse home visitation on children's criminal and antisocial behavior: 15 year follow-up of a randomized controlled trial. *Journal of the American Medical Association, 280,* 1238–1244.

Olweus, D. (1979). Stability of aggressive reaction patterns in males: A review. *Psychological Bulletin, 86,* 852–875.

Olweus, D. (1986). Aggression and hormones: Behavioral relationship with testosterone and adrenaline. In D. Olweus, J. Block & M. Radke-Yarrow (Eds.), *Development of antisocial and prosocial behavior: Research, theories, and issues* (pp. 51–72). Orlando, FL: Academic Press.

Patterson, G. R., & Bank, L. (1989). Some amplifying mechanisms for pathologic processes in families. In M. R. Gunnar & E. Thelen (Eds.), *Systems and development: The Minnesota Symposia on Child Psychology* (pp. 167–209). Hillsdale, NJ: Erlbaum.

Patterson, G. R., Capaldi, D. M., & Bank, L. (1991). An early starter model for predicting delinquency. In D. J. Pepler & K. H. Rubin (Eds.), *The development and treatment of childhood aggression* (pp. 139–168). Hillsdale, NJ: Erlbaum.

Patterson, G. R., Crosby, L., & Vuchinich, S. (1992). Predicting risk for early police arrest. *Journal of Quantitative Criminology, 8,* 335–355.

Peeples, F., & Loeber, R. (1994). Do individual factors and neighborhood context explain ethnic differences in juvenile delinquency? *Journal of Quantitative Criminology, 10,* 141–158.

Piquero, A. R. (2000). Frequency, specialization, and violence in offending careers. *Journal of Research in Crime and Delinquency, 37,* 392–418.

Piquero, A. R. (2008). Disproportionate minority contact. *The Future of Children, 18,* 59–79.

Piquero, A. R., & Brame, R. (2008). Assessing the race-ethnicity-crime relationship in a sample of serious adolescent delinquents. *Crime & Delinquency, 54,* 390–422.

Piquero, A. R., Diamond, B., Carriaga, M., Kazemian, L., & Farrington, D. P. (2012). Stability of aggression revisited. *Aggression & Violent Behavior, 17,* 365–372.

Piquero, A. R., Farrington, D. P., & Blumstein, A. (2003). The criminal career paradigm: Background and recent developments. In M. Tonry (Ed.), *Crime and justice: A review of research, Vol. 30* (pp. 359–506). Chicago: University of Chicago Press.

Piquero, A. R., Farrington, D. P., Welsh, B. C., Tremblay, R., & Jennings, W. G. (2009). Effects of early family/parent training programs on antisocial behavior and delinquency. *Journal of Experimental Criminology, 5,* 83–120.

Piquero, A. R., Hawkins, J. D., & Kazemian, L. (2012). Criminal career patterns. In R. Loeber & D. P. Farrington (Eds.), *From juvenile delinquency to adult crime: Criminal careers, justice policy, and prevention* (pp. 14–46). Oxford: Oxford University Press.

Piquero, A. R., Jennings, W. G. & Barnes, J. C. (2012). Violence in criminal careers: A review of the literature from a developmental life-course perspective. *Aggression and Violent Behavior, 17*(3), 171–179.

Piquero, A., & Tibbetts, S. G. (1999). The impact of pre/perinatal disturbances and disadvantaged familial environment in predicting criminal offending. *Studies on Crime and Crime Prevention, 8,* 52–71.

Raine, A. (1993). *The psychopathology of crime: Criminal behavior as a clinical disorder.* San Diego, CA: Academic Press.

Raine, A. (2008). From genes to brain to antisocial behavior. *Current Directions in Psychological Science, 17,* 323–330.

Raine, A., Brennan, P. A., & Farrington, D. P. (1997). Biosocial bases of violence: conceptual and theoretical issues. In A. Raine, P. A. Brennan, D. P. Farrington, & S. A. Mednick (Eds.), *Biosocial bases of violence* (pp. 1–20). New York: Plenum.

Raine, A., Moffitt, T. E., Caspi, A., Loeber, R., Stouthamer-Loeber, M., & Lynam, D. (2005). Neurocognitive impairments in boys on the life-course persistent antisocial path. *Journal of Abnormal Psychology, 114,* 38–49.

Rosenfeld, R., White, H. R., & Esbensen, F.-A. (2012). Criminal career patterns. In R. Loeber & D. P. Farrington (Eds.), *From juvenile delinquency to adult crime: Criminal careers, justice policy, and prevention* (pp. 118–149). Oxford: Oxford University Press.

Rubin, R. T. (1987). The neuroendocrinology and neurochemistry of antisocial behavior. In S. A. Mednick, T. E. Moffitt, & S. A. Stack (Eds.), *The causes of crime: New biological approaches* (pp. 239–262). Cambridge: Cambridge University Press.

Sampson, R. J., Morenoff, J., & Raudenbush, S. (2005). Social anatomy of racial and ethnic disparities in violence. *American Journal of Public Health, 95,* 224–232.

Sampson, R. J., Raudenbush, S., & Earls, F. (1997). Neighborhoods and violent crime: A multilevel study of collective efficacy. *Science, 277,* 919–924.

Schaeffer, C. M., & Borduin, C. M. (2005). Long-term follow-up to a randomized clinical trial of multisystemic therapy with serious and violent offenders. *Journal of Consulting and Clinical Psychology, 73,* 445–453.

Schweinhart, L. J., Barnes, H. V., & Weikart, D. P. (1993). *Significant benefits: The High/Scope Perry Preschool Study through age 27.* Ypsilanti, MI: High/Scope Press.

Smith, C., & Thornberry, T. P. (1995). The relationship between childhood maltreatment and adolescent involvement in delinquency. *Criminology, 33,* 451–481.

Snyder, H. N. (2001). Epidemiology of official offending. In R. Loeber & D. P. Farrington (Eds.), *Child delinquents: Development, intervention, and service needs* (pp. 25–46). Thousand Oaks, CA: Sage.

Stattin, H., & Magnusson, D. (1989). The role of early aggressive behavior in the frequency, seriousness, and types of later crime. *Journal of Consulting and Clinical Psychology, 57,* 710–718.

Stouthamer-Loeber, M., Loeber, R., Wei, E., Farrington, D. P., & Wikstrom, P. H. (2002). Risk and promotive effects in the explanation of persistent serious delinquency in boys. *Journal of Consulting and Clinical Psychology, 70,* 111–123.

Tate, D. C., Reppucci, N. D., & Mulvey, E. P. (1995). Violent juvenile delinquency: Treatment effectiveness and implications for future action. *American Psychologist, 50,* 777–781.

Thornberry, T. P., Huizinga, D., & Loeber, R. (1995). The prevention of serious delinquency and violence: Implications from the program of research on the causes and correlates of delinquency. In J. C. Howell, B. Krisberg, J. D. Hawkins, & J. J. Wilson (Eds.), *Sourcebook on serious, violent, and chronic juvenile offenders* (pp. 213–237). Thousand Oaks, CA: Sage.

Thornberry, T. P., Huizinga, D., & Loeber, R. (2004). The causes and correlates studies: Findings and policy implications. *Juvenile Justice, 9,* 3–19.

Thornberry, T. P., Krohn, M. D., Lizotte, A. J., Smith, C. A., & Tobin, K. (2003). *Gangs and delinquency in developmental perspective.* New York: Cambridge University Press.

Tremblay, R. E., Pihl, R. O., Vitaro, F., & Dobkin, P. L. (1994). Predicting early onset of male antisocial behavior from preschool behavior. *Archives of General Psychiatry 51,* 732–739.

Tremblay, R. E., Schaal, B., Boulerice, B., Arsenault, L., Soussignan, R., & Perusse, D. (1997). Male physical aggression, social dominance, and testosterone levels at puberty. In A. Raine, P. A. Brennan, D. P. Farrington, & S. A. Mednick (Eds.), *Biosocial bases of violence* (pp. 271–291). New York: Plenum.

Turner, A. K. (1994). Genetic and hormonal influences on male violence. In J. Archer (Ed.), *Male violence* (pp. 253–288). London: Routledge.

Wadsworth, M. E. J. (1976). Delinquency, pulse rates, and early emotional deprivation. *British Journal of Criminology, 16,* 245–256.

Wadsworth, M. E. J. (1978). Delinquency prediction and its uses: The experience of a 21-year follow-up study. *International Journal of Mental Health, 7,* 43–62.

Wasserman, G. A., Miller, L. S., & Cothern, L. (2000). Prevention of serious and violent juvenile off ending, *Juvenile Justice Bulletin,* Washington, DC: US Office of Juvenile Justice and Delinquency Prevention.

Wikstrom, P.-O. (1985). *Everyday violence in contemporary Sweden.* Stockholm: National Council for Crime Prevention.

Wikstrom, P.-O., & Loeber, R. (2000). Do disadvantaged neighborhoods caused well-adjusted children to become adolescent delinquents? A study of male juvenile serious offending, individual risk and protective factors, and neighborhood context. *Criminology, 38,* 1109–1142.

Zahn, M. (Ed.). (2009). *The delinquent girl.* Philadelphia, PA: Temple University Press.

Zingraff, M. T., Leiter, J., Myers, K. A, & Johnsen, M. C. (1993). Child maltreatment and youthful problem behavior. *Criminology, 31,* 173–202.

25 Gender, Racially, and Culturally Grounded Practice

Keva M. Miller, Ben Anderson-Nathe, and Jana L. Meinhold

■ Introduction

The U.S. juvenile justice system emerged more than a century ago to promote public safety and maintain youth accountability through rehabilitation rather than exclusively punitive responses to delinquent and criminal behaviors. Building on evolving understandings of developmental psychology, including the early-twentieth-century construction of adolescence as a developmental stage, the founders of this system recognized critical differences between adult and juvenile offenders. Consequently, they advocated for widespread reforms in the correctional system, calling for a separate and differently structured system for responding to juvenile delinquency and crime. This emergent juvenile court was designed to respond to youth offenders differently than how correctional systems dealt with adult offenders, authorizing decision-makers to utilize discretion and provide services informed by individualized and contextualized assessments (Abrams, Anderson-Nathe, & Aguilar, 2008; Nanda, 2012). The new juvenile justice system explicitly named juvenile rehabilitation, rather than punishment, as its central goal. While in recent years the system has created new and innovative approaches, its original intent has yet to be realized fully, and despite the juvenile correction system's original emphasis on rehabilitation and differentiated responses, policy reforms have increasingly missed the mark and many intervention modalities remain similar to those instituted by adult correction systems.

Despite the juvenile correction system's original intention of empowering differential treatment and individualized rehabilitation for juvenile offenders (as distinct from offenders in the adult corrections system), the juvenile court remains bound by the sometimes-competing principle of blindness in justice. Demographic trends in the current juvenile system, however, beg the question of how well the system has balanced these competing demands for individualized support on the one hand and consistency in law enforcement on the other. These trends—females entering the system in increasing numbers, significant advancements in the academic literature concerning the role of hegemonic masculine characteristics (e.g., competition, aggression, emotional stoicism) in perpetuating criminal behavior, and disparate corrections involvement among youth of color—present new challenges for programming and interventions within the juvenile justice system. An integrated and deliberate response to these challenges requires critical attention to the role of gender, race, and culture in the lives of juvenile offenders and in the intervention services provided to them.

Even in circumstances where rehabilitation and community reintegration remain principal features of state and local juvenile justice systems, these systems often fail to address the complex, individual needs of youth that may call for services and/or collaboration of services that are outside the juvenile justice purview. This is particularly true among young people who have involvement with multiple social service systems. Thus, there is a continued call to restructure services that effectively address youth delinquency and crime, respond to the parallels between involvement with juvenile justice and other systems, and interrupt the school-to-prison pipeline—all issues that could be addressed more effectively through gender, racially, and culturally grounded perspectives.

This chapter presents a brief overview of recent trends related to the role of gender, race, and culture in juvenile justice, including both entry into the system and intervention or disposition while under its supervision. Following our introduction of these trends and their associated challenges, we briefly point to innovations and responses already evident in different juvenile justice jurisdictions. In the final section, we have included vignettes to help illustrate some of the tensions the system and the youth it serves encounter as it strives to be attentive to these trends.

Gender in the Juvenile Justice System

Prior to the 1990s, the study of juvenile offending was dominated by masculinist ideologies, which neglected any consideration of the importance of gender, how gender constructs shape identities, attitudes, and behaviors, or how intervention responses for males and females may differ as a result of these constructs (Bergsmann, 1989; Chesney-Lind, Morash, & Stevens, 2008; Chesney-Lind & Pasko, 2013). In fact, from its earliest days, the juvenile justice system was explicitly oriented toward male offenders, based on gender schemas at the time that constructed criminality as an almost exclusively masculine character flaw (Abrams & Anderson-Nathe, 2013). For several decades, as these gender schemas were almost uniformly upheld as cultural norms, gender determined disposition when young people acted out: girls' misbehavior was construed as resulting from mental health concerns or immoral sexual expression, while boys' misconduct was interpreted as warranting the purview of the corrections system.

While much attention has focused recently on girls' increased presence in the juvenile justice system, even now this attention has been largely based on essentialized understandings of bodies and sex assignments (more than on gender or gender construction). Put differently, the field's attention has been on *girls* in corrections rather than on the role of *femininities* as they relate to female juvenile offending. More recently, Freiburger and Burke (2011) push the discussion of traditional sex-role perspectives of femininity when it comes to the adjudication and treatment of girls, with attention to the joint effects of race/ethnicity (Moore & Padavic, 2010). Expressions of conventional femininity, or the lack thereof, can benefit girls or make them targets of stigma, granting feminine girls access to preferential treatment in the system or keeping them out of the system altogether because "good girls" should not offend and those who do draw the attention of the courts.

By contrast, the past 10 years have seen a much more nuanced and critical examination of the role of gender as a social construct implicated in the offending behavior and treatment of young men in the system. More specifically, the

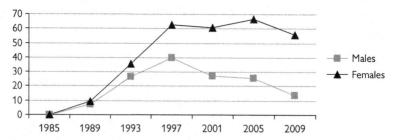

Figure 25.1 **Percentage increases and decreases in national estimates for all male and female court processing cases.**
Source: Adapted from the 2012 Puzzanchera, C. and Kang, W. *Easy Access to Juvenile Court Statistics: 1985–2009.*

corrections literature has begun to examine explicitly questions related to the role of hegemonic masculinities in contributing to and reinforcing boys' criminal conduct and complicating intervention and treatment programs within the system. In this section, considerations regarding sex-typed and gender construction, or the lack thereof, in juvenile justice policies and practices are discussed. We briefly examine the historical characterization of female delinquency, identify the shifts in types of female offenses and the resultant recent increases in girls' corrections involvement, as well as attend to the current feminist criminology trends that examine of pathways to female delinquency and crime. The discussion is then directed to new understandings of the role of hegemonic masculinity in contributing to and complicating treatment of boys' criminal behaviors.

Female Offenders

Female offenders have constituted a relatively small percentage of the overall juvenile justice population, which in part has contributed to juvenile justice criminologists' ongoing lack of or diminished attention to the unique challenges female offenders encounter (Funk, 1999). The traditional social expectation of female behaviors was evident in the historical context of the types of offenses girls were punished for in the juvenile justice system. For example, girls who came to the attention of juvenile justice systems were often portrayed as exhibiting abhorrent or immoral behavior (running away, perceived promiscuity). Violations of these social norms were judged harshly and the juvenile justice system served as a function for correcting such behaviors and preparing young girls for traditional gender-typed roles (Abrams & Curran, 2000; Chesney-Lind & Shelden, 2004; Freiburger & Burke, 2011; Odem, 1995; Sherman, 2012).

In recent years, the landscape of female offending has changed dramatically. Although females continue to represent a smaller percentage of the juvenile justice population than their male peers, female offenders are the fastest-growing juvenile offending population. In 1985, 19% of all delinquency cases were committed by females, as compared to 28% in 2009 (Puzzanchera & Kang, 2011). Thus, on average, the female delinquency cases grew approximately 3% per year, compared to a 1% growth in male delinquency cases, between over a 14-year span (Puzzanchera, Adams, & Hockenberry, 2012; Puzzanchera & Kang, 2011). The estimated percentage increases and decreases of all national male and female court processing cases from 1985 to 2009 are illustrated in Figure 25.1.

In addition to the increases in female delinquency offenses since the mid-1980s, America began to witness changes in the types of female arrests and referrals to juvenile courts—shifts that comparably resemble traditional male offenses (e.g., aggravated assault, property crimes, drug offenses) and have resulted in an increase in female offenders coming to the attention of juvenile justice systems. From 1985 to 2009, arrest rates for a number of categories (e.g., violent crime index, aggravated assault charges) rose dramatically for females, while male arrest rates increased by much smaller percentages or for some types of crimes decreased (e.g., property index crimes) as compared to female rates. As an example, from 1985 to 2009 the female violent crimes index increased by 82% compared to 16% for males, there was an 83% increase for aggravated assault female cases compared to a 21% increase for males, and the property crime index increased by 30% for females compared to a 43% decrease for males (Puzzanchera & Kang, 2012).

The increased involvement of girls in juvenile corrections presents challenges for local jurisdictions ranging from physical and structural requirements (such as those related to the capacity needs of sex-segregated residential facilities) to implications for attending to the unique and complex female offender issues that require individualized, contextualized sex-specific intervention responses. Recent research into criminal etiology among female youth offenders lends credence to current arguments in favor of intervention responses that emphasize gender and sex as salient considerations. In other words, young female offenders' criminal biographies (Goodey, 1997) differ in some significant ways from their male peers', which carries implications for service delivery and differentiated responses. In the context of juvenile corrections' long history, scholars have only recently begun to inquire about the link between exposure to traumatic life experiences and pathways of female delinquency, crime, and juvenile justice involvement (Bloom, Owens, Deschenes, & Rosenbaum, 2002; Chesney-Lind, Morash, & Stevens, 2008; Gavazzi, Yarcheck, & Chesney-Lind, 2006; Hennessey, Ford, Mahoney, Ko, & Siegfried, 2004). Studies have shown that prior to girls' involvement with the juvenile justice system they are disproportionately affected by emotional neglect, physical abuse, and sexual abuse/violence or sexual exploitation (Schaffner, 2007; Widom, 2000). They are also commonly exposed to domestic violence, multiple ephemeral foster care placements, parental substance abuse/dependence, and parental criminal behavior/

justice involvement (Acoca, 1998; Belknap & Holsinger, 2006; Gaarder & Belknap, 2002; Rodney & Mupier, 2004; Siegel & Williams, 2003). This is not to say that boys do not have similar experiences; rather, these traumatic occurrences are theorized to be much more common among girls, and the etiology of female crime and delinquency is a manifestation of exposure to such traumas (Cauffman, 2008; Funk, 1999; Pasko & Mayeda, 2011; Siegel & Williams, 2003). Therefore, the historical practices of approaching female and male offending similarly ignores critical complexities of female offenders' lives and needs to address the past and achieve a sustainable sense of self that allows them to access adaptive coping mechanisms to move forward.

Understanding the causal processes and challenges that the link between female victimization, abuse, violence, coercion, instability, loss, and the subsequent offending behaviors poses becomes essential to structuring services that effectively address female offenders' mental and behavioral health needs. Unfortunately, these inextricable links are difficult to comprehend fully and systems do not effectively address them. Sustained or acute traumatic events experienced by girls and their ensuing involvement with the juvenile justice system are too often addressed within the silos of either the mental health or juvenile justice system. Moreover, the principal factors of the traumatic experiences sustained by girls in the system are not routinely considered a priority in conceptualizing the most effective means to address female crime and delinquency (Schaffner, 2007).

Masculinities and Juvenile Crime

Over the past two decades, significant scholarly thought has emerged to analyze gender socialization, gendered identity development, and, to a slightly more limited degree, the interactions between gender socialization and criminality (Connell, 1987, 1995; Mac an Ghaill, 1994; Messerschmidt, 1993, 2000; Pascoe, 2007; Thompson & Pleck, 1995; West & Zimmerman, 1987). This literature has also taken up considerations of how race and class affect gender socialization, specifically with regard to masculinities and crime. Central to this literature is the understanding, clearly articulated in Paechter's (2007) notion of "communities of gendered practice," that gender is constructed and negotiated in context; the formation of gendered identities occurs in direct interaction with the social environment.

Although juvenile corrections has only recently drawn scholarly attention as a potential site of gender socialization (specifically for young men with regard to their performance of hegemonic masculinities), the implications for youth in corrections are significant (Abrams & Anderson-Nathe, 2013; Abrams, Anderson-Nathe, & Aguilar, 2008; Cesaroni & Alvi, 2010; Reich, 2010). It is clear that role modeling plays a significant part in shaping and granting legitimacy to gender identities and expressions; the models of adult masculinity young men are exposed to clearly influence those young men's pathways toward their own masculine identities and expressions (Majors & Billson, 1992; West & Zimmerman, 1987). Consequently, when young men witness and are rewarded for expressions of maleness that adhere to the expectations of hegemonic masculinity (including but not limited to competition, demonstrations of power and ownership, use of aggression to resolve or respond to conflict), these behaviors and values become clearly associated with their sense of self as young men (Abrams & Anderson-Nathe, 2013; Chu, Porche, & Tolman, 2005). The literature is also clear that significant associations exist between expressions of these and other features of conventional masculinity ideologies and behavior problems, including eventual involvement with the juvenile corrections system (Pleck, Sonenstein, & Ku, 1993).

These associations between demonstrations of masculinity that adhere to conventional male values and behaviors and criminal conduct are clear and hold significance for gender-specific programming in corrections facilities. Although "gender-specific" has often served as a proxy for "attentive to girls' issues, as well" in juvenile corrections, this association suggests that as the system strives to support young male offenders in achieving the system's stated goal of rehabilitation, it would do well to support those young men in challenging and transforming the narratives of masculinity that underlie much of their criminal conduct.

Programs such as The Council for Boys and Young Men®, as operationalized in the Ohio juvenile corrections system, seek to address these concerns related to hegemonic masculinity and boys' difficulty in adopting noncriminal behaviors and identities without also attending to their understandings of gender and masculine identity (Gray, 2012). Abrams and Anderson-Nathe (2013) have similarly called for gender-specific programming in juvenile corrections, geared toward supporting young male offenders in articulating and disentangling their criminal conduct from their understandings of what it means to be a young man. Commenting largely on the adult system, Goodey (1997) has suggested that rehabilitation and behavior change is strengthened by offenders' ability to articulate and rewrite masculine biographies to include a broader range of expressions and behaviors than those endorsed by hegemonic masculinity. Like their female peers, boys in the juvenile justice system also carry histories that both inform and complicate their criminal behaviors; gender socialization is one significant feature of those histories and juvenile corrections entities must be supported in developing programs and interventions to attend to these needs.

■ Race, Delinquency, and Crime

Racial disparity in the juvenile justice system has been a primary focus at national and state levels. In 1988, in response to the overrepresentation of youth

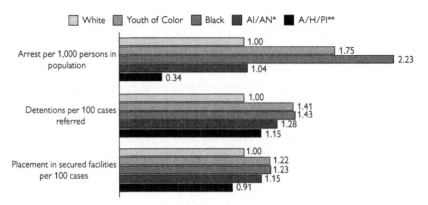

Figure 25.2   **Relative rate of index for delinquency offenses for youth 10–17 years old.**

Source: Adapted from the 2009 *National Disproportionate Minority Contact Databook.*
Developed by the National Center for Juvenile Justice for the Office of Juvenile Justice and
Delinquency Prevention.

*AI/AN: American Indian or Alaskan Native; **A/H/PI: Asian, Hawaiian, or Pacific Islander.

of color in America's juvenile justice system, Congress amended the Juvenile
Justice and Delinquency Prevention Act of 1974 (P.L. 93-415, 42 U.S.C. 5601
et seq.), which required that each state assess whether racial disproportionality existed; if this was found to be a problem, states had to implement strategies for corrective action. Despite these efforts, youth of color, specifically
African-American/Black youth, continue be disproportionately represented at
all stages of juvenile justice processing, from arrest to confinement in secure
facilities (Armstrong & Rodriquez, 2005; Bishop, 2005; Crutchfield, Skinner,
Haggerty, McGlynn, & Catalano, 2009; Shook & Goodkind; Rodriquez, 2007).
In 2009, the National Center for Juvenile Justice for the Office of Juvenile
Justice and Delinquency Prevention (OJJDP) reported that youth of color were
approximately 75% more likely to be represented among juvenile delinquency
arrest rates, 41% among juvenile detention rates, and 22% among juvenile
secure facility placement rates. In comparison to White youth, Black youth
had the greatest disparity: Black youth were 123% more likely to be arrested,
43% more likely to be detained, and 23% more likely to be placed in secure
facilities (Puzzanchera & Adams, 2012). Disparities are often reported using
the Relative Rate Index (RRI), a methodology that measures rate differences
between groups to estimate either the group's overrepresentation or underrep-
resentation. The RRI for non-youth of color represents 1, with an RRI greater
than 1 indicating overrepresentation and an RRI less than 1 suggesting under-
representation. The OJJDP 2009 RRIs for juvenile arrests, detentions, and
placements in secured facilities are illustrated in Figure 25.2.

The issues associated with racial disparity in the juvenile justice system
are complex and not easily deconstructed by attributing them to a single factor. Rather, racial disparity is multifaceted. However, it is evident from some

research that race has a direct and indirect effect on case outcomes that subsequently lead to racial disparity, particularly among Black youth (Bishop, 2005; Engen, Steen, & Bridges, 2002; Frazier & Cochran, 1986; Leiber & Fox, 2005; Pope & Feyerherm, 1992; Sampson & Laub, 1993; Rodriguez, 2010). Scholars have expressed concern that disproportionate exposure to the juvenile justice system and disparate outcomes once youth enter the system are due at least in part to biased decision making. This selection bias disadvantages youth of color differently than their similarly situated White counterparts (Bishop & Frazier, 1996). Racial profiling/stereotyping, individual bias on the part of arresting officers, juvenile justice decisions related to case processing and case outcomes, and decreased likelihood of court decisions to use diversion programs have contributed to the overrepresentation of youth of color within juvenile justice system (Bridges & Steen, 1998; Curry-Stevens & Nissen, 2011; Leiber, 2003; Wooldredge & Thistlethwaite, 2004). Scholars have also included within their discussion the role of youths' social context, thus providing an alternate theory to the existence of racial bias within the juvenile justice system (Bridges & Steen, 1998; Feld, 1999). There is acknowledgement that individual or structural racial bias may occur within the juvenile justice system; however, those instances are isolated occurrences. Rather, youth of color are more likely to be exposed to familial and community risks as well as racial segregation, concentrated poverty, and deindustrialization, all of which increase their vulnerability to criminal activity/behavior and lead to a greater propensity to commit more serious crimes (Bridges & Steen, 1998; Feld, 1999). Other scholars attribute racial disparity in the juvenile justice system to legal issues (Hindelang, 1978; Tracy, 2002).

Regardless of the factors that contribute to racial disparity in juvenile justice, the disparities that exist highlight a continued need to understand and address the context in which juvenile justice decisions are made, structural and institutional failures, and environmental and familial risks that increase youth of color's vulnerability to juvenile justice involvement. The juvenile justice system has articulated a need for a thorough analysis of the interlocking effects of the multiple factors associated with the involvement of youth of color with the juvenile justice system and the long-term implications for their futures. In addition, juvenile justice systems across the country have implemented various practices and policies to adhere to the system's stated priority for resolving race disparities at various decision points.

In recent years, juvenile justice policies have identified a need to adopt family inclusion practices to help address the behavioral and emotional concerns of its youth (Brown, 2012). Family inclusion practices could easily become a translatable culturally responsive practice that honors the juvenile justice system's priority for resolution of race disparities. For example, families and communities of color value preserving close ties with extended family, kin and non-kin alike, and accessing these resources allows for a collective responsibility for its youth (Miller & Bank, 2013; Miller, Gil-Kashiwabara,

Briggs, & Hatcher, 2010; Murry, Brown, Brody, & Simons, 2001). Thus, actively engaging families, not just the nuclear family but also those identified within the extended family and community, as collaborative partners is imperative to the well-being of these youth. While many systems nationwide have adopted family inclusion practices, these efforts have not consistently articulated how culture-specific programing would include extended family and community.

States such as Iowa, South Dakota, Colorado, Oregon, and Pennsylvania either have expressed a need for or implemented cultural sensitivity training for law enforcement, court officials, and juvenile justice personnel in hopes of reducing the disproportionate representation of youth of color within the juvenile justice system (Armour & Hammond, 2009). Cultural training has potential utility if checks and balances are also implemented such that follow-up training, system support through funding for ongoing training, and experiential application of concepts learned from the training are put in place. Law enforcement and juvenile justice system personnel each employ decision-making discretion at various points in the system that influences outcomes for youth. Therefore, training must examine how each of the decision-making points serves as a potential pathway for youth of color's entrance into the system or as a contributor to the *race effect*—that is, the predisposition of exposure that is perpetuated into a deeper involvement within the system. Moreover, corrections systems must examine how their practices and policy issues may disadvantage youth of color by making them more susceptible to involvement with and/or disparate treatment within the juvenile justice system. States that have implemented cultural sensitivity-responsive training have also effectively implemented policies that require any type of new legislation to analyze and report its impact on people of color (Brown, 2012). States such as Oregon, Colorado, and New Jersey have also implemented risk assessment instruments to reduce racial minority youth disproportionate contact. Risk assessments can help prevent the overuse of detaining youth in secure facilities, particularly youth who pose a low risk for future delinquency or youth awaiting trial for nonviolent activities (Armour & Hammond, 2009; Brown, 2012). Such enactments of practices and policies nationwide have the potential to begin to address racial disproportionality in the juvenile justice system.

■ The Intersection of Gender, Race, and Multiple System Involvement

Gender and Race

Disposition and treatment within the system also vary widely by race and gender. Freiburger and Burke (2011) have demonstrated that Black and Hispanic females and American Indian males are reported to experience harsher treatment throughout their involvement with the corrections system, likely due to the system's stereotypical perception of these groups. Compounding their differential treatment within the corrections system, these youth also experience the weight of systemic oppressions, like racism and sexism, beyond the walls of juvenile corrections facilities. Among young Black men, for instance, behaviors that may be interpreted as normative in the context of young people's development are often interpreted by authorities in schools and other settings as deviant, threatening, or even criminal (Pascoe, 2007). Coupled with existing literature demonstrating differential rates of discipline for Black youth in high schools, as compared to their White peers (Curry-Stevens, Cross-Hemmer, & Coalition of Communities of Color, 2010), these intersections present significant challenges for youth who encounter the corrections system.

Females, particularly females of color with prior referrals or records, are more likely to come to the attention of courts and be deemed to need deterrence of future bad behavior through court adjudication (Freiburger & Burke, 2011). The court's increased likelihood to adjudicate females of color for status offenses where White males would not be similarly adjudicated may play into recent increases in female cases. For example, Moore and Padavic (2010) examined the gender-role ideologies of female offenders and their possible contribution to the disproportionate numbers of racial and ethnically diverse females in the juvenile justice system. Their findings suggest that White females receive more lenience from the courts compared to Black females with the same offense, unless the White females' offenses are in a higher category of concern (crossing a threshold where courts are given the discretion to provide lenience). Thus, the juvenile justice system exercises considerable variability within the acceptable sentencing or conviction guidelines for females depending on racial group, with less tolerance granted to Black females with or without prior offenses. This increase in harsher treatment or intolerance of females of color is concerning, particularly given to the lack of appropriate and effective treatment for diverse female offenders in juvenile justice systems.

The complexities associated with gender and race in juvenile justice system involvement are complicated by disturbing trends that show parallels between concurrent or prior involvement with child welfare systems, mental health services, and/or substance abuse treatment. The challenge these systems encounter lies within the difficulty of viewing the systems as interconnected, as systems do not routinely seek partnerships to create a shared vision for the youth and families each simultaneously serves. Without interconnected system collaboration, youth are more susceptible to poor outcomes and greater difficulty resolving the issues that led to their systems involvement. Moreover, interactions with the juvenile justice system and combined interactions with other systems of care may serve as a pathway toward subsequent involvement with the adult correctional systems.

Substance Abuse and Mental Health Issues

Youth in the juvenile justice system also are identified as having substance abuse and mental health problems, or both, at rates higher than those of the general population. In fact, substance abuse increases youth's vulnerability to entrance and prolonged involvement with the juvenile justice system (Belenko & Sprott, 2002; Center on Addiction and Substance Abuse [CASA], 2004), a corollary of which is an increase in the chances of serious mental health concerns (Robertson, Dill, Husain, & Undesser, 2004; Nissen & Merrigan, 2011). Wasserman and colleagues (2010) found in their survey of 9,819 youth that 17% of the juvenile justice population at intake, 39% of detained youth, and 47% of youth in secure post-adjudication facilities had a substance abuse/use problem, as compared to 8% of youth in the general population. While no differences were found between male and female substance abuse/use, there were definite racial differences: African-American, Hispanic, and American youth were more likely to have substance abuse/use issues than their similarly situated White counterparts. In the same study, similar comparisons were examined concerning mental health problems. On average, youth in the general population experienced mental health concerns at an estimated rate of 20%, compared to 35% of the juvenile justice population at intake, 59% of youth in detention, and 54% of youth placed in a secure post-adjudication facility (Wasserman, McReynolds, Schwalbe, Keating, & Jones, 2010). Research has provided varying estimates on the prevalence of mental health problems among female offenders; however, female offenders, regardless of their race or age, experience mental health problems at higher rates than male offenders (Cauffman, 2004; Cauffman, Lexcen, Goldweber, Shulman, & Grisso, 2007; Espelage, Cauffman, Broidy, Piquero, Mazerolle, & Steiner, 2003; Wasserman et al., 2010). When mental health differences are examined according to race, youth of color, compared to White youth, have also been found to have a greater likelihood of experiencing mental health disorders (Wasserman et al., 2010).

Unfortunately, the co-occurring needs associated with addressing delinquency along with mental health and substance abuse needs are often difficult to treat and the treatment needs remain unmet (Heilbrun et al., 2000; Molidor, Nissen, & Watkins, 2002; Tripodi & Springer, 2006). Given that youth of color in the juvenile justice system experience higher rates of substance abuse and mental health concerns, these unmet needs increase their vulnerability to deeper involvement with the system and recidivism once and if they exit juvenile corrections. Similarly, female offenders are at risk for not having their mental health needs addressed. Thus, the intersectionalities of life experiences prior to a youth's entrance into the juvenile justice system, juvenile justice system involvement, and concurrent substance abuse and/or mental health needs with factors of race and gender complicate the issues. The system must make a concerted effort to increase the evaluation of needs. Moreover, youth within the juvenile justice system benefit if the system maintains a resolve to ensure sensitivity to the need for culturally responsive interventions.

Child Welfare Service Needs

Although it is difficult to enumerate the crossover cases between juvenile and social service systems due to the lack of national tracking practices that link youth in child welfare and juvenile justice systems (Pennell, Shapiro, Spigner, Bilchik, Osher, & Lee, 2011), research suggests that 9% to 29% of youth are dually involved with the juvenile justice and child welfare systems (Herz, 2010). According to a study by Washington State's King County, compared to youth with limited or no involvement with child welfare, youth with child welfare involvement experienced poorer outcomes (e.g., length of time in detention, recidivism rates), particularly females and youth of color (Halemba & Siegel, 2011). Examining the racial composition of the child welfare and juvenile justice systems, it is clear that there is an overlapping racial demographic, with an overrepresentation of youth of color within both systems. Therefore, it is important to invest in resources that collect and track data across systems (i.e., child welfare, juvenile justice) so that we can understand the extent that racial disproportionality and disparity affect youth across both systems as well as how the parallels affect youths' lives.

The intersectionality between child welfare and juvenile justice systems can be compounded by the previously mentioned need for services from mental health and substance abuse treatment facilities, which has the potential to present additional serious challenges. While juvenile and child welfare systems have identified the need to partner and address the unique mental health service needs for children with dual juvenile justice and child welfare involvement, neither system has consistently been successful in addressing the problem, either alone or working together. These unmet needs, in particular unmet mental health needs, may have the greatest impact on African-American youth with dual juvenile justice and child welfare involvement. African Americans, more than any other racial group, are identified to have the greatest need for mental health services (Baker, Kurland, Curtis, Alexander, & Papa-Lentini, 2007). Unfortunately, accessibility to culturally responsive mental health services in child welfare and juvenile justice systems does not meet the overwhelming demand. Once again, as a result the specific cultural needs of youth of color are often not addressed by service providers in either system (Briggs & McBeath, 2010; Risley-Curtiss, Combs-Orme, Chernoff, & Heisler, 1996).

■ Case Illustrations

The juvenile corrections system is often just one system of many involved in the lives of the young people who come under its jurisdiction. As we have illustrated, other services often intersect, including mental health, child welfare, and schools. The vignettes that follow represent composites of young people who have come to the attention of the juvenile justice system. Each vignette highlights some of the unique considerations outlined earlier in this chapter and invites readers to position themselves as juvenile justice workers or other helping professionals, articulating service needs, identifying pathways or considerations in the formation of the youth's criminal trajectory, and exploring possible interventions.

■ Vignette 1

Karina is a 13-year-old Latina whose recent testing revealed fifth-grade academic performance, a 2-year delay when compared to her seventh-grade peers. Despite these findings, Karina has not been screened for an individualized education program (IEP) or special education services; school officials attribute her academic performance to a simple lack of initiative. Since infancy, she has been exposed to drug activity in her home and community and has witnessed domestic violence perpetrated by a number of her mother's boyfriends. Karina's uncle, who lived in the home, began sexually abusing her when she was 5 years old. The abuse continued until child welfare became involved with the family when Karina was 8, at which time she was removed for substantiated neglect and her mother's failure to protect her. Karina was placed in a non-relative foster care home for 18 months, during which time she maintained contact with her mother. When she returned home, Karina experienced repeated sexual advances from her mother's live-in boyfriend. Karina first came to the attention of the juvenile justice system within months of returning home. By age 12, she had multiple encounters with the system for running away from home, truancy, and possession of marijuana. Karina was recently arrested on her fourth truancy charge and second possession of a controlled substance. She is currently in the county's short-term detention facility, awaiting a hearing to determine whether she will be placed on probation or detained in a longer-term juvenile facility.

■ Vignette 2

Larry is a 17-year-old African-America male who dropped out of school 3 years ago. His mother is single and works three part-time jobs to bring in enough income to care for her five children. Larry's maternal grandmother and aunt have on occasion provided financial assistance. Regardless, money is tight for the family. Larry has been involved in the juvenile justice system since he was 12 years old due to various auto theft, burglary, and gang-related assault charges. His older brother and sister have had similar involvement with the system; less than a year ago, Larry's oldest brother was sentenced to 25 years in prison for a gang-related murder. This prompted Larry to denounce his own gang involvement and start the process of having his gang tattoos removed. Larry completed probation 3 months ago but asked that he remain under the supervision of his probation officer and be allowed to continue his counseling until his 18th birthday. He is currently working toward his GED and receiving vocational training to become an electrician. A week ago, Larry and his friends were pulled over by the police for running a stop sign. The police searched the car and found marijuana. Larry and his friends were arrested for possession, but Larry adamantly denies that the marijuana was his and states that he was unaware that the marijuana was in his friend's car.

■ Vignette 3

Tasha, a 14-year-old White female, has been involved with the juvenile justice system since she was 10 years old. She has been picked up for running away, shoplifting, assaulting her mother, and truancy. She does not do drugs but drinks heavily, consuming two to five drinks per day. Tasha's relationship with her mother and stepfather has been strained for as long as she can remember. Both parents have been in and out of substance abuse treatment facilities for the past 7 years, leading Tasha to say that her parents "are basically never around and can't really be bothered to care" about her or her three siblings. Tasha recently ran away from her parents' home, but her mother did not report her as a runaway, stating that "Tasha takes off like this all the time—whenever she has a new boyfriend, she's up and gone. But she'll come back. She always does." During Tasha's most recent detention experience, 6 months ago, she was dually diagnosed with bipolar disorder and an alcohol abuse problem. Tasha recently found out that she is three months pregnant but has not disclosed the pregnancy to anyone except to a close friend, a fellow probationer who then shared the news with her P.O. Two weeks ago, when she learned the friend had disclosed the pregnancy, Tasha was arrested for assaulting the friend and the arresting officer. She is awaiting her hearing with the judge to determine whether she will be confined in a locked facility.

■ Vignette 4

Vu is a 16-year-old Vietnamese resident in a long-term correctional facility. Despite its geographic location in a predominantly White city, Vu is one of a large number of Vietnamese youth held in this facility. The program is structured in such a way that to advance in the program and earn enough levels to warrant release back to the community, residents must produce written reflections and reports (the program calls them "contracts") outlining the details of their offenses, their thinking errors, their family relationships, and their plans for avoiding criminal behavior upon release. Vu, having fairly recently come to the United States, struggles with spoken and written English; he routinely asks his Vietnamese peers, most of whom have been in the United States longer and are more bicultural than he is, for help with translation and understanding of the program's expectations. Recently, the only bilingual (Vietnamese-English) staff person left the facility; it is now against the rules for residents to speak with one another in Vietnamese, due to the staff's concern that they cannot understand what residents say to one another. Vu has tried and failed three times to successfully present his treatment contracts; they continue to be declined on the grounds that they don't "go deep enough" into his past. If he fails a fourth time, he runs the risk of being sent back to the county-run facility for noncompliance.

■ Vignette 5

Josh is a 15-year-old Latino male currently serving a 9-month probation sentence for possession of marijuana. He has lived with his maternal grandmother since his mother was arrested 2 years ago for multiple felony charges including theft, fraud, and extortion. Josh's mother was found guilty last week on all counts and is awaiting sentencing; she faces a prison term of 3 to 5 years in a women's prison far away from Josh's home city. Over the past 2 years, Josh has been expelled from three different schools for truancy, drug possession, and fighting. He is attending an alternative school across town, where he is one of few students of color. Josh has considered dropping out because, as he puts it, he would "rather hang with my friends and smoke weed than put up with crap from school." His grandmother and probation officer both believe the friends Josh mentions are actually members of a neighborhood gang; Josh has denied that this is the case. Josh's teachers have consistently commented on how highly gifted and intelligent he is and have suggested that he has potential to succeed academically if only he would refocus his attention and apply himself. Josh was recently referred to the juvenile justice system for a third time because of his participation in a fight at school with a peer assumed to be in a rival gang.

■ Vignette 6

Corrine, a 16-year-old biracial African American/American Indian female, was arrested for shoplifting diapers and baby formula from her local food mart. She has been arrested twice before, once for a fight at school and again for breaking the city's juvenile curfew. This most recent arrest is the first in nearly 2 years. Corrine's mother has been arrested and incarcerated in the county jail multiple times for misdemeanor charges. Her mother has also been in treatment for alcohol and drug abuse, and she has received inpatient care for major depression and suicidal ideation. During both of her mother's inpatient stays, Corrine bore the responsibility of maintaining the family home and taking care of herself and her sibling. Corrine dropped out of school a year ago and is currently the primary caregiver to her 2-year-old brother and 8-month-old daughter. Recently, Corrine applied for government daycare assistance so she can return to school and complete her high school degree or GED, with the hopes of eventually attending community college to become a nursing assistant.

Discussion Questions

We provide the vignettes outlined above as teaching cases, with the intention that students and other readers can use these examples as jumping-off points to begin transforming the discourse and practice of juvenile justice to better meet the changing needs of its constituents. Although it is beyond the scope of one chapter to outline intervention modalities or program designs to address each of the complexities we have outlined, we hope that these vignettes can spark imagination and conversation about what such interventions might entail and what barriers exist to their creation and implementation. In light of the diverse circumstances presented in each vignette, and the varied roles helping professionals might play in the lives of young people connected with the juvenile corrections system, consider the following questions and discussion prompts:

☐ What does each vignette suggest about the unique needs of the young person it highlights? How do their experiences prior to their encounters with juvenile justice shape their treatment within the system?

☐ From an intervention standpoint, what should probation officers, corrections officers, attorneys, judges, and other juvenile justice partners consider before moving forward?

☐ How does gender, race, or ethnicity affect these young people's experiences with the system or their treatment within it?

☐ What systemic issues within and outside of the juvenile justice system appear to pose barriers for these youth? Where is there the potential for the system to serve as a source for a positive outcome?

☐ What leverage/advantage points exist for possible systemic changes?

☐ How might multiple service systems work together to provide better treatment and intervention for these young people and their families? What might it look like for these systems to offer gender and culturally specific services?

Discussion/Implications

This chapter has presented data and case examples in support of an argument that the contemporary juvenile justice system is facing significant transformation in the populations it serves. Youth of color are disproportionately involved with and affected by the juvenile corrections system, and that system often lacks the culturally relevant services necessary to support these youths' rehabilitation and ultimately their successful re-entry into their communities. Similarly, more females are entering juvenile corrections than at any other point in the system's century-long history, and the historical male bias of corrections institutions, processes, and interventions has not met the needs of these females. Even with regard to male offenders, recent scholarly attention to associations between hegemonic masculine traits and juvenile crime has suggested that corrections institutions would provide better service for young men if gender-specific programming (inclusive of critical examinations of masculinity) were provided. Added to these demographic shifts is increased recognition of the complicated intersections of systems involvement and service needs for many young people in juvenile corrections, including the impacts of mental health and substance use issues, child welfare involvement, and complicated relationships with educational institutions.

We do offer some recommendations for the system. At the very least, the academic literature around gender and race in juvenile corrections points to the need for gender-inclusive and racially sensitive programming. In terms of gender, corrections institutions must reconsider their longstanding notions that the default juvenile offender is male and engages in criminal conduct solely due to behavioral issues (impulse control, conduct disorders, and the like) or learned behavior (parental histories of incarceration). For male offenders, attention must be paid to examining how they internalize and perform masculinity, and how those gendered performances may in some cases actively work against rehabilitation messages. For female offenders, our systems will do well to anticipate and design interventions and services that address the complex biographies of abuse and trauma that many girls bring into the system with them. Concerning racially sensitive programming, the juvenile system must continue to grapple with how racial bias in policing, arrest and conviction rates, and experiences of discipline and access to services for youth of color once they are in the system contribute to racial disproportionality and disparity. Further, juvenile corrections must do better in terms of building bridges between young people and their home communities, recognizing and interrupting the racial biases that may lead well-intentioned corrections officers to approach youth and communities of color with the same default assumptions and understandings they bring to White communities.

Given the juvenile justice system's explicitly stated central emphasis on rehabilitation and differential responses to the unique needs of its youth, the system must continue to extend beyond current policies and practices and thoroughly examine how the contexts of race, gender, and culture factor into the experiences of its youth. Policies and practices must reflect the complex needs of juvenile justice-involved youth with deliberate and multisystem integrated responses.

References

Abrams, L. S., & Anderson-Nathe, B. (2013). *Compassionate confinement: A year in the life of Unit C*. New Brunswick, NJ: Rutgers University Press.

Abrams, L., Anderson-Nathe, B., & Aguilar, J. (2008). Constructing masculinities in juvenile corrections. *Men and Masculinities, 11*(1), 22–41.

Abrams, L. S., & Curran, L. (2000). Wayward girls and virtuous women: Social workers and female juvenile delinquency in the progressive era. *Affilia, 15*(1), 49–64.

Acoca, L. (1998). Outside/inside: The violation of American girls at home, in the streets, and in the system. *Crime and Delinquency, 44*(4), 561–590.

Armour, J., & Hammond, S. (2009, January). *Minority youth in the juvenile justice system: Disproportionate minority contact*. National Conference of State Legislatures. Retrieved from http://www.ncsl.org/print/cj/minoritiesinjj.pdf.

Armstrong, G. S., & Rodriguez, N. (2005). Effects of individual and contextual characteristics on preadjudication detention of juvenile delinquents. *Justice Quarterly, 22*(4), 521–539.

Baker, A. J., Kurland, D., Curtis, P., Alexander, G., & Papa-Lentini, C. (2007). Mental health and behavioral problems of youth in the child welfare system: Residential treatment centers compared to therapeutic foster care in the odyssey project population. *Child Welfare, 86*(1), 97–123.

Belenko, S., & Sprott, J. B. (2002). *Comparative recidivism rates of drug and nondrug juvenile offenders: Results from three jurisdictions*. March Paper presented at the Academy of Criminal Justice Sciences Annual Conference, Anaheim, CA.

Belknap, J., & Holsinger, K. (2006). The gendered nature of risk factors for delinquency. *Feminist Criminology, 1*(1), 48–71.

Bergsmann, I. R. (1989). The forgotten few: Juvenile female offenders. *Federal Probation, 53*(1), 73–78.

Bishop, D. M. (2005). The role of race and ethnicity in juvenile justice processing. In D. F. Hawkins & K. Kempf-Leonard (Eds.), *Our children, their children* (pp. 23–82). Chicago: University of Chicago Press.

Bishop, D. M., & Frazier, C. E. (1996). Race effects in juvenile justice decision-making: Findings of a statewide analysis. *Journal of Criminal Law and Criminology, 86*(2), 392–414.

Bloom, B., Owen, B., Deschenes, E. P., & Rosenbaum, J. (2002). Moving toward justice for female juvenile offenders in the new millennium. *Journal of Contemporary Criminal Justice, 18*(1), 37–56.

Bridges, G. S., & Steen, S. (1998). Racial disparities in official assessments of juvenile offenders: Attribution stereotypes as mediating mechanisms. *American Sociological Review, 63*(4), 554–570.

Briggs, H. E., & McBeath, B. (2010). Infusing culture into practice: Developing and implementing evidence-based mental health services for African American foster youth. *Child Welfare, 89*(1), 31–60.

Brown, S. A. (2012). *Trends in the juvenile justice state legislation: 2001–2011*. National Conference for State Legislatures, Washington, DC.

Cauffman, E. (2004). A statewide screening of mental health symptoms among juvenile offenders in detention. *Journal of the American Academy of Child and Adolescent Psychiatry, 43*(4), 430–439.

Cauffman, E. (2008). Understanding the female offender. *The Future of Children, 18*(2), 119–142.

Cauffman, E., Lexcen, F. J., Goldweber, A., Shulman, E. P., & Grisso, T. (2007). Gender differences in mental health symptoms among delinquent and community youth. *Youth Violence and Juvenile Justice, 5*(3), 287–307.

Center on Addiction and Substance Abuse (CASA) (2004). *Criminal neglect: Substance abuse, juvenile justice, and the children left behind.* New York: Author, Columbia University.

Cesaroni, C., & Alvi, S. (2010). Masculinity and resistance in adolescent carceral settings. *Canadian Journal of Criminology and Criminal Justice, 52*(3), 303–320.

Chesney-Lind, M., Morash, M., & Stevens, T. (2008). Girls' troubles, girls' delinquency, and gender responsive programming: A review. *Australian & New Zealand Journal of Criminology, 41*(1), 162–189

Chesney-Lind, M., & Pasko, L. J. (2013). *The female offender: Girls, women, and crime (3rd ed.).* Los Angeles: Sage.

Chesney-Lind, M., & Shelden, R. G. (2004). *Girls, delinquency, and juvenile justice* (3rd ed.). Belmont, CA: Wadsworth.

Chu, J. Y., Porche, M. V., & Tolman, D. L. (2005). The adolescent masculinity ideology in relationships scale: Development and validation of a new measure for boys. *Men and Masculinities, 8,* 93–115.

Crutchfield, R. D., Skinner, M. L., Haggerty, K. P., McGlynn, A., & Catalano, R. F. (2009). Racial disparities in early criminal justice involvement. *Race and Social Problems, 1*(4), 218–213.

Curry-Stevens, A., Cross-Hemmer, A., & Coalition of Communities of Color (2010). *Communities of color in Multnomah County: An unsettling profile.* Portland, OR: Portland State University.

Curry-Stevens, A., & Nissen, L. B. (2011). Reclaiming Futures considers an anti-oppressive framework to decrease disparities. *Children and Youth Services Review, 33*(1), S54–S59.

Engen, R., Steen, S., & Bridges, G. (2002). Racial disparities in the punishment of youth: A theoretical and empirical assessment of the literature. *Social Problems, 49*(2), 194–220.

Espelage, D. L., Cauffman, E., Broidy, L., Piquero, A. R., Mazerolle, P., & Steiner, H. (2003). A cluster-analytic investigation of MMPI profiles of serious male and female juvenile offenders. *Journal of the American Academy of Child and Adolescent Psychiatry, 42*(7), 770–777.

Feld, B. C. (1999). *Bad kids: Race and the transformation of the juvenile court.* New York: Oxford University Press.

Frazier, C., & Cochran, J. (1986). Detention of juveniles its effects on subsequent juvenile court proceedings. *Youth and Society, 17*(3), 286–305.

Freiburger, T. L., & Burke, A. S. (2011). Status offenders in the juvenile court: The effects of gender, race, and ethnicity on the adjudication decision. *Youth Violence and Juvenile Justice, 9*(4), 352–365.

Funk, S. J. (1999). Risk assessment for juveniles on probation—A focus on gender. *Criminal Justice and Behavior, 26*(1), 44–68.

Gaarder, E., & Belknap, J. (2002). Tenuous borders: Girls transferred to adult court. *Criminology, 40*(3), 481–517.

Gavazzi, S. M., Yarcheck, C. M., & Chesney-Lind, M. (2006). Global risk indicators and the role of gender in a juvenile detention sample. *Criminal Justice and Behavior, 33*(5), 597–612.

Goodey, J. (1997). Boys don't cry: Masculinities, fear of crime, and fearlessness. *British Journal of Criminology, 37*(3), 401–418.

Gray, M. E. (2012). *"Man up": A longitudinal evaluation of adherence to traditional masculinity among racially/ethnically diverse adolescent inmates.* Unpublished doctoral dissertation, Portland State University.

Halemba, G., & Siegel, G. (2011). *Doorways to delinquency: Multi-system involvement of delinquent youth in King County (Seattle, WA).* National Center for Juvenile Justice. Retrieved from http://www.ncjfcj.org/sites/default/files/Doorways_to_ Delinquency_2011.pdf

Heilbrun, K., Brock, W., Waite, D., Lanier, A., Schmid, M., Witte, G., Keeney, M., Westendorf, M., Buinavert, L., & Shumate, M. (2000). Risk factors for juvenile criminal recidivism: The post-release community adjustment of juvenile offenders. *Criminal Justice and Behavior, 27*(3), 275–291.

Hennessey, M., Ford, J. D., Mahoney, K., Ko, S. J., & Siegfried, C. B. (2004). *Trauma among girls in the juvenile justice system.* National Child Trauma Stress Network. Retrieved from http://www.nctsnet.org/products/trauma-among-girls-juvenile-justice-system-2004

Herz, D. (2010). *Crossover youth practice model: Research summary.* Washington, DC: Center for Juvenile Justice Reform, Georgetown University Public Policy Institute.

Leiber, M. (2003). *The contexts of juvenile justice decision making: When race matters.* Albany, NY: State University of New York Press.

Leiber, M., & Fox, K. (2005). Race and the impact of detention on juvenile justice decision making. *Crime & Delinquency, 51*(4), 470–497.

Majors, R., & Billson, J. M. (1992). *Cool pose: The dilemmas of black manhood in America.* New York, NY: Touchstone.

Messerschmidt, J. W. (1993). *Masculinities and crime: Critique and reconceptualization of theory.* Lanham, MD: Rowan & Littlefield Publishers, Inc.

Messerschmidt, J. W. (2000). *Nine lives: Adolescent masculinities, the boyd, and violence.* Boulder, CO: Westview Press.

Miller, K. M., & Bank, L. (2013). Moderating effects of race on children's internalizing and externalizing behaviors who have mothers with child welfare and criminal justice involvement. *Children and Youth Services Review, 35*(3), 472–481.

Miller, K. M., Gil-Kashiwabara, E., Briggs, H. E., & Hatcher, S. (2010). Contexts of race, ethnicity, and culture for children of incarcerated parents. In J. M. Eddy & J. Poehlmann (Eds.). *Children of incarcerated parents: A handbook for researchers and practitioners* (pp. 141–157), Baltimore, MD: The Urban Institute Press.

Molidor, C. E., Nissen, L. B., & Watkins, T. R. (2002). The development of theory and treatment with substance abusing female juvenile delinquents. *Child and Adolescent Social Work Journal, 19*(3), 209–225.

Moore, L. D., & Padavic, I. (2010). Racial and ethnic disparities in girls' sentencing in the juvenile justice system. *Feminist Criminology, 5*(3), 263–285.

Murry, V. M., Brown, P. A., Brody, G. H., & Simons, R. L. (2001). Racial discrimination as a moderator of the links among stress, maternal psychological functioning, and family relationships. *Journal of Marriage and Family, 63*(4), 915–926.

Nanda, J. (2012). Blind discretion: Girls of color & delinquency in the juvenile justice system. *UCLA Law Review, 59*, 1502–1539.

Nissen, L. B., & Merrigan, D. (2011). Helping substance-involved young people in juvenile justice be successful: Conceptual and structural foundations of the Reclaiming Futures model. *Children and Youth Services Review, 33*(1), S3–S8.

Odem, M. E. (1995). *Delinquent daughters: Protecting and policing adolescent female sexuality in the United States, 1885–1920.* Chapel Hill, NC: University of North Carolina Press.

Pascoe, C. J. (2007). *Dude, you're a fag: Masculinity and sexuality in adolescence.* Berkeley: University of California Press.

Pasko, L., & Mayeda, D. T. (2011). Pathway and predictors of juvenile justice involvement for Native Hawaiian and Pacific Islander youth: A focus on gender. *Journal of Ethnic & Cultural Diversity in Social Work, 20*(2), 114–130.

Pennell, J., Shapiro, C., Spigner, C., Bilchik, S., Osher, T., & Lee, K. J. (2011). *Safety, fairness, stability: Repositioning juvenile justice and child welfare to engage families and communities.* Washington, DC: Center for Juvenile Justice Reform. Retrieved from http://cjjr.georgetown.edu/pdfs/famengagement/FamilyEngagementPaper.pdf

Pope, C. E., & Feyerherm, W. (1992). *Minorities and the juvenile justice system: Full report.* Rockville, MD: U.S. Department of Justice, Office of Juvenile Justice and Delinquency Prevention, Juvenile Justice Clearing House.

Puzzanchera, C. (2009). Juvenile arrests 2008. *OJJDP Juvenile Justice Bulletin.* Retrieved from https://www.ncjrs.gov/pdffiles1/ojjdp/228479.pdf

Puzzanchera, C., & Adams, B. (2012). *National disproportionate minority contact databook.* Developed by the National Center for Juvenile Justice for the Office of Juvenile Justice and Delinquency Prevention. Online. Available: http://www.ojjdp.gov/ojstatbb/dmcdb/

Puzzanchera, C., Adams, B., & Hockenberry, S. (2012). *Juvenile court statistics 2009.* Pittsburgh, PA: National Center for Juvenile Justice. Retrieved from http://www.ojjdp.gov/ojstatbb/njcda/

Puzzanchera, C., & Kang, W. (2012). *Easy access to juvenile court statistics: 1985–2009.* Online. Retrieved from http://www.ojjdp.gov/ojstatbb/ezajcs/

Puzzanchera, C., Sladky, A., & Kang, W. (2012). *Easy access to juvenile populations: 1990–2011.* Online. Retrieved from http://www.ojjdp.gov/ojstatbb/ezapop/

Reich, A. (2010). *Hidden truth: Young men navigating lives in and out of juvenile prison.* Berkeley: University of California Press.

Risley-Curtiss, C., Combs-Orme, T., Chernoff, R., & Heisler, A. (1996). Health care utilization by children entering foster care. *Research on Social Work Practice, 6*(4), 442–461.

Robertson, A. A., Dill, P. L., Husain, J., & Undesser, C. (2004). Prevalence of mental illness and substance use disorders among incarcerated juvenile offenders in Mississippi. *Child Psychiatry and Human Development, 35*(5), 55–74.

Rodney, H., & Mupier, R. (2004). The special needs of girls in trouble. *Reclaiming Children and Youth, 13*(2), 103–109.

Rodriguez, N. (2007). Juvenile court context and detention decisions: Reconsidering the role of race, ethnicity, and community characteristics in juvenile court processes. *Justice Quarterly, 24*(4), 629–656.

Rodriguez, N. (2010). The cumulative effect of race and ethnicity in juvenile court outcomes and why preadjudication detention matters. *Journal of Research in Crime & Delinquency, 47*(3), 391–413.

Sampson, R., & Laub, J. (1993). Structural variations in juvenile court processing: Inequality, the underclass, and social control. *Law & Society Review, 27*(2), 285–311.

Schaffner, L. (2007). Violence against girls provokes girls' violence: From private injury to public harm. *Violence Against Women, 13*(12), 1229–1248.

Sherman, F. T. (2012). Justice for girls: Are we making progress? *UCLA Law Review, 59*(6), 1584–1628.

Shook, J. J., & Goodkind, S. (2009). Racial disproportionality in juvenile justice: The interaction of race and geography in pretrial detention for violent and serious offenses. *Race and Social Problems, 1*(4), 257–266.

Siegel, J. A., & Williams, L. M. (2003). The relationship between child sexual abuse and female delinquency and crime: A prospective study. *Journal of Research in Crime and Delinquency, 40*(1), 71–94.

Thompson, E. H., & Pleck, J. H. (1995). Masculinity ideologies: A review of research instrumentation on men and masculinities. In R. F. Levant & W. S. Pollack (Eds.) *A new psychology of men,* (pp. 129–163). New York, NY: Basic Books.

Tracy, P. E. (2002). *Decision making and juvenile justice: An analysis of bias in case processing.* Westport, CT: Praeger.

Tripodi, S. J., & Springer, D. W. (2006). Mental health and substance abuse treatment of juvenile delinquents. In A. R. Roberts & D. W. Springer (Eds.), *Social work in juvenile and criminal justice settings* (3rd ed.) (pp. 351–365). Springfield, IL: Charles C. Thomas.

Wasserman, G. A., McReynolds, L. S., Schwalbe, C. S., Keating, J. M., & Jones, S. A. (2010). Psychiatric disorder, comorbidity, and suicidal behavior in juvenile justice youth. *Criminal Justice and Behavior, 37*(12), 1361–1376.

West, C., & Zimmerman, D. H. (1987). Doing gender. *Gender & Society,* 1(2), 125–151.

Widom, C. S. (2000). Childhood victimization: Early adversity, later psychopathology. *National Institute of Juvenile Justice Journal, 242*(1), 3–9.

Wooldredge, J., & Thistlethwaite, A. (2004). Bi-level disparities in court dispositions for intimate assault. *Criminology, 42*(2), 417–456.

VI

Juvenile Justice Reform

26 The Road Ahead: Progressive Possibilities and Challenges for Juvenile Justice Reform

Laura Burney Nissen

The juvenile justice system is a constantly evolving, ideologically diverse, and complex network of laws, programs, disciplines, and systems. Its genesis—indeed, its whole history—can be best understood as a reform of the adult criminal justice system, and a series of subsequent reforms seeking to focus and improve its efforts. In contrast, it also has a history of intermittent punitive shifts intended to strengthen its rigor and youth accountability. Its overall mission is to simultaneously protect the public and provide a rehabilitative environment in which young people have the best chance to change the trajectory of their lives (Fox, 1970).

The contemporary snapshot of the U.S. juvenile justice system reveals a network of structures and policies urgently in need of re-emphasized change efforts. The system has been described as "dangerous, ineffective, unnecessary, obsolete, wasteful and inadequate" (Mendel, 2011, p. i), and, despite the fact that youth incarceration rates are down dramatically (Sickmund, Sladky, Kang, & Puzzanchera, 2011), the United States continues to rank dramatically in first place among nations for rate of youth in confinement (Hazel, 2008). Further, the majority of incarcerated youth are being held for nonviolent offenses (Sickmund et al., 2011), and a disproportionate number are youth of color, despite many years of laws aimed at changing the trajectory (National Council on Crime and Delinquency, 2007; Office of Juvenile Justice and Delinquency Prevention [OJJDP], 2012).

The chapters in this volume attest to the creative and tireless work of U.S.- based advocates, social scientists, researchers, juvenile justice practitioners, community members, and families to improve outcomes for youth in the juvenile justice system. The variety of subjects covered further testifies to the complexities involved in the reform community's efforts to drive change in so many (albeit necessary) directions simultaneously.

This final chapter will provide an overview of the depth and breadth of juvenile justice reform as a specific phenomenon, as it operates now and sets the stage for future reforms. It will use an explicit social justice lens and consider the degree to which juvenile justice reformers have adequately articulated its importance. Four keys for effective reform, synthesized from the literature, are introduced: the concept of systems change, the role of leadership, the importance of cultivating political will, and the merits of using a social change lens in the deployment of a more enduring juvenile justice reform practice. Finally, it will conclude with an overview and analysis of expert projections for the immediate future agenda of juvenile justice reform and will offer some additional ideas for future development of the effort.

■ Defining the Scope and Breadth of Reform Now and into the Future

The term "juvenile justice reform" refers to all attempts to improve the performance, effectiveness, and/or fairness of juvenile justice practice. There are variations (from conservative to progressive) on this definition, depending on who is using it. Reform is encouraged by legal and community activists, social scientists, and local community members who identify and push for needed changes at every level of government and in every category of juvenile justice practice. It is impeded by bureaucracy, competing ideologies and juvenile justice practice priorities, and political processes, including inconsistent commitment from leaders besieged with differential priorities for other public interest issues. Juvenile justice reform is always an amalgam of two significant forces: (1) the independence and autonomy of individual state (and often individual county or jurisdictional) perspectives and authority, with (2) the sensibility of an integrated, national framework of model policy and practices that blend the most up-to-date evidence base and consistent constitutional protections. Tribal courts, of course, operate within a separate legal system in the United States and have their own variations on this theme (Cobb & Mullins, 2010), although Native American youth are overrepresented in the proportion of youth handled by the U.S. federal system (Motivans & Snyder, 2011).

In the 1970s, Congress took steps to create and authorize federal standards for the care and custody of young people in the juvenile justice system, as well as guidelines to prevent delinquency. The resulting Juvenile Justice and Delinquency Prevention Act (JJDPA) (as of this publication the JJDPA is overdue for a reauthorization from Congress) focuses on four "core protections": deinstitutionalization of status offenders, removal of juveniles from adult jails/lockups, sight and sound separation of juvenile and adult inmates, and disproportionate minority contact. The JJDPA includes formula grants as well as other limited discretionary funds for distribution in demonstration programs. The federal guidelines specifically add incentives for states that participate in particular ways, including creating citizen advisory boards to provide oversight and to recommend how funds should be spent, and participation in regular monitoring by the federal agency responsible for the funds, the OJJDP, an agency within the U.S. Department of Justice. Participation is guided by a state juvenile justice plan, which historically includes a platform of reforms to attend to local concerns and priorities. Each reauthorization cycle provides opportunities to strengthen the core protections, which can be thought of as reforms themselves (Act 4 Juvenile Justice, 2011). States are free to "reform" or to "innovate"—or some combination of the two—depending on local priorities and concerns.

This structure is vital to an understanding of the reform ecosystem, one in which federal guidelines are one aspect of the evolution of the system, and local juvenile justice authorities drive additional aspects. Many of the reforms in juvenile justice are connected to a strange contradiction in its complicated and longstanding history, which has always navigated tensions between redemption and punishment, and the degree to which constitutional protections apply to youth (Butts & Harrell, 1998). This becomes particularly complex when one realizes there are over 3,000 counties in the United States and a slightly smaller number of jurisdictions (Puzzanchera, Adams, &

Hockenberry, 2012), each engaged in its own interpretation of and variations on what we refer to singularly as "juvenile justice" practice. Indeed, there is no one "juvenile justice system" in the United States, but rather there are loosely connected jurisdictions all practicing in their own chosen manner. Only one state, Wyoming, elects not to participate in the JJDPA program, thus forfeiting federal funding to support its juvenile justice infrastructure.[1]

The breadth of recent juvenile justice reform in multiple arenas is truly remarkable. Particularly noteworthy were the following U.S. Supreme Court cases:

☐ *Roper v. Simmons*, 2005, which eliminated the death penalty for minors; this is universally considered one of the major successes of juvenile justice reform in recent history (Benekos & Merlo, 2008)

☐ *Graham v. Florida*, 2010, which eliminated sentences of life without the possibility of parole for youth in non-homicide convictions

☐ *Miller v. Alabama*, 2012, in which the Court ruled that juveniles convicted of murder cannot be subject to a sentence of life without parole (National Conference of State Legislatures, 2012)

Finally, the emergence of "risk assessment" science, which, though far from perfectly implemented, has clearly made the case that deinstitutionalization is a more cost-effective, humane, and just approach to juvenile justice than youth incarceration (Mendel, 2011).

But there are many more examples. In 2012a, the National Juvenile Justice Network prepared a report on successful reforms, including more than 250 examples of incremental policy changes and reforms, illustrating that though slow, change is happening throughout the United States. These reforms can be grouped into six categories:

1 Reforms that interrupt destructive emergent policies. This sometimes occurs through advocacy, sometimes through lawsuits.[2]

2 Reforms that focus on reducing the overrepresentation of youth of color

3 Reforms that incentivize alternatives to incarceration for the majority of young offenders who do not need it (per an abundance of literature cited elsewhere in this book and chapter) that allow them to stay at home, or near home, with better outcomes

4 Reforms that tackle the juvenile justice system itself and seek to combine multiple, simultaneous, and complementary reforms to achieve lower costs, improve success, and increase public safety

5 Reforms that focus on the "school-to-prison pipeline" (Edelman, 2007) and keep special focus on those mechanisms (primarily school and child welfare) where young people most often initially come to the attention of the system and where early interventions can be most effective

6 Reforms that address the overly punitive sexual offender registry system as it applies to young offenders who are at low risk of reoffending

Also in 2012, the National Conference of State Legislators compiled a 10-year retrospective analysis of state-level juvenile justice reforms and noted that most fell into the following categories: "distinguishing juvenile offenders from adults; due process and procedural issues; prevention and intervention; treating mental health needs of juvenile offenders, disproportionate minority contact; detention and corrections reform; and reentry/aftercare" (pp. 14–15).

Approaching the recent history of juvenile justice reform from a different perspective, Butts and Evans (2011) analyzed diverse efforts across multiple states from the 1970s onward to reduce juvenile incarceration. They concluded that these could be grouped into three types of reforms:

1 Resolution (direct managerial influence over system behavior)
2 Reinvestment (financial incentives to change system behavior)
3 Realignment (organizational and structural modifications to alter system behavior (p. ii)

Of the three strategies, they found that realignment may be the most durable over time; the other two are vulnerable to future generations of leadership and unexpected political/economic circumstances. The goal of realignment is reinforced by the reality that more expensive (and less effective) incarceration strategies are not feasible given dramatic budget shortfalls and cuts in federal, state, and local juvenile justice dollars, thus providing more incentives to interrupt the tradition of incarceration and promoting deinstitutionalization, while (it is hoped) not sacrificing valued programming (Coalition for Juvenile Justice, 2011; National Juvenile Justice Network, 2010).

Additional areas of reform relate specifically to previous sections of this volume but include, among others, such topics as actively addressing the over-representation of youth of color in the juvenile justice system (Bell, Ridolfi, Finley, & Lacey, 2009; National Council on Crime and Delinquency, 2007); maintaining a focus on the unique developmental dimensions of youth in the justice system, such as the inclusion of state-of-the-art developmental science; ensuring that gains made in new Supreme Court decisions relating to youth are incorporated at the state levels; raising the age of juvenile court jurisdiction; determining juvenile competency to stand trial; and reducing the transfer of youth into the adult system (National Conference of State Legislatures, 2012; Scott & Steinberg, 2008).

Further areas include increasing positive youth development as a focus of juvenile justice practice and infrastructure (Butts & Barton, 2008; Mackin, Weller, Tarte, & Nissen, 2005); increasing the availability and quality of services for girls (Watson & Edelman, 2012) and for LGBTQ youth (Garnette, Irvine, Reyes, & Wilber, 2011); increasing the trauma-informed capacity of the juvenile court and associated programs (Buffington, Dierkhising, & Marsh, 2010); building more evidence-based and culturally relevant behavioral health infrastructure (Grisso, 2007; Nissen & Merrigan, 2011; Nissen, Butts, Merrigan, & Kraft, 2006; Nissen & Curry-Stevens, 2012; Skowyra

& Cocozza, 2001); preventing gang activity (Howell, 2010); increasing the voices of crime victims and community stakeholders in a balanced and restorative justice framework (Bazemore, Schiff, & Hudson, 2004); increasing family engagement (Garfinkel, 2010; Osher & Hunt, 2002); increasing the availability and quality of youth mentoring resources (Tolan, Henry, Schoeny, & Bass, 2008); developing effective tribal youth courts (Melton, 2004); and protecting the right of youth to defense counsel (Friedman, 2010; National Juvenile Justice Network, 2010; Sterling, 2009). Other noteworthy reforms included the introduction of specialty courts (such as juvenile drug and/or mental health courts) (Marlowe, 2010); understanding and preventing the phenomenon of "crossover youth" who drift from the child welfare to juvenile justice systems (Herz, Lee, Lutz, Stewart, Tuell, & Wigg, 2012); focus on aftercare and transition programs for youth leaving confinement (Altschuler, 2008); concerns and legal issues about the experiences of very young children in the juvenile justice system (Dietch, 2009); and reform of juvenile detention (Holman & Zeidenberg, 2006).

Some reformers have worked on addressing the punitive laws aimed at easing the transfer of youth to the adult system (45 states now give judges the discretion to move a youth's case to the adult system) through rigorous advocacy, demonstrating the widespread ineffective outcomes associated with these policies (Mulvey & Schubert, 2000). Occasionally, an entire state will take on the challenge of particularly rigorous systemic transformation, as did Missouri in the late 1990s, when it unprecedentedly revised its vision and related practices. Missouri's simultaneous revision of its policy, practices, and skills has been influential in guiding other similar state reforms (Mendel, 2010). From a state-level perspective, other ways to consider reform include a deep analytical and political analysis of the sum total of reform projects (and their results) that have occurred in a given period, as was recently done in an analysis of New York state's juvenile justice system, revealing not merely the technical aspects of reform articulation and execution but the political ones as well (Newman, 2011/2012).

Reforms are often initiated from within the system voluntarily, but the United States also has a history of using lawsuits to reconcile dereliction of performance that often pertain to the conditions of confinement. At times, such lawsuits can persist for many years, essentially forcing and monitoring compliance with reforms set forth by a court authority (Justice Policy Institute, 2009). In a particularly dramatic turn, in 2008 Pennsylvania dealt with a case of corruption that was widely covered in the media, in which private juvenile institutions and juvenile court judges were found guilty of racketeering (among other charges) and a $2.8 million kickback scheme involving the cases of literally thousands of juvenile court participants. Far-reaching litigation and reform priorities emerged from the case (Ecenberger, 2012). This case brought to light the vulnerabilities associated with increased involvement of the private sector in corrections with minimal oversight from a monitoring authority, and it intensified the rigorous critique of privatization of the justice system, both in the United States and globally (Culp, 2010; Deitch, 2011; Muncie, 2005).

In almost all the arenas of reform mentioned above, successes can be found in local communities, but it is unclear how to turn short-term local successes into long-term systemic reform (Lipsey, Howell, Kelly, Chapman, & Carver, 2010) or how to take them "to scale" at broader implementation levels and to shift federal, state, local, and tribal policies to ensure consistency of effort while preserving a community's identity and authority.

Ultimately, the juvenile justice landscape is, at best, a patchwork of uneven and incomplete application of state-of-the-art approaches. Despite many years of reform, much work remains to be done to ensure that local innovation and advocacy gains knit together to shift state and federal policy, and where appropriate, that gains made at the federal level filter appropriately to the local level.

■ A Social Justice Lens in Juvenile Justice: Implied but Often Missing

In the field of juvenile justice, there remains a focus on accountability and concerns of appearing "soft on crime" that many have suggested impede greater progress in evolving the juvenile justice system (Scott & Steinberg, 2008). Continuing efforts and primary investments to deliver more evidence-based programs and protocols, while important and notable, have implied that a scientific "intervention-based" solution is the most appropriate to the challenge of juvenile justice. While there is no question that more of such services are needed (for they are often in short supply—rendering a distributive justice challenge) and that they can assist many youth and families, such a focus obscures other drivers of real-world juvenile delinquency—primarily social/economic injustice, health and education disparities, racism, and poverty. Many reforms concerned with procedural justice (access to defense counsel, overrepresentation of youth of color among them) imply a focus on underlying social justice issues—yet all too often, these very concerns are marginalized in the actual discourse regarding resolution.

Poverty has a particularly devastating impact on young people, summarized by a cumulative effect of lack of access to vital social resources; accumulation of individual, family, and community stresses; and increased marginalization from the public view (Eamon, 2001; Evans, 2004; Yoshikawa, Aber, & Beardslee, 2012). Worst of all, pervasive negative images of poor youth add to a sense of "disposability" and criminality in youth from poor backgrounds that prevents the development of broader social outrage regarding unprecedented levels of child poverty, hunger, and homelessness (Giroux, 2003). A public health lens, truly approaching juvenile justice from a sense of social determinants of youth well-being, as well as delinquency, has been introduced as a vehicle to guide dialogue and reform but is not pervasive in the United States (Myers & Farrell,

2008). One study underscored the tragedy by quantifying that the 7-year life outcomes of youth involved in the juvenile justice system in Los Angeles evidenced premature death, ongoing drug problems, continuing illegal activities, and over a third involved in either additional arrests or jail time (Ramchand, Morral, & Becker, 2009).

It has also been well documented that race and poverty continue to intersect at dramatically steep levels, especially in childhood, with staggering statistics documenting that 38% of African American, 35% of American Indian, 42% of Hispanic, and 14% of Asian/Pacific Islander youth are currently living in poverty (as compared to only 13% of White youth) in the United States (Annie E. Casey Foundation, 2013).

Although decades of study and rigorous methodology have delivered sound frameworks to guide reductions in the overrepresentation of youth of color in the juvenile justice system (Piquero, 2008; Armour & Hammonn, 2009), the reality is that racial disparities among youth of color in America's juvenile courtrooms and institutions remain among the most resistant to reform; rates remain unacceptably high (Bell, Ridolfi, Finley, & Lacey, 2009).

Even more sobering is the dramatic growth in frequency in which communities are designed as suffering from "concentrated poverty" (defined by Turner & Kaye [2006] as a community in which the concentration of poverty is above 40%). According to the most recent data, there has been a 25% increase in the number of youth growing up in this level of poverty across all states, with some states reporting dramatic spikes (Alaska: 400% increase; Colorado, 360% increase; North Carolina, 179% increase; Oregon, 200% increase) (Annie E. Casey Foundation, 2012). As such, Birckhead (2012) suggested the phenomenon of "delinquency by reason of poverty," which underscores the likelihood that poor youth experience all aspects of the cradle-to-prison pipeline differently due to an increased focus on the needs of the child versus the other normal aspects of justice proceedings (in other words, drawing poor youth further into the system to receive needed social services rather than based on the actual weight of their offense) and what most juvenile justice professionals have termed "net-widening." Even with increased attention to austerity and program cutbacks, the poorest of youth still find that they land in the juvenile justice system as the social service system of last resort—especially youth of color. This phenomenon, termed "accumulated disadvantage," is best illustrated by data clearly showing progressively higher representations of youth of color as one moves more deeply into the system. Data show that more youth of color are arrested, referred to juvenile court, detained, formally processed, adjudicated, waived to criminal court, and admitted to state prison (National Council on Crime and Delinquency, 2007). As a solution, Birckhead calls for earlier and more comprehensive safety-net mechanisms as a matter of human rights and justice for young people.

In short, despite the well-meaning efforts of progressive juvenile justice advocates and professionals, deep intersections of race, class, socioeconomic status, and other indicators cannot be easily resolved by incremental policy shifts or innovative programs on their own. Much can and should be improved about juvenile justice practice, but acknowledgment, as well as direct strategies related to these types of contextual elements that create a robust stream of youth into the system, would be a welcome start to a next chapter for juvenile justice reform. A broader linking of justice reform work with efforts to address community-wide poverty, public health, and community justice concerns would offer the most promising path to re-energized and creative inquiry, scholarship, and policy debate. To do this would require a more intentional inclusion of economic and racial injustice issues as centrally acknowledged barriers to success, and as pivot points for policy and practice interventions.

■ Four Keys for Successful Reform

To build the best possible foundation for reforms of the future, a clear focus on the ingredients of successful efforts is warranted. Often this is more than merely implementing a best practice; rather, reform is a complex tapestry of guiding, implementing, responding, troubleshooting, and engaging communities toward what are often very diverse goals over sometimes great ideological or political differences. This section will focus on four such elements: systems change; leadership, both collaborative and cross-sectional; political will; and social change.

Systems Change

The juvenile justice system is a perfect example of how a change in one part of a system does not automatically equal a reform, for it is too complex and multifaceted to achieve this. Further, as has been alluded to previously in this chapter, the juvenile justice system is but one system; it cannot "fix" the problem of delinquency in isolation from school, health, poverty, and other extra-community systems. Indeed, one might posit that a view of "youth- and family-serving systems" should be the true focus of juvenile justice reform, so that interconnected and interdependent opportunities and barriers can be identified and addressed, albeit in an often contentious and ideologically diverse community and political context.

In other words, "system change" is required; however, "system change" is a frequently used but underdefined concept that can live up to its potential only when coming into clear focus among the people engaged in the activity, as it involves not only the technical implementation of new ideas, but risk and teamwork (often across sectors). For some, it means changing the "existing structure, function and/or culture of a system" (Perison, Boydell, Ferguson, & Ferris, 2011, p. 308). Such changes often "require changes in dedicated resources, structural relationships, power arrangements and values" (Kreger, Brindis, Manael, & Sassaoubre, 2007, p. 301). Rolling back a zero-tolerance policy in a school system that routinely calls the police to send youth who act out into the juvenile justice system, a practice especially common in neighborhoods where students are predominantly youth of color, and instead using in-school mediation and programming to solve behavior problems closer to home can be thought of as a kind of systems change. Similarly, offering substance abuse assessment and intervention services, a common factor associated with delinquency (Chassin, 2008; Mulvey, Schubert, & Chassin, 2010), at the early stages of the juvenile justice system to ensure that young people with behavioral health challenges receive the help they need may also be thought of as a systems change. Tracking both cost savings and reductions in recidivism to promote the expansion of services and alternatives to incarceration and to defend against rollbacks of new approaches is a third aspect of possible systems change. Initiating all of these changes together in an integrated plan, with partners from all involved systems, in the same community, with data to prove that this more sensible and humane approach merits continuation and reinforcement, however, represents the best interpretation of true systems change.

System change requires new levels of dialogue and trust to approach problems from not a blaming perspective but a problem-solving perspective involving "honest and frank discussions that strive to generate new understandings about organizational and community life. Assumptions are then revealed and multiple, competing perspectives and solutions are explored, debated and valued" (Behrens & Foster-Fishman, 2007, p.5). It often involves a simultaneous blend of implementing new approaches, ending outdated and ineffective approaches, shifting policy and sometimes roles, sharing power and opportunity, and devising new ways of measuring outcomes at a more systemic level.

Leadership

To implement this type of systems change well, new variations in traditional hierarchical mental models of leadership are needed. Although most leaders throughout juvenile justice and other youth-serving systems may often simultaneously "lead" their own organizations or divisions as well as cross-system change efforts, systems change requires an ability to mobilize *many* leaders simultaneously, as well as to intentionally cultivate leadership in the rank and file, and in the community at large. This is often described as "collaborative leadership"—and a collaborative leader is defined as a person who "convene[s] in a broadly inclusive manner, provides good information, energizes and constructively facilitates a shared understanding of problems in a credible, open process, and collectively creates authentic visions and strategies for address-ing those identified concerns" (Chrislip. 2002, p. 146). Lessons from existing juvenile justice reform efforts (Nissen, Merrigan & Kraft, 2005) suggest the importance of acknowledging that collaborative leadership is a vital ingredient in systemic reform, and that it carries several features that are important in a juvenile justice environment:

☐ Leadership for change almost never needs to be created out of nothing; it is often already present in systems and communities, although perhaps unacknowledged.
☐ Change, even when desired, involves losses that are often challenging for organizations to deal with.
☐ Competition over scarce resources is often a reality.
☐ Conflicts are inevitable but hold the potential for productive and constructive bridge-building, if appropriately guided.

A recent guide to improving juvenile justice programming elaborates on the importance of leadership in driving important juvenile justice reform—typi-cally a long-term (rather than short-term) endeavor:

> Even when begun with vigor and commitment, change efforts often fizzle out ... It is the community consensus that creates the comfort to change practice and make the changes routine. Strong, consistent, adaptive agency leaders and champions who advocate in support of change appear to be key factors in achieving sustainability. These principles need to be recognized from the beginning and then form a continuing guide to implementation throughout the change process. A leader's personal, unwavering commitment to change tends to carry the day. A champion's ability to engage key public stakeholders in making a commitment to change is vital. Combined, these actions create a positive affect and social support around the change process. Successful leaders and advocates inspire hope, excitement, camaraderie, and a sense of urgent purpose. They celebrate the sheer joy of creating something meaningful together. (Lipsey et al., 2010, p. 48)

Cultivation of Political Will

Merely working together on shared goals is fruitless without a calculated plan to turn ideas into new policies and programs. Strategic reforms call for the explicit engagement of key stakeholders with adequate power and resources to guide change through the complexities of policy, organizational, and practice-level changes. "Political will" has been the term most frequently associated with this resource, and it has been defined as "the commitment of political leaders and bureaucrats to undertake actions to achieve a set of objectives and to sustain the costs of those actions over time" (Brinkerhoff, 2000, p. 242). Political will is the careful and painstaking process of converting a capacity for change into the actual change itself, through a combination of citizen participation and mobilization of leaders willing to engage in the process (Lezine & Reed, 2007; Malena, 2012). It also relies on a sound understanding of the current fiscal climate in the United States and the methods for making a strong cost-savings case for reform (National Juvenile Justice Network, 2010). Successful reform in the juvenile justice system operates in an ultimately political environment against other issues, concerns, and stresses and can succeed only with attention to this political dimension.

Social Change

Perhaps the least explored dimension of juvenile justice reform is the curious omission of robust discourse concerning the work not just as adjustments made to institutions, but as a *social movement* to accelerate and encourage change. Reform is most often described by such terms as "initiatives," "models," "programs," and the like, yet almost never with the associated community development factors (coupled with political will above) that most frequently result in meaningful change. Yet, in reality, "there is no community intervention that is neutral with respect to justice" (Sandler, 2007, p. 272), and thus, an explicit social justice relationship to social change (underscored with human rights sensibilities) may serve to accelerate momentum.

A brief historical analysis of successful U.S. social movements specific to vulnerable populations associated with large systems (e.g., deinstitutionalization of the mentally ill, passage of the Americans with Disabilities Act, abolition of the death penalty for minors) reveals that their success has clearly been due to a combination of factors, including but not limited to the organization of successful social movements (coupled with resultant changes in the views of population majorities), which ultimately contributed to desired change. Such changes were often provoked by moral outrage at a practice revealed after being submerged in the complexities of everyday routine.

Recently, social change language is beginning to surface in the context of juvenile justice policy, for example in a publication from the National Juvenile Justice Network entitled "Bringing Youth Home: A national movement to increase public safety, rehabilitate youth, and save money" (2011), which strongly suggests that "something beyond" individual local and state reforms needs to occur to link successes together meaningfully into a more dedicated strategy for broader and more enduring change.

Bringing attention to and naming the "cradle-to-prison pipeline"—with associated cross-sectoral institutional and community responsibilities to dismantle policies and practices that inhibit youth well-being and envision those that offer youth the best possible chances for success—is an instance where the phrasing of the problem is meant to inspire the transcendence of mere models and the inspiration of a social movement (Edelman, 2007).

Some scholarship within the United States has begun to introduce concepts, practices, and tools that may be helpful in expanding the impact of human rights frameworks on juvenile justice (Sarri & Shook, 2005), but it is not yet a dominant frame in U.S.-based juvenile justice practice.

Juvenile justice reform suffers from substantial stigma regarding youth behaviors that are often framed (imprecisely and inaccurately) in overwhelmingly negative and contentious terms, fueling punitive policy reactions despite the fact that most youth crime is at a low level and nonviolent (Dorfman & Wallack, 2009). Fortunately, public opinion tends to favor rehabilitation combined with community safety measures (Nagin, Paquiro, Scott, & Steinberg, 2006). Reformers inherit an opportunity to convert such energy, therefore (and some would say a responsibility), through use of the first three of the elements listed above—systems change, leadership, and political will—into community consensus on the waste, abuse, and inherent human rights violations associated with juvenile justice practices that should be changed. In this sense, juvenile justice reform is not just about implementing institutional change; it is about investing in the organizational and community conditions in which change will most likely occur. In this sense, such change is wisely focused as much outside the juvenile justice system as it is inside it, by partnering with a variety of community allies to fuel the social determinants of adolescent success, and, where necessary, redemption.

■ Philanthropy and Reform

No credible overview of juvenile justice reform covering the past 20 years could be complete without acknowledging the unique role that private philanthropy has played in creating "spaces" in which broader, courageous conversations could be entertained outside of the realm of everyday juvenile justice practice. During an era when there have been significant cutbacks to local juvenile justice from traditional sources (Coalition for Juvenile Justice, 2011), additional investments for reform and new kinds of transformative programming have been instrumental. At the national level, this includes the Robert Wood Johnson Foundation's investments in numerous juvenile justice efforts, chiefly including the Reclaiming Futures initiative (which focuses on creating a new standard of care for youth with behavioral health disorders in the juvenile justice system, www.reclaimingfutures.org) and Adolescent Portable Therapy at the Vera Institute of Justice, a practice also used in the juvenile justice system (http://www.vera.org/project/adolescent-portable-therapy); the Annie E. Casey Foundation's investments in the Juvenile Detention Alternatives Initiative (focused on reducing or eliminating the overuse and abuse of juvenile detention, especially for youth of color, http://www.aecf.org/MajorInitiatives/JuvenileDetentionAlternativesInitiative.aspx); and the MacArthur Foundation's investments in its Models for Change initiative (focused on cross-cutting, multiple, and overlapping state-specific reforms simultaneously intended to increase public safety, improve youth outcomes, and decrease juvenile justice costs, http://www.modelsforchange.net/index.html). Both Annie E. Casey and MacArthur have also made substantial investments in the Haywood Burns Institute's efforts to create new approaches to interrupting the overrepresentation of youth of color in the juvenile justice system by creating groundbreaking analytical tools tied to key decision points in juvenile justice processing (http://www.burnsinstitute.org/). Literally tens of millions of dollars and thousands of youth in the juvenile justice system (and their communities) have benefited from the learning laboratories and leadership opportunities made possible by these efforts. Innovation and research have followed and have documented progress and identified many areas of for additional reform (Annie E. Casey Foundation, 2011; Butts & Roman, 2007; Griffin, 2011; Hernandez & Fitzgerald, 2010), and more is under way. Although it can safely be said that untold numbers of young people have had improved experiences in juvenile justice due to these types of initiatives, what is less clear is how such evidence-based innovations that show such promise in their early years can be adopted on a large scale, or translate into improved standards at the federal level. OJJDP has welcomed these new frameworks to enhance juvenile justice practice; however, a systematic way of involving, engaging, and integrating the lessons learned has not been established. Juvenile justice reform of the future should benefit more intentionally from the availability of public–private partnerships to hasten innovation and take advantage of dissemination opportunities.

■ Expert Opinions

Table 26.1 provides an overview of some of the recent recommendations of experts across the juvenile justice policy and research arenas.

All agree that future reform should focus on increasing gains made to reduce the number of youth who are unnecessarily incarcerated, and to do so partly by continuing to focus on changing the financial incentives for doing so. It is also common to recommend that programs focus on youth-specific approaches, the inclusion of families, and reducing unequal justice and increasing equity. The Justice Policy Institute (2009) specifically advocates for the introduction of a new discourse to replace the "tough on crime" language of past eras, using instead a rigorous standard tied to the costs, benefits, and outcomes of interventions. Several of the experts mention the deployment of important treatment, education, and employment supports to prepare young people to succeed after their involvement in juvenile justice. Mendell (2011) urges attention to data to hold systems accountable. Given the size and complexity of the juvenile justice system as it has been described in this volume, this is among the most formidable of future shifts. Lispsy and colleagues

Table 26.1   **Priorities for Future Juvenile Justice Reform, as Cited by Experts in Recent Literature**

Nelson & Lubow (2009)	Justice Policy Institute (2009)	Mendel (2011)	Coalition for Juvenile Justice (2012)
• Respect the well-established differences between youth and adults. • End the indiscriminate and wholesale incarceration of juveniles. • Focus on the crucial role of families in resolving delinquency. • Halt the increasing propensity to prosecute minor cases in the juvenile court. • Rely on other systems for youth, rather than using the juvenile justice system as a dumping ground. • End system policies and practices that allow unequal justice to persist (p. 71).	• Incentivize counties to send fewer youth to secure residential facilities by shifting the fiscal architecture of the state system. • Invest in intermediate interventions, not buildings. • Invest in proven approaches to reduce crime and recidivism among young people. • Develop, support. and evaluate new and different approaches to reduce crime and recidivism among young people. • Re-examine policies and practices that have the consequence of sending more youth to the system. • Policymakers should take care to rely not on the "tough on crime" rhetoric of the past, but instead on the research that shows that locking up more youth does not keep our communities safe. • Invest in policies that increase employment, educational attainment, and treatment for those who need it (pp. 14–15).	• Limit eligibility for correctional placements. • Invest in promising nonresidential alternatives. • Change the financial incentives. • Adopt best practices for managing youth offenders. • Replace large institutions with small, treatment-oriented facilities for the dangerous few. • Use data to hold systems accountable (pp. 28–36).	• Affirm commitment to high standards of practice to protect and preserve youth and families who come in contact with the courts. • Ensure federal investments to leverage, inspire, and support state and local improvements as essential to increasing youth success and community safety, even in times of budget cutting. • Strengthen the federal government's juvenile justice infrastructure, via the OJJDP, to maximize resources and leadership (p. 2).

(2010) also suggest that intentionally working on the "culture" of juvenile justice agencies (and requisite affiliated policymakers and executive state leadership often appointed from adult criminal justice backgrounds) to foster environments of continuous learning and improvement in an era of budget cuts and unparalleled system stress is a great challenge, but one that must be undertaken. Finally, the Coalition of Juvenile Justice (2012) focuses on needs for strengthening federal infrastructure to provide an essential architecture for ongoing reforms and success.

■ Future Development

This chapter has taken an in-depth look at the concepts and practices surrounding juvenile justice reform. As the review and analysis concludes, several additional ideas for development are warranted to guide the field into the future.

First, more scholarship is needed on juvenile justice reform itself, akin to implementation science (Fixsen, Naoom, Blasé, Frieman, & Wallace, 2005) but more comprehensive in scale, so that rather than understanding how one program or practice implementation unfolds and is practiced, we can understand how making multiple shifts in complex ecosystems contributes to the relative success (or lack thereof) of more comprehensive change initiatives. Numerous research and evaluation reports are excellent starts for understanding how a single program performed (or even multiple variations of one); a few even map the breadth of successful reform at a glance (Willison, Mears, Shollenberger, Owens, & Butts, 2009), but tell little about the ingredients, drivers, inhibitors, and lessons learned in a way that is comprehensive and analytical. Butts and Evans' (2011) reform framework mentioned earlier in this chapter—resolution, reinvestment, and realignment—is also an important start in understanding "families" of reform types, and how each performs under different circumstances. Such knowledge could fuel and inspire another level of dialogue with federal officials and other important stakeholders about how to take juvenile justice reform to the next level, and move beyond grant-by-grant or lawsuit-by-lawsuit reforms that are inherently vulnerable and unsustainable to the degree they remain independent rather than strategic.

Secondly, a renewed commitment to the principles of balanced and restorative justice is called for. Popular and visible in the 1980s, 1990s, and early 2000s, a focus on principles of community-anchored dialogue, reconciliation, and offender engagement in repairing the harms of offenses in a meaningful way is now less common, although much needed. This framework (Bazemore, Umbreit, Klein, Maloney, & Pranis, 1997) continues to hold much potential to uphold critical variables associated with state-of-the-art juvenile justice reform, with the added benefit of significant community engagement and ownership of juvenile crime prevention and intervention. Because these approaches are most often combined with the inclusion of the voices of offenders, crime victims, and community members themselves, they have the additional benefit of renewing the literal humanity of the justice process in local communities.

Third, more innovation should be intentionally cultivated through ongoing partnerships between philanthropy and federal, state, and tribal governments.

Even the most impressive evidence-based practice continues to have room for improvement and evolution.

Finally, more federal commitment and integration is required to address the fragmentation of federal funding that shifts to many youth-specific and community programs all focused on similar groups of youth. OJJDP (mentioned earlier) now serves as the central federal policy and practice lead for juvenile justice policy and formula funds in the United States. Under its umbrella, responsibilities include a wide array of justice programming (including special grant programs and the oversight of state compliance with the JJDPA's core requirements). OJJDP has a unique ability to accelerate or inhibit reforms, yet it has experienced significant cuts over the past 10 years (Coalition for Juvenile Justice, 2011) and suffered from the lack of a permanent administrator throughout the entire first Obama administration (Coalition for Juvenile Justice, 2011)—although one has just been appointed, a welcome resolution to the agency's stalled momentum (Center on Juvenile & Criminal Justice, 2013).

That said, as described in this chapter, some reforms to boost the success of young people who are at risk of involvement or are already in the juvenile justice system are needed in ways that reflect cross-system, cross-agency, cross-disciplinary, and cross-policy reforms. While there is a federal Interagency Working Group on Youth Programs (www.findyouthinfo. gov) comprising representatives from 12 federal departments and five federal agencies that relate to youth programs in some way, its current budget, scope, and ultimate impact are limited. It would be more visible, mobilize greater resources, and have a more significant impact as a cabinet-level bipartisan office of the White House charged with inspiring a new type of dialogue and improving the status of young people in the United States (comparing, for example, the implications of state-by-state plans of various required interconnected youth- and family-focused agencies, such as education, child welfare, juvenile justice, welfare reform, and housing). Explicit focus on the ongoing and worsening human rights crisis of youth poverty and its resultant indicators would be a primary focus. This office could better chart a course for a new national dialogue on youth well-being, success, and, when necessary, reclamation. It would do so by advancing a more efficient, focused, and coordinated reform agenda—better integrating, comparing, and analyzing local reforms, state reforms, tribal reforms, and federal reforms—in a way that would hold the most promise of moving from mere reform to complete transformation of the system. As a White House office, it might also have the power to call for a new generation of data-management capability to identify gaps and create clear and compelling data about the relationship of local to national policy trends.

Juvenile justice reform is embedded in the culture of juvenile justice itself. As surely as juvenile justice is being practiced in every community in the United States, one can be assured that someone nearby is likely planning, implementing, or evaluating some type of reform. Some of these reforms are voluntary, and some of them are requirements of special grant funds, or the result of a consent decree or lawsuit concerning unacceptable practices of the past. The goal of most juvenile justice reform remains a careful balance of the autonomy and independence of state, tribal, and local perspectives on the one hand with evidence-based practices and the invocation of consistent constitutional protections on the other. While practicality is important, expansive thinking, a sense of new possibilities, and a renewed sense of urgency from a human rights standpoint are also invaluable to the cause. There is reason to celebrate the accomplishments of the juvenile justice reform field, but it can never rest on its laurels, as there is still so much more work to be done: youth throughout the United States need our diligent and dedicated energy to make these systems work better and more fairly.

Notes

1   For more information regarding the implications of Wyoming's decision to refrain from participating in the JJDPA, see John Kelly's article in *Youth Today*, June 29, 2009, available at: http://www.youthtoday.org/view_blog.cfm?blog_id=180
2   For a complete overview of lawsuits addressing emergent or longstanding problematic juvenile justice policies or practices extending back to 1978, see the Juvenile Law Center Legal Docket at: http://www.jlc.org/legal-docket/all/juvenile-and-criminal-justice

References

Act 4 Juvenile Justice (2011). *Juvenile Justice Delinquency and Prevention Act (JJDPA) recommendations and fact sheet*. Washington, DC: Juvenile Justice & Delinquency Prevention Coalition.

Altschuler, D. (2008). Rehabilitating and reintegrating youth offenders: Are residential and community aftercare colliding words and what can be done about it? *Justice Policy Journal, 5*(1), 4–26.

Annie E. Casey Foundation (2010). *Annual results report summary*. Baltimore, MD: Author.

Annie E. Casey Foundation (2012). *Data snapshot: High poverty communities*. Baltimore, MD: Author.

Annie E. Casey Foundation (2013). *Kids count data book: 2012*. Baltimore, MD: Author.

Armour, J., & Hammond, S. (2009). *Minority youth in the juvenile justice system: Disproportionate minority contact*. Washington, DC: National Conference of State Legislatures.

Barton, W. H., & Butts, J. A. (2008). *Building on strength: Positive youth development in juvenile justice programs*. Chicago: Chapin Hall Center for Children at the University of Chicago.

Bazemore, G., Schiff, M., & Hudson, J. (2004). *Juvenile justice reform and restorative justice*. Devon, UK: Willan Publishers.

Bazemore, G., Umbreit, M., Klein, A., Maloney, D., & Pranis, K. (1997). *Balanced and restorative justice for juveniles: A framework for juvenile justice in the 21st century*. Washington, DC: Office of Juvenile Justice and Delinquency Prevention.

Behrens, T. R., & Foster-Fishman, P. G. (2007). Developing operating principles for systems change. *American Journal of Community Psychology, 39*(3-4), 411–414.

Benekos, P. J., & Merlo, A. V. (2008). Juvenile justice: The legacy of punitive policy. *Youth Violence and Juvenile Justice, 6*, 28–46.

Bell, J., Ridolfi, L. J., Finley, M., & Lacey, C. (2009). *The keeper and the kept: Reflections on local obstacles to disparities reduction in juvenile justice and a path to change.* San Francisco: Haywood P. Burns Institute.

Birckhead, T. R. (2012). Delinquency by reason of poverty. *Washington University Journal of Law and Policy, 38*, 53–107.

Brinkerhoff, D. W. (2000). Assessing political will for anti-corruption efforts: An analytical framework. *Public Administration and Development, 20*(3), 239–253.

Buffington, K., Dierkhising, C. B., & Marsh, S. C. (2010). *Ten things every juvenile court judge should know about trauma and delinquency.* Reno, NV: National Council of Juvenile and Family Court Judges.

Butts, J. A., & Evans, D. N. (2001). *Resolution, reinvestment and realignment: Three strategies for changing juvenile justice.* New York: John Jay College of Criminal Justice.

Butts, J. A., & Harrell, A. V. (1998). *Delinquents or criminals? Policy options for young offenders.* Washington, DC: Urban Institute.

Butts, J. A., & Roman, J. (2007). *Changing systems: Outcomes from the RWJF Reclaiming Futures Initiative on Juvenile Justice and Substance Abuse. A Reclaiming Futures National Evaluation Report.* Portland, OR: Reclaiming Futures National Program Office, Portland State University.

Center on Juvenile & Criminal Justice (February 7, 2013). *Appointment of permanent OJJDP Director signals a positive step.* Online article downloaded on March 20, 2013, at: http://www.cjcj.org/post/juvenile/justice/appointment/permanent/ojjdp/director/signals/positive/step

Chassin, L. (2008). Juvenile justice and substance abuse. *The Future of Children, 18*(2), 165–183.

Chrislip, D. D. (2002). *The collaborative leadership fieldbook.* San Francisco: Jossey-Bass.

Coalition for Juvenile Justice (2011). *Historic federal funding chart.* Downloaded on March 26, 2012, at: http://www.act4jj.org/media/documents//document_159.pdf

Cobb, K. A., & Mullins, T. G. (2010). *Tribal probation: An overview for tribal court judges.* Washington, DC: Bureau of Justice Assistance.

Culp, R. (2010). Prison privatization turns 25. In K. Ismali (Ed.), *U.S criminal justice policy: A contemporary reader* (pp. 183–209). Boston: Jones and Bartlett Publishers.

Dietch, M. (2009). *From time out to hard time: Young children in the adult criminal justice system.* Austin, TX: The University of Texas at Austin, LBJ School of Public Affairs.

Dietch, M. (2011). *Oversight of private juvenile facilities.* Presentation to the NJJN Forum, July 28. Available at: www.utexas.edu/lbj/sites/default/files/file/ .../juvenilestexas—final.pdf

Dorfman, L., & Wallack, L. (2009). *Moving from them to us: Challenges in reframing violence among youth.* Berkeley, CA: Berkeley Media Studies Group.

Eamon, M. K. (2001). The effects of poverty on children's socioemotional development: An ecological systems analysis. *Social Work, 46*(3), 256–266.

Ecenbarger, W. (2012). *Kids for cash: Two judges, thousands of children, and a $2.8 million kickback scheme.* New York, NY: The New Press.

Edelman, M. W. (2007). The cradle to prison pipeline: An American health crisis. *Preventing Chronic Disease, 4*(3), A43–52.

Evans, G. W. (2004). The environment of childhood poverty. *American Psychologist, 59*(2), 77–92.

Fixsen, D. L., Naoom, S. F., Blasé, K. A., Friedman, R. M., & Wallace, F. (2005). *Implementation research: A synthesis of the literature.* Tampa, FL: University of South Florida, Louis de la Parte Florida Mental Health Institute, National Implementation Research Network.

Fox, S. J. (1970). Juvenile justice reform: A historical perspective. *Stanford Law Review, 22*(6), 1187–1239.

Friedman, B. E. (2010). Protecting truth: An argument for juvenile rights and a return to In re Gault. *UCLA Law Review, 57*, 165–177.

Garfinkel, L. (2010). Improving family involvement for juvenile offenders with emotional/behavioral disorders and related disabilities. *Behavioral Disorders, 36*(1), 52–60.

Garnette, L., Irvine, A., Reyes, C. & Wilber, S. (2011). Lesbian, gay, bisexual and transgender youth and the juvenile justice system. In F. T. Sherman & F. H. Jacobs (Eds.), *Juvenile justice: Advancing research, policy and practice* (pp. 156–173). New York: John Wiley and Sons.

Griffin, P. (2011). *Adding up Models for Change: Initial findings from the Models for Change database.* Chicago, IL: MacArthur Foundation.

Grisso, T. (2007). Progress and perils in the juvenile justice and mental health movement. *Journal of the American Academy of Psychiatry and the Law, 35*(2), 158–167.

Hazel, N. (2008). *Cross-national comparison of youth justice.* London: Youth Justice Board.

Hernandez, G., & Fitzgerald, M. S. (2010). *Tackling disproportionate minority confinement: An evaluation of Louisville metro's efforts to reduce DMC using the Burns Institute Model.* Oakland, CA: Planning for Change.

Herz, D., Lee, P., Lutz, L., Stewart, M., Tuell, J., & Wiig, J. (2012). *Addressing the needs of multi-system youth: Strengthening the connection between child welfare and juvenile justice.* Washington, DC: The Center for Juvenile Justice Reform and The Robert F. Kennedy Children's Action Corps.

Howell, J. C. (2010). *Gang prevention: An overview of research and programs.* Washington, DC: OJJDP Juvenile Justice Bulletin.

Justice Policy Institute (2009). *The costs of confinement: Why good juvenile justice policies make good fiscal sense.* Washington, DC: Author.

Kreger, M., Brindis, C. D., Manael, D. M., & Sassoubre, L. (2007). Lessons learned in systems change initiatives: Benchmarks and indicators. *American Journal of Community Psychology, 39*, 301–320.

Lezine, D. A., & Reed, G. A. (2007). Political will: A bridge between public health knowledge and action. *American Journal of Public Health, 97*(11), 2010–2013.

Lipsey, M. W., Howell, J. C., Kelly, M. R., Chapman, G., & Carver, D. (2010). *Improving the effectiveness of juvenile justice programs.* Washington, DC: Center for Juvenile Justice Reform.

Mackin, J., Weller, J., Tarte, J., & Nissen, L. (2005). Breaking new ground in juvenile justice settings: Assessing for competencies in juvenile offenders. *National Council for Juvenile and Family Court Judges Journal, 56*(2), 25–37.

Malena, C. (Ed.) (2012). *From political won't to political will: Building support for participatory governance.* Sterling, VA: Kumarian Press.

Marlowe, D. (2010). *Research update on juvenile drug treatment courts.* Washington, DC: National Association of Drug Court Professionals.

Melton, A. P. (2004). *Building culturally relevant youth courts in Tribal communities.* Lexington, KY: National Youth Court Center.

Mendel, R. A. (2010). *The Missouri model: Reinventing the practice of rehabilitating youthful offenders.* Baltimore, MD: The Annie E. Casey Foundation.

Mendel, R. A. (2011). *No place for kids: The case for reducing juvenile incarceration.* Baltimore, MD: The Annie E. Casey Foundation.

Motivans, M., & Snyder, H. (2011). *Tribal youth in the federal juvenile justice system.* Washington, DC: U.S. Department of Justice, Office of Justice Programs, Bureau of Justice Statistics.

Mulvey, E. P., & Schubert, C. A. (2012). *Transfer of juveniles to adult court: Effects of a broad policy in one court.* Washington, DC: U.S. Department of Juvenile Justice, Office of Juvenile Justice and Delinquency Prevention.

Mulvey, E. P., Schubert, C. A., & Chassin, L. (2010). *Substance abuse and delinquent behavior among serious adolescent offenders.* Washington, DC: Office of Juvenile Justice Bulletin.

Muncie, J. (2005). The globalization of crime control—the case of youth juvenile justice: Neoliberalism, policy convergence, and international conventions. *Theoretical Criminology, 9*(1), 35–64.

Nagin, D. S., Piquero, A. R., Scott, E. S., & Steinberg, L. (2006). Public preferences for rehabilitation versus incarcerations of juvenile offender: Evidence from a contingent validation study. *Criminology and Public Policy, 5*, 627–652.

National Conference of State Legislatures (2012). *Trends in juvenile justice state legislation 2001–2010.* Washington, DC: Author.

National Council on Crime and Delinquency (2007). *And justice for some: Differential treatment of youth of color in the juvenile justice system.* Washington, DC: Author.

National Juvenile Justice Network (2010). *The real cost and benefits of change: Finding opportunities for reform during difficult fiscal times.* Washington, DC: Author.

National Juvenile Justice Network (2011). *Bringing Youth Home: A national movement to increase public safety, rehabilitate youth, and save money.* Washington, DC: Author.

National Juvenile Justice Network (2012a). *Advances in juvenile justice reform: 2009–2011.* Washington, DC: Author.

National Juvenile Justice Network (2012b). *Seven ways to improve juvenile indigent defense.* Washington, DC: Author.

Nelson, D. W., & Lubow, B. (2009). A roadmap for juvenile justice reform. In C. W. Harman (Ed.), *Mandate for change: Policies and leadership for 2009 and beyond* (pp. 71–82). New York: Lexington Books.

Newman, S. A. (2011/2012). The past, present and future of juvenile justice reform in New York State. *New York Law School Law Review, 56,* 1264–1296.

Nissen, L. B., Butts, J., Merrigan, D., & Kraft, M. K. (2006). The RWJF Reclaiming Futures initiative: Improving interventions for justice-involved youth. *National Council for Juvenile and Family Court Judges Juvenile and Family Court Journal, 57*(4), 39–52.

Nissen, L. B., & Curry-Stevens, A. (2012). Evolving on purpose: Results of a qualitative study to explore how public youth system reform advocates apply anti-oppressive practice frameworks in a collaborative training and action process. *Action Research, 10*(4), 406–431.

Nissen, L. B., & Merrigan, D. (2011). Helping substance-involved youth people in the juvenile justice system be successful: Conceptual and structural foundations of the Reclaiming Futures model. *Children & Youth Service Review, 33,* S3–S8.

Nissen, L. B., Merrigan, D., & Kraft, M. K. (2005). Moving mountains: A leadership lens in national substance abuse and juvenile justice reform. *Child Welfare, 84*(2), 123–140.

Office of Juvenile Justice and Delinquency Prevention, U.S. Department of Justice (2012). *Disproportionate minority contact fact sheet.* Washington, DC: Author.

Osher, T., & Hunt, P. (2002). *Involving families of youth who are in the juvenile justice system.* Washington, DC: National Center for Mental Health and Juvenile Justice.

Piquero, A. (2008). Disproportionate minority contact. *The Future of Children, 18*(2), 59–79.

Puzzanchera, C., Adams, B., & Hockenberry, S. (2012). *Juvenile court statistics.* Pittsburgh, PA: National Center for Juvenile Justice.

Ramchand, R., Morral, A. R., & Becker, K. (2009). Seven-year life outcomes of adolescent offenders in Los Angeles. *American Journal of Public Health, 99*(5), 863–870.

Sandler, J. (2007). Community-based practices: Integrating dissemination theory with critical theories of power and justice. *American Journal of Community Psychology, 40,* 272–289.

Sarri, R., & Shook, J. (2005). Human rights and juvenile justice in the United States: Challenges and opportunities. In M. Enslaco & L. Majka (Eds.), *Children's rights.* New York: Rowan and Littlefield.

Scott, E. S., & Steinberg, L. (2008). Adolescent development and the regulation of youth crime. *The Future of Children, 18*(2), 15–33.

Sickmund, M., Sladky, T. J., Kang, W., & Puzzanchera, C. (2011). *Easy access to the census of juveniles in residential placeme\nt.* Online. Available: http://www.ojjdp.gov/ojstatbb/ezacjrp/

Skowyra, K. R., & Cocozza, J. J. (2001). *Blueprint for change: A comprehensive model for the identification and treatment of youth with mental health needs in contact with the juvenile justice system.* Delmar, NY: The National Center for Mental Health and Juvenile Justice.

Sterling, R. W. (2009). *Role of juvenile defense counsel in delinquency court.* Washington, DC: National Juvenile Defender Center.

Tolan, P., Henry, D., Schoeny, M., & Bass, A. (2008). Mentoring interventions to affect juvenile delinquency and associated problems. *Campbell Systematic Reviews* (16). Downloaded on March 28, 2013, from: www.campbellcollaboration.org/lib/download/238/

Turner, M. A., & Kaye, D. R. (2006). *How does family well-being vary across different types of neighborhoods?* Washington, DC: The Urban Institute.

Watson, L., & Edelman, P. (2012). *Improving the juvenile justice system for girls: Lessons from the states.* Washington, DC: Georgetown Center on Poverty, Inequality, and Public Policy.

Willison, J. B., Mears, D. P., Shollenberger, T., Owens, C. E., & Butts, J. A. (2009). *Past, Present, and Future of Juvenile Justice: Assessing the Policy.* Washington, D.C.: The Urban Institute.

Yoshikawa, H., Aber, J. L., & Beardslee, W. R. (2012). The effects of poverty on the mental, emotional and behavioral health of children: Implications for prevention. *American Psychologist, 67*(4), 272–284.

Glossary

Accountability: Providing information, in useful form, to others who must make decisions or take action regarding a person, case, situation, agency, or community. A social worker may be accountable to a supervisor, community, clients, the court, a board of directors, the profession, and others. Being accountable means being responsible for providing services in accordance with high standards.

Addams, Jane: Established Hull House, an early settlement house in Chicago during the 1880s to help wayward youths, homeless families, and new immigrants.

Adjudication: A juvenile who is *adjudicated* is judicially determined (judged) by an official juvenile justice agency (e.g., the county juvenile court) to be a delinquent or status offender.

Advocacy: To speak up, to plead the case for another, or to champion a cause, often for individuals and groups who cannot speak out on their own behalf. Types include self-advocacy, case advocacy (for a client), and class advocacy (advocacy on behalf of a group or category of individuals in similar circumstances).

Aggression Replacement Training (ART): A multimodal, psychoeducational intervention to promote skills acquisition and performance, improve anger control, decrease the frequency of acting-out behaviors, and increase the frequency of constructive, prosocial behaviors. The primary ART trainers for clients are teachers, counselors, social workers, childcare workers, and others who have direct responsibility for youths who frequently behave aggressively. The intervention is made up of three components, each of which the youth attends on a weekly basis: skill-streaming, anger control training, and moral education.

Anger Control Training (ACT): Its goal is teaching youths the techniques of anger control. The youth brings to each session a description of a recent anger-arousing experience (a hassle), which he or she records in a binder (hassle log). For 10 weeks the youngsters are trained to respond to their hassles with a chain of behaviors that include identifying triggers, identifying cues, using reminders, and using reducers.

Anger management: Techniques based on cognitive-behavioral restructuring are effective in helping individuals to recognize the antecedents of anger and its physiological indicators, to learn alternative coping skills to use when provoked, and to become comfortable using these strategies through role-playing and other exercises.

Attention-deficit/hyperactivity disorder (ADHD): ADHD is characterized by inattention, disorganization, hyperactivity, and impulsivity. Juveniles with this disorder often are easily distracted and inattentive, have difficulty concentrating, and have poor organizational skills. They demonstrate poor school performance, little patience, poor problem-solving skills, and difficulty attending to stimuli.

Balanced and restorative justice: This model addresses both individual and community responsibility by focusing on the repair of harm and requiring that both contribute to that repair.

Balanced approach: Mission addresses community demands for (1) sanctioning based on accountability measures that restore victims and clearly denounce and provide meaningful consequences for offensive behavior; (2) offender rehabilitation and reintegration; and (3) enhanced community safety and security. It does this by articulating three system goals directed toward the three primary "client/customers" of the system—the victim, the offender, and the community.

Behavior modification system: The primary element of an effective behavior management system is the systematic and direct reinforcement of appropriate behaviors. In many systems, the focus is on "shaping" new behaviors by reinforcing "small steps" along the process of change. The entire system is based on earning; nothing is taken away, but all privileges (type of visitation, bedtime, use of recreational items, amount and type of items allowed in room) must be earned.

Boot camps: Boot camps are used as a type of diversion for youth from typical residential facilities. Often they are used for first offenders to attempt to "shock or scare" them into appropriate behavior. Boot camps are usually 3 to 6 months long and are based on a military schedule and discipline. Rigorous physical training is part of the foundation along with education, but the majority of programs do not provide therapy, vocational training, or life skills training.

Brief treatment: An approach to working with clients that acknowledges upfront that there is a time limit to treatment. Models vary and may specify time limits (e.g., up to 12 sessions) or may limit the amount of time (e.g., up to 3 months). In other words, the treatment is not open-ended. See the quarterly international journal "Brief Treatment and Crisis Intervention" (www. brief-treatment.oupjournals.org) and Dr. Roberts's website (www.crisisinterventionnetwork.com).

Chicago Area Project: Initiated by the Institute for Juvenile Research and the Behavioral Research Fund in 1929, it was one of the best-known examples of a coordinated ecological program aimed at reducing juvenile delinquency. Clifford R. Shaw was the founder and director of the project, which consisted of a series of studies from 1929 to 1933 as well as a classic experiment in delinquency prevention at the local level that lasted until 1962. The studies conducted by Shaw and McKay (1972) concentrated on two areas: (1) the epidemiology of delinquency in different areas of Chicago and (2) the acquisition of delinquent beliefs and behavior from delinquent subcultures. Shaw and McKay found that a disproportionately large number of juvenile delinquents came from certain areas of Chicago. The high-rate sectors were termed *delinquency* areas.

Chronic offender: A youth offender who has been arrested four or more times during his or her minority. These youths perpetuate a significant portion of all delinquent behavior and do not age out of crime but continue their behavior into adulthood.

Cognitive-based interventions: Interventions include conflict resolution, peer mediation, social skills, and anger-management programs.

Cognitive-behavioral focus: If behavior change is to be "portable" (that is, to carry past the detention center program), youth need to make fundamental changes in how they see the world, themselves, and their response to situations around them. The cognitive focus shows youth how their thinking (their beliefs and attitudes) affects their behavior. The goal is to help youth change their thinking, and thus their behavior.

Cognitive-behavioral therapy (CBT): An approach that employs progressive relaxation, cognitive reframing, and communication skills. The approach presents clients with options that draw on these different interventions and then encourages them to correct distorted thinking and develop individualized anger-control plans using as many of the techniques as possible.

Comorbid psychiatric disorders: When a juvenile has two or more separate and distinct psychiatric problems at the same time. This situation poses significant theoretical, conceptual, diagnostic, and treatment planning difficulties. Comorbid conditions spawn confusion and questions with regard to the course of the disorders. For example, are observed symptoms part of one disorder or two? How does one disorder affect the occurrence or onset of another disorder? Did the disorders begin at the same time, or should one be considered primary? Treatment issues are challenging as well; for instance, should both disorders be treated simultaneously or should one disorder be treated first? If so, which one and with which types of interventions? In addition, how can disorders that seem to be polar opposites occur in an individual at the same time? Depression and conduct disorder are disorders that have very different symptomatology, yet they occur together frequently and warrant concern.

Conduct disorder (CD): Youth with CD persistently violate norms or rules and disregard the rights of others. They may be aggressive toward animals and people, and destroy property. These juveniles also have deficits in social skills and problem-solving skills, and they tend to see others' interactions with them as hostile. They are also impulsive and tend to lack empathy.

Conduct disorder diagnosis: The overriding feature of CD is a persistent pattern of behavior in which the rights of others and age-appropriate social norms are violated. The youth may exhibit aggressive behavior toward others, using a weapon, fire setting, cruelty to animals or persons, vandalism, lying, truancy, running away, and theft. The DSM-V allows for coding a client with one of two subtypes of CD: childhood-onset type (at least one criterion occurs prior to age 10) and adolescent-onset type (absence of any criteria prior to age 10). While an adolescent may be considered a "juvenile delinquent" after only one delinquent act, to warrant a diagnosis of CD that same adolescent must be engaged in a pattern of behavior over an extended period of time (at least 6 months) that consistently violates the rights of others and societal norms.

Conflict resolution: An approach emphasizing communication, anger-management, and perspective-taking skills, usually taught as a curriculum unit with a prescribed number of lessons. While some programs employ peer mediators, increasingly school district-wide approaches that teach conflict-resolution and mediation skills to all students are being used.

Crack cocaine: A freebase cocaine product produced by mixing cocaine salt with baking soda and water. The solution is then heated until a brittle form of cocaine is produced. This product is then broken into small, smokeable pieces of crack ("rock").

Delinquency offenses: Illegal acts that are considered crimes whether committed by an adult or a juvenile (e.g., aggravated assault, arson, burglary, drug-related offenses, theft, rape).

Dependency cases: A documented pattern of child neglect, physical abuse, and/ or sexual abuse and identification of a minor needing foster care or other residential placement outside the home.

Depression: A disturbance of mood marked by inability to enjoy activities and relationships, feelings of hopelessness and worthlessness, problems sleeping and eating, and thoughts of suicide.

Designer drug: A drug with properties and effects similar to a known hallucinogen or narcotic but having a slightly altered chemical structure, especially such a drug created in to evade restrictions against illegal substances.

Detention education: A number of detention education program operators believe that effective education must be more than rote academic maintenance and that detention education should respond to the juvenile's needs. Presented with students at multiple levels and with multiple needs, a quality detention education curriculum should provide a continuum of academic services ranging from special education to GED preparation to post-secondary options. The detention education curriculum should teach and reinforce prosocial behaviors that translate into success for the student at home, at school, in the community, or in a future placement. Youth in juvenile detention facilities need instruction in communication, problem solving, decision making, interpersonal relationships, values, critical thinking, and healthy lifestyle choices.

Diagnosis: A discrete process of determining through observation, examination, and analysis the nature of a client's illness or functional problems.

Diagnostic and Statistical Manual of Mental Disorders, Fifth Edition, Text Revision (DSM-V): The latest edition of the official manual of mental disorders used in the United States and many other countries, published by the American Psychiatric Association. It provides a listing of all the officially recognized mental disorders and their code numbers, as well as the diagnostic criteria used in identifying each disorder. The codes and terms are a subset of the mental disorders listed in the International Classification of Diseases, Ninth Revision, Clinical Modification (ICD-9-CM).

Diagnostic criteria: Detailed descriptions, called diagnostic criteria, are provided in DSM-V for each of the specific mental disorders. These specify the rules for inclusion and exclusion symptoms and other features when making each diagnosis.

Dialectical Behavioral Therapy (DBT): A gender-specific treatment model that focuses on emotional regulation. When used with severely disturbed female juvenile offenders, DBT was found to be effective in reducing certain behavior problems (e.g., aggression, parasuicidal behavior).

Direct calendaring: A "one family/one judge" approach that allows the judge to remain with the case for all stages of case processing. Direct calendaring is believed to result in courts making more consistent decisions because judges will be more familiar with the complexities of the family situation and its needs and expectations. Direct calendaring is also thought to make the family less likely to feel that a stranger who is not familiar with their situation is making life-altering decisions on their behalf. This is in contrast to master calendaring.

Discrimination: Being treated differently based on a group status rather than one's behavior or qualifications. Discrimination due to race or ethnicity occurs when one group is treated differently than another group based wholly or in part on its race or ethnicity. See *disparity* and *overrepresentation*.

Dismissed cases: Cases that are dismissed (including those warned, counseled, and released) with no further disposition anticipated.

Disparity: Disparity refers to different groups having different probabilities for a particular outcome due to their group status. See *overrepresentation* and *discrimination*.

Disproportionate minority contact (DMC): The overrepresentation of minority youth in the juvenile justice system, in proportion to their general population and as compared with White youth. Minority populations/youth of color include American Indian and Alaska Native, Asian, Black or African American, Hispanic or Latino, Native Hawaiian or other Pacific Islander, and persons of mixed race/ethnicity.

Disposition: The most severe action taken or treatment plan decided upon or initiated in a particular case. Disposition cases include waived, placement, probation, or dismissed.

Disruptive behavior disorders: ADHD and CD are termed *disruptive behavior disorders*. Youth diagnosed with ADHD and CD who have deficits in social skills and problem-solving skills and increased impulsivity are prone to have problems with law-abiding behavior. Faced with daily temptations to break the law, these youth cannot control their initial impulses or think clearly about the pros and cons and future consequences of their behavior. They are also more likely to surround themselves with negative peers and have difficulty refraining from peer pressure. Both disorders place youth at risk for school failure, school suspensions, and school violence.

Drug abuse: Any use of drugs that creates legal, social, emotional, family, or social harm as the direct result of behaviors of the individual taking the illegal drug.

Drug court: See *specialty courts*.

Drug trafficking: Doing or being concerned in any of the following: (a) producing or supplying a controlled drug; (b) transporting or storing a controlled drug; (c) importing or exporting a controlled drug.

Drug urinalysis: In practice, urinalysis refers to (1) macroscopic analysis, which includes the assessment of physical characteristics and (2) chemical analysis or microscopic analysis for formed elements.

Early childhood education: High-quality early childhood education can help prevent school violence. Several early comprehensive intervention programs have had favorable impacts on preventing delinquency and violence.

Empathy: Enables a person to feel what another is feeling and to understand why she or he is feeling that way.

Empathy training: A program designed to help an individual to feel a sense of connection with others. The juvenile delinquent is encouraged to see the victim as a human being, as someone's son or daughter, or mother or father. Several approaches to teach victim empathy currently exist.

Evidence-based practice: An approach to practice that requires the examination of research findings from systematic clinical research (e.g., randomized controlled clinical research) in making decisions about the care of a specific population with a specific problem. The process involves critically identifying and employing treatment or practice approaches that have the strongest basis of empirical support for attaining desired outcomes. An evidence-based practice is considered any practice that has been established as effective through scientific research according to a set of explicit criteria. The term *evidence-based practice* is also used to describe a way of practicing in which the practitioner critically uses best evidence, expertise, and values to make practice decisions that matter to individual service recipients and patients about their care. Evidence-based practice is the use of interventions that are based on rigorous research methods. Evidence-based practice involves integrating different studies and establishing the combined probative value. An example of an evidence-based practice approach to supporting and serving families and children would be based on the likelihood that certain types of supports and services can be shown to be more effective than other interventions.

Family systems theory: Family systems theory is the foundation of the majority of family treatment programs. This theory states that the family is the major socializing agent that influences and helps shape the child's attitude, values, behavior, and personality. Basic principles include the following: the family is seen as an organized whole; behaviors are seen as actions and reactions rather than one-way communication; families resist change unless it meets their needs; well-functioning family systems are less resistant to change and are more willing to adapt; and family systems comprise subsystems such as the parent subsystem or the parent–child subsystem. Lastly, family systems theories identify boundaries between individuals and subsystems, and interaction across these boundaries occurs based on rules and consistent behaviors.

Family-focused interventions: Programs that focus on the family as a whole, rather than only on the child or only on the parent. Comprehensive treatments that address the needs of the child, parent, and family have been found to be the most effective for youth with antisocial behaviors.

Fetal alcohol spectrum disorder: Often referred to as fetal alcohol syndrome (FAS) or fetal alcohol effects (FAE) and other alcohol-related birth defects. A pattern of mental and physical problems that may occur in some children whose mothers drank alcohol during pregnancy. While the baby is developing in the mother, alcohol the mother drinks is passed to the developing child. Drinking during any stage of pregnancy may cause FAS or FAE.

Forestry camps: Camps for juvenile delinquents that operated between 1933 and 1943; generally modeled after the Civilian Conservation Corps camps. The goal of those camps was to provide a treatment program that included conservation of natural resources in addition to employment and vocational training. These camps provided an open setting with no gates, bars, guns, or isolation facilities. Two basic types of camps developed in the late 1940s and early 1950s: senior forestry camps and junior probation camps. A senior forestry camp was for youths age 16 to 18. Emphasis was on work such as nursery, reforestation, maintenance and construction, brush clearance, and fire suppression. During World War II, the forestry camps added to their program training in the fundamentals of military life and drill (provided by the Army). A number of boys who received this training went directly from the camp into military service.

Formal assessment: Before a youth is placed within the juvenile justice system, a formal assessment should be conducted that includes a thorough history of the youth's development from birth to present day, including family, psychological, social, and academic history. Details regarding child abuse, alcohol and drug problems, lethality, family violence, traumas, and previous mental health issues are crucial. A formal assessment by the school for learning disabilities that may have previously gone unnoticed is also a must. The offending behavior must be explicitly identified in order to assess the severity and chronicity of the offenses.

Functional Family Training (FFT): Functional family therapy (FFT) has been found to be an effective practice in the mental health arena with families and troubled youth. It has also been found to reduce recidivism in youth involved in corrections and substance abuse and with very serious juvenile offenders. FFT has also been found to be effective with diverse youth in various geographical areas. Trained therapists using FFT work to modify the family's functioning and therefore the youth's symptoms that are thought to be a symptom of problematic family functioning. The emphasis for change and treatment is on the family as opposed to singling out or blaming the youth for all of the family's problems.

Gang suppression: Any intervention whose purpose is to intervene and to prevent gang violence and other gang activities.

Heroin: A substance produced via chemical processing of morphine. The result is a drug more potent than morphine. There is a resurgence of heroin abuse and addiction across the United States within urban areas.

House of Refuge: Opened in New York on January 21, 1825, it was the first prison for juveniles that was completely separate from an adult prison. Similar juvenile institutions opened in 1826 and 1828 in Boston and Philadelphia, respectively. Between 1845 and 1854, several other large cities established houses of refuge for juvenile offenders. These first houses of refuge were built to counteract the poverty, vice, and neglectful families that were considered breeding grounds for delinquency. The houses of refuge were supposed to provide a home for unruly and troubled children, where they would be reformed, educated, and disciplined. Children were put in such places for protection from the temptations of immoral, unfit, and neglectful families and vice-ridden, disorganized communities. In addition, juveniles in cities with houses of refuge would not have to be incarcerated in adult jails and prisons, so they would not be corrupted by repeat adult offenders. Houses of refuge were built as secure facilities. Some were surrounded by brick walls, and their interiors were designed to confine inmates securely while instilling order, respect for authority, and strict and steady discipline.

Intoxication: A transient state of physical or psychological disruption secondary to the ingestion of a mood-altering substance that impairs the functioning of the central nervous system (e.g., alcohol).

Judicial discretion: the power or right to make official decisions using reason and judgment to choose from among acceptable alternatives.

Juvenile aftercare plan: Upon release from a state training school, also known as a juvenile correctional institution, the juvenile may be ordered to undergo a period of intensive aftercare or parole. During this period the juvenile may be monitored or under the supervision of the juvenile court or the corrections department. Aftercare programs should include a continuum of services and scheduled activities, such as after-school recreational and creative arts programs, alternative dispute-resolution programs, mentoring and tutoring programs, career development and vocational training programs, religious group meetings, family counseling, volunteer work with the homeless and disabled, and neighborhood crime-prevention projects.

Juvenile assessment center (JAC): The first JAC was established in Hillsborough County (Tampa), Florida, in 1993. Most JACs share the following four characteristics: *single point of entry* (a 24-hour centralized point of intake and assessment for juveniles who have come into or are likely to come into contact with the juvenile justice system); *immediate and comprehensive assessments* (service providers associated with the JAC make an initial broad-based and, if necessary, a later, in-depth assessment of youths' circumstances and treatment needs); *management information systems* (MIS; needed to manage and monitor youth, to ensure that appropriate treatment services are provided, and to avoid duplication of services); and *integrated case management services* (JAC staff use information from the assessment process and the MIS to develop recommendations to improve access to services, complete follow-ups of referred youths, and periodically reassess youth placed in various services).

Juvenile court: The first juvenile court was established in Cook County, Illinois, in 1899, and it was viewed by the vast majority of social reformers as a milestone in the developmental process of American justice. The purpose and function of the court was to have been rehabilitation rather than punishment. During the first quarter of the 20th century, both the general public and public officials warmly and enthusiastically hailed the juvenile court movement as a panacea for the misbehavior, troubles, and social ills of children and youth. In recent years, judges and their chief probation officers have advocated for and developed restitution programs in the form of monetary and community work service assignments in order to hold juveniles accountable for their offenses. Juvenile offenders in property-related crimes are the most likely candidates for these restitution programs. In addition, during the current decade the threshold of public tolerance for violent juvenile offenders has decreased considerably. The result has been harsher handling by prosecutors and judges for violent and chronic juvenile offenders. To increase violent juveniles' accountability for their offenses, the strategy used with increasing frequency is to mete out harsher and more severe penalties.

Juvenile delinquency: A violation of state or federal law or municipal ordinance by a minor that, if committed by an adult, would constitute a crime such as burglary, robbery, simple assault, and aggravated assault.

Juvenile delinquent: A minor who commits one of many diverse forms of antisocial behavior. Most state criminal codes define juvenile delinquency as behavior that is in violation of the criminal code and is committed by a youth who has not reached adult age. This includes juveniles who have been arrested or contacted by the police, even though many of these individuals are merely reprimanded or sent home when their parents pick them up.

Juvenile detention: The temporary and safe custody of juveniles who are accused of conduct subject to the jurisdiction of the court who require a restricted environment for their own or the community's protection while legal action is pending. Juvenile detention provides a wide range of helpful services that support the juvenile's physical, emotional, and social development. They may include education, visitation, communication, counseling, continuous supervision, healthcare services, nutrition, recreation, and reading. Juvenile detention includes or provides for a system of clinical observation and assessment that complements the helpful services and reports findings.

Juvenile Detention Alternatives Initiative (JDAI): The Annie E. Casey Foundation established JDAI in 1992 to demonstrate that jurisdictions could establish more effective and efficient systems to accomplish the purposes of juvenile detention. In the largest detention reform effort to date, JDAI sought to reduce the inappropriate detention of youth in selected metropolitan jurisdictions around the country. JDAI had four basic objectives: (1) to eliminate the inappropriate or unnecessary use of secure detention; (2) to minimize failures to appear and the incidence of delinquent behavior; (3) to redirect public finances from building new facility capacity to responsible alternative strategies; and (4) to improve conditions in secure detention facilities.

Juvenile diversion: Any process that is used by components of the criminal justice system (police, prosecution, courts, corrections) whereby youths avoid formal juvenile court processing and adjudication. *Diversion* refers to the channeling of cases to nonjudicial community agencies or facilities, in instances where these cases would ordinarily have received an adjudicatory (or fact-finding) hearing by a court. The major goal of the first juvenile courts, established at the turn of the 20th century, was to provide an alternative to, and thereby divert youths from, the criminal court. The juvenile court was created to avoid the unfair and inhumane treatment to which juveniles were subjected when processed through the criminal court and incarcerated with adult felons. Diversion has also existed for a long time in the form of informal station adjustments and discretionary handling by police officers when they have given youths a warning and sent them back home. However, the development of formal programs for the purpose of diverting juveniles from adjudication in the juvenile justice system did not begin until the late 1960s. The main objectives of juvenile diversion are to (1) avoid labeling; (2) reduce unnecessary detention and incarceration; (3) reduce repeat offenses; (4) provide counseling and other services in the community; and (5) lower justice system costs.

Juvenile gang: A juvenile gang is tied together by common interests, has an identified leader, and generally acts as a group to achieve illegal, immoral, or harmful objectives.

Juvenile Justice and Delinquency Act of 1973: In 1980 President Carter signed the reauthorization of the Juvenile Justice and Delinquency Prevention Act into law. This revised act contained an historic amendment mandating the removal of juveniles from adult jails. Only those juveniles who are tried as adults for criminal felonies are allowed to be detained or incarcerated in adult jails. OJJDP focused attention on rural jails, which were often the only place police could detain juveniles.

Juvenile Justice and Delinquency Prevention Act of 1974: This legislation strongly discouraged status offenders from being held in secure juvenile correctional facilities, either for detention or placement. This important legislation and policy mandate are called *deinstitutionalization of status offenders*.

Juvenile justice processing: There are nine steps: initial contact by law enforcement agencies; law enforcement informal handling, diversion, arrest, and/or referral to the juvenile court; court intake via the juvenile probation intake unit or the prosecutor's office; pre-adjudication juvenile detention; prosecutors file a delinquency petition in juvenile court or waive to adult criminal court; investigation or predisposition report prepared by a probation officer; juvenile court judges adjudicatory decision and sanctions; participation and completion of mandated juvenile offender treatment program; juvenile aftercare plan.

Juvenile offender re-entry: Re-entry is the return of the offender from a placement outside of the home community back to the home community. For the juvenile justice community, re-entry expands the concept of reintegration. An overwhelming majority of youth released from juvenile facilities return home. Detention must address the physical and emotional component of re-entry since both are important to the crafting of a successful outcome. A systematic involvement of community-based programs throughout incarceration enhances the likelihood of successful community reintegration.

Juvenile probation: Professional probation officers provide juvenile offenders with supportive services and referrals that, depending upon the youth's needs, might include individual counseling, group counseling, referral to community mental health centers for outpatient treatment or inpatient psychiatric services, appropriate referrals to addiction treatment programs, family counseling, vocational training, assistance in finding employment, enrolling in alternative education programs, or preparing for the high school equivalency examination.

Juvenile sex offender: A juvenile found to have committed any violation of law or delinquent act involving juvenile sexual abuse. "Juvenile sexual abuse" means any sexual behavior that occurs without consent, without equality, or as a result of coercion. Juvenile sexual offender behavior ranges from non-contact sexual behavior such as making obscene phone calls, exhibitionism, voyeurism, and the showing or taking of lewd photographs to varying degrees of direct sexual contact, such as frottage, fondling, digital penetration, rape, fellatio, sodomy, and various other sexually aggressive acts.

Juvenile status offender: A juvenile who engages in deviant acts or misbehavior that, if engaged in by an adult, would not be considered crimes (e.g., truancy, incorrigibility, and running away from home). For status offenders, many states have separate legislation that views these juveniles as individuals "in need of supervision." An array of crisis intervention services, runaway shelters, youth service bureaus, addiction treatment programs, day treatment programs, and family counseling programs have been developed to serve these youths.

Labeling Theory: Labeling theory is the view of deviance according to which being labeled as a "deviant" leads a person to engage in deviant behavior. Originating in Howard Becker's work in the 1960s, labeling theory holds that deviance is not inherent to an act, but instead focuses on the tendency of majorities to negatively label minorities or those seen as deviant from standard cultural norms.

Learning disability: Includes specific learning disabilities, mental retardation, emotional disturbance, and health impairments (ADHD, epilepsy, etc.). Children who qualify for this category are eligible for special education services in the least restrictive environment possible. Most schools provide special education services and classes within their school building; however, some schools use alternative schools for children who have a disability but who are also exhibiting disruptive or offending behaviors. Juveniles exhibiting severe behaviors are often removed completely from the school system and placed in the juvenile justice system.

MAYSI-2: The Massachusetts Youth Screening Instrument was designed to evaluate psychological distress in youth entering the juvenile justice system. It does not focus on psychological diagnoses but rather on situational and characterological distress in youth in the juvenile justice system. The instrument has seven subscales: alcohol and drug use, angry-irritable, depressed-anxious, somatic complaints, suicidal ideation, thought disturbance, and traumatic experiences. Scores above the cutoff warrant mental health referrals. The easy-to-score instrument has been proven reliable and valid with youth in the juvenile justice system. It has only 52 items and can be completed in 10 minutes.

Methamphetamine: A stimulant that can be taken by snorting or injecting.

Mental health court: See *specialty courts*.

Mood disorders: Mood disorders include depressive disorders as well as bipolar disorder. Depression is characterized by depressed or irritable mood, diminished interest in activities, difficulties with concentration, and fatigue. Manic episodes are characterized by grandiosity, talkativeness, distractibility, and decreased need for sleep. Youth with bipolar disorder that includes cycles of depression as well as mania may exhibit delinquent and risk-taking behaviors during the manic phase. During this phase, youth often feel invincible and cannot comprehend future consequences of their behavior.

Multisystemic Therapy (MST): A family- and community-based treatment approach that is theoretically grounded in a social-ecological framework and family systems. A basic foundation of MST is the belief that a juvenile's acting-out or antisocial behavior is best addressed by interfacing with multiple systems, including the adolescent's family, peers, school, teachers, neighbors, and others. Services are delivered in the client's natural environment, such as the client's home or a neighborhood center. MST aims to improve parental discipline practices and family relations, decrease the youth's contact with deviant peers, improve the youth's academic performance, and develop support systems to maintain the changes. The main goals are to divert the youth from juvenile justice and mental health residential placements and to help the youth and family progress toward their life goals.

Needs assessment: A formal process that identifies needs as gaps in results between "what is" and "what should be," prioritizes those gaps on the basis of the costs and benefits of closing versus ignoring those needs, and selects the needs to be reduced or eliminated. Needs assessments serve to identify gaps between current and desired results that occur both within an organization (at the micro level of results) as well as outside (at the macro and mega levels of results) in order to provide useful information for decision making.

Nonpetitioned delinquency cases: Informally handled cases in which duly authorized court personnel screen for adjustment prior to filing a formal petition. Such personnel include judges, referees, probation officers, other officers of the court, and/or an agency statutorily designated to conduct petition screening for the juvenile court.

Office of Juvenile Justice and Delinquency Prevention (OJJDP): Created in 1974 within the Law Enforcement Assistance Administration (LEAA) to coordinate efforts to control delinquency (P.L. 93-415). For the fiscal years 1975 through 1977, 89,125 OJJDP formula grants to state and local agencies were approved. Since LEAA became defunct in 1981, OJJDP is now part of the Office of Justice Programs of the U.S. Department of Justice.

Oppositional defiant disorder: Defined by a pattern of negativity, noncompliance and defiance to authority figures (e.g., parents, teachers, and other adults), and temperamental outbursts that impair a child's ability to function effectively in home, school, and peer environments. This maladaptive pattern of behavior must have endured for 6 months or longer for the diagnosis to be made accurately. The DSM-V is careful to note that these behaviors must occur more often than in peers of comparable age and developmental level.

Outcome: Measurable change in daily practice.

Outcome measures: Outcome measures help staff make specific decisions about program change. Outcomes that are closely linked to day-to-day management can be used routinely to monitor strengths, weaknesses, or trouble spots. (This requires ongoing assessments of the conditions of confinement.) Outcome measures provide assurance to administration, staff, and the public that the total program functions with reasonable effectiveness.

Overrepresentation: Having more youth from a particular racial or ethnic group represented in the juvenile justice system than would be expected based on their proportion in the general population. See *disparity* and *discrimination*.

Parens patriae: A principle enabling the court to act in lieu of parents who were found to be unwilling or unable to give their child appropriate guidance. This paved the way for the juvenile court in the United States to assume jurisdiction for dependent and neglected children. The principle evolved from a 1772 English court case, *Eyre v. Shaftsbury*. There has been some confusion between the terms *parens patriae* and *in loco parentis*. The former refers to the responsibility of government to serve the welfare of the child, not (as the latter might suggest) to replace the parents. The doctrine of *parens patriae* was used to free the juvenile court judge to accept social and psychological evaluations and provide informal proceedings, thus departing from due process of law. It also justified the court's right to "save" children who had committed non-criminal offenses, such as disobeying parents, truancy, and associating with immoral and criminal persons.

Persistently Dangerous School and Unsafe School Option: Part of the No Child Left Behind Act of 2001 (U.S. PL 107–110, Title IX, sec. 9532), it emphasizes physical acts of violence. Each state receiving funds under the Act must "establish and implement a statewide policy requiring that a student attending a persistently dangerous public elementary school or secondary school, as determined by the state in consultation with a representative sample of local educational agencies, or who becomes a victim of a violent criminal offense, as determined by State law, while in or on the grounds of a public elementary school or secondary school that the student attends, be allowed to attend a safe public elementary school or secondary school within the local educational agency, including a public charter school." Thus, the onus is on school administrators to demonstrate that they are providing safe environments in which students can learn, or those students can take their business elsewhere.

Petitioned cases: Formally handled cases that appear on the official court calendar in response to the filing of a petition or other legal instrument requesting the court to adjudicate the youth a delinquent-status offender or dependent child or to waive the youth to criminal court for processing as an adult.

Placement cases: Cases in which youth are placed out of the home in a residential facility housing delinquents or status offenders or are otherwise removed from their home.

Posttraumatic stress disorder (PTSD): PTSD is usually caused by an overwhelming or traumatic event outside the range of ordinary human experience. Individuals suffer from intrusive recollections, avoidant/numbing symptoms, flashbacks, nightmares, and hyperarousal for at least 1 month.

Preventive approaches: Teaching skills and ways to alter the school environment that will decrease the likelihood of violent events occurring. Preventive approaches offer much more promise as a strategy of reducing school violence. These approaches can be as simple as installing metal detectors or can involve more complicated interventions such as social skills training, conflict resolution training, and organizational changes. Preventive approaches are based on the belief that there are identifiable risk factors associated with violence, and interventions that address these risk factors are likely to reduce violence. Many components of school violence prevention models can serve as points of departure for interventions with the perpetrators.

Probation: A legal status created by order of the sentencing court as an alternative to incarceration. The term *probation* is derived from *probare*, meaning "to prove"— that is, it allows the offender the opportunity to prove himself or herself.

Property crime: A category of crime that includes, among other crimes, burglary, larceny, theft, motor vehicle theft, arson, shoplifting, and vandalism. Property crime involves only the taking of money or property and does not involve force or threat of force against a victim (in contrast to violent crime).

Psychiatric hospitalization: Adolescents are more likely to be hospitalized if they appear psychotic, remain homicidal, or need intensive psychopharmacological management. Inpatient treatment can be particularly helpful in stabilizing the youth, redirecting suicidal, self-destructive, or homicidal impulses and reducing internal conflict. It can also provide an optimal setting for evaluating the youth, assessing his or her potential for continued violent behavior, and understanding the family system of which he or she is a member. Unlike the homicidal child, who is typically viewed as psychologically disturbed, an adolescent killer is generally regarded as antisocial and is likely to be institutionalized in a facility for juvenile delinquents or adult criminals.

Quasi-experimental designs: Experimental designs in which people are not randomly assigned to different forms of the program. Quasi-experimental designs can compare different forms of the program that naturally occur or can use procedures such as matching or waiting lists to form quasi-control or comparison groups.

Randomized controlled trial: An outcome study of treatment effectiveness measured using an experimental design. Such designs usually involve assessments of client and system functioning before and after the intervention and random assignment of clients to treatment and to alternative conditions such as no treatment, standard care, or placebo treatment.

Reactive approaches: An approach to school violence that relies on tough disciplinary action and punishment. The recent public frenzy over school violence has influenced the type of approach that is taken toward school violence. Many concerned parents, educators, and politicians advocate "get tough" and "zero tolerance" policies for youth responsible for school violence. These catch phrases translate into reactive and punitive disciplinary actions.

Recidivism: Recurrence of criminal delinquent behavior in an offender. The recidivism rate refers to the general frequency of reoffense or re-adjudication in a particular group of offenders after a specified follow-up period.

Restitution: Restitution is sometimes incorporated as part of a post-adjudication court order. It often takes one of three forms: *monetary restitution,* or paying back the victim for losses or damage suffered; *community service,* in which the juvenile is ordered to perform a given number of work hours at a private nonprofit or governmental agency; or *direct services to victims,* victim-offender reconciliation programs, in which trained staff bring the victim, if willing, together with the offender. See also *victim-offender mediation.*

Restorative justice: Emphasizes three goals: (1) identifying the obligation created by the juvenile's offense and ensuring that he/she is held responsible for it (accountability), (2) returning the offender to the community competent to interact in a successful prosocial manner (competence), and (3) ensuring that the community is not further injured by the juvenile's delinquent behavior (public safety). Restorative justice is based on the assumption that none of the essential functions of the justice system—rehabilitation, community protection, sanctioning, and victim restoration—can be accomplished without the joint involvement of victims, offenders, and the community. It is based on the belief and value statement that justice is best served when victims, offenders, and the community receive balanced attention and gain tangible benefits from their interactions with the juvenile justice system. Restorative justice also speaks directly to the need for societies to make allowances for offender repentance or forgiveness and to make possible and encourage offender reintegration following appropriate sanctioning.

Retributive justice: Gives priority to punishment through incarceration as the primary means of sanctioning offenders for violations against the state.

Risk factors for delinquency and mental health problems: Individual risk factors include substance abuse, mental health problems, poor social problem-solving skills, learning disabilities, and cognitive impairments. Family risk factors include poor parental supervision, poverty, paternal criminality, family history of psychiatric disorder, intense marital conflict and dysfunction, ineffective discipline practices, and exposure to domestic violence. School risk factors include truancy, poor academic achievement, and untreated learning disabilities. Peer risk factors include association with delinquent peers and gang membership. Community risk factors include exposure to violence and drug dealing. These risk factors can assist personnel in understanding the severity and potential severity of problems the youth may have. For instance, a youth who has only two risk factors for mental illness will have less of a chance for developing these problems than one who has seven risk factors. The age of the youth in combination with the known risk factors should shed light on where the youth should be placed and treated.

Runaway youth: Youth who have left home without parental/caregiver permission and stay away for one or more nights. A runaway episode has been defined as being away from home overnight for youth under 14 (or older and mentally incompetent) and for two or more nights for youth 15 and older. Research suggests that running away from home is often episodic rather than chronic, with youth running away for short periods and returning home, in some cases multiple times.

School violence: Encompasses an array of behaviors ranging from verbal taunts to bombing persons in a school building. These behaviors are overt, aggressive acts that result in physical or psychological pain, injury, or death. Violence includes behaviors that aggress against property as well as persons, so school vandalism can be seen as a form of school violence. Most of the literature relating to this issue limits the scope of the concern to behaviors on school grounds. Physical acts of violence are much easier for school officials to document; they demand attention by virtue of their visibility and tendency to provoke outrage. Nonphysical acts of violence involving feelings of intimidation or fear are difficult to document and less likely to be reported.

School-to-prison pipeline: Policies and practices that push schoolchildren, especially at-risk ones, out of classroom and into the juvenile and criminal justice systems. This pipeline reflects how incarceration has a higher priority than education.

Skill streaming: An intervention in which a 50-skill curriculum of prosocial behaviors is systematically taught to chronically aggressive adolescents and younger children. The skills fall into one of six families: beginning social skills, advanced social skills, skills for dealing with feelings, alternatives to aggression, skills for dealing with stress, and planning skills.

Social skills: A complex set of skills that facilitate interactions between peers, parents, teachers, and other adults. The "social" refers to interactions between people; the "skills" refers to making appropriate discriminations—that is, deciding what would be the most effective response and using the verbal and nonverbal behaviors that facilitate interaction.

Specialty courts: Specialty courts handle cases where the defendant has an underlying problem and will benefit from services directed toward solving that problem; there are mental health, drug, and family courts.

Status offenses: Deviant acts or misbehavior committed by a juvenile that, if engaged in by an adult, would not be considered crimes (e.g., truancy, incorrigibility, curfew violations, and running away from home). See also *juvenile status offenders*.

Statutory exclusion: One of the ways that a juvenile case can be transferred to adult court. Statutory exclusion, also known as *legislative exclusion,* refers to cases that are defined in state law as automatically being referred to adult criminal court. See judicial waivers for a contrasting approach.

Street youth: "An individual who (A) is (i) a runaway youth; or (ii) indefinitely or intermittently a homeless youth; and (B) spends a significant amount of time on the street or in other areas that increase the risk to such youth for sexual abuse, sexual exploitation, prostitution, or drug abuse" (Title 42, The Public Health and Welfare; Chapter 72. Juvenile Justice and Delinquency Prevention; Runaway and Homeless Youth; General Provisions).

Training school: A large, state-operated institution for long-term incarceration of juvenile delinquents.

Transfer: The process of certifying and waiving a juvenile into the adult criminal court. This can be done only through a legislative judicial waiver.

Teen courts: Also referred to as youth courts, they provide a method for diverting juveniles from the formal justice system.

Therapeutic jurisprudence: A legal reform theory that considers the law as a therapeutic agent, without displacing due process. It considers how legal rules, legal actors, and legal procedures act as social forces that can affect legal outcomes, including the emotional and psychological well-being of the parties involved.

Throwaway youth: Youth who have been asked, told, or forced to leave home by parents or caregivers with no alternate care arrangement.

Uniform Crime Reports: The annual Federal Bureau of Investigation (FBI) statistical report of all arrests taking place annually in the United States, based on police department reports.

Victimization surveys: Victimization studies have been completed in many cities throughout the United States. These studies have been conducted as joint efforts by the U.S. Bureau of Justice Statistics and the Bureau of the Census. The best-known victimization survey is the National Crime Victimization Survey (NCVS), a massive, annual, house-to-house survey of a random sample of 60,000 households and 136,000 individuals. The NCVS provides annual estimates of the total number of crimes committed by both adult and juvenile offenders. The six types of crime measured are rape, robbery, assault, household burglary, personal and household larceny, and motor vehicle theft. Based on the survey data, it has been estimated that 40 million serious crimes occur each year in the United States.

Victim-offender mediation: A process that provides interested victims (primarily those of property crimes and minor assaults) the opportunity to meet their offenders in a safe and structured setting. The goal is to hold offenders directly accountable while providing important support and assistance to victims. With the assistance of trained mediators, the victims are able to let the offenders know how the crime affected them, receive answers to their questions, and be directly involved in developing a restitution plan that holds the offenders financially accountable for the losses they caused. See also *balanced approach; restitution;* and *restorative justice.*

Violent crimes: The FBI's UCR considers violent crime to include four offenses: murder and nonnegligent manslaughter, forcible rape, robbery, and aggravated assault. Violent crimes are defined in the UCR as offenses that involve force or threat of force.

Violent Crime Control Act of 1994: The largest crime bill in the history of the country; it provided for 100,000 new police officers, $9.7 billion in funding for prisons, and $6.1 billion in funding for prevention programs that were designed with significant input from experienced police officers. The Act also significantly expanded the government's ability to deal with problems caused by criminal aliens. It provided $2.6 billion in additional funding for the FBI, DEA, INS, U.S. Attorneys, and other Justice Department components, as well as the Federal courts and the Treasury Department.

Voice DISC-IV: The National Institute of Mental Health Diagnostic Interview Schedule for Children, Version 4, is a highly structured diagnostic interview used to assess psychiatric diagnoses of children and adolescents. It was designed to be administered by interviewers with no formal clinical training following the rules and conventions outlined in the DISC training manual.

Wilderness programs: Provide adjudicated and troubled youths with a rigorous physical and emotional challenge unlike anything they have ever known. In small, closely supervised groups, the juvenile offenders learn to follow instructions and to work cooperatively with other youths to accomplish a series of difficult physical challenges, thereby enhancing their own self-esteem. Most programs also strive to strengthen the youths' academic skills by incorporating aspects of learning directly related to outdoor living (e.g., map reading and compass skills). Present-day wilderness programs for juvenile offenders evolved from two separate directions: forestry camps for youthful offenders and the Outward Bound model created in Wales during World War II.

Wraparound programs: Wraparound programs provide an array of formal and informal services to youth and their families while maintaining youth in their community. These programs are effective for low-risk or first-time offenders, since community safety must always be ensured. Wraparound programs focus on the youth and family's strengths and build on the natural supports that exist within the family. They expect family involvement in the treatment and use individualized service plans.

Youth service bureaus: A type of community-based juvenile diversion program that has a full array of structured after-school and evening programs such as field trips to museums, ping-pong tournaments, billiards, volleyball, basketball, chess tournaments, and so on. During the 1970s, major federal funding for youth service bureaus was provided through the Law Enforcement Assistance Administration. The modern-day version of a coordinating council is a community-based youth service bureau. Developed to provide and coordinate programs and services for both delinquent and nondelinquent youths, these youth service bureaus have five basic goals: divert juveniles from the juvenile justice system; fill gaps in service by advocating for and developing services for youths and their families; provide case coordination and program coordinating; provide modification of systems of youth services; and involve youth in the decision-making process.

Youth shelter: A short-term residential facility to house status offenders and younger juvenile delinquents who can benefit from being detained and cared for in a social services-oriented setting.

Zero tolerance policies: A zero-tolerance policy in schools is a policy of punishing any infraction of a rule, regardless of accidental mistakes, ignorance, or extenuating circumstances; any policy that allows no exception.

Index

abatement strategies, 354
abnormal brain
    development, 132–36
abortion, 64
abuse. *See also* substance abuse
    chronic, 135
    emotional, 21, 474
    exposure to, 134
    physical, 21, 48, 54
academic failure, 282
academic interventions, 281–82
academic performance. *See* school
    performance
accumulated disadvantage, 614
ACT. *See* anger control training
Act 4 Juvenile Justice, 139
acupuncture, 41
Adam Walsh Child Protection and
    Safety Act of 2006, 535–36
Addams, Jane, 152
ADHD, 379. *See also* conduct
    disorder
adjudication
    decisions, 50, *51*
    of females, 583, 591
    juvenile court intake and,
        10–11, *13*, 184
    juvenile detention, 11
    for juvenile sex offenders,
        537, 545
    national estimates of, 50
    options, 16
    procedural safeguards in, 44
    residential placements, 17
    for substance abuse, 30
    in teen courts, 44
adjudicatory judicial hearings,
    11–12, 47, 187, 591
adolescence, definition of, 131
adolescence-limited offenders, 96

adolescent competence
    below-average intelligence
        and, 174
    counsel waivers and, 181–82
    determination, 174
    developmental psychology
        and, 170–71
    diminished, 182, 227
    emotions and, 171
    geographic disparities
        in, 182–83
    guilty plea and, 182
    impulsive behavior, 177
    legal standards and, 172–74
    Miranda rights and, 176, 177
    procedural safeguards
        toward, 169
    risk perception and, 171
    self-control and, 171
    to stand trial, 173–74
    to waive or plead guilty,
        179–184
Adolescent Coping with
    Depression Course, 426, 432
Adolescent Development and
    Juvenile Justice (ADJJ), 170
adolescent-limited offenders,
    133, 134
Adolescent Portable Therapy, 619
adult correctional facilities, 39,
    40. *See also* correctional
    facilities
adult criminal court
    data challenges, 255
    ethnic disparities in, 248–49
    national estimates of youth
        processed in, 242
    offense limitations for
        youth, 245
    proceedings in, 249

racial disparities in, 248–49
recidivism of juveniles
    transferred to, 254
state policies, 258–59
statutory minimum age
    limitations, 243
transferring youth to, 243–47,
    244–45, 258–59, 612
adult judge model for teen court,
    230. *See also* teen courts
advocacy strategies, 129–130
AFDC. *See* Aid to Families with
    Dependent Children
African Americans
    arrest rates for, 6, 197–98,
        522, 588
    attitudes toward police, 155
    detention estimates for, 49, 588
    disposition disparities
        for, 590–91
    gang members, 341
    incarceration rates of, 6, 248
    juvenile crime rates and, 25
    juvenile justice population of,
        389, 488
    mental health services and, 593
    police encounters with, 158
    poverty and, 614
    racial disparities, 588
    re-entry needs of, 373
    referral rates to juvenile
        court, 562
    risk assessments and, 400, 540
    risk factors for
        delinquency, 113
    school environment, 268, 271,
        274, 282
    screening and assessment of,
        419–420
    sex offenders, 540

African Americans (*Cont.*)
  substance abuse among, 592
  transfers to adult
    court, 488–89
  violence and homicide
    composition by, 566
  women, 513
Aftercare for Indiana through
    Mentoring, 368–69
aftercare interventions. *See also*
    re-entry interventions
  case management approach
    to, 366–67
  individual approach to, 367–69
aftercare plans, 14
aftercare services. *See also* re-entry
    programs
  definition of, 364
  goal of, 364
  national estimates of, 364
after-school recreational
    programs, 14
age
  juvenile court jurisdiction
    limits and, 18–20,
    42–43, 44
  juvenile crime rates and, 25
age-crime curve, 567–68
age of jurisdiction laws, *19–20*,
    247, 494
aggravated assault
  as adult felony, 20
  arrest rates for, 66, *67*, 72
  crimes cleared, *67*, 68, *68*
  deterrence theory and, 81
  of homeless youth, 467
  male vs. female ratio of, 519
  social science theories and,
    80, 560
  victimization survey
    findings on, 30
  as violent crime, 23
aggression
  antisocial behavior and, 103
  cognitive impairments
    and, 133–34
  covert, 520
  drug abuse and, 104–5
  physical, 520, 556
  school-based interventions
    and, 303
  self-reported, 556

testosterone levels and, 563–64
  violence and, 556
Aggression Replacement
    Training, 427
aggression replacement training,
    328, 331
Agnew, Robert, 89, 97
AIDS. *See* HIV-AIDS
Aid to Families with Dependent
    Children, 513
Alaska, 209–10
alcohol abuse. *See also*
    substance abuse
  homeless youth and, 465
  petitioned cases involving, 50
  school-based interventions
    and, 300
  self-report surveys of,
    28, 30, 92
  by status offenders, 21
aliens, juvenile detention and, 43
AL offenders, 96
alternative dispute resolution
    programs, 14
alternative education
    programs, 21
Amber Alert system, 535
American Academy of Child and
    Adolescent Psychiatry, 129
American Bar Association, 129,
    495, 512
American Civil Liberties Union
    (ACLU), 253
American Correctional
    Association, 207–8
American Indians. *See* Native
    Americans
American Medical Association,
    125, 129
American Psychiatric
    Association, 129
American Psychological
    Association, 534
Amnesty International, 42–43
amygdala, 172
Anderson, Elijah, 93
anger control training, 328
Annie E. Casey Foundation, 135,
    619, 620
anti-gang programs
  classification of, 345–49, *348*
  community-based, 345

dispositional theories, 347
Gang Resistance Education and
    Training program, 345, 349
gang-suppression
    programs, 352–53
home nurse visits, 349–350
justice reinvestment
    innative, 351
for members, 352
neighborhood targeting, 344
parent education
    programs, 349
prevention programs,
    345, 352–53
situational crime theories, 347
that target community
    resources, 351
theory-driven, 347
antisocial behavior
  abnormal brain development
    and, 133
  aggression and, 103
  as early-onset delinquency
    predictor, 103–4
  gender effects on, 566
  juvenile delinquency and, 7
  school-based interventions
    and, 300, 303
  theft and, 103
  vandalism and, 103
anxiety, 303, 414, 416, 417,
    466, 518
APA. *See* American Psychological
    Association
Apprendi v. New Jersey (2000), 186
Arizona, 251, 255, 259, 515
Arizona Supreme Court, 156–57
arrests
  crime clearances and, 66
  definition of, 10
  disparity in rates of, 6
  of female offenders, 54
  national estimates of, *70*
  official statistics on, 22–26, 46
  rate of, 4, 68–70
  statistics, 62
arson
  arrest rates for, 23, *67*
  crimes cleared, *67*
  as designated felony, 20
ART. *See* aggression replacement
    training

Asian Americans
arrest rates of, 6
juvenile justice population of,
389, 488
poverty and, 614
risk and protective factors, 496
assault. *See* aggravated assault
assessments. *See* risk assessments;
screening and assessment
at-risk youth, 269, 277
attachment, 85, 105–6
attention-deficit/hyperactivity
disorder, 379. *See also*
conduct disorder
Attorney General, U.S., 257
attorneys. *See also* counsel
adjudicatory hearings
and, 11–12
as aggravating factor in
sentencing, 183–84
court-appointed, 183–84, 502
juvenile interrogations and, 179
presence in juvenile courts,
180–81, 182
right to counsel and, 43–44,
153, 156, 157
Austin, Texas, 471
automatic waiver, 246–47
auto theft, 8, 23, 30

balanced and restorative
justice, 622
Baltimore, Maryland, 251
Bayh, Birch, 40
Beccaria, Cesare, 81
behavioral genetics, 136–37
behavioral therapies. *See*
cognitive-behavioral therapy
behavior disorders. *See*
attention-deficit/
hyperactivity disorder;
conduct disorder; disruptive
behavior disorders
behavior interventions,
school-based, 280–82
belief, 85
Berrien County Juvenile
Center, 209
best friend delinquency, 107
bias
gender, 54
racial, 419, 496, 503, 589

against women (*See* female
offenders)
Big Brothers/Big Sisters, 162
biomarkers, 136, 139
biosocial theory, 95–97
bisexual youth. *See* LGBTQ youth
Bitsche, Ray, 197
BJS. *See* Bureau of Justice
Statistics, U.S.
blended sentencing, 255
Blueprints for Violence
Prevention, 298
Blueprints Model
programs, 425–26
boot camps, 41
Bosket, Willie, 127, 128
boys. *See* males
brain development. *See*
neuroscience; teenage brain
brain over-claim syndrome, 129
brain research. *See* neuroscience;
teenage brain
brain scans, 130, 136–37
Breed v. Jones (1975), 168
Bringing Youth Home, 618
British National Survey of Health
and Development, 561, 563
Brook, Carol, 196
Brown, Jordan, 242
bullying, 89, 273, 281, 302, 398,
563, 571
Bureau of Justice Statistics, U.S.,
30, 40, 69, 74, 252
burglary. *See also* robbery; theft
arrest rates for, 23, 67
crimes cleared, 67
drug use as factor in, 30
sentencing issues and, 250
Butts, J., 126

California, 224, 255, 274
California Corrections
Standards, 316
California Department of Juvenile
Justice, 364
Cambridge-Somerville Youth
Study, 560, 564
Cambridge Study of Delinquency
Development, 556–57
Campus Sex Crimes
Act, 535
cannabis. *See* marijuana use

capital punishment. *See* death
penalty
career development programs, 14
Carter administration, 40, 45
car theft, 23, 30, 67
case management aftercare
programs, 366–68
case management for
drug-involved offenders, 41
Catalano, David, 293
CBT. *See* cognitive-behavioral
therapy
CD. *See* conduct disorder
CDC. *See* Centers for Disease
Control and Prevention
celerity of punishment, 82, 84
Census Bureau, U.S., 30, 71
Center for Restorative Justice, 283
Center on Addiction and
Substance Abuse, 592
Centers for Disease Control and
Prevention, 254
CHAPTERS model to good
detention practice, 197
Chesterton, G.K., 210
Chicago, Il., 195, 205, 352
Chicago Area Project
program, 351
Chicago Youth Development
Study, 560
child abuse, 561
child prostitution, 469
children in need of services
(CINS), 9
children in need of supervision,
9, 467–68
Children's Bureau, U.S., 7, 23, 46
Child Savers movement, 509
child welfare
crossover youth and, 375–77,
593, 598, 612
gender and race issues, 591
juvenile status offenders
and, 21
legal issues with, 399
and mental health, 402–3
multidisciplinary teams
and, 422
multisystemic therapy and, 433
racial composition of, 593
referrals from, 15
child welfare agencies, 15, 21

child welfare systems, 402–3
CHINS. *See* children in need of supervision
chronic disruptive behavior, 295
chronic offenders. *See* SCV offenders
Civil Rights movement, 153
Coalition of Juvenile Justice, 622
cocaine, 30
Cochrane Collaboration, 296–97
cognitive-behavioral therapy, 126, 209, 426
cognitive development, 103–4, 131–32, 133–34
collaborative leadership, 616–17
collateral consequences, 186
collective bargaining agreements, 207
Colorado, 251, 258, 259, 590
Colorado Blueprints for Violence Prevention, 298
Columbine High School (Littleton, Colo.), 38, 154
Columbus Dispatch, 204–5
commitment, 85
common law, 20
community
　compositional perspective of, 346
　contextual perspective of, 346–47
　definition of, 343
　delinquency prevention programs, 42
　homeless youth and, 468
　influencing crime in, 344–45
　neighborhood programs and, 14
　street gangs and, 343–44
community agencies, 16
community-based care, 126
community-based interventions
　aggression replacement training, 328, 331
　characteristics of, 322–23
　clinical issues of, 324–25
　criminogenic need principle, 319–321
　effectiveness of, 323
　functional family therapy, 327–28
　for juvenile offenders, 314–15

legal issues with, 323–24
　model for, *321*
　multidimensional treatment foster care, 326–27
　multisystemic therapy, 221, 325–26, 571
　responsivity principle, 321
　restorative justice programs, 328–330
　risk-need-responsivity model, 317–322
　risk principle, 319
community-based programs
　crime prevention, 345–47
　detention vs., 195
　introduction of, 153
　justice reinvestment initiative, 351
　restorative justice and, 283
　sex offender registration, 186, 538
　substance abuse treatment, 216–17
community crime theories, 344–45
community disorder theory, 344
community empowerment theory, 344–45
community mental health programs, 16
community organization models, 38
Community Prevention Services, 254
Community Protection Act of 1990, 534–35
community re-entry services. *See* re-entry programs
community regeneration theory, 344–45
community reintegration, 582
community service
　restitution and, 15
　as sanction, 15, 17
comorbid conduct disorder, 433
competence. *See* adolescent competence
competency determination, 174
Comprehensive Crime Control Act of 1984, 39
concentrated poverty, 614
concurrent jurisdiction, 246

conditional dispositions, 12
conduct disorder, 416
confidentiality, 448
confinement. *See* juvenile detention
Connecticut, 80, 258
consent decrees, 199–200
constitutional law. *See* due process; Eighth Amendment; Supreme Court, U.S.
control. *See* anger control training; impulse control
control theory, 84–88, 97
co-occurring mental disorders, 225–27, 416, 424, 431
Cook County Juvenile Detention Alternatives Initiatives, 195
Cook County Juvenile Temporary Detention Center, 197, 205, 403
Copenhagen Perinatal Project, 556, 564
Coping Power Program, 299
correctional facilities. *See also* incarceration; juvenile correctional facilities
　for adults, 39, 40
　confinement of youth in, 242–43
　jail removal programs and, 40
　as psychiatric hospitals, 415
correctional liability, 198
Correctional Program Assessment Inventory, 323
Council for Boys and Young Men, 587
counsel. *See also* attorneys
　adjudicatory hearings and, 11–12
　as aggravating factor in sentencing, 183–84
　court-appointed, 183–84, 502
　presence in juvenile courts, 180–81, 182
　right to, 43–44
　waivers of, 181–82, 187
counseling. *See also* family counseling
　in groups, 21
　as informal case disposition condition, 10
　for status offenders, 21

court-appointed lawyers, 183–84, 502
court-appointed referees, 11
Court for Individualized Treatment of Adolescents, 224
court-ordered change in juvenile detention, 199
court orders, 199–200, 205
court order violations, 15
court referrals and dispositions. *See also* juvenile justice processing
  characteristics of, 162
  by juvenile courts, 16, 46–47, 51–52, 159
  for minor crimes, 161
  for minority juveniles, 158
  from parents, 15
  police discretion and, 158, 159, 162
  from probation departments, 15
  from schools, 15
  from victims, 15
  violent crimes and, 15
court system. *See* criminal courts; family courts; juvenile courts; juvenile justice processing; Supreme Court, U.S.; tribal courts
crack cocaine, 30, 64, 153
cradle-to-prison pipeline, 618
creative arts education, 14
crime. *See* criminal offenses; *specific crimes*
crime clearances, 66–68
Crime in the United States (annual report), 69
crime rates
  increase in, 62
  Merton's theory on, 90–91
criminal courts. *See also* adult criminal court; juvenile courts
  age of offender and case processing by, 18, 42–43
  delinquency case processing and, 10–11, 15–16, *16*, 17, *489*, 511
  juvenile case transfers to, 39

juveniles tried as adults in, 38–39, 44, 242
criminal diversion program, 161–62
Criminal Justice Legal Foundation, 134
criminal offenses, 44. *See also specific offenses*
criminogenic need principle, 319–321, *320*
Crisis Intervention Services Project (CRISP), 352
crossover youth, 375–77, 402–3
cross-systems partners, 432
"cruel and unusual punishment" clause, 43
crystal-meth, 30
cultural sensitivity training, 590
cumulative risk effect, 102
curfews, 9, 10, 15, 229, 353
custodial dispositions, 12
custodial interrogations, 175
Cuyahoga Hills (OH) Juvenile Correctional Facility, 207
CWD-A. *See* Adolescent Coping with Depression Course

Dallas Police Department, 162
Dalton (GA) Regional Youth Development Center, 203, 207
Dama, Rich, 209
DARE program. *See* Drug Abuse Resistance Education (DARE) program
"dark figure of crime," 28
dating violence prevention, 302–3
day treatment programs, 16, 17
DBT. *See* Dialectical Behavior Therapy
death penalty. *See also* Roper v. Simmons
  Eighth Amendment and, 43
  neuroscience and, 128, 250
decarceration of juvenile facilities, 126–27, 129
Decker, Tim, 208
decriminalization of status offenses, 38
deinstitutionalization of status offenders, 15, 21, 38, 39–40
Delaware, 231

delinquency. *See* juvenile delinquency
delinquency convictions, 186
delinquency hearings, 46
delinquency offenses
  case processing of, 492
  case processing summary rates for, *493*
  definition of, 32
delinquency petitions, 11–12
delinquency prevention programs. *See also* prevention programs
  Coping Power Program, 299
  federal funding of, 38, 42, 45–46
  risk and protective factors, 293–95, *294*
delinquency proceedings, 185
delinquent behavior
  formal reprimand, 161
  neighborhood effects and, 371–72
  parental attitudes and, 442
  sanctions for, 161–63
  warning and release, 161
delinquent child, definition of, 8
delusions, 30
Denver Youth Survey, 519, 558
departments, U.S. *See* key word, e.g. Justice Department
dependency cases, 32, 46
deportation hearings, 43
depression, 303, 414, 417, 431, 518
deprivation, 87, 91
designated felonies, 20
Desktop Guide to Good Juvenile Detention Practices, 197
detached worker program, 352
detention facilities. *See* juvenile detention
deterrence theory, 81–84, 97
developmental psychology
  false confessions, 177
  juvenile's ability to exercise rights, 175–76
  law and, 170–71
developmental taxonomy, 96–97
deviance, secondary, 21
deviant peer relationships, 107

Diagnostic Interview Schedule for Children, 415, 420
Dialectical Behavior Therapy, 427
differential association theory, 92
differential location in the social structure, 94
differential social location, 94
differential social organization, 94
digital divide, 473
diminished competence, 182
diminished responsibility, 170
direct file, 246
disability status, 104
DISC. *See* Diagnostic Interview Schedule for Children
discretion
    police, 157–58, 497
    prosecutorial, 8, 42
dismissed cases, 50
disorderly conduct, 229
disparity
    equal justice vs., 55
    racial and ethnic, 6, 53
disposition hearings, 12, 16–17
dispositions
    arrest and detention, 163
    collateral consequences, 186
    custodial, 12
    definition of, 12
    delinquency convictions, 186
    disparities in, 590–91
    gender stereotyping, 590–91
    informal, 10, 15
    juvenile case processing and, 12, 15–17, 248
    national estimates of, 51–52
    prior convictions and, 186
    probation as use of, 414
    racial disparity in, 53
    types of, 12
disproportionality, definition of, 488
disproportionate minority confinement
    biological factors to, 494
    challenges to, 197–98
    compliance with, 490
    data challenges, 497
    definition of, 488
    educational factors to, 495
    familial factors to, 494–95
    legal issues with, 489–491

mandate implementation, 500
measurement of, 491–92
political factors to, 495
psychological factors to, 494
racial factors to, 496
reduction of, 195, 490, *491*, 499, 501
relative rate index, 492
representation index, 491–92
social factors to, 495
spiritual factors to, 496
technical assistance manual, 490, 492
themes to address, 496–97
trends in addressing, 499–500
disruptive behavior disorders. *See* attention-deficit/hyperactivity disorder; conduct disorder
diversion programs. *See* juvenile diversion
DMC. *See* disproportionate minority confinement
DMC Technical Assistance Manual, 490, 492
domestic violence, 48. *See also* child abuse
double jeopardy clause, 168
Dow, David, 290
downward departure, 124
drinking. *See* alcohol abuse
drop-in centers for youth, 476
dropout rates, 17, 221, 272, 274, 292
drug abuse. *See also* alcohol abuse; substance abuse; *specific drugs and drug types*
    aggression and, 104–5
    of homeless youth, 467
    intervention and treatment programs for, 41
    petitioned cases involving, 50
    self-reports of, 30
    by status offenders, 21
    treatment facilities, 16
    types of drugs and, 30
Drug Abuse Resistance Education (DARE) program, 154
drug education, 10
drug-related crimes, 8
    deterrence theory and, 81
    increase in, 153

national estimates of, 47, 48
    self-reports of, 30
drug treatment facilities, 16
due process
    juvenile's right to, 155–57
    lack of, 153
    mental illness and, 227
    revolution of, 168
    right to counsel and, 43–44
Duncan v. Louisiana (1968), 184
Dunedin Birth Cohort Study, 556, 566
Dunlap, Earl, 196, 205
Durant, Gary, 124, 125, 130, 134

early childhood development, 135, 297
early chronic disruptive behavior, 295
early life stress, 134–35
early-onset Delinquency, 105–6
economic deprivation, 87, 105, 113
Ecstasy (drug), 30
Eddins, Neil, 209
education
    about drugs, 10
    creative arts, 14
Eighth Amendment, 43, 256
electronic monitoring, home-based, 16
Elmira Prenatal/Early Infancy Project, 570
emotional abuse, 21, 474
emotional and cognitive development, 103–4
emotional disability, 377
employment for homeless youth, 468–69
England. *See* Great Britain
Enhanced Mental Health Services Initiative, 423
environmental influences. *See* situational factors
equal justice, need for, 54–55
Estimate of Risk Adolescent Sexual Offense Recidivism (ERASOR), 398–99, 541–43
ethnic groups. *See* minority groups
ethnic heterogeneity, 87

evidence-based prevention
 programs. *See also*
 school-based interventions
adolescent coping with
 depression course, 426, 433
in classroom setting, 304
clinical issues of, 304–5
"combination" models, 424
confinement and, 200–201
for co-occuring disorders, 424
Coping Power Program, 299
in correctional settings, 426–27
cost-benefit analysis of, 297
description of, 297–99
dialectical behavior
 therapy, 427
evaluations, 323
functional family
 therapy, 327–28
Good Behavior Game, 299–300
in home-based settings,
 428–430
implementation issues, 304,
 424–25, 432
with juvenile offenders,
 317–322
Lazarus' multimodal
 theory, 433
LifeSkills Training, 300–301
Mendota Juvenile Treatment
 Center Program, 426–27
motivational enhancement
 therapy, 427
multidimensional treatment
 foster care, 326–27, 427–28
multimodal therapy, 433
multisystemic therapy, 221,
 325–26, 429–430
in outpatient settings, 428
PAX Game, 299–300
Positive Action, 301–2
Project ALERT, 298, 306
in residential settings, 427–28
resources to identify, *298*
in school environment, 295–97
Seattle Social Development
 Project, 114–15
sequenced approach to, 424
social context of, 200–201
theoretical eclecticism, 433–34
trauma focused cognitive
 behavioral therapy, 428

executions. *See* death penalty
ex parte Crouse, 509
expulsions, 268–69, 270, 277

Faith and Service Technical
 Education Network
 (FASTEN), 369
false confessions, 177
false identification, 28
families. *See also* family-focused
 interventions
breakdown in, 153
in colonial times, 151
communication within, 443
delinquency factors and, 29
dysfunction of, 152
home nurse visits to, 349–350
number of children in, 106
single-parent, 29, 106
as source of negative
 behavior, 152
of status offenders, 21
stepparent, 106
structure of, 106
substance abuse treatment
 and, 217
support from, 89, 221–22
training programs for, 570
violence in (*See* child abuse;
 domestic violence)
Family and Youth Services
 Bureau, 476
family counseling
juvenile aftercare plans and, 14
status offender treatment and, 21
family courts, 509
family-focused interventions. *See
 also* family therapy
case examples, 449–455
collaboration models and, 316
confidentiality and, 448
evidence-based practice, 126
functional family therapy,
 327–28, 370–71, 428–29,
 445–46, 449–452
in home-based settings,
 428–430
for homeless youth, 477
legal issues with, 447–49
multidimensional treatment
 foster care, 326–27, 427–28,
 446–47, 453–55

multisystemic therapy,
 221, 325–26, 370–71,
 443–44, 571
recidivism reduction with, 455
re-entry programs, 370–71
Family Group Conferencing, 329
family inclusion practices,
 589–590
family integrated transitions,
 370, 424
family services, 14–15
family structure. *See* families;
 single-parent households
family therapy. *See* functional
 family therapy
Fare v. Michael C. (1979),
 175, 179
Farrington, David, 555
Fast Track Prevention Project, 115
FBI. *See* Federal Bureau of
 Investigation
FBI Uniform Crime
 Reports, 22, 30
fearlessness theory, 563
Federal Bureau of Investigation,
 22–23, 30, 66, 67, 74
federal government
 juvenile detention
  regulations, 10
 juvenile policy shifts by, 38
 presidential commission
  recommendations and, 38
 prevention program funding
  by, 38, 42, 45–46
feeder schools, 277–78
female offenders. *See also* females
 arrest rates for, 54
 characteristics of, 515–16
 criminal biographies
  of, 585–86
 delinquency case processing
  and, 585
 detention in, 512–13
 discrimination against, 512
 expectations of, 514
 juvenile justice system and,
  511–12, 584–86
 mental health needs of, 592
 race and ethnic impact, 513–15
 recidivism rates, 512
 as victims of sexual abuse, 48,
  54, 402, 516

females. *See also* gender; mothers
as abuse victims, 48, 54, 111
aggressive behavior and,
518–523
arrest rates for, 441–42
court adjudications, 591
as crime victims, 54
decreased adjudication
rate of, 50
delinquency case processing
and, 511
detention estimates for, 48–49
discrimination against, 512
diversion program referrals
for, 162
entering juvenile justice
system, 389–390, 508
as gang members, 341
homeless, 466, 473–74
immorality and, 509
immoral sexual expression
in, 583
incarceration rate of, 372, 510
juvenile justice system history
of, 508–10, 584–86
as juvenile offenders (*See*
female offenders)
juvenile offending and, 48,
54, 372
lesbian and bisexual, 475
life experiences,
negative, 517–18
multidimensional treatment
foster care, 446–47
pathways perspective, 517–18
petitioned case decrease
for, 49
placement case decrease for, 52
re-entry needs of, 372–74
referral rates to juvenile
court, 562
risk assessments and,
401–2, 405–6
risk factors for
delinquency, 111–13
school suspension rates of, 276
sentencing practice of, 510
services for, 586
traumatic experiences,
112–13, 586
as violent offenders, 48, 442,
518–523, 562

waived case rate changes
for, 52
femininities, role of, 583
feminist criminology, 516–18
FFT. *See* functional family therapy
Fifth Amendment, 43, 157,
168, 172
fighting. *See* aggression
financial hardships, 105
fines, payment of, 15, 16
firearms. *See* guns
fire-setters. *See* arson
first-generation (1G) risk
assessments, 393
First Offender Program (Dallas,
Texas), 162
Fish, Albert, 533
FIT. *See* family integrated
transitions
Florida, 54, 134
Flynn, John, 157
Formula Grants program, 492
for-profit companies, 41
foster care, 16, 326–27,
427–28, 446–47
Fourteenth Amendment, 179
Fourth Amendment, 256
fourth-generation (4G) risk
assessments, 394, 404
Freiburg Cohort Study, 568
functional family therapy,
327–28, 370–71, 428–29,
445–46, 449–452
funding
for cultural training, 590
of delinquency prevention
programs, 38, 42, 45–46
disproportionate minority
confinement, 492
Formula Grants program, 492
fragmentation of federal, 623
gender bias programs, 54
homeless youth priorities
with, 473
for juvenile drug courts, 217
for juvenile justice
infrastructure, 610
juvenile sex offenders and,
532, 535, 536, 547
policy issues of, 45–46
for re-entry and aftercare
services, 380

GAIN-I, 421, 422, 432
GAIN-SS, 418–420, 422, 432
Gallegos v. Colorado (1962),
174, 179
"gambler's fallacy," 83
gang activity. *See* street gangs
gang prevention programs. *See*
anti-gang programs
Gang Resistance Education and
Training program, 345, 349
gangs. *See* street gangs
gang-suppression programs,
352–53. *See also* anti-gang
programs
gay youth. *See* LGBTQ youth
gender. *See also* females; males
adjudication rate decrease
and, 50
attitudes toward police in, 155
changed waived case rates
and, 52
detention estimates and, 48–49
disparities in juvenile justice
system, 391–92
diversion program referrals
for, 162
juvenile delinquency referrals
and, 48
in juvenile justice
system, 583–87
petitioned case decrease
and, 49
placement case decrease
for, 52
police discretion and, 158
racial differences in violent
behavior by, 566
re-entry needs for, 373
referral rates to juvenile
court, 562
risk assessments by, 400
socialization, 586
gender gap, 512–13, 562
gender identity, 478
gender socialization, 586
General Accounting
Office, 180–81
"general" deterrence, 82. *See also*
deterrence theory
general responsivity, 321
general strain theory
(GST), 89–90

General Theory of Crime, A
(Gottfredson), 85
genetics, behavioral, 136–37
Georgia Department of Juvenile
Justice, 203
"get tough" policy, 153, 159, 169
girls. *See* female offenders;
females
Glaser, D., 135
Goldstein, Arnold, 328
Good Behavior Game, 299–300
Gottfredson, M., 85
Graham v. Florida (2010), 127,
134, 170, 250, 256, 610
Great American Crime
Decline, 65
Great Britain
common law in, 20
social disorganization
theory in, 87
Great Depression, 152
GREAT program. *See* Gang
Resistance Education and
Training program
Greene County (OH), 232
Grisso, Thomas, 175–76
group counseling, 21
group homes, 16, 511
group treatment, *321*
Gun-Free Schools Act of
1994, 273
guns
availability of, 64–65
buyback programs, 350
exposure to violence with, 108
street gangs and, 340

Haley v. Ohio (1948), 174, 179
hallucinations, 30
handguns. *See* guns
Hare Psychopathy
Checklist: Youth
Version, 398
Hawkins, Richard, 293
Haywood Burns Institute, 620
Head Start, 135
hearings. *See* disposition hearings
Heywood Banks Institute, 197
High/Scope Perry Preschool
Project, 570
Hindelang Criminal Justice
Research Center, 30

Hirschi, Travis, 85
Hispanics. *See* Latinos
HIV-AIDS, 222, 468–69,
472, 479
Holder, Eric, 536
home-based electronic
monitoring, 16
home-based interventions, 370,
428–430, 443–44. *See also*
family-focused interventions
Homeboy Industries, 352
home environment. *See* families;
situational factors
homeless shelters for youth, 365
homeless youth. *See also*
runaways
accessing technology, 472–74
arrest rates for, 467
case management services
for, 477
child prostitution and, 469
drop-in centers for, 476
employment for, 468
estimates of, 464
intervention programs
for, 476–78
justice interventions for, 476–78
law enforcement and, 467
LGBTQ, 474–75, 478
mental health challenges, 466
origins of, 465–66
peer networks for, 469–470
as public health issue, 464
recidivism and, 124
runaway shelters, 475–76
services for, 475–76
sexual health
interventions, 477–78
sex work for, 468–69
social network technology
and, 473–74
social support and, 469
status offenses for, 467–68
street survival behavior, 472
substance abuse and,
465–66, 477
transient nature of, 470–72
transitional living
programs, 476
as victims, 468–69
vocational training
programs, 477

homicide. *See* juvenile homicide
homosexuality, 534. *See also*
LGBTQ youth
horizontal violence, 520–21
hospitalization, psychiatric, 40
Houses of Refuge, 509
houses of refuge, 151–52
Houston, Texas, 65
Hughes, Bobby, 203
Hull House movement, 152
Human Rights Watch, 253

IAP. *See* Intensive Aftercare
Program
IDEA. *See* Individuals with
Disabilities Education Act
of 1997
Illinois, 231, 258, 259, 415
immorality, 509
impulse control, 172
incarceration. *See also* correctional
facilities; juvenile
correctional facilities;
juvenile detention
aftercare services, transition
to, 367–68
confinement issues, 252–54
crime rates and, 64
criminogenic nature of, 127
increase in, 153
of juveniles in adult
facilities, 40
minority group rates of, 6
national estimates of, 269
risk factors for youth, 252–53
school referrals, 269–270
of young women, 510
incorrigibility, 9
individual adolescent
development, 103–5
individualized education plan
(IEP), 281–82
Individuals with Disabilities
Education Act of 1997, 377
informal control, 88
informal probation, 10–11, 15
inhalants, 30, 300
Initial Security Classification
Assessment, 424
injuries, to crime victims
"in need of supervision," 9, 32
In re Christopher H. (2004), 182

In re Gault (1967), 43, 152–53,
156, 168, 172, 179, 388
In re Javier A. (1984), 44
In re Winship (1970), 43, 168
institutional anomie theory
(IAT), 90–91
institutionalized treatment, 16
intake officers, 10, 15
intelligence testing, 136
Intensive Aftercare
Program, 367–68
intentional bias, 496
Interagency Working Group on
Youth Programs, 623
Internet technology, 472–74
interrogations, police, 174–79
intervention programs
academic support, 281–82
anti-gang (*See* anti-gang
programs)
behavior, 280–82
to block gang activity, 354
case management services for
youth, 477
cognitive-behavioral, 209
collaboration models,
316–17
community-based (*See*
community-based
interventions)
confinement and, 200–201
cost-effective, 329
court-ordered, 205
for crossover youth, 375
evidence-based prevention
programs, 114–15
family-focused (*See*
family-focused
interventions)
general responsivity, 321
home-based, 370
for homeless youth, 476–78
for LGBTQ youth, 478
protective factors for
Delinquency (*See* protective
factors for Delinquency)
risk factors for delinquency
(*See* risk factors for
delinquency)
risk-need-responsivity model
(*See* Risk-Need-
Responsivity model)

school-based (*See* school-based
interventions)
school environment, 114
for SCV offenders, 568–571
sexual health, 477–78
social science theories, 201
specific responsivity, 321
that improve community
resources, 353
involvement, 85
Iowa, 590
isolation, 252–53

Jackson v. Hobbs (2012), 170
Jacob Wetterling Crimes Against
Children and Sexually
Violent Offender Registration
Act of 1994, 535
jails. *See* juvenile detention
Jajoura, Roger, 368–69
James D. and Catherine
T. MacArthur Foundation,
169, 170, 249, 425–26, 500,
619–620
JDAI. *See* Juvenile Detention
Alternatives Initiative
J.D.B. v. North Carolina (2011),
175, 179, 256
Jessica Lunsford Act of 2005
(Florida), 535
JINS (juveniles in need of
supervision), 9
JJDPA. *See* Juvenile Justice and
Delinquency Prevention Act
of 1974
JLWOP. *See* life-without-parole
John D. and Catherine
T. MacArthur Foundation,
169, 170
Johnson Youth Center Treatment
Unit, 209–10
JRAS. *See* Juvenile Risk
Assessment Scale
JSO. *See* juvenile sex offenders
J-SOAP-II. *See* Juvenile Sex
Offender Assessment
Protocol-II
J-SORRAT-II. *See* Juvenile Sex
Offense Recidivism Risk
Assessment Tool-II
judges, juvenile court
adjudicatory hearings and, 11

client interactions with, 223
counsel advisory and, 181–82
counsel presence as aggravating
factor, 183–84
criminal justice policies of, 81
dispositional hearings and,
11, 181
fact finding by, 185–86
judicial waivers and, 246
juvenile dispositions, 248
life-without-parole
sentencing, 250–51
racketeering and, 612
sanctioning by, 12–14,
16–17, 217
transfer or waiver hearings and,
15–16, *244–45*
judicial waiver, 246
jury trials, 43, 185–86, 187
"just desserts" philosophy, 42–43
justice. *See* balanced and
restorative justice; restorative
justice
Justice Department, U.S.
arrest rates, 69
racial disparities in justice
system, 249
settlement agreements, 202–3
treatment of youth
lawsuits, 490–91
Justice Policy Institute, 620
justice reinvestment innative, 351
juvenile, definition of,
63, 150–51
juvenile aftercare plans, 14
juvenile apprentices, 151
juvenile correctional facilities
costs per day for, 572
decarceration, 126
delinquency case processing
and, 13–14
evidence-based prevention
programs for, 426–27
gender socialization, 586
juvenile aftercare plans
and, 14
life imprisonment in, 127
masculine identities and
expressions in, 586–87
medication management
in, 430–32
private, 40, 41

status offender
deinstitutionalization and,
15, 21, 39–40
juvenile court counselors, 502
juvenile courts. *See also* juvenile
drug courts; juvenile justice
processing; juvenile mental
health courts; teen courts
attorney presence in, 180–81
counsel presence as aggravating
factor, 183–84
counsel waivers and, 181–82
delinquency case processing
and, 10–11, 511
detention intake and (*See*
juvenile detention)
establishment of, 152,
388, 509
forensics and, 324–25
guilty plea in, 182
informality of, 185–86
jury trials and, 185–86
justice by geography, 182–83
maximum/minimum
age for jurisdiction of,
18–20, 43, 44
number of cases handled by, *18*
probation development and
(*See* probation)
procedural safeguards in, 174
referrals and dispositions by,
16, 46, 51–52, 159
referral to, 162, 272–74,
315, 414
reform for, 611
rehabilitative approach
with, 168
school referrals to,
272–74, 275
status offenses and, 510
transfers to adult court (*See*
adult criminal court)
waived cases (*See* adult
criminal court)
Juvenile Court Statistics (report
series), 46
juvenile death penalty. *See* death
penalty
juvenile delinquency. *See also*
juvenile justice system;
juvenile offenders; SCV
offenders

arrest rates for, 4, 6, 46, 414,
492, 588
biological variables in, 95–96
Chicago Area Project
program, 351
during childhood, 555–56
confinement conditions,
200–202
consequences of, 291–92
as coping strategy, 90
courts and (*See* juvenile courts)
crime incidence decline and, 4
definition of, 7–8, 32
distrust of police, 154
early-onset, 105–6
evidence-based programs
for (*See* evidence-based
prevention programs)
family dysfunction and, 152
family situation and, 29,
89, 442
female offenders and, 48, 54
feminist criminology
and, 516–18
fiscal amount related to, 291
gang related (*See* street gangs)
learning disabilities, 104
major policy shifts for, 38–39
official and unofficial statistics
on, 22–27, 46–47
pathways perspective
to, 517–18
peer, 92–93
pleasure in, 104, 172
police force, attitude
toward, 155
police interrogations
and, 174–79
poverty and (*See* poverty)
protective factors for (*See*
protective factors for
Delinquency)
punishment vs., 82–83
punitive policies toward,
38–39, 42–43
rate decline in, 306
repeat violent offenders and, 21
risk factors for (*See* risk factors
for Delinquency)
self-protection and, 108
self-report studies of,
22, 27–29

situational factors (*See*
situational factors)
social science theories (*See*
social science theories)
social stimuli, 95
social support and, 89–90
types of, 8
variance in, 95
variations in, 80
juvenile delinquency offenses
age as determining factor in, 18
case processing of, 9–14
definition of, 5, 32
status offenses vs., 32
juvenile detention. *See also*
juvenile correctional facilities
in adult facilities, 242–43
collective bargaining
agreements and, 207
confinement conditions,
199–200, 252–54
correctional liability, 198
court-ordered change in, 199
court-ordered interventions
and, 205
crowding concerns for, 194
developmental strategies
for, 210–11
disproportionate minority
confinement, 195, 197–98
evidence-based prevention
programs for, 426–27
external change processes, 199
female offenders and, 54
gender gaps in, 512–13
hearings and, 11
internal change processes, 199
juvenile removal programs, 40
LLC approach to
confinement, 201–5
mental health and, 417
national estimates of, 49, 194
opponents of, 196
performance-based
standards, 206–7
personnel training for, 253
practitioner resources for, 197
pre-adjudication, 10–11
quality assurance, 206–7
racial disparities in, 53
rates, 588
rates for, 194–95

juvenile detention (*Cont.*)
  rational behavior training, 209
  reform, 195–97, 612
  secure custody and, 194
  sex offenders and, 547
  sexual assault in, 252
  sexual misconduct of
    personnel, 204–5
  social science theory and
    research perspective on, 201,
    202, 205–6
  standards for, 196–97,
    199–200
  suicide risk in, 252
Juvenile Detention Alternatives
  Initiative, 135, 513, 619
Juvenile Detention Alternatives
  Initiative Self-Assessment
  Standards, 208
juvenile diversion
  as policy innovation, 39–40
  referrals to, 161–62
juvenile drug courts
  components of, 217–18
  contingency management, 221
  definition of, 216
  description of, 216–220
  dropout rates, 221
  effectiveness of, 220–21, 235
  family support for, 221–22
  history of, 217
  implementation
    failures, 222–23
  judge-client interactions, 223
  logic model of, *219*, 220
  multidisciplinary teams
    and, 423
  multisystemic therapy, 221
  participant outcomes, 223
  phase structure of, 216–17,
    219–220, *219*
  program attrition, 221
  recidivism and, 423
  sexual behaviors of youth, 222
  strategies for, 217, *218*
  treatment programs, 222–23
juvenile executions. *See* death
  penalty
juvenile homicide
  arrest rates for, 23, 66, *67*, 72
  crimes cleared, 67–68, *67*, *68*
  as designated felony, 20

increase in, 153
juvenile victims of, 23
male vs. female ratio of, 519
rate decline in, 62, 63–65
sanctions for, 82
in school settings, 38
social science theories
  and, 80, 82
street gangs and, 340
juvenile institutionalization. *See*
  institutionalized treatment
juvenile intake units, 10–11, 15
juvenile justice agencies, 9. *See*
  also specific agencies
Juvenile Justice and Delinquency
  Prevention Act of 1974, 15,
  38–40, 42, 54, 153, 249,
  488, 609. *See also* Office
  of Juvenile Justice and
  Delinquency Prevention
juvenile justice policy. *See*
  juvenile justice system
juvenile justice processing.
  See also juvenile courts;
  juvenile detention; juvenile
  justice system
  court referrals and dispositions
    in, 46–47, 51–52
  death penalty and, 43
  female offenders and,
    513–15, *584*
  geographic disparities
    in, 182–83
  mental health in, scope of, 417
  mental health
    practitioners, 324–25
  Miranda rights and, 155–57
  petitioned vs. nonpetitioned
    cases (2001-2009), 49–50
  police interrogations
    and, 174–79
  race and ethnic impact, 513–15
  sanctions during, 161–63
  screening and assessment,
    418–422
  state policies, 258–59
  transfers to adult court,
    258–59, 488–89, 612 (*See*
    also adult criminal court)
  waived cases (*See* adult
    criminal court)
  of young women, 511

juvenile justice reform
  balanced and restorative
    justice, 622
  collaborative
    leadership, 616–17
  comprehensive change
    initiatives, 622
  definition of, 608–9
  federal commitment to, 623
  history of, 127–130
  innovation and research for, 620
  philanthropy and, 619–620
  political will for, 617–18
  priorities for, *621*
  public-private partnerships,
    619–620, 622–23
  realignment, 611
  reinvestment, 611
  resolution, 611
  scope of, 608–13
  social movement
    toward, 618–19
  state-level analysis, 611
  systems change, 615–16
juvenile justice system
  accountability of, 613–15
  adjudication decisions and, 50
  change in, 615–16
  child welfare and, 375–77
  collaboration models
    and, 316–17
  community reintegration
    and, 582
  cultural sensitivity
    training, 590
  definition of, 6–7
  demographics, 389–390, 582
  disabled youth and, 377–79
  disparities in, 6,
    52–54, 391–92
  diversion and
    deinstitutionalization
    programs and, 39–40
  dual system youth, 375–77
  due process and, 43–44
  effective treatment for
    offenders, 314–15
  equal justice as goal of, 54–55
  family inclusion practices
    within, 589–590
  female history in,
    508–10, 584–86

female offenders and, 54,
372, 508
flowchart, *13*
funding for, 45–46
gender, role of, 54,
517, 583–87
gender-specific services in, 373
geographic disparities
in, 182–83
goals of, 582
history of, 151–53, 508–11
interpretations of, 609–10
jail removal programs and, 40
"just desserts" philosophy
and, 42–43
Latina girls growing visibility
in, 514
LGBTQ youth and, 475
major shifts in, 38–39
mental health disorders
and, 365
mental health system
collaboration with, *318*
mission, 608
new approaches to, 41 (*See also*
juvenile justice reform)
offense statistics and, 46–47
personnel training for, 590
police discretion and, 157–58
policies toward, 38–39,
589–590
policy reforms, 582
prevention program funding
and, 42
primary care of youth, 317
priority setting for, 609
privatization of, 612–13
procedural safeguards in, 169
racial bias, 419, 496, 503, 589
racial disparities in (*See* racial
disparities)
racialized patterns of, 514
recent trends in, 47–48
recommendations for, 54–55
schools and, link between,
269–270, 274
sexual behaviors of youth
in, 222
state policies, 258–59
structure of, 609
substance abuse disorders
and, 365

tribal courts, 609
unconstitutional treatment of
youth, 490–91
juvenile life without parole. *See*
life-without-parole
juvenile mental health courts
co-occurring disorders, 225–27
description of, 224–25
diversion program
referrals, 423
effectiveness of, 225, 235
legal issues with, 227
multidisciplinary teams
and, 423
screening and assessment,
226–27, *226*
juvenile murderers. *See* juvenile
homicide
Juvenile Offender law
(New York), 128
juvenile offenders. *See also*
juvenile delinquency;
juvenile sex offenders; SCV
offenders; status offenses
classification of, 554
deinstitutionalization of, 17,
21, 39–40
effective treatment for, 314–15,
317–322, 429–430
female (*See* female offenders)
handling of, 21–22
police discretion with, 157–58
referral rates to juvenile
court, 562
rehabilitative approach with,
161, 390
sexual misconduct of, 510
teen court referrals, 229
violent (*See* SCV offenders)
juvenile-police interactions
dispositions, 160–63
with gangs, 154
one-on-one, 159
police discretion and, 157–59
preventive approaches
and, 164
in school environment, 153–54
variations in, 159
juvenile probation. *See* probation
Juvenile Risk Assessment Scale
(JRAS), 543
juveniles. *See* youth

Juvenile Sex Offender Assessment
Protocol-II, 399, 539–541
juvenile sex offenders (JSO)
Amber Alert system, 535
definition of, 532
Estimate of Risk Adolescent
Sexual Offense Recidivism
(ERASOR), 398–99, 541–43
false negatives, 545
funding for research, 532, 535,
536, 547
history of, 533–37
legislation regarding, 534–37
Megan's Law, 535, 543
as mental illness, 533
Multiplex Empirically
Guided Inventory of
Ecological Aggregates
for Assessing Sexually
Abusive Adolescents and
Children, 544
policies, 532–33, 547–48
public registry for, 535–36
recidivism rate for, 545
risk assessment for, 399,
532, 537–38
risk assessments tools for,
538–547
risk factors for, 532–33
sex offender registration,
186, 538
Juvenile Sex Offense Recidivism
Risk Assessment Tool-II
(J-SORRAT-II), 399, 541
Juveniles Taken into Custody
(OJJDP 1991 report), 40
juvenile status offenders. *See*
juvenile offenders; status
offenses
juvenile superpredators, 242
juvenile training schools, 21, 511

Keller, Thomas, 369
Kelly, Ralph, 202–3
Kentucky, 231
Kent v. U.S. (1966), 43,
152–53, 246
kidnapping, 20
King, Jane, 209

Lanza, Adam, 80
larceny, 8, 23, 30, *67*

Latino Hills Project, 352
Latinos
    attitudes toward police in, 155
    classification of, 497–99
    disabled, 378–79
    disposition disparities
        for, 590–91
    female, 513, 514
    gang members, 341
    incarceration rate differences
        and, 248
    juvenile justice population
        of, 389
    poverty and, 614
    psychotropic medication use
        on, 430–31
    risk and protective factors, 496
    risk assessments and, 401, 540
    school environment, 282
    school suspension rates for,
        268, 274
    sex offenders, 540
    substance abuse among, 592
    violence and homicide
        composition by, 566
"law and order" philosophy, 38
law enforcement agencies
    crime reporting by, 22, 23
    cultural sensitivity
        training, 590
    gang-related homicides
        and, 340
    gate-keeper function of, 150
    homeless youth and, 467
    juvenile justice processing and,
        10, 15, 150
    personnel training for, 590
Law Enforcement Assistance Act
    of 1965, 45. See also Office
    of Juvenile Justice and
    Delinquency Prevention
law violation, 92
lawyers. See attorneys;
    prosecutors
Lazarus, Arnold, 433
LCP offenders, 96
leadership, collaborative, 616–17
lead poisoning, 124, 135
learning disabilities, 104, 377
learning theory, 91–95, 97
legal competence, 173. See also
    adolescent competence

legal rights, 43–44
legislative exclusion. See statutory
    exclusion
legislative waiver, 246–47
lesbian youth. See LGBTQ youth
Lessons from Death Row Inmates
    (Dow), 290
Level of Service/Case
    Management Inventory, 394
Level of Service
    Inventory-Revised, 394
LGBTQ youth, 474–75, 478
life-course persistent offenders,
    96, 133, 134
life experiences, negative, 105
LifeSkills Training, 300–301
life-without-parole, 134, 170,
    242, 250–51, 256
limbic system, 172
LLCL approach to confinement,
    201–5, 207–8
local education agencies
    (LEAs), 378
Loeber, Rolf, 555
Lombroso, C., 86
loneliness, 107
Los Angeles, Calif., 352
Los Angeles school system, 154
LS/CMI. See Level of Service/Case
    Management Inventory
LSI-R. See Level of Service
    Inventory-Revised
Luzerne County, Penn., 196

MacArthur Foundation. See
    James D. and Catherine
    T. MacArthur Foundation
macro-level social science
    theories, 80
magnetic resonance imaging
    (MRIs), 139
males. See also gender
    adjudication rate decrease
        for, 50
    detention estimates for, 48–49
    diversion program referrals
        for, 162
    entering juvenile justice
        system, 389–390
    homosexual, 534
    identities and expressions
        of, 586–87

as juvenile apprentices, 151
and juvenile crime, 586–87
juvenile delinquency
    referrals of, 48
juvenile drug courts and, 221
petitioned case decrease of, 49
placement case decrease for, 52
police discretion and, 158
risk factors for
    delinquency, 112–13
school suspension rates of, 276
self-reports of delinquency, 28
waived case decrease in, 52–53
maltreatment, 106, 561
mandatory sentencing laws, 242,
    250, 259
marginalized youth, 274
marijuana use
    homeless youth and, 465
    peer involvement in, 92
    school-based interventions
        and, 300
    self-reports on, 28, 30, 92
Martinek, Terry, 209
Martinez, Orlando, 203
Maryland, 232
masculine identity, 586–87
Massachusetts, 258
Massachusetts Youth Screening
    Instrument, 405, 415,
    419–420, 422
maturity gap, 96
MAYSI-2. See Massachusetts
    Youth Screening Instrument
McKeiver v. Pennsylvania (1970),
    43, 152–53, 168, 184–85
mediation, 41
MEGA. See Multiplex Empirically
    Guided Inventory of
    Ecological Aggregates for
    Assessing Sexually Abusive
    Adolescents and Children
Megan's Law, 535, 543
men. See males
Mendota Juvenile Treatment
    Center Program, 426–27
mental health disorders
    anxiety, 303, 414, 416, 417
    depression, 303, 414, 417
    diagnostic patterns of, 416
    girls and, 402
    homosexuality and, 534

in juvenile justice
processing, 417
juvenile justice system
and, 365
prevalence rates for,
415–18, 433
probation disposition and, 414
psychiatric, 416
recidivism, 404
risk assessments, 402, 403
screening for (*See* screening
and assessment)
mental health system
collaboration with juvenile
justice system, *318*
community programs and, 16
personnel, 317
treatment responsibility of, 317
mental illness. *See also* juvenile
mental health courts; mental
health system
challenges, 466
co-occurring disorders,
225–27, 416
court proceedings and, 249
diagnosis of, 224
disorders (*See* mental health
disorders)
evidence-based prevention
programs for, 426–430
females and, 592
homeless youth and, 466
homosexuality and, 534
juvenile justice population
with, 592
juvenile sex offenders, 533
prevalence rates for, 466
psychiatric hospitalization
and, 40
remediation of, 322
risk assessments, 403–4
screening and assessment for,
226–27, *226*, 405, 415,
418–422
mental retardation, 377
mentoring, 14, 111, 368–69, 612
Merton, Robert, 90
MET. *See* Motivational
Enhancement Therapy
metal detectors, 160
methamphetamine, 30, 301
Miami, Florida, 65

micro-level social science
theories, 80
Mid-Atlantic Juvenile Defender
Center, 495
middle-class status, 88–89, 139
Miller v. Alabama (2012), 170,
250, 256, 610
Minnesota, 183
minority groups. *See also* African
Americans; Hispanics; Native
Americans; racial groups
arrest rates for, 6, 198
classification of, 497–99
crime rates and, 65
elementary-age interventions
and, 301
equal justice for, 55
incarceration rate differences
and, 6, 248–49
juvenile justice population of,
389, 488
juvenile justice system
disparities for, 52–53
police encounters with, 158
school discipline and, 160
school environment, 272, 274
minority overrepresentation. *See*
disproportionate minority
confinement
MINS (minors in need of
supervision), 9
Miranda, Ernesto, 156
Miranda rights, 156, 169, 175,
177, 179, 187, 256
Miranda v. Arizona (1966), 156, 175
Mississippi, 8, 258
Missouri, 208–9
Missouri Approach, 208–9
MJTCP. *See* Mendota Juvenile
Treatment Center Program
mobility, residential, 87
Model Risk Assessment tool, 393
Models for Change initiative,
619–620
"Models for Change: System
Reform in Juvenile Justice"
report, 425–26, 500
Moffit's theory on delinquent
behavior, 133
Moffitt, T., 133–34
Moffitt's developmental
taxonomy, 96–97

monetary restitution, 15
Montana, 8
Montreal
Longitudinal-Experimental
Study, 563
Moore, Alvin, 156
moral behaviors, 131–32
moral depravity, 136
moral reasoning, 328
mothers. *See also* single-parent
households
delivery complications, 564
depressed, 565
smoking and/or drinking, 570
motivation, universal, 81–82
Motivational Enhancement
Therapy, 427
MST. *See* multisystemic therapy
MTFC. *See* multidimensional
treatment foster care
multidimensional treatment
foster care, 326–27, 427–28,
446–47, 453–55
multimodal therapy, 433
Multiplex Empirically Guided
Inventory of Ecological
Aggregates for Assessing
Sexually Abusive
Adolescents and Children
(MEGA), 544
"multi-systemic" therapies, 126
multisystemic therapy, 221,
325–26, 370–71, 429–430,
443–44, 571
Muncie, John, 132
murder. *See* juvenile homicide
Murray, Albert, 203

National Academy of
Sciences, Juvenile Justice
Committee, 131
National Association of School
Resource Officers,
159–160
National Association of Youth
Courts, 228
National Bar Association, 512
National Center for Juvenile
Justice, 4, 22, 46, 588
National Center for Mental Health
and Juvenile Justice, 403,
404, 415–16

National Coalition for the
Homeless, 477
National Coalition of State
Juvenile Justice Advisory
Groups, 40, 389
National Collaborative Perinatal
Project, 565
National Comprehensive Gang
Model, 154
National Conference of State
Legislators, 611
National Council of Juvenile and
Family Court Judges, 206
National Council on Crime and
Delinquency, 197,
488–89
National Council on
Disabilities, 377–78
National Crime Victimization
Survey, 22, 30–31
National Household Survey on
Drug Abuse, 29–30
National Incident-Based
Reporting System (FBI), 22
National Institute of
Corrections, 198
National Institute of Juvenile
Justice and Delinquency
Prevention, 29
National Institute of Mental
Health, 29, 139
National Juvenile Justice
Network, 129, 610, 618
National Partnership for Juvenile
Services, 196
National Registry of
Evidence-Based Practices
and Programs, 297–98
National Survey of Children's
Exposure to Violence, 108
National Survey of Drug Use and
Health, 216
National Youth Court
Guidelines, 230
National Youth Gang Center, 340
National Youth Gang Survey, 341
National Youth Survey, 22,
29, 519
Native Americans
arrest rates of, 6
disposition disparities
for, 590–91

incarceration rate differences
and, 248–49
juvenile justice population of,
389, 488
poverty and, 614
risk and protective factors, 496
risk assessments and, 401
substance abuse among, 592
tribal courts, 609
natural disasters, 105
NAYS. See National Youth Survey
NCCD. See National Council on
Crime and Delinquency
NCJFCJ. See National Council
of Juvenile and Family
Court Judges
NCJJ. See National Center for
Juvenile Justice
NCLB. See No Child Left Behind
Act of 2002
NCMHJJ. See National Center for
Mental Health and Juvenile
Justice
NCVS. See National Crime
Victimization Survey
negative emotions. See specific
emotions
neglect, 134
neighborhood crime prevention
programs, 14, 345–47,
354, 538. See also
community-based programs
Network on Adolescent
Development and Juvenile
Justice, 249
neuroscience
brain biomarkers, 136, 139
brain development research,
129–130
brain over-claim
syndrome, 129
case studies, 124–25
causal links between
risk-taking behaviors
and, 125–26, 130,
139n3, 556–57
death penalty and, 128
impulse control, 172
legal defense strategy
and, 128–29
magnetic resonance imaging
(MRIs), 139

policy discussion of, 137–38
prefrontal cortex (PFC), 172
punishment/treatment
and, 135–36
risk-taking behaviors and, 132
SCV offenders and, 564
sentencing issues and,
249–250
serotonin, 563
Nevada, 259
New Jersey, 590
New Mexico, 231, 233
New York (state)
crime rates and, 65
designated felonies, 20
juvenile offender law, 128
maximum/minimum age for
juvenile status, 18, 128
reform efforts, 258
settlement agreements, 203
NHSDA. See National Household
Survey on Drug Abuse
NIBRS. See National
Incident-Based Reporting
System (FBI)
NIMH. See National Institute of
Mental Health
No Child Left Behind Act of
2002, 271–72, 273, 304
nominal dispositions, 12
nonchronic violent offenders, 554
nonpetitioned cases, 15, 49–50
normal brain
development, 131–32
North Carolina, 18, 258
NREPP. See National Registry of
Evidence-Based Practices
and Programs
nuisance abatement, 354
NYGS. See National Youth Gang
Survey

obedience to authority, 176
observational studies, 27
"offending" brain, 132–33, 137.
See also teenage brain
offenses, distribution of, 47.
See also criminal offenses;
juvenile delinquency
offenses; status offenses
Office of Juvenile Justice and
Delinquency Prevention

arrest reporting by, 4
criminal justice statistics
    collection by, 23, 30
delinquency case
    estimates, 364
gang model, 154
juvenile incarceration
    findings, 40
mission, 488
program funding, 45–46
school-based interventions
    and, 303
Office of Sex Offender
    Sentencing, Monitoring,
    Apprehending, Registering,
    and Tracking (SMART), 536
Office of Youth Development, 23
Ohio, 8, 203–4, 224, 231,
    251, 516
Ohio Correctional
    Institution Inspection
    Committee, 204–5
Ohio Department of Youth
    Services (DYS), 204
OJJDP. *See* Office of Juvenile
    Justice and Delinquency
    Prevention
*Oklahoma Publishing Co. v. District
    Court in and for Oklahoma
    City* (1977), 43
Omnibus Crime Control and Safe
    Streets Act of 1968, 45
"once-an-adult/always an adult"
    statute, 247, 259
Oregon, 258, 590
Oregon Youth Authority, 365, 377
out-of-home placements, 52,
    180–81, 417, 443, 447. *See
    also* placement cases
out-of-school suspension
    policies, 109
outreach, 479
OxyContin (oxycodone), 30

Pam Lychner Sexual Offender
    Tracking and Identification
    Act of 1996, 535
parens patriae, 43, 160–61, 234,
    388, 509
parental attachment, 105–6, 560
parent education programs,
    349–350

parents/parenting. *See also*
    families; mothers
abuse by, 89
attitudes toward delinquent
    behavior, 442
convicted, 565
interrogations, presence at,
    175, 179
interventions and, 281, 327
juvenile court referrals
    from, 15
LGBTQ children and, 474
maternal cigarette smoking, 96
middle-class status of,
    88–89, 139
removal from (*See*
    placement cases)
self-control and, 86
single-parent households, 29,
    106, 494–95, 561
skills, 570
supervision by, 560–61
teenage, 105
teen court programs and, 230
training, 299, 570
pathways perspective approach to
    delinquency, 517–18
PAX Game, 299–300
PAXIS Institute, 299
PC DISC v.3.0, 421
PCL:YV. *See* Hare Psychopathy
    Checklist: Youth Version
Peacemaking Circles, 329
peer bonding, 558
peer delinquency
    controlling, 94–95
    personal vs., 92–93
    risk and protective factors, 495
    risk assessments and, 401
    risk factors for, 106–8, 557
peer domain, 110
peer jury model for teen
    court, 230
peer networks, 469–470,
    472, 478–79
peers
    approval from, 174
    homicide of, 519
    influence on re-entry
        services, 366
    prosocial, 110
    rejection of, 107–8

relationships with, 443
    as role models, 228
    in school environment,
        109, 300
    teen courts and, 228, 234
penal system. *See* correctional
    facilities; incarceration;
    juvenile correctional facilities
Pennsylvania, 590
Pennsylvania Supreme Court, 509
performance-based standards
    (PbS) movement, 206–7
persistent offending, 133
person offenses, 47, 48, 54
persons in need of supervision
    (PINS), 9, 467–68
petitioned cases
    disposition of, 15–16
    national estimates of, 49–50
    racial disparities and, 53
pharmacotherapy, 430–32, 433
Philadelphia Biosocial
    Project, 564
Philadelphia Birth Cohort, 562
philanthropy and reform,
    619–620
physical abuse
    female offenders as victims
        of, 48, 54
    status offender exposure to, 21
Piaget, Jean, 131–32
PINS (persons in need of
    supervision), 9, 467–68
Pittman, Christopher, 250
Pittsburgh Youth Development
    Study, 561, 565, 567–68
placement cases
    female juvenile offenders
        and, 54
    national estimates of,
        51–52, 53
    racial/ethnic disparities in, 53
pleasure
    from delinquency
        involvement, 104
    neuroscience and, 172
*Police and Criminal Evidence Act of
    1984* (England), 176
police discretion, 157–58, 164
police force. *See also* law
    enforcement agencies
    arrest and detention by, 163

police force (*Cont.*)
in colonial times, 151
court referrals by, 162
DARE program, 154
discretion with juveniles, 157–58, 164
false confessions, 177
function of, 150
history of, 151–53
interrogations, 174–79
juvenile attitudes toward, 155
juvenile interactions with, 153–54
juvenile relations and, 151–53
minority youth and, 163
police-juvenile interactions
dispositions, 160–63
with gangs, 154
one-on-one, 159
police discretion and, 157–59
preventive approaches and, 164
in school environment, 153–54
variations in, 159
political will, 617–18
Portland State University, 369
Positive Action, 301–2
Positive Behavioral Intervention and Support (PBIS), 280–82
positive punishment effect, 83–84
Positive Youth Development, 210
posttraumatic stress disorder, 406, 428, 466, 518
poverty, 113, 153, 155, 557, 613–14, 623
PREA. *See* Prison Rape Elimination Act of 2003
preadjudication juvenile detention, 10–11
predisposition reports, 16
prefrontal cortex (PFC), 172
pregnancy, 564, 570
preschool-age prevention programs, 570
President's Commission on Law Enforcement and Administration of Justice, 28
prevention programs. *See also* evidence-based prevention programs
anti-gang (*See* anti-gang programs)

community (*See* community-based programs)
delinquency, 38, 42
federal funding for, 45–46
during pregnancy, 570
during pre-school years, 570
to reduce recidivism, 4
school-based (*See* school-based interventions)
for SCV offenders, 569, 570
universal, 114
preventive approaches. *See also* Juvenile Justice and Delinquency Prevention Act of 1974
evidence-based, 114–15
maternal smoking and/or drinking, 570
program funding and, 42, 45
screen and intervene programs, 135–36
prevocational programs, referrals to, 16
Pride school confidential questionnaire, 30
prior convictions, 186
Prison Litigation Reform Act (PLRA), 200, 203–4
Prison Rape Elimination Act of 2003, 198, 257–58
prisons. *See* correctional facilities; jails; juvenile correctional facilities; juvenile detention
privatization of justice system services, 41, 612–13
probation
case disposition estimates (2001-2009), 52, 53
decrease in, 17
informal, 10–11, 15
sanctions involving, 12–14, 16–17
sentencing vs., 251
use of, as disposition, 414
violations of, 15
probation departments, 15
probation officers
girl behavior and, 515
investigation/predisposition report preparation by, 12, 16
juvenile court intake and, 10–11, 15

program capacity, 323
program content, 323
Project ALERT, 298, 306
Project Exile, 353
Promoting Alternative Thinking Strategies, 302
Property Crime Index offenses, 66
property-related crimes
arrest rates for, 23–24
clearances, 66
crimes cleared, 67
national estimates of, 47, 48
rate decline in, 4, 48, 63
self-report surveys of, 28
prosecutorial discretion, 8, 43
prosecutors, 43, 246
prosocial peers, 110
prostitution, 30, 467
PROTECT Act of 2003, 535
protective factors for Delinquency
characteristics of, 110
definition of, 102, 110
mentoring, 111
non-parent adult, 111
psychiatric disorders. *See* mental health disorders
psychiatric hospitalization, 40
psychological abuse, 303, 516. *See also* emotional abuse
psychological disorder. *See* mental health disorders
psychology, developmental, 170–71
psychosis, 466
psychosocial day treatment programs, 16
psychotic episodes, 30
psychotropic medication use, 430–31
PTSD. *See* posttraumatic stress disorder
public-defender offices, 183
public order offenses, 47, 48
public-private partnerships, 619–620, 622–23
public schools. *See* school environment
punishment. *See also* death penalty; sanctions; sentencing
capital (*See* death penalty)
delinquency vs., 82–83

deterrence theory and, 82
disparities in, 153
"just desserts" philosophy
   and, 42–43
non-abusive, 85
perceived threat of, 82
preventive approaches to, 135
severity of, 84
speed of, 84

queer youth. See LGBTQ youth

racial disparities, 53–54,
   248–49, 275–76, 391–92,
   587–590, 614
racial groups. See also African
   Americans; minority groups
adjudication rate increases
   and, 50
attitudes toward police in, 155
bias of, 419, 496, 503, 589
classification of, 497–99
detention rates and, 49
discrimination against, 113
disparities in justice system
   (See racial disparities)
disposition disparities
   for, 590–91
equal justice for, 55
and gender differences in
   violent behavior, 566
juvenile crime rates and, 25, 65
juvenile justice system
   disparities and, 52–53
petitioned cases and, 51
placement case increase
   and, 53
police discretion and, 158
referral rates to juvenile
   court, 562
substance abuse among, 592
waived cases and, 52–54
racial identity, 113–14
racialized gender
   expectations, 514
racketeering, 612
Rand Corporation, 351
rape
in adult facilities, 252
arrest rates for, 23, 66, 67, 532
crimes cleared, 67, 68
as designated felony, 20

Miranda rights and, 156
victimization survey
   findings on, 30
rational behavior training, 209
RBT. See rational behavior
   training
Reagan administration, 39, 153
reasonable doubt standard, 43,
   156, 168
recidivism
aftercare services and, 368
decline in rate of, 4
girls' rates of, 512
homelessness and, 124
impact on, 220–21
increase in rate of, 196, 319
JRAS score and, 543
juvenile drug courts and,
   220–21, 235
for juvenile sex offenders, 545
in juveniles transferred to adult
   court, 254
mediation programs and, 41
mental health disorders
   and, 404
multidimensional treatment
   foster care, 447
multisystemic therapy
   intervention and, 444
neighborhood factors to, 372
predicting, 546–47
privatization and, 41
reduction of, 329, 369, 455
re-entry services and, 364
for sex offenders, 399,
   536–37, 540–41
teen court participation and,
   231, 235
Reclaiming Futures initiative, 619
recreational programs, 14
re-entry interventions. See also
   aftercare interventions
individual approach to, 366–69
mentoring and, 368–69
re-entry programs. See also
   aftercare services
barriers to, 365
for crossover youth, 375–77
definition of, 364
disabled youth and, 377–79
family integration and, 366
goal of, 364

neighborhood effects, 371–72
social challenges to, 365–66
strengths-based approach
   to, 368
referees, court-appointed, 11, 16
reform. See juvenile justice reform
reinforcement theory, 209
relative rate index (RRI), 492, 588
religious group meetings, 14
religious services, 29, 496
Reno v. Flores (1992), 43
reparations, 283
repeat juvenile offenders, 21
reprimand, formal, 161
"resetting effect," 83
residential mobility, 87
residential placements, 17
residential treatment programs,
   13–14, 16, 315, 427–28
responsivity principle, 321, 390
restitution
community service as, 15
as informal case disposition
   condition, 10, 15
mediation programs and, 41
of money, 15
restorative justice and, 283
as sanction, 16, 17
restorative justice, 41, 228,
   283–84, 328–330. See also
   balanced and restorative
   justice
reverse waivers, 247–48,
   255, 259
review hearings, 14
right to counsel, 43, 103, 156,
   157, 495, 612
right to jury, 185
risk assessments
administering, 397
advantages of, 544–45
African Americans and, 400
characteristics of, 395–96
child welfare and, 402–3
definition of, 388
disadvantages of, 545–46
English as a second language
   and, 405
Estimate of Risk Adolescent
   Sexual Offense Recidivism,
   398–99, 541–43
false negatives, 545

risk assessments (*Cont.*)
first-generation of, 393
format of, 392
fourth-generation, 394, 404
gender and, 400
for girls, 401–2
guidelines for, 395–96
Hare Psychopathy
Checklist: Youth
Version, 398
instruments, 393
of juvenile offenders, 390
Juvenile Risk Assessment
Scale, 543
Juvenile Sex Offender
Assessment Protocol-II, 399,
539–541
Juvenile Sex Offense
Recidivism Risk Assessment
Tool-II, 399, 541
for Latino youth, 401
legal issues with, 399–402
measurement equivalence
of, 405
MEGA, 544
mental health problems
and, 400
Model Risk Assessment, 393
Native Americans and, 401
recidivism predictions
from, 546–47
Salient Factor Score, 393
second-generation, 393–94
selection standards for, *396*
for sex offenders, 538–547
sexual
behavior-specific, 398–99
short-term, 542
Structured Assessment
of Violence Risk in
Youth, 397–98
third-generation, 394
tools for, 390–91, 590
uses of, 390–93
for violent and non-violent
behavior, 396–98
Youth Level of Service/
Cases Management
Inventory, 396–97
risk factors for Delinquency
academic performance, 108–9
behavioral, 555–57, *558*

bias as, 496
biological, 494, 562–64, *564*
brain structure and function
as, 130
during childhood, 571
community-related, 559
convicted parent, 565
cultural, 496
definition of, 102
educational, 495
family, *112, 294*, 494–95,
560–61, *561*, 565
Fast Track Prevention
Project, 115
by gender, 111–13
generational, 567–68
HIV-AIDS, 470, 472
homelessness and, 470
individual, 103–5,
112, 294
maternal smoking and/or
drinking, 570
mental illness, 225–27
neighborhood environment,
108, *294*
neuroscience and, 132, 172
parents, 560–61, *561*
peer relationships, 106–8,
112, 294
perception of risk, 171
political, 495
psychological, 494,
555–57, *558*
by race, 113–14
racial, 496
school environment, 108–9,
112, 294, 295, 559
Seattle Social Development
Project, 114
social, 495, 557–560, *559*
socioeconomic conditions,
557, 560
spectrum of, 102
spiritual, 496
street survival behavior, 472
structural, 495
types of, 392
violence and aggression, *391*
Risk-Need-Responsivity model,
317, 318–322, 390
risk perception, 171
risk principle, 319

risk-taking behaviors, 86,
125–26, 130, 132, 139n3,
294, 295, 556–57, 563
RNR model. *See* Risk-Need-
Responsivity model
robbery. *See also* burglary; theft
arrest rates for, 23, 66, *67*,
72, 467
crimes cleared, *67*, 68, *68*
drug use as factor in, 30
of homeless youth, 467
negative life events and, 105
rate decline in, 62, 65
social science theories and, 80
victimization survey of, 30, 31
Robert Wood Johnson
Foundation, 619
Rochester Youth Development
Study, 558, 560, *561*, 566
Roe v. Wade (1973), 64
Roper v. Simmons (2005), 39,
44, 127, 128, 153, 170,
256, 610
Rose, Nikolas, 136
RRI. *See* relative rate index
rule violations, 103
runaways. *See also*
homeless youth
abused females as, 54
estimates of, 464
federal policy for, 38
LGBTQ youth and, 474–75
reclassification as
delinquents of, 40
regional differences in, 471
street survival behavior, 472
transience of, 470–72
runaway shelters, 475–76

"safe" climate at school, 109
Safe Dates, 302–3
Salient Factor Score risk
assessment, 393
SAMHSA. *See* Substance Abuse
and Mental Health Services
Administration
sanctions
criminal diversion
program, 161–62
delinquency case processing
and, 12–14, 16–17
deterrence theory and, 82

formal reprimand, 161
in juvenile drug courts, 217
for sex offenders, 536–37
teen court, 230–31
teen jurors and, 233
warning and release, 161
Sandy Hook Elementary
School, 80
*Save the Children from a Life of
Crime* (Welsh), 306
SAVRY. *See* Structured Assessment
of Violence Risk in Youth
Schall v. Martin (1984), 43
school attendance, 10. *See also*
truancy
school-based interventions
aggressive behavior and, 296
behavior prevention, 280–82
Coping Power Program, 299
DARE program, 154
delinquency
prevention, 293–95
developmental approach
to, 292–93
efficacy of, 296
evidence-based prevention
programs, 295–97
Gang Resistance Education and
Training program, 345, 349
Good Behavior Game,
299–300
implementation issues, 304
PAX Game, 299–300
Positive Action, 301–2
Promoting Alternative
Thinking Strategies, 302
Safe Dates, 302–3
school-to-prison pipeline
and, 279
Seattle Social Development
Project, 114
Second Step, 303
suspensions and, 272
teacher delivery of, 304
three-tiered approach
to, 304–5
school-based prevention
programs. *See* school-based
interventions
school bonding, 109, 282
school dropouts, 29
school engagement, 109, 282

school environment. *See also*
school-to-prison pipeline;
state training schools
attendance rates, 278, 474–75
characteristics of students in,
277–78, 278
discipline, 160, 268, 270
expulsions, 270
incarceration referrals from,
269–270
interventions (*See* school-based
interventions)
juvenile court referrals
from, 15
juvenile-police interactions
in, 153–54
for LGBTQ youth, 474–75
metal detectors, 160
PBIS approach to, 281
police presence in, 153–54,
159–160
removal from, 270–71
restorative justice and, 283–84
risk and protective factors, 495
risk factors for delinquency,
108–9, 112, 294, 295, 559
students with disabilities, 271
suspensions (*See* school
suspensions)
violence in (*See* school
violence)
zero-tolerance policies, 109,
160, 268, 271, 273, 616
school exclusions, 270–72
schoolhouse-to-jailhouse
track, 268
school performance, 282
school resource officers (SROs),
153–54, 159–160, 275,
279–280
school suspensions
of African-Americans, 271
categories for, 273–74, 273
factors associated with, 272
national estimates of, 274
policies, 109
prevention programs
and, 301–2
rates of, 271, 276
school-to-prison
pipeline, 268–69
student behaviors and, 273

of students with
disabilities, 271
school-to-prison pipeline
brain development and, 137
definition of, 268
expulsions, 268–69
Path 1 (indirect model),
279, 282
Path 2 (direct model), 279–280
pathways from, 268–69, 269
restorative justice, 283–84
school exclusion
research, 270–72
from school
perspective, 276–79
suspensions, 268–69
zero-tolerance policies, 283–84
school violence
decline in, 274
gun-related, 38, 154, 159
high-profile examples of, 38
school resource officers and,
153–54, 159–160
screening and assessment
Diagnostic Interview Schedule
for Children, 420–21, 422
GAIN-I, 421
GAIN-SS, 418–420
instruments, 418–422
juvenile justice processing, 418
juvenile justice system, 418
Massachusetts Youth Screening
Instrument, 405, 415,
419–420
mental health courts and,
226–27, 226
for mental illness, 226–27, 226,
415, 418–422
risk factors for delinquency
(*See* risk assessments)
standardized diagnostic
instruments, 420–22
substance abuse, 616
SCV offenders
behavioral and psychological
risks, 555–57, 558
biological factors to, 562–64,
564, 567
during childhood, 555–58
classification of, 554
community-related risk factors
for, 559

SCV offenders (*Cont.*)
family factors toward,
560–61, *561*
generational period
factors, 567–68
heart rate of, 563
intervention programs for,
568–571, 572
maternal complications during
delivery, 564
parental attachment and, 560
physical aggression of, 556
rate increase in, 554–55
referral rates to juvenile
court, 562
risk factors for, 559, 565–68
serotonin levels of, 563
social factors of, 557–560,
559, 565
testosterone levels of, 563–64
uniform crime report facts
on, *555*
Seattle, Washington, 350
Seattle Social Development
Project, 114
secondary deviance, 21
second-generation (2G) risk
assessments, 393–94
Second Step, 303
secure custody. *See* juvenile
detention
secure residential treatment
programs. *See* residential
treatment programs
self-control, 104, 138, 169, 171
self-control theory, 85–86, 88
self-esteem, 107, 301
self-fulfilling prophecy, 21
self-identity, 104, 478
self-incrimination, privilege
against, 43, 156, 157, 168,
172, 174
self-mastery, 131
self-protection, 108
self-report studies of delinquency,
22–23, 27–29
sentencing. *See also* death penalty
arbitrary, 153
attorney presence and, 180–81
blended, 255
counsel as aggravating factor
in, 183–84

for designated felony
convictions, 20
female, 510
jury trials and, 185
for life imprisonment, 127
life-without-parole, 134, 170,
242, 250–51, 256
mandatory laws for, 242,
250, 259
state policies and, 44
teenage brain and, 249–251
in teen courts, 230
for youth waived to adult
court, 254
serious, chronic and violent
(SCV) juvenile offenders. *See*
SCV offenders
serotonin, 563
settlement agreements,
199–200, 202–3
sex, as work, 468–69
sex offender registration,
186, 538
Sex Offender Registration Act of
2011 (New York), 124
Sex Offender Registration and
Notification Act (SORNA).
See Adam Walsh Child
Protection and Safety Act
of 2006
sex offenders. *See* juvenile sex
offenders
sexual abuse
by detention personnel,
204–5
female offenders as victims of,
48, 54, 402, 516, 520–21
homeless youth and, 466
negative life events and, 105
as risk factors for
Delinquency, 111
status offender exposure to, 21
suicidal behavior and, 518
trauma, 428
sexual aggression. *See* rape
sexual assault
in adult facilities, 252
sentencing issues and, 250
sexual behaviors, 111, 222,
301, 398–99
sexual health
interventions, 477–78

sexual interests/attitudes/
behaviors scale, 542
sexually transmitted diseases,
222, 468–69, 472, 477–78,
479, 524
sexual misconduct, 510
sexual orientation, 478
shame, 104
Shaw, Clifford, 351
sheriff's departments. *See* law
enforcement agencies
shoplifting, 28, 229
SH v. Reed, 203–4
single-parent households, 29,
106, 494–95, 561
situational factors. *See also*
families; risk factors for
delinquency
altering environments, 96–97
lead poisoning, exposure to,
124, 135
maternal cigarette smoking, 96
risk factors for
delinquency, 113
toxins, exposure to, 96, 124
Sixth Amendment, 157, 179
skill streaming, 328
smoking, 301, 465
Snyder, Howard, 69
social bonds, 85
social cognitive processes, 104
social control theory, 293
social development model, 293
social disorganization theory,
86–87, 88, 344
social learning theory, 293
social movements, 618–19
social networks, 87, 344–45, 367,
469–472, 478–79
social network technology,
472–74, 479
social science theories
biosocial theory, 95–97
control theory, 84–88, 97
definition of, 80–81
deterrence theory, 81–84, 97
differential association
theory, 92
general strain theory, 92
institutional anomie theory, 92
learning theory, 91–95, 97
macro-level, 80

micro-level, 80
Moffitt's developmental
    taxonomy, 96–97
strain theory, 88–91, 97
social science theory and research
    perspective, 201, 202,
    205–6, 208–10
social services, 15, 21
social stress, 105
"Social Structure and Anomie"
    (Merton), 90
social studies. *See* predisposition
    reports
socioeconomic conditions, 105,
    155, 301, 557, 560. *See also*
    poverty
solitary confinement, 252–53
SORNA. *See* Adam Walsh Child
    Protection and Safety Act
    of 2006
*Sourcebook of Criminal Justice
    Statistics*, 30
South Dakota, 590
special education services, 300
"specific" deterrence, 82. *See also*
    deterrence theory
specific responsivity, 321
speed. *See* methamphetamine
spouse abuse. *See* domestic
    violence
SROs. *See* school resource officers
SSDP. *See* Seattle Social
    Development Project
SSTR. *See* social science theory
    and research perspective
standard metropolitan statistical
    areas (SMSAs), 91
Stanford v. Kentucky (1989), 43
state juvenile codes and statutes,
    7–9, 18, 42–44
state training schools
    juvenile aftercare plans of, 13
    status offenders and, 21
State University of New York,
    Albany, 30
status offenders. *See* juvenile
    offenders
status offenses. *See also specific
    offenses*
    bootstrapping, 512–13
    case processing of, 14–15
    decriminalization of, 38

definition of, 5, 32
females, 512–13
homeless youth, 467–68
juvenile delinquency and, 9
protective supervision
    for, 514
runaway (*See* runaways)
sexual misconduct, 510
truancy, 9, 28, 108–9, 272,
    301, 468
statutory exclusion, 246–47
STDs. *See* sexually transmitted
    diseases
stealing. *See* theft
Steinberg, Laurence, 137, 250
stepparent families, 106. *See also*
    families
Steward, Mike, 208
St. Louis, Mo., 350, 471
stolen property offenses, 47
strain theory, 88–91, 97
street gangs
    arrest rates for, 352
    behavior of, 340
    community crime
        theories, 344–45
    community influence
        on, 343–45
    criminal activity of, 341–42, 344
    death rate of members, 340
    definition of, 339–340
    female members, 341
    intervention programs
        for, 352–53
    joining, 342
    juvenile justice reform
        and, 611–12
    leaving, 342–43, 352
    national estimates of, 340
    police interaction with, 154
    poverty and, 153
    profile of, 341
    programs against (*See*
        anti-gang programs)
    serious crime and, 558–59
    suppression tactics, use of, 352–53
street survival behavior, 472
street youth, 471
stress
    chronic, 113
    exposure to, brain development
        and, 134–35

of interrogations, 177
    social, 105
Structured Assessment
    of Violence Risk in
    Youth, 397–98
student courts, 228
substance abuse. *See also*
    alcohol abuse; drug abuse;
    marijuana use
    aggression and, 104–5
    arrest rates for, 216
    diagnostic patterns of, 416
    homeless youth and,
        465–66, 477
    as juvenile crime factor, 30
    juvenile justice population
        with, 592
    juvenile justice system
        and, 365
    LGBTQ youth and, 475
    LifeSkills Training and,
        300–301
    mental health disorders
        and, 414
    peer rejection and, 107
    petitioned cases involving, 51
    rates of, 416
    as risk factors for delinquency,
        104, 111, 475
    school-based interventions
        and, 296, 300–301
    screening instruments, 418–422
    self-control and, 86
    social science theories and, 80
Substance Abuse and
    Mental Health Services
    Administration, 297–98,
    303, 464. *See also*
    drug abuse
suicidal behavior
    drug use as factor in, 30
    homeless youth and, 466
    mental health and, 416, 466
    school-based interventions
        and, 300
    sexual abuse and, 518
suicide risk, 252
Supreme Court, U.S.
    abortion ruling, 64
    judicial waiver ruling, 246
    juvenile death penalty rulings,
        20, 39, 43, 44, 127, 153

Supreme Court, U.S. (*Cont.*)
life without parole ruling,
134, 250
right to counsel ruling, 43, 44,
156, 157, 168
rulings regarding youth,
256–57, 610
suspensions. *See* school
suspensions
Sutherland, Edwin, 92

technology and homeless
youth, 472–74
teenage brain. *See also*
neuroscience
abnormal development
of, 132–36
developmental stage
monitoring, 132
normal development
of, 131–32
research of, 129
sentencing issues and,
249–250
teenage engagement, 132
teenage parenthood, 105
teen courts
adult judge model, 230
completion rates, 231
confidentiality and, 232
definition of, 228
description of, 229–231
effectiveness of, 231–32, 235
eligibility criteria, 229
history of, 228
peer and student, 228
peer jury model, 230
programs, 230
recidivism rates, 231
retention rates, 231
sanctions involving, 230–31
satisfaction in, 233
sentencing in, 230
teen jurors, impact on, 233–34
tribunal model, 230
youth judge model, 230
youth offenders' perceptions
of, 232
testosterone, 563–64
Texas, 21, 251, 253–54, 258, 423
TF-CBT. *See* trauma focused
cognitive behavioral therapy

theft. *See also* burglary; robbery
antisocial behavior and, 103
arrest rates for, 67
auto, 8, 23, 30
crimes cleared, 67
deterrence theory and, 81
drug use as factor in, 30
of homeless youth, 467
punishment for, 82
self-control and, 86
social science theories and, 80
theoretically defined structural
variables, 94
Theory of Social Structure and
Social Learning (SSSL), 94
therapeutic jurisprudence, 324
third-generation (3G) risk
assessment, 394
Thomas, Clarence, 134
throwaway youth, 465. *See also*
homeless youth
"tough on crime," 128, 129,
297, 620
toxins, exposure to, 96
transfer hearings, 15–16, 51. *See
also* adult criminal court
transgender youth. *See*
LGBTQ youth
transience, 470–72, 479
transitional living programs, 476
trauma. *See also specific types*
as risk factors for Delinquency,
111, 112–13, 402, 406, 586
sexual abuse, 428
trauma focused cognitive
behavioral therapy, 428
Treatment for Adolescents with
Depression study, 431
tribal courts, 609
tribunal model for teen court, 230
truancy, 9, 28, 108–9, 272,
301, 468
tutoring, 14
"tyranny of non-experts," 201

Uniform Crime Reporting (UCR)
program, 66, 492
Uniform Crime Reports (FBI), 29,
30, 532, 555, 566
unintentional bias, 496
United Kingdom. *See* Great
Britain

universal motivations, 81–82
universal prevention
programs, 114
University of Chicago, 86
"unsafe" climate at school, 109
U.S. departments and agencies.
See key word, e.g. Justice
Department
U.S. Supreme Court. *See* Supreme
Court, U.S.
Utah, 259

vandalism
antisocial behavior and, 103
social science theories and, 80
Vasquez, Steven, 124–25, 126,
128, 133, 134, 135, 138
Vera Institute of Justice, 619
victimization
female, 586
girl-to-girl, 521
of homeless youth, 468–69
negative life events and, 105
sexual, 518
sexual assault and, 520
surveys of, 22, 27, 30–32
victim-offender mediation,
329–330
victims
juvenile court referrals, 15
of sexual abuse, 48, 54
of violent crimes, 31
Violence Initiative Project, 139
violent behavior. *See also*
domestic violence; school
violence
aggression and, 556
biological factors on, 567
child abuse and, 561
childhood predictors of, 565
maternal complications during
delivery, 564
peer rejection and, 107
racial differences in, 566
serotonin levels and, 563
testosterone levels and, 563–64
Violent Crime Control Act of
1994, 41
violent crimes. *See also* juvenile
homicide; SCV offenders
arrest rates for, 23–24,
62, 70–76

during childhood, 555–56
clearances, 66–67
crimes cleared, 67
decline in, 4, 71
drug use as factor in, 30
female offender referrals for, 48
increase in, 72
learning theory and, 93
media attention to, 5
national estimates of,
    62–65, 63
rate decline in, 554
rate increase in, 62–63
referral rates to juvenile
    court, 562
repeat juvenile offenders
    and, 20–21
in schools (See
    school violence)
victims of, 31
violent offenders. See SCV
    offenders
Virginia, 251, 258
vocational training programs, 14,
    21, 477
Voice DISC-IV, 416, 420, 421,
    430–31, 432
volunteer work, 14
VOM. See victim-offender
    mediation

waived cases. See also adult
    criminal court
Miranda waivers, 175
national estimates of, 51–52
racial disparities in, 53–54
reverse waivers, 255
waiver hearings, 15–16, 51
waiver of counsel, 181–82, 187
wardship (ward of the
    court), 11–12
warning and release sanction, 161
Warren, Earl, 157
Washington (state), 42, 231,
    251, 534
Washington State Institute for
    Public Policy, 329
weapons, 62. See also guns
Wetterling Act of 1994, The, 535
Wilson, James Q., 128
Wisconsin, 427
witnesses, 43
women. See females; mothers
wraparound services, 316–17

YLC. See Youth Law Center
YLS/CMI. See Youth Level of
    Service/Cases Management
    Inventory
YMCA, 162
youth. See also females; males

crossover, 375–77
definition of, 63
with disabilities, 377–79
dual system, 375–77
homeless (See homeless youth)
isolation of, 153
marginalized, 274
tried as adults, 242 (See also
    adult criminal court)
violence (See SCV offenders;
    violent crimes)
Youth Center of the High
    Plains, 209
youth courts. See teen courts
youth drop-in centers, 476
youth homicide. See juvenile
    homicide
youth judge model for teen
    court, 230
Youth Law Center, 197
Youth Level of Service/Cases
    Management Inventory,
    366–67, 396–97
Youth Risk Behavior Surveillance
    System (YRBSS), 519–520

zero-tolerance policies, 109,
    160, 268, 271, 273,
    283–84, 616
Zimring, Franklin, 65, 537

CPSIA information can be obtained
at www.ICGtesting.com
Printed in the USA
BVOW07*0912310118
506320BV00007B/4/P